PLANTSMAN'S PARADISE
Travels in China

ROY LANCASTER

Cardiocrinum giganteum variety *yunnanense* flowering in 1987 in the woodland garden of the Royal Botanic Garden, Edinburgh, grown from seed collected on the Cangshan in 1981. The dark stem is typical of the Yunnan variety. (June)

PLANTSMAN'S PARADISE
Travels in China

ROY LANCASTER

GARDEN • ART • PRESS

First published in 1989 by The Antique Collectors' Club Ltd.
Reprinted 1989, 1993 (with addendum)

ISBN 978-1-85149-515-3

British Library Cataloguing-in-Publication Data:
A catalogue record for this book is available from the British Library

---

ENDPAPERS

Front: *Pinus yunnanensis* in the Western Hills above Lake Dianchi (see p157)

Back: *Rhododendron redowskianum* on the Baitou Shan (see p469)

Printed in China for Garden Art Press, an imprint of The Antique Collectors' Club Ltd.,
Woodbridge, Suffolk IP12 4SD

To the late Marianne Beuchert, a dear friend and fellow student of the Chinese flora whose encouragement and gifts of treasured books have considerably enriched my appreciation of China's Green Heritage

Also, to Mikinori Ogisu, botanist, horticulturalist, plant explorer and friend whose generous spirit and extensive travels in China's wild places have played a significant part in our understanding and enjoyment of its flora.

Acknowledgements

The role played by my wife in the preparation of this book has already been acknowledged in the Dedication. Despite the daily demands of running a home and family she somehow made time to type the manuscript and encourage me in many other ways. To Andrew Lauener, until his recent retirement a senior botanist at the Royal Botanic Garden, Edinburgh, I owe a great debt of gratitude. Not only did he check the manuscript from a botanical standpoint, he answered in detail countless queries concerning the nomenclature of Chinese plants in cultivation. His erudition, patience and good humour have been a constant source of encouragement to me. The manuscript has also been read by San Chwee Choo, who kindly checked all references to Chinese place names. He also checked the various maps, making many helpful comments and suggestions.

My old friend and former colleague at the Hillier Arboretum, Hatton Gardner, has done his usual thorough job in compiling the indices, a tedious task which he nevertheless enjoys. In addition, a lot of friends and correspondents have obliged me at various times with information or have helped me in other ways. They include Professor J McNeil (Regius Keeper), Dr David Chamberlain and Ron McBeath, all of the Royal Botanic Garden, Edinburgh; Peter Green, Brian Mathew, Brian Halliwell, Miss Susyn Andrews and Miss Marilyn Ward, all of the Royal Botanic Gardens, Kew; Tony Schilling (Deputy Curator of the Royal Botanic Garden, Kew) in charge of Wakehurst Place; John Bond (Keeper) and Martin Gardner, both of the Savill and Valley Gardens, Windsor Great Park; Dr Norman Robson of the British Museum (Natural History); Jerry Cross of the Ministry of Agriculture, Fisheries and Food (ADAS); Dr Brent Elliot, Librarian RHS Lindley Library; Keith Rushforth, Alan Mitchell, Victoria Hallet; Dr D V Geltman and Dr M E Kirpicznikov of the V L Komarov Institute, Academy of Sciences, USSR; Dr P Bamps of the Jardin Botanique National de Belgique; Heino Heine; Harry J van de Laar; Dr Charles Nelson of the National Botanic Gardens, Dublin; Dr Stephen Spongberg of the Arnold Arboretum, Massachusetts; Paul Meyer of the Morris Arboretum, Philadelphia; Mrs Holly H Shimizu; Wang Wen-tsai of the Institute of Botany, Academia Sinica, Beijing; Guan Kaiyun of the Yunnan Institute of Botany, Academia Sinica, Kunming; Wang Dajun, Curator at the Shanghai Botanical Garden. To all of these I record my thanks and appreciation. My thanks also to Raoul Moxley for providing the means by which many of my dreams were realised.

My publishers deserve a special thanks for allowing what was originally envisaged as a book of 180 pages to expand to the present 500. It was a difficult not to say brave decision which, however, was surely made easier by the choice of Cherry Lewis as editor. I could not have wished for a better guide through the complexities of the text. She has been like a robin with the eyes of an eagle, friendly, patient, encouraging, gently critical and possessed of a sixth sense for inaccuracies and inconsistencies. If any weaknesses or mistakes remain they are solely my own.

Last but no means least, a warm thanks to the many friends and companions with whom I have shared these journeys. Without their camaraderie, support and enthusiasm, these experiences would not have tasted as sweet.

Acknowledgements for the new Edition

Once again I record my thanks and appreciation to the following individuals, friends and colleagues who, in one way or another have contributed to the preparation of this new edition, most importantly my wife Sue who, as before, has been responsible for dealing with my handwritten notes and making them more presentable for my editor. They are Tony Aiello, David Alderman, Olivier Colin, Allen Coombes, Kenneth Cox, Peter Cox, Philip Cribb, Gary Dunlop, Brent Elliott, Raymond Evison, Alnos Farjon, Mark Flanagan, Maurice Foster, Jim Gardiner, Martin Gardner, Chris Grey-Wilson, David Howells, Diane Wyse Jackson, Jim Jermyn, Tony Kirkham, Paul Meyer, Kim Jung Myung, Seamus O'Brien, Mikinori Ogisu, Martyn Rix, Keith Rushforth, Brian Schrire, Stephen Spongberg, Carla Teune, Peter del Tredici, Malcolm Walker, Peter Wharton, Bleddyn Wynn-Jones, and the late Marianne Beuchart. In addition, I wish to thank all those institutions, arboreta and gardens who have welcomed my visits and assisted my research, in particular the RHS Garden, Wisley where both Garden and Botany Department staff have been most patient with my enquiries, so too, the staff at the Royal Botanic Gardens Edinburgh and Kew and the Sir Harold Hillier Gardens and Arboretum.

I also thank all those many individuals too numerous to mention but remembered, with whom I have shared conversations about Chinese plants in gardens and the wild. Their knowledge, enthusiasm and unending curiosity serves to remind me how fortunate I am to be a plantsman.

Finally, I thank my publishers, the Antique Collectors' Club Ltd., in particular Diana Steel for deciding on this new edition and sticking with it to the end, my editor Susannah Hecht whose professionalism, patience and willingness to please has been like music to my ears, and Sandra Pond whose design skills and flair have provided the finishing touch.

Photographic Acknowledgements

I wish to thank the following institutions, organisations and individuals for making important photographs available for use in this book.

China Today Magazine: p.50 (bottom)

Peter Cox: p.481 (middle)

Raymond Evison: p.41 (bottom right)

Mark Flanagan: p.72 (top right)

Jeanette Fryer: p.137 (bottom right)

Martin Gardner: p.99 (top left and right)

Harvard College, President and Fellows ©: p.343 (bottom), p.345 (bottom), p.349 (top left and right), p.356 (right), p.486 (bottom), p.491 (middle and bottom), p.492 (top and middle), p.495 (bottom)

Hugo de Vries Laboratory, University of Amsterdam: p.489 (middle)

Hunt Institute for Botanical Documentation, Carnegie Mellon University, Pittsburgh, USA ©: p.487 (middle)

Institute of Botany, University of Vienna: p.485 (bottom)

Jim Jermyn: p.248 (bottom left), p.258 (top)

Andrew Lauener: p. 483 (second from top)

Kim Jung Myung: p.468, p.469

Mikinori Ogisu: p.16 (top right), p.19 (bottom left), p. 67, p.84 (top), p.88 (top right), p.341 (top), p.346 (top right and left), p. 370 (top right and bottom right)

National Botanic Gardens, Glasnevin, Dublin: p.486 (middle)

Barbara Phillips: p.346 (bottom)

Martyn Rix: p.359 (bottom)

Royal Botanic Garden, Edinburgh: p.110 (bottom), p.112 (bottom), p.160 (top), p.161 (top right), p.164 (top left and right), p167 (bottom), p.168 (all), p.172 (top), p.177 (bottom), p.194 (top right), p.205 (bottom), p.213 (top left), p.219 (top right, bottom left and right), p.220 (top left), p.221 (bottom), p.222 (top left), p.223 (bottom), p.225 (bottom left), p.228 (bottom), p.257 (bottom), p.267 (top and bottom), p.268, p.269 (bottom), p.296 (top and bottom), p. 479 (middle), p.480 (bottom), p.484 (middle and bottom), p.493 (middle)

Royal Botanic Gardens, Kew: p.479 (top and bottom), p.480 (middle), p.481 (top), p.483 (bottom), p.485 (middle), p.486 (top), p.487 (top and bottom), p.488 (top and bottom), p.489 (top), p.490 (middle and bottom), p.491 (top), p.492 (bottom), p.493 (top), p.494 (top and bottom), p.495 (top)

Royal Geographical Society: p.51 (bottom), p.83 (top)

Tony Schilling: p.122 (top right)

Brian Schrire: p.331 (right)

Frits Smit: p.399

Société des Missions Etrangères de Paris: p.269 (top), p. 480 (top), p.481 (bottom), p.482 (top, middle and bottom), p.483 (top and third down), p.485 (top), p.488 (middle), p.489 (bottom), p.490 (top), p.493 (bottom)

Société Jersiaise: p.144 (bottom)

Stephen Spongberg: p.352 (bottom left)

Travel and Tourist Bureau of Yunnan Province: p.165 (bottom), p.166 (bottom), p.262 (top)

Vilmorin Family: p.494 (middle)

Donat Walder: p.165 (top left)

Mario Zanferdino: p.101 (bottom right)

Contents

Opposite: Rich broad-leaved deciduous and coniferous forest in the Song Hua river valley
of the Changbai Shan Reserve in China's Jilin province. (July)

Introduction

There must be few gardens in Britain that do not contain at least one plant of Chinese origin, and I suspect the same may also be true of gardens in Europe and North America. If this be so, then my first contact with a Chinese plant most probably occurred in the 1940s, in the garden of my childhood home in Bolton, Lancashire. The identity of the plant - even if I could remember it - is irrelevant, for at that time my interests lay elsewhere and the first plants to capture my attention were those which grew wild in the waste places and countryside around my home.

It was not until I left school and began work for the Bolton Parks Department that garden plants came into my life. The first two years I worked in Moss Bank Park where, among other attractions, there was a walled area which had been planted as a so-called 'Old English Garden'. It was full of interesting plants, including a vast colony of *Senecio tanguticus* (now *Sinacalia tangutica*), a splendid Chinese ragwort with boldly cut leaves and large conical plumes of yellow flowers in autumn. On two occasions I was given the job of reducing this colony to a more manageable size, and far from cursing it I came to admire its tenacity and reliability. In the same garden grew a Golden rain tree or Pride of India - *Koelreuteria paniculata*, another Chinese native. It was a rare tree in Lancashire at that time and keen local gardeners came to the park specially to see it. I remember this tree as much for its desultory performance as for its exotic English names, for in ten years acquaintance I never once saw it flower, lacking, no doubt, the warm summers of its homeland in northern China and Mongolia.

Not far from the walled garden was an impressive limestone rock garden of the kind Reginald Farrer, author of the classic *The English Rock Garden,* would have approved. It boasted a wide range of alpine and rock plants as well as a scattering of shrubs, small flowering trees and slow-growing conifers. In a perimeter border there flourished a suckering clump of *Aralia elata,* the Angelica tree from China and Japan. Its tall pithy stems were fiercely armed with sharp spines and in winter, to my untutored eyes, they looked decidedly dead. Their true state I discovered to my cost. Given the task of digging and cleaning the border I zealously pruned the stems to ground level, receiving for my trouble a cuff around the ears and a reprimand from the foreman in charge. As it turned out, far from killing it, my pruning only encouraged it to sucker even more vigorously which, in retrospect, is probably what my foreman had feared.

Happily, not all my early endeavours ended this way, and it is to Moss Bank Park, its plants and plantsmen that I owe my initiation to the Chinese flora. Here it was that I began to appreciate its rich variety and its popularity with gardeners, an appreciation confirmed by the regular appearance of the names 'chinensis' and 'sinensis' on garden labels and in nursery catalogues.

During the succeeding years my encounters with Chinese plants increased, and with familiarity came a desire to know more about their origins and histories. As any keen gardener appreciates, knowing a plant's name is to possess a key which opens the door to a wealth of information. The importance of plant names as a source of information was thoroughly drummed into me during two years as a student gardener at the University Botanic Garden, Cambridge, under its Director at the time, the late John Gilmour. Then began a long association with the well-known nursery firm of Hilliers of Winchester, first as horticultural botanist, later as Curator of the Hillier Arboretum. For eighteen years I was exposed to one of the world's largest collections of woody plants in which those of Chinese origin were heavily represented. At the same time I enjoyed the benefits of the knowledge and experience of the late Sir Harold Hillier, one of the world's greatest and most respected dendrologists. Not surprisingly, my interest in Chinese plants increased as a consequence and my thirst for information concerning their origins became a passion - fuelled by the writings of those fortunate enough to have visited China.

I first read of the plant hunters in my late teens. The travels of these fascinating individuals who often risked, and sometimes lost, their lives in search of plants to ornament our gardens captured my imagination, and the exploits of Ernest Wilson and George Forrest particularly attracted me. Both had spent a significant amount of time in China and were responsible for the presence in our gardens of a large number of ornamental plants. Their names I frequently encountered in the names of plants they had introduced, of which *Berberis wilsoniae, Magnolia wilsonii, Pieris formosa* variety *forrestii* and *Iris forrestii* were but four examples. The first of these, as it happens, is named after Wilson's wife, though he was responsible for its first introduction.

As my knowledge of the subject increased, I came to realise that the history of plant hunting in China was like a rich tapestry, the diverse threads representing the efforts and achievements of a great number of people, Chinese as well as foreign. This knowledge, however, did nothing to encourage my own ambitions in that direction. Ever since

1949 China had been closed to all but a few westerners and I had reluctantly come to accept that the opportunity of seeing her flora at first hand would not come in my lifetime. Then all that changed.

Following the chaos of the Cultural Revolution (1966-1976) and its subsequent reverberations, China reopened its doors to foreigners and tourism gradually became an accepted part of the country's attractions. In the spring of 1979 I received, from out of the blue, an invitation to accompany, as guest lecturer, a cultural tour to China. I accepted immediately.

I must admit that I was, to put it mildly, somewhat surprised and a little puzzled by the invitation. As far as I could tell, our tour would be concerned with recent aspects of Chinese history and present day activities rather than with her wild or garden flora. In the event, I was required to comment on crops seen from train or bus, in addition to which I delivered a couple of lectures. The greatest satisfaction of the tour for me, though, was that it allowed me to set foot in China and make that all-important first contact.

Having spent two days in Hong Kong, the tour took us by train to Guangzhou (Canton), thence to Hangzhou (Hangchow) and Shanghai in the east where I made my first Chinese gardening friend, Wang Dajun, Curator of the Shanghai Botanical Garden. We left Shanghai by steamer, crossing the Yellow Sea to Qingdao (Tsingtao) on the Shandong Peninsula. The final part of the tour we spent in Beijing (Peking) where we experienced a rich slice of an ancient culture with visits to the Imperial City, Summer Palace and, of course, the Great Wall. On several occasions during the tour I was able to examine the native vegetation and meet with Chinese botanists.

The following year I was invited to lead a botanical tour for a specialist travel concern based in London. This time the interests of the group were more akin to my own and the tour more enjoyable and exciting as a consequence. We started the tour in Beijing in October, moving down country to Chengdu (Chengtu) in Sichuan (Szechuan). Two days later, I realised an ambition when our party climbed Emei Shan (Mt Omei) and I at last trod in the footsteps of Ernest Wilson. Emei Shan was for me an astonishing experience, followed closely by Kunming in Yunnan where our group next spent an enjoyable few days. A hugely successful tour was concluded by a visit to Xiqiao Hill, south west of Guangzhou in Guangdong province.

If the 1980 tour fulfilled an ambition, then 1981 was the cream on the cake. In the spring of that year I again found myself in China, this time as a member of the Sino-British Expedition to the Cangshan, a range of mountains in west Yunnan previously known as the Tsangshan or, more evocatively, the Tali Range. Here, in George Forrest territory, my excitement and sense of fulfilment reached new levels as an incredibly rich flora was revealed to us over an all too brief period of five weeks. Added to this was the immense pleasure and satisfaction of working with Chinese botanists on a joint venture.

In the autumn of the same year I accompanied a party of plant enthusiasts on a short expedition into western Sichuan close to a mountain called Gongga Shan or Minya Konka. Although a mere three weeks in duration, the trek led us into the mountains and valleys of an area not visited by any of the old western plant hunters, except perhaps Joseph Rock, and introduced us to a treasure house of familiar plants as well as those less so.

In spring 1983 I accompanied another botanical tour, this time to the Wudang Shan (Wudang Mountains) of north-west Hubei (Hupeh). To reach them, we journeyed through the Yangtze Gorges, disembarking at Yichang (Ichang) where, over eighty years before, Ernest Wilson, acting on information provided by an Irish customs official, Augustine Henry, began his quest for the Chinese dove tree - *Davidia involucrata*.

My next visit to China took place in 1984, when I accompanied a small group of enthusiasts on a botanical trek to the Changbai Shan (Changbai Mountains) in north-east China on the border with North Korea. This was another exciting experience among plants familiar and new, including two dandelions new to science!

My most recent adventure in China took place in September 1986, when I accompanied another group of enthusiasts first to Jiuzhaigou 'a Chinese fairyland' - north of Songpan in north-west Sichuan, and thence to the fabled Jade Dragon Mountains (Yulongshan) above Lijiang in north-west Yunnan. But that is another story.

How unpredictable fate and how fleeting opportunity. At the beginning of 1979 my knowledge of Chinese plants was based solely on those I had seen in cultivation, yet within the short space of five years I had visited four of the most famous capitals in Chinese plant hunting history - Yichang (Ichang) in Hubei, Dali (Tali) in Yunnan, Kangding (Tachienlu) in Sichuan and, of course, Beijing (Peking) itself. To have travelled in these areas and to have experienced at first hand the wealth of plants to be found there has been for me not only a dream come true but also an experience which has considerably enriched my life.

If the following accounts encourage others to follow the 'China Trail', or if they simply rekindle or strengthen an interest in China and her beleaguered green heritage, then I shall be well satisfied. I use the word beleaguered intentionally for, as those who have recently travelled in China's wild places will know, the erosion of her forest, first noted and lamented by Augustine Henry and others a hundred years and more ago, continues unabated and its future should be the concern of us all.

Notes to the New Edition

Travels in China had been out of print for several years when Diana Steel of the Antique Collectors Club rang me one day about the possibility of a reprint. It was soon agreed that this would not be a simple reprint but something much more: not just a new format in full colour throughout and all my original slides digitally rescanned to produce illustrations of far better quality, but also hundreds of extra images. The results I hope, speak for themselves, I believe they have contributed substantially to this new edition.

It was only natural that we consider updating such things as nomenclature as well as information concerning the introduction of plants described into Western cultivation. Many plants seen in China in the 1980s, but not known to be in cultivation in the West at that time, are now here and in some cases well established. It is 18 years since this book was first published, in which time many changes have occurred in China especially those concerning roads and transportation and therefore access to once remote areas. I never would have dreamed, for instance, in 1980, that our journey by truck and foot to the summit of Emei Shan (Mt. Omei) in Sichuan would be supplanted by a metalled road all the way to the summit plus a gondola ride. Likewise, the journey from Chengdu to Kangding, which in 1981 took us several days, can now be achieved in a matter of hours.

The enormous increase in tourism and all that that implies has turned some byways into highways and provided many a small town with western-style hotels. Even more dramatic developments such as the Three Gorges Dam on the Yangtze have changed (some would claim destroyed) entire landscapes together with their associated wildlife and flora. I do not intend here discussing the merits or otherwise of these changes as far greater minds and expertise have addressed the subject. Suffice it to say that, as it affects this book, I have decided to leave the accounts of my travels unchanged as they describe situations as I found them at the time and, hopefully, will be judged in an historical context rather than an ongoing one.

Corydalis flexuosa at the Royal Botanic Gardens, Edinburgh. This striking perennial caused a sensation in the garden world when introduced in the 1970s, originally by Compton, D'Arcy and Rix. (May)

Plant Exploration in China

When E H Wilson, one of the most successful of plant hunters referred to China as the 'Mother of Gardens' he was speaking from a rich and personal experience. His four expeditions during the first decade of the twentieth century helped make available to western gardeners the fruits of a botanical paradise. But Wilson is only one of many names in the history of plant exploration in China. His was a single albeit important contribution to the study of the Chinese flora, a study which began long before his exploits and which continues today. Indeed, it must be said that the Chinese themselves were the first to collect, cultivate and chronicle their native plants. Naturally, these were mainly plants of economic value rather than those of ornamental merit only. Interestingly, many plants grown originally by the Chinese

for economic use later became appreciated for their aesthetic value, two of the most famous examples being the bamboo and the lotus. Even today, for most Chinese, the food or medicinal potential of a plant is often more important than its aesthetic value, though this is not to say, of course, that the Chinese do not appreciate the latter.

I well remember climbing a mountain in Hubei province accompanied by a Chinese guide who spent the whole day pointing out to me those plants used in Chinese traditional medicine. Exactly the same thing happened to me once in the mountains of Jilin province in north-east China. Lu and Hueng, writing in the 'Botany' account of Edward Needham's monumental *Science and Civilisation in China* (1986), remind us that "...anyone who knows Chinese literature is aware that there was not a single century

13

Asarum magnificum at the Wushan Botanic Garden, China. This magnificent species is now widely grown by connoisseurs in the west. (May)

Aspidistra fungilliformis, in the author's garden. One of a growing number of species recently introduced to the West. (November)

Epimedium epsteinii, in the author's garden. A striking species in flower and now widely available in the West. The name commemorates the late Harold Epstein, a well-known American gardener and collector of alpines and woodland plants, especially epimediums. Introduced by Darrell Probst in the 1990s. (April)

Betula insignis at the Howick Arboretum, Northumberland. A handsome birch in leaf and catkin increasingly available in the West from specialist suppliers. (April)

Bergenia emeiensis, in the author's garden (flowered under glass). A most ornamental species now widely available and already a parent of several hardy hybrids in Western cultivation. Introduced by Mikinori Ogisu in the 1990s. (March)

between AD100 and 1700 that did not see the appearance of at least one new and original work on pharmaceutical natural history and some which saw many..." In other words, Chinese botany had no Renaissance, though it had no 'dark ages' either. The first foreign plants introduced and cultivated by the early Chinese appear to have been cereal crops such as rice, remnants of which have been found in Zhejiang province dating to 7,000 years ago, while wheat culture dates to at least 4,000 years ago.

The first Chinese plant hunter, so history records, was Chan Chien who, during a term as an ambassador of the Han dynasty to the 'western territories' in 126BC, is said to have introduced to China the fodder crop alfalfa and the grape vine. During the following centuries many other economic crops were introduced into China from abroad, especially by merchants along the famous 'Silk Route' through Central Asia. The process of plant introduction to China has continued up until the present day. Anyone who has travelled in China cannot help but have noted the great number of foreign trees planted in urban areas, especially

along roads, railways and field margins. Among the most notable are eucalypts and casuarinas from Australia, Swamp cypress, pines and poplars from North America, and London planes from Europe. In many northern and eastern areas especially, the North American False acacia *Robinia pseudoacacia*, and the shrubby False indigo *Amorpha fruticosa* have been planted in vast numbers, the former since the end of the nineteenth century.

Fascinating though this story is - with its reversal of the commonly-held assumption that ornamental or useful plants only come *out* of China, this book is more concerned with Chinese native plants and their introduction to the western world. Here again the Chinese have played a part, particularly during the last hundred years, exploring little known areas of the country, especially in the west, studying, recording and collecting, slowly piecing together the jigsaw of plant distribution. Vast quantities of dried material have resulted from this activity, much of it deposited in the various provincial botanical institutes and in Beijing.

Fargesia denudata, in the author's garden from N.W. Sichuan. Introduced in 1986 and now grown by many bamboo enthusiasts. (July)

Impatiens omeiana, in Charles Cresson's garden, Philadelphia. A creeping perennial forming colonies when happy. Its pale yellow flowers are eclipsed by the ornamental foliage. (July)

Helleborus thibetanus in the wild in Baoxing, W. Sichuan, China. Now a firm favourite with hellebore enthusiasts and a parent of several garden hybrids. It was introduced by Mikinori Ogisu and others in the 1990s. (March)

Before the founding of the People's Republic in 1949, China supported just two botanic gardens, the Sun Yat-Sen Botanic Garden in Nanjing (established 1929) and the Lushan Botanic Garden in Jiangxi (established 1934). By 1983 the number (including arboretums) had risen to twenty-one distributed across the country. Today (2007), the number listed on the database of Botanic Gardens Conservation International (www.bgci.org) totals 140. Some, at least, of these institutions, whatever else they may be involved in, are concerned with maintaining a representation of the Chinese native flora and to this end regularly dispatch teams into the more remote areas for the purpose of collecting dried and living plants and seed. Some of this seed is made available to western institutions via annual lists (Index Seminum) published by the Chinese institutions concerned. By this means, a regular supply of plants, some of which are new to western cultivation, find their way each year into the gardens of Europe, North America and elsewhere, a refreshing and positive example of the continuing goodwill shared by China and the western world.

But to return to the history of plant exploration in China by the West, a subject with which every plant enthusiast, especially the gardener, is at least, in part, familiar. It is a long and detailed story, the telling of which has been attempted in varying degrees by a host of authorities and authors, the two most notable accounts (in their different ways) being those of Emil Bretschneider and E H M Cox. A truly comprehensive account from the very beginnings to the present day has yet to be published and will require the talents of a remarkable and dedicated person in the mould of a Joseph Needham, editor of Science and Civilization in China. Interestingly, although a comparative handful of well-

Lonicera calcarata, in the author's garden. A powerful climber to 15m or more, notable for its spurred flowers, which change in colour from white through peach to orange. Introduced by Mikinori Ogisu. (June)

Mahonia bodinieri, in the author's garden. A bold foliaged species of recent introduction. It is capable of making a small tree. (September)

Michelia maudiae, in the author's garden. One of the hardiest and most ornamental of several recently introduced species to Western cultivation (May)

Parratia subaequalis, in the author's garden. An erect growing tree compared with the commonly cultivated form of *P persica*, its smaller leaves are capable of rich autumn tints. (October)

Podophyllum delavayi, Tregrehan, Cornwall. A recently introduced species and one of the most exciting foliage perennials for woodland gardens. Here grown in a conservatory. (May)

Podophyllum delavayi, Tregrehan, Cornwall. The curious flowers are borne beneath the foliage and are powerfully if pungently scented. (May)

known plant collectors are responsible for a large proportion of Chinese plants in present-day cultivation, there remain a good many plants which were introduced by individuals of whom we know little or nothing. Sea captains, doctors, customs and legation officials, travellers, missionaries, engineers, merchants and home-based patrons and institutions have all played a part in the introduction of Chinese plants into western cultivation. Some of their names are commemorated in the names of plants they were directly or indirectly responsible for introducing. Other individuals may never be remembered though their introductions continue to bring pleasure.

In passing, it is worth pointing out that a good number of Chinese native plants arrived in western cultivation and continue to do so indirectly via other countries, in particular Japan. Examples include the Foxglove or Goddess Tree *Paulownia tomentosa*, the so-called Sacred bamboo *Nandina domestica*, the Roof iris *Iris tectorum* and, more recently, the several colourful, flowered cultivars of *Loropetalum chinense*. Some of these plants have been cultivated in Japan for centuries, having originally been introduced there by Buddhist monks and others.

Of the major pioneer plant collectors I need say little here. Their exploits have been recorded many times, by themselves or by others, and their legacies fill our gardens today. However, to help readers appreciate the many references to these plant explorers and others in this book, those whose names are especially associated with Chinese

Paeonia decomposita in the wild in W. Sichuan, China. This recently introduced tree peony is noted for its much divided leaves and rose to rose-purple flowers. (May)

Saruma henryi, in the author's garden. Originally discovered by Augustine Henry in the 19th century and now established in Western cultivation from more recent introductions. The generic name is an anagram of *Asarum*. (April)

Pittosporum crispulum, in the author's garden. A small evergreen tree introduced from W. Sichuan in the 1980s. The specific epithet refers to the crisped leaf margins. (April)

Sinocalycanthus chinensis, in the author's garden. This plant was first introduced to Britain as seed from the Shanghai Botanic Garden in 1983. It is presently (2007) 3 x 3m. (June)

Clematis urophylla, in the author's garden (flowered under glass). Originally introduced by Martyn Rix, this has proved to be an excellent winter-flowering climber for a conservatory or outside in warmer regions. It is closely related to *C yunnanensis*. (January)

plants and plant exploration are listed in Appendix 4, along with short biographical details, their main areas of activity or achievement together with an example of a plant named after each. It must be stressed that this is a select list and I regret the omission of those individuals, mainly Chinese, for whom I have been unable to obtain personal details.

This begs the question, what of modern day plant exploration in China? In the last thirty years a great deal has taken place both on the botanical and horticultural front. The Chinese themselves have continued to expand their botanical exploration throughout the country collecting huge numbers of herbarium specimens and publishing their findings in a wide range of journals and books, including a new *Flora of China* both in Chinese and English editions. They have also made extensive collections of living material especially seed, much of which has been grown in the gardens and research collections of the various scientific institutions. Some at least of the seed collected has been made available to institutions and gardens abroad, including in Britain, Europe and N. America.

The number of visits made to China in the same period by foreign botanists and horticulturists, both professional and amateur, has also considerably increased, resulting, among other things, in a new wave of introductions of such magnitude that it would be invidious of me to even attempt to chronicle them. The following brief list, however, is given as an example of the rich temperate flora that continues to surprise and delight both the botanical and horticultural fraternity worldwide as this great country continues to reveal its green secrets: *Acer wuyuanense, Aconitum episcopali, Amentotaxus argotaenia, Asarum magnificum, Aspidistra fungilliformis, Betula insignis, Begonia taliensis, Bergenia emeiensis, Camellia chekiangoleosa, Celtis choseniana, Clematis urophylla, Corydalis flexuosa, Cotoneaster ogisui, Daphne aurantiacus, Disporum longistylum, Epimedium epsteinii, Fargesia denudata, Helleborus thibetanus, Hepatica yamatutai, Impatiens omeiana, Liquidambar acalycina, Lithocarpus variolosus, Lonicera calcarata, Mahonia bodinieri, Michelia maudiae, Melliodendron xylocarpum, Paeonia decomposita, Parrotia subaequalis, Pittosporum crispulum, Pterocarya macroptera* var. *insignis , Podophyllum delavayi, Rhododendron sinofalconeri, Ribes davidii, Saruma henryi, Sinocalycanthus chinensis* and *Tilia chingiana*.

About this book

This is not a history of plant exploration in China though it does contain references to many of the characters who have played a major part in the story. Neither is it a general account of the Chinese flora though over one thousand native plants are described. Rather is it a personal account of the journeys I have made and the plants I have seen principally on six visits to this great country. Its seven chapters are devoted to areas I have visited as leader of botanical treks and tours and once as a member of an expedition. Some plants seen on three subsequent visits have also been included where it was felt appropriate or relevant. The book is aimed as much at gardeners as at those more botanically inclined and I hope enough of general interest is included to amuse both real and armchair travellers.

Due to the diversity of the intended readership I feel it is necessary to explain some aspects of the text:

The country

One of the largest countries in the world, China is just roughly similar in size to Europe or the United States. Its main land mass stretches from latitude 20^0 to 54^0 N, and from longitude 73^0 to 136^0 E, while a myriad of southern islands continue China's territory almost to the equator at 3^0 N. From north to south her territory measures over 5,500km (3,418 miles), and from east to west over 5,000km (3,107 miles), giving a total land area of approximately 9.6 million sq km (3.7 million sq miles).

Contained in this vast expanse is an enormous range of physical features and climatic types, from sea shore to high mountains and plateaux, from rain forest to desert, from near arctic to the tropics. It is said that when the sun rises over the Wusuli river in Heilongjiang province in the north east, it is still dark over the Pamirs in the west, and that when blizzards wrap the north in winter, spring sowing is already underway in Hainan province in the south. Mountains, such an impressive and important feature in China's landscapes as well as in the history of plant exploration, make up around a third of her territory, whilst Highlands in excess of 4,500m (14,765ft) account for another fifth. According to one recent assessment, China boasts 12 million hectares (29 million acres) of lakes, plus 13 million hectares (31 million acres) of marsh, bog and coastal saltmarsh. Peter Wharton

provides an excellent account of China's mountain ranges in *The Natural Landscapes of China and Bordering Regions – A Botanist's View* in *The Jade Garden* (2005).

The flora

Estimates vary as to the extent of China's native flora, though most available opinion places it close to 30,000 species of higher (flowering) plants (including 7,000 species of trees) representing 2,988 genera and 300 families, approximately one eighth of the world total. One mountain alone - Emei Shan (Mt Omei) in Sichuan province - is said to support 3,000 different plants. Because of the great physical and climatic diversity of the land, together with man's influence over the centuries, the native plants of China are unequally spread. There are, for instance, many areas such as deserts and the upper regions of high mountains where the native flora is comparatively limited. The same might be said of those vast areas of cultivation where cereal and other crops are so intensively grown that only the most resilient native plants survive, usually as weeds.

Fortunately, there are considerable areas of the country, especially in the mountains, where the native flora is still as rich as ever it was (though even here it is under increasing pressure) and where there is ample opportunity for western plant enthusiasts to see and experience for themselves some of the 'wondrous things' that thrilled the plant explorers and travellers of old.

Choice of plants

Clearly, it would have been a massive if not impossible task to have attempted to describe in this book all the plants I have seen growing wild in China. I have had to be selective. Most of the plants described are possessed either of ornamental merit or botanical interest. Many are familiar from western cultivation, having been introduced from China, sometimes via Japan or another country, during the last two hundred years or so. Others are rarely or not at all represented in western cultivation. Apart from Chinese native plants actually seen, I have referred to numerous other native plants as well as non-Chinese plants where their inclusion is relevant to the discussion. There are also many references to cultivars (garden varieties) of Chinese plants raised in Chinese, Japanese or Western cultivation.

Zheduo Pass above Kangding, a magnificent mountain landscape with the Minya Konka range to the right. It is in these alpine pastures that on 18th July 1903 E.H. Wilson first set eyes on *Meconopsis integrifolia*, the yellow poppywort. (September)

Plant descriptions

In describing plants already well known in cultivation, eg *Buddleja davidii*, I have generally restricted my remarks to those features considered variable, such as flower size and colour, leaf size, habit, etc. Plants rare or little known in the West, *Keteleeria evelyniana* for instance, have generally been given more detailed descriptions, as have those plants which in western cultivation have been a source of confusion or misidentification, eg *Betula costata* and *Pleione forrestii*. Technical terms have been avoided except where their use clarifies an important point. A Select Glossary of such terms may be found at the end of the book.

Measurements

Wherever possible, the approximate height of a plant seen in the wild state has been given, especially in the case of trees considered to be of exceptional size. Measurements are given in metric with the approximate Imperial equivalent in parentheses.

Measurements of leaves, flowers and other parts of a plant have mostly been taken with a rule, while figures for the height overall of trees and shrubs including the length of climbers are estimated. Where both height and girth or width are given, the height appears first. Measurements given for Chinese trees in British cultivation have mainly been taken from Bean's *Trees and Shrubs Hardy in the British Isles* (8th edition revised) and are largely the work of the late Alan Mitchell – dendrologist and tree measurer extraordinaire. More recent measurements have been provided by the Tree Register of the British Isles (TROBI) in 2006, and from *Champion Trees of Britain and Ireland* (Owen Johnson ed., 2003).

Habitat

So often one is familiar with a plant in cultivation, while knowing little if anything about its native conditions; for example, *Lonicera rupicola* is often unkempt and of little merit in cultivation, very different from the dwarf, compact berry-studded mounds of its native mountains where it is grazed and wind-pruned to shape. I have tried, therefore, to give some indication of the habitat of plants seen in the wild, especially in relation to aspect, altitude and soil as well as to associated plants, in the belief that this may be of use to fellow gardeners in providing the best conditions for such plants in cultivation.

Nomenclature and classification

Wherever possible, I have used those names which currently appear to command the majority opinion. In some instances this has been difficult if not impossible to determine. Where these plants are in British cultivation I have been guided by the current edition of the *RHS Plant Finder*, which is revised annually. For woody plants I have also consulted Bean's *Trees and Shrubs Hardy in the British Isles*. I have also taken into account those volumes so far published of *Flora Reipublicae Popularis Sinicae* and the continuing volumes in English of the *Flora of China*. Recently published accounts and monographs have helped with certain genera such as *Rhododendron*, *Roscoea*, *Hypericum*, *Sorbus* and *Buddleja*. These and other publications and papers consulted are listed in the Bibliography. The scientific names of Chinese native plants described, together with the names of the authorities responsible for first

23

publishing them, are listed in the Index of Plants, Synonyms[1] and Common Names.

For those unfamiliar with the terms used in plant classification, the following simplified explanation given to me by the late Professor W T Stearn may be of some help in understanding the status of plants described in this book.

In our everyday life we are all used to organising related items into convenient groups. Take spoons for instance; there are soup spoons, table spoons, tea spoons and so on. They all have a common characteristic which makes them a spoon but each has its own particular shape and use. Change the bowl of the spoon into a blade and it is no longer a spoon but a knife, and here again there are endless variations on a theme. So it is with plants. For the purposes of this book the highest grouping we need concern ourselves with is that of family. Just as spoon, knife and fork might be said to belong to the cutlery family, so plants such as crab apple (*Malus*), rose (*Rosa*) and bramble (*Rubus*) belong to *Rosaceae*, the Rose family.

In this book families are always spelt with a capital initial and appear in italics, eg *Rosaceae* (Rose family), *Betulaceae* (Birch family), *Magnoliaceae* (Magnolia family) and *Orchidaceae* (Orchid family). The groups within each plant family, eg. *Malus, Rosa, Rubus*, etc, are known as genera (genus singular). Just as spoons are divided into types according to their characteristics and uses, so plant genera are divided into species. Thus, a large genus such as *Rosa* contains numerous species, while some smaller genera contain but a few, in the case of *Kerria* for instance, only one - *Kerria japonica*. The name of a species comprises two words, the first of which is the genus, eg: *Rosa gigantea, Rosa moyesii, Rosa koreana*. The name of the genus is spelt with a capital initial, while the specific epithet (the second word) is spelt with a lower case initial. Both parts of the name appear in italics, eg 'On the hillside stood a tall specimen of *Pinus armandii* rising above a thick scrub in which *Rhododendron decorum* was dominant'.

An exception to this rule concerns those generic names used in a colloquial sense which usually, as in this book, appear in Roman type with a small initial, eg: 'We saw here several rhododendrons and a rather fine spiraea with red flowers'.

A combination of the two might read as follows: 'We saw here several rhododendrons among which *Rhododendron decorum* was dominant'. Where a plant described has a well-known English name this has generally been preferred to a colloquialised generic name, eg: 'The forest supported a mixture of deciduous and evergreen trees including three different pines, the most common of which was *Pinus armandii*'.

Where I describe a plant which I have been unable to identify as to species, it appears in one of two ways, eg: 'Here we found a most unusual species of *Lonicera*' or 'Here grew an unusual *Lonicera* species'.

Variations within a species are sometimes considered significant enough to treat separately under one of three categories. In order of importance these are subspecies,

variety (correctly *varietas*) and forma (usually anglicised as form), and these terms are used in full throughout this book.[2]

It is worth pointing out certain pitfalls which can trap the unwary. In English everyday language, the words variety and form are commonly used in a loose sense to describe any variation from the normal, while variety again is used by many amateurs as a general term in referring to species. Strictly speaking, the term variety (or *varietas*) should be reserved for plants of wild origin while those of garden origin or those specially selected from the wild (many of which have fancy names in English), should be referred to as cultivars. Cultivar names in this book appear with a capital initial and in roman type in single quotation marks, for example *Sophora japonica* 'Pendula'. To illustrate the use of the various categories described above here are a few examples:

Acer	*Acer griseum*
(genus)	(species)

Rhododendron arboreum ssp *delavayi*
(species)　　　　　(subspecies)

Pieris formosa var *forrestii*
(species)　　(variety)

Rosa sericea f *pteracantha*
(species)　(forma)

Sophora japonica 'Pendula'
(species)　　(cultivar)

x placed between the generic name and the specific epithet indicates a plant of hybrid origin, eg *Populus x canadensis*

Two of the most helpful popular accounts in English of plant classification are *Flowering Plant Families of the World*, revised edition (2007) by V H Haywood, R K Brummit, A Culham and O Seberg, and *The Botanical Garden* (2002) by Roger Phillips and Martyn Rix. An invaluable reference of its kind is D J Mabberley's *The Plant Book - A Portable Dictionary of the Higher Plants*. For an explanation of the correct nomenclature of plants and other organisms I can do no better than recommend Charles Jeffrey's book *Biological Nomenclature*, while for those who wish to know more about botanical terms, including the meaning of genus and species, I recommend *The Penguin Dictionary of Botany*.

There are many gardeners who do not appreciate the use of Latin and Greek in the scientific names of wild plants. Why, goes the argument, can't English names be used? English names are fine if one is discussing well-known plants with another English-speaking gardener, but try asking a non-English-speaking Chinese or Russian if he or she knows, for instance, the Trident maple or the Boston ivy, and likely as not you will be met with a blank expression. Ask them if they know *Acer buergerianum* or *Parthenocissus tricuspidata*, which are the scientific names of the two plants, and if your listener is a botanist or a keen gardener the names will more than likely be met with a nod of recognition. I always regard the scientific names of plants as a sort of international botanical language, a botanical esperanto, and I can think of a number of occasions abroad when in using such names I have established at least an initial rapport with non-English-speaking people, including Chinese and Japanese horticulturists and botanists.

Apart from their importance as a means of reference and contact, scientific names are in themselves a fascinating subject, the study of which leads one into many other realms. There are a number of books presently available listing scientific names together with their pronunciation and meaning, and I recommend that such a book be treated by the beginner as an essential pocket companion on all visits to gardens or wild places.

Place names

In general, the Chinese place names mentioned in this book follow the Pinyin system while, for more important locations, the Wade-Giles or Post Office names used in older western produced English language atlases and books have been given in parentheses where necessary. A brief explanation of the Pinyin/Wade-Giles/Post Office systems, together with examples, may be found under Chinese Place Names, Appendix 1.

Plant Collecting in China Today

It will be clear to anyone reading this book that I have been involved in introducing plants from China to western cultivation. I have always tried to do this on a scientific basis, the object being safely to establish in cultivation a particular stock, first for purposes of botanical study and secondly, where appropriate, for ornamental use. A seedling or a pinch of seed has been my preferred method of introduction and I have endeavoured to place such

material in the hands of those persons best qualified to succeed in establishing it. Botanic gardens and specialist collections have been the first to benefit from these introductions on the basis that, should it ever be deemed necessary or wise, plants would be available to return to the wild. Most of my collections have, accordingly, been carefully documented and I have done my best to maintain records of their performance in cultivation.

There is no doubt, however, that the days of plant collecting in the old sense are over and any intelligent person cannot be surprised at this. Forrest's 'mule loads of seed' and Wilson's 'basket loads of bulbs' are, or should be, a thing of the past. In the last twenty-five years the Chinese authorities have realised what collective effect the plant pickings of tourists can have on the flora of certain popular locations, and the digging up of plants and their removal from China is now illegal.

Despite this, large quantities of rare and desirable species dug from the wild continue to find their way (via various channels) to specialist suppliers in Japan and the West. No true plantsman or gardener should encourage or condone this commercial traffic in rare plants, nor should the tourist involve himself in indiscriminate collecting, much of which inevitably ends in disappointment. It simply is not worth it. Far better to use a camera to obtain a permanent record of plants seen in China and to obtain living plants via a legitimate source of supply. Many nurseries offer Chinese plants from stock long established in cultivation, while some specialist nurseries offer plants raised from seeds or plants legally collected or received more recently via reputable sources. Readers are recommended to consult *The RHS Plant Finder*, which includes current sources of supply of many Chinese plants.

1. Synonyms are invalid names, that is, names by which plants were previously known. Where relevant, these are shown in the text in parentheses immediately following the valid or currently accepted names, eg *Viburnum nervosum (cordifolium)*.

2. Species, subspecies, variety and forma may also be abbreviated as follows: species: sp (singular), spp (plural); subspecies: ssp (singular), sspp (plural); variety: var (singular), vars (plural); forma: f (singular), ff (plural).

RUSSIA

MONGOLIA

Amur River

Songhua River

Harbin

Mudanjiang

Jilin

Changchun

Tumen

Antu

Changbai Shan

Heavenly Lake

NORTH
KOREA

Chifeng

Fushun

Tonghua

Shenyang

Jinzhou

Anshan

Dalian

SOUTH
KOREA

Fragrant Hills

Huang He River

BEIJING

Tianjin

Weihai

Yinchuan

Shijiazhuang

Taiyuan

Jinan

Tai'an

Qingdao

CHINA

Xining

Lanzhou

Zhengzhou

Xi'an

Luoyang

Xuzhou

Huaian

Zaozhuang

Nantong

Nanjing

SHANGHAI

☐ 1

Shiyan

Xiangfan

Han River

Wudang Shan

Wushan

Wuhan

Hangzhou

☐ 2

Yangtze River

Wanxian

Yichang

Yangtze River

Chengdu

Nanchang

Shangrao

Wenzhou

Leshan

Chongqing

Gongga Shan

Luzhou

Changsha

Linchuan

Nanping

Fuzhou

Mekong River

Salween River

Yulong Shan

Hengyang

Guiyang

Gan River

INDIA

Lijiang

Cang Shan

Er-hai

Xiaguan

Dali

Kunming

Anning

Lake Dianchi

Liuzhou

Zhangzhou

Xiamen

TAIWAN

Shantou

Guangzhou

BURMA

Yu Jiang River

Nanning

HONG
KONG

VIETNAM

Hong River

Pingxiang

Zhanjiang

LAOS

HAINAN

Haikou

PHILIPPINES

THAILAND

0   500   1000 Miles

0   500   1000   1500 Kilometres

26

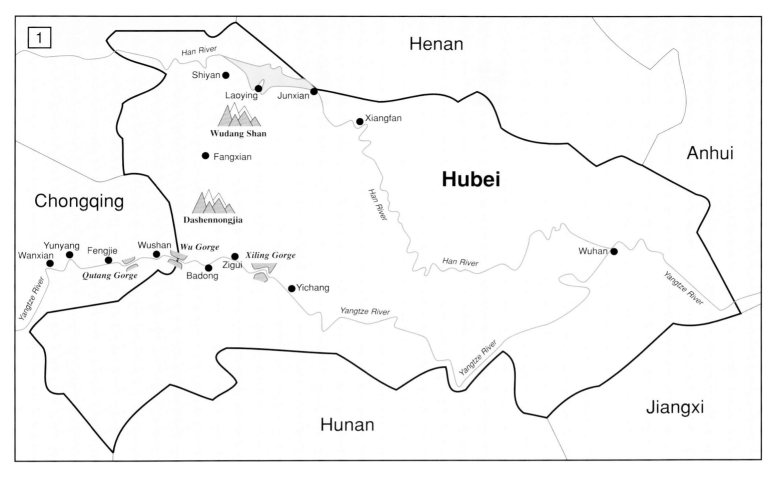

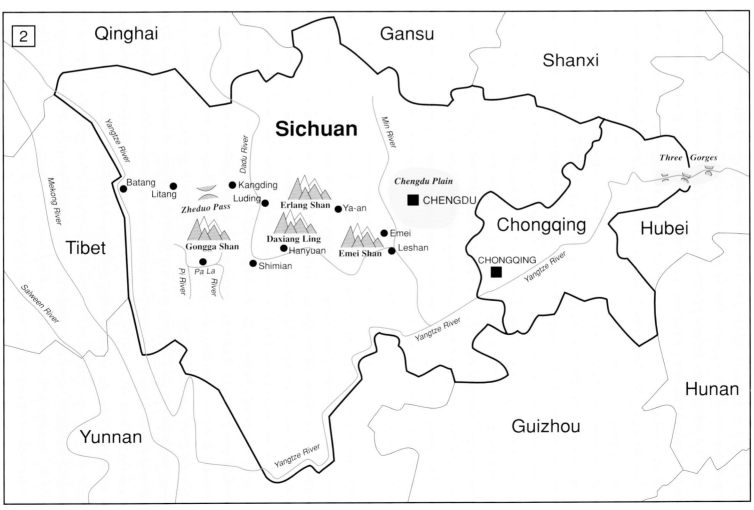

Chapter One

The Hills of Beijing

The Great Wall Express on which we travelled in May 1979

China's capital Beijing (Peking) is situated in the north east of the People's Republic in Hebei province, formerly known as Hopei or Chihli. It is one of only three municipalities, the other two being Shanghai and Tianjin. Approaching the city by air from the south one can see the North China Plain, a vast area stretching seemingly without end to the south and east. Much of this plain, which is intensively cultivated, is less than 50m (164ft) above sea level, while Beijing itself, lying on its northern fringe, is a mere 43m (141ft) above sea level. It often comes as a surprise, therefore, to the first-time visitor, to see range upon range of hills and mountains rising out of the plain to the north and west of the city. Seen from a great height these hills look to be arid and devoid of vegetation, certainly not places likely to interest a plantsman.

The true situation, however, is quite another matter. The hills of Beijing are composed mainly of granite and gneiss with, in the north, some limestone. They range from between a few hundred to 1,000m (3,280ft) high and are part of the ranges connecting the Greater Jingan Mountains to the north and the Taihang Mountains to the south. This series of ranges forms the eastern rim of the Inner Mongolian and Loess plateaux whence the dust storms, a depressingly reliable feature of Beijing winters and springs, originate.

The hills support brown forest or mountain soils of neutral or slightly alkaline reaction, yellowish-brown in colour, well-drained and relatively fertile. In broad terms Beijing, on a similar latitude to Ankara, Madrid, Philadelphia and Denver, enjoys a Continental climate of cold winters and hot summers with four clear-cut seasons. Spring arrives in April giving way to summer at the end of May or early June. Most of Beijing's rain, 625mm (24½ in) per annum, falls in summer when temperatures are at their highest. Autumn lasts from September through to mid-November, when winter intervenes bringing dry, cold weather with infrequent light snowfalls. This pattern holds good for much of the Beijing municipality with slight local variations in the hills. The maximum temperature in summer is 39.5°C (103°F) with a minimum of 10.5°C (51°F). In winter the maximum temperature is 14.5°C (58°C) with a minimum of -19°C (-2°F). July is the hottest month with an average of 25°C (77°F), while January, with an average of -5.5°C (22°F), is the coldest.

At one time Beijing's hills were covered by a deciduous broad-leaved forest in which oaks of several species predominated. The area was part of the most extensive forest community of eastern Asia outside the tropical regions, and in China it extended from the Yangtze Valley to south-eastern Siberia. From earliest times this forest has been subject to indiscriminate felling to provide fuel, building materials or simply to make space for cultivation or construction. Destruction of the forest on the hills of Beijing has continued over many centuries until fairly recent times, accelerated periodically by the needs of war.

In the 1950s tremendous tree planting programmes were initiated by the authorities in an attempt to reclothe the denuded hills. As a result, large tracts of land now support a variety of young trees, mostly species that were once natural features of these hills and an inspiration to poets and emperors.

Bearing in mind the climatic conditions pertaining to the Beijing area, and indeed to north China generally (long hot summers and cold dry winters) it is surprising that so many plants native to the region should be satisfactory in British cultivation. True, the performance of some woody plants is lessened by lack of a regular and thorough summer ripening, but these are comparatively few in number. Even the problem of early bud break, common to many woody plants from the more northerly regions, is of limited occurrence in plants from the Beijing Hills, *Deutzia grandiflora* being a notable exception.

It is now possible for foreign visitors to visit several areas in the hills around Beijing, but far and away the two most popular are those around the Great Wall at Ba-da-ling north of the city, and the famous Fragrant Hills to the west. They may not necessarily be the best but they are easily accessible and fairly representative, supporting as they do a wide selection of interesting plants.

The Great Wall at Ba-da-ling north of Beijing. One of the wonders of the world, it has also been described as one of the greatest pieces of eccentricity. (October)

The Great Wall at Ba-da-ling

Almost everyone knows of the Great Wall. As a schoolboy I vividly remember being shown pictures of this faraway barrier snaking its way up and down interminable hills, nor was I alone in believing the myth that the Great Wall was the only man-made structure on earth visible from the moon. In those days I never even imagined that I would one day see it for myself.

We travelled to the station below the Great Wall at Ba-da-ling by rail and those who have travelled on Chinese trains will know the comfort and enjoyment involved. We sat in large canvas-clad settees with white lace antimacassars. Each settee was mounted on a swivel base giving one the option of sitting in the conventional forward position or, by a flick of a lever, facing the window – as I was when I saw my first Chinese wild spiraea. Having left the plain, the railway track forces its way through the hills along a steep-sided ravine, and here the rocky slopes were splashed with white from the flowers of *Spiraea trilobata*, so called because the small green leaves generally have three main lobes. It is a small shrub, usually forming a mound up to 1m (3ft), occasionally more. In May and June the flowers are borne in domed clusters along the uppersides of the

Spiraea trilobata, a small deciduous shrub, is common in the hills north of Beijing, its flower clusters creating white splashes on stony hillsides in late May, early June. (June)

29

Rhaponticum uniflorum, a bold perennial, its flowerheads resembling those of a giant knapweed (*Centaurea nigra*) and attractive to a wide range of insects. (June)

Caragana sinica, a small loose-habited shrub commonly found on the same slopes as *Spiraea trilobata*. Its small yellow pea-flowers turn brownish-orange with age. (May)

slender hairless branches. Although introduced into cultivation in Britain as long ago as 1801, it has never been common, nor does it flower with quite the same abandon as in its native hills.

Another spiraea found in these hills is *S pubescens*, differing markedly from the other in its diamond-shaped leaves that are boldly toothed above the middle and, in some forms, covered beneath with a dense white pelt of hairs. Even the arching shoots are downy, at least when young. It has white flower clusters in May and June similar to *S trilobata*. Plants from seed collected recently in these hills and elsewhere in north China are vigorous small shrubs with leaves lacking the white pelt. Some have coloured well in autumn before leaf fall.

Growing with the spiraeas were two yellow flowered shrubs with weakly thorny stems. The first of these, *Berberis poiretii*, was an elegant shrub up to 2m (6ft) with arching stems densely clothed with bright green narrow leaves freshly emerged. From each leaf cluster hung a raceme 5-8cm (2-3in) long of pale yellow cup-shaped flowers. This is a most attractive species, uncommon in western cultivation, although first introduced by d'Incarville in the middle of the eighteenth century. Its berries in autumn are slender and bright red. Just as plentiful here is *Caragana sinica* (chamlagu) a loose-habited shrub up to 1.5m (5ft), with arching angular

stems and leaves composed of two pairs of leaflets, the upper pair the larger. The golden yellow pea-flowers turn brownish-orange with age and are carried singly from the leaf axils in May and June.[1] This species is rare in cultivation in Britain, preferring a more Continental-type climate.

At one point our train came to an unscheduled halt and many passengers, Chinese and foreign, climbed down from the carriages to stretch their legs along the side of the track. I lost no time in scrambling up a steep slope above. Here grew a bold perennial, *Rhaponticum uniflorum*, with a rosette of deeply-lobed leaves from the centre of which rose an erect downy stem 30-75cm (12-30in) high bearing, at its summit, a bold pink flowerhead. With it grew a blue flowered ornamental sage, *Salvia miltiorrhiza*, which opens its two-lipped flowers on an interrupted spike. An unusual species this, with leaves separated into paired leaflets. I cannot recollect having seen it in western cultivation. I later saw it being grown in the medicinal plant garden of a village hospital near Guangzhou, where I was told that it is called Dan-shen (red-root sage) by the

1. At the Arnold Arboretum near Boston, Massachusetts, it is said to be the first pea-flowered shrub to open – usually in May. The oldest specimen in the Arboretum grown from seed collected by William Purdom in 1909 is 1.5m (5ft) tall and 4m (13ft) across, forming a tapering mound.

Rehmannia glutinosa, a glandular hairy herb whose long-tubed flowers have a sombre attraction. (June)

Rehmannia glutinosa is widespread in the Beijing area. (June)

Chinese and is used for invigorating the system, to treat inflammation, palpitations and insomnia as well as a cancer remedy.

Another plant commonly used in Chinese traditional medicine is *Rehmannia glutinosa*, a perennial herb with erect stems 30-60cm (1-2ft) high.[2] It is a member of the foxglove family producing racemes of nodding, long-tubed, two-lipped flowers varying in colour from yellowish-buff with purplish veins to purplish-red with creamy-buff on the inner face of the spreading lips. While they cannot be described as colourful, they do possess a dusky attraction that cannot be ignored. The entire plant is covered with a dense pelt of sticky hairs. A number of plants grew in the rubble close to the railway track and we later found it very common in several of Beijing's historical sites including the Old Summer Palace and the Forbidden City where it sprouts from cracks and chinks in walls and paving.

The shrill sound of a guard's whistle disturbed my short sojourn on the hillside and I reluctantly returned with the others to the train, which then moved on to the end of the line at Ba-da-ling, some twenty minutes walk away from the Great Wall. We had already seen the wall, or rather fragments of its numerous subsidiaries, on our way through

the mountains, but the excitement of these glimpses paled by comparison with the main wall. Known in China as the 'Ten Thousand Li Wall', it stretches for some 3,460km (2,150 miles), with a further 2,865km (1,780 miles) of branches and spurs, through the mountains of northern China, from Jiayuguan Pass in Gansu province in the west to Shanhaiguan Pass on the shores of Bohai Bay in Hebei province in the east. Sections of the wall were begun in the Warring States period (fifth century BC) when several Chinese states in the north were fighting not only each other but occasionally the 'barbarians' (nomadic tribesmen) from north of the mountains, especially from what is now Inner Mongolia. According to one Chinese account, the barbarians (a word once used by the Chinese for all foreigners), were excellent horsemen and archers who 'struck and vanished like the wind'. Standing on the wall today, it is not difficult to imagine these wild cavalrymen galloping through the pass that connects the once barren north with the fertile plain to the south. It was to prevent these incursions that the Emperor Qin Shi Huang, under whose reign the empire was united in 221 BC, ordered the various sections of wall to be linked up and extended. It is said that over 300,000 soldiers and 500,000 peasants, many of them press-ganged into service, worked for ten years to complete the project, countless thousands dying in the process. Not surprisingly, considering its great length, its remoteness and the difficulties associated with its manning and maintenance, the wall did not prove totally effective, being breached many times, most notably by Genghis Khan in the 13th century.

2. First recorded in Beijing by d'Incarville around the middle of the eighteenth century, *Rehmannia glutinosa* was probably introduced to Europe some years later by another French Jesuit, Pierre Martial Cibot, who sent seed to the Botanical Garden in St Petersburg. It was reintroduced to the same garden by Bunge early the following century. In cultivation it is usually grown as a pot plant in the cool greenhouse or conservatory and, crossed with *R henryi* has produced an attractive hybrid *R x kewensis*. The genus was named in honour of Joseph Rehmann (1779-1831), a physician of St Petersburg.

Pinus tabuliformis, the North China pine, is native over a wide area and has been replanted on the Beijing Hills in vast numbers. The clusters of male flowers (strobili) in June are conspicuous above the rich green needles. (June)

For the next thirteen centuries the wall suffered long periods of neglect in between programmes of restoration. Today, on gaining access to the wall at Ba-da-ling, one has only to walk for half an hour in either direction to find the wall broken and in some places almost razed to the ground.

Plant enthusiasts visiting the wall have two options: they can climb the wall east or west and gain access to the hillsides beyond the rebuilt sections or via exits on the way up, or they can make straight for the hills from the road below. Either way, a treat awaits. Although little if any of the original forest cover remains, a number of what one assumes to have been the original tree species have, since the 1950s, been planted – sometimes on an impressive scale. None of these are as yet large but they are at least established and already help to soften the otherwise arid-looking hillsides. Most frequent among these are pine, elm, apricot and sumach. The first of these is *Pinus tabuliformis*, the North China pine, which has a wide distribution in the wild from the mountains of western China down to sea level in the plains of the north. This is to north China what *P massoniana* is to the south and is the old and often gnarled pine commonly associated with temples and other sites of religious or historical significance, such as the Forbidden City in Beijing and the Yu Yuan in Shanghai. It is also much

planted in city areas in parks, avenues and around railway stations and airports in the north.

Above Ba-da-ling *P tabuliformis* stains the hillsides dark green and is the only evergreen present in any numbers. Its rich green needles are densely set on the shoots. They are from 7.5-15cm (3-6in) long and borne in pairs, or occasionally in bundles of three. Its solitary cones are ovoid, up to 6cm (2½ in) long, and cling to the branches for several years. The seeds they contain are edible and are sometimes offered for sale along with those of sunflower, lotus and other favourites.

The common elm is *Ulmus pumila*, a small often scrubby tree here but in suitable situations capable of 20m (65ft) or more eventually.[3] In cultivation in Britain, where this species is not common, there are several trees in excess of 10m (33ft), the record being held by a tree of 22m (72ft) in Mote Park, Kent (1995). It is easily recognised by its dark, almost blackish, rugged bark (on older trees certainly), and small, dark green, coarsely-toothed leaves up to 7.5cm (3in) long. These are usually evenly tapered or rounded at the base, unlike those of most other elms, including the equally small-leaved *U parvifolia*, which are unequal-sided. The flowers of *U pumila* are borne on the naked twigs in early spring and are replaced in May by clusters of green, disc-like fruits notched at the apex. One of

Pinus tabuliformis as a planted tree is commonly associated with temples and other sites of religious or historical importance as well as railway stations and airports in the north. Here old and carefully trained specimens in the Forbidden City in Beijing well demonstrate the meaning of the scientific name *tabuliformis* - 'flat topped'. (June)

our Chinese guides on a subsequent visit told me that the fruits are edible when young and are mixed with wheat flower and made into pancakes. The tree was extensively planted in North America, especially in the mid-west where it was much in demand by farmers and others because of its ability to resist neglect, drought and extremes of temperature. Anyone having travelled in northern China, experiencing the winter cold and summer heat, will not be surprised by this. More recently, this elm has shown resistance to Dutch elm disease, *Ceratocystis ulmi*, although, in America certainly, its leaves are beloved by insect pests. Rural areas apart, U *pumila* is considered by many to be an inferior ornamental and landscape tree compared with that other small-leaved Asiatic elm U *parvifolia*.

Another elm commonly found in these hills is *Ulmus macrocarpa*, native over a wide area of north-east Asia.[4] It is usually seen as a large shrub but is capable of making a tree up to 13m (42ft) or more. Its distinguishing characteristic is the three year old shoots, which are hairy and often furnished with two corky wings. The leaves are distinct in being extremely

harsh to the touch (like sandpaper), due to a coating of short bristles on both surfaces. The fruits, too, are roughly hairy and measure 2-3cm (¾ - 1¼ in) long, the largest in the genus.

Ulmus macrocarpa is usually seen as a small tree or large shrub; the winged branchlets of this Chinese elm are a characteristic feature. (October)

3. *Ulmus pumila* has a very wide distribution in the wild, from Korea across Siberia and north China to central Asia, and was in cultivation in the West by the middle of 19th century. In North America it is associated (or should be) with Frank Meyer who, during the early part of the 20th century, introduced great quantities of scions and seed of this tree via the US Department of Agriculture.

4. *Ulmus macrocarpa* has been known to western botanists since Père David's collections in the mid-1800s, but was apparently first introduced in 1908 by Frank Meyer to the Arnold Arboretum. It is an interesting elm without, however, being especially ornamental.

Prunus armeniaca flowering on a hillside below the Great Wall east of Ba-da-ling in early spring. The pale pink blossoms brighten the otherwise drab landscape and are welcomed by the Chinese as a sign that warmer days are here. (April)

Prunus davidiana. The white or pink flowers of this handsome wild peach appear before the leaves in late winter, to be followed by small green downy fruits. It is plentiful in the Beijing area, both wild and cultivated, and is particularly common on the site of the Old Summer Palace where this picture was taken. (June)

If one visits the Ba-da-ling area in early spring it is to see the hillsides painted with a delicate colourwash of pink, for this is the flowering season of the wild apricot, *Prunus armeniaca*, which has been planted here in tens of thousands.[5] Already, it looks quite at home with the native vegetation if, indeed, it is not itself a native of these hills. Here it is shrubby, occasionally forming a round-headed tree to 5m (16ft) though capable of twice that size elsewhere. The flowers are normally pale pink or blush, and are produced singly on short spurs from the shoots of the previous year. This early flush of beauty is replaced by the comparatively subdued though polished green of summer leafage, only to come alive again in autumn when the leaves, which are rounded and abruptly pointed, take on colourful tints of red, orange and copper. The rounded downy fruits, 3cm (1¼ in) wide, mature to a yellowish shade sometimes tinged red. As far as I am aware the fruits of the wild apricots are not eaten, being rather fibrous and harsh in flavour, although an oil is, or used to be, expressed from the fresh kernels. It is significant that Frank Meyer, that 'hawk eye' of a fruit and seed collector, made no

collections of this apricot in China. The medicinal value of the fruits is another story. The dried kernels of the apricot have long been used in China as a herbal remedy for cancer, the common cold, coughs, asthma, constipation in old men, and following childbirth in women.

The closely related Japanese apricot, *P mume*, is also cultivated in the Beijing area, though only as a pot plant or as penjing (bonsai). In the wild, according to Yü, it is mainly distributed in southern China, where it is also extensively cultivated for its edible kernel. It was introduced to Japan at a very early date and became so popular there that, according to a recent authority, over three hundred garden varieties have been named.

In cultivation in England, the above two are best grown against a south- or west-facing wall where *P mume* certainly will flower tolerably well in February or March, scenting the air around. Of the several forms of *P mume* occasionally

5. According to Professor T T Yü, *P armeniaca* is represented in north China by several garden or cultivated varieties (cultivars) most of which are grown for their edible fruits. The truly wild form he believes should be referred to as variety *ansu*. Botanically, it differs only in minor characters from the cultivated tree, although its kernel is said to be edible.

available in Britain, 'Alphandii' (semi-double pink), 'Omoi-no-mama' (semi-double white) and 'Beni-shidare' (double, rich, madder-pink, strongly fragrant) are the most satisfactory, although others of equal merit may from time to time become available.

Staying with prunus, I shall never forget my first sight of the so-called 'Père David's peach', *Prunus davidiana*, flowering one February in the old Winter Garden at the University of Cambridge Botanic Garden. I was a student then and both the rose-pink flowers of forma *rubra* and the white flowers of forma *alba* were included in one of our regular plant identification tests. Both trees were rather erect in habit, some 6m (20ft) tall each on a 2m (6ft) stem. It has never been a common tree in British cultivation partly, I suppose, because the early blossoms are doubly susceptible to frost and bullfinches. Given a sheltered position, however, and a warm summer to ripen growth it is a tree well worth considering. *Prunus davidiana* is a native of north China and is particularly common in the hills of Beijing where it occurs both wild and planted.

It was first collected here in 1865 by the missionary after whom it is named, Père Armand David. On the site of the Old Summer Palace north west of the capital, this peach is abundant, and on a visit there in June 1984 I collected a handful of fruits. These resulted in seedlings of two distinct kinds, one with reddish young shoots, which I take to be the pink-flowered type, and another with pale green shoots, which I suspect will have white flowers. The leaves are lance-shaped, tapering gradually to a slender point like some elegant willow. Frank Meyer, the American collector who saw this tree many times on his travels through north China in the early part of the twentieth century, reported that it was very resistant to drought and alkaline soil and that it was extensively used by the Chinese as a stock on which to graft flowering peaches and plums as well as small bush cherries and apricots.

Until my first visit to the Great Wall I always thought of *Cotinus coggygria*, the Smoke tree or Venetian sumach, as being a native of central or southern Europe. I first saw it on the sun-baked hills of northern Greece where, from a distance, its grey plumose inflorescences bore a fanciful resemblance to puffs of smoke. Its distribution, however, is much greater and extends eastwards to the drier areas of the Himalaya and into central and northern China where it is said to be represented by *Cotinus coggygria* variety *cinerea*, though how this differs from the typical form is hard to discern. On the hills above Ba-da-ling it thrives, forming large clumps and thickets with occasional individuals tree-like up to 5m (16ft). The rounded or obovate leaves are typical, and where branches have been cut the wood is seen to be yellowish; certainly in Europe a yellow dye used to be obtained from the branches of this plant. It covers large areas of hillside on both sides of the wall often mixing with *Prunus armeniaca*. Like the apricot, its leaves offer

Cotinus coggygria variety *cinerea*. The fiery foliage of this hardy sumach is a spectacular feature of the Beijing Hills in autumn. Here in the hills below the Great Wall at Ba-da-ling it is joined by the equally rich tints of *Prunus armeniaca*. (October)

no great attraction in summer but give exceptional red and orange tints in autumn. On a visit in October 1980 I was spellbound by the combination of the prunus and sumach painting the hillsides with bold bands and splashes of fiery orange and red. Seen against the rich green of the pine and the neutral clay colours of the surrounding landscape it created an unforgettable picture.

On our approach through the hills that October day, we saw in several places the unmistakable scrambling growths of a most ornamental deciduous climber the Chinese bittersweet – *Celastrus orbiculatus*. Its rounded leaves had already turned a rich yellow, while the pea-sized yellowish fruits were splitting to reveal the brilliant scarlet-coated seeds. Here it clothed steep banks or clambered over hillside scrub, but given the necessary support it can reach a great height. Indeed, the finest specimens I know of still grow in the garden planted by Lord Swaythling at Townhill Park, Southampton. There two exceptional plants, with twining

35

Iris lactea flowering freely in a dry sunny bed in the Summer Palace near Beijing. Of wide distribution in the wild, from Kazakhstan in Russia, east to south-east Siberia, north, central and west China. (June)

Iris ruthenica variety *nana* - a dwarf form of this variable species, its flowers preceding the narrow leaves. (May)

stems as thick as a man's arm, have reached 18m (59ft) at least in a large English oak, their combined branches forming a vast tapestry in the oak's crown, hanging in long curtains and streamers that turn the colour of the sun in autumn. Being dioecious in function, one of these giants is a male the other female, and so it must normally be if this climber is being considered for its bright fruits. There are in cultivation, however, hermaphrodite forms (with perfect flowers) that are propagated by cuttings or grafting. Beautiful though this climber is, especially when its fruits spangle the stems from November through to January, it is rampant and suitable only for the largest gardens and parks where it is best trained into an old or declining tree. If male and female forms are planted these can be placed together in the same hole.[6]

But to return to my first visit in early June 1979. Having laboured up the steeply inclined wall for half an hour or so I came to a place where it was broken, affording easy access to the hillside and an abundance of interesting plants. At this time of the year the weather is already warm, 25°C (77°F) on average, and the ice cream and drink vendors of the valley do a steady business with the large numbers of tourists, Chinese and foreign, arriving by bus, car and train. Surprisingly, and fortunately, few of them venture from the wall and one can botanise in comparative peace. The first plant I noticed was an *Iris* species with clumps of green grassy leaves rising above single, slate-blue, fragrant flowers on short stems. It proved to be I *ruthenica*, a widely distributed species from Korea westwards across China and Asiatic Russia to eastern Europe. Not surprisingly it is variable, and four years later in early May

I found on the hillside above Ba-da-ling station a dwarf form, possibly *Iris ruthenica* variety *nana*, whose deep blue flowers were opening almost as soon as they emerged from the ground. The flowers, of course, are not plain, the falls carrying a tracery of blue, lavender or violet on a white ground, while the standards and styles are violet or slate-blue without variegation. It grows commonly on the hills and is especially plentiful at the base of the wall, where grows another species, I *dichotoma*, now generally considered as belonging to the genus *Pardanthopsis* of which it is the only species (P *dichotoma*).

There is no possibility of confusing the two, P *dichotoma* having clumps of glaucous green leaves 2.5cm (1in) across carried in fans like those of a bearded iris. From the leaf fan rises an erect stem, much branched and up to 1m (3ft) high. The flowers, however, are of no great ornament, being small for the size of plant, short-lived and, in the case of the Great Wall plants, a creamy, almost dirty white with purplish brown spots and streaks on the falls. It is uncommon in cultivation, which does not surprise me, but in America it has been crossed with another Chinese relative of iris – *Belamcanda*, to produce, according to Brian Mathew of Kew, some extraordinary intermediates some of which are ornamental.

Another perennial we found flowering both on and below the Great Wall in June 1979 was *Thalictrum petaloideum*,

6. Although first recorded and collected by Sir George Staunton during Lord Macartney's mission in 1793, C *orbiculatus* was not successfully introduced to western cultivation until some seventy years later via Japan by the Russian botanist Maximowicz. A further introduction was effected in 1882 when Emil Bretschneider sent seed he had collected in the Beijing Hills to several western gardens.

Ziziphus jujuba (ziziphus), a curious form of the jujube with spiralling shoots. A cultivated plant in the Imperial Garden of the Forbidden City. (October)

Once a summer retreat of emperors, the Summer Palace near Beijing is now a popular venue for the Chinese people who specially enjoy boating on the Kumming Lake. Although the first palace was built here in the twelfth century, the present buildings date only from the late nineteenth century. (June)

a clump-forming plant with much divided fern-like leaves and erect flowering stems to 76cm (30in). These were branched above and flourished numerous small flowers which, despite their lack of petals, were rendered conspicuous by their clusters of white stamens. It was a most attractive plant and, as far as I am aware, was not represented in western cultivation until a seedling was given to the Royal Botanic Gardens, Kew in 1980. Its nearest relation appears to be T aquilegiifolium.

After the trees already mentioned, the dominant vegetation on the hills above Ba-da-ling is the scrub layer, a fascinating mixture of shrubs most of which are undoubtedly native, having in some instances survived many times being cut to the ground for firewood and fodder. One of the most plentiful shrubs is the jujube – Ziziphus jujuba. Its cultivated thornless form (variety inermis) can be seen in many a garden and backyard in the Beijing area, but in the hills the thorny-stemmed wild plant (variety spinosa) prevails, usually forming a dense low tangle with occasional specimens to 3m (10ft) high. The arrangement of the spines in pairs, one long and straight the other short and decurved, is characteristic and

incidentally plays havoc with bare flesh or looseknit clothing. The small, fleshy damson-shaped fruits produced singly in the leaf axils ripen to a brownish-red and have a pleasant acid taste when fresh. They are more palatable, however, when dried. The dried ripe seeds are used in Chinese traditional medicine for anxiety, insomnia, night sweats and dizziness, and for what is quaintly referred to as 'hand and foot' fever.[7]

Despite evidence of man's activities, the mountains north of Beijing have a wild, rugged appearance which is only slightly softened by a green film of low vegetation. (June)

7. The abundance of Ziziphus jujuba (ziziphus) in the Beijing Hills was noted by several early collectors, including, on his visit in 1861, Robert Fortune, who referred to it as a species of buckthorn – Rhamnus, to which of course Ziziphus is related. In fact, a true buckthorn, Rhamnus globosa, is commonly found growing with the jujube but is easily recognised by its small single spines, densely branched, often compact habit and clusters of tiny blackish fruits. R parvifolia is similar and also common in these hills. Neither of the buckthorns are, to the best of my knowledge, in western cultivation. Ziziphus, of course, has long been grown in those countries enjoying warm summers. There is a large specimen in the garden of La Mortala near Ventimiglia on the Italian coast, and another of 6 x 7.5m (20 x 25ft) in the Brooklyn Botanic Garden, New York. Both fruit freely.

Vitex negundo variety *heterophylla*, the form most commonly represented in the Beijing Hills, with jaggedly toothed leaves. (June)

flowering later than in the wild. In colder areas it makes an attractive if not spectacular subject for a sheltered, south-facing wall where it should be pruned in the same way as one would prune *Buddleja davidii* (ie cutting back the old flowering shoots in March). The introduction of *V negundo* variety *heterophylla* from north China to Europe is generally acknowledged to have been made by Pierre d'Incarville from Beijing to Paris, and thence, in 1758 or thereabouts, to London and Philip Miller at the Chelsea Physic Garden by Monsieur Richard, gardener to Louis XV at Versailles.

From the Beijing Hills, d'Incarville also introduced *Lycium barbarum* (*halimifolium*), the Chinese boxthorn or wolfberry.[8] The purple flowers are scattered all along the arching, occasionally spiny shoots giving way to bright scarlet or orange egg-shaped berries, up to 2.5cm (1in) long, which are said to be sweet and to have various medicinal uses. Indeed, it is cultivated as a crop in parts of northern China, especially in Ningxia province. According to a recent report, the dried ripe fruit and root bark are used in China in the treatment of cancer as well as for impotence and backache. It is not uncommon in British cultivation, thriving best on light soils especially by the sea and, given a warm summer, crowds its many branches with colourful berries. A word of warning, however; once established in ideal conditions it suckers freely to form a large thicket, ideal if one needs to arrest soil erosion but bad news where less aggressive neighbouring plants are involved.

In the hills of Beijing, as elsewhere in China, soil erosion is a problem and any plant that helps arrest or prevent it is important. Another such plant is *Myripnois dioica*, a low-growing deciduous shrub that suckers to form dense patches. It is an interesting plant botanically, a member of the groundsel family – Compositae, with small privet-shaped leaves 2-4cm (¾ -1½ in) long and small flowerheads in the axils of the leaves. These are dioecious (male and female on separate plants), the females having parachuted seeds like those of a dandelion. Interesting it is, ornamental it most certainly is not, a criticism one would not level at *Deutzia grandiflora*, another shrub abundant in these hills. In June 1979 it was past flowering, but on my visit in early May 1983 it was at its best. From a distance, it reminded me of a snowy mespilus or juneberry, *Amelanchier* species, its flowers appearing with or before the new leaves, creating white splashes on the landscape. Produced singly or in twos or threes, these flowers at 2.5-3cm (1-1¼ in) across are the largest of any deutzia and also the earliest to appear. It can reach 2m (6ft) in the wild and a large bush in full flower is a lovely sight, its petals often washed a faint blush as they open. *D grandiflora* is, unfortunately, a sight rarely seen in cultivation in Britain where it is not normally the happiest of shrubs. Like certain other woody plants from

Another plant that first caught my eye in June 1979 was *Vitex negundo*, a loose-stemmed shrub occasionally growing to 3m (10ft) high, but usually half this height in the hills, where it is very common. The leaves are divided into five leaflets, which are sharply toothed, while the tiny violet-blue or pale blue flowers are carried from late spring through summer in slender interrupted spikes or panicles at the ends of the branches. In the wild *V negundo* is distributed from India and Sri Lanka to China and, not unnaturally, is variable in leaf shape and flower colour. Most if not all the plants I have seen wild in the Beijing Hills belong to *Vitex negundo* variety *heterophylla* (*incisa*) in which the leaves are smaller and the leaflets deeply-toothed or cut, presenting a more delicate, sometimes lace-like, effect. Even this variety is variable and individuals can be found with leaves resembling in form (but not colour) those of the fern-leaved maple *Acer palmatum* 'Dissectum'.

Because of the need for summer sun to ripen its growths, *V negundo* is less common in British cultivation than its attractions would merit, although summers of the late 1970s and early 1980s did much to enhance its credibility here. In gardens it makes a wide-spreading shrub, generally

8. This plant was acquired by Miller for the Chelsea Physic Garden. At the time of its arrival in England there were some who mistakenly believed this to be the plant from which tea was made. One such was Archibald Campbell, 3rd Duke of Argyll (1682-1761), who had a notable tree collection on his estate at Twickenham, London. Presumably from this association arose another English name for the plant – 'Duke of Argyll's tea tree'.

Deutzia grandiflora. Its flowers, which appear with or before the leaves, are the largest in the genus, creating splashes like snow clouds on the otherwise tired brown hillsides. (May)

Deutzia grandiflora is common on slopes and among rocks in the Beijing Hills. Here it is pictured below the Great Wall at Ba-da-ling. (May)

north China it comes into growth too early with us and is all too frequently checked by frost. It was first collected by Bunge in the vicinity of Beijing and is said to occur in Hubei and Shaanxi provinces as well as in north China.

Another deutzia found in these hills, though less common and less ornamental than *D grandiflora,* is *D parviflora.* As the name suggests, its individual flowers are much smaller and carried in branched heads at the ends of the shoots in May or early June. I have seen it on two occasions, once in a small ravine growing with *Philadelphus pekinensis,* the local mock orange. From an ornamental standpoint the latter is rather ordinary compared with most other members of the genus. In some ways it resembles the European *P coronarius,* having similar racemes of cream-coloured, fragrant flowers 2.5cm (1in) across produced in late May to early June.

In the same ravine in October 1980 I saw *Euonymus alatus* variety *apterus,* the smooth-stemmed version of the winged spindle, an elegant shrub of some 2m (6ft) with slender arching green shoots and leaves already displaying a crimson autumn suffusion. While in western cultivation *E alatus* is fairly common, variety *apterus* is less so and mainly confined to specialist collections. A splendid example can be seen in the woodland garden at Knightshayes Court in Devon, where

one of two specimens measures 2.5 x 4.5m (8 x 15ft) and is a charming picture in early winter when the leafless branches are strung with orange-seeded red capsules.

Euonymus alatus variety *apterus.* Differing from the typical plant in its unwinged branchlets, this attractive shrub is frequent in the Beijing Hills. The plant pictured grows in the gardens of Knightshayes Court in Devon. (November)

Euonymus bungeanus cultivated plant in France demonstrating the characteristic pale yellow almost straw colour of autumn leaves. (October)

Euonymus bungeanus is a small tree of elegant arching growth with characteristically slender-pointed leaves. The pale pink capsules crowd the branches in autumn. Photographed in the wild at Ba-da-ling. (October)

Clematis tubulosa, here photographed by Raymond Evison in the hills N.E. of Beijing. (September)

Different again is *Euonymus bungeanus*, named after the Russian botanist Alexander von Bunge and first introduced to Britain by Bretschneider in 1883 from north China. In the valleys south of Ba-da-ling I have seen it as a large shrub or small tree to 7m (23ft) high, its leaves in autumn a pale lemon yellow against which the yellowish or pinkish white capsules and orange seeds are shown to good effect. It is a popular street tree in some northern cities and there are several excellent examples in the vicinity of the Forbidden City in Beijing. There is no question that it does best in a continental climate, enjoying a long hot summer when it will fruit abundantly, an event which, in Britain, is all too infrequent.

The genus *Clematis* is better represented in China than elsewhere and several species are found in the Beijing Hills. At Ba-da-ling the visitor may expect to see four of these, *C tubulosa*, *C aethusifolia*, *C brevicaudata* and *C hexapetala*, flowering at

Clematis aethusifolia, a fragile, slender-stemmed species scrambling over low scrub in the Beijing Hills. (October)

Clematis hexapetala, an herbaceous species common in the Beijing Hills where it grows among rough grass and scrub. (May)

Boehmeria nivea, a non-stinging relative of the nettle once commonly cultivated in China for its fibre, one of the strongest known. It is frequently found as a weed in towns and cities and in waste places. The leaves are silvery white beneath. Forbidden City, Beijing. (May)

different seasons. *Clematis aethusifolia* is a fragile, slender-stemmed plant scrambling through and over low vegetation. Its leaves are downy and finely divided, indeed, as the name implies, not unlike those of the fool's parsley – *Aethusa cynapium*. In late summer the flowers appear, small, slender, pale yellow nodding bells each on an erect slender stalk. Plants grown from seed collected by the Great Wall have flowered in Britain. It is a charming if unspectacular species, suitable for training over a low support such as a shrub or trellis where its stems are capable of reaching 2m (6ft) or more. By comparison, *C brevicaudata* is less ornamental and rarely seen in cultivation. Indeed, the only plants I have encountered in Britain are from recent seed introductions. It is a woody climber and in the Beijing Hills is quite commonly seen scrambling over neighbouring shrubs and into the lower branches of trees. Its leaves are coarser than those of *C aethusifolia* and its small flowers, borne in dense panicles, are star-shaped with conspicuous stamens after the fashion of our native Traveller's joy – *C vitalba*.

Very different in effect is *C tubulosa*, a sub-shrubby or herbaceous species of 1m (3ft). The leaves are large and coarse, made up of three leaflets, the terminal one being by far the largest. The flowers, too, are unusual, being tubular with a swollen base and four spreading lobes resembling those of a florist's hyacinth. They are blue and borne in clusters in the joints of the shoots from late summer into early autumn.

Previously known as *C heracleifolia* var. *davidiana*, this handsome clematis was introduced as seed from the Beijing area to France by the Abbé David in 1863. It differs from the related *C heracleifolia* with which it is commonly confused in gardens in its larger, upright, strongly fragrant

flowers in bunched axillary clusters, male and female flowers on separate plants (dioecious), (monoecious in *C heracleifolia*). *C tubulosa* is more commonly cultivated in Western gardens and is a parent of several garden hybrids, such as 'Campanile', 'Cote d'Azur', 'Crepuscule', 'Mrs Robert Brydon' and 'C x jouiniana'. Well known in Britain, 'Wyevale' is a darker blue selection of *C tubulosa*. All are valuable for their hardiness and late summer to autumn displays.

The Great Wall is being refurbished at Ba-da-ling to give visitors some idea of its original state. It was built wide enough to allow five horsemen or ten soldiers to move along abreast. (June)

Lilium pumilum. A member of the Martagon or Turk's-cap group, it is widespread throughout north China, occurring on stony slopes in grass or scrub and on the margins of woodland, usually in full sun. (June)

Lilium pumilum. A typical plant with flower buds almost open in late June. The slender grass-like spiralling leaves are characteristic. (June)

The highest watch tower at Ba-da-ling stands on a hilltop and is reached only after a steep climb – which the Chinese equate with 'climbing a ladder to heaven'. In late June 1984 I slogged up the 'heavenly ladder' to show several members of a group I was leading some of the plants I had seen on previous occasions. It is worth mentioning at this point that such is the variety of the flora of the Beijing Hills that, in four visits to Ba-da-ling, I have each time encountered new (to me) and interesting plants. On this occasion we were lucky enough to find a lily and a day lily in flower, both in fair quantity. The lily was *Lilium pumilum* (*tenuifolium*), a member of the Martagon group with a slender wiry stem up to 50cm (20in) high clothed with numerous slender grass-like green leaves. The nodding flower is slender and tapered in bud, the petals gradually peeling away and strongly recurving to assume the familiar Turk's cap shape. I examined several flowers and they measured on average 5cm (2in) across and from one to three per stem. Their colour – a clear brilliant sealing wax scarlet – was an absolute giveaway, otherwise we should not have seen this little lily among the herbs and scrub in which it grew. The same might be said for the day lily *Hemerocallis minor*, although its leafy clumps are more substantial and obvious. Its arching leaves, green and strap-shaped, are topped by the 50-75cm (20-30in) stem bearing three or more flowers. Only one flower opens at a time and this is yellow and trumpet shaped with spreading segments. We could see the day lilies from the wall top, some clumps growing right against its base, sometimes in association with *Iris ruthenica* in fruit at the time.

In 1976, during a tour to China by Peter Green and John Simmons, Deputy Director (now retired) and Curator respectively of the Royal Botanic Gardens at Kew, a visit was made to the Great Wall at Ba-da-ling where many plants were noted. Among them was a lilac – *Syringa pekinensis.* At the beginning of May 1983, when visiting the same area, I resolved to try and find it for myself. On the day of my visit, a Chinese holiday, the Great Wall was swarming with visitors and rather than face the inevitable hassle I decided to climb into the hills from the road.

Hemerocallis minor. The flowers of this day lily can often be seen from the Great Wall in June and July. (June)

Syringa pekinensis. Resembling a privet in many ways, the white flowerheads of this large shrub stand out among the plantations of North China pine on a hillside above Ba-da-ling. (June)

Syringa pubescens. This lilac was first found in the Beijing Hills by Russian collectors in 1831. Its flowers are sweetly fragrant. (May)

flower well. Naturally it fares better on the continent of Europe and in North America than in Britain. It is slow in growth to start with, and seedlings I have from seed collected in 1983 had grown no more than 7 or 10cm (2¾ or 4in) in the first two years, and flowered for the first time in May 1988.[9]

Peter Green, who is a noted authority on the family *Oleaceae*, which includes *Syringa*, kindly examined and identified my Great Wall lilac the year before he retired from Kew and I then took the opportunity of asking him where exactly he had seen *Syringa pekinensis*. With his instructions in my head I once again climbed the 'heavenly

It was a bright sunny day and both *Deutzia grandiflora* and *Caragana sinica* were at their best, a fact which did not escape the notice of Chinese visitors, some of whom carried bunches of their flowering shoots from picnics in the hills. I followed a promising ravine for some distance, hearing but not seeing the activity on the nearby wall. Suddenly I spotted the unmistakable flowers of a lilac on the slopes above and I rejoiced. Only one thing puzzled me, these flowers were lilac, violet in bud, and very different from the white-flowered *Syringa pekinensis*. On reaching the spot I found several bushes 1.5m (5ft) high clothed with broad-based (ovate) leaves to 6cm (2½ in) long. The flowers were borne in dense conical or rounded trusses after the fashion of *S vulgaris*, the common lilac, only smaller. As expected, they were deliciously fragrant. I carried one truss down triumphantly, to share with my colleagues, but it was not until my return home that I was able to have it identified as *Syringa pubescens*. Dwarfed on the hills, by frequent cutting perhaps, this species is capable of 3-4.5m (10-15ft) in cultivation where it requires a long summer ripening to

9. *S pubescens* is widespread in northern China and was first collected (as herbarium specimens) in the Beijing Hills by the Russians Bunge and Kirilov in 1831. Its first introduction as seed to western cultivation is attributable to Bretschneider, who collected it in the same hills fifty years later.

Syringa oblata is a native of north China and commonly cultivated, as on this railway station south of Ba-da-ling. (May)

Two of the twelve stone human statues, a military mandarin and a civilian mandarin lining The Sacred Way to the Ming Tombs. These symbolise the loyal cortège of the dead emperor and date from the 15th century. Beijing (June 1979)

ladder' in late June 1984 and, when only a short distance from the highest watchtower, saw the Pekin lilac on the hillside below to my left. It took me but a few minutes to climb down from the wall and descend the steep slope to

where the lilac grew. There were several small bushy trees of some 2-3m (6-10ft) with lenticelled, cherry-like bark on the main stems. The leaves were small, broad-based and abruptly pointed. The privet-like, creamy-white flowers were carried in dense shapeless heads and gave off a mealy, fungus-like smell, not unpleasant but certainly no match for *S pubescens*. Its flowers were almost blown but enough remained to help us spot this tree as clumps and individuals scattered over a wide area. Like *S pubescens*, *S pekinensis* was first introduced to the West by Bretschneider and shares the same liking for long hot summers, although, surprisingly, it is free flowering at Kew and elsewhere in Britain, though it is by no means common.

Lilacs apart, some of the most interesting plants of the Great Wall area are those which require one to get down on hands and knees in order fully to appreciate their beauty. Among these are a creeping thyme – *Thymus mongolicus*, very much like our own *T serpyllum*. But for me, pride of place goes to the Chinese pasque flower, *Pulsatilla chinensis*, which is widely distributed in these hills. It is similar in flower to our native species *P vulgaris*, the blooms emerging from the still brown grass on a silky hairy stem. As the silky leaves expand, the royal-purple flower is seen looking up as it opens to reveal a handsome boss of golden stamens through which the purple brush of styles protrude. It is a gem of a plant and when I first saw it in

The site of the Old Summer Palace was once a magnificent pleasure ground for the Imperial court. Built by the Emperor Qian Long between 1740 and 1747, the many palaces and landscaped gardens were destroyed by British and French forces in 1860. The planted pines are *Pinus bungeana*. A wild peach, *Prunus davidiana* also grows here. (June 1979).

Pulsatilla chinensis. The rich purple flower with its corona of golden stamens moved Reginald Farrer to name this plant the 'Purple Emperor'. (May)

Pulsatilla chinensis, the Chinese pasque flower, is widely distributed in the Beijing Hills. The leaves enlarge greatly after flowering. (May)

early May 1983 it was in full flower, its richly-coloured stars studding the grassy places on the hillsides, descending even to the roadside by the Ba-da-ling railway station. By late June the fluffy white seed heads have developed on elongating stems and, with its considerable broadly-lobed leaves, it bears little resemblance to the flowering plant of spring.[10]

Although there is undoubted comfort in travelling to the wall at Ba-da-ling by train there are decided advantages in taking the alternative route by road. While roadworks and city traffic may slow one down initially, the benefits of being able to stop, however briefly, on the journey through the hills make the delays more tolerable. I have done this on two occasions, each time stopping at different locations to discover plants not seen at Ba-da-ling. The ravine with the euonymus and philadelphus was one such place. In 1984 we stopped at another, by the old entrance gate to the pass that lies to the right of the road where it begins to climb through the hills. The gate is of white marble and inside are bas-reliefs of Buddhist themes with inscriptions in Chinese

and other languages thought to date from the fourteenth century. Nearby is an easily accessible ravine whose flora no doubt is typical of hundreds of others in these hills.

On a rock face near the mouth of the ravine grew two unusual ferns one of which, *Cheilanthes argentea*, had tufts of small, finely divided fronds with silver backs. It sprung from tiny crevices, those on the exposed surface of the rock dry and shrivelled but soon reviving in wet weather. The second fern, *Pyrrosia petiolosa*, had a creeping, fleshy rootstock that formed dense mats on the rock surface. Even more interesting were the fronds, which were oblong, entire, 3-7cm (¼ -¾ in) long and evergreen, the brown spore bodies in rows densely covering the lower surface. The ferns shared their situation with a small member of the *Gesneria* family – *Boea hygrometrica* – which, however, preferred the cool shady underbelly of the rock. The hairy crimpled leaves are borne in tight, flattened rosettes from which in summer arise one or more slender stems carrying a loose head of small, lavender, two-lipped flowers. It is widely distributed in China and is one of a large number of Chinese rock gesneriads, few of which are in cultivation.

Passing through the bottom of the ravine was a small stream almost but not quite dried out. Its damp margins shaded by trees supported a number of herbaceous plants, including *Astilbe chinensis* showing its much divided leaves and remnants of the previous year's seed heads. The only colour was provided by *Sedum aizoon* with its dense flattened heads of golden yellow flowers on fleshy leafy stems. It is plentiful in

---

10. *P. chinensis* was referred to by Reginald Farrer as the 'Purple Emperor' of the pulsatilla group. In his classic *The English Rock Garden*, under the synonym *P. sinensis*, he refers to it growing in the valley of the Ming Tombs near Beijing, a site included on most tourist itineraries today – I first saw this species there in 1979. In typical style Farrer tells us that it 'blooms in spring between the flagstones of dead emperors' graves, in March, the only sign of life in that silent mountain valley of death where the ancient sovereigns of China rest'. It is rare in cultivation and not at all easy, Farrer complained, having proved so unsatisfactory that 'gardeners have come to suspect the plant of being a vampire, drawing the blood of its imperial glory only from the dust of dead emperors'.

A view through a ravine south of the Great Wall at Ba-da-ling. Shrubs and trees growing here include *Pyrus ussuriensis, Euonymus bungeanus, Philadelphus pekinensis* and *Prunus armeniaca*. (October)

these situations and looks no different to the plant at present in British cultivation. On the drier slopes of the ravine *Leptodermis oblonga* was plentiful with *Indigofera bungeana* and *Abelia biflora*. The first of these is a dwarf shrub 1m (3ft) high, of dense twiggy habit with clusters of small, downy, tubular flowers varying in colour from pale to deep reddish-purple. It is a north Chinese representative of a genus almost unknown in British gardens due, no doubt, to its liking for hot summers. Some species are more ornamental than others and would be worth introducing, if only on a trial basis, in our drier counties – Cambridgeshire for example. *Indigofera bungeana* is similar to *I potaninii* with tapered racemes of small rose-coloured pea flowers on stalks longer than the corresponding leaf stalk. It is, however, much smaller than that species, rarely reaching above 1.5m (5ft) and of comparatively neat compact appearance.

Indigofera bungeana, one of many plants named after Alexander von Bunge, a Russian botanist of German extraction who collected in the Beijing area in 1831. (June)

A pagoda in the Fragrant Hills with an ancient specimen of *Pinus tabuliformis* to its right. (October 1980)

The Fragrant Hills

One of the loveliest areas in the Western Hills, the Fragrant Hills (Xiangshan) are a favourite with Beijing people who go there to exercise, picnic or simply to enjoy the scenery. They are situated northwest of the city and can be reached in about one hour by car. An area of 1,600 hectares is now designated as a park, but it was formerly an Imperial estate known to the rulers of the Qing dynasty (AD 1644-1911) as the Garden of Serene Beauty. It is well named and is worth visiting whatever the season. Autumn, however, is generally acknowledged as being the most satisfying, for then the hills are alight with the rich tints of dying leaves.

As in the northern hills around the Great Wall, much of the colour is provided by the sumach *Cotinus coggygria* variety *cinerea* and the apricot *Prunus armeniaca* and its variety *ansu*, which, aside from any native survivors, have been planted in great numbers since the 1950s. Bold plantings of contrasting evergreens are provided by conifers, in particular *Pinus tabuliformis* and *Platycladus orientalis*, which once

The steep track which climbs to the highest point in the Fragrant Hills at 580m (1,904ft). Conifers planted here include *Pinus tabuliformis*, *P bungeana* and *Platycladus orientalis*. (October 1980)

Scabiosa comosa. Although comparatively small, the flowerheads of this Chinese scabious are beautiful in close up. It is common in the Beijing Hills. (October)

Dianthus chinensis, the wild ancestor of the 'Indian' or 'Chinese' pinks of western gardens, is common in the Beijing Hills. (October)

existed here as native stands and which, according to some authorities, still persist in some valleys, particularly in places to which access is difficult.

My first visit here was in October 1980. I was accompanying a group of twenty-two keen amateur and professional horticulturists representing five countries. For all but a few it was a first visit to China and everyone was naturally in good spirits. We were driven by bus to a village outside the park and at the foot of the hills. From here we passed through the main entrance pausing only to study a plan of the park fixed to a nearby wall.

The lower area nearest the village is in parts a rather formal garden with trees, pools and colourful bedding displays. Very soon, however, we were following a steep track that runs inside the northern boundary wall, now in a poor state of repair, and climbs a ridge to the summit of the park's highest hill, Fragrant Hill itself, which is 580m (1,904ft) above sea level. Many of the shrubs seen in the hills at Ba-da-ling and elsewhere in the Beijing region are common here and include *Vitex negundo* variety *heterophylla*, *Spiraea trilobata*, *Deutzia grandiflora* and *Myripnois dioica*. Most common however is *Grewia biloba*, a large deciduous shrub with slender branches and roughly hairy leaves up to 12cm (5in) long. The flowers are small and creamy yellow and borne in axillary clusters in summer. These are replaced by small, two-lobed, orange or yellowish fruits.[11]

Almost as common as the grewia was a shrubby member of the pea family, *Lespedeza bicolor*. It is a freegrowing shrub up to 3m (10ft), though normally much less, with long slender shoots clothed with small trifoliolate leaves. In late summer and early autumn these shoots are lined with short racemes of small pea-shaped flowers that vary in colour from pale to dark purple, self or bicolour. *L bicolor* is common in north and northeast China as well as in Japan and was first introduced

to Europe in 1856 by the Russian botanist Maximowicz. The flowers of lespedeza are borne on the shoots of the current year and, in common with the related indigofera, it responds best, in British cultivation certainly, to an annual pruning of the old shoots in late winter or early spring. This encourages the production of stronger shoots with greater flowering potential. In Britain, too, the lack of regular summer heat impedes ripening, while shoots are frequently cut back by frost – another reason for hard pruning.

On our way up the Fragrant Hill we had occasion to cross the wall and explore the grassland and rough herbage on the other side. Our attention had been caught by a small, blue or bluish-lilac flowered scabious – *Scabiosa comosa*, and growing with it we found a pretty annual pink which turned out to be *Dianthus chinensis*. The pink was fairly plentiful over a wide area, a slender-stemmed, rather straggling plant of 23-30cm (9-12in) with linear leaves and a single flower 2.5cm (1in) across. The petals, boldly toothed in the outer margin, were a rich, almost purplish-pink with a slightly darker basal area separated from the outer margin by a purplish-red irregular line giving a distinct 'eyed' effect to the flower. Plants grown from seed have flowered in my garden, but its slender fragile habit of growth necessitates it being planted where it is supported by neighbouring perennials or dwarf shrubs. One plant which has persisted for several years has threaded its way through a small rock rose – *Cistus* species, and its flowers combine attractively with the grey foliage of the latter.[12]

The pinks and the scabious were not the only herbs to attract our attention that day in the Fragrant Hills. Growing in the middle of a colony of myripnois, we found a

11. The north Chinese form belongs to the variety *parviflora* (small flowered), and although it was introduced to Britain in 1888 it has remained rare in cultivation requiring a warmer climate than we generally enjoy. As seen in the wild it is a shrub entirely without ornamental merit, although it is of interest if only because it belongs to the same family as the limes or basswoods (*Tilia*).

12. While the wild form is not in the front rank of ornamental pinks it is interesting from a historical point of view. *D chinensis* was one of the first Chinese plants named by the great Swedish naturalist Linnaeus in 1753. It was cultivated much earlier by Philip Miller at the Chelsea Physic Garden, having first been introduced to the Jardin des Plantes in Paris in 1705 by French missionaries in China. It is now rarely seen in its wild form, having given way soon after its arrival to a whole range of double forms whose cultivation has continued to the present. In gardens today the 'Indian' or 'Chinese' pinks, as they are known, are represented by a host of colourful varieties and strains, single and double, of easy cultivation grown from seed sown under glass in February or March or sown *in situ* in early April. In cultivation, as in the wild, they love a sunny, well-drained position.

Sophora flavescens, a herbaceous relative of the Pagoda tree (*S japonica*). Its dried roots are used by the Chinese in traditional medicine. (June)

perennial whose leaves bore a slight resemblance to those of a hellebore. The leaf blade, circular in outline and up to 20cm (8in) across, was divided to the base into numerous narrow segments creating, when expanded, one of the most unusual pleasing effects of its kind I have ever seen. These leaves were borne on erect stalks up to 30cm (12in) high or so, several leaves forming a bold clump. Above the leaves rose another stem two to three times as tall, bearing a few heads of parachuted seeds, clearly placing this mystery plant in the *Compositae* or dandelion family. We found several clumps in a small area of scrub and have since seen it in the shade of trees elsewhere in these hills. The mystery might have ended there had I not collected a few seeds, which the following year germinated to provide plants for distribution. It has since flowered in several gardens in July and August, its flowers small, in cylindrical clusters, white with black protruding styles enclosed in a sheath of pink-tinted bracts, like tiny shaving brushes. The flowers added nothing to the plant's attraction but it at least enabled me to identify it as *Syneilesis aconitifolia*. I have grown a plant in my garden for several years now and this has enabled me to observe its extraordinary leaf growth. In early spring the soil above the clump is broken by what appear to be small mushrooms. As these develop they are seen to be covered in silvery silky hairs. Gradually the leaf stalk lengthens and the blade expands finger-like until, by late spring, it is fully expanded and an object of extraordinary beauty. So far it is proving quite hardy, and I have no reason to doubt that it

will eventually take its place in gardens among those plants grown principally for foliage effect. Many other herbs grow in the Fragrant Hills including a small Chinese edelweiss – *Leontopodium leontopodioides*, which is of no special garden merit, a bellflower relative – *Adenophora polymorpha*, which is as rampagious in the garden as the dreaded *Campanula rapunculoides*, and a small herbaceous sophora – *Sophora flavescens*, the dried root of which has been used by the Chinese as a herbal remedy for cancer.

Syneilesis aconitifolia. A member of the family *Compositae*, this unusual perennial herb is noted for its striking, deeply dissected leaves, especially attractive on first emerging. The small pinkish groundsel-like flower heads on 30-90cm stems are of little ornamental merit. Here seen in the Asian Garden, University of British Columbia Botanic Garden. (April)

Begonia grandis ssp *evansiana*. A hardy perennial and one of the hardiest species in British gardens, given winter protection. Here growing in the Dell Garden, Bressingham, Norfolk. (October)

All these enjoy open sunny situations, but in the shade of the trees, especially in the sheltered gullies, there are other perennials some of which are most certainly garden worthy. One of these, *Begonia evansiana*, now correctly *B grandis* subspecies *evansiana*, has been in cultivation in Britain since the beginning of the nineteenth century.[13] I have often marvelled at the hardiness of *Begonia evansiana*; no other can compete on this score and seeing this plant flourishing in a relatively dry, shady gully in north China resolved me to experiment with it in similar situations in cultivation. Its handsome leaves, which are reddish beneath, and its showers of pale pink flowers from red buds are worthy of a wider audience than it at present enjoys. It is the hardiest Begonia species and I have it on good authority that it is perfectly hardy in New Jersey and perhaps elsewhere in the New York area. It can easily be propagated by seed or by bulbils that occur in the leaf axils; once established it will produce a regular supply of young plants from both sources. There is also a white flowered form.

13. *Begonia grandis* ssp. *evansiana* has the honour of being the first begonia to be featured, in 1812, in Curtis's *Botanical Magazine*. It is named after Thomas Evans of the East India Company in London who was instrumental in introducing this plant from China in 1808. It is also native to Japan. Evans is said to have devoted almost his whole income to the acquiring of new and rare plants principally from China and the West Indies.

The woods of the Fragrant Hills are home to a most impressive relative of our native whorled Solomon's seal. *Polygonatum sibiricum* is a giant of its kind with erect stems up to 1m (3ft), the long narrow leaves carried in whorls at intervals and bearing in their axils clusters of nodding tubular whitish flowers. It is an impressive perennial rare, if at all present, in cultivation in the West.

When, in 1980, we finally made it to the summit of Fragrant Hill we were surprised to find there a man selling apples and haws. The latter were heaped on a blanket and looked like small deep red crab apples 2.5cm (1in) or more in diameter. We recognised them as belonging to *Crataegus pinnatifida* 'Major', a Chinese thorn that we found as scattered individuals in the Western Hills. The fruits are eaten raw or prepared as a sweetmeat, in which case they are skewered on sticks and sold on the streets of Beijing and elsewhere where they are a popular winter delicacy, especially with children.[14]

Having toiled to the top of the Fragrant Hills we were surprised to find apples and haws being offered for sale. The haws belong to *Crataegus pinnatifida* 'Major' which is cultivated in the region. (October)

Sweetmeats on sale in a Chinese market. These are a popular winter delicacy especially in Beijing and are made from the fruits of *Crataegus pinnatifida* 'Major'

A temple in the Fragrant Hills surrounded by a rich assortment of vegetation. Most of the smaller trees have been planted since 1950. (October 1980)

The dried ripened fruits are also used medicinally in China for the treatment of diarrhoea and stomach ache. Typical C *pinnatifida* is a smaller, bushier tree or large shrub with thorny branches and smaller leaves and fruits. It is a native of north and north-east China, east Siberia, and North Korea. C *pinnatifida* 'Major' is normally a small tree and, according to E H Wilson, is not known in a wild state. He believed it to have been developed by selection and long cultivation. It is one of my favourite ornamental trees and deserves to be grown far more widely than at present. I first encountered it in the old West Hill Hillier nursery in Winchester. Here it grew in a border, a round-headed tree of some 10m (33ft) with bold, lustrous green, broad-lobed leaves, up to 13cm (5in) long, that turned a rich red before falling. This cultivar is also characterised by its thornless or sparsely thorned branches. Unlike the fruits, its white flowers are similar in size to those of the type being 2cm (¾ in) across and produced in clusters (corymbs) in May or early June. Like all thorns it is tough and hardy and adaptable to most soils and situations, being especially suitable for urban areas.[15]

Interestingly, growing not far from the apple vendor on the hilltop, we found a bush cherry, *Prunus tomentosa*, not uncommon. A native in these hills, it is also much cultivated by the Chinese for its edible red cherry-like fruits.[16] I have grown this shrub, which can reach 3m

(10ft), with slender, downy (tomentose) stems, in a garden on the chalk soil of Winchester and elsewhere. Its small white blush-tinted flowers produced in late March are pretty without being exciting. My plant was one of a number grown from stones extracted from bear droppings found in a Kashmir forest reserve where this plant is naturalised. The bear's digestive system proved more than equal to the cherry stone's woody shell and, incidentally, provided me with an unusual after-dinner story.

The Fragrant Hills Park has a long and colourful history. It was once a wild area used for hunting by a succession of emperors, including the famous Qian Long (1736-1796) who added pavilions, pagodas and temples to make it one of

Remnants of native woodland as well as ancient planted trees can usually be found in the vicinity of temples, a fact well illustrated in this photograph taken in the Western Hills by William Purdom in 1914-15

14. Their use as sweetmeats was noted by Bretschneider who sent seeds of this and the typical tree to both Kew Gardens and the Arnold Arboretum between 1860 and 1880.

15. The American collector Frank Meyer found it cultivated as orchards near Boshan in Shandong province. In 1905 he sent fruits to the US Department of Agriculture with the comment: 'A fine fruit for preserves and a very ornamental tree; is simply loaded in the fall with red berries and keeps its glossy-green leaves until late in autumn'.

16. Meyer in 1913 despatched 42,000 stones of this 'promising bush cherry' to be tested in North Dakota. Despite this enormous quantity (typical of Meyer's industry) I am not aware that his introduction established a new orchard industry in America.

Populus tomentosa. Two fine specimens of this poplar growing in the courtyard of a temple in the Fragrant Hills. Sitting at their feet is Harry J van de Laar, a Dutch horticulturist. (October 1980)

Morus alba, a multi-stemmed tree or large shrub in the Fragrant Hills, the leaves deeply and attractively lobed. (October)

the most beautiful parks in the empire. He also had the perimeter wall built and is said to have reintroduced game for hunting. The nineteenth and twentieth centuries saw the park in decline and considerable damage was done in 1860 by the Anglo-French forces and in 1900 during the Boxer Rebellion. More recently, the Fragrant Hills played host to the late Chairman Mao Zedong who, after the liberation of Beijing in 1949, stayed here in the Shuangqing Villa directing the continuing war of liberation. Most of the buildings remain and are now in various stages of restoration. They make a pleasant change from the formal gardens below and the scrub covered hillside above, especially in summer when the sun is at its strongest. They are also worth visiting for another reason – their trees. It is well known that in areas where native forest has been regularly cut over or even destroyed, the best place a plantsman can head for is the nearest temple or pavilion. In the vicinity of such places remnants of native forest, or at the very least individual trees that owe their survival to the proximity of a religious building or artefact, are generally to be found. Quite often trees have been deliberately planted there because of some real or imagined religious significance.

The temples and pavilions of the Fragrant Hills have their share of such trees some of which are notable specimens. There are, for instance, a pair of poplars, *Populus tomentosa*, outside one temple that are the largest of their kind I have yet seen. They tower to at least 30m (100ft) high, with impressive trunks and powerful spreading crowns. Their boldly-toothed leaves are large and rounded or broad ovate, finely grey pubescent becoming glossy dark green above, and pale downy becoming green and glossy beneath. Mature leaves of variable form are to be found at the same time on the same tree. The origin of *P tomentosa* is something of a mystery. It has variously been known as *P alba* variety *tomentosa* and *P pekinensis*, and bears more than a passing resemblance to the European grey poplar *P canescens* considered a hybrid of *P alba*, the white poplar, and *P tremula* the aspen.[17] Trees seen in Beijing in the second half of April appear to represent two clones, one of which is female, the long slender fruiting catkins draping the already leafy branches. Other trees,

17. The Polish botanist S Bialobok reached just such a conclusion in 1964, suggesting its most likely parentage as being the eastern race of *P alba* and the Chinese aspen *P tremula* variety *davidiana*. I have never seen it in a truly wild state and it is mostly seen planted as a city or suburban tree in north China, being particularly abundant on the roads and streets of Beijing and its neighbourhood. It was known to Bretschneider, and is said to have first been introduced to Europe (Paris) by the French agronomist and botanist G E Simon in the 1860s.

Acer truncatum. Commonly planted in the Fragrant Hills and on Beijing streets, this handsome Chinese maple is still not well enough known in western cultivation. Here a young tree in the Hillier Arboretum, Hampshire shows rich autumn tints.[19] (October)

often interspersed with the latter in avenues, are distinctly later leafing and presumably male, the spent catkins having already been shed. For such a splendid ornamental tree, this poplar is curiously scarce in western cultivation, and I know of only one example, at the Forestry Commission Research Station, Alice Holt, Surrey, which in 2001 measured approximately 19m (62ft) high with a diameter at chest height of 65cm (25in).

The variety of trees growing in the Fragrant Hills is one of the most interesting if not fascinating aspects of exploration there – which and how many of these have been planted is difficult now to ascertain, as many are species previously native here. Some indeed, according to local experts, are relics of those earlier forests or descendants of them. Whatever their true origin, the present day forests are at least representative of an original state and as such are worthy of study. I have already mentioned the trees that contribute the famous autumn tints, but there are others whose dying leaves add colour, if only locally. One of these is the white mulberry *Morus alba*, a tree native in north China though cultivated since time immemorial.[18] The importance of this tree to man lies in its leaves on which the larvae of the silkworm moth (*Bombyx mori*) feed. In China it is commonly planted along field margins where it is regularly lopped to encourage younger, stronger shoots and larger leaves. In cultivation in Britain this tree is not common, the black mulberry (*M nigra*) being preferred.

Having seen old specimens of both I have to confess that, to my eye, the latter tree has the more pleasing habit. Added to this are its dark, sweet, juicy fruits, compared with which those of *M alba* are pale and insipid. *M alba* does, however, have a bonus in its autumn foliage, which is a most appealing clear yellow, creating in the Fragrant Hills splashes of brightness in the otherwise evergreen or red tinted canopy. The dried leaves, roots, twigs and fruits of this mulberry figure strongly in Chinese traditional medicine. In one combination or another they are used for colds, coughs, headaches, dizziness, insomnia, diarrhoea and in the treatment of cancer.

The only maple found in any quantity in the Fragrant Hills now is *Acer truncatum* whose leaves in November turn rich yellow-orange, sometimes with red tints. Since my first sight of this species, in 1979, it has become one of my favourite maples and one I constantly recommend to tree lovers in Europe and the United States. In the Fragrant Hills it makes a tree of some 8m (26ft) with a rounded crown, bearing usually five-lobed leaves 7.5-12.5cm (3-5in) wide.

18. *Morus alba* was named in 1753 by Linnaeus who thought it was native to Italy, though it had, apparently, been introduced to Tuscany from the Middle East in 1434. It was already in Britain by 1596 and was cultivated by the herbalist Gerard.

19. In a poem, *A Visit to the Hill*, written during the Tang dynasty (AD 618-907), the poet Du Fu wrote: 'Sitting in my chariot I enjoy the maple leaves in late autumn. They are more beautiful than flowers in February'

The base of the blade is often straight, hence the name – *truncatum* (ie truncated) and both surfaces are more or less smooth and shining green. It always strikes me as a healthy looking tree, its foliage glistening green until well into autumn when it assumes much warmer tints. The greenish-yellow flower clusters are unusual in being erect and appearing with the young leaves in spring. The fruits that follow often have reddish or bronze tinted wings and crowd the branches. It is a favourite street tree in urban areas of north China, especially in Beijing – which is hardly surprising considering its many qualities. The largest specimen in the British Isles is a tree in the Royal Botanic Gardens, Kew, which measured 13m (45ft) in 2001.

The Chinese are fond of collecting wild herbs in the Western Hills for use in traditional medicine. This old man had been collecting and preparing them for much of his life

The forests of the hills contain representatives of many familiar tree genera and we were pleased in 1980 to find, among other things, *Quercus dentata* with its large boldly lobed leaves, and the equally attractive though far more graceful Mongolian lime – *Tilia mongolica*, a small tree here with relatively small, boldly-toothed leaves that are unlike those of any other species. Because of its small size, compact habit and its neat and unusual leaves this lime is being increasingly noticed in western cultivation where it is still not common, though there are good specimens in

several arboreta and specialist collections. If it has a weakness it is the vulnerability of its branches to wind damage, but this should not rule out its planting in sheltered sites. T *mongolica* is capable of becoming 12-20m (40-65ft) high eventually and there is a specimen of 20m (65ft) in the Royal Botanic Gardens, Kew. In the wild it is native to north China and the Russian far east. It was first discovered by Père David in 1864 and reached cultivation (in Paris) sixteen years later.

In case readers are reaching the conclusion that the Fragrant Hills must be visited in autumn if they are to see trees at their best, let me describe two that display their floral charms during summer, indeed, when I saw them in late June 1984 they were reaching their peak of perfection. Neither may ever have occurred naturally in these hills but they are now so well established that it is hard to imagine it otherwise. The first of these, *Albizia julibrissin* – the Pink Siris, is a member of the legume family in the same subfamily as the acacias and mimosas. It is capable of reaching 15m (50ft) in time but is normally much less in the hills with wide-spreading branches developing a rather flat-topped or shallowly domed crown. Its leaves are large – 25-45cm (10-18in) long, and much divided (bipinnate), and have a fern-like effect that

A group of plant enthusiasts climbing the Fragrant Hills in 1980. In the centre is Gloria Barretto, Curator of the Kadoorie Botanical Gardens, Hong Kong, Ruy Barretto her son is far left, Peter Addington far right, author second from right. (October 1980)

Tilia mongolica. The sharply lobed and toothed vine-like leaves characterise this species, which is also noted for its rich yellow autumn tints. Here taken at Chateau de Courson, France (May)

provides ideal backing for the short- stalked flower clusters whose main attraction are the numerous thread-like pink stamens. They resemble fluffy pink shaving brushes and cover the upper sides of the branches creating a lovely effect. They are followed by flattened seed pods up to 12.5cm (5in) long. Growing on steep hillsides, it is possible to look down on the albizias and so better appreciate their flowers. This tree was first introduced into Britain in 1745 from western Asia.

Enjoying the same slopes, and common in all the hills around Beijing including those at Ba-da-ling, is *Koelreuteria paniculata*, known to many western gardeners as the Golden Rain Tree or Pride of India, names also used to describe *Laburnum anagyroides* and *Lagerstroemia speciosa* respectively. Introduced to Britain as long ago as 1763, it is a distinctive tree at all seasons especially in late summer when the rich yellow flowers are borne in bold heads (panicles) at the ends of the branches. Even after flowering the show is not over, for then the fruits develop, conspicuous bladder-like pods which turn from pale green to pink then brown as they age. Even the leaves are attractive, pinnate, like those of an ash, with boldly and attractively toothed and lobed leaflets, sometimes changing to golden yellow before falling in autumn. They were at one time used in north China to obtain a black dye. The largest trees I have seen in the Fragrant Hills were in the region of 12m (40ft) tall, but it is capable of 18m (60ft) in sheltered ravines and in cultivation. Its flowers create a bright splash on the hillsides and I shall never forget one sunny day in June 1984, breasting a hill south of Ba-da-ling and gazing down upon a tree in full bloom, its canopy a yellow cloud attracting bees and insects in variety. It seemed light years away from a small tree struggling to survive in a relatively sunless Lancashire park of my youth.

There is no doubt about the preference of both koelreuteria and albizia for sun and a long hot summer to ripen their growth. In Britain the unripened summer shoots of young trees certainly suffer die back or frost damage and disease sometimes follows. The best trees of koelreuteria I have seen in Britain grew in southeast England, a region which most approximates to the continental climate beloved by these trees. Indeed one of the most notable specimens (though not the largest) grows in the Chelsea Physic Garden in London. *K paniculata* makes a superb lawn tree and is well worth considering for all but the coldest, sunless areas. *Albizia julibrissin* is best considered as a wall shrub except in the warmest or driest areas. Both will bring a hint of the subtropical to the garden, especially the albizia whose leaves make it a popular subject in 'subtropical' bedding schemes. In the United States albizia is popular in the south, but even

Koelreuteria paniculata is a native of north China and is commonly planted in the Beijing Hills. The curious inflated seed capsules in August (top right) are as ornamental as the flowers in June (below right)

there it is now under attack from a vascular wilt disease that kills the top growth. Many plants survive only as root sprouts. It is also subject to attack there from webworm, which causes severe defoliation. Koelreuteria, on the other hand, is relatively trouble free and is very popular especially as a lawn specimen. In colder areas it is unrivalled for its late flowers.

Before moving on to pastures new I should like to mention a few of the climbers found in the Fragrant Hills, some of which make a major contribution to the landscape there. Most common are two vines – *Vitis amurensis* and *Ampelopsis aconitifolia*. The first of these is a bold, vigorous scrambler with shoots, grey woolly when young, climbing by means of branched tendrils that coil around a support. Its leaves are five lobed, sometimes deeply so, downy beneath and 10-25cm (4-10in) or occasionally more across. In a wild state the leaves often give rich autumn tints of red or purple but this is not always the case in cultivation, especially in mild areas. It was at one time regarded as a variety of the common grapevine *V vinifera*, but few who have seen it in these northern hills would immediately relate the two. Its powerful growths clothe the ground in clearings and on open hillsides, scrambling over lesser vegetation and into the tree canopy. *V amurensis* is native over a wide area of north-east Asia. The fruits, which I have not seen, are said to be black and quite small, about 8mm (⅓ in) across. Although introduced to Europe around the middle of the nineteenth century, it has remained uncommon in cultivation, in Britain at least. It ought to be more widely grown if only for its bold foliage and autumn tints.

The Chinese are fond of bright colours in their flower gardens and city parks. This striking red dahlia grew in the Forbidden City, Beijing. (October)

Viola mandshurica is a common violet in the hills around Beijing. It is easily recognised by its slender leaves and richly coloured flowers. Below Great Wall at Ba-da-ling. (May)

Punica granatum. An unusual golden version of the normally red-fruited pomegranate cultivated in the Forbidden City, Beijing. (October)

Parthenocissus tricuspidata showing the delicate tints of early autumn on the wall of the author's house. (October)

seem thoroughly at home and established. The parthenocissus, which is certainly native to Japan and east China, climbs the stems of some of the tall trees in the ravines and when I saw it in October 1980 was close to its peak, the reddish-orange, maple-like leaves creating smouldering columns in the gloom. Commonly referred to as the Boston ivy, because of its ivy-shaped leaves and its free use as a wall cover in the American city of that name, this deciduous vine, unlike those already described, climbs by means of branched tendrils equipped with tiny sucker pads that remind me of something in a science fiction film. There can be no denying its excellence as a wall cover, winter excepting of course, but it is equally valuable and spectacular when planted to grow into a tall tree such as an oak or a pine. A well-established plant so grown is unforgettable. Its long, searching stems having reached the canopy tumble down through the branches forming long streamers and curtains ever shifting and changing, burnished bronze or copper in spring, shining green in summer, firecracker red in autumn. It is worth pointing out to those who still refer to this vine as Virginia creeper that this name correctly belongs to a closely related American species – *P. quinquefolia*, similarly climbing, whose leaves are divided into five, occasionally three, distinct leaflets, never ivy-shaped as are the adult leaves of *P. tricuspidata*.

Ampelopsis aconitifolia could not be more different. Its stems, while fast growing, are more slender than those of *Vitis amurensis* and quite smooth (glabrous). Even more characteristic are the leaves, which are long stalked, 10-12.5cm (4-5in) across and composed of five lance-shaped, deeply divided leaflets. Indeed, it was once named *A. dissecta* in reference to the finely-cut leaves, which are, nevertheless, variable in the depth to which the leaflets are lobed and toothed. Some extreme forms in the wild are nearly as effective in leaf as the fern-leaved Japanese maple *Acer palmatum* forma *dissectum*. The rather insignificant flowers are produced in late summer to be replaced by orange-coloured fruits about 6mm (¼ in) across. In the Beijing area *Ampelopsis aconitifolia* is a common vine, scrambling over rocks and bushes by means of twining tendrils into the branches of small trees. When covering its support it is a most elegant and luxurious climber. Considering its hardiness and tolerance of difficult situations it deserves a wider recognition in western gardens than it enjoys at present, though it was introduced to the West around the middle of the nineteenth century.

Growing in the same woods as the last are two climbers that are as familiar to gardeners in the West as the others are unfamiliar. One is a vine – *Parthenocissus tricuspidata*, the other the exquisite, ubiquitous wisteria – *Wisteria sinensis*. Whether either is native to the Fragrant Hills is doubtful, yet both

Parthenocissus tricuspidata, the best known and most commonly cultivated of all Chinese vines. Known in America as the Boston ivy, its slender tendrils with sucker pad tips enable it to cover almost any surface. Here it creates a spectacular autumn display on a public house in Hampshire, England. (October 1964)

Like the previous climber, *Wisteria sinensis* in the wild is most often found in trees or swamping lesser fry on forest margins or peripheral scrub. In the Fragrant Hills it grows into and over a variety of trees in the ravines and it is easy there to see the anti-clockwise direction of its twining stems, those of the Japanese wisteria – *W floribunda* twining in a clockwise direction (ie stems ascending left to right towards the growing point). It might be necessary to lie on one's back and imagine oneself as a growing shoot to understand this. Sorting out this characteristic on some of the old plants in cultivation, however, is not always a simple matter.

There are few rivals to a wisteria as a hardy flowering deciduous climber, and when seen covering a wall, its branches hidden from view in late May by a multitude of hanging lilac-blue racemes, it lays strong claim to being

the world's most beautiful. Although it will continue to be planted on warm sunny walls where it undoubtedly flourishes, the wisterias, Chinese and Japanese, should also be considered for training into suitable trees, which they will eventually, once a year, transform into a thing of exceptional beauty. In Britain I have seen wisterias trained into English oak, Scots pine and Lawson cypress, all substantial trees and once, in the Hillier Arboretum, into a 8m (26ft) Pussy willow – *Salix caprea*. In this latter case, the wisteria chosen was 'Multijuga', a form of *W floribunda* with extra long racemes of bicoloured flowers in June.

It would be more than remiss of me to leave the hills of Beijing, and the Fragrant Hills in particular, without reference to what many regard as one of the most beautiful trees of its kind – the Lacebark pine, *Pinus bungeana*, named

Entrance to Forbidden City, Beijing with portrait of Mao Zedong. (October 1980)

Juniperus chinensis is both native and commonly planted in China especially in the vicinity of temples. There are several veteran trees in the courtyards of the Forbidden City in Beijing. (October 1980)

Above. A trail in the Fragrant Hills, near Beijing. The vegetation consists of a dense scrub of trees and shrubs, heavily replanted since 1950, beneath which many perennials thrive. (October 1980)

Top left. Detail of *Pinus bungeana* showing the flaking bark. The varied colours and tones exhibited are truly breathtaking, even more so when wetted by rain. Forbidden City, Beijing. (October)

Left. *Pinus bungeana*. The flaking bark of this tree is its chief claim to fame, the beautiful marbled effect giving rise to its English name Lacebark pine. (October)

Pinus bungeana a magnificent veteran of 30m. or so, which, when photographed in October 1980, appeared to be dead. (Yu Hua Yuan, Forbidden City, Beijing)

after the Russian botanist Alexander von Bunge who first collected specimens of this tree near Beijing in 1831. P *bungeana* is said to be native to the mountains of Gansu, Shanxi, Shaanxi and south to Hubei where Augustine Henry first found it in the 1880s. Its true status in some areas, however, is difficult to ascertain because of its long history as a planted tree especially in the vicinity of Buddhist temples and monasteries. In the Fragrant Hills are many examples of this pine planted over the last few decades but, according to some accounts there once existed much older, larger specimens. Indeed, Robert

Fortune, the Scottish plant hunter on a visit to these hills in the autumn of 1861, found a Lacebark pine that had a thick trunk that rose from the ground to a height of 1m (3ft), at which point some eight or ten stems sprung out, rising perpendicularly to a height of 24-30m (80-100ft).

Fortune, who had earlier introduced seed of this pine to England from a garden in Shanghai, described the bark of this giant as peeling like an arbutus, while the bark of the secondary stems was of a milky white colour. It is the bark that is this pine's chief claim to fame, though its general habit and lightness of canopy add much to its overall beauty. Frank Meyer, who saw it many times in China, thought it 'beautiful and serene enough to worship'. After having encountered it in Gansu he was moved to write: 'the more one sees of them, the more one loves them – in rain, bright sunshine, soft moonlight, or snow laden, their exquisite appearance cannot fail to exert an uplifting influence on one's mind'. If this seems a little far fetched, one has only to stand beneath a large specimen of this pine to experience the special magic of which Meyer (and others) have written.

I am not aware that old trees still exist in the Fragrant Hills but there are such trees in Beijing, especially in the Bei Hai Park, the Jing Shan (Coal Hill Park) and the Forbidden City. In the Yu Hua Yuan, or Imperial Garden in the Forbidden City, are several magnificent specimens one of which must be at least 30m (100ft). When I last saw the latter tree it appeared to be dead, possibly as a result of the compaction caused by the trampling of millions of feet since this garden was opened to the public. The bark of the young stem and branches is certainly milky pale in this continental climate, though less so in British cultivation. The bark of the main trunk and major branches peels like that of a plane producing a remarkable marbling of greys, silvers, yellows and greens. It is a fascinating patchwork pattern which changes with the hour, the weather and the season.

In cultivation in Britain P *bungeana* is hardy but slow, the largest specimen at Kew (2001) being a multi-stemmed tree of 11m (36ft). Though by no means common there are a number of specimens in other gardens many of which have developed a low, multi-stemmed habit up to 6m (20ft) or more.

Pinus bungeana, surely one of the most beautiful of all pines rivalling if not excelling the plane and the gum tree in the brilliance of its bark effect. Forbidden City, Beijing. (October 1980)

Chapter Two

Sacred Emei Shan

If there is one mountain in China calculated to set a plantsman's pulse racing it is Emei Shan or Mt Omei in Sichuan province. The reasons for this are twofold. To begin with, it supports a rich flora, estimated by the late Professor Wen-pei Fang, the great authority on the Sichuan flora, to be in excess of three thousand species. Just imagine, three thousand different native plants on a single Chinese mountain. Compare this with the two thousand or so native in the whole of the British Isles! The second reason for its fame in the West lies in the publicity it has received from travellers and plant hunters, and one plant hunter in particular – E H Wilson who first visited the mountain in 1903.

One of China's four most sacred mountains, Emei Shan (latitude 29° 28′N, longitude 103° 41′E) is situated some 160km (100 miles) south-west of Chengdu, capital of Sichuan (formerly Szechuan) province in west China. It stands on the eastern flank of a series of high mountain ranges that run north-south through western Sichuan and Yunnan. Approached from the east across the Chengdu Plain, these mountains present a continuous, seemingly impenetrable barrier.[1]

As mountains go Mt Omei is not impressive to look at, certainly not from a distance. There are no peaks and no permanent snow. Approached from the east across the plain, and when not wrapped in cloud or mist, it looms on the horizon like a sleeping beast. Its shape, when seen across the plain, has been described as that of a couchant lion decapitated close to the shoulders, the fore feet remaining in position. The down-cleft surface forms a fearful, well nigh vertical precipice, considerably over 2,000m (1¼ miles) in height. These magnificent cliffs, on the north-east face, are in sharp contrast to the more accessible slopes of the south face. They are made of limestone, probably magnesium, which forms the basic rock, while in the valleys are mud shales notorious for causing frequent landslips after heavy rain.

According to figures published by the Chinese, the average annual precipitation on Emei Shan is 1,938.5mm (76.3in). Rain occurs mainly in the three month period July-September, July being the wettest month and also the warmest with an average temperature of 12.6°C (54.6° F). This is followed by a comparatively dry period which lasts

Davidia flowers like no other in the temperate world

from November to April. January is both the driest month, with an average precipitation of 10.5mm (about ½ in), and the coldest, with an average temperature of -4°C (25°F).

Large areas of the lower mountain are cultivated with wild intrusions in the steep ravines and along the sharp ridged crests. Above 1,220m (4,000ft), however, the native vegetation gradually assumes control until the steepening slopes become dominated by evergreen forest beneath which shrubs and perennials in infinite variety hold sway. In many places, bamboo forms dense thickets through which grow isolated trees and shrubs.[2]

The lower half of the mountain, up to 1,828m (6,000ft), enjoys a warm temperate climate and supports evergreen forest in which the Laurel family (*Lauraceae*) predominates, with genera such as *Machilus*, *Lindera* and *Litsea* well represented. These give way above to evergreen oaks which occur well into the upper region. Other tree genera found in this region include *Idesia*, *Emmenopterys*, *Euodia* and *Carrieria*, all deciduous. This region also supports a rich perennial layer with ferns and fern allies particularly plentiful in the moist shady ravines. The upper region, from around 1,828m (6,000ft) to the summit, enjoys a cool temperate climate with deciduous trees and shrubs dominant, and evergreens mainly represented by rhododendrons and silver fir above and evergreen oaks lower down.

The first botanist to climb Emei Shan, in 1887, was a German missionary, the Reverend Dr Ernst Faber, who collected a large number of dried specimens, seventy of which proved new to science. He was followed in 1890 by A E Pratt, a naturalist whose interests lay mainly with reptiles, mammals, birds, insects and fish. He did, however, make a collection of plants some of which proved to be

1. Indeed, the main ranges are known as the Hengduan Mountains, 'hengduan' meaning 'cut across', ie blocking east-west travel. Anyone who has travelled through this land of high mountains and deep valleys will readily appreciate the point. Compared with its neighbours to the west, one of which, Gongga Shan (Minya Konka), is 7,590m (24,900ft), Emei Shan is relatively small. It was originally estimated at 3,353m (11,000 ft), but a more recent calculation places it at 3,099m (10,167ft). It appears larger because of its position – separated from and forward of the main mass – on the western rim of the Chengdu Plain, itself only 400m (1,312ft) above sea level and above which Emei Shan steeply rises.

2. Wilson described the floristic zones of Emei Shan in *A Naturalist in Western China*, where a chapter devoted to his exploration of the mountain is as fascinating as it is disappointingly brief. His rough grouping of the mountain's flora into two main regions still holds good and, while the boundaries between the two are perhaps not as clear cut as he suggests, the change from one to the other should be apparent to anyone who climbs the mountain.

Emei Shan seen through the haze rising from the Chengdu Plain. As mountains go, it is not impressive to look at, not from a distance certainly, but it qualifies as one of China's treasure houses for plants, supporting over three thousand different kinds. (October)

new. Three years later, in 1893, Emei Shan was visited by the celebrated Russian traveller and botanist G N Potanin during his fourth and last Chinese expedition.

The activities and collections of all these men were well known to E H Wilson when he made his first visit to Emei Shan in October 1903 during his second expedition for the nursery firm of Veitch in Chelsea. Wilson returned on several subsequent occasions making a large number of collections including seed and living material. From Wilson's Emei collections, many ornamental plants, some of them new species, were introduced for the first time into western cultivation.

Wilson was followed in 1914 by a German teacher and botanist, Dr Wolfgang Limpricht, who concerned himself only with collecting dried specimens for the herbarium. Surprisingly, since Wilson's time, Emei Shan has received very little attention from Western plant hunters. It may well be that others, aware of Wilson's reputation for thoroughness, assumed the mountain to have surrendered all its treasures and gone elsewhere. Whatever the reason, it is obvious today that Wilson could not possibly have seen every worthwhile plant there, and this is borne out by the number of new species subsequently found by Chinese botanists and others. Since the 1920s Chinese collectors have regularly been visiting Emei Shan and studying and recording its flora. These have included some of the most respected authorities such as F T Wang, T T Yü, W C Cheng and S S Chien. But there is one name which, more than any other, will be associated with the botany of Emei Shan — that of the late Professor Wen-pei Fang who had a special affection for the mountain.

For fifty-five years until his death in 1983 he studied its flora, visiting it on many occasions at different seasons. No one knew it better or appreciated it more than he.

It was to Professor Fang I wrote in November 1979 when I was asked to accompany a botanical tour to China the following year. Part of our time was to be spent on Emei Shan and it seemed natural to seek an audience with 'the master'. And so it was on 10 October, 1980 I arrived with a party of twenty-two plant enthusiasts at Chengdu airport on a flight from Beijing. The Professor was accompanied by his son Dr Min-yuan Fang and Mikinori Ogisu, a young Japanese man who has since become an authority on the Sichuan flora.

For over an hour, over cups of green tea, he talked to us of Emei Shan and the plants we could expect to see there. He then proceeded to hand out to our group copies of Volume 1, Numbers 1 and 2 of *Icones Plantarum Omeiensium*, a classic of its kind edited by Professor Fang in 1942 and 1944 respectively. The first number was prepared by the Professor as a member of the National Szechuan University at their wartime headquarters at Emei and, considering the difficulties of the time, it is an impressive publication containing descriptions of some fifty plants found on Emei Shan, each description in English and Chinese and accompanied by an exquisite line drawing.

Even though the day was by then well advanced, our preparation for Emei Shan was not yet over, for after dinner we gathered in the room of Mikinori Ogisu to hear what he had to relate about the mountain whence he had

Clerodendrum bungei a common roadside plant at lower levels in Sichuan and a popular garden subject in Britain where it is usually treated as an herbaceous perennial, its soft woody stems frequently damaged by winter frosts. (October)

Left. The statue of the Great Buddha at Leshan is carved from a sandstone cliff above the Min river. It is said to have taken ninety years to carve and to have been completed in AD 713. Note the tiny figures in the top right hand corner. (October)

returned only that day. His descriptions confirmed our wildest dreams and we went to our beds that night excited and filled with curiosity for the morrow.

Another surprise meeting awaited me at breakfast when I found Dr Shiu-ying Hu of the Arnold Arboretum, Massachusetts, at an adjoining table. I had met her in January 1976 when visiting Boston to lecture and I remembered having a most enjoyable meeting in her office discussing the Chinese flora and listening to stories of her life in China. It transpired that she was to be in Chengdu for several months teaching at the University of Sichuan.

En route for Emei Shan

Having seen our baggage loaded into a truck, we left Chengdu in a small bus, heading south through the sprawling suburbs and into the plain. We passed through fields of intensive cultivation, principally rice which was being harvested. Along the edges of many fields mulberries were planted which appeared to be a large-leaved form of *Morus alba*. Their stems had been pruned to produce strong shoots with correspondingly large leaves for silkworm culture.

Late that morning we arrived at the city of Leshan, once known as Chiating. It stands at the confluence of three rivers the Min, the Dadu (Tung) and the Qingyi (Ya). In the old days an important route to Emei Shan brought travellers and traders from the Yangtze up the Min to Leshan, while even more continued up the same river to Chengdu.

Leshan was once an important centre of the silk trade as well as of timber and insect white wax. It is also the site of the famous statue and temple of the Great Buddha. The statue has been cut into the face of a sandstone cliff across the Min river from the city. It is colossal – a sitting figure 71m (233ft) from top to toe; it is said to have taken ninety years to carve

and to have been completed in AD 713. I had an amusing reminder of this statue on a subsequent visit to China when I was taken to see a thriller film, a sort of Chinese 'whodunit', which began with someone being pushed to his death from the statue's head. The film improved considerably, for me certainly, when lengthy sequences depicting secret meetings between the film's main characters were set in the unlikely location of Emei Shan. Most of the film I spent trying to identify the rhododendrons and other flowers which, of course, were incidental to the plot.

Our visit to the giant statue was accomplished in a coal-fired ferry which nosed its way through a flotilla of river craft, several of which differed little in appearance to those depicted in some of E H Wilson's photographs from the beginning of the 20th century.

After a splendid lunch in a Leshan restaurant we set off on our final leg heading west out of the city and across the plain. The Chengdu Plain is some 130km (80 miles) long and 105km (65 miles) wide, with an average altitude ranging from some 550m (1,800ft) to 610m (2,000ft). It is, however, only part of a much greater depression known as the Sichuan Basin which extends for almost 259,000 sq km (100,000 sq miles). About 135 million years ago the entire area was occupied by a lake the waters of which subsequently escaped during a period of upheaval. Now the region is bounded on all sides by high mountains. The greater part of the basin is broken up into a network of low rounded or flat-topped mountains averaging 914m (3,000ft). It enjoys hot summers with an abundance of rain and mild winters with frequent mists. Not surprisingly, considering its extensive irrigation and its fertile red soils, it is green all the year round and supports an abundance of crops. It is these red soils that account for another name for this region – the Red Basin,

Camellia oleifera is commonly cultivated in Sichuan and elsewhere in China for the oil in its large seeds. (October)

River craft on the Min at Leshan have changed little in the past hundred years. This one was seen during a visit in October 1980

which was coined by the Prussian geologist and explorer Baron von Richthofen who visited here in 1817.

From the summit of hills over which our road passed we had occasional glimpses of Emei Shan and its neighbouring mountains and, anxious though we were to reach our destination before nightfall, we could not resist asking for two unscheduled stops in order to explore the vegetation on the roadside. We had already seen thickets of *Clerodendrum bungei* in flower and we were able to examine this shrub more closely when we made our first stop. Its suckering, pithy, purplish stems here reached 2m (6ft) and were well clothed with large heart-shaped leaves which gave off a nauseous odour when crushed. Most stems ended in a domed head of purplish-red scented flowers, creating a striking effect against the green or purple-suffused leaves. This is a handsome plant in gardens, and its late flowering means it attracts a wide range of insect visitors, especially bees and butterflies. Sadly it is too rarely seen in British cultivation, due possibly to the tendency of its stems to be damaged by severe frost – often to ground level. In these circumstances it is best treated as a herbaceous plant and, if need be, in colder areas its rootstock can be protected in winter by a layer of bracken, leaf mould or some other, preferably organic, material.

The clerodendrum is a common roadside plant at lower altitudes throughout Sichuan and shares these sites with several other common shrubs including two roses – *Rosa multiflora* and *R laevigata*. The former is usually seen as a wide-spreading bush with long unruly stems to 3m (9ft) or more clad with small but wickedly hooked thorns. It is easily recognised in summer by its gland-fringed stipules and branched heads (panicles) of small white or blush-pink flowers 2.5cm (1in) across with a pleasant fruity fragrance. These are followed by equally characteristic pea-sized hips which are red and smooth when ripe. The typical form of this rose is native to Japan and Korea and is represented in China by several forms some of which have double flowers. It is much cultivated by the Chinese. The typical plant is less common in European cultivation than it is in American and has long been used by nurserymen as an understock on which to bud named hybrids.

R laevigata may or may not be native in Sichuan but it is frequently met with in the Red Basin and was recorded by Wilson in the Yangtze Gorges to the east. Given the opportunity, its long green rambling stems will clamber into nearby trees and frequently swamp lesser fry. In one place we found this species and *R multiflora* growing together over the same bush, an unfortunate pyracantha. *R laevigata* is readily detected by its variously sized reddish-brown prickles and its glossy green (often evergreen) leaves which are divided clover-like into three leaflets. I have not seen the large, solitary, deliciously fragrant creamy-white flowers in the wild

Gordonia acuminata. A handsome evergreen tree with its large camellia-like flowers, we found growing in a steep gully below the road from Leshan to Emei. (October)

but I have seen the characteristic bristle-clad hips which are red when ripe, 2cm (¾in) across, and crowned by the persistent green sepals. In cultivation this rose requires a warm sunny position with plenty of room for its powerful stems. It is best seen in southern Europe and in the southern United States, in which country it has long been naturalised, earning for itself the name Cherokee rose. In fact, so common is it in Georgia that it was chosen as the State flower.

Even more interesting was our second roadside stop, which occurred on a steep slope scored with deep gullies. The common plant here was *Camellia oleifera*, an evergreen shrub up to 3m (9ft) with finely-toothed, pointed glossy green leaves 2.5-5cm (1-2in) long. The flowers were borne singly 5-7.5cm (2-3in) across with white petals, the outer ones pink flushed, surrounding a bold brush of yellow-tipped stamens. This camellia is widely cultivated in southern China and elsewhere in south-east Asia for the oil in its seeds, which, as 'tea oil', is used in cooking and in toiletries such as soap and shampoo.

In common with several other economic plants, the extensive cultivation of this camellia over many centuries has blurred the extent of its native distribution. It is said to occur wild in woods and thickets in many places and I was interested to note a Wilson reference to its wild nature in the sandstone ravines of north-central Sichuan. Although introduced to Britain as long ago as 1820 (earlier in a semi-double flowered form known as 'Lady Banks' Camellia'), it remains uncommon in cultivation here and is found mainly in specialists' collections. Like its Japanese relative *C sasanqua* it flourishes best in a continental climate where long hot summers ripen the growths. Like *C sasanqua* too, it is winter flowering in Britain and is best given a sheltered wall in all but the warmest areas.

Descending one of the gullies we found ourselves walking beneath a grove of straight-stemmed evergreen trees up to 9m (30ft) or more high and bearing lance-shaped leaves to 23cm (9in) long, glossy green above and glaucous beneath. The young leaves were an attractive coppery-red. The flowers, many of which were strewn on the ground, were large and camellia-like, creamy-white with a central boss of yellow-anthered stamens. We decided that it was *Gordonia acuminata*. Unfortunately, although I photographed the flower, I gathered no voucher specimen.

We arrived at the town of Emei in late afternoon and were taken to our quarters for the night at Red Spider Lodge, a guest house situated at the foot of the mountain among trees of many kinds. In the last half hour before dark we explored the immediate vicinity of the lodge finding plenty to interest us. The sloping ground behind the lodge was clothed in a dense continuous carpet of *Iris japonica*, alas not in flower. We later saw vast areas of this same species in the valleys around Emei Shan, the bold fans of glossy green strap-shaped leaves almost smothering lesser vegetation. Although the predominantly white or pale lavender frilly flowers do not compare with more gaudy members of the genus, these great

A large rock fall blocking the road in a river valley below Emei Shan. Such falls and slides are frequent here after heavy or continuous rain. (October)

drifts must nevertheless look quite impressive at the height of their season in April and May. A plant collected from this area received a Preliminary Commendation when shown before the Royal Horticultural Society in 1982.

Another plant frequent in this area is the pale yellow flowered *Hedychium omeiense*, commonly found along the water courses in the lower reaches of Emei Shan. Another yellow-flowered species *H panzhuum* Z Y Zhu sometimes accompanies it. Both are now regarded as synonyms of *H flavescens*.

After breakfast next morning our party boarded the bus and drove to Bao Guo Monastery. Built in the sixteenth century, this impressive building lies at the foot of the mountain and is where most visitors begin the long journey to the summit. I shall remember it for two other reasons. In the first courtyard grew three splendid columnar specimens, one 6.5m (22ft) high of *Fokienia hodginsii*, a unique conifer, the only species of its genus. It is native to the provinces of Guizhou (Kweichow), Fujian (Fukien) and Zhejiang (Chekiang) and was first discovered by a Captain A Hodgins in about 1904. Five years later it was introduced to Britain by Admiral Clinton-Baker. It remains a rarity in cultivation due, most likely, to its rather tender nature. The best specimen I have seen grows in the garden on Garinish Island, Co Cork, Ireland, an old but sprawling bush of 2m (6ft) by 3m (9ft) or more. A smaller specimen grows almost unseen in the woodland at Exbury in Hampshire. *Fokienia* is said to be intermediate in character between a *Calocedrus* and *Chamaecyparis*, having foliage and seeds similar to the former and cones similar to the latter. The foliage is borne in flattened sprays and is most distinctive, especially beneath with the striking white stomatal V-shaped markings.

The monastery supported a small shop where paintings, silks and similar gifts could be purchased. Many of our party bought walking sticks made from a most interesting bamboo that, according to the monks, grew somewhere on the mountain. Our curiosity was aroused by the peculiar form of these canes, which were yellowish-brown in colour with prominent raised, sharp-edged nodes. We later discovered that the canes belonged to *Qiongzhuea tumidinoda* (with tumour-like nodes), one of three species of a genus described and published for the first time in 1980. Some authorities now regard *Qiongzhuea* as belonging to the genus *Chimonobambusa* and the above species as *C tumidissinoda*. It is found in the wild in N.E.Yunnan and S.W. Sichuan in the mountains either side of the Yangtze river. Here it commonly forms extensive thickets often covering the summits of lower mountains between 1,500 and 2,100m (4,921 and 6,889ft.) altitude. It

Chimonobambusa tumidissinoda growing on a wooded hillside in Leibo County, S. Sichuan. Note the characteristic swollen nodes. Photographed by Mikinori Ogisu. (April)

normally occurs in broad-leaved evergreen and deciduous forest and in Leibo County in S. Sichuan I have seen it growing beneath a mixture of *Tetracentron sinense*, *Cercidiphyllum japonicum*, *Davidia involucrata*, *Carpinus fangiana* and the evergreen *Castanopsis platyacantha*. Conditions said to be enjoyed by this bamboo include warmth and abundant rainfall, mist, little sun, snow in winter and an acid soil. The green canes are from 2-6m (7-20ft.) tall and are characterised by their strongly swollen nodes which form a circular ridge like two dishes placed face to face. The leaves are narrowly lance-shaped up to 15cm (6in) long and up to 12mm (½ in) wide, green above, paler beneath. It is said to flower in April, its fruits ripening in May. No reference is made to the regularity of flowering, although flowering and fruiting material was collected apparently in 1965 and 1976.[3]

Accompanied by two guides from the China International Travel Service, we left the monastery in four jeeps driving along a dirt track which skirted the slopes before entering a deep valley. We drove through a fine grey drizzle, the accompanying mist obscuring our view of the higher slopes. Solitary Chusan palms (*Trachycarpus fortunei*) loomed out from the mist and these, together with China fir (*Cunninghamia lanceolata*), were the only trees to catch our attention as we slowly ascended the snaking road. We had been driving for about half an hour when, on rounding a bend, we were brought to a sudden halt by a large rock fall blocking the road ahead which had been brought down by the heavy rain the previous night. We all piled out of our jeeps to examine the situation, some of us wondering if our adventure was to be

3. Although only recently named, this famous bamboo has a long history in China going back to the Han Dynasty (206 BC-AD 220). Qiongzhu sticks, as the canes are known, were exported to central Asia and India, carried there by way of the Silk Route. They also found their way into Europe and Africa. Selected canes have also been used for tobacco pipes. It seems that large quantities of Qiongzhu canes are cut each year for both domestic use and export, and such is their importance and vulnerability that a move is underway to protect the native stands from over-exploitation. First introduced to the West (England) by Peter Addington in 1987 it is now well represented in cultivation, in warmer areas certainly where its fast spreading tendencies can cause problems. .

The beginning of an unforgettable ride. Members of our group watch pig carcasses being loaded onto the coal truck.

Anemone hupehensis f *alba*, a late flowering herbaceous perennial, brightens the scrub covered hillsides and field margins beneath heavily lopped specimens of the China fir. (October)

short lived. There was no way that the obstacle could be cleared that day, but on the other side of the fall we could see an empty coal truck in the same predicament. We dispatched our guides to negotiate an arrangement with the truck driver to take us back the way he had come and to our relief he agreed. Within ten minutes we had collected our belongings from the jeeps and crossed the rock fall to the awaiting truck.

On my way over the fall I found a most interesting *Viburnum* species, which had been carried down from the steep hillside above. It was a shrub of some 3m (9ft) with leaves not unlike those of *V rhytidophyllum* in size and shape but without the characteristic puckered (bullate) appearance and woolly undersurface. Luckily some of the branches carried bunches (corymbs) of red fruits, some of which I was able to introduce to Britain. A seedling was eventually grown at the RHS Garden Rosemoor in Devon.[4]

From collectors' notes, it appears that this species is not uncommon on Emei Shan, where it is found as a shrub or small tree up to 5m (16ft) high in woods and thickets at lower altitudes of between 518m and 1,200m (1,700 and 4,000ft). This casts some doubt on its likely hardiness in British cultivation, but I am hopeful that, given a sheltered position, it will succeed at least in the warmer counties. Interestingly, growing in the same valley as the viburnum and common in the roadside thickets was a hydrangea – *Hydrangea strigosa*, or *Hydrangea aspera* subspecies *strigosa* as one

4. It was a specimen taken from the Rosemoor plant that enabled Heino Heine of the Paris Museum to identify it as *V ternatum*, a name given by Dr Alfred Rehder in 1907, presumably to an original Wilson collection. Wilson collected this species during his second expedition for Veitch, and although there is some confusion regarding its exact locality, it would most certainly have been in west Sichuan. Subsequently, *V ternatum* was collected in several locations, mostly on Emei Shan by the Chinese botanists F T Wang and, of course, Wen-pei Fang. Together with specimens of the above collections in the Paris Museum is one from Yunnan collected in 1901 by the French missionary Père Ducloux.

authority prefers it. In its erect habit and lance-shaped leaves it seemed identical with the shrub we grew for many years under this name in the Hillier Arboretum. This shrub carried no number but Harold Hillier always believed it to be a Wilson collection. The Hillier plant grew well enough in a sheltered border but it occasionally suffered frost damage and, more to the point, it proved extremely shy of flowering. Indeed, in my fifteen years as Curator of the Arboretum I only ever saw this shrub flowering twice and then only in October/November after a long hot summer. The tender nature of this particular plant in cultivation is consistent with its low altitude in the wild on Emei Shan. For general cultivation in Britain this group of Lace-cap hydrangeas are best represented by selected forms of *H aspera* such as 'Macrophylla' and the Kawakami Group and the plant long grown as *H villosa* now known as *H aspera* Villosa Group.

Our party of eleven shared the open-topped coal truck with five villagers, three pig carcasses, a heap of native cucumbers and a basketful of nervous chickens. The journey that followed is one I am never likely to forget and several coal-smudged pages of my notebook will forever serve to remind me of the event.

A wealth of plants both new and familiar presented themselves as our truck charged along a pock-marked, winding and ever-ascending dirt road, engine snorting, gears crashing. People in the fields and children in doorways looked on, wide eyed, as we sped through hamlets, crossing precarious log bridges over torrents and a threshing river. China fir became frequent though increasingly more bedraggled in appearance due to overzealous pruning for firewood. Later, higher up the mountain in the forest, we saw trees of better shape. Beneath the trees on the slopes an

Hydrangea aspera subspecies *strigosa*, a common shrub at low altitudes in the mountains of western Sichuan. The narrow leaves and late flowering habit are characteristic. (October)

Kalopanax pictus was common in the valleys of Emei Shan often planted in the vicinity of villages. Photo taken at the Arnold Arboretum Massachussets. (October)

attractive late flowering perennial occurred, *Anemone hupehensis* f *alba*, up to 1m (3ft) high, the flowers white, flushed pink on the back of the tepals.

A tree commonly seen in the vicinity of villages as well as along the roadside was *Kalopanax pictus* (*K septemlobus*), a species widely distributed in eastern Asia, especially in Japan, and commonly planted in the Chengdu Plain and the valley bottoms in the mountains of Sichuan. It is generally a gawky tree when young with relatively smooth bark beset with stout, broad based yellowish prickles. It improves, however, as it matures and we saw several well balanced and handsome specimens of 20m (65ft) or more. The largest recorded specimen in British cultivation is a tree at Emmetts in Kent, which in 1984 measured 21m (68ft). Mature trees develop a dark deep ridged and furrowed bark, the prickles being mainly confined to the branches. The leaves are large and shallowly five-lobed but in variety *maximowiczii* they are deeply lobed and, as a consequence, more impressive. The tiny white flowers are borne in large branched heads in late summer giving way in autumn to small black berry-like fruits not unlike those of

Aralia elata. Like the last named it is a member of the ivy family, *Araliaceae*, and its flowers are just as attractive to insects as its fruits are to birds. In Britain, its unripened shoots are subject to damage in severe winters and it is undoubtedly more suited to a continental climate with its warmer summers. Not surprisingly, it is much admired in North America where it is planted as a shade tree. According to Michael Dirr, it has survived temperatures of -22°C (-7.5°F) in Wisconsin.

The Butterfly bush, *Buddleja davidii*, was abundant but seed collected from several plants has yet to produce anything of merit, most flowers being in the lavender-blue range. Despite this, I am pleased to have seen this commonly cultivated shrub in a wild state where its seeds are spread with the same abandon as in Britain, seedlings sprouting in the most unlikely places except in the forest's shade. As Wilson noted, it is, in the wild, a shrub of river valleys and associated slopes in the scrub layer. In very cold areas, such as are found in some of the northern states of the United States and Canada, this shrub behaves as a herbaceous plant, sprouting anew each spring from the base.

Buddleja davidii, the well-known Butterfly bush here seen with *Sinacalia tangutica* formerly known as *Senecio tangutica*, a bold yellow-flowered perennial growing by a stream in Sichuan. (September)

Clerodendrum trichotomum here represented by variety *fargesii* a most handsome shrub or small spreading tree both in flower and fruit as seen here. at Altamont, Ireland. (November)

Another shrub I had long wished to see in a wild state was *Clerodendrum trichotomum*. Here it was fairly common in the roadside scrub. The characteristic cat-like odour of its bruised leaves, unpleasant to some, we occasionally detected as our truck brushed by them, and the equally characteristic heads of scented star-shaped white flowers protruding from their maroon inflated calyces were still present on some bushes though faded on others. This is one of my favourite shrubs and is valuable for its late flowering. Equally effective are the bright blue pea-sized, berry-like fruits with richly coloured star-shaped maroon calyces lasting into early winter, eventually turning black when ripe. Widely distributed in China as well as in Japan, *C trichotomum* is not as common in British cultivation as it deserves. Although its pithy branches are often cut back in severe winters it readily sprouts anew in spring and sometimes produces suckers from the roots. It is best grown in full sun and is equally happy on acid or alkaline soils.[5]

After a while the road narrowed into little more than a track which in places passed through dense thickets of bamboo and mixed scrub. Roses and brambles with long thorny tentacle-like shoots raked the lurching truck and there was pandemonium aboard as we ducked to avoid being lashed and torn. At one point a villager was pinned to the tailboard by a falling carcass, while the sound of the chickens, who never ceased complaining, reached a crescendo at each hump in the track. Meanwhile, the cucumbers, a short rounded variety, rolled across the truck floor like balls on a snooker table, half of them bruised if not already burst. Cotoneaster,

berberis, acanthopanax and aralias appeared in rapid succession along the route, some hanging their fruits temptingly within reach. I was especially pleased to see the long, curved, leaden-blue pods of *Decaisnea fargesii* carried in heavy drooping bunches beneath large ruffs of deeply divided (pinnate) leaves.[6] The pods up to 15cm (6in) long are filled with a greyish slimy pulp in which the black flat circular seeds are set one on top of another like a pile of miniature dinner plates. On drying, the pulp takes on the consistency of plaster of Paris, making seed extraction all the more difficult.

This uncommon shrub is worth growing for its handsome foliage alone, the unusual fruits being a bonus. The yellowish-green flowers in June are comparatively dull. Its stout stems can reach 5m (16ft) and it lends an imposing summer presence to the shrub border, associating well with small- to medium-sized rhododendrons among which its foliage provides a striking contrast. It is quite hardy and tolerant of any well drained soil, acid or otherwise. According to Alfred Rehder, who identified many of Wilson's plants, its

5. Indeed, in the Arnold Arboretum, Massachusetts, it behaves almost as an herbaceous perennial, regularly producing each summer dense rounded mounds of young shoots with bold foliage. One of the best specimens I ever saw grew on the shallow chalk soil of the Hillier West Hill Nursery in Winchester. It was a broad spreading short-stemmed tree no more than 5m (16ft) high, but almost twice as much across. It belonged to the variety *fargesii*, a hardier plant than most others.

6. Its name commemorates two famous plantsmen – Joseph Decaisne, a Belgian botanist and one-time Director of the Jardin des Plantes in Paris, and the missionary Paul Farges who first discovered this species in north-east Sichuan. It was introduced to the West as seed from the same source in 1895.

7. It is named after the Reverend B Ririe of the China Inland Mission, and a friend of Wilson.

Our party prepares to leave the coal truck at the end of an incredible botanical drive in pouring rain on Emei Shan. (October)

Decaisnea fargesii, a striking shrub when in fruit with leaden blue pods in drooping bunches. It was common in mixed scrub on Emei Shan. Here it is seen in cultivation at Maurice Mason's garden, Larchwood, Norfolk. (November)

fruits although insipid are edible and eaten in China, though I have no personal experience of this and cannot say which part of the fruit is eaten unless it be the pulp. Professor Fang told us that the fruits are certainly eaten by monkeys on Emei Shan. He also told us a local name for this shrub which refers to the fruits resembling the excrement of cats, we could only assume that the creatures in mind were of some giant breed! The only other member of the genus is *D insignis* which is described as having golden-yellow fruits. Native of Yunnan and the Himalaya west to Nepal it is extremely rare in cultivation and I have yet to see it fruiting.

The variety of trees and shrubs appearing now on all sides read like a catalogue. It was like driving through the pages of *Rehder's Manual* or through all four volumes of *Bean*! Eventually, we reached a point in the track, now a road again, where several wooden dwellings stood, smoke pouring from every joint and aperture. Here the road levelled before curving away and out of sight. It was the end of the ride and we clambered down from the truck feeling a mixture of relief and regret. From this point, some 2,100m (6,889ft) above sea level, we faced a hard climb to the mountain's summit. Our route lay initially along a steep muddy track that snaked its way through dense bamboo, heading for a ridge high above. We made slow progress plodding through the mud but, when the track emerged from the bamboo and travelled over rocky ground, the going became easier.

To attempt to describe all the plants seen during our stay on Emei Shan would require a book of its own. What follows, therefore, is a string of highlights, a handful of pebbles from a beach.

Our route lay initially along a steep muddy track that snaked its way through dense bamboo thickets. (October)

We had already encountered our first rhododendron – *Rhododendron ririei* [7] on our way through the bamboo. First discovered here by Wilson in 1903, its pale magenta-purple flowers were long past and we had to content ourselves with the striking contrast between the leaf surfaces, dark green above, white beneath. Similar in effect are the silver-backed leaves of *R argyrophyllum* subspecies *omeiense*, a pink-flowered shrub that, on Emei Shan, is often found in association with *R ririei*.

Rhododendron calophytum. Left, an old tree of around 7.5m. (25ft.) dominates a trail through bamboo on Emei Shan. (October). Seed (L.470) from this tree produced a seedling, right, flowering for the first time in the Savill Garden. (Photograph by Mark Flanagan. (March)

Even more impressive, however, is *Rhododendron calophytum* which we found quite common in the bamboo and elsewhere.[8] It is easily recognised by its more or less smooth, rich-green leaves, which are long and comparatively narrow – 20-30cm (8-12in) long by 5-9cm (2-3½ in) wide and even larger on young plants or on vigorous shoots. The loose trusses of white or pink flowers in March or April are a bonus. Like others of its kind, *R calophytum* enjoys a sheltered, preferably woodland site in cultivation and this is borne out by its occurrence in the wild. By far the best specimens were those growing in deep gullies and ravines and similarly sheltered situations. In such places specimens of 9m (30ft) were not uncommon and one single-stemmed specimen of 10m (32ft) must have been two hundred years old or more. Even larger specimens were recorded by Wilson and others.

Of all the ornamental trees in cultivation I have always had a soft spot for maples and rowans or Mountain ash, especially in autumn when the leaf tints of one and the fruits of the other provide our gardens with a wealth of colour. I had long been familiar with the many species of both genera grown in collections like the Hillier Arboretum, but not even this prepared me for the galaxy of talent on Emei Shan. Two sorbus in particular attracted instant attention by their fruits. One of these, *Sorbus sargentiana*, occurred here as a low, widely-branched tree with typically bold foliage and equally large heads (corymbs) of small orange-scarlet fruits. Just as characteristic are the conspicuous buds in winter, which

Sorbus sargentiana is one of the most spectacular and easily recognised of its kind, especially in autumn when the small fruits are borne in large dense heads. This photograph was taken in the Hillier Arboretum in Hampshire of a tree derived as a graft from a tree collected as seed (L.470A) on Emei Shan in 1980. (October)

8. Although first discovered by Armand David elsewhere in Sichuan in 1869, this noble species was first introduced to Britain by E.H. Wilson in 1904.

Sorbus setschwanensis; the attractive pearl-white fruits of this most ornamental shrubby mountain ash. Later the leaves turn a rich crimson. A specimen in the author's garden grown from Emei Shan seed (L.492). (October)

Sorbus setschwanensis; the young foliage and flower buds of this Chinese rowan in early summer is possibly the most elegant of all *Sorbus* species. Here growing in the author's garden. (June)

resemble red versions of the familiar 'sticky buds' of Horse chestnut (*Aesculus hippocastanum*).

Another Wilson discovery, this magnificent rowan commemorates Charles Sprague Sargent, first Director of the Arnold Arboretum who financed Wilson's third and fourth Chinese expeditions. In cultivation, this species requires a sunny site with plenty of elbow room if it is to develop to its full stature. The finest specimens I ever saw, both over 10m (32ft), grew as a pair in the Silk Wood extension to the Westonbirt Arboretum in Gloucestershire. Sadly, one has since died.

The other mountain ash we saw growing in some numbers on the mountain was *Sorbus setschwanensis*, a white-fruited species closely related to *S koehneana*. It was a small tree or shrub of about 5m (16ft), with elegant arching branches,

dainty fern-like leaves, and small pure white fruits in loose bunches. Koehne, who named this species, claimed it to be the smallest leaved of all sorbus. In *Bean* it is given faint praise but young plants grown from seed collected on Emei Shan are full of promise. These are shrubby in growth with slender, arching stems while the leaves are the smallest and neatest of any I have seen, making even those of *S vilmorinii* seem coarse by comparison. They are copper coloured when young, turning a rich crimson in autumn. A plant in my garden has regularly attracted favourable comment from visiting plantsmen and others and I am confident that it faces a bright future in cultivation. It associates well with dwarf rhododendrons or heathers and should make an ideal specimen tree or shrub for the smaller garden. The small crowded heads (corymbs) of white flowers set in red calyces contribute to the charm of this species in early June. Like many of its relatives, it is less satisfactory in dry conditions and appears to do best in areas of higher rainfall which is not surprising considering its native climate.

Growing with the mountain ash on Emei Shan was *Sorbus pallescens*, a relative of our native whitebeam, a handsome tree of 5-8m (16-26ft) with undivided leaves, white downy beneath. Its fruits were the size of small crabs, green in colour with a red 'cheek'. A true crab was also present in *Malus yunnanensis*.

Of maples we saw six, possibly seven, species including the big leaved *Acer franchetii*. By far the most common was *Acer campbellii* subspecies *flabellatum*, a form of the Himalyan *A*

Acer campbellii subspecies *flabellatum* with its seven-lobed leaves on red flushed stalks is a common maple on Emei Shan. (October)

The Pilgrim's Path on Emei Shan is an ancient route to the summit. Here it passes through dwarf bamboo, possibly *Bashania faberi* (fangiana) a food source of the panda, beneath silver fir (*Abies fabri*), the stems of the latter swaddled in moss. (October)

campbellii. Here it was a tree 12-15m (40-50ft) high occurring singly or in groves. The leaves, carried on reddish stalks, were rounded in outline, sharply toothed and with seven abruptly pointed lobes reaching a third of the way to the base. They looked at their best having turned red or yellow, brightly staining the hillsides around. Rare in cultivation, *A campbellii* subspecies *flabellatum* is sometimes represented there by the variety *yunnanense*, which is generally less hardy.

The maple I was most pleased to see, however, was *A davidii*, named after Armand David, who first found it in the Baoxing (Mupin) district of Sichuan.[9] On Emei Shan *A davidii* reached 9-12m (30-40ft) with typically striated bark. A small tree in my garden grown from Emei Shan seed has rich red polished young shoots and silver-grey striations on the older wood. It is strong growing and bold foliaged, in character not unlike those found by Forrest in west Yunnan. In cultivation in Britain *A davidii* is popular and among the best known of the 'snakebark' group of maples. It is less common in North America outside of arboreta and botanic gardens. The tallest recorded British specimen is a tree in the Winkworth Arboretum, Surrey, which in 2000 measured 20m (65ft).

9. It was later introduced to England by Charles Maries from the Yichang (Ichang) area of Hubei province, but the most important collections were those made by Wilson from Hubei and Sichuan and by George Forrest and Kingdon-Ward from Yunnan.

The Pilgrim's Path

During our wanderings on either side of the track, we had gradually been moving up the mountain until, without warning, we joined one of the two stepped paths that ascend the mountain from the Bao Guo Monastery. Higher still the two paths unite for the final journey to the Golden Summit. Known as the Pilgrim's Path, this ancient route up Emei Shan represents an impressive feat, many thousands of stone steps (22,000 according to one estimate) climbing up and down several spurs of the mountain before ascending the final ridge. In places the steps are shallow, elsewhere deep, making the climb doubly trying for all but the fittest. No slope appears to have been too steep for the step builders and there are several almost vertical pitches, which are best described as stone ladders. Of the two routes, that together form the Pilgrim's Path, the northern route at 44 kilometres (27½ miles) is the shorter. It is also wider and easier to follow. The southern route is more winding and more exhausting to follow, stretching some 63.5 kilometres (39½ miles) from monastery to summit, a journey that would normally take from three to four days depending on one's fitness. Next day, at the summit we met two young Japanese visitors who claimed to have taken only two days for the climb, presumably by the northern route. Having seen Japanese and Chinese youths jogging up similar mountains elsewhere I was not really surprised.

In years gone by the Pilgrim's Path was the scene of great activity. Many thousands of pilgrims came annually from all parts of the Empire to worship at the Golden Summit, stopping at the many temples and shrines on the way. In 1903 Wilson found up to seventy Buddhist temples (monasteries) on Emei Shan, most of them on the main route to the summit where they occurred every 5 li (2.5km/1½ miles). They were controlled by abbots and contained upwards of two thousand monks and acolytes. Today only a handful of temples remain, mostly in the care of elderly monks whose duties are as much towards the needs of tourism as to those of religion. Pilgrims still visit Emei Shan and later, on descending the mountain, we met a Tibetan and his wife approaching the summit with a mixture of reverence and anticipation in their eyes. They had been on the road for several weeks and had reached their destination a short while before an old woman with an incurable disease whose frail body was supported in a chair strapped to a porter's back. These pilgrims were just three of

many for whom the mountain still retains its original significance and appeal.

Although the stepped track made the going easier underfoot, its regularity reminded us of the steepness of our climb and our progress slowed but not only because of the steep ascent, we also made frequent stops to examine the wayside plants that continued to bedazzle by their variety. Two cotoneasters appeared in the thicket, both large shrubs with distinctive puckered (bullate) leaves. They differed principally in their fruits, those of *Cotoneaster moupinensis* shining black, those of *Cotoneaster bullatus* brilliant red. Hardy and handsome, these two are not as commonly cultivated in Britain as one might have expected considering the merits of their fruit and foliage. Because of their eventual size – 3m (9ft) or more – they are best suited to medium- to large-sized gardens where they excel either as 'back of the border' subjects or alternatively as specimens in the lawn. Both were originally first introduced to France towards the end of the last century. Even better than *C bullatus* is the variety *floribundus*, which is the form generally represented in gardens. It has up to three times the number of flowers – and therefore fruits – in the cluster, though the flowers of both species are not worthy of praise.[10]

Pilgrims still visit Emei Shan. Here a Tibetan family climb the long path to the summit temple. (October)

10. Since these descriptions were written the plant whose seeds I collected as C bullatus has been described by Fryer and Hylmo as a new species C emeiensis whilst the black-fruited plant thought to be C moupinensis could well have been the recently named C lancasteri.

Above. An old man we met climbing the Pilgrim's Path on his way to the summit of Emei Shan

Above. *Cotoneaster lancasteri* (L.1527), a recently described species which might well have been the plant seen on Emei Shan in 1980 and thought to be *C moupinensis*. Photographed in the author's garden. (September)

Left. *Cotoneaster emeiensis*, a newly described species from Emei Shan previously thought to be *C bullatus*. Its seed was introduced (L494) in 1980 and this species is now established in cultivation. Here it is photographed in the author's garden. (October)

Growing with the cotoneasters and elsewhere on the mountain we found a mock orange (*Philadelphus* species). It was a shrub of lax habit 2-2.5m (6-8ft) in height with minutely downy young shoots and distinctive slender-pointed leaves. Seed was collected and in 1985 some of the resultant plants flowered for the first time. In 1986 a plant flowered in my garden from late June into July, the flowers borne in elongated clusters (racemes or racemose panicles) on short leafy shoots along the upper ends of the arching branches. The individual flowers were relatively small, 2-2.5cm (¾ -1in), across and cup shaped, the white petals backed by a downy cream-coloured calyx and enclosing a cluster of golden anthers. Their small size is compensated for, however, by a sweet fragrance. In most characters this shrub answers to *Philadelphus subcanus*, agreeing in all but minor details with plants grown under this name at Wakehurst Place in Sussex and mentioned in Bean's work.

At a height of some 2,500m (8,200ft) we reached a small wooded plateau known as Lei-dong-ping or Thunder Cave Terrace. In this area, plants continued to dominate. *Rosa sericea* subspecies *omeiensis* was the common rose, a shrub of 3m (9ft) with fern-like leaves and stems densely clad with bristles and small flattened thorns. The small, pear-shaped, red and yellow hips had already fallen.

A lilac, which I mistook for *Syringa reflexa* was more likely *S komarovii*. The two are closely related, being similar both in height, 4m (13ft) or more, and foliage. Both have long densely packed cylindrical or narrowly conical arching or nodding inflorescences. Those of *S reflexa*, however, are generally longer, more slender and more recurved, as well as having other minor botanical differences. Besides this, the two species occur in the wild in different areas. *S komarowii* is restricted to west Sichuan (including Emei Shan) while *S reflexa* is native to Hubei province in central China. Both are easy and hardy in cultivation and are useful at the back of the shrub border or as specimens in the lawn. Their flowers in June are fragrant, varying in colour from dark to light pink, sometimes with a lilac or purple tinge.

Many years ago, as a young man, I remember being taken to see a large neglected garden on an exposed hillside on the moors north of my home in Lancashire. It had been planted some fifty years earlier with a wide variety of trees and shrubs, most of which had since run riot and presented a jungle-like appearance. For me it was a magical place, a treasure house of new and unusual plants to which I frequently returned over a period of years. On one visit I found a small tree with unusual prickly leaves. Its identity puzzled me for a long time until one year it produced bright red fruits not unlike those of the English holly but smaller. At last, with the help of a dear friend, Jack Barber, my gardening 'guru', I traced its identity to that of a Chinese holly – *Ilex pernyi*, named after Paul Perny a French missionary who first discovered it. Perny worked in the province of Guizhou (Kweichow) between 1848 and 1862,

At Lei-dong-ping, or Thunder Cave Terrace, the only dwelling we could see was a small wood-framed tea house (or, more correctly, shack) with bamboo matting walls. In such dwellings E H Wilson and others occasionally sought lodgings for the night. (October).

Syringa komarowii. A handsome Chinese lilac related to *S reflexa* with characteristic narrow drooping flower-heads. Here seen in the author's garden from seed (L.490) collected on Emei Shan. (May)

travelling there, according to Bretschneider, disguised as a Chinese beggar. I have since seen *I pernyi* in several collections, notably in the Hillier Arboretum where it fruited profusely after the drought of 1976. One can perhaps understand my delight, therefore, when I found this species not uncommon in the woods at Lei-dong-ping. Here it was a small tree, up to 8m (26ft) high, and its distinctive oblong, five-spined, leathery, evergreen leaves borne along either side of the branches recalled the memory of my original discovery and I could not resist sharing the story with my companions.

The Abbé Perny's holly is not the only species of its clan present on Emei Shan. There are several more and we found at least five others including *I ciliospinosa, I purpurea, I diplosperma, I fargesii* and *I yunnanensis.* The last two I remembered from the Hillier Arboretum as forming part of a holly collection, which was at that time (1970s) the most comprehensive of its kind in Europe.

On banks above the path and elsewhere at Lei-dong-ping, grew an interesting selection of perennials among which *Podophyllum hexandrum* variety *chinense* seemed little different from the typical species so common in the mountains of Kashmir and elsewhere in the Himalaya. *Anemone davidii* reminded me of our native woodland species *A nemorosa*, though perhaps with slightly less delicate flowers and a more erect habit. A plant in my garden grown from seed collected on Emei is forming a colony by means of its slender creeping underground stems. Its leaves are purple flushed beneath when young. Very different in appearance was *Rodgersia aesculifolia* with its bold colonies of long-stalked, rugged, horse chestnut-like leaves. Unfortunately, it was well past flowering but it must present quite a spectacle when its creamy-white plumes are at their best in summer. Here it grew in moist places, and it enjoys similar sites in cultivation where it is hardy and readily available. It was seen on Emei by Wilson but had first been discovered over thirty years earlier in the Baoxing (Mupin) area of Sichuan by Armand David.

Several ground-covering plants occurred in the woods at Lei-dong-ping and no doubt elsewhere on the mountain. Two of these, *Rubus fockeanus* and *Euonymus mupinensis*, are now in cultivation from Emei Shan. The rubus, or rather its name, has long been a source of confusion in gardens. It is a small plant with clover-like (trifoliolate) crinkly leaves and small inclined white-petalled flowers. It resembles a miniature strawberry in appearance, except that the leaves are dull green and the fruits like small raspberries. It spreads like a strawberry, too, its slender runners covering a large area in time. Not many years ago the name *R fockeanus* was commonly used in cultivation for a species with shallowly five-lobed, but otherwise undivided, puckered leaves, a very distinctive plant fully evergreen, quite prostrate and comparatively slow growing.

The following simplified story illustrates just one of the ways nomenclature can cause confusion in the garden. When compiling the *Hillier Manual* (published 1971), quite by accident we came across *R fockeanus* (as we then named and grew it) in a book – *The Woody Flora of Taiwan.* The description confirmed our plant not as *R fockeanus*, but as *R calycinoides.* In the *Manual* we adopted this name, which had been published for this species by the Japanese botanist Hayata in 1913. All should have been happy ever after, but it was not. Subsequently, I learned that the name *R calycinoides* was invalid for the Taiwan species as it had previously been used and published (in 1879) by the German botanist Kuntze for an east Himalayan species. The next available

Euonymus mupinensis (L.551), a far-reaching, low-growing evergreen species forming carpets on the woodland floor. Here seen in cultivation in the author's garden. Note the shining green leaves and slender-stalked flowers pressed close to the leaf upper surface. (June)

Standing on the edge of the precipice above Lei-dong-ping, a wooded plateau on the Pilgrim's Path, we observed a series of remarkable limestone cliffs, their faces softened by a colourful mosaic of autumn foliage. (October)

cultivation it seems set to follow the same lifestyle.

Climbing above Lei-dong-ping the path skirts the edge of a high vertical cliff. Standing on the very lip of the abyss we observed a remarkable sight. Across to our left rose a magnificent limestone precipice, part of a huge spur running down from the main mountain towards the north east. The spectacle was made all the more impressive by the presence of mist or cloud (or both) several hundred metres below, obscuring the full extent of the precipice's height. It was an awesome sight, this vast rock wall softened only by the vegetation that filled gullies and ledges over its entire visible

name for the Taiwan species appears to be R *pentalobus*, originally published in 1909, again by Hayata, for a plant that proves to be no more than a growth form of the Taiwan species. To sum up, the small leaved creeping Chinese species of *Rubus* seen on Emei Shan should be referred to under the following name: R *fockeanus* Kurz. The Taiwan plant meanwhile, common in cultivation and by far the most ornamental of its kind is now correctly known as R *rolfei*.

Whether true R *calycinoides* is in cultivation I cannot say but, in 1971, I was party to introducing two other creeping species into cultivation from east Nepal. One of these was R *calycinus* with lobed leaves, the other R *nepalensis* with leaves trifoliolate like those of true R *fockeanus*. I should love to say that these are likely to be the last words on the subject, but somehow I doubt it.

Euonymus mupinensis is an evergreen spindleberry with long green stems that lie on the ground rooting where conditions permit. Its leaves are rather broad with toothed margins. On Emei Shan, it formed extensive carpets in the shade of rhododendrons and associated shrubs, climbing for several metres the stems of neighbouring trees. In

The Pilgrim's Path supports a regular traffic of porters carrying supplies to the Temple of the Golden Summit. The wooden frame supports the load above this porter's back, while the T-shaped stick in his hand supports him or his load when resting. (October)

Two of Emei Shan's loveliest trees, both conifers, are the dome-crowned *Tsuga dumosa* (left), and the flat-topped *Abies fabri* (right).

face. Many of the trees and shrubs there were in autumn leaf presenting a colourful mosaic of green, red and yellow against the grey of the limestone. I could not help thinking of the interesting plants, some possibly undescribed, for which this precipice and others like it was a home. Eventually, I turned away; to climb such walls would test an experienced rock climber let alone a plantsman.

Steep flights of steps followed and ascending them was exhausting work despite the many stops to examine plants. An evergreen tree which had been with us for some time now became dominant. *Abies fabri*, named after Ernst Faber who first collected it, is one of several silver firs found in the mountains of western China. It is a magnificent tree of 30m (100ft) or more, conical when young, becoming more or less flat-topped with the upper branches ascending towards the tips in maturity. It has the dark blue or bluish-black cones so typical of its group, standing on the upper sides of the shoots. The shining dark green leaves are silvery-white beneath, the margins slightly recurved. One of our party on Emei Shan was Keith Rushforth, who has made a detailed study of *Abies* – the Chinese species in particular. He was delighted to have the opportunity of examining *A fabri* in its classic location, and has since written about the confusion surrounding this species and the closely related *A delavayi* from west Yunnan, upper Burma and north-east Thailand. According to Rushforth, *A fabri* differs from *A delavayi* in a number of ways, more especially in the shorter, barrel-shaped rather than cylindrical cones with reflexed (not spreading or

erect) cusps. The shoots too, are paler, fawn-brown or yellow-brown as against the maroon or, less often, red-brown or orange-brown of *A delavayi*. E H Wilson, who also saw and collected seed of this tree on Emei Shan (though he called it *A delavayi*), declared that 'no more handsome conifer exists in all the Far East'. Praise indeed, and one detects more than a hint of sadness when he went on to point out that those temples on the higher parts of the mountain were constructed almost entirely from the wood of this fir. In British cultivation *A fabri* is rare, the tallest tree being found at Benmore, Argyll, which in 1991 measured 28m (92ft).

There is another conifer on this mountain that, though apparently fewer in numbers, is equal in my eyes to the silver fir. This challenger for the conifer crown is a hemlock fir *Tsuga dumosa* (*yunnanensis*). Unlike its rival, this tree did not appear to be anywhere dominant, although we saw the occasional group or small grove. In the areas we passed through it was mainly represented as isolated individuals, some specimens every bit as tall as the fir, but differing from afar in their wide-spreading habit with graceful downcurved branches. Even mature trees growing close to firs of similar age could easily be recognised from a distance by their domed crowns. In British and Irish cultivation, *T dumosa* grows best in western areas, the tallest being in Ireland. A tree labelled *T yunnanensis* at Borde Hill in Sussex had reached a height of 10m (32ft) in 1981.

The autumn colours were superb on these upper slopes. Bright splashes of yellow, gold, crimson and scarlet

Above. The brilliant tints of deciduous trees and shrubs including maples, Enkianthus, *Lindera* and *Sorbus*, stand out in the dark canopy of rhododendrons, oaks and other evergreens on the upper slopes of Emei Shan. (October)

contributed mainly by species of *Acer, Betula, Sorbus, Malus, Viburnum, Berberis* and *Enkianthus*. The last named was the most brilliant of all, a sheet of flame in the thickets. Once as we rounded a corner, its sudden appearance and effect on the pathside stopped us in our tracks. It was *Enkianthus deflexus*, a species with pendulous clusters of comparatively large, bell-shaped, cream-coloured flowers flushed and striped red in June. It is a large shrub, occasionally a small, erect-branched tree 5m (16ft) or more high, distributed in the wild from east Nepal to west China.

It was while admiring the enkianthus that we were reminded of the lateness of the hour, and with a long climb still before us we decided to resist the temptation of further exploration in order to catch up those of our colleagues who were by now well ahead. Typically, our resolve did not last long. After climbing a hundred metres or so (300ft), a large *Viburnum nervosum (cordifolium)* confronted us with its bold oval leaves tinted red and yellow, while in the vicinity lurked a host of Rhododendron species including *R ambiguum, R strigillosum, R pachytrichum, R davidii* and *R wiltonii*. The last named we found particularly impressive with its handsome leaves up to 10cm (4in) long, shining green and puckered (bullate) above, covered beneath with a thick pelt of brown woolly hairs. This species is only known from a few mountains in west Sichuan and was another of Wilson's original discoveries. It is uncommon, though not difficult, in cultivation where it is admired as much, if not more, for its leaves than for its clusters of white or pink bell-shaped flowers in April or May.

Rhododendron wiltonii poised on the edge of a precipice. Beyond is a spectacular series of limestone cliffs. (October)

Enkianthus deflexus growing by the Pilgrim's Path on Emei Shan, its leaves a sheet of brilliant colour. This species is rarely seen in western cultivation. (October)

A view at dawn looking west from the summit of Emei Shan. In the middle distance is the territory referred to by E H Wilson as the Laolin, or Wilderness, while dominating the horizon are the snow covered mountains of the Gongga Shan or Minya Konka range and the mountains above Kangding on the Tibetan border. In the foreground a fringe of *Abies fabri*, many of them in poor condition.(October)

The Golden Summit

It was inevitable that dusk should find us still in the thicket, and following a determined climb up the remaining steps we finally achieved the Temple of the Golden Summit (Jin Ding) as darkness fell. The present wooden building is but the latest in a line of temples, most of which are reputed to have been destroyed by fire or lightning. We entered through an open door stumbling wearily through echoing unlit passages where the occasional sound of chanting voices was the only indication that we were not alone. Eventually, a monk clutching a tiny butter lamp greeted us and we gladly followed him up interminable wooden stairs and along further corridors to where rooms had been prepared for our use. Large bowls of steaming hot water were placed in an adjoining room and once washed and changed and wrapped in voluminous padded overcoats we began to feel comfortable and more aware of our surroundings. After a while, our monk reappeared to lead us out of our quarters and across a small courtyard, where incense smoked at the feet of a genial pot-bellied Buddha, into a large room filled with tables and chairs. Despite the butter lamps, so dim was the interior that I very much doubt if any of us knew what we ate for supper that night. I do remember, however, peeping through a doorway into the kitchen, there to behold a scene medieval in its effect. Cauldrons and woks with bubbling or sizzling contents stood on various fires

while cooks and assistants, bodies glistening with sweat, moved in attendance.

That night, we slept in our greatcoats in huge wooden beds, listening to the rain beating a tattoo on the corrugated iron roof above. Next morning we were up before dawn intent on seeing the sunrise. It was cold and dark as we stood some distance from the temple stomping our feet and swinging our arms in an effort to keep warm. The sun eventually emerged, shining brilliantly for several minutes before disappearing into low cloud but leaving us with an all too brief memory of a rose-painted landscape. It was replaced by a sea of grey cloud, punctured in places by neighbouring mountains among which the distinctive flat-topped bulks of Wa-Shan and Wa-wu Shan were recognisable.

Close to the present temple is a fearsome precipice estimated as being over 1,610m (1 mile) high, from the brim of which Emei's most famous spectacle, the 'Fo-guang' or 'Glory of Buddha', a phenomenon similar to the 'Spectre of the Brocken', can be seen when certain weather conditions prevail. Baber and Wilson among many famous visitors failed to see the phenomenon, but A E Pratt was luckier, seeing it twice during his visit to the mountain in 1890. On the days in question the sky was clear with a bright sun and there was a layer of cloud some 610m (2,000ft) below the edge of the precipice. 'This extraordinary phenomenon', Pratt wrote, 'is apparently the reflection of the sun upon the upper surface of the clouds beneath, and has the appearance of a golden disc surrounded by radiating bars bearing all the colours of the rainbow. These are constantly moving, and scintillate and change colour in a very remarkable manner'. Devotees believed this phenomenon to be an emanation from the aureole of Buddha and an outward and visible sign of the holiness of Emei Shan. Sometimes, according to other accounts, the shadow of the onlooker is projected on to the disc.

The precipice in question is known as the 'Great Leap', and for a very good reason. In times gone by religious zealots when exposed to the 'Glory of Buddha' were so overcome by excess of religious feeling that they would throw themselves over the precipice into the clouds upon which the 'Glory' appeared, their bodies as a rule, according to Pratt, 'falling on an inaccessible spur covered with forest, perhaps a mile or more below'. Being less bold, yet nevertheless keen to learn what those rocky ledges supported, I crawled on my stomach to the edge of the brink only to find the cliffs concealed by cloud and mist. On withdrawing, however, I was impressed to note that the patch of ground on which I had irreverently lain contained no less than one dwarf rhododendron (R *nitidulum* variety *omeiense*), a new dwarf *Cotoneaster* species (C *chengkangensis*), a flattened *spiraea* (*Spiraea myrtilloides*), a blue gentian, a yellow saxifrage and for good measure an edelweiss. Of all these, the last named was the most impressive with its clusters of small flowerheads surrounded by large, white, flannelly, long-pointed bracts creating a star-shaped effect. It has since been identified as *Leontopodium calocephalum*, the second name deriving from the Greek kalos: beautiful and *cephalos*: head – 'beautiful head'. Later, we found it again on a rock face forming bold clumps 25cm (10in) high. As far as I am aware this species is not in cultivation at the present.

We spent a little time after breakfast examining further the edge of the precipice and were interested to find a number of trees and shrubs of gnarled form pruned by wind and exposure. These included *Rhododendron ambiguum* again and R *faberi*, one of Faber's original discoveries, distinct on account of the hairs (indumentum) on the leaf undersurface. These occur in two layers, the upper layer loose and rust-red in colour eventually wearing away to reveal a lower layer that is white, dense and persistent. Another find here was a *Sorbus* species, probably S *helenae*, a small tree with distinctive broad oblong leaflets with rust-coloured hairs beneath. It is related to the white-fruited, east Himalayan S *insignis* and was first discovered by Wilson after whose wife, Ellen, it is named.

The 'Great Leap', foreground, a fearsome precipice close to the Temple of the Golden Summit. From here, in days gone by, religious zealots jumped to a certain death. Photographed by H L Richardson early 1900s.

With the morning advancing, we reluctantly left the Golden Summit to begin the long descent. For our return journey we planned to follow the Pilgrim's Path almost to its source and we had two and a half days in which to achieve it, allowing for two overnight stops in monasteries and as many botanising forays as we could squeeze in. We made good time to Lei-dong-ping just beyond which we stopped to botanise. Here grew *Stachyurus retusus*, a shrub of some 2-3m (6-9ft) with deciduous leaves broader towards the apex (obovate), at which there occurred a distinct notch. The flowers are said to be greenish-yellow. This was the first of six species seen on the mountain, and it is perhaps worth mentioning the others here even though they occur at lower altitudes – under 1,980m (6,500ft). Three evergreen species, all from around 1,200-1,300m (3,900-4,300ft), are of considerable merit, more for their foliage than their flowers. One of these, S *yunnanensis*, had slender-pointed leaves up to 13cm (5in) long and droopy spikes of greenish-yellow flowers in March or April.

Leontopodium calocephalum, an impressive Chinese edelweiss near the summit of Emei Shan. The name *calocephalum* derives from the Greek - kalos: beautiful, and *cephalos*: head. Beautiful head - a most appropriate description! (October)

Stachyurus yunnanensis, an evergreen species of little ornamental merit in flower. Photographed on Emei Shan by M. Ogisu. (March)

Its close relative, S *obovatus*, we found even more plentiful in the forest. This was a shrub of some 2-3m (6-9ft), with toothed, glossy-topped, leathery, evergreen leaves, dark shining green above, broader towards the apex (obovate or oblanceolate) where they abruptly contract to a distinct tail-like point. The greenish-yellow flowers in March are borne in short, drooping axillary spikes.

Growing in the same situation as the last was S *salicifolius*, a shrub of similar dimensions but more graceful, with slender arching or drooping branches and narrow, finely-toothed leaves up to 13cm (5in) long by 8-12mm (¼ - ½ in) across. The greenish-yellow flowers are borne in drooping axillary spikes in May. None of the above three would I describe as truly hardy, though they would be well worth trying in milder areas. All have been introduced from Emei Shan in recent times, and S *salicifolius*, a most

distinct and attractive foliage shrub is presently thriving in my garden.

S *himalaicus* is a vigorous deciduous shrub up to 3m (9ft) or more with bold foliage and, in late winter, drooping spikes of flowers, which vary from yellow to rose-pink in colour. It is distributed in the wild from China and Taiwan to east Nepal, from which latter country an expedition, of which I was a member, introduced it as seed in 1971. A form with rose-pink flowers was previously in cultivation in Britain from a Forrest or Kingdon-Ward collection and I well remember a specimen flowering for the first time against a sheltered north wall of Jermyns House, home of the late Sir Harold Hillier, in the 1960s. Its flowers were greeted with great excitement by Hilliers staff, not for their beauty, which was negligible, but because of their unusual colour. Unfortunately S *himalaicus*

Stachyurus salicifolius, a most handsome evergreen with narrow, willow-like leaves in lush sprays. The flowers in May are pale yellow in narrow drooping spikes. Author's garden. (October)

Euonymus cornutus variety *quinquecornutus*, a slender-stemmed spindleberry with narrow leaves and ornamental fruits hanging from the branches like Christmas baubles. (October)

is not fully hardy out of doors in Britain and the Jermyns House plant later succumbed in a severe winter. Another deciduous species is S *chinensis* which is equal in merit to its Japanese counterpart S *praecox*, though rarely seen in cultivation.

On the Pilgrim's Path we encountered a man with an antique long-barrelled, short-stocked musket. Later we heard him discharging it in the bamboo thicket

On Emei Shan S *chinensis* occurs at varying altitudes, and plants grown from seed collected there reflect this. Those from lower elevations are semi-evergreen and subject to damage by frost, due to the tendency of their shoots to continue growing late into the year. The hardier forms, however, are excellent medium- to large-sized shrubs for the garden on all but badly drained soils. Their flower spikes are initiated in autumn, opening the following spring before the leaves. The small pale yellow cup-shaped flowers have no discernible scent but they are very effective in decorating the naked shoots at a time when few other flowering shrubs are active. There is in British cultivation a *Stachyurus* called 'Magpie' with boldly white-margined leaves, which originated as a thousand-to-one chance in a box of seedlings in the Winchester Nursery of Hilliers in 1948. It might well be a hybrid of S *chinensis* with S *praecox*.

The skimmias are a group of evergreen shrubs represented in cultivation mainly by the Japanese *Skimmia japonica* and its various forms and hybrids. The brilliant red fruits of female plants are well known and it came as a surprise to me, therefore, to find on Emei Shan a skimmia with shining black fruits. This was S *laureola*, a low-growing shrub 1m (3ft) or less, which formed colonies in the shade of the trees. Surprisingly, the fruits are quite ornamental and should provide a striking contrast to the red-fruited skimmias in cultivation.[11]

At one point the path passed through a dense thicket of bamboo in which we found *Lonicera nitida* and *Kerria japonica*, both well known to us from cultivation. We found ourselves musing on the vast numbers of the former shrub

11. This species was originally introduced from west China, by Wilson certainly, under the name S *melanocarpa* (meaning black fruited), but it occurs in the wild as far west as east Nepal, where it was collected by the late Len Beer in 1975 and, more recently, by Tony Schilling and Nigel Taylor of Kew. The Emei Shan skimmia introduced as seed by the author and Harry van de Laar was designated S *laureola* subspecies *lancasteri* by Taylor, 1989. It is represented in cultivation by both male and female plants.

A quiet pool near the summit of Emei Shan, its banks crowded with rhododendrons, enkianthus and juniper. (October)

sold for hedging by western nurserymen since Wilson's original introduction in 1908. It must run into millions. The kerria is better known in cultivation in its double flowered form 'Pleniflora', first introduced from a Guangzhou (Canton) nursery by the Kew collector William Kerr in 1850 and originally named *K japonica*. The single-flowered wild plant is just as hardy and ornamental though half the height of the other and more densely branched. The most interesting find here, though, was a spindleberry – *Euonymus cornutus*, its slender green stems reaching 2m (6ft) supported by a bamboo. The long, narrow, paired leaves up to 15cm (6in) long were sparsely placed, the upper pairs producing from their axils horned red capsules, which hung like baubles on slender stalks. An uncommon shrub in cultivation, this species should be given the support of other shrubs or even bamboo to enable its fruits to be seen to advantage. The typical plant has flowers with four petals and capsules with four horns. Plants in my garden grown from seed collected on Emei Shan have flowers with five purplish red petals and capsules with five horns. It is aptly named *Euonymus cornutus* variety *quinquecornutus*.

Halfway down a long flight of steps we met a man carrying an antique long-barrelled, short-stocked musket. He grinned when asked, through our guide, if it really worked, before continuing on his way up the mountain. A short while later we

heard a loud report and we assumed the man to be firing at the pheasants we had heard, but not seen, in the bamboo thickets. Later still, one of our party caught up with us, white faced and visibly shaken. He told us he had been 'rooting around' in the bamboo, apparently searching for seeds, when he heard the gun being fired not more than a few metres from his position. It was not until he heard the shot rattling through the canes above him that he realised he had been mistaken for a pheasant. He had not waited for the hunter to reload or investigate, and had made a hasty retreat following a circuitous route back to the safety of the Pilgrim's Path.

Our path now followed a tortuous course, up and down spurs and ridges and around crags into ravines and gullies. Eventually we arrived at Xixiangchi, or Elephant Bath Temple, which occupies a commanding site at a height of about 2,100m (6,890ft) above sea level. According to local legend, when the Buddha Samantabhabra mounted the Golden Summit on an elephant, he stopped here to wash his mount in a pool. The difference in altitude between this point and our overnight stop at Jiulaodong, Nine Elders Cave, is 540m (1,768ft), yet it took us the whole of an afternoon to cover the distance following the Pilgrim's Path. This was due partly to the irregular route of the path, and partly to the incredible richness of the forest between the two. One comparatively short stretch of steps on a steep

Meliosma veitchiorum. Above. It is not uncommon in the woodlands on Emei Shan. Here a cultivated tree derived from an E.H. Wilson introduction is seen in flower at Nymans, Sussex. (May). Right. A young tree in the same garden. Note the handsome foliage

slope took us an hour to descend as first one and then another treasure called for investigation.

Tilia nobilis, a lime new to me, was a tree of some 12m (40ft), with leaves similar in some respects to those of *T platyphyllos*, but larger and smoother. A tree close to the path was in fruit but most of these were found on investigation to be empty. Two exceptions have produced seedlings that, together with trees grown from scions grafted on *T x europaea*, should establish this rare tree in cultivation. Close by the lime and of a similar size grew *Meliosma veitchiorum*, an uncommon tree in western cultivation where it is admired for its large, deeply divided (pinnate) leaves on red stalks. These are concentrated towards the ends of the stout branches where they form bold ruffs, colouring yellow or gold before falling in autumn. The small greenish-white flowers borne in large heads (panicles) are of marginal interest to the gardener. It is a hardy tree suitable for woodland cultivation or as a lawn specimen where space permits. It was originally introduced by Wilson from west Sichuan in 1901 and trees, possibly of this introduction, are to be found at Kew (near the ferneries) and at Nymans in Sussex. When I last saw the Kew tree it appeared to be on the decline but the Nymans tree, a larger specimen, appears to be in excellent health and there are other younger trees.

Clematis fasciculiflora, the author in February 2005 examining a flowering plant of this late winter-flowering species growing on a wall at the National Trust garden Overbecks in Devon.

Cornus chinensis, a Chinese relative of the European *C mas* here photographed (above) flowering on Emei Shan by M. Ogisu (November) and (left) in leaf on a tree that once grew in the Ventnor Botanic Garden on the Isle of Wight. (June)

A third tree which caught our attention in this area was a curious dogwood – *Cornus chinensis* (not to be confused with *C kousa* variety *chinensis*). One tree, a densely branched specimen of some 9m (30ft) or more, grew conveniently close to the steps, making examination that much easier. It is closely related to *C mas*, the so-called Cornelian cherry of Europe, having similarly shaped but much larger leaves and flower clusters borne on the naked twigs in winter. It is, however, less hardy and requires a sheltered situation in the milder areas of Britain. The only specimens of this tree I ever saw in cultivation grew in the Hillier Arboretum, the Savill Garden, Windsor, and the Ventnor Botanic Garden on the Isle of Wight. The Hillier tree grew outside on a south-facing wall and, when it finally succumbed in a severe winter, had reached about 5m (16ft) without ever having flowered. This plant originated as a cutting from the Savill tree, which flourishes still in the temperate house. Here it has flowered, while just as spectacular are the handsome, beautifully ribbed leaves, some of which have reached as much as 30 x 17.5cm (12 x 7in).[12] The Ventnor tree was supplied by Hillier in 1975. Ten years later it had made a broad spreading specimen of 6m (20ft) and as much or more across, its typically bold leaves with their tail-like points (drip tips) creating a subtropical effect. It was planted in a sheltered glade, flowering each year in February and March. Sadly, this tree perished in the severe winter of 1986/87.

The trees on Emei Shan were still in partial leaf but the flower clusters were already plump, their protective bracts under pressure. Indeed, in several instances the bracts had already parted revealing their bright yellow stamens.

Smaller trees associated with the dogwood included *Lindera obtusiloba*, *Rhododendron pingianum* and *Stranvaesia davidiana*, the last named, in my opinion, one of the most underrated evergreens in cultivation. Usually seen in gardens as a large shrub with spreading branches, this species responds well to pruning and can be trained to a more compact tree-like habit if so desired. The old leaves turn crimson and linger on the branches for some time before falling, while the bright red fruits hang in bunches well into winter, untouched by birds who find them on the dry side. Tolerant of drought as well as shade, hardy and easy on most soils, *S davidiana* has much to commend it and I was delighted to find it in the wild growing where no less a personage than E H Wilson found it in 1903. It had, however, already been introduced to the West from nearby Baoxing (Mupin) by Armand David (whose name it bears) in 1869.

Chinese ivy *Hedera nepalensis* variety *sinensis* clothing the stem of a silver fir (*Abies fabri*) on Emei Shan. (October)

Some experts consider *Stranvaesia* to be insufficiently distinct botanically from *Photinia* and unite them under the latter name. The plant described above then becomes *Photinia davidiana*. There is a rather handsome orange-yellow fruited form in cultivation whose full name (if the above change is followed) is *Photinia davidiana* variety *undulata* 'Fructu Luteo'. It also differs from the typical plant in its shorter, wavy-edged leaves. It was raised by the Slieve Donard Nurseries in Co Down, Northern Ireland in 1920. The red and yellow fruited forms planted together make a striking informal hedge or screen.[13]

Interestingly, in order to reach seed of the *stranvaesia*, I had to push my way through an extensive colony of a Chinese mugwort, *Artemisia lactiflora*, which is grown, though not commonly at present, in herbaceous borders in Britain. Its erect leafy stems reached 2m (6ft) high, the leaves jaggedly lobed, topped by large plume-like heads of tiny creamy-white flowers. This plant certainly was first introduced to cultivation by Wilson.

An important element of the forest on Emei Shan are the climbing plants representing a range of families. The greatest variety is to be found in the warmer lower regions of the mountain. In the upper regions the selection is considerably less and *Clematis* species are dominant. One of these, by the way, probably *C fasciculiflora*, is an interesting species and has been introduced, possibly for the first time, into western cultivation. Seed collected of this plant has produced progeny that are fast growing with trifoliolate leaves, the leaflets bearing a distinct silver or grey-green central splash. In contrast to the attractive leaves, the flowers are bell shaped, greenish-white and borne in drooping axillary clusters on the old wood.

Photinia davidiana, a most handsome evergreen shrub or small tree noted for its bold foliage and drooping clusters of crimson fruits that last from autumn through winter. Here seen in the woodland garden at Stanage Park. (October)

The middle zones of the mountain support some of the most interesting climbers from a garden point of view including a Chinese ivy, *Hedera nepalensis* variety *sinensis*. This we found common on a range of trees, especially silver fir, as well as forming a ground cover in dense shade. Its leaves were less variable than those of the English ivy, although lobed and unlobed forms were encountered. The latter were broad based tapering to a blunt point. This species differs most obviously from our black-fruited native species in its orange fruits, which, as is usual in ivies, are only produced on the adult

12. It was grown from seed collected by Kingdon-Ward in Tibet in 1950. He came across the tree in flower on a hillside where he had made camp, and the colour of the flower clusters (much larger than in *C mas*) he described as 'a luminous sulphur yellow'. Shortly thereafter, this same hillside slid into the valley as a result of the great Assam earthquake. Kingdon-Ward barely escaped with his life and among the collections he carried with him was seed of the dogwood. Of the six plants that germinated, only the Savill Garden plant survives.

13. *Photinia davidiana* is now less grown in cultivation due to its susceptibility to the bacterium known as 'Fire Blight', though the occurrence of this disease in Britain is scattered.

growth. Interestingly, on our climb the previous day, we had seen this ivy forming mounds of adult growth over boulders and old tree stumps. In some areas these mounds were quite plentiful with handsome glossy entire or few-lobed leaves. Plants from several recent seed collections are now established in cultivation and a seedling in my own garden from Emei Shan produces young leaves of a charming shining chocolate colour.

Fruits of a very different kind are borne by the long hairy-stemmed *Actinidia deliciosa*, the so-called Chinese gooseberry. It is frequent in the forests of Emei Shan, particularly in the vicinity of some of the temples where it may well have been planted in the past. Wilson saw it here and elsewhere during the early years of the 20th century and introduced it as seed to Britain where it was and still is grown, mainly as an ornamental vine for its bold foliage. Although both Wilson and Augustine Henry before him wrote on the uses of the edible fruit in China and recommended its potential as a commercial crop in the West, it was not seriously exploited until the 1950s, by which time a few orchards had been established in New Zealand. By the end of 1983 Kiwi fruit orchards covered over 8,000 hectares (20,000 acres) in that country alone.

Actinidia deliciosa is in nature dioecious: bearing male and female flowers on separate plants. All the plants from

Rubus henryi, a deeply lobed form growing in an Oxford garden. Even more ornamental is the variety *bambusarum* with leaves composed of three distinct finger-like leaflets. (July)

Wilson's first introduction distributed by the nursery firm of Veitch were male. Female plants were later introduced and made available to the public in 1912. Nevertheless, Britain's inclement climate has not helped in the development of the Chinese gooseberry as a commercial crop, although it is at present being established on Guernsey in the Channel Isles in the glasshouses built for a once thriving tomato industry. The plant is hardy enough, but the pollination process as well as the fruit ripening is undoubtedly encouraged by a long hot summer.

The most exciting ornamental climbers in the middle zones of Emei's forest are the climbing hydrangeas, two species of which we saw on our descent. Both are deciduous and woody stemmed, climbing by means of aerial roots in the manner of an ivy. *Hydrangea anomala* appears to be the most common and, in general appearance, resembles its better known (in cultivation) variety *petiolaris* (*H petiolaris*), a native of Japan, Korea and Taiwan. In this case, the flowerheads are of lace-cap form, a flattened or dome-shaped arrangement of tiny greenish fertile flowers with several large white sterile ray florets around the margin. In the closely related *Schizophragma integrifolium*, the flowerheads (cymes), which can be as much as 30cm (12in) across, are composed almost entirely of small, insignificant greenish fertile flowers. Terminating each division of the flowerhead, however, is a single sterile flower consisting of a large, dark-veined white bract up to 9cm (3½ in) long that acts as a flag to passing insects. The hydrangea climbed up a range of trees reaching at least 20m (65ft) on some. The schizophragma also climbed trees, indeed one specimen had so swamped a dead stump that it resembled a tree in its own right (one often sees a similar situation with ivy in Britain), but nowhere did we see it climbing as high as the hydrangea, 15m (50ft) being the maximum, and on several occasions we saw it clothing shady rocks and cliffs in deep ravines.

Harry van de Laar with a seeding specimen of *Schizophragma integrifolium*, a magnificent deciduous climbing hydrangea relative on Emei Shan. The conspicuous bracts are past their best. (October)

Schizophragma integrifolium, a fine individual in flower on the laboratory wall at the RHS Garden, Wisley. Sadly, this plant no longer exists. (June)

Neither of these climbers is common in cultivation, not surprisingly in the case of *H anomala*, which has nothing to recommend it over the variety *petiolaris*. *S integrifolium*, however, although slower growing, is a magnificent flowering climber, suitable for walls, stumps or tree trunks. A large established plant on a tall tree is an impressive spectacle in July when the huge flowerheads are set against the handsome foliage. It differs from the Japanese *S hydrangeoides* in its much larger flowerheads and bracts and its larger, longer-stalked leaves which are entire or sparsely toothed.

No mention of climbers on Emei Shan would be complete without the mention of *Rubus*, better known to western gardeners as the brambles, blackberries and raspberries. In addition to prostrate *R fockeanus*, already mentioned, several more species are found here at all altitudes. In three days we found *R cockburnianus*, *R pinfaensis*, *R setchuenensis*, *R irenaeus*, *R parkeri*, *R ichangensis* and *R henryi* — and this list is by no means the end of the story. Not all of these climb, of course, and those that do are more scramblers and ramblers than true climbers. *R henryi*, here represented by variety *sozostylus*, synonyms (*R sozostylus*), (*R fargesii*), is a

typical rambler with its long prickle-clad stems that clamber over and into neighbouring scrub and small trees often reaching several metres high, its stems eventually hanging like curtains above the path. In this species the evergreen leaves are shaped like those of a maple, boldly three lobed, sometimes with an extra, much smaller, basal pair. Dark shining green above, they are covered beneath with a dense pale-brown or yellowish-grey felt, white on young leaves. The fruits are black.[14] Very different in appearance is *R setchuenensis*, a strong-growing scrambler with close-felted thornless shoots and large, long-stalked, rounded deciduous leaves with toothed and scalloped margins. The pink flowers are small and insignificant but they are replaced by black edible fruits of good flavour. The growth of this bramble is prodigious, a plant in my garden sending up shoots 5m (16ft) or more long in a single season.

14. First discovered in Hubei province by Augustine Henry, after whom it is named, it was introduced to cultivation by Wilson in 1900. A plant grown from Emei seed is now established against a fence in my garden where, in February 1985, it was subjected to temperatures of -10°C (14°F) without distress.

Carla Teune examines the bold autumn foliage of *Viburnum nervosum* on Emei Shan. (October)

Epimedium acuminatum, a seedling from Emei Shan seen in flower at Blackthorn Nursery in Hampshire. It is a most striking form with large arrow-shaped leaflets and large bi-coloured, long spurred flowers appearing over an extended period. (May)

I have always been a keen advocate of 'bringing back the birch', not the punishment, I hasten to add, but the tree. China supports a great number of species, some of which are equal if not superior to our common native species *Betula pendula*. In the lower and middle zones of Emei Shan grew a birch with yellowish-grey bark, darkening and flaking with age. It was not a particularly tall tree, less than 15m (50ft) on average with many specimens between 7 and 9 metres (22 and 30ft), and I must confess that I took it to be a poor form of *B utilis*, which is rather common in western China. A sample of seed was collected and later distributed, and one of the resultant seedlings initially grew away strongly in my garden. The bark is shining amber brown, flaking with age, while the shoots are densely short, downy (pubescent). In size the leaves can be as much as 10cm (4in) on young shoots, but average 8-9cm (3-3½ in) with a slender point and sharp teeth. Dull green above, the lower surface has a sprinkling of tiny shining glands best seen with a hand lens. The veins are in nine to twelve pairs and are conspicuously raised below. It is a distinctive birch, though not one of the most ornamental, and has been identified as *B luminifera* which some authorities regard as a subspecies of the Himalayan *B alnoides*. Like *B alnoides*, *B luminifera* is decidedly tender in British cultivation and has since perished.

B luminifera was first discovered in eastern Sichuan by the French missionary Farges, but its presence in western cultivation is mainly as a result of E H Wilson's introductions. Accompanying this birch in several places on Emei Shan was *Viburnum nervosum* (*cordifolium*), a shrub of 4.5-6m (15-20ft) whose large handsome leaves had turned a

most gorgeous orange and red and which shone through the occasional patches of mist like a smouldering bonfire.

Towards the end of our second day on Emei Shan we encountered a whole range of interesting and ornamental plants growing on both sides of the Pilgrim's Path. Indeed, at one point, so rich was the flora, that to blink was to risk missing something new and we found ourselves descending the steps a few at a time with frequent stops for detailed observation.

In 1928 *Rehderodendron macrocarpum* was first discovered on Emei Shan by Professor Fang. A tree of some 6-9m (20-30ft) with racemes of white flowers, it represented a new genus of the *Styrax* family (*Styracaceae*). The original tree was found growing by the Pilgrim's Path along which Wilson travelled over twenty years previously. 'The history of this genus also shows that even so diligent and observant a plant collector as Wilson may sometimes be caught napping', wrote one pundit at the time. Having experienced the plant riches of Emei Shan for myself, I can well understand Wilson having missed this tree and no doubt many others as well. A botanist would need to live on the mountain for many years, if not a lifetime, to have any chance of seeing every plant found there.

We did not see *Rehderodendron* that day either, but we did find a rather handsome *Osmanthus* species, a large evergreen shrub or small tree with lance-shaped dark green leathery leaves margined with slender pointed teeth almost prickly to the touch. Some individuals in the forest were 5m (16ft) or more high. A specimen shown to Professor Fang on our return to Chengdu was given the name *O omeiensis* but, according to Peter Green, an authority on these plants, this name correctly belongs to a rather distinct and tender species of a different group to our plant. In my opinion, the above plant is more likely to have been *O serrulatus*, which was originally introduced from west China by Wilson in 1910. Seed collected in 1980 produced several strong young plants in several European collections and in Britain certainly these are proving hardy, strengthening my belief as to their likely identity. *O serrulatus* is uncommon in British cultivation, where it is usually seen as a dense rounded bush of slow compact growth, at least when young. Several specimens in the Hillier Arboretum planted in the 1960s were approximately 4m (13ft) high and as much through in 1986. The white sweetly-scented flowers are borne in clusters in the leaf axils in spring.

In one shaded gully above the path we found two fascinating perennials, neither of which I had encountered or heard of before. The first of these was *Begonia limprichtii* (*houttuynioides*), which preferred moist places and was especially fond of steep banks where the rock surface was lubricated with a thin film of water. The flowers were over but the most striking feature about this plant was the leaves, which were rounded and fleshy, purple beneath and emerald green above with a distinct metallic sheen. They contrasted most effectively with the large, much divided leaves of a bold perennial – *Astilbe grandis*, whose plumes of white flowers on 1.5m (5ft) stems had now faded to green, though not without charm.

Not far from the begonia we found colonies of an *Epimedium* species with lance- or arrow-shaped slender pointed leaflets, glaucous beneath, shining dark green above, and edged throughout with short bristle-like teeth. Seedlings of this epimedium have been introduced to Britain where they are now well established. On their first flowering in 1982 they were identified by Professor W T Stearn as *Epimedium acuminatum*, confirming the opinion of Professor Fang, with whom we had consulted on our return to Chengdu. It was first discovered apparently by the French missionary Paul Perny in the 1850s. The flowers are striking both in size and colour, although the latter character is variable; plants with yellowish flowers are probably hybrids. A plant in my garden carries flowers up to 5cm (2in) across, coloured a dusky plum-purple, paling to white at the tips of the long curved, spreading spurs. The four sepals are a contrasting white, the two smaller sepals purple tinted on the back. Numerous flowers are produced in a long arching panicle, each flower suspended on a thread-like stalk. In

Epimedium acuminatum 'Galaxy' flowering for the first time at Blackthorn Nursery. The white flowers have faintly yellow tipped spurs. (April)

Nine Elders Cave Monastery on Emei Shan. In the woods around this building the Chinese Dove tree (*Davidia involucrata*) occurred in some numbers. (October)

Davidia involucrata variety *vilmoriniana*, (above) a fine specimen flowering in the lower valley at Trebah in Cornwall (June); and (left) in a public garden in Vancouver, Canada (June). The two conspicuous white bracts give rise to the English names Dove Tree and Pocket-handkerchief Tree.

cultivation, in a normal year flowering begins in April continuing through May into early June. Several other *Epimedium* species occur on Emei Shan as well as hybrids.[15]

At the end of a long and memorable day we wearily entered the Nine Elders Cave Monastery (Jiiu-lao-dong) at 1,800m (5,900ft), but not before the forest had yielded one more surprise. The Chinese Dove tree, *Davidia involucrata*, is reputedly the main reason E H Wilson was commissioned by the English nurseryman Sir Harry Veitch and his nephew James Herbert Veitch to travel to China in 1899. The story of Wilson's experiences on the trail of this tree is, perhaps, too well known to bear repeating here. Suffice to say that Wilson eventually succeeded in his endeavour and, from his seed introductions, *Davidia involucrata* was firmly established in western cultivation. Interestingly, seed of a variety of *Davidia involucrata* named *vilmoriniana*, after the French nurseryman Maurice de Vilmorin,

15. In 1993, from seed collected from an E *acuminatum* in S. Sichuan, several seedlings were raised by Robin White of Blackthorn Nursery, one of which I named 'Galaxy' for its yellow-tipped white flowers. Another, with handsome, crimson, mottled foliage has been named by Robin, 'Persian Carpet'

One of many wooded ravines on Emei Shan. Wild and exciting, such places are crowded with a rich variety of flora and fauna. (October)

had been sent to Paris in 1897 by the missionary Paul Farges. From this seed a single seedling was raised at the Arboretum des Barres near Paris, which flowered in 1906. By a strange irony, in 1901 while Wilson was in China collecting seeds of his davidia, a rooted cutting of the Vilmorin tree was received at Kew. On learning of this, Wilson naturally, was disappointed regarding it as 'one more little cup of bitterness to drain'. If he had not been the first, at least he could take credit for having assured its future in our gardens. From his four expeditions to China, Wilson introduced large quantities of seed mostly of variety *vilmoriniana* to the West. The tallest specimen of *D involucrata* in British cultivation is a tree planted at Hergest Croft in Herefordshire in 1903, which was 16m (52ft) tall in 1995. The tallest specimen of variety *vilmoriniana* is also at Hergest Croft, measuring 21m (69ft) in 2002. Similar trees can be found at Frensham Hall in Surrey and Fosbury Manor in Wiltshire. In a recent survey it has been estimated that 80% of

the davidias grown in Britain and Ireland belong to the variety *vilmoriniana*, which is reputedly the most cold-hardy.

Both the typical tree and its variety occur on Emei Shan and must have been seen by Wilson. On our descent that October day, we had caught sight of isolated Dove trees in various parts of the forest, but it was not until the end of the day that our excitement really took flight. For some time we walked through an area of forest not too far from the path, where Dove trees were plentiful, with specimens of 15-18m (50-60ft) or more growing in the company of a Chinese horse chestnut, *Aesculus wilsonii*, of equal proportions. The hairy leaves of these Dove trees suggested the type species, though trees seen the next day probably belonged to the variety *vilmoriniana*. For some ten to fifteen minutes after most of my colleagues had trooped into the monastery, I sat on the steps in the gathering gloom quietly watching as the Dove trees gradually faded into the shadows of the forest.

Carpinus fangiana fruiting for the first time in the author's garden. Note the large, boldly veined and ornamental leaves. (October)

Idesia polycarpa is not uncommon on Emei Shan. Here the spectacular fruits are borne on a female tree in cultivation. (October)

Morning found us eager to be on our way, wondering what new treasures lay in store. On our first long descent our eyes were assailed by a stream of interesting trees of which *Carpinus fangiana*, named after Professor Fang, was the most unusual. It was a tree of some 15m (50ft) here, with conspicuous large pointed buds and boldy-veined leaves most of which had already fallen. Its impressive fruiting catkins, which we did not see, are 20-27cm (8-10½ in) long, rarely 35cm (14in), and a tree in full fruit must present an astonishing spectacle. Close by grew a 10m (32ft) specimen of *Tetracentron sinense*, with leaves similar to those of *Cercidiphyllum japonicum* but larger, more pointed and borne alternately along the shoots. One of the finest specimens of this rare tree I have seen in cultivation (probably a Wilson original) grows at Caerhays in Cornwall and is a large spreading specimen, which in 1975 measured 12m (40ft) high. The first I ever saw was a much smaller tree growing on the chalk in the Winchester nursery of Hilliers when I first joined that firm in 1962. It was still there in 1985, although the site is now maintained as a small public garden. The tallest specimen in British cultivation, incidentally, is a tree at High Beeches in Sussex, which in 1982 measured 14m (46ft). Sadly this was blown down in the great gale of 1987.

The Chinese version of the Japanese *Cercidiphyllum japonicum* is known as variety *sinense*[16] and, among several specimens seen on the mountain, was a tree of some 25m (82ft) with three stems. It grew quite close to the path, its branches spreading high above our heads. *Cornus chinensis* occurred again, one specimen with a trunk diameter of 60cm (24in) at the base.

Far more impressive was *Idesia polycarpa*, a large deciduous tree, in leaf and aspect not unlike a handsome poplar such as *Populus lasiocarpa*. The leaves were heart shaped, dark green above, glaucous and thickly coated with a pale grey down beneath. They were borne on stalks that carried two conspicuous raised glands towards their apex. These glands are a characteristic of this tree. The fragrant yellowish-green flowers are carried in loose drooping terminal heads (panicles) in summer, male and female on separate trees (dioecious). In themselves, they are of little or no ornamental merit, but the females when pollinated produce pea-sized berries, which ripen to a brilliant orange-red. These hang from the branches in conspicuous grape-like clusters at which time the tree is at its most spectacular. Even the males are rendered attractive by their bold leaves on reddish stalks. None of the trees I saw on Emei Shan that day carried fruit. They varied in height from 10.5-15m (35-50ft) and seemed in excellent health.

16. Current Chinese opinion does not recognise the Chinese tree as significantly distinct from the typical species as found in Japan.

Cercidiphyllum japonicum, a large old multi-stemmed tree by the Pilgrim's Path on Emei Shan. Carla Teune and
Harry J. van de Laar admire its size. (October)

A native of Japan as well as China, *I polycarpa* was first
recorded in the former country by the Kew collector
Richard Oldham in 1862/3, it was introduced to
cultivation a few years later by the Russians. From the
downy nature of the leaf undersurface, I concluded that the
Emei Shan trees we saw belonged to the variety *vestita*,
which was first collected in west Sichuan by Wilson in
1908. According to Professor Fang, both the typical tree
and its variety grow on Emei Shan, the latter apparently
growing at a higher altitude than the other.

A tree grown from Wilson's seed once grew in Hillier's
old Winchester nursery, West Hill. It had attained 12m
(40ft) or so in 1962 when I first saw it. Some years later,
in preparation for a possible transplanting operation, I was
given the job of thinning out the branches and generally

cleaning up the tree; I could not help noticing how pithy
the young stems were. It is a hardy tree but one that
obviously enjoys a long warm summer to ripen the shoots
and encourage berry production and display. The largest
specimen in British cultivation is a tree at Stourhead in
Wiltshire, which in 1980 measured 17.5m (58ft). In
January 1985 in North Island New Zealand I saw this tree
planted as an avenue outside a Kiwi fruit farm. Although
no more than 6m (20ft) high, many of the trees were
loaded with berry clusters. Its name commemorates
Eberhard Ides, a German or Dutch explorer in northern
Asia, who was in the employ of Tsar Peter the Great of
Russia between 1691 and 1695.

The most exciting find of the morning, however, was
made in a shady ravine some distance below our previous

Mahonia eurybracteata, a specimen under glass at Blackthorn Nursery bearing dense clusters of bloomy black fruits. Note the sea-green colour of the leaflets on this seedling. (April)

Mahonia eurybracteata; a seedling of this rare species growing in the author's garden. The leaf colour is variable among seedlings, but most are ornamental in effect. (June)

night's accommodation. Here grew two shrubs, both mahonias, neither of which I had seen or heard of before. The taller of the two, *Mahonia eurybracteata (confusa)*,[17] varied from 1-2m (3-6ft), its slender erect stems sporting handsome pinnate leaves. These consisted of from nine to seventeen narrow spine-toothed leaflets 7-10cm (2¾ - 4in) long by 1.5-2.5cm (½-1in) wide, the terminal leaflet long-stalked. In colour they were an attractive bluish-grey or greyish-green above, paler below. Other plants I noticed had leaflets of a pale green above. The second species, *Mahonia gracilipes*,[18] was even more distinct, a smaller suckering shrub up to 1m (3ft) with leaves comprising five to seven leaflets 5-13cm (2-5in) long by 1.5-4.5cm (½ - 1¾ in) wide. These were dark green above and chalk white beneath, a striking contrast. Both forms of M *eurybracteata* as well as M *gracilipes* have been introduced to Europe and are grown in a cool greenhouse at the Savill Garden, Windsor, where M *gracilipes* has already produced suckers, while M *eurybracteata* has flowered and produced viable fruits. Seedlings derived from the latter plants exhibit the two distinct leaf colours of the original introductions.

In the autumn of 1983 I planted out one of the grey-leaved seedlings in my garden where it came through the following winter without damage. In 1984 I added two green-leaved

Mahonia gracilipes. Above. The cup-shaped flowers are unique in colour and not unlike those of certain epimediums in effect. Right. Showing the chalk white undersides of the leaflets and the curious flowers borne in loose sprays. Photographed by Martin Gardner at RBG Edinburgh. (October)

seedlings and I was delighted to note that all three survived the severe weather of February 1985 when temperatures dropped to -10°C (14°F). They have also survived the equally severe conditions of January and February 1986. Hopefully these two species will prove satisfactory in all but the coldest gardens, although to be on the safe side I would suggest they be given woodland or at least sheltered conditions, preferably in an acid or neutral loam. So far I have had no reports of their performance on chalk or limy soils.

M *eurybracteata* produces slender, erect racemes up to 12.5cm (5in) long of yellow flowers at any time from July to November. The flowers of M *gracilipes*, on the other hand, are unique in being purple or reddish-purple in colour with a creamy-yellow inner cup, not unlike an epimedium in effect. They are borne in thin, lax, often branching racemes up to 30cm (12in) long from July to October. M *gracilipes* has flowered at the Savill Garden and Boskoop,

both plants under glass, while a plant outside in my garden flowered for the first time in 1987.

It would appear to be the only non-yellow-flowered mahonia and this, together with its chalk-white leaf undersurfaces and dwarf habit, makes it unique and a potentially exciting addition to those species long in cultivation. It should make an interesting parent for hybridising.[19]

Mahonia eurybracteata x gracilipes. Note the red-budded flowers. A handsome but variable hybrid, this original Savill seedling in the author's garden leaning more to the former (male) parent in character. (October)

17. M *eurybracteata* was first discovered in the Yichang (Ichang) area of Hubei province by Augustine Henry in 1887 and Wilson later collected it from the same area as well as from Emei Shan. It is also recorded from Guizhou province.

18. M *gracilipes* is recorded from Sichuan and N.E. Yunnan. It was first discovered by Ernst Faber on Emei Shan and later on the same mountain by Wilson, who collected seed. Amazingly, neither of these mentioned its flower colour, nor did the Reverend Ahrendt when describing it in his work on the genus.

19. In 1986, seeds were collected from the Savill Garden M *gracilipes* and, following successful germination, plants flowered for the first time in August 1988. Several of these proved to be hybrids with M *eurybracteata*, showing leaf and inflorescence characteristics of the latter and flower colour intermediate between the two. Such hybrids have occurred elsewhere, both in cultivation and the wild. Both M *eurybracteata* and M *gracilipes*, together with their hybrids, are now proving hardy in cultivation, given a sheltered situation.

Aucuba omeiensis. Above. A plant of this magnificent foliage shrub growing in the author's garden. The leaves can reach 30cm (12in) in length, while in the wild plants are capable of attaining 5m (16ft) or more in height. Left. This plant produces male flowers. (June)

similar potential. Examples of this bold foliage plant are at present in cultivation under glass in the Savill Garden, Windsor. They have been grown from cuttings taken from a single seedling and once they are sufficient in number will be tested outside in sheltered woodland and protected situations. It may even have a future as a foliage plant for indoor cultivation. Plants are now being grown elsewhere, outside in sheltered situations including a 3.6m (12ft) example in my own garden. This bears greenish-yellow male flowers.

Many years ago, on my first visit to the Royal Horticultural Society Garden at Wisley in Surrey, I came across a handsome evergreen spindleberry growing in a border. It must have been 2-3m (6-9ft) high and at least that much across. Apart from its attractive leathery, sharply toothed leaves, I remembered it for the yellowish capsules that crowded its branches. Some of these had already split to reveal the brilliant orange-scarlet coated seeds. Since that time *Euonymus myrianthus*, as it proved to be, has occupied a special place in my affections and, because it is uncommon in western cultivation, I never tire of singing its praises. I mention it here because it grew in the general hugger-mugger of shrubs and herbage above the track on Emei Shan that day, its appearance causing me a great deal of pleasure. It is a hardy shrub and, apart from its fruits, which last into winter, it has attractive greenish-yellow, four-petalled flowers in dense clusters. Like most of its clan, it is happy on most soils, acid or alkaline, but flowers and, therefore, fruits best in a sunny situation. The word myrianthus, by the way, means 'very many flowers'.

Two woody plants regarded by Wilson as among his favourite introductions are *Staphylea holocarpa* and *Emmenopterys henryi*. It was fitting, therefore, that we should find both growing within a few yards of one another on Emei Shan, seventy-seven years to the day of Wilson's first visit. Wilson's first collections of these trees, however, were

Staphylea holocarpa variety *rosea*. The delicate pink flowers emerge with the young growth. Hillier Arboretum. (April)

Native to Sichuan only, and first found on Emei Shan, is the magnificent *Aucuba omeiensis* (*A chinensis* ssp. *omeiensis*), a rare evergreen, with thick, leathery dark green, boldly-toothed leaves up to 30cm (12in) long, the teeth being tipped with small hard points (mucros). Plants we saw in the forest carried green fruits 2.5cm (1in) long, which would ripen to bright red. One specimen was a small tree of 5m (16ft) high while other younger specimens showed

Euonymus myrianthus. A distinct and distinguished evergreen species here in the RHS garden, Rosemoor, Devon. (June)

made elsewhere during his third expedition. Neither were in flower in October but this did not lessen the thrill of seeing them ourselves for the first time in the wild. The staphylea or Chinese bladdernut, is a large shrub or small tree averaging 5m (16ft) in height, and occasionally growing up to 10m (32ft) on Emei Shan. It is distinct with its pendulous clusters of flowers, which emerge with the leaves in spring. The colour of the flower varies from white to pink and a cultivated form with larger pink flowers is known as variety *rosea*. This is certainly one of the loveliest shrubs of its kind, both in the wild and in cultivation,

although in some gardens its flowers are subject to damage by frosts. Given some shelter, such as that provided by other trees and shrubs, it eventually becomes a wide-spreading specimen of subtle beauty in spring. One of the finest specimens of variety *rosea* grows in the woodland at Caerhays Castle in Cornwall and is probably an original Wilson introduction. It is tolerant of a wide range of soils, acid or alkaline, so long as they are not waterlogged.

Emmenopterys henryi Wilson regarded as 'one of the most strikingly beautiful trees of the Chinese forests, with its flattish to pyramidal heads [corymbs] of white, rather

Emmenopterys henryi. The impressive base of a tree growing in the gardens of Villa Taranto on the shores of Lake Maggiore, Italy. Here being measured by Manfred Walder. (April)

Emmenopterys henryi flowering at the Villa Taranto on the shores of Lake Maggiore in northern Italy. Wilson regarded this as 'one of the most strikingly beautiful trees of the Chinese forests'. (June)

Cotoneaster glabratus, a seedling from Emei shan flowering in the author's garden. (July)

large flowers and still larger white bracts.' Unfortunately, although this tree has been in cultivation in the West since 1907, there has been only one recorded flowering in Europe – in the gardens of the Villa Taranto, Pallanza, Italy, in 1971. I saw this famous specimen for the first time in 1986, by which time it was a magnificent multi-stemmed tree in excess of 15m (50ft) high, having been planted as a 1m (3ft) specimen in 1937. Since 1971 it has flowered most years and obviously benefits from the consistently high summer temperatures of the Lake Maggiore region.

In Britain, as indeed in Europe, it is a rarity, occasionally to be seen in the more notable collections as a large shrub or small- to medium-sized tree of rather spreading habit. The tallest specimens in Britain, over 15m (50ft), grow at Caerhays Castle in Cornwall, and there is another fine specimen in the National Botanic Gardens at Glasnevin in Ireland. Like the staphylea, *E henryi* appears adaptable to varying soils although it grows best on a deep loam slightly on the acid side. I first saw this tree on the shallow chalk soil of Hilliers West Hill nursery in Winchester where it grew very slowly. Indeed Harold Hillier once told me that it was

an original Wilson introduction and yet it had grown less than 6m (19ft) in fifty years. Its distinctive oval leaves are quite attractive, bold and fleshy, up to 23cm (9in) long on red stalks borne in pairs especially towards the ends of the branches. They are at their best in spring when they emerge a striking bronze colour. The tallest specimen we saw on Emei Shan was a 12m (40ft) tree growing on a steep bank above the path. Both Henry and Wilson however reported seeing trees of 24m (80ft) in Hubei province.

In contrast to the above rarity were two cotoneasters, both of which occurred frequently on steep banks and cliffs. *Cotoneaster salicifolius* was first collected here by Wilson in 1904, while *C glabratus* he introduced four years later. Both are large shrubs with long arching branches and narrow evergreen leaves, those of the latter whitish (glaucous) beneath and lacking the dense pelt of hairs so typical of the other. Indeed, the leaves of *C glabratus* are comparatively smooth by contrast and have a less 'veiny' appearance with a polished upper surface. Both species were in fruit, the tiny red fruits in dense bunches; from seed collected at the time, both are now established in cultivation.

For lunch that day we stopped at Hongchunping, or Spring Crag Monastery, set in a densely wooded ravine. As so often in China the monastery has benefited through the centuries from the planting of an interesting variety of trees, many of which are now exceptional specimens of their kind. Just outside the monastery on a deep slope, grew two magnificent ginkgoes (*Ginkgo biloba*) of about 30m (100ft) reputed to be 1,500 years old. They appeared to be a male and a female and the ground beneath was littered with fallen fruits from most of which the seeds had already been extracted by pilgrims and other travellers. A western visitor may take some convincing that the foul smelling ripened fruit of a ginkgo contains an edible fleshy seed, yet this is so, and those who take meals at any of the monasteries on Emei Shan may expect to find the seeds of ginkgo included on the menu, usually in stews or roasted. They are used in cooking throughout China, of course, and one may buy them canned in Chinese stores in any western city. The seeds are also used in Chinese medicine in the treatment of colds and asthma.

Two other large trees, both conifers, grew above the Pilgrim's Path near the monastery. *Podocarpus neriifolius* was represented by a specimen of some 25m (82ft) high, its long spreading and drooping branches clothed with narrow (linear) shining green leaves up to 15cm (6in) long. It is a handsome tree but, unfortunately, it is too tender for cultivation out of doors in Britain, except perhaps in the mildest areas. This is probably the same tree as that seen by Wilson in 1903 when it was 16m (52ft) high. This species was once commonly planted around temples in Sichuan and has a wide distribution in the wild from Nepal to Taiwan and south to New Guinea and Fiji.

Right. *Ginkgo biloba*. One of two impressive examples growing near the Spring Crag Monastery on Emei Shan. Standing in awe is Carla Teune. (October)

Magnolia officinalis. Above. In flower in the Hillier Arboretum in Hampshire (June). Left. A young tree growing in a courtyard at Hongchunping or Spring Crag Monastery. (October)

Even more impressive was a specimen of the Funeral or Weeping cypress – *Cupressus funebris*, which must have been between 35 and 40m (115-130ft) high, its long pendulous branchlets creating a green curtain effect similar to that of the Bhutan endemic *C corneyana*. This species is truly native to central China and, in particular, to west Hubei and east Sichuan, though widely cultivated elsewhere. It was first reported to the West by Sir George Staunton, a member of Lord Macartney's Embassy to the Qian Long Emperor in 1793. He recorded it as being commonly planted in graveyards in the Vale of Tombs near the city of Hangzhou, in Zhejiang province. Curiously, it was not introduced to Britain until some fifty-five years later when Robert Fortune sent seeds to the Bagshot Nursery of M Standish. Fortune's seed had been gathered from trees growing in the green tea country, some two hundred miles south west of Shanghai. He later found it in great abundance in the mountains south west of Ningbo (Ningpo) in Zhejiang province. Many other travellers in China have remarked on its use as a graveyard tree in the same way that the yew is used in Britain. Sadly, it is not a hardy tree and there are few specimens of note growing out of doors in Britain or Ireland, though it was formerly popular as a pot plant in conservatories where its elegant foliage was much admired.

One other tree, growing in a courtyard in the monastery, is worth special mention. This was *Magnolia officinalis*, a handsome specimen of 7m (22ft) with stout branches and

A poisonous caterpillar; one of Emei Shan's most colourful inhabitants, it is best left well alone. (October)

A raised walkway winds through a ravine in the lower reaches of Emei Shan. Here grew many mosses, ferns and other plants revelling in shade and moisture. (October)

bold ruffs of large leaves up to 53cm (21in) long. In cultivation in Britain this species is uncommon and usually represented by its variety *biloba* in which the leaves have a distinct and characteristic notch in the broad apex. Several trees of this variety, varying in age, grow in the Hillier Arboretum in Hampshire where they flourish, opening their large saucer-shaped fragrant white flowers from the tips of leafy young growths in early summer. It is mainly suited to medium- or large-sized gardens on acid soils where it is hardy enough, especially if given the shelter (but not the shade) of other trees. Apart from the tree at Hongchunping, we saw several specimens growing in villages in the Emei area. Few of these exceeded 7m (22ft), but it is capable of reaching 15m (50ft) in suitable situations.

M officinalis was first introduced to cultivation by Wilson in 1900. Even he, despite his extensive travels in wild and inaccessible areas, was unable to find this tree in a wild state, but only in cultivation in villages and around temples. For centuries this magnolia has been cut down in the wild for the bark of its stems and roots as well as for its flowers, all of which are considered by Chinese herbalists to be a potent medicine in the treatment of several ailments. Because of this destruction it is possible *M officinalis* no longer exists in a wild state, which makes all the more important its continuing cultivation in the West.

After leaving Hongchunping we continued our descent, still following the steps of the Pilgrim's Path through deep gullies and ravines. At one point we trod the boards of a raised walkway that squeezed its way through the bottom of a narrow canyon, whose gloomy fern-clad walls towered above us dripping water on our heads. On another section of the path we found large hairy caterpillars, which our guides warned us not to touch because of their reputedly poisonous nature.

Wanniansi, the main courtyard with its well-stocked gardens. Here we found an interesting collection of penjing (bonsai). (October)

Nearby grew a tree of some 15m (50ft), its branches heavy with tiny, warted red fruits. This has since been identified as *Euodia baberi*, named after Sir Edward Colborne Baber. Seedlings of this species in Britain have grown strongly, producing large deeply divided (pinnate) leaves with a characteristically pungent aroma when bruised. Having in mind its location on the lower slopes of Emei Shan, I expect this tree to prove too tender in all but the mildest areas of Britain.

On a damp shady bank above the track, one of my colleagues found *Begonia wilsonii*, a fleshy-stemmed rhizomatous perennial to 30cm (12in) with bold toothed leaves and a cluster of pink flowers on an erect stem. It was interesting without being startling and I am not aware that it is in present day cultivation.

Towards the end of the day we reached our overnight lodgings at Wanniansi (Ten Thousand Year Monastery), which is situated in a relatively open position at about 1,041m (3,414ft). There are two things in particular for which I shall remember this monastery. One is the meal we had shortly after our arrival. More of a banquet, it consisted of some seventeen dishes including wild fungi and ginkgo 'nuts' ending, as is traditional in China, with boiled rice. The second is the monastery garden, a small area enclosed by a low, clipped box hedge. The box was an

Wanniansi, or Ten Thousand Year Monastery, and the genial Abbot Guan Ming, who showed us round the gardens. (October)

Buxus bodinieri. A handsome narrow-leaved box here growing in the author's garden where it is proving hardy. (August)

unusual species with leaves narrowed to the base and was probably *Buxus bodinieri.* This is now in cultivation and a plant in my garden has survived several winters without harm including temperatures of -10°C (14°F) in February 1985. What struck me as being unusual about this garden was its plant content and design. Apart from several examples of penjing (bonsai) in porcelain trays, the rest of the planting was more western, both in its informality and in its curious mixture of plants – a real plantsman's selection – including *Hypericum patulum* and a fine group of the giant lily *Cardiocrinum giganteum* variety *yunnanense.* Both were in fruit and we were invited to take a pinch of seed from each of them by a delightful smiling 'gardener', one of the monks who, dressed in a blue tunic and tightly wrapped puttees, might have stepped straight from the pages of a Chinese history book. (I later learned that our 'gardener' was none other than the Abbot Guan Ming.) The lily seed germinated after two to three years but plants have yet to flower. *Hypericum patulum* is also well established and is so far proving hardier than previous collections. In my garden it has made a shrub of relatively neat, compact habit to 1m (3ft), with arching reddish branches and two-

ranked leaves. The cup-shaped golden-yellow flowers, 4-4.5cm (1½ -1¾ in) across, are carried on short lateral shoots and face outwards and are slightly nodding rather than erect. It is certainly free-flowering, beginning later than most others and is at its best from late August to October.

Even the penjing in the monastery garden contained a few surprises. One was a rare dwarf rhododendron – *R dendrocharis,* which occurs in a wild state on Emei Shan as an epiphyte on forest trees. Even more interesting was *Ribes henryi,*[20] an unusual evergreen gooseberry, a dwarf thornless shrub with hairy shoots and rounded leaves. Like the closely related *R laurifolium,* its greenish-yellow flowers are produced in February and March, male and female on separate plants.

Our tour of the garden took place after breakfast on our final morning. We had been woken by the sound of bells,

20. *Ribes henryi* was first discovered in Hubei by Augustine Henry, after whom it is named. Its introduction into cultivation is accredited to E H Wilson, even though Wilson at the time knew nothing about it. A single seedling turned up in a seed pan of *Sinowilsonia henryi* introduced by Wilson from west Hubei in 1908; this has given rise to all the plants in cultivation, not that it is in any way common.

A wooded ridge settled in mist and cloud. Such places are teeming with flora and fauna. (October)

gongs and voices chanting somewhere below. Apart from our meeting with the gardener we had no contact with the monks other than an occasional glimpse of them as they attended to their duties. How different it must have been a hundred years ago when Baber visited the mountain. In an account published after his return to England, he describes several meetings and conversations with the abbots and monks of Emei Shan, one of which in particular intrigued me. He was told by one of the abbots, that 'often during the ascent of the mountain have pilgrims been beguiled by the chant of invocations and the pleasant tolling of bells in lone spots where no monastery lies, and straying from the path towards such sounds, have lost their way. On a sudden, in the thickest part of the forest, they have described coming upon immense halls in which images of purest gold are seated on jewelled thrones; there they have been daintily fed and delicately lodged by ministering priests, and guided on the morrow back to the main path, but never after their return from the Golden Summit have they been able to find the mysterious abode of their hosts'. 'Sometimes', continued the abbot, 'a pilgrim strays into the mouth of a cave from which issues a gleam of no earthly splendour; and lighted by the ray mile after mile without fatigue through stupendous chambers of which he never divulges the unutterable secrets, he at length falls asleep, to awake on the top of Emei gazing at the Glory of Buddha'.

The abbot told Baber that he would see the 'Glory of Buddha' when he reached the Golden Summit. Baber did not see it and neither did we. Nor did we see those stupendous chambers or jewelled thrones, though the sounds of bells and incantations had been real enough.

From a plantsman's point of view though, the woodlands of Emei Shan are filled with treasures and wondrous sights and I can well believe that to stray from the well-worn paths would bring even greater delights. Our visit had been all too brief and yet the experience far exceeded our wildest dreams.

Leaving Wanniansi, we parted from the Pilgrim's Path which had brought us from the summit and, with the sun already warming our faces, we made our way down through hamlets and fields to where our bus awaited us in the valley. Before climbing aboard I risked one last look at the mountain. Its green lower slopes were plain enough, but the cliffs and crags were already lost from view and I was left with only my notes and memories to remind me that I once visited paradise.

A covered bridge crosses a stream in the lower reaches of Emei Shan. Here the woodland was dense, unspoilt and rich in species. (October)

Chapter Three

City of Eternal Spring

Over 2,000 years old Kunming, or Yunnan-fu as it was previously known, is the capital of Yunnan province in south-west China. It is a large sprawling city situated in the middle of the Yunnan Plateau at 1,894m (6,213ft) above sea level. By British standards this is high indeed – Ben Nevis is 1,343m (4,406ft), but Kunming, at latitude 25° 04′N and longitude 102° 41′E, lies just north of the Tropic of Cancer and roughly on the same latitude as Nassau in the Bahamas, the Florida Keys and Luxor in Egypt. It enjoys, therefore, a warm temperate climate[1] with short, dry, sunny winters, warm springs, warm summers and warm autumns. Not surprisingly it has earned itself the title City of Eternal Spring, although the city landscape is drab.

The city is surrounded by mountains to the north, east

Pavilion in the Western Hills above Kunming

and west, while to the south lies Lake Dianchi (also known as Kunming Lake or Lake Tienchih), at 310 sq km (120 sq miles), the largest in Yunnan and the sixth largest freshwater lake in China. It was referred to by Marco Polo on his visit to Kunming – or rather its early predecessor, Yachi – in 1280. He remarked on its size, some hundred miles in circumference, 'in which are found a vast quantity of fish, the best in the world, of great size and of all kinds'. The mountains, some of which reach 3,000m (10,000ft) or more, are mainly rounded in outline and composed mostly of limestone that outcrops over vast areas. The soil is typically red earth, which, incidentally, covers a greater area in China than any other soil type. Except for local variations these soils are slightly acidic in nature with a pH of 6.6 and are capable of supporting a rich flora. Originally they were covered by forest in which broad-leaved evergreens prevailed, especially *Quercus*, *Castanopsis* and *Lithocarpus* species. Remnants of this forest remain but, as elsewhere in China, they are mainly restricted to relatively inaccessible places, except where religious activities have afforded local protection. Most of the forest in the Kunming Hills was destroyed before liberation in 1949, and during the 'Great Leap Forward' in the 1950s.

Interestingly, these mountains have attracted few major foreign plant collectors, although Kunming (then Yunnan-fu) was visited by several distinguished plantsmen, including George Forrest, who was there towards the end of his eventful first expedition in 1906. Not surprisingly, he preferred the higher mountains of west and north-west Yunnan, which proved far richer in novelties. The same can be said for that other great name in Yunnan plant exploration, the French missionary Jean Delavay. He stayed in Kunming prior to leaving for Dali (Tali-fu) in 1882, and there he died on 30 December, 1895.

Two other names that readily come to mind when the history of botanical exploration in the Kunming area is discussed are those of Frenchmen Père François Ducloux and E Maire, both of whom lived and worked there in the

Lake Dianchi from the Western Hills. Photograph taken by Joseph Rock in the early twentieth century

1. January is the coldest month, if cold is the word, with an average temperature of 9.5°C (49°F), while July qualifies as the warmest month with an average temperature of 20.9°C (70°F). Average annual precipitation is 1,015mm (40in) most of which falls between June and October.

Fields of winter wheat in a valley north of Kunming. Within a few weeks the wheat will have been harvested and the fields prepared to receive a crop of rice. The hillsides, long since denuded of woodland, are now badly eroded in places, supporting mainly scrubby growth of shrubs and lopped saplings. (April)

early years of the present century. Maire in particular collected extensively in the hills around the city, though his collections, as far as I am aware, were almost entirely restricted to herbarium specimens. The same must be said of the German botanist Camillo Schneider and the Austrian Handel-Mazzetti who collected widely in Yunnan, including the Kunming area, between 1914 and 1918. Since then these mountains have been subject to a great deal of botanical study by Chinese botanists, many of them staff members of the Yunnan Institute of Botany in Kunming. One of these, Professor Guo-mei Feng, was our guide when I visited Kunming as a member of the Sino-British Expedition to the Cangshan in spring of 1981, though my first introduction to these mountains had taken place in October the previous year.

On that occasion we had left Chengdu in Sichuan after a memorable visit to Emei Shan, catching the train to Kunming. It is a journey of some twenty-four hours, the line passing in places along deep river valleys running through the high mountains of the Sichuan-Yunnan borderlands. The construction of this line has been described as one of the greatest engineering feats of modern times, the 1,094km (680 miles) of track passing through 427 tunnels and over 653 bridges.

During our brief stay we visited three areas of interest to the plantsman: the famous Western Hills, an area in the

The construction of the Chengdu-Kunming railway has been described as one of the greatest engineering feats of modern times. Here it passes along one of the many river valleys in the mountains of the Sichuan-Yunnan borderlands. (October)

hills to the north west known as Hua Hong Dong, and the famous Stone Forest to the south east.

The following spring I was again in the Western Hills and Hua Hong Dong, as well as two new areas: Da Shao and Anning. Each of these areas appears to have its own specialities as well as a great number of plants common to all. Most of the hill regions visited appear barren from a distance and, in spring especially, conditions are dry.

With a few notable exceptions, trees are confined to ravines, steep hillsides and protected areas, especially around temples. The shrub element, however, is well represented and, in suitable situations, forms dense scrub in which roses, cotoneasters, pyracanthas, berberis, viburnums and hypericums are common. Their tolerance of exposed, dry and, at times, drought conditions, and their ability to withstand regular browsing, hacking and sometimes burning has enabled the shrubs of the Kunming Hills to survive where many trees have perished.

On a practical note, because of the generally balmy climate prevailing in this area, many of the plants flourishing here are not suitable for growing out of doors in Britain except in the milder areas of the south and west. The warm, dry, well-drained soil conditions are also few and far between in Britain. Having said this, a surprising number of plants from these hills are familiar garden plants in the West. In discussing each of the areas visited, readers will understand that it has been impossible to describe more than a fraction of the total number of plants seen.

Elsholtzia species, Hua Hong Dong, Western Hills, Kunming. (October)

The Western Hills

A half hour drive from Kunming brings one to the Western Hills or Xishan. Viewed from Lake Dianchi, four main hills – Huating, Louhan, Taihua and Taiping – can be seen providing a contour resembling a sleeping Buddha, hence the alternative name Shui Fo Shan [Sleeping Buddha Hills]. Much of their beauty is derived from their position rising above the north-west shore of the lake.

Leaving the lakeside, the road winds its way for 7km (4½ miles) into the hills through woods and across steep rocky hillsides, ending at Dragon Gate or Longmen at an altitude of 2,200m (7,215ft). From this point a narrow path cut into the rock continues across the face of a high cliff passing through the so-called Pavilion Reaching Heaven (Datiange) on to a small cave. The views over the lake from this path are tremendous, especially in the morning when the colours of the east-facing hillsides reflected in Lake Dianchi are at their most intense. The path, and associated carvings, was completed in sixty-three years, between 1781 and 1843, by a Taoist monk – Wu Laiqing, with the help of several stonemasons.

From the entrance to Dragon Gate one can follow a track that leads ultimately to the main summit. This takes two to three hours and makes for an enjoyable half-day or even full-day excursion. But there is also a wealth of plants to be seen on the slopes above the road. Indeed, a worthwhile day can be spent taking a bus or taxi to Dragon Gate and then walking back down the road.

Growing not far from Dragon Gate is a small round-headed tree of some 9m (30ft) with slender branches and prettily toothed and veined leaves 5-8cm (2-3in) long. In November 1980 it was in fruit, the small nodding clusters of green nuts with attendant bracts being typical of a hornbeam – *Carpinus* species. It reminded us of C *turczaninowii*, a native of north China and Japan, but when we saw it again the following year we were told by Professor Feng that it belonged to the closely related C *pubescens*. This species is now in cultivation in Europe from seed collected from this isolated tree, and in 1985 a plant in my garden was growing strongly despite winter temperatures of -10°C (140F). Even larger plants 3m (9ft) or more from the same source were growing in the Research Station at Boskoop, which I visited

The Western Hills from Lake Dianchi. Photograph taken by Joseph Rock in the early Twentieth century

A small cave in a high cliff above Lake Dianchi is approached by a narrow path beyond Dragon Gate. From this precarious perch a spectacular view may be had across the lake to Kunming and the hills beyond. (October)

in 1984. These specimens, however, had been given winter protection. The young leaves are an attractive coppery-red.

The hornbeams are a comparatively neglected group of trees in Britain. Apart from the European C betulus and its cultivar 'Fastigiata', they are rarely seen outside specialist collections. This is a pity, as the genus contains a good many trees and a few shrubs of ornamental merit. What they lack in flower they amply make up for in leaf, habit and, in my experience certainly, rich yellow autumn colour. The fruit clusters of several species are also ornamental. There are close on a dozen species recorded in British cultivation and twenty-five species native to China, few of which are known in the West.

I shall never forget my first sight of Ilex macrocarpa fruiting in the Hillier Arboretum. This holly is distinct on two counts, one of which is its deciduous nature, its thin textured elliptic leaves up to 10cm (4in) long, toothed and, like the shoots, quite smooth (glabrous). Its main claim to

A seated figure looks out from a niche in the cliff face above Dragon Gate, Western Hills. (October)

Ilex macrocarpa grows in woods in the Western Hills. It is a deciduous holly best appreciated in winter when the cherry-like shining black fruits stud the naked branches of female trees. Photographed in the Hillier Arboretum. (October)

Lake Dianchi from the Western Hills. Beside a yellow-tiled pavilion the unmistakable column of *Cupressus duclouxiana*, the Chinese equivalent of the Italian cypress. (October)

Cupressus duclouxiana. The relatively large rounded cones 2.5cm (1in) across stud the branches like miniature soccer balls. (October)

fame, however, rests on its cherry-like shining black fruits borne singly on short stalks from the leaf axils of female trees. For the layman it is hard to believe that this tree is really a holly. Fruiting apart though, it has little to offer as an ornamental. Several trees of around 10m (32ft) grew in the woods above the road in the Western Hills and had it not been for Professor Feng pointing them out we should doubtlessly have passed them by. Not surprisingly, I suppose, *I macrocarpa*, although first introduced by Wilson in 1907, is a rare tree in western cultivation where it is quite hardy. The largest specimen in Britain is a tree in the Westonbirt Arboretum, which measured 13m (42ft) in 2002.

Other trees found in the vicinity of Dragon Gate, and no doubt elsewhere, include *Cercis glabra*, *Celtis biondii*, and *Catalpa fargesii* forma *duclouxii*. The *Cercis* is a rather splendid Chinese version of the Judas tree, *C siliquastrum*, of the eastern Mediterranean region. It is, however, quite distinct from the common species in its greater size and larger, more pointed, glossy, green leaves. One specimen, seen in April 1981, was a single-stemmed tree of 8m (26ft) with remarkable heart-shaped leaves up to 18cm (7in) long, of a shining green, almost lacquered, appearance above. Another even taller tree (near a temple at Anning, south west of Kunming) measured 12m (40ft). It is most nearly

related to *C chinensis*, producing its pink pea flowers in clusters on the older shoots in May.

Catalpa fargesii forma *duclouxii*[2] occurred as scattered trees up to 15m (50ft) high, the ridged bark forming small plates. As seen in the wild, both *C fargesii* and the form *duclouxii* are handsome large-leaved ornamental trees, capable of great height. *C fargesii* forma *duclouxii* differs from the type principally in its non-hairy leaves, shoots and inflorescences. Both have lavender, bell-shaped flowers with a flared mouth, stained yellow and with brownish-red spots in the throat. They are excellent hardy trees for medium- to large-sized gardens, flowering in mid-summer. Neither are as wide spreading as the American *C bignonioides* nor are they, in my experience, as gaunt in appearance as Bean's comments suggest. A specimen of forma *duclouxii* in the Hillier Arboretum formed a narrow-crowned tree of pleasing appearance regularly attracting admirers in June with its delicately tinted flowers, which, on maturity, were shed to form a carpet on the ground.

François Ducloux is remembered in another tree commonly found in the hills of Kunming. This time it is a conifer, *Cupressus duclouxiana*, that bears his name.[3] It is a distinctive blue-grey cypress of tight columnar habit, a Chinese version of the Italian cypress *C sempervirens* 'Stricta',

Above. *Gentianella grandis*, a slender-stemmed, grassy-leaved annual, is common in the Western Hills. Its flowers in autumn need searching out in the low, dried herbage. (October)

Left. *Sarcococca ruscifolia*, 'Dragon Gate' growing at Liss Forest Nursery. Grown from seed (L.660), collected above Dragon Gate in the Western Hills. (August)

and is unmistakable on the slopes of the Western Hills and elsewhere in the vicinity. It is also much planted in the gardens and parks in the city, and a specimen in the grounds of a Government guest house in which we stayed in 1981 contained three trees of 18m (60ft) or more. Despite Ducloux's introduction, his cypress has never been plentiful in western cultivation, due perhaps to its reputed tenderness when young. Certainly most, if not all, of the best specimens in the British Isles are in Ireland in gardens such as Mount Usher, Kilmacurragh and Headfort. The tallest specimen in British cultivation is a tree of 19m (63ft) at Rowallane, Co. Down (2000). The cones of this species are distinct in being 2.5cm (1in) across, globular, the scale bosses having small cusps; at Hilliers, where this conifer was grown in pots, the cones always reminded me of miniature soccer balls. Seed collected from the Western Hills in 1980 has established a new population of this cypress in western cultivation. As to its hardiness, a 2m (6ft) specimen in my garden is growing strongly and was undamaged by chill winds and temperatures of -10°C (14°F) in February 1985. Other seedlings elsewhere in Britain were similarly unharmed.

It was originally found by another French missionary, Delavay, but Ducloux sent seeds of it to the Paris nurserymen Vilmorin in about 1905 and from this it became established in cultivation. In places below Dragon Gate one can climb

on to the hillside above the road and clamber about the rocks where a rich selection of shrubs and perennials are to be found, including *Sarcococca ruscifolia* variety *chinensis*, a well-known evergreen in British cultivation. From seed collected at the time, I raised a form with narrow, slender-pointed leaves, which is now established in cultivation under the name 'Dragon Gate'. In October 1980 we found a number of perennials in full flower including a slender-stemmed gentian, *Gentianella grandis*, with grass-like leaves and funnel-shaped blue or bluish flowers. Blue was also the colour of the flowers of *Codonopsis convolvulacea*, a tuberous-rooted perennial with slender, trailing stems, pairs of small ovate leaves and a single terminal flower with five spreading lobes. Reginald Farrer, author of *The English Rock Garden* and a plant hunter himself, described this species as 'a most beautiful but almost unprocurable rarity, with bells of a lovely clear blue, even outside'. That was in 1919 and, while

2. Its name commemorates two French missionaries, Paul Farges and François Ducloux. Farges first discovered the type tree, *C. fargesii*, in east Sichuan where it was also seen by Augustine Henry. Later still, in 1901, E H Wilson found it in west Hubei and introduced it to cultivation as seed. The form *duclouxii* was collected by both Delavay and Ducloux in Yunnan and introduced to cultivation from Hubei by Wilson in 1907. Unfortunately, Wilson's seed (W 640) was distributed wrongly as *C. fargesii* and it was some years before the mistake was discovered.

3. It was originally found by another French missionary, Delavay, but Ducloux sent seeds of it to the Paris nurserymen Vilmorin in about 1905 and from this it became established in cultivation.

Leontopodium sinense, a big, bold-flowered edelweiss that grows in stony places, often by roads in the Western Hills. (October)

Aconitum vilmorinianum, a strong climbing monkshood, is frequent among scrub and woodland margins in the Western Hills. It is not yet known in western cultivation. (October)

it is certainly available from specialist growers today, its fragility caused at least one alpine nurseryman, no less an authority than Will Ingwersen, to recommend it be given alpine house treatment.[4] It is a familiar feature of these hills and has a wide distribution in the province.

We found blue of another variety in the flowers of an extraordinary monkshood: *Aconitum* species. This differed from those tall clump-forming monkshoods of our herbaceous borders in being a climber, its long green stems twining their way 3-4m (9-13ft) or more into tall shrubs, sometimes scrambling over low scrub. Its leaves were typically deeply divided and dark green, while its flowers were bold blue or violet-blue, high-crowned helmets up to 5cm (2in) long with black, anthered stamens bunched just inside the mouth. These flowers are borne singly on stalks from the same axis, the whole forming an erect, branched head. Sometimes, having reached the top of a bush, the monkshood's stems tumbled down under the weight of the flowers. This is quite the most handsome monkshood I have ever seen, far more impressive than the better-known *A hemsleyanum*, a similarly climbing species from the Altai Mountains. According to Andrew Lauener, an authority on

the genus, our Kunming plant was *Aconitum vilmorinianum*. We also found it at Hua Hong Dong and, previously, had seen it on Emei Shan in Sichuan province.

Contrasting with these blues were the flowers of several herbs, which, like the monkshood, were new to me. One of these was a fleshy stemmed stonecrop – *Sedum bracteatum* – that sprang from sunny rock crevices to form low hummocks of yellow flowers, made more distinct on account of the conspicuous narrow, spreading, leaf-like bracts attending the flower clusters. This plant, probably an annual, was quite outstanding of its kind, the flowers produced in such numbers as to obliterate the stems and leaves. As far as I am aware, it is not in western cultivation.

Equally impressive was an edelweiss, *Leontopodium sinense*, a bold leafy perennial with erect stems of 30-60cm (1-2ft) terminating in small clusters of tiny flowerheads made conspicuous by the presence of numerous, long, spreading bracts. The entire plant was powdery-grey felted, a regular 'dusty miller'. It was fairly common, even growing on the roadside in places, and it was while photographing one particularly handsome specimen that I spotted a little primula flowering in the shady crevice of a nearby rock. *Primula duclouxii* is a member of the same group as that

Sedum bracteatum is a common sight in autumn in the Western Hills where it sprouts from crevices in rocks and cliffs, forming hummocks and pads of brilliant yellow, starry flowers. (October)

4. To *C convolvulacea* belongs the honour of being the first recorded introduction of a Yunnan plant to Britain. This was achieved by a medical officer and naturalist John Anderson in 1868. Unfortunately, his introduction via Calcutta was restricted to a herbarium specimen.

greenhouse favourite *P malacoides* and has similar, though smaller, pink flowers with a yellow eye. Like *P malacoides*, it is an annual, though much smaller in stature, reaching 5 or 6cm (2 or 2½ in) high. Indeed, when I saw this plant I believed it to be a rather poor specimen of *P malacoides*, which is a plant of marshy ground – Forrest found it growing on the edge of irrigation channels and rice fields elsewhere in Yunnan. In no way comparing with *P malacoides* as an ornamental, *P duclouxii* is, nevertheless, a dainty little species that, according to Stephen Haw, is only known from this location. In an account of this species in the *Alpine Garden Society Bulletin* for March 1983, Haw refers to its site as limestone cliffs and to its flowering in January and February, which suggest that the single plant seen here in October 1980 was an isolated early-flowering individual.

Another unusual inhabitant of rock crevices here, this time in sun or semi-shade, is a small gesneriad, *Corallodiscus bullatus* (not unlike a *Haberlea* at first glance), which formed flattened rosettes of remarkably puckered (bullate) leaves. It seemed a hot, dry situation for such a plant, but no doubt the roots are safe enough in the cool crevice. Over a period of years the rosettes multiply to form substantial clumps when they appear most impressive. In October 1980 when I saw them, these plants had long since flowered, but in May 1983 a plant from this source flowered in the alpine house of Barry Starling in Essex, England. The flowers were shaped like miniature foxgloves, pale violet on the outside, paler or nearly white within, and were borne several together in a loose cluster atop a slender stalk. Mr Starling exhibited his plant at the 1983 Chelsea Flower Show, where it received a Certificate of Preliminary Commendation as a plant for foliage and flower in the alpine house.

A close associate of the corallodiscus in the rock crevices was a peculiar fern relative, *Selaginella tamariscina*. I

Selaginella tamariscina, a curious relative of the ferns, is found in rock crevices in many areas of Yunnan. In the Western Hills it is quite plentiful and most attractive with its *Thuja*-like fronds. In periods of drought these curl upwards to help reduce water loss. (October)

Corallodiscus bullatus, a member of the *Gesneria* family, grows in rock crevices, slowly forming tight, crowded rosettes of puckered leaves. It is common in the Western Hills. (October)

have seen a good number of *Selaginella* species, from the jungles of Malaysia to the temperate forests of New Zealand, and I know how variable they can be, but this species on the limestone rocks of the Western Hills I found far and away the most fascinating. From a stout rootstock delving deeply into the rock crevice there rises a bold rosette of densely overlapping bright green fronds. The whole rosette has the appearance of a small, flattened conifer, though the second name refers to its resemblance to a tamarisk (*Tamarix* species). In times of drought, the fronds curl upwards and the rosette closes to help reduce water loss. With the return of moist conditions the fronds unfold and the plant resumes its former state.[5]

Several true ferns were also present among the rocks, including *Pyrrosia calvata*, a creeping carpeting fern with long

5. This characteristic it shares with *Selaginella lepidophylla* the famous Rose of Jericho or Resurrection Plant, which is native to the Americas, from southern USA, south to Peru.

tapering strap-shaped fronds and, surprisingly, *Botrychium virginianum*. Anyone familiar only with our native moonwort, *B lunaria*, would find this comparatively bold species quite startling. I was certainly surprised to see it, not that it was new to me, having been shown it for the first time in April 1980. What really puzzled me was what it was doing here in China, when I had so recently seen it wild in Virginia, from which American state it takes its name. I was later to learn that the Rattlesnake fern, as it is known in North America, is found in many parts of North America and thence across Europe into Asia as far as China and Japan.

In the bottom of a dry stream bed below the road we found the seed heads of the giant *Lobelia seguinii*. This extraordinary plant at first produces a rosette of large, finely-toothed, green leaves. Once the plant has reached maturity it sends up a tall fleshy pyramidal or columnar flowering stem as much as 5m (16ft) high. This stem bears numerous ascending branches carrying small blue or bluish-white flowers. Being monocarpic the parent plant dies after flowering but not before it has scattered its tiny seeds all around. Plants from seed collected at the time were grown in several gardens including the Royal Horticultural Society's Garden at Wisley, but I fear that this stock has since died out.

Buddleja crispa sprouting from the wall of a monastery in the Western Hills. It is variable both in leaf size and shape as well as in its flowering period. (April)

Botrychium virginianum is a larger, bolder version of the European moonwort (*B lunaria*). Originally described in the eighteenth century from Virginia, this curious fern has a remarkable distribution in the wild from North America eastwards across Europe and Asia to China and Japan. It is not uncommon in the Western Hills. (October)

For anyone with a special interest in shrubs, these hills are a paradise. Many of the familiar garden genera are represented here, including *Buddleja* with several species. Most plentiful is a species formerly known as *B caryopteridifolia*, an evergreen or semi-deciduous shrub growing to 3m (9ft) high or more and as much across, the young shoots as well as the soft, flannelly leaves covered with a loose white or pale greyish felt. The leaves are ovate or triangular, with a tapered or heart-shaped base and can be as much as 15cm (6in) long – even longer on vigorous shoots. The lilac, sweetly-scented flowers are produced in dense axillary whorls on short terminal heads (panicles) during summer. I remember plants under this name being grown at the Hillier Arboretum and, although originating from several different sources they all appeared to have close affinities with *Buddleja crispa*, a native of Afghanistan and the Himalaya. Interestingly, *B caryopteridifolia*, as well as several other former species, notably *B farreri*, *B sterniana* and *B thibetica*, is now regarded by Dr A J M Leeuwenberg of Wageningen, Holland, as being part of the variable *B crispa*. If this opinion is accepted, B *crispa* is represented in western cultivation by a number of distinct clones differing in leaf size and shape as well as in form and time of flowering. One well-known form with small leaves flowers in Britain in July, while another, with larger leaves, flowers twice a year, once in spring before the leaves and again in late summer on short leafy branchlets. In the Western Hills B *crispa* thrives on the dry, boulder-strewn slopes and, in true buddleja style, seeds itself into walls and on the roofs of nearby temple buildings.

Another shrub common in these hills is *Berberis wilsoniae*. I was particularly pleased to see the real McCoy in view of its seeming scarcity in present day cultivation. It was first collected and introduced to the West from west Sichuan in 1904 by E H Wilson after whose wife it is named. Over the years it must have been propagated by the million, especially for use in parks and town and city plantings. It was the first berberis I learned to recognise on starting work for a parks department in the north of England. Easily propagated from cuttings it has also been grown from seed, which is produced in abundance, and therein lies the problem. Berberis of this group are promiscuous when grown in proximity in cultivation and seed-grown plants can be expected to vary. B *wilsoniae* is known to have contributed to the complex swarms of hybrids grown under the names B x *carminea* and B x *rubrostilla*, and seed-grown B *wilsoniae* has for many years been offered by the nursery trade in Britain if not in Europe and the United States. Whilst most of these seedlings have fulfilled the expectations of buyers in terms of habit, fruit and autumn leaf, they have gradually come to look less and less like the original species. B *wilsoniae* as commonly sold is a mounded shrub of fairly compact habit to 1.2m (4ft) with generally green leaves and rounded or ovoid red or salmon red berries. As we saw it in the Western Hills of Kunming it forms a compact shrub less than 1m (3ft) high. Its small, sea-green, obovate to oblanceolate leaves are less than 2cm (¾in) long and are rather glaucous beneath and, like the shoots,

covered above with a pale bloom. The red fruits are ovoid or rounded and carry a thin bloom. The dwarf, compact habit and grey, bloomy foliage are its most outstanding features and some plants in cultivation from seed collected at the time have retained this essential character and, incidentally, have proved to be semi-evergreen. It is interesting to read Wilson's comments in *Aristocrats of the Garden* published in 1926: 'A low growing and decidedly ornamental plant for rockeries in particular is the new B *wilsoniae* from the China-Tibetan borderland, which bears globose, brilliant salmon-red fruits'; and again: 'Another low growing species is B *wilsoniae* with dense twiggy branches, grey-green semi-persistent leaves which become beautifully tinted in the late fall, and masses of yellow flowers succeeded by brilliant salmon red globose berries'.

Right and above right. *Berberis wilsoniae*, a plant in the author's garden grown from seed collected in the Western Hills. Many plants (seed grown) in western cultivation are of hybrid origin. (July)

Myrsine africana, a densely twigged evergreen shrub, the female with dark blue fruits is a common constituent of the scrub layer in the Western Hills. It is also found on the mountains of east and southern Africa. (October)

Differing from the last in almost every respect is *Myrsine africana*, a frequent companion of the berberis in the Kunming Hills. It is a densely twigged evergreen shrub growing to 1.5m (5ft) with masses of small, shining, dark green leaves that are toothed in their upper half. The tiny insignificant flowers are dioecious (male and female on separate plants), the females when fertilised giving rise to tiny, dark blue, rounded berries in the leaf axils. It is rare in cultivation, which is surprising considering its relatively compact habit and neat foliage. It is especially attractive in spring when its reddish-coppery young growth adds a decided sparkle to the glossy but otherwise dark foliage. More interesting is its occurrence in the wild, for it has what botanists term a disjunct distribution. Native of south-west China and the Himalaya, it leaps across western Asia and mainland Europe with a stopover in the Azores to reappear on the mountains of eastern and southern Africa (hence the name).

During the summer months the hills around Kunming are filled with the flower and fragrance of roses, of which there are several species. Most common is *Rosa banksiae* in its wild variety *normalis*. This forms large mounds of long, arching, prickly stems that scramble over surrounding scrub and rocks. The small, yellow-stamened, single, white flowers flood the branches from April into May casting a sweet fragrance in the air. When I saw this rose flowering in the spring of 1981 it evoked happy memories of an office I occupied for several years at the Hillier Arboretum in Hampshire. Growing on the office wall was a single white Banksian rose and every year in spring, when the increasing warmth caused me to open wide my windows, the rose would each day fill my room with the sweet smell

of violets. Banksian roses, whether they be the single white, the single yellow ('Lutescens'), the double white ('Alba Plena') or the most commonly seen double yellow ('Lutea'), demand in cultivation a warm sunny wall – and the warmer the conditions the better they will flower.

In October 1980 we saw at Hua Hong Dong a plant of *R banksiae* that carried a few late flowers. Interestingly, these were white, double and rather small, not unlike those of the original Lady Banks' rose on which the name *R banksiae* was founded. The last named was originally introduced to England by the Kew collector William Kerr, who found it in a Guangzhou nursery in 1807. It was named after the wife of the then director of Kew, Sir Joseph Banks.[6] It is not known how or where the double white Banksian rose originated, whether as a seedling or branch sport, and without a detailed comparison of material I am not even sure that the plant now referred to as *R banksiae* 'Alba Plena' is the same as the one we found in Yunnan. However, I have since been told by other travellers to Yunnan that the double white Banksian we saw at Hua Hong Dong is not uncommon elsewhere on the Yunnan Plateau and in the warm valleys of the north-west of the province.[7] Whether this rose has been planted I do not know, but its history would make a fascinating study. Indeed, the history of all roses cultivated in China by the Chinese would be well worth documenting.

Even more impressive than the wild Banksian rose is *Rosa gigantea* or *R odorata* variety *gigantea*, as some people prefer it. In these hills it forms a bold, wide-spreading shrub with stout thorny arching stems, bedecked in spring with large cream-coloured flowers 10cm (4in) or more across, with a bold central mass of golden stamens. These are powerfully and deliciously fragrant enabling one to detect the presence of this rose in thick scrub long before it is located. *R gigantea* ranges in the wild from Yunnan through upper Burma into north-east India and is variable in size as well as hardiness. In Burma it is recorded as climbing as high as 18-24m (60-80ft) into forest trees. Sir Henry Collett, from whose collections this rose was named in 1888, described having found it in the Shan Hills, having first spotted it in flower at a distance of two miles through his field glasses. Much later,

6. There is evidence that *R banksiae* variety *normalis* was already in cultivation in Britain several years before William Kerr's introduction of the double white-flowered form in 1807. A rose of this description was introduced from China to his home, Megginch Castle, Strathtay, Scotland, by Robert Drummond in 1796. About a century later, cuttings of this rose, which grew unhappily, never flowering on the castle wall, were taken by a descendant to Nice where, not surprisingly, it flourished and flowered. This rose is now a familiar and well-established feature of Mediterranean gardens. Drummond's introduction would almost certainly have originated from a Chinese garden or nursery.

7. What must have been the first discovery of this rose in a wild state by a European was made by Delavay in Yunnan in 1884, and was followed, a year later, in west Hubei and east Sichuan, by Augustine Henry. According to Henry it is a common feature of the Yangtze Gorges and their subsidiary glens, its stems tumbling in long curtains of blossom from the steep slopes and cliffs providing an impressive spectacle in spring. It was from these same gorges that this rose was reintroduced to the West as seed by E H Wilson in the early years of the 20th century. Interestingly, although I have not examined this rose in Hubei, the one commonly referred to as *R banksiae* variety *normalis* by the Chinese in Yunnan has prickly stems, while the form long grown in cultivation in the West has unarmed – or sparsely thorned – stems.

Above and below. *Rosa gigantea* growing on a hillside at Da Shao north of Kunming. It is a vigorous shrub with long, arching, thorn-clad stems. (April)

Rosa longicuspis is one of the most commonly occurring roses in the Western Hills and elsewhere on the Yunnan Plateau. It is a strong-growing species forming dense mounds of arching, thorny stems clothed with polished green leaves and plastered in spring with sweet-scented flowers. (April)

in 1948, it was reintroduced from Manipur by Frank Kingdon-Ward. It is widespread in Yunnan where it is extremely variable in size, specimens as little as 1.5m (5ft) having been described by George Forrest. It is these smaller forms of R *gigantea* that some authorities, notably Graham Thomas, believe may have contributed, together with the wild R *chinensis*, to the tea-scented roses of Chinese gardens and, through them, to the hybrid teas and other groups of today's gardens in the West.

In cultivation in Britain R *gigantea* is predictably a plant for warm sunny walls and is only satisfactory in the milder areas where, incidentally, it is evergreen or semi-evergreen except in severe winters, its rich glossy green leaves providing a bonus. A third rose, with scrambling stems and fragrant white or pink-tinted flowers, is *Rosa longicuspis*, which will be more fully discussed in the next chapter. Suffice to say that it is common in the Kunming area.

121

Left. *Hedychium yunnanense*. The ripened fruits are an attractive feature in autumn, shown here in the author's garden. (October)

Right. *Hedychium yunnanense*. This species was common in the Western Hills above Kunming. Here the original introduction is seen flowering under glass at Wakehurst Place in Sussex. (July)

Another plant frequent in this area, and gathered later in full flower by one of our party, was a ginger lily *Hedychium* species. It was a leafy plant with a flowering stem up to 1m (3ft), the spike filled with cream-coloured flowers with a yellow tube and a long curving red stamen. In 1984 this plant flowered in a cool greenhouse at Wakehurst Place in Sussex and was identified at Kew as belonging to *Hedychium yunnanense*, a native of Yunnan, south east to Vietnam and possibly Laos. Grown under glass initially, this introduction is proving quite hardy in many gardens in Britain, including my own and the RHS Gardens Wisley.

A group of flowering shrubs commonly found in the Western Hills, indeed throughout Yunnan, are the hypericums. There are probably a greater number of woody species in Yunnan than in any other province. In October 1980 I collected seed from several apparently different hypericums growing in both the Western Hills and at Hua Hong Dong further north. These were supplemented by herbarium specimens collected at the same time and again in April the following year prior to the Sino-British Expedition to the Cangshan. These specimens were given to Dr Norman Robson of the Botany Department of the Natural History Museum in London. A botanist of wide interests and expertise, he has made a special study of the family *Guttiferae*, in particular the genus *Hypericum*, and is now regarded as a world authority on the subject. Over the last few years Dr Robson has paid special attention to the herbarium specimens recently collected in south-west China and these have been supplemented by plants now flowering in cultivation from wild collected seed. His conclusions, published in a British Museum Bulletin in 1985, contain a great deal of information of importance to both botanist and plantsman. The hypericums he describes

include several new species and subspecies based on material examined from Chinese and western herbaria together with cultivated material of wild origin.

Based on Robson's conclusions the following are among the shrubby hypericums found in the hills of Kunming. All have yellow flowers in summer. *Hypericum beanii* is a bold shrub up to 2m (6ft) high, though usually much lower, with star-shaped flowers 3-4.5cm (1¼ -1¾ in) across. We found this variable species growing in dry stony places in the Western Hills above Dragon Gate, at Hua Hong Dong, Da Shao and in the Little Stone Forest south east of Kunming. It is restricted in the wild to Yunnan and west Guizhou and was first discovered near Mengzi (Mengtze) in south Yunnan by Augustine Henry in about 1897. It was also collected in the Kunming area by Maire in 1906. It is a most attractive though uncommon shrub in cultivation, first introduced as seed by Henry in 1898. Plants from recent collections are strong growing and free flowering in July and August with occasional flowers later. In common with *H forrestii* and *H pseudohenryi*, it was originally given the name *H patulum* variety *henryi*, a most confusing 'kettle of fish' finally resolved by Dr Robson in 1970.

Very different is *Hypericum acmosepalum*, which we found growing at Da Shao in 1981. This is a strong growing shrub with erect slender stems to 2m (6ft). The leaves are oblong or narrowly elliptic and the flowers 3-5cm (¼-2in) across, deep yellow, sometimes tinted red on the outside. The stiff erect habit, narrow leaves and clusters of star-shaped flowers with conspicuous stamens make this an easily recognised species. Added to this are its sharply pointed sepals, giving rise to its name *acmosepalum*, which means literally 'with sharply pointed sepals'. It is distributed through four provinces of south-west China

Hypericum acmosepalum at Santaipo, near Xiaguan, west Yunnan. A strong-growing shrub of erect habit, its narrow leaves and comparatively small flowers with conspicuous stamens are characteristic. (May)

Right. *Hypericum beanii* growing in the Western Hills. One of several species common in the hills around Kunming, it was first discovered in south Yunnan by Augustine Henry and is named after W J Bean, a famous curator of Kew Gardens. (April)

and was first introduced by George Forrest to western cultivation, where it is still rather rare but is worth considering for its profusion of flowers, its bright red seed capsules and its neat semi-evergreen leaves, which often colour red in autumn and winter.

More elegant in habit is H *henryi*, a slender-stemmed shrub capable of 3m (9ft) in a suitable situation but most often 2m (6ft) or less. It is a distinct species on account of its branchlets arranged in herring-bone or frond-like fashion, gracefully arching and clothed with small, neatly arranged leaves. In many ways it resembles the Himalayan H *uralum* and has similar small, cup-shaped flowers 3-4cm (1¼ -1½ in) across. We found this distinctive species at Hua Hong Dong and plants are now in cultivation from seed collected at the time.[8] The plant described above is the typical form. Another form, subspecies *uraloides*, is described in the next chapter.

8. Like many other hypericums in cultivation in Britain, it was damaged by the severe winters of 1985 and 1986, suffering in my garden temperatures of -10°C (14°F). Happily, it recovered fully and in 1985 flowered freely from August to October. Apparently this species was previously in cultivation in California (1959) and Scotland (1977), probably from seed collected in 1937 by George Forrest's collectors who continued to be employed after Forrest's death by the Hon H D McLaren of Bodnant in North Wales.

Hypericum lancasteri growing in the Western Hills. This species was named after the author by Dr N K B Robson of the British Museum (Natural History) in 1985. (April)

Left. Hypericum lancasteri flowering in the author's garden from seed collected in the Western Hills in 1980. The wide-spreading sepals, which are red tinted in the bud stage, add to the flowers' attraction. It performs best in a warm, sunny, well-drained situation.(July)

Two other hypericums were found in the Western Hills in 1980 and 1981. The first of these, a small shrub up to 1m (3ft) with neat, pointed (oblong-lanceolate) leaves 3-6cm (1¼-2½in) long and erect, star-shaped to slightly cup-shaped flowers, has been named *Hypericum lancasteri*. The flowers are from 3-5.5cm (1¼-2in) across, backed by a star-shaped arrangement of five spreading or recurved sepals that are reddish in bud.[9] In cultivation *H lancasteri*, which is named after the author, has retained its relatively dwarf, mounded habit and produces its flowers freely through the summer months into early autumn. It is suitable for a sunny border or scree and is now being propagated by several sources in Britain. Unfortunately, it appears to be rather less hardy than some other species and was killed or damaged in a number of gardens during the severe weather of January and February 1986.

9. Specimens of this newly-named species were first collected in the Kunming area by Maire in 1913 and were until recently regarded as another species – *H stellatum*. It has also been collected by the Chinese botanist Zhao (1978) in south-east Sichuan and in west Yunnan by the Sino-British Expedition to the Cangshan in 1981.

Hypericum curvisepalum. The young growths of this recently named species, related to *H lancasteri* are red flushed in spring. It occurs frequently in the hills around Kunming and elsewhere on the Yunnan Plateau. Here it is seen on a hillside in the Cangshan. (May)

Tea house of the Great Flower Monastery in the Western Hills. As elsewhere in China, native woodland has survived in the vicinity of the monastery including several trees of great size and age. (April)

Very similar is *Hypericum curvisepalum*, a slightly larger shrub with distinct cup-shaped flowers 2-4cm (¾-1½ in) across. Like H *lancasteri*, this too has relatively narrow leaves while the narrow, wide-spreading, recurved sepals are purplish in bud and fruit. One of the most appealing characteristics of this species is the reddish-purple of its young growth in spring. In the wild, H *curvisepalum* occurs in north Yunnan, south Sichuan and west Guizhou. Specimens were first collected by Maire in Yunnan in 1913, but, like H *lancasteri*, it was long regarded as belonging to H *stellatum*.

About 1.5km (1 mile) down the road from the Dragon Gate is situated the Great Flower Monastery or Taihuasi. The original temples were built early in the fourteenth century and contain, among other things, nineteen bronze statues of the Buddha accompanied by clay statues of the arhats (disciples). The temple is famous for its gardens, which contain many notable trees as well as flowering shrubs and perennials. On our visit in April 1981 we saw some lovely peonies, mainly *Paeonia lactiflora* as well as its variety *trichocarpa* (P *yui*), which differs from the typical plant in its hairy ovaries. It was represented here by white and red double-flowered forms. From a dendrologist's point of view the most impressive features of Taihuasi are the many fine trees, some of great age, growing in the vicinity.

Paeonia lactiflora variety *trichocarpa*. A double white form of this uncommon variety growing in a garden in the Great Flower Monastery. (April)

Ehretia corylifolia. The Ehretias are woody members of the Borage family (*Boraginaceae*), which includes the more familiar herbs forget-me-not and comfrey. Shown here are the fragrant flowers of a tree in the Western Hills above Kunming. (April)

In October 1980 *Alnus nepalensis* was in flower with long yellow catkins borne in heavy, drooping swags at the ends of the branches. The leaves were equally impressive being over 20cm (8in) long and a lustrous dark green above. It was fairly common in the area, one magnificent specimen was 24m (80ft) high having a girth of 220cm (87in). It is a pity that this species is not hardy enough for general cultivation in the British Isles, where it would be warmly welcomed by tree lovers. It is one of only three autumn-flowering alders.

In 1981 we were able to examine and measure many more trees in the monastery environs. They included a veteran *Ginkgo biloba*, which was said to be six hundred years old and was 15m (50ft) high with a girth of 406cm (160in) at chest height. An equally imposing – 24m (80ft) – specimen of *Celtis yunnanensis* had a girth of 295cm (116in), while not far away was a *Cupressus duclouxiana* of at least 30m (100ft) with a girth of 220cm (87in). The celtis, to my knowledge, is unknown in the West, yet it would be a tree well worth introducing to areas enjoying a warm climate. Apart from its potential size, its main characteristic is the long, drawn out point to the leaf, which makes this, together with the peculiar jagged-ended leaf of the Korean *Celtis koraiensis*, one of the most easily recognised species in the genus.

Other trees measured include: *Catalpa fargesii* forma *duclouxii* 21m (70ft); *Albizia mollis* 24m (80ft) with a girth of 382cm (150in) (tree dying); *Pinus armandii* over 30m (100ft); *Hovenia dulcis* 15m (50ft); *Eriobotrya japonica* 10.5m (35ft) with a girth of 46cm (17in); *Alangium chinense* 12m (40ft), with leaves both entire and three-lobed; *Calocedrus macrolepis* 12m (40ft) with a girth of 65cm (26in), and *Ehretia corylifolia* 6.5m (22ft). There were also three

Celtis yunnanensis, a native nettle tree with characteristic taper-pointed leaves. A large specimen of some 24m (80ft) was growing by the Great Flower Monastery in the Western Hills. (April)

specimens of *Populus yunnanensis* all over 24m (80ft) with girths of 223cm (88in), 228cm (90in) and 240cm (94in).

The ehretia in particular interested me, with its compact rounded crown, rounded hairy leaves resembling those of a hazel (*Corylus* species) and its dense terminal heads (panicles) of fragrant, creamy-white flowers. It is common in the Kunming area and no doubt elsewhere in Yunnan as well as in west Sichuan, Jiangxi, Hubei and Guangdong, and seems quite tolerant of dry conditions. The only tree of this species I ever saw in cultivation was in the Botanic Garden of the Black Sea town of Sokhumi in Georgia in 1979.

Behind the monastery the native woodland is fascinating and, one presumes, typical of the forest once widespread in these hills. Two pines are present, one in particular, *Pinus armandii*, being plentiful and represented by some particularly tall-stemmed trees of 22m (72ft) or more. Named after Père Armand David, who first found it in the mountains of Shaanxi (Shensi) province in 1873, it is a most lovely tree in the wild with its drooping blue-green needles up to 15cm (6in) long carried in bundles of five. In some respects it resembles the Himalayan *P wallichiana* differing, however, in its relatively broad, stumpier cones, greener young shoots and shorter leaves. It is less satisfactory in cultivation than *P wallichiana*, in Britain certainly, the latter being preferred for its vigour, blue-grey needles, long cones and general all-round performance. *P armandii* enjoys a wide distribution in the wild from central and west China to north Burma, with outlying populations in Taiwan and Korea, and it is probable that some introductions might prove more satisfactory than others. Even so, trees in excess of 20m (65ft) are known in Britain and Ireland, the largest being at Cosfort Castle in Co. Armagh, which in 2000 had reached a height of 30.5m (just short of 100ft). Two trees from the original introduction by Augustine Henry from south Yunnan in 1897 are still growing at Kew.

With *P armandii* grew *Pinus yunnanensis* (*tabuliformis* variety *yunnanensis*), which is very different with its stout shoots and branches and shining, dark green needles up to 20cm (8in) – longer on young trees or vigorous shoots – borne in pairs or, occasionally, in bundles of three. As a young tree, it is fast growing and spectacular with bold, densely-needled branches, but gradually, as it matures, it becomes more open branched and is less impressive. The cones, up to 10cm (4in) long, are normally borne singly, although I have seen tight clusters of cones clinging tenaciously around the branch in the manner of the Monterey pine, *P radiata*, of California. When ripe, the cones are a warm orange-brown, like the shell of a hazel nut, and are most appealing especially when carried on young trees at eye level. In the wild *P yunnanensis* is plentiful in west China, particularly in Yunnan where it is also locally planted on hillsides. It is capable of reaching 30m (100ft). Judging by its performance in the Western Hills and in similar locations

elsewhere, it seems remarkably tolerant of dry conditions and, if it were not for its unsatisfactory habit as a mature tree, it would be worthy of wider planting in the West. The largest specimen in Britain, is a tree at RBG Kew, which measured 16m (52ft) in 2001.

Quite as plentiful as the pines in the Western Hills are the various species of evergreen oak, large trees – many of them 18m (60ft) plus – with stout trunks and heavy canopies. Of these *Quercus senescens* possesses thick, leathery, broad, entire leaves 5cm (2in) long, pale and densely hairy (pubescent) beneath, while in *Q gilliana* the thinly-downy, green leaves of similar size are armed with spine-tipped teeth that are especially noticeable on the leaves of juvenile and sucker growths.

By contrast the leaves of *Lithocarpus dealbatus* are lance-shaped up to 12.5cm (5in) long (occasionally more), with smooth margins and a slender, pointed apex. The green upper surface contrasts effectively with the greyish or whitish, hairy lower surface (*dealbatus* means 'whitened'). More attractive, however, are the recently emerged young growths, soft and drooping and of a pale suede colour, like the ears of a spaniel pup.

I had encountered none of these oaks previously, but a fourth species, *Q glauca*, I did recognise. Chinese botanists refer this species to a separate genus, *Cyclobalanopsis*, as *C glauca*, and there are many other species. They differ from *Quercus* in several details, of which the most obvious are the scales of the acorn cup (involucre), which are united (connate) and arranged in concentric rings.

The leaves of *Q glauca* are variable in shape but usually taper from the middle to a slender point. They average 10-13cm (4-5in) in length and are distinct in their parallel venation, boldly toothed (serrate) margins and minutely hairy and grey-green (glaucous) undersurfaces. The newly-emerged coppery or bronze coloured leaves are as limp and fragile as the mature leaves are firm and leathery. This species has a wide distribution in the wild in east Asia, from Japan in the east to the Himalaya in the west.[10]

Lithocarpus differs from *Quercus* principally in its mode of fruiting, for it bears numerous acorns in sessile clusters in an erect spike. Some of these fruiting spikes are quite heavy when mature and fall to the ground with a thump, clattering through the canopy on their way. The name *lithocarpus* is derived from the Greek lithos – a stone, and *karpos* – a fruit – alluding no doubt to the hard acorns that would surely test the patience of a squirrel.

To complete a trio of oak relatives we found *Castanopsis*, represented by two species, *C orthacantha* and *C delavayi*. *Castanopsis* is allied both to *Castanea* (sweet chestnut) and *Quercus* (oak), having nuts enclosed in a prickly case as in the chestnut, but taking two years to ripen as in some oaks. All

10. The earliest introduction to British cultivation was from Nepal in 1804, but the few established trees in the milder areas of Britain probably originated from Wilson's or Forrest's seed. In British cultivation it is rare and frequently confused with *Q myrsinifolia*.

Pinus yunnanensis is easily recognised by its long, shining, green needles in pairs (occasionally in threes) and its orange-brown cones, which cling tenaciously to the branches. Western Hills. (April)

The steep slopes of the Western Hills above Lake Dianchi are well-wooded in places, both deciduous and evergreen trees being present. Evergreen oaks of the genera *Quercus*, *Castanopsis* and *Lithocarpus* are particularly plentiful. (April)

the species are evergreen and I was particularly pleased to see the above two, having first encountered them in the famous woods above the castle at Caerhays. The two trees in question are probably the only specimens of any size in western cultivation having been introduced as seed by George Forrest, probably in 1924. The Caerhays *C orthacantha* was 15m (50ft) when measured in 1984. In the woods in the Western Hills *C orthacantha* reaches 18m (60ft) or more, and has leathery pointed leaves 10cm (4in) or more long, toothed usually in the upper half. Characteristically, they are equally green on both surfaces, hence the synonymous name *C concolor* under which it is, or once was, grown at Caerhays. The fruits are borne in tight prickly clusters in an erect spike. The leaves of *C delavayi* are of similar size, if not slightly longer, and are often coarsely toothed. In contrast to those of the *C orthacantha*, the undersurface is silvery-grey or whitish.

These are but a handful of oaks and oak relatives in a province well endowed with them. In a recent account Yunnan is accredited with no less than twenty-four species

of *Quercus*, thirty-six species of *Cyclobalanopsis*, sixty-six species of *Lithocarpus* and thirty-eight species of *Castanopsis*. Not counting varieties, that makes 164 species in total. In Britain we have two, both *Quercus* species!

At first glance the relatively dry Western Hills, and others like them hereabouts, would not strike one as being a promising site for rhododendrons and yet several species find a home here. Two of the most frequent are R *decorum* and R *microphyton*, the former of wide distribution in Yunnan as well as Sichuan and western Guizhou (Kweichow). It seems to favour drier situations and is a common component of hillside scrub and open forest, often tolerating repeated lopping and burning. Not surprisingly, considering its distribution and range of locations, R *decorum* is variable in hardiness as well as in leaf and flower. Those in the Western Hills are not among the hardiest and seed collected in 1981 has been widely distributed to gardens in different climatic zones on the basis that some will succeed somewhere. Its flowers are large and trumpet shaped, varying from pink to white. They are

Rhododendron microphyton is a common evergreen azalea in the Western Hills where it grows on sunny slopes as well as in woodland shade. (April)

possessed of a rich fragrance and are borne (in the best forms) in bold trusses at any time from April to July depending on form and location. In the spring of 1981 one of my colleagues, Peter Cox, collected seed from these and many other populations in Yunnan, the notes on his seed packets – 'late flowering', 'early flowering', 'good white', 'pale pink, deeper flush' and 'large leaves' – indicating the range of variation.

Very different is *Rhododendron microphyton*, a member of the *Azalea* group. This is a small twiggy shrub, often of dense habit, the slender shoots crowded with evergreen leaves 1-3cm (½ -1¼ in) long. The small funnel-shaped flowers are borne in terminal clusters in April and May, varying in colour from pale to deep mauve, pink or purple. In the Western Hills it shares the same dry slopes as *R decorum*, equally hacked about though capable of 1.5-2m (4-6ft) when left alone in a sheltered gully or on a woodland margin. Restricted in the wild to Yunnan, it is of borderline hardiness and is rarely seen in cultivation outdoors in Britain.

Besides these, two other species of *Rhododendron* are common in the hills of Kunming. *Rhododendron spinuliferum* is another variable shrub, up to 2.5m (8ft) in height with downy and bristly shoots and leaves up to 7.5cm (3in) long, tapering to the base, downy and scaly beneath. The flowers, too, are distinct in being tubular, 2.5cm (1in) long, and narrowing to the mouth, out of which the stamens protrude. They are found in varying shades of red and are produced in March and April in terminal clusters as well as in the axils of the upper leaves. Closely related is *R scabrifolium*

variety *spiciferum* (*R spiciferum*), a smaller, open-habited shrub of 1-2m (3-6ft), first found in these hills by Delavay in 1891. In this case the leaves are narrow, up to 3cm (1¼ in) long, and covered above, as are the young shoots, with a mixture of hairs and bristles, while the lower surfaces are

Rhododendron spinuliferum, a variable species with bristly shoots and leaves and clusters of tubular flowers from which protrude the stamens and style. Western Hills. (April)

131

The large cones of *Keteleeria evelyniana* turn a rich brown on ripening, remaining attached to the branches after shedding their seed. (April)

covered with hairs and scales. The widely funnel-shaped flowers only reach 1.5cm (⅗ in) and are borne in small clusters from the upper leaf axils in March and April. They vary in colour from pale to deep pink or almost white. It is not the hardiest of rhododendrons in British cultivation.

R scabrifolium itself, a taller, lank-habited shrub growing to 3m (9ft) and with larger leaves, we found common in the hillside scrub further to the west of Kunming towards Xiaguan. In the Kunming Hills in April 1981, we found two different plants that were regarded by the rhododendron experts in our party as hybrids between *R spinuliferum* and *R scabrifolium* variety *spiciferum*. Both plants occurred in scrub in the presence of the parents and had a few deep pink flowers remaining.[11] From the evidence in the Kunming Hills, all these rhododendrons seem remarkably tolerant of hot sun and dry soil and are able to withstand frequent browsing, cutting and burning, not that this is a prerequisite of their successful cultivation.

The list of plants we saw in the Western Hills in 1980 and 1981 is enormous and I have mentioned but a fraction. Before moving on to pastures new, however, I would mention just one more, a tree that both puzzled and fascinated us when first seen. It is a conifer, *Keteleeria evelyniana*, which is native to these dry hills and in similar places elsewhere in Yunnan. On first seeing it in 1980, I thought we had found a species of *Abies* because the leaves and erect cones are not unlike those of a fir. The cones of *Keteleeria*, however, remain intact when ripe, falling in one piece whereas those of *Abies*, of course, break up at maturity, the scales and seeds falling like so much brown

confetti. In *Keteleeria*, too, the male catkins are borne in stalked clusters (umbels) rather than singly.

Previously unknown in western cultivation *K evelyniana* is perhaps worth describing in some detail here. It is a most distinguished conifer, dense and conical as a young tree becoming more spreading with age. In the Western Hills it is found on the lower slopes often mixed with *Pinus yunnanensis*. We later saw it dominant on hills further to the west. Specimens of 25m (80ft) or so are not uncommon and, according to one Chinese source, it is capable of as much as 40m (130ft) in suitable locations. The third year and older branches have a grey and brown flaking bark, while the young shoots are green with scattered glandular hairs. The leaves are spread either side of the shoot and are erect above, with a narrow V-shaped depression. They are narrowly strap-shaped (linear) averaging 5cm (2in) long, ending with a short point (mucro). Green above, they are marked below with two broad bands of grey-green stomata either side of a prominent, raised, green midrib. When the leaves finally are shed they leave behind on the shoot a small raised scar, in size midway between that of an *Abies* and the plug of a *Picea*.

The crowning glory of this species, however, are the cones. Borne on the top side of the upper branches, these are cylindrical in shape tapering to a rounded or flattened summit. They vary in size from 15-20cm (6-8in) and are composed of tapering scales that curve outwards at the tip revealing the wing tips of the seeds, two behind each scale. When young, the cones are green, later becoming purple, the scales oozing a clear resin that turns white on drying. This was the state of the cones when we saw them in October 1980. They are quite the most beautiful I have ever seen, crowding the branches like richly ornamented sticky candles. By the following April they had matured to a rich brown and had lost most of their beauty. At that time I climbed into a tree to collect some samples that clung tenaciously to the branches and I had to use a sharp knife to cut them away. Most of the seed had already been shed and much of what remained had already been eaten or damaged by weevils. My colleagues and I spent the best part of an evening laboriously breaking up the cones in order to extract a small heap of apparently good seed, and, to my knowledge, only a few have resulted in seedlings.

Having since seen this species in the dry inner valleys of west Sichuan, I can support Bean's statement in *Trees and Shrubs Hardy in the British Isles* that the failure of these trees (*Keteleeria*) to flourish in Britain is perhaps due to insufficient summer heat. Comparatively mild winters would also appear to be a contributing factor.

Keteleeria evelyniana, a fine specimen of over 20m (65ft) in the Western Hills attended by saplings of *Pinus yunnanensis* and *Cupressus duclouxiana*. It was first discovered by the Irish botanist and plant collector Augustine Henry at Yuanjiang, Yunnan in 1898 and named for his life-long friend Evelyn Gleeson of Dublin.

11. Such hybrids are not uncommon in these hills and have been referred to as R x duclouxii by Chinese botanists.

Low hills of outcropping limestone above a rich, red earth at Hua Hong Dong, north west of Kunming. *Cupressus duclouxiana* and *Juniperus formosana* are plentiful here with a rich variety of shrubs and herbs, including *Berberis*, *Cotoneaster*, *Pyracantha* and *Stellera*. (April)

Hua Hong Dong

Some 13km (8 miles) north west of Kunming is the Qiongzhu or Bamboo Temple, said to be the most famous ancient Buddhist temple in Yunnan. It lies on a wooded hillside known as Jade Hill or Mount Yufeng and is easily reached by road from the city. The first monastery on this site is known to have been built in the early years of the Mongol reign (AD 1280-1368), and some believe the site to have been occupied much earlier. Indeed, one story recorded on a tablet in the Hall of the Laughing Buddha has it that the first temple on the site was built in AD 638. According to the legend, two brothers went hunting in the Western Hills. While they were chasing an escaped rhinoceros they encountered a group of strange looking monks who, on the brothers' sudden appearance, disappeared as if by magic. All that the brothers could find of the monks' presence was a bamboo stick stuck in the ground. The very next day the bamboo stick started to grow, rapidly increasing until it formed a dense grove. Startled by this, the brothers came to the conclusion that the monks must have been the spirits of the mountains and, in recognition of this, they built a temple on the site to show their gratitude for this miraculous encounter.

In 1419 the temple was destroyed by fire and rebuilt three years later. Later still, in the 1880s, it was extensively restored. Apart from an impressive statue of Buddha, the temple is renowned for its collection of statues depicting arhats (disciples). The halls are full of them, rank upon rank, five hundred in all. Measuring 1m (3ft) high, they were made by moulding clay over a wooden model or

Leucosceptrum canum, a shrubby member of the mint family *Labiatae* growing at Hua Hong Dong. (October)

Juniperus formosana at Hua Hong Dong. This is a bright green, prickly-leaved shrub of dense, erect habit, sometimes developing into a small tree. (April)

Pyracantha fortuneana flowering on a hillside at Da Shao. This is the most commonly occurring firethorn in the Kunming area, producing in autumn reddish or orange-yellow fruits. (April)

frame. To achieve this it took Sichuan sculptor Li Guangxiu, working with five assistants, seven years – from 1883 to 1890 – to complete. The remarkable thing is that each figure is different in dress and facial expression, while all the social strata – warriors, officials, scholars as well as craftsmen and peasants – are represented, some stern, others smiling; indeed, all the emotions can be seen as one scans the rows of faces.

The sculptors drew their inspiration for their models from the people of the region. Li Guangxiu, so it is said, opened a small tea house where he studied the features of his customers, no doubt sketching them prior to modelling them in clay. The sculptures on the middle tier, apparently better than the rest, were done by Li himself, while those of the upper and lower tiers were done by the apprentices under his instruction.

In one of the temple courtyards are two cedar trees, *Cryptomeria japonica*, reputedly six hundred or so years of age, while before the Hall of Arhats stand two ancient evergreen magnolias, *Magnolia delavayi*, whose short-lived flowers fill the temple with fragrance during summer.

Beyond and above the temple the road climbs to a rough limestone plateau, at approximately 2,200m (7,217ft), that is dissected by gullies and supports the occasional hill. The

location is known as Hua Hong Dong and is notable for the variety of plants growing in its red soil. Visits to the area in October 1980 and April 1981 revealed a wealth of interesting and unusual plants of which, for reasons of space, I shall describe only a very few.

The two most common trees, both conifers, are *Cupressus duclouxiana* and *Juniperus formosana*, the former scattered over a wide area, their dark columns lending a Mediterranean aspect to the landscape. The juniper reaches 11.5m (38ft) when undisturbed, but most of the plants we saw were bushy in habit (through browsing, presumably), with several main stems, the loosely spreading and ascending branches heavy with the prickly, spine-tipped foliage. Despite its name *formosana* (of Formosa or Taiwan), this juniper is widespread in China but it is rare in cultivation in the West.

Other trees, including *Keteleeria*, *Juglans* and various evergreen oaks, occurred more sparingly and mainly in ravines and other sheltered locations. The scrub vegetation here is incredibly varied and contains a great many shrubs familiar from western cultivation. In 1981 the firethorns (*Pyracantha* species) were at their best, the branches of *Pyracantha fortuneana* in particular smothered with white flowers. This is a hairless, green-leaved species, its flowers replaced in autumn by masses of small reddish or orange-

Above. *Cotoneaster insolitus* in the hills around Kunming. This specimen in the author's garden was raised from seed collected at Hua Hong Dong. (November)

Left. *Pyracantha angustifolia* often grows with *P fortuneana* in the hills around Kunming. Its orange-yellow fruits and white or grey felted leaf undersurface are characteristic. (October)

yellow berries. The other species at Hua Hong Dong, *Pyracantha angustifolia*, has narrowly oblong and more or less entire leaves, which are clothed beneath, like the young shoots, with a dense almost woolly greyish-white down. The flowers of this species do not compare in effect with those of P fortuneana, but in autumn it is a different story, for then the orange-yellow berries stud the branches, almost glowing against the dark green and grey of the foliage. In cultivation it, not surprisingly, performs best in a warm sunny position and is especially productive against a sheltered wall where it will berry freely most years, the berries, by the way, remaining firm and coloured on the branches long after those of most other pyracanthas have turned brown or fallen.

In the same family as the pyracanthus (*Rosaceae*), are the cotoneasters, represented in these hills by several species, including *C mairei* (referred to by the Chinese as *C dealbatus*), which resembles and is related to the well-known *C franchetii* of gardens. A second species is the small-leaved, slender-stemmed *C amoenus*, which is less common in cultivation. In addition, there occur a number of smaller, even dwarf cotoneasters with smaller leaves, referred to by the Chinese as *C buxifolius*, a neat and compact species in cultivation, but, as far as I can ascertain, restricted in the wild to the Nilgiri Hills of Kerala in SW India. Seed was collected from several plants and examples are now established in cultivation.[12]

Rivalling the cotoneaster in berry in October 1980 was *Berberis wilsoniae*, which we had already seen in the Western Hills above Lake Dianchi. At Hua Hong Dong, however, it was joined by two other species, both evergreen with blue-black berries covered by a white or grey bloom. B pruinosa (*pruinose* meaning glistening as though frosted over) is a free-growing large shrub 3m (9ft) or more high with erect and spreading branches, fierce triple spines at each node and clusters of polished green leathery spine-toothed leaves that are dull green or sometimes greyish-white beneath. The slightly fragrant yellow flowers in late April or May are borne in short-stalked clusters from the leaf axils and are then most conspicuous and attractive. This handsome evergreen is not uncommon in collections in Britain but rarely offered by the nursery trade, which is surprising considering that it was first introduced from Yunnan to the West by Delavay as long ago as 1894. Plants in cultivation from Hua Hong Dong seed (L.692) are growing freely and flower well in May.

The other evergreen berberis, a slender leaved erect shrub with yellow flowers, was referred to by Chinese botanists in 1981 as *Berberis kunmingensis*. Since then, Dr David Chamberlain at the Royal Botanic Garden, Edinburgh, has renamed it B *ferdinandi-coburgii* variety *vernalis*. A young plant in my garden is fairly stiff and erect in habit with long, narrow, green, spine-toothed leaves and clusters of pale

12. One of these cotoneasters is a dwarf evergreen shrub of up to 1m (3ft) with small, neat, oval leaves to 1.5cm (½in) long, dark green above, and silky, pale and hairy beneath. The branches in June are crowded with small, white flowers and studded in autumn with small, orange-red fruits. It is quite hardy. According to Jeanette Fryer this is *C insolitus*. The name *C vandelaarii* has been given to another species found at Hua Hong Dong by H J van de Laar (VdL 80671) in October 1980. This is an evergreen shrub up to 1.5m (5ft) high, of wide, spreading habit with crinkly, shiny leaves up to 5.5cm (2in) long, and large clusters of pinkish flowers in June and July. The pale, orange-red fruits are fully ripe by Christmas, remaining until the following spring.

Myrica nana at Hua Hong Dong. Left. The male form of this dwarf evergreen shrub with flower spikes long spent. Right. The female form with fruiting heads well developed. It is rare, if present at all, in British cultivation. (October)

Cotoneaster vandelaarii. Below. (VdL 80671) Autumn berries, (November). Right. In flower (June). This most ornamental species honours the Dutch horticulturist and plantsman the late H.J. van de Laar

Michelia yunnanensis is a common companion of *Myrica nana* in the hills around Kunming. A small- to medium-sized evergreen shrub, its leaves are thick and leathery, covered beneath when young, as are the young shoots and flower buds, with a pelt of ferruginous hair. Da Shao. (October)

Michelia yunnanensis, a larger-flowered form growing outside in the Quarry Hill Botanic Garden, California. (April)

yellow flowers, but it has proved to be less than hardy, having been severely damaged in two consecutive winters.

Evergreens are in plentiful supply at Hua Hong Dong and two in particular attracted my attention. One was *Myrica nana*, a species commonly 1m (3ft) high in this area, but capable of twice this in ravines and similarly sheltered places. It is a relatively compact shrub with stiff erect branches and dark green, leathery leaves 2.5-8cm (1-3in) long, toothed and broadened towards the tip. Male and female flowers are carried on separate plants (dioecious) in the axils of the upper leaves in spring, the males in dense yellowish erect catkins, reddish-brown in bud, the females in rounded heads. The latter develop into small green bauble-like fruiting heads 1.5cm (½ in) across, which darken to reddish-brown when ripe.

A common companion of the myrica both here and elsewhere in the Kunming Hills is *Michelia yunnanensis*. Like the

myrica, this is fairly dwarf in exposed areas but taller growing, as much as 4m (14ft) in shelter. A multi-stemmed shrub, its leaves are 4-8cm (1½-3in) long, broader in the upper half, of thick leathery texture and entirely without teeth. Of a dark green appearance above, they are initially covered beneath, like the young shoots, with a ferruginous hair (indumentum). The cup-shaped flowers are borne singly in the leaf axils on a short, thickened stalk (peduncle). In the bud stage they are enclosed in an envelope (spathaceous bract), which is covered by a rich pelt of ferruginous hair. Gradually the buds swell, burst, then shed the bracts, allowing the creamy-white tetals to expand. The flowers are at their best in April or May, but the most satisfying effect comes in the earlier stages when both buds and expanded flowers create a striking contrast among the dark green foliage. *M yunnanensis* is native to Yunnan, most closely related to the banana-scented *M figo* (*fuscata*) occasionally seen under glass or outside in

Stellera chamaejasme forma *chrysantha*, a herbaceous member of the *Daphne* family, common throughout the Yunnan Plateau. The fragrant, yellow flowers of this Chinese form are a startling contrast to the normally white flowers of the better known Himalayan plant. (April)

bud. A long established plant will develop into a mound 20-30cm (8-12in) high and as much or more across. This description refers to the typical form, which occurs in the wild from north-west India (Uttar Pradesh) to central Nepal, Bhutan, through Tibet to north China and Siberia at altitudes between 2,700 and 4,300m (8,850 and 14,100ft). At Hua Hong Dong, as elsewhere in Yunnan, a form of *Stellera chamaejasme* occurs, forma *chrysantha*, in which the flowers are a rich yellow, a lovely contrast with the pink-stained buds. It is plentiful across the exposed rocky plateau and is a fine sight from April to June when in flower. According to Polunin and Stainton (*Flowers of the Himalaya*) the roots of *Stellera* are used in Tibet in the manufacture of a crude paper, in the same way, no doubt, as is the bark of *Daphne bholua* in Nepal. It is, however, as an ornamental on which its fame rests in western cultivation.[14]

Stellera was not the only plant at Hua Hong Dong suitable for rock garden or scree cultivation. In April and May a small skullcap, *Scutellaria amoena*, is widespread, its creeping stems turning up at the ends to support 10-15cm (4-6in) spikes of erect lavender-blue or pale violet flowers each with a bold, white marking on the lip. It tends to form small mats or tufts and is well named *amoena*, meaning pleasant or delightful. It combined effectively in

warm areas in Britain, and more commonly planted outside in southern Europe and in the south east of the United States. Several times I have received seeds from Yunnan and, although distributed to growers of proven skill, I have yet to hear of germination. Perhaps seed has been allowed to dry out before being sent to me, but some day someone will succeed and I look forward to seeing it in British cultivation.[13]

Myrica nana is similarly inclined and I cannot help thinking that in colder countries both these evergreens would make interesting container subjects for the cool house or conservatory.

If there is one plant designed to set the mouths of alpine plant enthusiasts watering it is the *Daphne* relative *Stellera chamaejasme*, named in honour of George W Steller (1709-1746), a German naturalist and traveller in Siberia after whom the extinct Steller's sea-cow is also named. *S chamaejasme* is a herbaceous perennial, sending up annually from a stout tap root clumps of erect, unbranched, densely leafy stems terminating in domed clusters of sweet-scented, tubular, white flowers varying from green to reddish in

13. In recent years *M yunnanensis* has been successfully established in warm, sheltered gardens in Britain and Europe and in the Pacific coastal areas of North America.

14. Rarely seen in gardens and seldom mentioned in horticultural literature, *Stellera* is one of the most desirable and difficult of plants in cultivation and, except from seed, apparently impossible to propagate. Even seed collecting can be frustrating as the seeds are borne without a fleshy coat and, when ripe, fall at the slightest touch. Small plants of the typical form from Nepal are at present at Wisley, Kew and the Royal Botanic Garden, Edinburgh, grown from seed and seedlings collected by Ron McBeath in the Marsyandi Valley in 1983. In addition, Edinburgh have old flowering specimens from seed collected by Colonel Donald Lowndes in Nepal and Ludlow and Sheriff in south-east Tibet.

Scutellaria amoena, a choice little perennial skullcap plentiful at Hua Hong Dong. The name is particularly apt for this species, *amoena* meaning 'pleasant or delightful'. (April)

Bauhinia brachycarpa variety *microphylla*, a deciduous shrub enjoying sun and warmth. Hua Hong Dong, Kunming. (April)

places with a dwarf shrubby species of *Bauhinia*, which proved to be *B brachycarpa* variety *microphylla*, quite an attractive shrub not unlike an amelanchier at a glance, with five-petalled, white flowers 2.5cm (1in) across, no match, however, for the large purple or white flowers of its more exotic relations, such as *B purpurea*, *B variegata* and *B blakeana*. The genus, which is mainly found in the tropics, takes its name from the brothers Johann and Caspar Bauhin, famous Swiss botanists of the sixteenth and early seventeenth century. They are amusingly represented in the characteristic two-lobed leaf.

In October 1980 we found two gentians growing on stony slopes at Hua Hong Dong. *Gentiana rigescens* was a perennial species with blunt-tipped leaves and erect or ascending stems to 30cm (12in). The funnel-shaped flowers 2.5cm (1in) or slightly more in length were borne at the ends of the stems in a six to ten flowered cluster, and, instead of the usual blue, were a distinctive rose-purple. Some plants bore several stems, their clustered flowers darkly attractive against the pale limestone.

Very different was *Gentianella grandis*, a slender-stemmed annual species with grassy leaves and sporting long-tubed flowers of a rich blue or bluish above the low dried herbage. These flowers with four spreading lobes had a curious quadrangular calyx tapering from the base to four long, pointed segments each with a conspicuous midrib.

I doubted that either of the above gentians were in present-day cultivation, whereas I held no such reservations about another blue-flowered plant that we found abundant in the Kunming area and elsewhere on the Yunnan Plateau. This was *Cynoglossum amabile*, a relative of our native Hound's tongue (*C officinale*) and, like this species, characterised by its fruits (nutlets) covered in tiny barbed spines or bristles. Like this species also, *C amabile* is

a biennial herb differing in this respect from the popular Himalayan *C nervosum* of our herbaceous borders, which is perennial. *C nervosum* and *C amabile* do, however, have an important characteristic in common in that their flowers are of a rich blue, outstanding enough on its own, but stunning when combined in the garden with low-growing, yellow-leaved perennials such as *Origanum vulgare* 'Aureum' or the less hardy *Helichrysum petiolatum* 'Limelight'.

The typical form of *Cynoglossum amabile*[15] is a fast-growing, freely-branched hairy herb producing a bold clump of downy leaves from out of which rise the flowering stems to form a wide-spreading head up to 60cm (2ft) high.[15] The flower colour has been described as celestial blue – a fair claim, and the flowers are similar in shape to those of forget-me-not, but slightly larger. From June onwards, earlier in the wild, they are carried in long sprays opening in succession and giving, therefore, an extended display. Various selections of this Hound's tongue have been made over the years, of which 'Firmament' has a compact bushy habit, to 45cm (1½ ft), with indigo blue flowers, though there are also pink selections.

In June 1981, while waiting for our bus to take on petrol in a town between Xiaguan and Kunming, I took the opportunity of gathering a great armful of this plant in fruit. I spent the next hour or so of our journey extricating myself and my helpers from the myriad clinging nutlets much to the amusement of our Chinese colleagues who regard this plant as a weed. Notwithstanding, enough seed was gathered to supply a large number of friends and others on my return home and the results brought pleasure to innumerable gardeners, one of whom achieved an impressive display by interplanting *C amabile* with Evening primrose (*Oenothera biennis*), the pale lemon flowers of the latter providing the perfect contrast.

Gentiana rigescens, a low-growing perennial species flowering in autumn at Hua Hong Dong. (October)

15. *Cynoglossum amabile* was first introduced into cultivation in Britain by A E Pratt in 1889-90 and by the French missionary Soulié three years later. From the beginning it seems to have been a favourite with gardeners and has remained so ever since, an ever-present member of the seed catalogues.

Sapindus delavayi, a handsome foliaged deciduous tree growing at the Caoxi Temple, Anning, south-west of Kunming. The small yellowish-green flowers are carried in dense conical heads. (April)

Anning

Some 40km (25 miles) to the south west of Kunming, along the Burma Road, lies the town of Anning through which flows the Cao River. In April 1981, we visited Anning in order to see the Caoxi Temple, which is situated on a hillside above the river at approximately 2,000m (6,561ft). The present temple was probably built some eight hundred years ago, certainly the three wooden Buddha figures have been dated to the Song Dynasty (AD 960-1280) and experts believe the buildings also to be typical of that period. If this is true, it is the only remaining Song Dynasty temple in the Kunming area. The earliest temple on this site is said to have been built in AD 502 by a monk whose title was Zhiyao. Zhiyao found that water at the Caoxi confluence of Shaozhou Prefecture smelt and tasted good. Believing that the source of the water must be a sacred place, he decided to build a temple there, and went on to predict that 170 years afterwards a supreme power would emerge at the site. His prophecy was fulfilled in the early Tang Dynasty, in the shape of a monk with the title of Huineng (AD 638-713), who developed Zen doctrines and founded the Caoxi Zen sect, which exerted great influence on Buddhism in China. The area is well known for its hot springs, the Anningwenquan [First or Top Spring in China], being one of China's most famous.

The hills around the temple are clothed with forest, though few trees of a large size remain except in the vicinity of the temple complex. This forest shows a predominance of evergreens in which *Keteleeria evelyniana* is prominent with some *Pinus yunnanensis* and the usual oaks. In places *Keteleeria* formed pure stands but the trees were mostly of a similar size and age though there was some regeneration. Nevertheless, the contrast between the Anning hills and similar hills elsewhere in the area, was quite noticeable. Here they were at least green, while elsewhere almost desert conditions prevailed and I was interested to be told by a Chinese colleague that when the Austrian botanist Handel-Mazzetti collected in the area between 1914 and 1918 he found extensive forests with trees in great variety and often of a large size. Large trees certainly flourished in the protected environment of the temple and included a magnificent Chinese pistachio, *Pistacia chinensis*, of 30m (100ft) at least, with a girth of 463cm (182in) at chest height. *Firmiana major* was represented by a twin-stemmed specimen to 25m (82ft) with large, lobed (palmate) leaves. This is said to differ from the better known and more commonly planted F *simplex* in its smooth grey (not green) bark and red (not creamy) flowers. *Sapindus delavayi* was a 20m (65ft) tree resembling a sumach (*Rhus* species) in general appearance, with downy, pinnate leaves 30cm (12in) or more long. The small, yellowish-green flowers are carried in large, branched, conical heads (panicles) at the ends of the shoots. Equally impressive were the many trees of *Cupressus duclouxiana*, one of which was easily 30m (100ft) high with a girth of 194cm (76in) at chest height.

Pistacia weinmanniifolia. The young growths are an attractive ruby-red becoming glossy green in maturity. Anning. (April)

Viburnum punctatum. Little if at all known in western cultivation, this is a handsome shrub with evergreen glossy-topped leaves that are marked beneath with pale brown sunken scales, hence *punctatum*, meaning spotted. Anning. (April)

Pistacia chinensis, mentioned above, is not unknown in western cultivation having first been introduced by von Bunge from the Beijing area in the 1830s. Both Père David and E H Wilson later introduced it from Sichuan (Szechwan). It is said to be native to central and western China but is commonly cultivated elsewhere, and I recall seeing it growing apparently wild in the hills above Qingdao (Tsingtao) on the Shandong Peninsula in 1979. According to Wilson, the wood of this tree made the best rudder posts for the larger boats, while the young shoots and leaves were, and perhaps still are, cooked and eaten by the Chinese as a vegetable. It is the young shoots that, in British cultivation certainly, provide probably the most ornamental feature of this tree. They emerge ruby-red, similar in effect to those of the evergreen *Photinia x fraseri* 'Red Robin' now so popular in gardens. Later, as the leaves expand, they lose their colour but remain a cheerful glossy green until autumn when, if conditions are suitable, they

again colour richly before falling. Through the growing season the young growths continue to please and at any one time from spring until early autumn, or later in warmer climates, each leafy branch has a terminal tuft of red. In shape the leaves are pinnate (like an ash) with nine to thirteen narrow leaflets, the terminal one generally absent. In the wild it is often seen growing in dry rocky places and is very tolerant of drought. It has long been grown, though not as commonly as its qualities would suggest, in the southern states of the United States, especially in California, and it has been strongly recommended there for its relative freedom from pests and diseases and its suitability as an urban tree. Curiously, in Britain it is rarely seen except in botanical gardens and specialist collections, where it makes a small- to medium-sized tree. It has been represented at Kew since 1897 and seems quite hardy and happy there, although it undoubtedly grows best in those countries enjoying warm dry summers.

Pistacia chinensis, an ancient tree growing at the Caoxi Temple, Anning. Over 30m (100ft) in height, this magnificent specimen has a trunk girthing 463cm (182in) at chest height. Standing at its base is Bob Mitchell, Curator of the University Gardens, St Andrews, Scotland. (April)

The pistachios are a small but well distributed clan, represented in southern Europe and Asia as well as in North and Central America and include the pistachio nut of commerce, *P vera*. In the dry hills around Anning we found another species, *P weinmanniifolia*, quite common. This is an evergreen shrub or small tree, dense and bushy in habit, here reaching 5.5m (18ft) in the shelter of the forest but capable of more. As with *P chinensis*, the young growths are an attractive red, but it is the mature leaves that attract. These are smaller than those of *P chinensis* with comparatively broad leaflets and a narrowly winged rachis. Both these species carry inconspicuous flowers in panicles or spikes, male and female on separate plants. The small fruits, like peppercorns, are said to be reddish at first becoming bluish on ripening.

We were impressed by the number of trees and shrubs seen in the woods above Anning that were completely new to us, though we usually recognised the genera to which they belonged. *Crataegus scabrifolia*, a small tree up to 6m (19ft) with a thorny trunk and shiny, hairy leaves was one, while another, *Viburnum punctatum*, was an evergreen shrub of 3m (10ft) with leaves glossy green above, 5-8cm (2-3in) long, bluntly toothed and with sunken, pale brown

Pittosporum brevicalyx, a small evergreen tree with a spreading crown growing in the woods around the Caoxi Temple at Anning, south-west of Kunming. (April)

scales beneath. Its creamy-white flowers were carried in dense terminal heads. A *Pittosporum* species reminded us of the strong Chinese representation of a genus we normally associate with New Zealand. This was *Pittosporum brevicalyx*, a 4.5m (15ft) tree of wide spreading habit with evergreen obovate, abruptly pointed leaves up to 12cm (5in) long. These were mainly gathered towards the ends of the branches providing ideal backing for the dense terminal clusters of fragrant, mustard-yellow flowers. I am not aware that this attractive species is represented in western cultivation, but if seed were available it would certainly be worth trying in the warmer areas such as the west coast of America and in the milder areas of Britain and Ireland. There are many other Chinese species of which the same could be said and, indeed, a *Pittosporum crispulum*, introduced as seed from Emei Shan (Mt Omei) in 1980 is growing well in my garden having endured -10°C (14°F) in the winter of 1984/85. This plant was received from a Dutch friend Harry van de Laar of Boskoop, where it has proved frost tender.

The *Aralia* family is very well represented in Yunnan and I was particularly interested in two examples frequent in the woods at Anning. One of these was *Pentapanax henryi*, an erect stemmed shrub up to 8m (26ft) with felted (tomentose) young shoots, leafless except for terminal tufts of

William Mesny in Chinese apparel

glossy, chocolate-purple, young growths that later expand into green leaves with three to five, toothed leaflets. The buds of this plant, according to our Chinese colleagues at the time, are used in traditional medicine to treat stomach ache, while the young leaves are cooked in oil and eaten as a vegetable.

Very different in appearance is *Nothopanax delavayi*, reaching 2-3m (6-9ft) in the woods, but capable of 5m (16ft) elsewhere. Its erect stems are clothed with long-stalked, evergreen leaves that are divided into seven narrow, slender-pointed leaflets up to 12cm (5in) long. If only this evergreen could be introduced to western cultivation it would, I am sure, become very popular. Like *Pentapanax henryi*, it would only be suitable for mild areas of Britain and countries enjoying a warm climate, though in colder areas it would make a most handsome and pleasing pot plant for the home. On emerging, the young growths are like tufts of glistening bronze filigree, paling as they expand into bold green plumes of fine-fingered foliage. We saw this species again in woodland clearings in the Western Hills above Kunming where, bathed in shafts of sunlight, it was an impressive sight.[16]

On his first visit to China in 1899, E H Wilson journeyed into southern Yunnan in order to confer with Augustine Henry who was then stationed at Simao (Szemao) close to the border with what is now Laos. It was an uncomfortable journey to say the least, and because of the virtually subtropical nature of the vegetation Wilson collected

16. This species has since been introduced to the West and is now established in several woodland gardens in mild areas of Britain if not Pacific N America.

17. The name *mesnyi* commemorates a Jerseyman, William Mesny (1842-1919), who first discovered this jasmine in Guizhou province in 1880. He was an extraordinary character, a true adventurer of the Victorian era who, over a period of thirty years or more, travelled through most, if not all, the provinces of China, eventually becoming a Major-General in the Chinese Imperial Army. In 1895, by now retired and living in Shanghai, he edited a weekly periodical, *Mesny's Chinese Miscellany*, giving a mass of useful information on China and notes derived from his experiences.

18. *O yunnanensis* was originally discovered by Delavay but was first introduced to British gardens by Forrest in 1923. It grows vigorously in light woodland at the Hillier Arboretum in Hampshire and has attained 10m (32ft) or more at Caerhays in Cornwall and Hidcote in Gloucestershire.

comparatively little in the way of seed or plants. One plant he did introduce from this area, however, and that is still with us today is *Jasminum primulinum*, now more correctly *Jasminum mesnyi*.[17] He collected this near Mengzi (Mengtze) on the return journey to Hanoi, and as there was no seed of it to be found he apparently collected plants, which he sent by the overland route to Hong Kong. Considering the difficulties of this operation it says much for Wilson's ability that these plants arrived in England alive and well, and it is to this original introduction that we owe most, if not all, of the plants of *J mesnyi* in western cultivation today. I was reminded of this story in April 1981 when, in the woods near the Caoxi Temple at Anning, we found *J mesnyi* forming dense piles of tangled growth covering a considerable area. Some of the typically semi-double, primrose-yellow flowers were present, but what is more to the point is that occasional shining black berry-like fruits were found. According to Bean (*Trees and Shrubs Hardy in the British Isles*), Wilson collected plants of this jasmine as it had never been found bearing seed. The seed we collected that day subsequently gave us plants, one of which, in my cool greenhouse, produced a few single flowers, and seedlings that flowered at the Royal Botanic Garden, Edinburgh, are likewise single. In Britain, *J mesnyi* is most often seen as a cool greenhouse or conservatory subject and only succeeds out of doors in milder areas. In countries enjoying warm summers it thrives and I will never forget seeing it in 1982 on the sun-baked slopes beneath the Acropolis in Athens where it had been planted along a perimeter fence, its long angular green stems smothered in flower.

In the main courtyard of the Caoxi temple stood an ancient specimen of a wild apricot, *Prunus mume*, reputedly seven hundred years old and dating from the Yuan Dynasty.

Nothopanax delavayi, an evergreen shrub of the ivy family with elegant leaves and green or yellowish-green flowers. It occurs in areas of woodland around Kunming, especially at Anning and in the Western Hills. (April)

Jasminum mesnyi, named after a Jerseyman who became a Major-General in the Chinese Imperial Army. It is now commonly planted in warm areas of Europe and North America. This specimen was photographed in Athens. (April)

Nearby grew a hundred-year-old tree of *Magnolia delavayi* and an impressive specimen of *Juniperus formosana* 13.5m (45ft) high with a girth of 83cm (33in) at chest height.

As we were leaving the temple area, we detected a delicious sweet perfume being carried by a breeze from the nearby woodland. We discovered its source to be several scattered trees of *Osmanthus yunnanensis* (*forrestii*), 6m (20ft) high with wide-spreading crowns. The long, evergreen, dull green leaves were 22cm (8½ in) long, and varied in having the margins either entire or prickly toothed, both kinds on the same tree, the latter mainly on the lower branches or sucker shoots. The sweet fragrance came from the small creamy-white flowers borne in crowded clusters in the leaf axils. We saw this species again later in the Cangshan above Yangbi in west Yunnan.[18]

Rumex hastatus. This small sub-shrubby sorrel covers extensive areas of dry river valley on the Yunnan plateau, staining the landscape red. Da Shao, Kunming. (April)

Da Shao

Some 40km (25 miles) north of Kunming lies an area known as Da Shao. In April 1981, in company with our Chinese colleagues, we spent half a day in the hills there at approximately 2,400m (7,873ft). There appeared to be no virgin forest and much of the area was regularly cut over for firewood. *Pinus armandii* was dominant on some ridges and in sheltered gullies, having been planted some seventeen years before. It was commonly accompanied by *P yunnanensis* and *Keteleeria evelyniana*, nowhere very large. Much of the woody vegetation comprised scrubby evergreen oaks including *Quercus* species, *Lithocarpus dealbatus* and *Castanopsis delavayi.* The whole area was cruelly coppiced but rich in species and provided more than enough to keep a plantsman busy and happy.

I was particularly interested in an aspen poplar. It did not actively seek the moister valley bottoms and gullies but occurred widespread across the slopes. Like the rest of its woody-stemmed colleagues, it was subject to regular pruning, but because of its stronger growth and rejuvenative powers it could often be seen as a 5-6m (16-19ft) sapling. Its leaves were rounded in outline, shallowly scalloped and carried on typically long, slender, flattened stalks allowing

the leaf blades to tremble in the slightest breeze. At the time, our Chinese colleagues referred to this tree as *Populus bonatii,* later changing their minds and renaming it *P rotundifolia* variety *duclouxiana*[19] – our friend Ducloux again!

At Da Shao grew many of the shrubs seen previously at Hua Hong Dong and in the Western Hills, and, indeed, this glorious mix is typical of the Yunnan Plateau. *Pyracantha, Cotoneaster, Rhododendron, Rosa, Hypericum, Michelia, Myrica* and *Pieris* were the main components, the latter represented by *P formosa,* which was very different in these dry exposed hills to the trees we saw later in the forests of the Cangshan. For here the *Pieris* was comparatively small, 2-3m (6-9ft), and kept in check by the local villagers, though its branches,

Populus rotundifolia variety *duclouxiana,* a common aspen in Yunnan, especially in the hills around Kunming where it rarely attains full size due to frequent lopping by villagers. Pictured is a female specimen, the fruiting catkins almost ripe. Da Shao. (April)

19. Alfred Rehder, in his *Manual of Cultivated Trees and Shrubs,* 1940, recognised the distinctiveness of this Chinese aspen, *P rotundifolia* (which is actually east Himalayan in distribution), but, in his famous bibliography published nine years later, he preferred to regard it as a synonym of another Chinese species, *P adenopoda.* The Sino-Himalayan aspens are a complex group varying in botanical detail but, from an ornamental point of view, no different and certainly no better than the European *P tremula* or the North American *P tremuloides.*

20. *C saluenensis* is widely distributed in Yunnan. It has been collected (as herbarium specimens certainly) by many people, including Maire, Schneider and Handel-Mazzetti in the Kunming area. George Forrest's original seed introductions in 1917 and later, some of which J C Williams used at Caerhays to breed some of the now famous Williamsii camellias, *C x williamsii,* were collected in west Yunnan in the Shweli-Salween-Tengchong (Tengyueh) area.

The trees on these dry hills at Da Shao are mainly planted pines – *Pinus armandii* and *P yunnanensis*, with scattered *Keteleeria evelyniana*. Beneath them flourishes a rich scrub layer in which roses, pyracanthas, cotoneasters, rhododendrons and heavily pruned evergreen oaks predominate. Here too grows *Camellia saluenensis* and *C pitardii* variety *yunnanica*. The highest point on the ridge is 2,700m (8,858ft). (April)

nevertheless, were filled with flowers mostly still in bud.

Many other flowering evergreens, including camellias, accompanied the *Pieris* and, had I not not seen them with my own eyes, I should have found it hard to believe that camellias could flourish in such conditions. The most abundant was *Camellia saluenensis*, densely leafy bushes of 2-3m (6-9ft).[20] We found none in flower although, according to Professor Feng, flowers are produced over a long season from November until April. From the evidence of lush growth and numerous fruits, this species seemed quite at home and free flowering on these sunny slopes where wind and human activity created a dusty soil surface with little or no permanent leaf litter. How different these conditions are to the comparatively lush, leafy, moist, shady woodland gardens of southern and western Britain, especially gardens like Caerhays and Trewithen in Cornwall where *C saluenensis* and its numerous hybrids flourish. The other camellia we found both here and in the Western Hills was *Camellia pitardii* variety *yunnanica*, similar in size to *C saluenensis*, but differing in its generally larger, long, pointed (acuminate) leaves, which were placed less densely on the branches than is normally the case with the other. Later we found *C pitardii* variety *yunnanica* in west Yunnan in the forests of the Cangshan where one bush had produced a late, pink, funnel-shaped flower. These camellias, some of which seemed quite old, having been regularly coppiced for generations, presumably enjoyed shadier, more sheltered conditions before the forest was destroyed; if the forest was allowed to re-establish, the changes in vegetation would make for a fascinating study.

Heinrich von Handel-Mazzetti, the Austrian botanist, who travelled extensively over the Yunnan plateau in 1914, was commemorated in, among other plants, a large evergreen shrub *Eurya handel-mazzettii*, which appeared fairly widespread in the Da Shao area. It is related to *Camellia*,

Camellia pitardii variety *yunnanica* is not uncommon at Da Shao where it may be found sharing the same slopes as the better known *C saluenensis*. Although flowering takes place in late winter the occasional bloom may be found in spring. (April)

Vaccinium fragile, a dwarf evergreen shrublet of neat habit. Hua Hong Dong, Kunming (April)

borne in the upper leaf axils. In some plants the flowers were pure white, but, in the main, they were variously tinted pink or red, particularly around the mouth, the effect heightened by the red bracts. This species has been introduced several times into western cultivation, most notably by Forrest from west Yunnan. Wilson also found it in west Sichuan and it is probable that these collections, from higher elevations than the Kunming plants, are hardier in British gardens. Having said that, I cannot recall having seen this species in cultivation, and though it once grew at Exbury Gardens in Hampshire, it must now be rare if at all represented in this country. It was not grown by Hillier during my years with that firm, yet was once offered by Marchant's Nursery of Wimborne, Dorset, and described in their 1937 catalogue as not being hardy in Midland gardens. Although I have yet to see them, the berries are said to be black and, according to George Forrest, are, in their season, the principal food of the common pheasant of Yunnan. It is a choice little shrub and its reintroduction is long overdue.

Similarly rare in cultivation is *Lyonia ovalifolia*, which, in the hills around Kunming, is commonly a small shrub, achieving a large shrub or small tree in more sheltered situations. Both at Da Shao and Hua Hong Dong we found it flowering in great profusion, the white, nodding, narrowly pitcher-shaped flowers crowded in short racemes terminating the lateral branches. The individual flowers were quite substantial, 1-1.5cm (½ in) long and, together with the glossy green leaves and the polished brown stems, gave an impressive show. Most of the Kunming plants were later identified as variety *hebecarpa*, with downy seed capsules. The most interesting member of the *Ericaceae*, however, at Da Shao, belonged to a species and a genus quite new to us. *Craibiodendron yunnanense* was a large evergreen shrub, regular lopping preventing it from assuming its normal size, which, in ideal conditions, can be 8m (26ft) or more. Its leaves are variable in size, glossy green, tapering abruptly to a blunt tip. It was, however, the young leaves that caught our attention, for these were coloured a brilliant coppery-red, as impressive in their own way as those of the best selections of *Photinia x fraseri*. None of the plants we examined showed any sign

being in the same family – *Theaceae*, but bears no comparison in flower, these being tiny and inconspicuous, male and female on separate plants. Here, too, occurred several members of the rhododendron family *Ericaceae*. *Rhododendron* itself was represented by several species already described elsewhere, with the addition of *R siderophyllum*, a shrub of 2-3m (6-9ft), closely related and similar to *R yunnanense*. From seed collected at the time, Peter Cox is currently growing plants with white flowers in dense trusses, It is, however, a rather tender species most suited to relatively dry and hot areas.

Quite different in appearance was *Vaccinium fragile*, a dwarf evergreen shrub up to 30cm (12in) high by as much or more across. This was a gem of a plant, of compact habit with densely bristly shoots, small finely-toothed pointed leaves less than 2.5cm (1in) long, and arching or drooping hairy racemes 5cm (2in) long of pitcher-shaped white flowers

Craibiodendron yunnanense is a rare relative of *Pieris formosa* with which, incidentally, it is often found in the wild. An evergreen tree, often shrubby, its main claim to ornamental fame are its beautiful young reddish-bronze or coppery-red leaves in spring. It was common in Dao Shao where lopping encourages a regular crop of attractive growth. (April)

Right. *Lyonia ovalifolia* is plentiful at Da Shao and elsewhere on the hills around Kunming. It is normally encountered as a low shrub due to frequent lopping and browsing, reaching tree size in sheltered or woodland sites. In spite of its ornamental value, it is rarely seen in western cultivation. (April)

of flower, but these are described as greenish-white, small and borne in erect terminal panicles; from a colour drawing I have seen in a book on Yunnan plants they do not appear to be very striking. Seed collected from an uncut specimen in the forests of the Cangshan in west Yunnan have given us several plants, some of which have already been distributed to gardens in the milder areas of Britain and Ireland where, it is hoped, this species will stand the best chance of establishing itself outside.[21]

We could have spent many days wandering the hills at Da Shao, but time, as always, was not on our side. Every hillside seemed to support not only plants we had not seen before, but also the regular appearance of those we had seen previously and that we knew from cultivation: *Rubus biflorus* with its white-bloomed stems; *Viburnum foetidum* (not to be confused with the

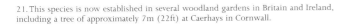

21. This species is now established in several woodland gardens in Britain and Ireland, including a tree of approximately 7m (22ft) at Caerhays in Cornwall.

Sophora viciifolia, which was common in the dry hills above Kunming and elsewhere on the Yunnan Plateau. It was planted as a rough hedge around farms and villages. Here photographed at the RGB Kew. (June)

winter flowering west Himalayan *V foetens*) with its small, red fruits and boldly toothed or lobed semi-evergreen leaves, pungently scented when crushed; *Sophora davidii*, prickly-stemmed and used as a living fence around village plots; the small red-flowered *Jasminum beesianum*; and the dwarf creeping *Pachysandra stylosa*. All were represented in good number.

One of the last plants we examined before leaving the area was a rare member of the cotoneaster family, *Rosaceae*, with an almost unpronounceable name. *Dichotomanthes tristaniicarpa* looks like a larger leaved version of *Cotoneaster pannosus* with its slender, arching shoots and pointed, silky-backed leaves up to 10cm (4in) long. Even the flowers in May and June are cotoneaster like, small and white and borne in terminal clusters up to 5cm (2in) across. It is in its fruits that the difference is to be seen and even this is only apparent to the trained eye. In *Cotoneaster* the fruit is a small berry-like pome with a fleshy pulp containing two to five nutlets. In *Dichotomanthes* the fruit, in reality a tiny dry oblong capsule, has a persistent calyx, which enlarges, ultimately covering all except the tip in a fleshy coat. It appears as a small, downy, reddish berry with the black capsule protruding from the tip.[22]

22. Predictably, it is rare in cultivation where, in Britain certainly, it is subject to damage in cold winters. A specimen flourished for many years on a sheltered wall in the Hillier Arboretum where it reached 2m (6ft) with long arching and drooping branches. It attracted little attention from the public, however, and when it eventually perished in a severe winter, it was missed only by a few. In 1986, I saw a magnificent specimen of 5m (16ft) by as much across in the Strybing Arboretum of Golden Gate Park, San Francisco. There is currently, in the author's garden, a plant of some 4.5m (15ft) that was raised from seed (L.1641) collected in the Kunming area in 1986.

Dry hills above Kunming, where a rich variety of flora can be found, including *Cupressus duclouxiana*, *Juniperus formosana*, *Pinus yunnanensis*, *Pyracantha fortuneana*, *Cotoneaster* species, *Stellera chamaejasme* variety *chrysantha*, *Michelia yunnanensis* and *Sophora davidii*. (April)

The Stone Forest and the Little Stone Forest hold many attractions for plant enthusiasts. A rich flora finds a congenial home among the rocks and in other places inaccessible to grazing animals. Lunan, south-east of Kunming. Both *Pinus yunnanensis* and *P armandii* occur here with *Cupressus duclouxiana*. (October)

The Stone Forest

The Stone Forest, or Shilin, of Lunan is one of the principal attractions for tourists in Yunnan if not China. It is situated some 126km (78 miles) south east of Kunming in what is officially termed the Lunan Yi Nationality Autonomous County, and it is in the 'forest' that Shilin village, a scattering of pink adobe dwellings belonging to the Sani people, a branch of the much larger and more widespread Yi nationality, is found. The Yi were once fierce warriors who developed an aristocratic society in which even the slaves had slaves and with its own language. They long ago evolved a religion based on sacred writings believing, among other things, that everything under the sun has a spirit.

The 'forest', which lies at an elevation of about 1,800m (5,900ft), is an area of rock formations, pillars, pinnacles and top heavy towers, a typical karst-like landscape, which from a distance, bears a fancied resemblance to a forest of old pines. The whole area was once an ocean bed. Then, about 270 million years ago, it was thrust to the surface by the movement of vast subterranean plates. At that time it was covered in a layer of limestone that was gradually eroded by the action of rain and wind, until the present formations took shape. The whole area is said to cover some 26,000 hectares (64,247 acres), but the most frequently visited and spectacular formations are concentrated into 80 hectares (197 acres) comprising the Stone Forest and the Little Stone Forest, both areas open to visitors. Despite the claim of one well-known guide book that some of the formations are as tall as California redwoods, the tallest stone tower is just under 30m (100ft). Nevertheless, the formations are certainly impressive whether one views them from below, passing through a labyrinth of stone corridors, or from above from one of the high vantage points. There are caverns and pools to add to the general interest.

For plant enthusiasts the Stone Forest has additional attractions in the flora that finds a congenial home among the rocks and in the open areas between. In October 1980 we visited this area on our last day before leaving Kunming

Clematis armandii, 'Snowdrift'. A selected form growing in a garden in Hampshire. (April)

for Guangzhou (Canton). It had rained for much of the three-hour journey from the capital and the sticky clay soil (marl) of the 'forest' area clung to our boots in great lumps as we wandered through the rock formations. Most visitors seemed to be heading for the main area, so with two Dutch companions, Harry van de Laar of the Research Station, Boskoop, and Carla Teune of the University of Leiden Botanic Garden, I decided to explore the less frequented Little Stone Forest. Here we found many old friends from European cultivation waiting to greet us.

One of these was *Clematis armandii*, its powerful growths clambering over rocks often hanging from a height of 6m (19ft) in great, shining, dark green curtains. It was well past flowering, of course, but its handsome evergreen leaves, each comprising three prominently three-veined and glossy leaflets, were ample compensation.[23] What a sight this climber must present in spring when the fragrant white flowers fall like snow across these dark stones. There are a number of closely related evergreen species that, although rare in cultivation, have been confused with C *armandii*. These include C *finetiana* and C *meyeniana*, both of which, however, are earlier flowering with smaller, less impressive flowers. C *armandii* is not suitable for cold areas and thrives best in Britain on a south or west facing wall or

23. Fairly widespread in central and south-west China, *Clematis armandii* is named after the French missionary and naturalist Armand David who first found it in Baoxing (Mupin) in west Sichuan, introducing it as seed to the garden of the Paris Museum in about 1873. It was introduced again in 1900 by E H Wilson and the plants from this collection were distributed by the Veitch firm from their Coombe Wood Nursery.

Clematis armandii, growing in the UBG Cambridge. (April)

fence or on a pergola or similar structure. Two named selections are most generally available from nurserymen, 'Snowdrift' with pure white flowers and 'Apple Blossom' with pink-tinted flowers. In both the flowers are 5cm (2in) or more across and produced in April and May, earlier in mild areas. In the wild the flowers of C armandii are rarely as large as this, and it is possible that those two selections belong to the variety *biondiana*. In cultivation there are plants purporting to be one or other of the selections that are most likely seedlings. Their flowers are variable in size and form and mostly white. True 'Apple Blossom' and 'Snowdrift' should be vegetatively propagated

Old man and grandchild at the Stone Forest, Lunan.

and, apart from their flowers and adult foliage, are worth growing for their young leaves, which are a most attractive shining copper or bronze-purple colour.

We found two other *Clematis* species here. One was the extremely vigorous C brevicaudata or something similar, another *Clematis ranunculoides*, a charming species with lax or trailing stems up to 2m (6ft) and leaves divided into three to nine leaflets. The nodding, bell-shaped flowers had four white, slightly spreading lobes stained rose or rose-purple on the back, especially noticeable in bud. Occasional plants had all-white flowers. Flowers were borne singly on erect slender stalks from the joints

A colourful shield bug in the Little Stone Forest in Lunan. (October)

Left. *Clematis ranunculoides*, an unusual late flowering species with its nodding bell-shaped flowers, is common in the Stone Forest. (October)

153

Above. In the Stone Forest we encountered numerous spiders' webs 1m (3ft) or more across, their occupants with most colourfully marked abdomens and slender legs. (October)

Right. A Praying Mantis in the Little Stone Forest. (October)

Below. *Mahonia mairei* flowering in the Hillier Arboretum, Hampshire. (March)

Mahonia mairei, a bold-foliaged, strong-growing species, here growing in the Hillier Arboretum. (June)

(nodes) of the current year's growth. Some plants we found were quite small, 30cm (12in), and yet well flowered and we agreed that they would make attractive pot plants for the cool greenhouse or conservatory as we doubted their hardiness. This variation in growth form, from dwarf shrub to 'vine', is shared by several other *Clematis* species, notable among them C *chrysocoma*.

A most handsome foliage shrub grew in the Little Stone Forest and was very much at home in the shelter of the rocks and stone pillars. This was *Mahonia mairei*, an erect multi-stemmed shrub 2-3m (6-10ft) high with leaves to 60cm (2ft) long comprising nine to thirteen or more spine-toothed leaflets. There were no flowers apparent at the time, but they are described as being yellow and carried in several lax terminal racemes up to 20cm (8in) long. It was

first discovered in the Kunming area by Maire in the early part of the 20th century and was named after him.[24]

Equally spiny in a different way was *Zanthoxylum multijugum*, a tall, almost scandent shrub to 5m (16ft) with long green stems, a few of which were branched and armed with scattered straight thorns. The leaves were long and narrow with numerous pairs (twenty-five or more) of small oblong or elliptic leaflets each with a tiny point. One plant was heavy with clusters of tiny, peppercorn-sized, red fruits.

One of the most welcome scents in the late winter garden belongs to those dwarf relatives of the box, *Sarcococca*. Indeed, it was John Gilmour, my old Director at

24. In the recently published *Flora of China*, M *mairei* is regarded as a synonym of M *duclouxiana*, a variable species ranging in the wild from SW China to Thailand and Assam.

The Little Stone Forest. Many strange, often amusing, rock formations were fashioned when the original limestone became eroded by the action of rain and wind. (October)

the University Botanic Garden, Cambridge, who, I believe, first coined for them the name Christmas box. In a mild winter some species will flower at Christmas if not before, but they are normally at their best in the New Year, in January or February, when the dark green, leafy branches are flooded with tiny, white flowers. Although small and without petals the flowers are crowded into dense axillary clusters and give off a sweet fragrance that pervades the still winter air. They are hardy evergreens, generally less than 1m (3ft), and spread by suckering to form ultimately, in some species, large clumps or colonies a metre or more across. They are also shade tolerant and are among the few flowering shrubs that can be grown in the dry shade of a yew. One of them, S ruscifolia variety chinensis, was common in the Little Stone Forest and plants grown from the red fruits collected that day are thriving and flowering in my garden and elsewhere in Britain. Not surprisingly, considering their location in the wild, the above plants come into growth early and are subject to frost damage. They are also narrower-leaved than the plants already in cultivation under this name. The sarcococcas in general cultivation on the other hand are hardier and less subject

to damage. Indeed, the plants of S ruscifolia variety chinensis most commonly grown are derived from a Wilson collection in Hubei (Hupeh) province at a higher elevation probably than those we saw in Yunnan where it is plentiful across the Yunnan Plateau. Sarcococcas, once established, are ideal for cutting for the home and stems cut in bud and brought indoors will open their flowers in the warmth, filling the room with fragrance, not to everyone's enjoyment.

Growing with the sarcococca was Rhaphiolepis indica, another low-growing evergreen shrub. Its leaves were narrow and leathery while the small dark coloured fruits were all that remained of the clusters of pink-centred, white flowers of summer. A tender plant in British cultivation, this shrub is less often grown than its hardier and more ornamental Japanese relative R umbellata. Even more ornamental is the hybrid between the two: R x delacourii, with its rose-pink flowers, even darker in the selection 'Coates Crimson'.

Trachelospermum bodinieri, which was common in the Little Stone Forest. Here it smothers an old stump in a woodland near Hangzhou in Zhejiang province. (May)

The Yunnan pine, *Pinus yunnanensis*, once occurred in natural stands in the mountains above Kunming. Now it mostly occurs as a planted tree like this young specimen in the Western Hills above Lake Dianchi. (October)

Two of the most common trees in the Little Stone Forest are the Yunnan pine, *Pinus yunnanensis*, and *Populus yunnanensis*. Both are probably planted here although, obviously, they are native to the province. From the lower branches of these trees, especially the pine, and in the taller scrub layer, we encountered numerous spiders' webs, quite large and measuring 1m (3ft) or more across. In the centre of each web was a fairly sizeable spider of a most striking colour. The large oblong or ellipsoid abdomen was a combination on top of red, yellow and black, while the underside was marked with an oblong pattern depicting a curious serpent-like shape rising from a stretch of water, or so it appeared to my eye. The long slender black legs had pale yellow bands at intervals. It really was a most remarkable arachnid and one well worth viewing at close quarters despite the difficulties of extricating oneself from its sticky net.

Apart from *Clematis armandii* previously mentioned, the high rock faces provided a home for several other climbers including two self clingers: one the Chinese ivy, *Hedera nepalensis* variety *sinensis*, the other *Parthenocissus himalayana*, a long

way from the Himalaya, but native here all the same. The most interesting climber, however, was *Trachelospermum bodinieri*, a twining shrub that here found its way into obliging trees and shrubs and crevices of the rock. It was not in flower, but its glossy, green, paired leaves were most attractive all the same. In May 1979 I remember seeing this species at Hangzhou (Hangchow) in Zhejiang (Chekiang) province climbing 6.5m (22ft) or more into trees, its white flowers filling the woods with a rich fragrance. *T bodinieri* is closely related to the well-known *T jasminoides*, which was first introduced to England from a Shanghai nursery by Robert Fortune in 1844. For many years thereafter it was treated as a greenhouse subject, valued for its sweet scent. It can, however, be grown outside in the warmer counties where it should be given a sheltered wall or similar support. I have yet to see it grown up a tree. It is also commonly grown outside in the southern United States, especially in the south east where it is known as Confederate or Star jasmine. As far as I am aware, *T bodinieri*, which is equally ornamental, is not presently grown in Western cultivation.

Chapter Four

In the footsteps of Forrest

The main pagoda at Chong Sheng (Temple of the Three Pagodas) near Dali. Dating from the Tang Dynasty (9th century), it is 69m (226ft.) high and comprises 16 storeys. (May)

'These mountains bear a flora which, apart from its intense botanical interest, is composed of those natural orders and genera most rich in plants of horticultural and economic value'. So wrote George Forrest about the mountains that lie to the west and north of Dali (Tali-fu) in western Yunnan. These mountains, among the most famous in the annals of plant hunting, have attracted some of the greatest plant collectors that ever lived. Delavay, Forrest, Kingdon-Ward and Rock were all tempted by the lure of these high places and, once bitten, they found it difficult to stay away.

It is hardly surprising then, that when in 1980 I was offered the chance of visiting these mountains as a member of a joint Sino-British Expedition, I could hardly believe my luck. The invitation came through my friendship with Peter Cox, nurseryman and writer of Glendoick, Perth. Peter's father Euan (E H M Cox) had accompanied the plant collector and writer Reginald Farrer on his expedition to upper Burma and later wrote of this experience in *Farrer's Last Journey*.

Peter Cox had been hankering after a trip to China for years and in the late 1970s, with encouraging signs of a new attitude towards foreigners by the Chinese Government, the time seemed ripe for an approach. Peter formed a team consisting of Sir Peter Hutchison, an amateur biologist and geographer, Bob Mitchell, Curator of the University of St Andrews Botanic Garden, David Chamberlain, a botanist at the Royal Botanic Garden, Edinburgh, and myself. Tony Schilling, Deputy Curator in charge of Kew's 'garden in the country', Wakehurst Place, Sussex, was to have completed the team, but was forced to withdraw at the eleventh hour due to peritonitis.

Obtaining the necessary permission from the Chinese took a very long time, and if it had not been for the help of dendrologist James Russell we might not have been successful. Jim Russell introduced the team to the late Sir John Keswick whose long experience and good standing with the Chinese was instrumental in having our request considered, while Sir John Addis, British Ambassador in Beijing, and the Great Britain-China Centre in London also offered considerable assistance in the preliminary stages.

Several locations for possible exploration had been suggested to the Chinese but it was not until the beginning of 1981 that we received confirmation of our destination. We were told that we should be heading for the Cangshan (pronounced Tsangshan) or Diancangshan, a range of mountains above Dali in western Yunnan and known to Forrest and his contemporaries as the Tsangshan or Tali Range. Its importance, botanically, lies in its position as an isolated massif to the east of the main range of mountains that runs through west and north-west Yunnan, and the adjacent provinces of north-east Burma and south-east Tibet. Because of this, several geographical elements of the flora of south-west China have outlying representatives on the Cangshan. In addition, there are several species that are almost endemic (found nowhere else) to this range.

The expedition was arranged through the Royal Society and the Academy of Sciences of China and was to be the first joint project of its kind between the two countries. Its ultimate success was mainly due to the detailed local planning carried out by our hosts, the Yunnan Institute of Botany in Kunming whose director, Professor Chen-yih Wu, joined us later in the field.

The aims of the expedition were twofold; first, to bring to Britain live material, both as seeds and plants, for further study. Secondly, to make a general collection of herbarium specimens to augment previous collections from this area both in China and in the West. A number of institutions and societies as well as individuals contributed generously to our budget and some of them later received samples of seed collected.

Having spent an exciting few days botanising in Hong Kong and the New Territories, we continued via Guangzhou (Canton) to Kunming, Yunnan's capital, where we were greeted by our hosts: Professor Guo-mei Feng (joint leader), Tien-lu Ming, Mrs Ruizheng Fang, Tao Deding and Guan 'Clyde' Kaiyun, who was to be our principal interpreter.

We stayed at a guest house for foreign visitors close to Kunming Zoo and from here, over the next few days, we set out on field excursions into the surrounding hills. Certainly for the British members this was an exciting time and, having already visited some of the areas the previous

Members of the Sino-British Expedition to the Cangshan, gathered on the steps outside the Yunnan Institute of Botany, Kunming, prior to departure. They are, back row, left to right: Peter Cox, Gaby Lock (student), David Chamberlain, unidentified; middle row, Peter Hutchison, He Qungan (driver), Tien-lu Ming, Tao Deding, Guan Kaiyun (interpreter); front row, Lu Zhenwei, the author, Guo-mei Feng (joint leader), Bob Mitchell (joint leader), Mrs Ruizheng Fang

autumn, I was fascinated by the floral changes spring had brought. These forays also provided an opportunity for getting to know one another. The Chinese, I suspect, were pleasantly surprised that their British visitors, only two of whom had been to China before, should recognise and have some knowledge of their native plants. Not all were familiar to us, of course, but between us we were able to identify a good number of species and nearly always the genus of the plants we encountered. From the first day Professor Feng demonstrated his wide knowledge of the Yunnan flora and there were few plants he could not immediately recognise. His specialist interests were *Rhododendron* and *Camellia* and he was always ready to share with us stories of adventures he had had while searching for these plants in the wild. One evening he treated us to a show in which he discussed most of the *Rhododendron* species of Yunnan illustrated by a succession of stunning colour

slides. Mountains, valleys, forests and plains – there was hardly an inch of the province he had not explored in his sixty years as a botanist in Yunnan.

His interest in *Rhododendron* was shared by Mr Ming and Mrs Fang, both of whom had published papers on the subject. Indeed, if the expedition could be said to have one specialist interest it had to be *Rhododendron*. This is not surprising since Yunnan is considered to be the cradle of the genus with over two hundred species represented there. We were looking forward to studying the species in the wild and seeing to what extent, if any, they hybridised, and the expedition was well equipped to do this for, apart from the Chinese input, the British team had its own expertise in David Chamberlain who, with his colleague James Cullen at the Royal Botanic Garden, Edinburgh, had recently published a revised *Rhododendron* classification, while Peter Cox had published two notable works on the genus in cultivation.

The main expedition was preceded by several days botanising in the hills around Kunming, during which we quickly established an excellent relationship with our Chinese colleagues. Here, in the field at Da Shao, Professor Feng, in the centre wearing a cap, is relating an amusing incident from one of his previous expeditions. (April)

In the days before powered vehicles, the journey from Kunming to Xiaguan took two weeks. Taken by George Forrest in the early 1900s, he captioned this photograph 'A good Chinese road and cultivated areas between Yunnan-fu [now Kunming] and Tali [now Dali]'

To Xiaguan

The plants seen in the Kunming area during our first week I have discussed in Chapter Three. Our next move was to take us from the capital, north west along the Burma Road to Xiaguan, a 402km (250 miles) drive by bus. The journey with stops took thirteen hours, nothing compared with the same journey in the 1800s before powered vehicles, when two weeks had to be allowed. Our expedition travelled in a modern Japanese mini-bus, while our belongings followed in a covered truck. By this time our party had expanded to include drivers, a cook and a liaison officer as well as a German exchange student from the University of Heidelberg, Miss Gaby Lock.

We set out on the last day of April, a bright windless morning, and headed through the hills to the town of Anning, which we had visited on a previous day. For much of the journey we passed through dry hilly country with little in the way of forest except for scattered stands of *Keteleeria evelyniana* and Yunnan pine, *Pinus yunnanensis*. Roses tumbled down the roadside banks, their long flower-bedecked stems vying for our attention with those of a firethorn − *Pyracantha fortuneana*.

In the vicinity of Anfengyin, a village some 69km (43 miles) out of Kunming, we saw a rare conifer, *Calocedrus macrolepis* (*Libocedrus macrolepis*), growing on the eroded banks by the road. On our return in June we stopped to examine this tree more carefully. Its bark was a pale greyish-brown colour with long shallow vertical fissures, the flattened ridges in between peeling away from the base with age. Nowhere did we see a tree with 'remarkably white' bark as reported by Augustine Henry. The scale-like leaves, bright green above with bluish-white stomatal markings beneath,

Calocedrus macrolepis, a rare conifer, here growing by the main Kunming to Xiaguan road near the village of Anfengyin. The lower branches of these trees have been lopped by villagers. (June)

A village between Kunming and Xiaguan, photographed by George Forrest in the early 1900s. In the vicinity of many such villages the Tallow tree, *Sapium sebiferum*, has long been cultivated

Thalictrum delavayi. Here photographed in a garden in Philadelphia, U.S.A. It is a handsome species previously known as *T dipterocarpum*. (June)

were borne in large vertically flattened sprays. The cones, cylindrical though broad-based, consisted of six green scales covered in a pale whitish bloom and, at first glance, were not unlike those of *Platycladus orientalis*. Despite the high degree of activity, grazing, cultivation and erosion, it was gratifying to see signs of regeneration with seedlings mostly occupying ditches. It was a most distinctive tree with its dense crown of sea-green foliage. Left alone it probably develops a broad conical habit but here it was heavily lopped at the base. Some individuals were 15m (50ft) at least, with substantial trunks. Apart from those by the roadside, we saw trees in villages and graveyards, and on field margins and the slopes of low hills, individuals and small groups mostly, occasionally in more sizeable groves. Professor Feng told us that this tree is also to be found in south-west Yunnan and it was from there, near Simao (Szemao), that Wilson introduced it on his visit to see Augustine Henry in 1899 (curiously, this was Wilson's only venture into Yunnan). Although this conifer received a First Class Certificate from the Royal Horticultural Society in 1902 (as Bean remarked 'rather in excess of its merit'), it has remained rare in cultivation, being only suitable out of doors in the mildest areas in Britain and Ireland.

We drove on through hills scantily clad with trees, mainly conifers and patchy scrub, meeting a regular flow of traffic ranging from tractors and trucks to carts drawn by weary ponies or mules. At regular intervals we encountered timber trucks heavily laden, grinding slowly up steep inclines or thundering downhill and lurching from side to side in a most alarming manner. According to Professor Feng they had come from the forests of the Yulong Shan (Likiang range) in north-west Yunnan and were carrying logs of *Picea likiangensis* and *Larix potaninii*.

For much of our route the road was lined with eucalyptus trees from Australia, while the widely distributed shrub *Dodonaea viscosa* was frequently planted on dry roadside banks, where it commonly grew with the native *Sophora davidii* (*viciifolia*). The latter shrub forms a dense thicket of thorny branches and is commonly planted in country areas as a hedge or barrier around vegetable plots or compounds holding chickens or livestock. It is certainly effective for this purpose and in addition looks quite attractive in May and June when crowded with its clusters of small pale blue pea flowers. It is not commonly grown in Britain, where it thrives best in drier areas such as East Anglia. Indeed, the first time I ever met this shrub was in 1960 in the University Botanic Garden, Cambridge, its greyish downy young branches and silky hairy pinnate leaves giving the bush a grey, almost silvery, appearance.

The sophora shared many a dry hillside above the Burma road with an evergreen shrub of the cotoneaster family (*Rosaceae*) called *Osteomeles schweriniae*. Here the osteomeles was mainly small and bushy to 1.5m (5ft) but it can reach almost twice this in sheltered sites. It is a distinctive shrub with small pinnate leaves comprising seventeen to thirty-one grey-downy leaflets, while the small white flowers are borne in clusters in June. These are succeeded by small dark red fruits maturing to black, not unlike small versions of certain cotoneasters in appearance but not so ornamental. It is common throughout the plateau region of Yunnan and in the warmer valley bottoms of the more mountainous north west as well as in similar locations in Sichuan. Not surprisingly, it enjoys a warm sunny site in western cultivation.[1]

Five years after the Cangshan expedition, I again passed this way on my way to Dali, this time in September, and among the bushes of osteomeles I had seen previously I was surprised to see the star-like purple and white flowers of *Thalictrum delavayi* (*dipterocarpum*). They were borne in large magnificent heads (panicles) on stems fully 2m (6ft) high.

1. It was first introduced to western cultivation via Paris by Delavay in 1888. In British cultivation it is usually represented by the variety *microphylla*, differing in its smaller, smoother leaves and denser habit.

Pyrus pashia is common in the dry hills between Kunming and Xiaguan, its small fruits when well ripened being collected and eaten by villagers. (June)

Quercus variabilis. A common deciduous oak in dry areas of the Yunnan plateau between Kunming and Xiaguan. Here photographed at the Hillier Arboretum. (July)

Pyrus pashia was common in these dry hills, the small rounded brown fruits being picked and eaten by the villagers when ripe – or rather overripe (bletted), as are medlars.

Another fruit enjoyed by the locals is the Chinese chestnut *Castanea mollissima*,[2] which is commonly grown as orchards in the vicinity of villages where it is usually seen as a tree of 9-12m (30-40ft). It differs from the European sweet, or Spanish, chestnut (*C sativa*), in its persistently downy shoots and short-stalked leaves, some of which are clothed beneath in a close white felt. It is certainly native to Sichuan, and is widely cultivated over a large area from north-east to south-west China.

Another tree commonly cultivated in Yunnan and elsewhere in south China is the Chinese Tallow tree, *Sapium sebiferum*. At a casual glance this could be mistaken for a small-leaved poplar, in particular a smaller, more compact version of the black poplar *P nigra*, but the leaves lack the

gloss. To my mind they look even more like a dull-surfaced version of the leaves of the Bo tree, *Ficus religiosa*, with the same tail-like points. The tiny yellow-green flowers are borne in early summer in crowded tail-like spikes from the tips of the shoots. It has long been cultivated in warmer parts of China and in other countries enjoying a similar climate. The tallow, which surrounds the seeds, is removed by a process of steaming and is used in the manufacture of candles, while some at least finds its way to Europe where it is, or used to be, an essential ingredient in certain types of soap. An excellent account of this tree and its economic uses is given by E H Wilson in his book *A Naturalist in Western China*. Wilson also mentions the rich colours shown by its leaves in autumn, a feature unlikely to be seen in Britain where it is only occasionally grown under glass in botanical collections. The situation is very different in the south-east of the United States where, in the coastal plain from South Carolina to Florida and Louisiana, it has found conditions so much to its liking that, since its introduction in 1850, it has gone wild almost to the point of becoming a nuisance.

At one point, near the town of Yipinglum, the Burma road passes through a series of gorges thickly clothed with tall scrub and fairly sizeable trees of various kinds in the more inaccessible places. Two deciduous oaks, *Quercus dentata* and *Q variabilis*, were among them while another was *Catalpa ovata*, a tree here of 9m (30ft) high, usually broader in the crown with three-lobed leaves up to 25cm (10in) broad on

2. Apparently first introduced to the West in the mid- to late nineteenth century, *Castanea mollissima* was again introduced from Beijing by Charles Sargent, Director of the Arnold Arboretum in 1903. It was later sent back by E H Wilson to the same institution in 1908 and by Frank Meyer to the US Department of Agriculture in 1913 and 1915. It was Meyer who confirmed the Asiatic origin of the chestnut blight (*Endothia parasitica*), which devastated the North American species *Castanea dentata*. Meyer also introduced to America blight-resistant selections of the *C mollissima*, which has replaced the native tree as an ornamental, especially in hot dry regions, and is even more valued for its fruits, there being commercial orchards in Maryland and Georgia. Chinese chestnuts are said to be sweeter than the European version, but not so sweet as the sadly missed American chestnut. There are several selections grown for their larger nuts or because they are more prolific, including 'Nanking', 'Orrin' and 'Crane'. *C mollissima* is also cultivated in Britain, though not as commonly as its ornamental merit deserves.

Catalpa ovata, a common tree in the Yunnan plateau and in villages between Kunming and Xiaguan. Here photographed in flower in a Winchester garden. (June)

Albizia mollis, a small- to medium-sized tree with a broad-spreading head clothed with handsome ferny foliage. Its many-stamened flowers are attractive to a wide range of insects. (April)

strong or sucker shoots. In places it formed thickets of erect young stems, presumably sucker growths from old stumps. We were too early for the flowers, which are inferior in ornamental effect to those of the American species C *speciosa* and C *bignonioides*, the Indian Bean tree.

Spectacular in flower here was *Albizia mollis*, a small- to medium-sized tree with wide-spreading branches, in time developing low-domed crowns. Its leaves are finely divided and fern-like in the manner of its clan, while the creamy-white to yellow fluffy flowers (really dense clusters of stamens) crowd the upper sides of the branches. On the day we saw them, the air above the flowers was filled with large blackish butterflies attracted to the glistening nectar.

To the rhododendron enthusiast, these apparently dry, sun-baked hills might, at first glance, appear the last place to find members of this lovely genus thriving, but we saw several species, mostly those found earlier in the Kunming area. In addition, there was *Rhododendron pachypodum*, new to

us and spectacular in flower. It is a member of the Maddenii subsection and closely related to R *ciliicalyx*, differing in minor details, especially the flowers, which are sprinkled with scales all over the outside instead of just on the lobes. In these hills it was fairly common, scattered in the scrub, usually on steep hillsides where it made a loose stemmed bush of 1-1.5m (3-5ft). The bold terminal trusses of funnel-shaped flowers measured 6cm (2½ in) across the flared mouth. They were slightly scented, white, sometimes pink flushed on the lobes, and possessed a yellow blotch in the throat.

We seemed to have arrived at an opportune time as flowering was at a peak and we could spot the bushes at a distance. Interestingly, this species was still producing flowers on our return a month later. On scrambling to our first plant above the road we were struck by the dusty condition of the earth in which it grew. Presumably its ultimate roots had found sufficient moisture to keep it alive and flourishing through the dry spring period. In the

Rhododendron pachypodum, a member of the Maddenii subsection, is fairly common on dry slopes and cliffs in the hills between Kunming and Xiaguan. The white flowers, which are slightly fragrant, have a yellow blotch in the throat. Unfortunately, it is not hardy out of doors in Britain. (April)

163

A village on the main road between Kunming and Xiaguan, photographed by George Forrest in the early 1900s. Note the sedan chairs in the background, the normal means of transport for people of rank. One of these may well have been for Forrest's use

A bridge on the road between Kunming and Xiaguan photographed by George Forrest in the early 1900s. Fields under cultivation can be seen in the background

following rainy season, I imagine, much of the water would run off the surface on these steep slopes. This species also grows on forest margins and in glades, where it is recorded as reaching as much as 4m (13ft). Unfortunately, it is not hardy out of doors in Britain except in the mildest locations. It would, however, make an unusual (though tending to be leggy) pot plant for the cool house or conservatory.

We crossed several hills of around 2,500m (8,200ft), the landscape changing from dry slopes dotted with trees and scrub to broad fertile valley bottoms, then back to dry hills again. Seen from a speeding bus, the changing scenery reminded me of the landscapes of well-known artists. Thus, the hillside villages with their squat ochre-coloured dwellings blending into the earth that gave them birth resembled the canvases of a Cézanne or Van Gogh, while the spindly heavily-lopped pines on many a hillside could have come straight from a painting by Lowry. Best of all, though, were the village scenes, which put me strongly in mind of those by the Flemish artist Pieter Brueghel, now

so popular with Christmas card manufacturers in the West.

I lost count of the number of villages through which we passed that day but each of them seemed a hive of activity. Most fascinating were those villages in the fertile valleys. Here we could see men and women in the fields tending crops, weeding, harvesting with sickles or clearing irrigation ditches. Elsewhere men were ploughing with water buffalo while, on the distant hillsides, stone was being quarried and carted to the village for splitting and final dressing into blocks for building. All but the very old and the very young were out and about and even the infirm were busy minding the babies and toddlers. In many ways, what we saw in these villages was a medieval society in action. Only an occasional small tractor or truck reminded us that we were actually in the late twentieth century.

We had arrived in Yunnan at a very busy time for the farmers. In late April into May the winter wheat is being harvested and most able-bodied villagers are engaged on this work, or its aftermath. Cleared of wheat, the fields are then flooded and ploughed ready for replanting with rice. In

Bai women planting rice near Dali. Before flooding, these fields were planted with wheat. (May)

Musella lasiocarpa photographed in his father's garden in Switzerland by Donat Walder. (June)

Musella lasiocarpa. A handsome relatively dwarf banana relative, native to north-west Yunnan, and much cultivated in the Xiaguan area. (April)

addition to the wheat, barley and rye are grown. Around the villages various vegetable crops were being cultivated, among them plots of *Vicia villosa*, a blue spiked vetch similar to our native tufted vetch (*V cracca*). However, it was the cultivation of a more exotic plant that caught our attention: a relative of the banana,[3] *Musella lasiocarpa* is native to the Jinshajiang Valley (from Yongshan to Lijiang) in north-west Yunnan. The leafy stems are not unlike those of a small banana and develop after flowering. The flowers, too, are similar to a banana's, borne in a large conical head comprising a mass of large colourful fleshy bracts. There is one striking difference, however, in that these flowerheads are terminal on a short, erect, leafless stem. Towards the end of October the leafy stems are sliced into sections and, after boiling to remove a poisonous principle, are cooked and eaten.[4]

We reached our destination, the city of Xiaguan, that evening and were taken to the guest house that was to be the expedition's base. As we headed across an open space towards our accommodation, we looked towards the western sky. In the darkness, an even darker shape loomed and we knew in our hearts that it was the Cangshan.

Marco Polo was the first European to see the Cangshan when he visited Dali (then the capital of western Karajang) in 1273. In chapter fifty of his second book he describes the country around as being 'wild and hard of access, full of great woods and mountains which it is impossible to pass, the air is so impure and unwholesome and any foreigner attempting it would die for certain'. Were he to return to this area today he would find the situation somewhat changed. The mountains remain, though the

3. Some authorities now treat it as a *Musa* species.

4. This handsome foliage perennial is now being grown as an ornamental in Britain though it needs winter protection in all but the warmest gardens.

The town of Xiaguan, our first base and the Cangshan looming above it. (May)

The Cangshan seen across Er-hai from Er-hai Park. The summit ridge averages 3,658-3,962m (12,000-13,000ft), with seventeen minor scattered peaks, none above 4,121m (13,520ft). (May)

great woods are gone and, while the country is still wild in the physical sense, air and rail links with Kunming have made it more easily accessible.

Let us consider the Cangshan, or Diancangshan as it is sometimes called, in more detail. Formerly known as the Tsangshan and to western plant hunters and rhodo-dendron enthusiasts as the Tali Range, it stretches on a north-south axis for some 50km (31 miles), its jagged summit ridge averaging between 3,658-3,962m (12,000ft-13,000ft) with seventeen minor peaks, none above 4,121m (13,520ft). According to geologists, it was formed as a result of a granite intrusion through limestone

Er-hai, or Ear Lake, situated at 2,050m (6,723ft) above sea level is, by any standards, a beautiful stretch of water and contains a variety of fish

Er-hai Lakeside scene. Note the men fishing in the background with a large bamboo-framed net. (May)

strata and, at areas of pressure and heat, the rocks have melted and reformed to give a great variety of differing types including marble in many colours and formations. The Cangshan is the only granite-influenced range in this large area; the remainder are predominantly of limestone, although limestone crags and buttresses are present in the Cangshan at higher altitudes. In geological terms the Cangshan forms part of the Mekong fold belt which extends for 1,126km (700 miles) from an area north-west of Yangbi County, south-eastwards along the Mekong river and across the border into Laos and Vietnam. It is bordered to the west by the massive Himalayan fold system and to the east by the South China Platform.

The two main flanks of the Cangshan show a striking difference in their vegetation due to the variable precipitation. Rainfall on the western flank is higher, to 1,016mm (40in), most of which falls during the period June to September inclusive. By the time the moisture laden south-west winds clear the high ridges they have already deposited much of their load and the eastern flanks, as a consequence, receive comparatively little.

To the east of the Cangshan, and separated from it by a 5km (3 miles) wide strip of land, lies Erhai Lake, correctly Er-hai (Ear Lake), which is situated at 2,050m (6,723ft) above sea level. It debouches at its southern end through Xiaguan and thence westwards via a narrow defile to the Yangbi river, which in turn flows south to the Mekong river. Aligned, like the mountain range, north and south, Er-

hai is some 61km (38 miles) in length and 8km (5 miles) at its widest point. It is by any standards a most lovely sight, especially on a calm clear day when its blue waters mirror the mountains above its shores.

It was several centuries after Marco Polo's visit that Europeans once again travelled this way. The nineteenth century saw a steady trickle of foreign government officials and others, attracted by the possibilities that the province held for trade. Starting in about the middle of the century,

Harbour on Er-hai east of Dali, photographed by George Forrest in March 1906

167

George Forrest, the Scottish plant hunter who collected in the Cangshan on several occasions between 1904 and 1930, making a particularly thorough exploration of the range in 1914

Another photograph of George Forrest. He is standing with his dogs in a moon gate in Tali-fu [now Dali], where he often stayed when exploring the Cangshan region

the traffic gradually increased as missionaries, engineers, explorers, naturalists and, of course, plant hunters appeared on the scene, including Père Jean Marie Delavay, Prince Henri d'Orléans, Frank Kingdon-Ward, Joseph Rock and George Forrest.[5]

In China the provinces are divided into prefectures or regions which are subdivided into counties. Xiaguan (Tsia-kuan), where our expedition was based, is the capital of the Dali Bai Autonomous Prefecture, while Dali itself is the capital of Dali County. On the night of our arrival we had met with the elders of Xiaguan who officially welcomed us to their city and prefecture and extended to us their best wishes and any assistance we needed. It was the Xiaguan

elders who provided us with several important personnel including a doctor and an armed guard.

The next day, being May Day, was a public holiday and we were taken to Er-hai Park, created in 1977 along a stretch of hillside above the southern end of the lake.

Packing cases containing seed, and possibly plants, collected by Forrest in north-west Yunnan, and ready for dispatch to Rangoon and thence by ship to England and J C Williams of Caerhays Castle, Cornwall. Photograph taken by Forrest in the early 1900s

5. From 1882 Père Jean Marie Delavay, the distinguished French missionary and botanist, was stationed for close on ten years in a small town north-east of Er-hai. For much of this time he collected in the mountains west, north and north-east of the lake sending to the herbarium of the Paris Museum more than 50,000 dried specimens representing over 4,000 species, all from Yunnan, for the greater part from the Dali and Lijiang (Likiang) areas of which a third proved to be species new to science. Delavay also collected and sent to Paris the seeds of plants, some of which were later to become established in our gardens.

The French explorer Prince Henri d'Orléans stayed here in 1895 at the beginning of his remarkable second expedition to the upper reaches of the Mekong, Salween and Irrawaddy rivers. Although his stay in Dali was short, he managed to collect at least a few specimens. Both the English explorer Frank Kingdon-Ward, between 1911 and 1922, and the American Joseph Rock, from 1922 onwards, passed through Dali several times on collecting expeditions. Scottish plant hunter George Forrest visited Dali and the Cangshan on several occasions between 1904 and 1930, making a particularly thorough exploration of the area in 1914. Delavay and Forrest are commemorated in the names of a great many plants native to this area.

168

Several methods of fishing are practised on Er-hai. This net suspended on a bamboo framework is lowered into the water and retrieved by means of a rope. (May)

Cormorants are still used by some fishermen on Er-hai. A small band placed around the bird's neck prevents the catch from being swallowed. The restriction is removed when the bird is not fishing. (May)

Styrax limprichtii growing on the dry hillside above the southern shore of Er-hai. This species was considered one of the very best of its kind by George Forrest who collected its seed on at least one occasion. (May)

People were out in great numbers enjoying themselves, picnicking and strolling in the sun.

A large number of people were involved in fishing, and we were fascinated by the variety of methods employed, some from the shore others from a boat. One method employed a square net approximately 3m (9ft) across and suspended on a bamboo framework, which was lowered into the water and then pulled up at intervals by means of a rope. It was being used from a static position at the end of a small stone pier jutting out from the shore, as well as from an isolated rock reached, presumably, by boat.

The most curious and impressive method employed cormorants. Two or three boats not too far from the shore were accompanied by flotillas of these sleek, glossy birds, which dived at intervals, occasionally returning to deposit a catch. Apparently it takes only a year to train a cormorant to this system and there appears to be no cruelty involved. The bird has a small band placed around its neck, which merely prevents the catch from being swallowed. The restriction is removed when the bird is not fishing.

There had been considerable planting in the park but it was the native vegetation that ultimately claimed our attention and we were pleased to find the small pale blue-flowered *Ceratostigma minus* growing quite commonly in dry places together with *Styrax limprichtii (lankongensis)*, a shrub of 2m (6ft) here, though possibly cut over. The axillary clusters of nodding white flowers are quite substantial for the size of the shrub and, if it were to be introduced into cultivation, I have no doubt it would become much sought after especially for gardens in the warmer or Mediterranean regions of the West. It was collected at least once by Forrest who considered it one of the very best, but if it was ever introduced to gardens it has long since been lost. It has recently been re-introduced to British cultivation from Er-hai. In a wooded area nearby we found an ancient *Buxus bodinieri* measuring 1.8m (6ft) x 3m (10ft).[6]

6. This species is once again in British cultivation from a recent collection, though it is of slow growth.

Cangshan — the western face photographed from Camp 1 above the town of Yangbi. The highest point is Malongfeng 4,121m. (13,520ft.)(May)

To Camp 1

It was planned that we should explore the Cangshan from four main camps. Camps 1 and 2 would be situated on the western slopes, Camp 3 on the eastern slopes above Dali, and Camp 4 towards the northern end of the range based on the village of Huadianba. Accordingly, the next morning we set off from Xiaguan heading for the village of Yangbi on the other side of the range. Our route took us south west along the Er or Erh river, which runs for several kilometres through a narrow gorge called Lung Wei Kuan or Dragon's Pass. At one time, before the Burma Road was constructed, passage along this gorge was interesting to say the least, and even now the experience is impressive. We did not stop during our drive through the gorge but we did see many interesting plants, one of which, a wild banana, claimed by the Chinese to be *Ensete wilsonii*, grew quite commonly in steep gullies and ravines above the road forming bold leaved clumps 3m (9ft) tall.

Even more exciting was the evergreen *Magnolia delavayi*,

Magnolia delavayi. Photographed in Dunloe Castle Gardens, Co. Kerry, Ireland. The bold leaves are a perfect backing for the fragrant blooms, which last for only 12 hours or so. (August)

equally wild and occupying similar sites as well as finding a living on the more exposed slopes. Most appeared to have been butchered and formed mounds of sea-green leafy shoots 3-5m (9-16ft) high, but the occasional older, stout-stemmed specimens were also seen.[7] The slopes on which it grows are steep and support a dense scrub layer. In dry periods, as in April-May, conditions here are hot and dusty and we could understand why this tree is so tolerant of drought in cultivation. In Britain and Ireland it is usually seen in the milder areas and its performance in the Cornish woodland gardens led the great authority on woody plants, W J Bean, to consider it the finest of all evergreen flowering trees, high praise indeed though not one I share. Its large chunky buds open to reveal a cup of ivory coloured tepals and a rich scent of ripened watermelon. They are not as impressive as those of its American counterpart M *grandiflora*, and disappointingly fleeting, opening at night and lasting for only twelve hours or so before they begin to fade. Without some protection it is liable to be cut back in severe winters as was our experience at the Hillier Arboretum in Hampshire.

Yangbi is the capital of the county of that name and belongs to the Dali Bai Autonomous Prefecture. It lies to the south west of the Cangshan at an altitude of 1,600m (5,247ft) and, as an example of the warm temperate almost subtropical climate pertaining here, there grows in the town near the meeting room a large specimen of the Cotton tree — *Bombax ceiba* (*malabaricum*). Native over a wide area from India to south China, Malaysia and tropical Australia, this tree is commonly planted for the cotton-like material in which the seeds are embedded. This is used for stuffing pillows and cushions, while the dried flowers are

7. It is interesting that the banana and the magnolia should grow together here in west Yunnan, for both have connections with E H Wilson whose main collecting areas were far to the north in Sichuan and Hubei. The former he presumably collected at the beginning of his first expedition on his journey to see Augustine Henry in south Yunnan. The magnolia certainly belongs to this period, and although originally discovered by Delavay north west of Dali in 1886, it was Wilson who first introduced it into cultivation in 1899.

Paddy fields above Yangbi, the still waters of the flooded fields reflecting the clouds above. (May)

used as a medicine for reducing inflammation. The Yangbi tree was 21.5m (71ft) high with a girth of 200cm (79in) at chest height, and must have been a magnificent sight earlier when in flower. The large bell-shaped red flowers appear in clusters along the leafless branches in April.

The Burma Road runs almost all the way to Yangbi before veering south of the town, which is reached by a secondary road. According to C P Fitzgerald (*The Tower of Five Glories*), work on the Burma Road was started in December 1937, and in late autumn the following year was opened to traffic. Considering the terrain and the difficulties of the period, it was a major feat, built by forced labour as a war

A farmer in his fields above Yangbi, Cangshan. His bamboo basket is almost certainly home-made. (May)

Farmer's son in the fields above Yangbi, on the Cangshan's eastern slopes. (May)

A villager resting in the fields above Yangbi. He gave us directions to the right track into the hills. (May)

Fish dam on the Yangbi river, photographed by George Forrest in the early 1900s

measure and completed in two sections. The first, from Kunming to Xiaguan, was finished in the spring of 1938. It crosses five major passes and winds for long distances on the crests of mountains. This section we had already travelled. The second section, from Xiaguan to the Burmese border at Namhkam, is slightly longer, about 467km (290 miles), and passes through much more difficult country. The mountains on this section are both higher and steeper, and two great rivers, the Lancang (Mekong) and the Nu (Salween), are crossed. This section was also built by forced labour, the inhabitants of districts up to 160km (100 miles) from the road being brought to work on it, camping in shelters made of boughs and turf. Fitzgerald believed that not far short of 100,000 men and women were employed on building the road. It was meant to replace what, for centuries before, had been the major pack route between Burma and China, a route which became known to western travellers as 'China's Back Door'.

In the days before the road was built, travellers heading for Dali or Kunming made their way to Bhamo in upper Burma, thence north to Myitkyina and across the border to Tengchong (Tengyueh) where Forrest lies buried, and on to Baoshan (Yung-ping) and Yangbi.

Kingdon-Ward, for obvious reasons, referred to the Burma Road as the 'Ambassador's Road', and travelled it himself many times as did Forrest. In those days the journey from Tengchong to Dali (Tali-fu) took approximately fourteen days, and for the keen observer, especially the naturalist, it was a journey filled with interest. Kingdon-Ward, in *The Land of the Blue Poppy*, writes of green parrots flashing screeching overhead, of Amherst's pheasants with handsome tails, as well as of the many lovely flowers along the way. Although Kingdon-Ward possibly, and Forrest

certainly, would have stayed in Yangbi when exploring the western flanks of the Cangshan, neither their names nor those of any other British plant hunter was remembered by the town elders whom we met at a welcoming ceremony on our arrival. One old man, however, did recall a westerner staying in Yangbi in 1948. He told us that this man had spoken English and because of ill health had employed some of the villagers to collect plant specimens in the mountains. We guessed this to have been the American collector Joseph Rock, who was the last major western collector to leave China in 1949. If this was so, we were the first western plant explorers since Rock to have stayed in Yangbi. It was quite a thought to go to sleep on.

Early the next day, after a breakfast of rice soup and eggs, we left the town in a convoy of vehicles heading for the village of Xieshanhe (Snow Bank) where we prepared for the long trek to Camp 1. Yangbi is one of the main centres of the Chinese walnut industry and the hills above the town are said to support 260,000 trees, all of which are numbered and recorded. Some of these are quite sizeable and the largest we saw growing by the track from Dapingdi to Mofanggou, altitude approximately 2,450m (8,038ft), measured around 30.5m (100ft) with a girth of 372cm (146in) at chest height.

As we later found, the nuts of these trees are of excellent quality and are exported to many countries, including Britain, where they are sold, each marked with a little red stamp, at Christmas time. Indeed China, with 118,000 metric tons in 1977, is the world's third largest producer of walnuts after the United States (185,972 tons) and Turkey (135,000 tons). Like most commonly

Mules and ponies on trail from Yangbi to Camp 1 on the western flank of the Cangshan. (May)

Walnut trees (*Juglans regia*) planted on the hills above Yangbi. Nuts from this source are exported to markets in Europe. (May)

cultivated fruits, the walnut is hard to place as a true native. Known in the West as the Persian or English walnut, *Juglans regia* is almost certainly native in west Asia and possibly south-east Europe, too, but it has been so widely cultivated for so long that its wild status elsewhere is mainly guesswork. In the dry inland valleys of western China, especially in Yunnan and Sichuan, one could well believe it to be native. It has certainly been known in China since the earliest written records and its superiority over native walnuts, such as *J cathayensis* and *J mandshurica*, is undisputed.

Apart from their nutritional value, the nuts are valued for the sweet oil they contain and for their medicinal properties. E H Wilson remarked on the value of the wood for rifle stocks, a use so popular in the early years of the 20th century that demand exceeded the supply. In China, too, where the cricket is regarded as lucky, musically trained 'singing' crickets were once carried around in intricately carved walnut shells. Even today halved shells, sometimes lacquered and housing tiny carved figures, are commonly sold in Chinese souvenir stores.

We were particularly grateful for the walnut trees of Yangbi, as they provided welcome shade on what proved

to be one of the hottest days on record. The track climbed steadily upwards through scattered remnants of former forest and areas of scrub. These slopes are very different to the 'thickly wooded hills' reported by the English traveller E Colborne Baber in 1876. In the lower elevations the natural flora is all but gone, though the situation improves with altitude. Pools of rich green in an otherwise parched landscape proved on examination to be *Iris tectorum*, forming extensive patches of broad ribbed leaves in fans above the thick partially exposed rhizomes. Some plants were in flower, large and frilly and of a pale violet-blue, white or pale lilac at the base with darker splashes and a conspicuous crest on the falls. They were carried singly on erect stems just level with or slightly clearing the foliage. This popular species, known as the Roof iris in Japan, where it is commonly grown on thatched roofs and wall tops, is native to central and south-west China and, supposedly, upper Burma. It is not uncommon in cultivation in Britain, having a liking for a warm sunny position, not surprising considering its sun-baked home above Yangbi. A plant established from this collection at the Royal Botanic Garden, Edinburgh, has proved strong

Iris tectorum formed rich, green, leafy 'pools' on the otherwise parched hillside above Yangbi. The flowers bear a conspicuous pale crest on the falls. (May)

Colony of *Iris tectorum*, on the trail above Yangbi, Cangshan. (May)

growing and free flowering, and it has performed similarly elsewhere, including the gardens of Holyrood Palace.

The scrub areas and pockets of forest contained a preponderance of evergreens, several of which we had already seen on the plateau areas near Kunming. Newcomers included the milky-white flowered *Gaultheria forrestii*, *Phoebe neurantha* and *Mahonia longibracteata*. There were familiar plants, too, in *Belamcanda chinensis* with its

characteristic fanned Iris-like foliage, *Philadelphus delavayi* and *Colquhounia coccinea*, an old friend from Kashmir and Nepal. We tried to keep ahead of the main group but as we climbed higher so the vegetation increased in variety and our progress slowed as a result. We were quite an impressive sight, the Chinese and British wearing white sun hats, followed by a dozen or more ponies and mules heavily laden with food and equipment. Some at least of

Philadelphus delavayi. This strong-growing mock orange with its deliciously scented flowers was frequent in the dry hills above the village of Yangbi. (May)

the muleteers were of the Lisu minority with rounded faces and a ready smile. They were fond of their pipes and would sit around camp at the end of the day, smoking contentedly while watching the antics and strange habits of us Europeans.

Camp 1 at Dapingdi was situated on a west-facing hillside above the village of Zhongshan at an altitude of 2,550m (8,366ft). It was set in a bracken-covered depression looking over a deep forested ravine in which grew conifers and broad-leaved evergreens together with a

Gaultheria forrestii. A common scrub component in the hills above Yangbi, the milky-white inflorescences are characteristic. (May)

Porter smoking home-made pipe in Camp 1 at Dapingdi. (May)

Chinese cooks preparing food at Camp 1 with Guan Kaiyun ('Clyde'), second from right, looking on. (May)

A muleteer at Camp 1 whose hat appeared to serve the dual role of summer shade and winter warmth. (May)

sprinkling of deciduous trees. The bracken was an Asian version (variety *wightianum*) of the cosmopolitan *Pteridium aquilinum*, which I first encountered on the pennine moors above my childhood home. It was, however, the preponderance of evergreens for which we shall remember this camp. For a start, the campsite was dominated by two of them – *Keteleeria evelyniana* and *Quercus gilliana*. The former tree, its base damaged by fire, measured 17.5m (58ft) with a girth of 219cm (86in) at chest height, while the oak was even larger at 21m (70ft) and a girth of 500cm (197in). Nearby was a *Lithocarpus dealbatus* of 20m (65ft) and 200cm (79in). Just as spectacular was *Rhododendron delavayi*, now regarded as a subspecies of the Himalayan

A shepherd girl at Dapingdi with flowers of the tree rhododendron, *Rhododendron arboreum* subspecies *delavayi*, which was quite common around Camp 1. In her hair is a flower of *Rhododendron yunnanense*. (May)

Rhododendron arboreum. It was common and scattered throughout the area, sometimes heavily lopped or fire damaged, but remarkably tolerant of stress and magnificent as a single stemmed tree up to 9m (30ft) or more with a girth of 164cm (64in) at chest height. It did not appear to have been a particularly prolific flowering year and the best was already past, but sufficient late trusses of the glowing crimson flowers remained to remind us of what had gone before. Even without flower, this rhododendron is handsome with its lance-shaped leathery leaves, shining dark green above and silvery white beneath, a striking contrast to the paler-coloured young growths emerging like candles from the tips of every branch.

We spent five days at Camp 1 exploring the hillsides and valleys above. It was a paradise and our notebooks

almost smouldered from the frequency and rapidity of our scribbled entries. Very quickly we established a routine: having breakfasted on rice soup and eggs, we would move out of camp at around 8am, carrying our packed lunches as we set off for an area decided upon the previous evening. We would return to camp at the end of the afternoon and gather round the camp fire or nearby to go through the specimens collected in the plant presses during the day, discussing each one and recording its details in a field notebook specially designed for the purpose. Mrs Fang kept the Chinese notebook, while I was in charge of the British version. Considering that all questions and answers had to be put via Clyde, our interpreter, we quickly established a good understanding and I looked forward to these sessions each evening as a schoolboy does a regular treat.

David and Bob helped sort out the specimens and prepare them for another press, a tedious job that had to be repeated for all specimens morning and evening. Without this regular change of drying paper most specimens would very quickly have rotted and, as it was, we had to take extra care in pressing thick-stemmed or fleshy specimens. Professor Feng supervised these sessions with all the skill born of experience. Some specimens would remind him of a previous encounter, which was then translated so that we all could enjoy the story.

The two Peters, meanwhile, took care of the seeds and living plants collected. They had had experience of this from previous expeditions in the wild and the fact that so much

Rhododendron arboreum subspecies *delavayi*. A late truss of crimson flowers on a tree above Camp 1. (May)

Young growths of *Rhododendron arboreum* subspecies *delavayi* in Santaipo, Weishan County. The silvery young growths are a striking contrast against the old foliage. (May)

Schima yunnanensis. An evergreen tree, a member of the *camellia* family *Theaceae*, was frequent in the forest above Camp 1. It is photographed here in flower. (May)

Joseph Rock, the American plant hunter, with *Rhododendron arboreum* subspecies *delavayi* on a ridge of the Cangshan in May 1922. Here the normally tree-like species has been dwarfed by exposure.

of what we collected is now established in cultivation says a great deal about their qualifications for this important task.

One of our first forays was into the wooded ravine near the camp. It was here that we found *Craibiodendron yunnanense*, again with its striking young leaves, which we had already seen at Da Shao near Kunming. There were several trees, one of 7.5m (25ft) from which seed was obtained.[8] *Schima yunnanensis* accompanied it, its evergreen lance-shaped leaves up to 12cm (5in) long and glaucous beneath. There were

trees of 15m (50ft) but, as yet, no sign of the ivory-white flowers. Oaks of several kinds were plentiful, mostly evergreens, including a huge spreading specimen of *Quercus* (*Cyclobalanopsis*) *glaucoides* of 37m (123ft) with a girth of 342cm (135in). A common deciduous oak was *Q aliena*, a most handsome tree with obovate leaves regularly and

8. Plants from this seed are now well established in several gardens in the milder areas of Britain and Ireland, including Caerhays Castle in Cornwall.

Camp 1 above Yangbi, with *Alnus nepalensis*, the deciduous tree in background. Here we spent five glorious days. (May)

boldly lobed and toothed. Other deciduous trees included *Betula utilis* with dark orange-brown peeling bark, and *Alnus nepalensis*. Growing on the branches of the latter and on those of the evergreen oaks was the evergreen *Agapetes mannii*, an epiphytic member of the *Rhododendron* family

Ericaceae. From its swollen and turnip-like woody base hung slender densely leafy stems to 1.5m (5ft) long.

Inevitably, the *Ericaceae* was well represented here with several species of *Vaccinium* including *V delavayi*, a dwarf evergreen shrub with small notched leaves 1.5cm (½ in)

Vaccinium delavayi. A dwarf shrublet with pink-tinted white flowers growing in the forest above Camp 1. (May)

Vaccinium sprengelii. This unusual species achieved large shrub or small tree size in the forest above Camp 1. (May)

Rhododendron yunnanense, appropriately enough, was abundant around Dapingdi, as elsewhere in the Cangshan. It varies in flower colour from pale lavender-pink to rose shades and white, with a flash of reddish, occasionally green, spots on the inside. (May)

Skimmia laureola subspecies *multinervia*, a remarkable tree skimmia growing in the woods above Camp 1 at Dapingdi. This specimen is a male with ornamental greenish-yellow flowers. (May)

long crowding the shoot and terminal clusters of pink-tinted white flowers.[9]

A vaccinium of a very different kind was *V sprengelii*, an evergreen shrub or small tree to 5m (16ft) or more with larger pointed leaves of an attractive coppery-red when young. This, too, had short racemes of white flowers tipped red in bud, heightened by the small red-tinted sepals. Rhododendrons, however, increasingly claimed the limelight and none more so than *Rhododendron yunnanense*, which was everywhere abundant and at the peak of flowering.[10] It was generally a tall shrub up to 6m (20ft) and mainly occurred as scattered individuals or small groups in forest clearings and in thickets. In flower colour it was variable, mainly pink and rose shades with a flash of red spots on the inside, and we also saw the occasional white with red or sometimes green spots. These were borne in loose terminal trusses and were very effective *en masse*, especially when seen across a valley on a far hillside. Growing with R *yunnanense* in one place we found R *irroratum*, like the former capable of 6m (20ft) or more.

Unfortunately, flowering in this species was almost over, but the few flowers that remained ranged from white to very pale yellow, flecked purple within and, in the opinion of Peter Cox, much more desirable than most of the various pinky shades seen in cultivation.

The skimmias are well enough known in cultivation and are among the most popular small evergreens for their red fruits in winter. Imagine my surprise, therefore, when I first set eyes on *Skimmia laureola* subspecies *multinervia*, a tree of 5m (16ft) or more growing in the depths of the forest. I was with Mr Ming at the time and he seemed more surprised at my surprise that such a skimmia should exist. The long pointed leaves were mainly gathered towards the

9. This species was first found in the Cangshan by Delavay and later introduced to cultivation by Forrest, a not uncommon occurrence, much as E H Wilson introduced so many of the plants previously discovered by Augustine Henry.

10. It has a wider distribution in China than its name would suggest, although it was first found in north-west Yunnan by Delavay who introduced it into cultivation via Paris. The present garden stock, however, is said to derive from later introductions by Forrest, Kingdon-Ward and Rock, some of Forrest's collections coming from the Cangshan, plus those of more recent introductions.

ends of the wide-spreading slender branches, at the tips of which occurred loose clusters of pale or yellowish-green flowers, male and female on separate trees. Once treated as a species in its own right, this is now considered to be a tree form of the dwarf S laureola, both having black fruits. Seedlings from the Cangshan and from eastern Nepal have been introduced into British cultivation in recent years but, because of its taller habit, black fruits and less hardy nature, it presents no threat to the popularity of S japonica and its selections.

We had just made our way up a steep treeless area of hillside to the lip of a deep valley, when one of our Chinese colleagues found a lovely ground orchid – Pleione yunnanensis. It occurred fairly commonly both in the scrubby margin of the forest and in grassy places in full sun. The single flowers with segments spreading widely like a starfish were lilac-pink in colour with purplish markings on the lip (labellum). It was borne on a slender reddish stalk 10-15cm (4-6in) tall from beneath a conical green pseudobulb. We saw this species several times later, on both flanks of the Cangshan, and noted a variation in flower colour from pale almost washy lilac or pink to a rich rose-pink. Once, on tussocky grass slopes high above Dali, it occurred in such numbers that it reminded me of pink crocuses from a distance. At one time this orchid was thought only to occur in Yunnan but plants considered to be the same species have been found in northern Burma, southern Sichuan and western Guizhou (Kweichow).[11]

The pleiones are among the loveliest in a family famed for its exotica. They are fairly easily cultivated in pots or pans in a free draining compost and are ideal subjects for the cool greenhouse, requiring no heat other than that necessary to keep out frost. The more vigorous kinds may even be grown on a windowsill, ideally in the bathroom or kitchen where the moist atmosphere is to their liking. Indeed, I remember the late Jack Brice, Head Gardener at

Pleione yunnanensis was fairly abundant on grassy slopes above Dapingdi, from a distance looking like a swathe of crocus. (May)

the Hillier Arboretum, who for several years regularly carried away the first prize at his local spring flower show with a large pan of a cultivar of P formosana called 'Blush of Dawn'. He grew it on his bathroom windowsill and at showtime it invariably carried over a hundred blooms, a magnificent sight that never failed to impress the judges.

Whenever Professor Feng found something of interest he would call out 'Come! Come!' and we would all gather round to view his prize. Once it was a rhododendron seedling perhaps three years old. Nothing unusual in that except that the leaves were as big as paddle blades and silver-grey underneath. He chuckled when he saw our faces, mine certainly, staring in amazement at Rhododendron sinogrande. A short search revealed several trees of this magnificent species growing in the shelter of the forest margin. It was in flower, or at least a few trees were, the majority having flowered the previous year. The flowers were bell-shaped, creamy-white to pale yellow, sometimes with a small basal red blotch, and were carried in large terminal trusses. One superb specimen at the bottom of a ravine had a truss at the end of almost every branch and must have measured at least 12m (40ft). Another tree of similar size had a single stem to 4.5m (15ft) with a girth at chest height of 110cm (43in) and was covered with a rich brown flaking bark. One leaf we measured was 57cm (22in) long by 24cm (9½in) broad, and there were larger leaves on several seedlings and young plants.

On one occasion, sheltering from rain while eating our lunch, I climbed into one of the larger specimens and sat astride a stout branch some 6m (20ft) from the ground. It was an exhilarating feeling, the rain rattling on the canopy around me and running in ever-swelling rivulets down the track. I could not help but wonder what those head gardeners of old would have thought of me sitting eating my lunch in a giant R sinogrande on a hillside in Yunnan.[12] In the good (bad?) old days when non-Cornish visitors to that county were regarded as "foreigners", plant enthusiasts wishing to gain entry to certain of the famous woodland gardens were almost required to produce a passport before an application was considered. In many such gardens R sinogrande was the pride and joy of its owners and was treated with due reverence, perhaps a favoured visitor being allowed to turn a leaf. Thus, my antics in a tree of such proportions in its homeland (holy ground indeed!) might have drawn from its admirers an acid stare at the very least.

11. It was first discovered in 1895 in alpine pastures near Mengzi (Mengtze) by William Hancock, an Ulsterman employed by the Chinese Imperial Customs Service, and shortly after was collected in the same area by Augustine Henry. Forrest also collected it on several occasions in north-west Yunnan.

12. George Forrest was the first to discover and introduce this species, in 1912, and its introduction not surprisingly caused a sensation in British rhododendron circles. Curiously, there are no records of his having found it in the Cangshan (which incidentally is the farthest south and east it has been recorded), but further to the west and north west. It is without doubt a most noble species in habit, foliage and flower and can be admired in many woodland gardens in the south and west of Britain as well as in Ireland.

Guan Kayun ('Clyde') our interpreter (left) and Professor Feng expedition leader (right), in forest above Camp 1. The professor invariably had a smile on his face. (May)

Rhododendron sinogrande. A 12m (40ft) specimen of this magnificent species growing in a sheltered ravine above Dapingdi. This location proved to be the furthest south and east this species has been recorded. (May)

Professor Feng with his prize specimen, a branch of Rhododendron sinogrande growing in the woods above Dapingdi. The huge leaves are silvery-grey beneath. (May)

Rhododendron sinogrande, derived from an original Forrest collection, here flowering in the woodland garden at Tregrehan, Cornwall. (May)

Arisaema echinatum, a curious yet elegant aroid with numerous slender leaflets arranged at the top of the leaf stalk like the spokes of an umbrella. It was frequent in the woods above Dapingdi. (May)

Arisaema elephas. Its flower presented a bizarre appearance in the dark depths of the woods above Dapingdi.

Meanwhile, the ground flora in the forests above Dapingdi was every bit as varied and as interesting as the woody vegetation. Particularly abundant were those curious relatives of our native Cuckoo pint (*Arum maculatum*) the arisaemas. We found several species including *Arisaema echinatum*, an all green plant, slim and erect with long-stalked leaves divided to the base into numerous long narrow (linear) segments. The flower had a long cylindrical tube with pale parallel striations spreading, above the mouth, into a sail-like limb with a long tail-like point. Both tail and rim of mouth and limb were a rich purple, a fine dark edge to the pale chartreuse.

Compared with the cool refinement of the above species, *Arisaema elephas* has a bizarre, almost obscene appearance. It is a shorter, stockier plant with leaves composed of three rather coarse leaflets marked with purple blotches. The flower, borne on a stout green stem, is shaped like a funnel, widening towards the mouth and sporting above that a broad blunt-tipped limb. The ground colour is white with greenish markings, but the major part of the limb is a dark liver-purple, the colour extending down into the throat in several tapering stripes. That is not all. Contrasting with the green swollen drumstick spadix of *A echinatum*, that of *A elephas* is long and tapering, rising from deep in the throat and arching like a swan's neck before hanging to the ground. It resembles a dark purple rat's tail

and measures 25-30cm (10-12in) long. Both these species grew in light shade, often on slopes, in a rich leafy moist but well-drained topsoil. To the best of my knowledge, neither are at present in cultivation although the genus as a whole is enjoying a resurgence of popularity among cultivators of the unusual. For many plant enthusiasts they hold a strange fascination with their often stunning, if somewhat sombre, colour combinations.[13]

Many years ago, when botanising in a wood on the limestone of north Lancashire, I found several plants of a peculiar perennial member of the lily family called Herb Paris (*Paris quadrifolia*). It was not particularly impressive in flower, but it did strike me as being unusual and I have never forgotten it. I was reminded of this in the forest above Dapingdi when we found not one but two species of *Paris*, each in its own way very different in appearance to the plant of my childhood. One of these, *Paris violacea*, was smaller in size than *P quadrifolia*, up to 15cm (6in) tall and, instead of four egg-shaped plain green leaves in a whorl, it possessed five lance-shaped wavy-edged leaves of dark green with silvery veins. The flower was similar in some respects to that of *P quadrifolia*, but with three leaf-like sepals, silver veined like the leaves. It was fairly common in similar situations to the arisaemas and was later found

13. Both the above species are now in Western cultivation.

Paris polyphylla variety *yunnanensis* forma *alba* growing in an area of scrub close to Camp 1 on the eastern flanks of the Cangshan above Dali. This proved to be a form new to science – note the white ovaries hence forma *alba*. (May)

Paris violacea, a little known relative of the European Herb Paris, *Paris quadrifolia*, growing in the woods above Dapingdi. The bold leaf venation is its principle ornamental attraction. (May)

again above Camp 2. This species is now in cultivation, possibly for the first time, at the Royal Botanic Garden, Edinburgh and elsewhere.

The second *Paris* species is one I first encountered in east Nepal in 1971, its name – P *polyphylla* – referring to the many leaves. Here we have a taller plant up to 40cm (16in) or more, very distinct in the numerous (up to twelve), comparatively narrow, green, long, pointed leaves with paler midribs arranged in a handsome ruff at the summit of the stem. Above this rises a slender stalk bearing the flower surrounded by a whorl of six long-pointed leaf-like sepals resembling a smaller version of the leaf whorl. In this species both stamens and petals appear identical, yellow with slender filament points. It was plentiful in wooded areas throughout the Cangshan and was represented by three varieties, variety *appendiculata*, variety *yunnanensis*, one plant of which, above Camp 2, reached 1m (3ft), and most commonly by *Paris polyphylla* variety *thibetica*, which had the narrowest leaves and bracts and was a plant of distinction. By some authorities these varieties are treated as species, namely P *delavayi*, P *yunnanensis* and P *thibetica* respectively.

In a scrub area near Camp 3 we later found a most striking paris, which had broader leaves in whorls of six to seven, five, occasionally four, large conspicuous yellow leaf-like sepals, five thread-like petals, a white ovary and styles and ten narrow yellow anthers. It was without doubt the most colourful of its clan we had ever seen and when our Chinese colleagues said it was new to them we fully expected it to be declared a new species. Bob was especially excited with this find as paris was one of his specialities. New it certainly was, but we were a little disappointed, and more than a little surprised, to hear from Mrs Hen Li of the Institute of Botany in Kunming that she regarded it as no more than a form of *Paris polyphylla* variety *yunnanensis*, for which she has proposed the name forma *alba*.[14]

Several of the above paris are now in cultivation in Britain and for maximum performance they require a moist but well-drained humus-rich soil preferably in semi-shade. In time they spread by means of rhizomes to form substantial clumps when they can easily be divided. The new form *alba*, in particular, has settled in well and is

Paris polyphylla variety *thibetica*, worth growing for its handsome ruff of leaves alone. The flowers are followed by shining red fruits in a terminal cluster. Here growing in the woods above Dapingdi. (May)

14. In a paper published in the American journal *Brittonia*, the eminent Russian taxonomist Armen Takhtadjan presented a revision of the Paris species under the genera *Paris*, *Kinugasa* and *Daiswa*. According to the author: '*Kinugasa* and *Daiswa*, especially the latter, differ from *Paris* in a number of taxonomic characters so important that we have every reason to recognise them as separate genera. The most obvious and important difference lies in the fruit – a poisonous bluish-black non-splitting berry in *Paris*, a non-poisonous (edible) dark purple non-splitting berry in *Kinugasa*, and in *Daiswa* a capsule, splitting when ripe to reveal dense clusters of seeds with a fleshy, juicy, bright scarlet coat. The rhizomes of *Paris* are slender and creeping while those of the other two are thick. The ovaries too differ, roundish with slender styles in *Paris*, angular with slender styles in *Kinugasa*, angular with thick styles in *Daiswa*'. Under Takhtajan's treatment, both *Paris polyphylla* and P *violacea* should be regarded as belonging to *Daiswa*, but not all authorities agree with him.

Pinus armandii in cone, above Dapingdi. This was a common pine in the Cangshan and is also extensively planted here. (May)

spreading in the Peat Garden at the Royal Botanic Garden, Edinburgh. According to Ron McBeath it produces stems 30cm (12in) high and has every appearance of a plant of distinction.

A common component of the scrub and forest margin above Yangbi were the buddlejas. On the sunny slopes at lower elevations *Buddleja delavayi* was still in flower (some specimens at least), the shrubs up to 3m (9ft) high with elliptic leaves and fragrant lilac, orange-throated flowers in loose terminal heads (panicles). Above Camp 1 *B forrestii* was more frequent, a greener plant with quadrangular shoots and larger, lance-shaped, long pointed leaves. A specimen on the south wall of my house raised from seed collected at the time has reached 2.5m (8ft) and flowers from September into October, the fragrant lilac, orange-throated flowers borne in loose drooping tapering clusters.

Our last full day in Camp 1 proved to be one of the

So rich was the flora above Dapingdi, by the end of a day the plant presses were bulging with specimens. (May)

most exciting and productive of the entire expedition. Peter Cox and David had decided to follow a track which led steeply up on to a ridge with the intention of making as much height as possible in the time available. Some of the Chinese accompanied them as guides and they were rewarded with several rhododendrons not previously seen by us including *Rhododendron lacteum*, *R heliolepis* and *R cyanocarpum*. The rest of the group, led by Professor Feng, headed straight up the valley above camp. At a height of 2,955m (9,696ft) we passed through an area of woodland in which two conifers, *Pinus armandii* and *Tsuga dumosa* (*yunnanensis*) were plentiful, both in cone. In places *Rhododendron sinogrande* occurred in groves, its stems clothed with moss and lichen creating a gloomy damp world beneath. Mosses carpeted the woodland floor and coated rocks and fallen trees in a thick spongy emerald-green pelt in which flourished clumps of the dwarf box-leaved evergreen *Vaccinium delavayi* and extensive colonies of a most attractive fern, *Plagiogyria taliensis*, which resembled a robust silver-backed Hard fern (*Blechnum* species).

Rhododendron rubiginosum occurred frequently, but was past flowering; the few late flowers we did see were considered by David and Peter Cox to be average to below average in merit compared with the best forms in cultivation. A red-flowered parasite *Scurrula parasitica* was common on a number of hosts including *Rhododendron yunnanense*. I remember having seen a related species, *S elata*, in east Nepal in 1973.

Also found in a rhododendron (*R arboreum* subspecies *delavayi*), some 3m (9ft) from the ground, was an epiphytic orchid, *Coelogyne corymbosa*. It formed a large clump of plump green pseudobulbs, each with two leaves at the tip. From the base of several pseudobulbs rose pale green stems with three to four large flowers 5-6cm (2-2½ in) across. These were cream in bud and, except for an orange-bordered yellow stain on the lip, were pure white when fully open imparting a delicious fragrance to the air around. They were quite extraordinary and, in the forest's gloom, reminded me of ghostly moths hovering about the branches. We saw several colonies of this species and found it again on the Cangshan's eastern flank above Dali. It mainly grew on the moss-covered branches of trees, but on at least two occasions we found it on mossy rocks.

Apart from the orchid, other scents pervaded the forest including one whose special sweetness seemed familiar from gardens. A short search revealed *Osmanthus delavayi*, which must be one of the most popular of all scented evergreens in cultivation. Here it formed a spreading bush of 3m (9ft) high and as much or more through. Later, we found even taller specimens in thickets. The numerous clusters of small white tubular flowers crowded the leaf axils all along the arching branches and one could imagine the pleasure a bush in full flower must have given its original discoverer Père Delavay, after whom it is named.[15]

Coelogyne corymbosa, an epiphytic orchid growing on a moss-covered boulder on the Cangshan's eastern flank. It is also often found in trees in the forest. The flowers are deliciously scented. I have previously seen this species in E. Nepal and Bhutan. (May)

The typical plant in cultivation has leaves up to 2.5cm (1in) long and half as wide, while those of the Cangshan plants seemed narrower and more sharply toothed. There is also a form more rarely seen in British cultivation, in which the leaves are larger and broader. This form also more naturally assumes a taller tree-like habit. It grows in some of the Cornish gardens, including Caerhays, where it may have originated from Forrest seed. It was at one time offered by Hilliers of Winchester under the cultivar name 'Latifolius'.

If we had been in these forests earlier in the year we should have enjoyed the fragrance of another evergreen that occurs here in some quantity, *Sarcococca hookeriana* variety *digyna*. This is also a popular shrub in western gardens and, to the best of my knowledge, is mainly represented by plants introduced as seed from west Sichuan by E H Wilson in 1908. I am not aware of any Forrest introductions from Yunnan, although one imagines he must have encountered it – if not in the Cangshan then elsewhere. Here it formed clumps and colonies with shoots up to 60cm (2ft) densely clothed with narrow leathery shiny-topped leaves 7.5cm (3in) long. Interestingly, the stems of most plants we saw

were purple and put me in mind of a similar plant in cultivation at the Hillier Arboretum in the 1960s, which we named 'Purple Stem'. Together with S *confusa*, this is the most highly scented of all the sarcococcus in gardens and among the top ten winter flowering shrubs, easily grown and suitable for most soils and situations.

While searching a particularly dense thicket in an area of mossy boulders we made the surprising discovery of a large stump of magnolia from which suckers some 6m (20ft) high had grown. Judging by the size of the stump, some 388cm (153in) in girth, it must once have been a sizeable tree and when we took the leaf characters into account (they were freshly emerged) we agreed that it could only be *Magnolia campbellii* subspecies *mollicomata*. Later, from an exposed ridge track, we saw in the forest below a mature specimen of the same tree, its branches still relatively bare, supporting a few incredibly late (early May)

15. He first sent seeds to the French nurseryman Maurice de Vilmorin in 1890 and out of all those distributed only one germinated. Fortunately, as it developed, this seedling was propagated by grafting on to stocks of privet and *Phillyrea latifolia*, and this charming shrub gradually found its way into cultivation. It was again introduced as seed, and more successfully, by George Forrest.

Magnolia campbellii subspecies *mollicomata* is one of George Forrest's most spectacular and popular introductions. It is seen here flowering in the famous Cornish garden Trewithen. (March)

pink flowers, which we were able to see quite clearly through our binoculars.

George Forrest first discovered this magnolia in the spring of 1904 on the western flank of the Mekong river valley. It was flowering in colonies. 'I got within a mile of them', he wrote in his diary, 'from which distance the masses of pink blossoms showed up distinctly'.[16] Nowhere in the Cangshan did we come across this tree forming colonies; all we saw were scattered individuals that, apart from the one described, had all been felled, whether for their timber, which I doubt, or for some medicinal property of their bark – as indeed is the case with M *officinalis*, I do not know, nor were our Chinese colleagues able to enlighten us on the matter. One similarly sprouting stump we found above Huadianba in the north of the Cangshan had young leaves of a lovely purplish hue. In fairness to Forrest, he later described M *campbellii* subspecies *mollicomata* as 'a plant of the open forests, growing singly or two or three together and always on the west flanks of those ranges where the monsoon rainfall is greatest'. This is certainly in line with our comparatively limited experience in 1981.

Magnolia campbellii subspecies *mollicomata* 'Lanarth', a superb richly-coloured form collected in north-west Yunnan in 1924 by George Forrest under his number F 25655. This specimen, flowering in the Hillier Arboretum in 2000, is a descendant of the original seedling tree at Lanarth, Cornwall. (February)

Aristolochia moupinensis. A twining climber with curious liver purple coloured flowers. (May)

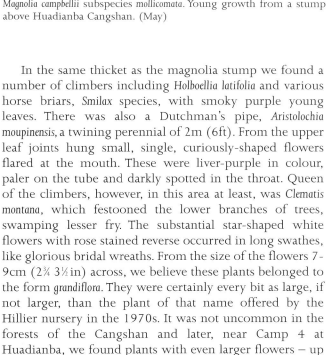

Magnolia campbellii subspecies *mollicomata.* Young growth from a stump above Huadianba Cangshan. (May)

Clematis montana, a large flowered form possibly *grandiflora* in the forest above Camp 1. Some flowers achieved 11cm. (4⅓in.) across. (May)

In the same thicket as the magnolia stump we found a number of climbers including *Holboellia latifolia* and various horse briars, *Smilax* species, with smoky purple young leaves. There was also a Dutchman's pipe, *Aristolochia moupinensis,* a twining perennial of 2m (6ft). From the upper leaf joints hung small, single, curiously-shaped flowers flared at the mouth. These were liver-purple in colour, paler on the tube and darkly spotted in the throat. Queen of the climbers, however, in this area at least, was *Clematis montana,* which festooned the lower branches of trees, swamping lesser fry. The substantial star-shaped white flowers with rose stained reverse occurred in long swathes, like glorious bridal wreaths. From the size of the flowers 7-9cm (2¾ 3½ in) across, we believe these plants belonged to the form *grandiflora.* They were certainly every bit as large, if not larger, than the plant of that name offered by the Hillier nursery in the 1970s. It was not uncommon in the forests of the Cangshan and later, near Camp 4 at Huadianba, we found plants with even larger flowers – up to 11cm (4½ in) across.

By midday we reached the top of a long steep wooded slope to find ourselves faced with a potentially exciting prospect. Directly ahead lay a steep-sided valley, its belly filled with virgin forest, while above was bare rock and precipices. It was a hidden valley, hidden that is, from the

Camp and to the best of our knowledge, unexplored. Even Professor Feng had not visited it and that made the prospect even more exciting. It was one of those situations that all plant explorer's have experienced, when bells ring and green lights flash in the mind, indicating that something special is in store. The valley was, in reality, more of an amphitheatre and, after gazing at it for some minutes, we plunged into the forest. Never have I seen forest like this. Trees, some well over 30m (100ft) soared skywards causing us to strain our necks in an effort to see their crowns. They were mainly evergreen oaks, among which *Lithocarpus leucostachyus* was prominent, with impressive stout trunks. A lower layer was rich in species including *Taxus yunnanensis* and *Rhododendron sinogrande* both of which were common, with individuals up to 13.5m (45ft). Even *R yunnanense* excelled itself here with at least one

16. Forrest successfully introduced this magnolia in 1924 from the Shweli-Salween divide near the Burma frontier and elsewhere. From these collections, it became firmly established in cultivation and an admired early flowering tree in large gardens, especially in the south and west of the British Isles as well as in Europe and the warmer areas of North America that border the Pacific. From one batch of Forrest's seed (F 25655), three seedlings were raised, one of which was grown in the famous garden at Lanarth on the Lizard Peninsula in Cornwall. This particular tree produced flowers of a stunning deep lilac-purple red, and when a grafted plant from the tree flowered for the first time in the Hillier Arboretum in 1975, it drew admirers from far and near. For several mercifully frost free days in February of that year staff, hardened to the unusual and rare, came to pay homage to this remarkable sight. Similar seedlings were raised at Werrington in the same county and at Borde Hill in W. Sussex.

Juniperus recurva variety *coxii*, an elegant juniper with branches and branchlets drooping at the extremities, was frequent on the Cangshan although no trees of good size were seen. This variety, first found in Upper Burma in 1914, is named after Peter Cox's father Euan, who with Reginald Farrer made the first introduction to cultivation. (May)

specimen of 10.5m (35ft). The yew T *yunnanensis* is related to the Himalayan species T *wallichiana* but differing, among other things, in its shorter leaves, which are blunt ended except for a small point (mucro).

More impressive than the yew, however, was the weeping juniper, *Juniperus recurva*, which occurred as scattered individuals throughout the area, one specimen 12m (40ft) high by as much through and with a girth of 64cm (25in) at chest height. The Chinese referred these trees to the variety *coxii* and I was inclined to agree with them.[17] The needles were certainly longer than those of the type, to 1.5cm (½in), and a rich green in colour. This, together with the strongly pendulous nature of the branches, reminded me of the several large specimens of variety *coxii* I have seen in cultivation in Britain. Later, high above Camp 2, we found a younger, smaller specimen of the same plant forming a dense relatively compact pyramid. Elsewhere, we saw plants more in keeping with J *recurva* with shorter needles of a variable hue.

From the scattered occurrence of this tree in the Cangshan and the scarcity of sizeable specimens, I suspect it was once more abundant and has suffered drastically at the hands of man. Its aromatic wood was once much in demand by the Chinese

It was its presence in the same general area of J *recurva* that led me to agree with current opinion that variety *coxii* is connected by intermediates to the type and is not distinct enough to be given specific rank as some have mooted. Even where variety *coxii* does not occur, as in east Nepal, J *recurva* is still a most variable species in habit, foliage colour and form and, therefore, in ornamental merit. Many seedlings, for instance, grown from seed collected in east Nepal in 1971 by the University College of Bangor Expedition are untidy in habit with multiple stems from the base and foliage of indifferent hue. Others seen in the wild, but not successfully introduced, were highly decorative with compact conical habit and with foliage including some good greens, greys and, once, silvery-blue like the colour of J *squamata* 'Blue Star'. A final word on J *recurva* variety *coxii*: I was interested to read in *Flora of Bhutan* by Grierson and Long that this variety occurs in Sikkim, and I think it not beyond the realms of probability that it awaits discovery in Bhutan and east Nepal and that its distribution follows that of the type.[18]

Several maples flourished here including *Acer forrestii*, while new rhododendrons included R *neriiflorum*, R *facetum*, R *rex* subspecies *fictolacteum* and R *anthosphaerum*, of which the first

17. *Juniperus recurva* variety *coxii* was first discovered in upper Burma by Kingdon-Ward in 1914. It was left to E H M Cox, Peter's father, after whom it is named, and Reginald Farrer to introduce it to cultivation six years later. Farrer described this juniper as growing always at altitudes of over 3,048m (10,000ft) in a region 'where the summer is wet and sunless, the winters of Alpine cold, and the springs late, ungenial and chilly'. Certainly our junipers grew from just below to well above the 3,048m (10,000ft) contour on the wetter western flanks of the Cangshan.

18. The tallest specimen of J *recurva* variety *coxii* in British cultivation is a tree of 18.5m (60ft) at Drenagh, Co. Derry, Northern Ireland (1983).

Rhododendron neriiflorum with its silvery backed leaves and waxy red flowers was not uncommon above Camp 1 at Dapingdi. (May)

Illicium simonsii. An attractive evergreen shrub flowering in the forest above Camp 1 at Dapingdi. (May)

and last were in flower: *R neriiflorum* with brilliant red funnel-shaped flowers borne in loose trusses beneath the silver backed foliage, while *R anthosphaerum*, with specimens of 9m (30ft), had already dropped its flowers, which appeared to be pink, heavily spotted with a darker shade.

I was delighted to see several plants I had first met with at the Hillier Arboretum, including *Viburnum atrocyaneum*, here up to 6m (20ft), *Meliosma cuneifolia* and *Neolitsea sericea*, with its evergreen silver-backed leaves and beautiful silky hairy young growths like small pointed spaniel's ears. *Illicium simonsii* was quite new to me, an evergreen shrub of 2m (6ft) or more with clusters of pale yellow flowers in the upper leaf axils. This species would be well worth introducing into cultivation where it would, I am sure,

189

prove popular in sheltered places and woodland gardens in the milder areas.[19]

One group of trees I was not in the least bit surprised to see, considering the habitat, was the sorbus, mainly represented here by those with undivided leaves. True, we did see one mountain ash – possibly *S pseudovilmorinii* – but by far the most common was one that our Chinese colleagues later identified as *S aronioides*. It was a small tree reaching 9m (30ft) on average, with leaves 8-12.5cm (3-5in) long, less than half as wide, toothed, glossy-green above, paler beneath. The flowers were creamy-white in dense terminal heads (corymbs). It is now in cultivation in Scotland from seedlings collected in the Cangshan, the colour of the new growths a beautiful shining chocolate.

And so it continued, trees and shrubs constantly changing in variety as we steadily climbed out of the valley,

our track now barely visible in an undergrowth rich in ferns, *Paris* species, cobra-like arisaemas and trailing thornless brambles. Once we found a large colony of the giant lily *Cardiocrinum giganteum* variety *yunnanense*, its dusky stems still several weeks from flowering but striking enough above the lush piles of glistening green foliage. Non-flowering rosettes were scattered over a wide area. Not far away, in a wet shady ravine, we found a splendid golden saxifrage, *Chrysosplenium davidianum*, which made our native species seem weedy by comparison. It formed low carpets of long-stalked kidney-shaped leaves above which were carried flattened heads of tiny yellow flowers with yellow-tinted bracts.[20]

19. This species is now in cultivation and well established in gardens like Tregrehan in Cornwall.

20 This species is now established in Western cultivation.

Chrysosplenium davidianum, a carpeting perennial in damp woodland shade above Camp 1. It is related to *Saxifraga*. The fern (top right) is *Plagiogyria taliensis*. (May)

Cardiocrinum giganteum variety *yunnanense* flowering in 1987 in the woodland garden of the Royal Botanic Garden, Edinburgh, grown from seed collected on the Cangshan in 1981. The dark stem is typical of the Yunnan variety. (June)

It was now late afternoon and the track, having taken us into a ravine and out on the other side, disappeared into a dense thicket of dead bamboo, killed, it seems, by a fire the previous year. We were somewhere in the middle of the bamboo when we detected a rich, almost spicy aroma. It seemed to be coming from a point above and ahead of us, and so, like the 'Bisto kids' on the gravy-browning packet, we followed our noses, intent on locating the source of this delicious smell. We did not have too far to go. Suddenly we emerged from the bamboo into a clearing. From the track a series of exposed rock slabs slanted away at a steep angle to the edge of a dark ravine from whence came the deep distant sound of a torrent. Our position was approximately 3,100m (10,171ft) above sea level. The joints between the slabs were filled with an assortment of low herbage and dwarf shrubs and it was here we found the object of our search – *Rhododendron edgeworthii*, several specimens of this shrub being 1-1.5m (3-5ft) high with handsome leaves boldly puckered

(bullate) above and covered beneath, like the young shoots, with a soft dense tawny or foxy-brown pelt of curly hairs. At the tips of several stems were carried loose trusses of large funnel-shaped flowers, flared and 10cm (4in) across the mouth. These were white, stained rose-red on the outside and in bud. From the flowers emerged the powerful scent that filled the glade and beyond.

R edgeworthii has a wide distribution in the wild, from Sikkim eastwards to south-west China. It usually occurs as an epiphytic shrub as much as 2.5m (8ft) tall on trees or rocks, often in a bed of moss. The Chinese plants were originally known as *R bullatum*, a name given by the French botanist Franchet to specimens collected by Père Delavay in the Cangshan in April 1886. Forrest introduced it to cultivation several times, as did Kingdon-Ward, Joseph Rock and others. Some of these introductions have proved hardier than others, but nowhere can it be described as hardy, except in the milder areas of Britain, and even there it has been known to suffer damage in

Rhododendron edgeworthii. The large fragrant flowers and bold foliage are a winning combination. It is not, however, a hardy species in British cultivation, though it has been grown out of doors in the milder areas and in warm situations elsewhere. (May)

Rhododendron sulfureum. A small loose-limbed shrub found as an epiphyte on rocks and stumps in the Cangshan. (May)

Pleione bulbocodioides - a fine dark form. Previously regarded as a species in its own right (*P delavayi*), it was first discovered in the Cangshan by the French missionary/botanist Jean Delavay. (May)

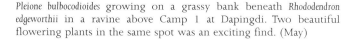

Pleione bulbocodioides growing on a grassy bank beneath *Rhododendron edgeworthii* in a ravine above Camp 1 at Dapingdi. Two beautiful flowering plants in the same spot was an exciting find. (May)

severe winters. It can, however, be grown in a pot or tub in well-drained compost in the cool house or conservatory where it provides a stunning talking point when in flower.[21]

Associated with R *edgeworthii* on the rock slabs above Dapingdi was another epiphytic rhododendron – R *sulfureum*, a very different species with small leaves and much smaller saucer-shaped flowers of rich yellow with an area of greenish speckles and no fragrance.

Exciting though the rhododendrons were, our 'Aladdin's Cave' was by no means exhausted. Growing on several grassy or mossy banks or rills on the slabs was the most beautiful pleione. One colony carried at least three dozen blooms, which rose above the leafless green flask-shaped pseudobulbs on 5-15cm (2-6in) stems. The blooms were a striking cyclamen-purple paling to white on the outside base of the lip and with darker magenta blotches on the inside. The marginal fringe and the five-crested keels (lamellae) of the lip were white tipped, a breathtaking combination. This species was first found in Cangshan by Delavay after whom it was named as *Pleione delavayi*. Recent opinion, however, has assigned it to the more widespread and variable *Pleione bulbocodioides*, where it must, for the time being at least, remain as a distinct and desirable form.

In the spring of 1906 George Forrest, collecting in western Yunnan, discovered a new *Pleione* species, which was subsequently named *Pleione forrestii*. Under his number, F 4859, he described the flowers as bright orange with brown markings. He found the new species growing between 2,743 and 3,048m (9,000 and 10,000ft) on moss-covered boulders and cliffs in a shady side valley on the eastern flank of the Tali Range (Cangshan). The 'Golden

Pleione', as it has become known, was one of several plants we hoped we might find in the Cangshan, but our chances seemed slim. Imagine our surprise and delight, therefore, when we spied it growing on the same rock slabs as *Rhododendron edgeworthii*.

We had photographed the two rhododendrons and the purple pleione, and were standing in a group in the centre of the slabs feeling, if my memory serves me correctly, rather dazed by the experience. Suddenly we saw a bold clump of the 'Golden Pleione' in a mossy niche and were by its side in seconds, ignoring our perilously close position to the edge of the ravine. There were several colonies, one 30cm (12in) across, with ten open flowers. These had sepals and petals of a paler colour than the rich canary-yellow lip. The latter was copiously fringed and wavy-edged with a conspicuous apical notch. Contrasting with the yellow was an extensive area of reddish blotches over the lip surface.

It seemed ages later that we heard Professor Feng calling for our return. He seemed a long way off and so he was, but he patiently listened to our story of the pleiones before urging us to make haste and return to camp before night descended. We subsequently found P *forrestii* several times above Camp 1. Once, a little shepherd girl with rhododendron flowers in her hair, brought us a group of three flowering plants on a pad of moss she had gathered from a fallen tree in the forest. On another occasion we found it growing in rock crevices and on the surface of a limestone cliff. The shrubs and herbage here had been scorched by a fire that had razed a bamboo thicket

21. Peter Cox grows this species best in his Argyllshire garden where it flourishes on old log piles covered in moss or else on mossy rocks. In the drier, colder conditions at Glendoick it survives in a raised bed between two minimally heated greenhouses.

Pleione forrestii, the fabulous 'Golden Pleione', growing in the mossy niche of a ravine above Dapingdi. It was originally found in the Cangshan by George Forrest in 1906, but the true species was not introduced to western cultivation until 1981. (May)

Pleione forrestii, the 'Golden Pleione', photographed by George Forrest in the Cangshan in 1906. Curiously, this plant was not introduced to western cultivation or, if it was, it was lost. The yellow pleione, a survivor of Forrest's introduction, grown for many years as P forrestii, has proved to be a hybrid P x confusa

at the foot of the cliff but the pleiones were still intact.

The story, however, does not end here. In 1924 George Forrest introduced plants of his 'Golden Pleione' into British cultivation from the Shweli-Salween divide in the far west of Yunnan, north west of Tengchong (Tengyueh). Pseudobulbs were sent to J C Williams at Caerhays in Cornwall who passed on stock to the Royal Botanic Garden, Edinburgh. What became of the Caerhays stock no one seems to know, but by the end of the Second World War the Edinburgh stock had

Shepherd girl with *Pleione forrestii* on a moss pad she had found in the forest above Camp 1 at Dapingdi. (May)

been reduced to a single pseudobulb. Principally as a result of the patience and care of E Kemp (then Curator), the stock was slowly built up again until material could be made available to the nurserymen W E Th Ingwersen of Sussex who introduced it commercially.

Now for a curious twist in the tale. For several years prior to the Cangshan expedition, certain authorities on the genus, notably Dr David Harberd, had become suspicious regarding the identity of the Edinburgh P forrestii. Finally, in 1979, its true status was proven beyond any shadow of doubt: it was a natural hybrid the result of true P forrestii crossing with the recently described P albiflora, the two parents sharing the same distribution, altitude, range and habitat in the wild. By way of confirmation a plant collected by us from above Dapingdi has proved to be the same hybrid though, obviously, a different clone. Appropriately, given its history, the hybrid has been named P x confusa. It differs from true P forrestii in its slightly larger, paler yellow flowers, which have deeply cut (dissected) ribs (lamellae) on the lip.

Samples from several of the P forrestii populations we found in the Cangshan in 1981 were introduced to cultivation and are growing at Edinburgh and Kew as well as in several other places. Our stock appears to have been the first introduction of the true species into the West and it was gratifying, therefore, to see a flowering plant originating from the rock slabs above Dapingdi receiving in April 1985 an Award of Merit when shown before the Royal Horticultural Society. Ron McBeath at Edinburgh describes the true P forrestii as being 'superb with smaller flowers [than the hybrid] of a deeper yellow'.

In addition, both the rich purple P bulbocodioides and P yunnanensis were introduced from the Cangshan in 1981 and a plant from the former collection flowering at Edinburgh recently for the first time has been confirmed as another hybrid – P bulbocodioides x P yunnanensis (this has since been described under the name P x taliensis). If nothing else, it confirms the remarkably promiscuous tendencies of these orchids, a fact that has not escaped the notice of specialist growers who have already raised many attractive hybrids.

Our trek from Camp 1 at Dapingdi north to Camp 2 at Shangchang led us through hot dry hills where erosion had turned the once fertile soil to dust. Here we found several *Hypericum* species, *Prinsepia utilis* and *Elsholtzia* species. (May)

To Camp 2

We left our camp at Dapingdi on 6 May with the sun climbing the sky. We were heading due north across the western flanks of the Cangshan, our track following the contours except for the occasional steep drop into a valley and an equally severe haul up the other side. Unlike the forested slopes above Camp 1, these were relatively treeless, cultivated mainly in the vicinity of villages. It was a hot tiring trek and, with few plants of interest to relieve the monotony, we found ourselves, as on the climb to Dapingdi, looking towards the walnut's precious shade. Scrubby areas were plentiful containing a mixture of shrubs in which *Hypericum*, *Rubus*, *Colquhounia*, *Elsholtzia* and *Coriaria nepalensis* were dominant. The latter is a large shrub with stout almost scandent stems to 5m (16ft) or more. It is a widespread species ranging from Kashmir in the west, eastwards through the Himalays to north Burma and west China. It has little garden value, though the young growths of plants hard pruned in spring have some merit. Even in this, however, they are surpassed by the Japanese *C japonica* whose branches are frondose in effect. The fruits of all three are ultimately black or purplish-black and no match for the much smaller Himalayan red-fruited *C terminalis*, especially in its yellow fruited variety *xanthocarpa*. As a genus, *Coriaria* has a far-flung distribution in the wild for, apart from Asia, it is represented in Europe (*C myrtifolia* being common in the Mediterranean region), Mexico, Chile and in New Zealand, where there are several species including the charming creeping *C plumosa*.

The common hypericum of these hillsides is a shrub originally described by Alfred Rehder of the Arnold Arboretum as a species, *H uraloides*, but which Dr N K B Robson of the British Museum now regards as a subspecies of the variable *H henryi*. To a plantsman's eye, subspecies *uraloides* differs in no great detail from the typical *H henryi*, although plants in cultivation grown from seed collected above Yangbi are variable in habit and size of leaf and flower. Of three seedlings growing in my own garden two are so late in flower and the flowers so sparse that I doubt I shall keep them, even though one has a pleasant frondose habit and both have narrowly ovate leaves, neatly arranged in two ranks along the slender stems. In a mild winter these are retained at least into the new year. The third seedling flowers well with pale yellow cup-shaped flowers 3-4cm (1¼-1½in) across, similar in effect to those of *H uralum* to which this subspecies is closely related. Two years after planting, all three seedlings put up strong arching shoots to 1.5m (5ft) in 1985.

Another shrub we encountered above Yangbi was *Prinsepia utilis*, its long arching green stems armed with stout spines up to 5cm (2in) long. The small damson-like fruits were strung beneath these stems and though edible we found them rather tart, the taste lingering for much of the day. It is an indication of the warmth enjoyed by these valleys that these fruits had already ripened in early May from flowers that must have opened in winter. In cultivation in Britain, the small white

A friendly family in the Lisu village above Yangbi, who offered us green tea and a most unusual soup. (May)

A Lisu woman on her way to work in the fields that cling to the steep slopes above Yangbi. (May)

fragrant flowers in short racemes normally appear in March, though mild weather will open them in February or earlier.

Around midday we stopped at the small village of Zaimen at 2,300m (7,545ft) and ate our lunch in the shade of a walnut tree. The fields here sloped to an alarming degree and yet some cultivation had been attempted for, among other crops, we noticed potatoes being grown. The villagers were of the Lisu race, jovial, generous, and hard working. It amazes me how these mountain farmers of Yunnan survive. Their fields are hacked from steep hillsides and their daily routine most westerners would consider a penance. Wind blows away the top soil in the dry season (April-May) and rain washes it into the streams during the summer. What soil remains they till with crude tools including a large bladed drag hoe.

For some time we watched as a tiny figure on the slope below gradually toiled towards us. Eventually, the figure, an old

man, reached the track and sat on the ground at the foot of a wall some metres away. He was short and fragile, his bent frame clothed in a much-mended and patched blue cotton tunic over which he wore a threadbare waistcoat, while on his head he wore a cap around which was wrapped a length of black cloth. He carried a reddish brown fibre poncho of a kind we had seen several times worn by farmers and hill porters. This fibre is stripped from the leaf base of the Chusan palm, *Trachycarpus fortunei*, which is cultivated in most of the villages in Yunnan. Sown on to a cotton base it makes a rough, thick, highly-protective outer garment – waterproof, windproof and warm.

The old man's face was haggard and deeply scored, and he had both a moustache and a wispy grey goatee beard, and although beads of sweat glistened on his brow he showed no other signs of his exertions. He regarded us for a while with the interested, innocent look of a child before climbing to his feet, shouldering his hoe and, with a smile

A log beehive in a village on a hillside above Dapingdi. The ends are sealed with dried mud. (May)

Our Chinese colleagues gathering flowering specimens of a mighty *Decaisnea fargesii* on a hillside above Dapingdi. (May)

Rhododendron virgatum subspecies *oleifolium*, a small shrub growing in a dusty gully by the track between Dapingdi and Shangchang above Yangbi. It is generally too tender for outside cultivation in Britain. (May)

and a nod, continuing on his way.

Not long after, we passed through another small hamlet where the sound of bees caught our attention. Here we found a cluster of curious beehives, which appeared to be hollow walnut logs, some 60cm (2ft) in diameter laid horizontally on low stone platforms. The ends of each log were sealed with dried mud, while a hole low down at one end allowed the bees access. The roof of each log had been cut away and replaced by a large piece of bark which, apart from allowing ready access to the honey, overlapped the hive sufficiently to provide shelter from sun and rain. A large stone had been placed on each bark roof to prevent it blowing away.

We continued our journey across a wide hillside, the temperature now somewhere above 25°C (77°F). Our excitement on finding a new plant was tempered by the thought of lingering in the heat and dust and several plants we collected without stopping. One of these was a rather pretty rhododendron, *Rhododendron virgatum* subspecies *oleifolium*, which grew in a gully by the track.[22] It was a small shrub to 1m (3ft) in height, with narrowly oblong green leaves sprinkled with brown scales beneath. The pale almond pink flowers up to 2.5cm (1in) across were carried singly or sometimes in pairs from the upper leaf axils.

Not far from this we came across a multi-stemmed specimen of *Decaisnea fargesii* some 5.5m (18ft) high. Intermingled with its handsome leaves were the drooping heads (panicles) of yellowish-green flowers. This shrub grew on a steep hillside down which we descended, partly on our backsides, in a cloud of grit and dust. A bold evergreen chestnut relative, *Castanopsis orthacantha* occurred here as

22. This rhododendron was first discovered by Delavay around 1884 under the name R *oleifolium*, and I remember seeing the typical R *virgatum* in east Nepal in 1971 where it grew on equally dry hillsides at similar altitudes. It is too tender for cultivation out of doors in the West, except in a warm dry climate.

Castanopsis orthacantha. An evergreen chestnut relative displaying its conspicuous male flowerheads above Dapingdi Camp 1. (May)

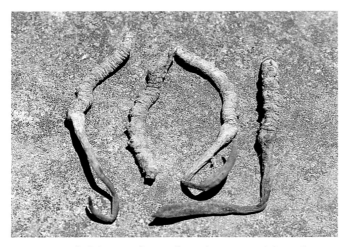

The mummified larvae of a Swift moth parasitised by a fungus, *Cordyceps sinensis*. These are considered an important item of Chinese traditional medicine and can often be found in village markets. They were known to the plant hunters and travellers of old as 'Ch'ung-tsao' or 'Tchong-tsao' (pinyin: Chongcao). (May)

scattered individual trees of 10m (32ft), the pointed leaves topped by bouquets of long arching string-like male catkins, which were a bright yellow and conspicuous from afar.

Eventually we attained a ridge that stretched seemingly endlessly above us. Climbing this in the sun's unremitting glare was purgatory. We each carried small packs, water bottles and camera gear, no great weight, but our strength was sapped by the heat and, in our minds, the climb became more a matter of survival than a botanical treat. Along the route we had occasion to pass several small farms, which were invariably guarded by fierce dogs that ran out to challenge us. Curiously, they often made for Peter Cox who warded them off with a deft wave of his ice axe, which doubled as a walking stick.

By late afternoon we reached a small Lisu village where we sank gratefully to the ground in the shade of a wooden porch. Our water had long since been used up and we were thankful to be offered refreshment by the villagers. The green tea when it arrived was scalding hot and was served in glass tumblers making handling and drinking an awkward business. We were in no hurry to move on, however, even though the site of Camp 2 was still some distance away. After the tea we were offered some soup, an unexpected treat, and the British team members could hardly wait to begin. We were each handed a bowl containing a hot clear liquid in which floated particles of vegetables, rice and curious brown twig-like objects 4-5cm (1½-2in) long. These we tucked into, Peter Cox eating six in no time at all. They were rather crunchy, but possessed no flavour I could describe. If it had not been for the look of expectancy on the faces of our Chinese colleagues we would probably have thought no more about it, but they were obviously waiting for some reaction. 'Okay', I said to Clyde, 'what are they?' Clyde thought for a moment, searching for an English translation before announcing that the 'twigs' were known as 'winter worm, summer grass'. 'Worms!', we exclaimed, 'please explain'. Clyde did.

In the mountain pastures between 3,660 and 4,570m (12,000 and 15,000ft) a Swift moth *Hepialus amoricanus* lays its eggs in the ground. On hatching, the larva, a fat cream-coloured caterpillar, moves through the soil feeding on the roots of grass. Some of the caterpillars, the unlucky ones, inadvertently take in the spores of a fungus that then germinates and grows, eventually killing the caterpillar, which is by now overwintering underground. At the end of spring and in early summer, the fungus produces a nail-shaped spore body, greyish or blackish in colour and some 4-5cm (1½-2in) long, which grows from the mouth of the dead caterpillar and projects above the ground. Certain country people, the equivalent to truffle hunters in Europe, knowing when and where to find these fungi, collect them in baskets or bags, taking care to remove caterpillar and fungus intact. These are then dried, the caterpillar becoming orange-brown, the fungus 'body' greyish-black, often bending at the tip like a shepherd's crook. This then was the source of our mysterious 'twigs'.

The fungus, *Cordyceps sinensis*, is one of many species parasitising caterpillars, beetles and similar hosts. In Britain we have *C miliaris*, whose orange club-shaped fruiting body I once found on a moth chrysalis in a heap of leaf mould. Caterpillars infested with the fungus mycelium are regarded as a great delicacy and an important tonic food in China, where they fetch high prices. Sichuan province is especially famous for these caterpillars, which are sent from there to other Chinese provinces tied in small bundles of about ten or twelve. They are, or used to be, sold in village markets and are available from practitioners in native medicine. They were known to most of the old plant hunters and E H Wilson remarked that, under the vernacular name 'Ch'ung-tsao' or 'Tchong-Tsao' (pinyin Chongcao or Dongchong xiacao), the infested caterpillar with the fungus body attached was esteemed for a variety of purposes: 'Boiled with pork it was employed as an antidote for opium poisoning and as a cure for opium eating, also with pork and chicken it was taken as a tonic and a mild stimulant by convalescent persons, rapidly restoring them to health and strength'. It is true that on leaving our Lisu hosts we experienced renewed energy for our climb, but I think that this was more the result of a rest and the thought of reaching camp than from any effect the caterpillars might have had. If nothing else, the incident gave our Chinese hosts something to chuckle about over the next few days.

It was with considerable relief that we hobbled into camp that evening, sinking wearily to the ground, quite happy to wait for supper and a tipple of Professor Feng's infamous spirit, Moutai, before pitching our tents. It had taken us nine hours to walk approximately 35km (22 miles) from Camp 1 at Dapingdi: nine hot, dusty, leg weary, unforgettable hours.

Our new camp, in a place called Shangchang, was

A view down the ridge above Camp 2 at Shangchang. The campsite lies hidden from view at the foot of the densely-wooded west-facing slope looking out across a large open grassy area long since cleared of trees for grazing purposes. The small town of Yangbi lies off the picture to the left middle distance in the Yangbi river valley. (May)

The site of Camp 2 at Shangchang. The summit ridge of the Cangshan can be seen in the distance. The woodland above the camp was full of good things, including maples, sorbus, styrax, rhododendrons, peonies, daphnes, roses, as well as numerous perennials, especially ferns. (May)

situated at approximately 2,745m (9,000ft) on the edge of an open grassy area at the foot of a wooded slope. The slope had a north-westerly aspect and the woods differed markedly from those at Dapingdi in being predominantly of broad-leaved deciduous trees with a scattering of evergreens and the usual rhododendron understorey. The cleared area was partially covered with bracken and grazed by goats, cattle and pigs, which were brought up each day from the villages below. Water was obtained from a spring just above camp, while essential food and provisions were brought up daily by ponies that then returned to Yangbi with dried herbarium specimens. It was an idyllic spot and during the next three days we had a happy time exploring the secondary ridges, on one occasion climbing to the main ridge itself. Much time was spent in the woods where trees of great variety flourished, especially maples, ash and styrax. The ash was *Fraxinus paxiana*, up to 21m (70ft) high, the leaves with petioles swollen at base and from nine to eleven narrow glossy green and smooth (glabrous) leaflets. It is a member of the Ornus group of flowering ashes,

Acer davidii, a justifiably popular snake-bark maple in western cultivation, is widespread in the wild in western and central China. (May)

Acer forrestii, with its characteristic three-lobed leaves on rhubarb-red stalks, is less often seen in cultivation than *A davidii*. Both this flowering specimen and that of *A davidii* were found in the woods near Camp 2. (May)

though we could detect no flowers in its high canopy.

Of *Styrax* we found two species, S *shweliensis*, now included by the Chinese in S *perkinsiae*, and S *grandiflora*, the latter a 10.5m (35ft) tree with white flowers in the leaf axils. S *perkinsiae* was a tree of similar size with pointed downy leaves 8-10cm (3-4in) long and glaucous beneath. It was not in flower, but the flower buds were covered in reddish-brown hairs and carried in the leaf axils on the new shoots. Neither, to my knowledge, are in cultivation in Britain where they would probably require a sheltered woodland situation in the south or west.

Maples were plentiful and included *Acer tetramerum*, one tree being 20m (65ft) with a girth of 247cm (97in) at chest height. A tree of similar height grows in the Royal Horticultural Society's Garden at Wisley in Surrey. Other maples included *A flabellatum* variety *yunnanense* and the sycamore-like *A franchetii* with its large leaves. The Chinese form of the Cappadocian maple, *A cappadocicum* variety *sinicum*, was also apparent with its pale bronze young foliage especially attractive when caught in the shafts of early morning or evening sun.

It was two maples of the so called snake-bark group, however, that caused most comment. One of these *Acer davidii*, I had admired on Emei Shan in west Sichuan the previous year, and here in the Cangshan it again impressed. It occurred as scattered individuals averaging 9m (30ft), with one exceptional specimen of 13.5m (45ft), the bark boldly striated and the branches upswept at first, then spreading widely, and curving down at their extremities to form a crown of great elegance. Leaves were variable in size and shape, occasionally to 15cm (6in) in length, sometimes with two small lobes towards the base. These lobed leaves were most predominant on young trees or on vigorous shoots of older trees. The mature trees we saw almost invariably had unlobed but double-toothed leaves tapering to an abrupt point and carried on green or slightly pink-tinged stalks, and when we turned them over we could see tufts of reddish-brown hairs at the base of the midrib. The trees were in flower at the time, the tiny pale greenish flowers borne on long slender tassels held horizontally above or slightly drooping beneath the leaves.

Equally attractive, and just as common here, was *Acer forrestii*, which was originally discovered by George Forrest on the Lijiang range (now the Yulong Shan) to the north of Dali. Some authorities, Bean included, suggest that there is little botanically to separate this species from *A laxiflorum* and that the differences between the two are slight. Having since seen the last named in Sichuan I have no hesitation in saying that the two are distinct and could not be mistaken for each other. Other maples are sometimes found in cultivation under the name *A forrestii*, and I once remember checking out the trees so labelled in the Hillier Arboretum – trees received from several sources – to find that out of ten trees only three were correctly named. The true species

Hedera nepalensis variety *sinensis* was common in the woods above Camp 2, its evergreen growths covering the ground and the stems of trees. Its orange-yellow fruits were particularly attractive. Note the entire adult leaves. (May)

is a most handsome tree and those we saw in the woods of the Cangshan were typical in every detail of Forrest's original introduction, the largest of which, in the British Isles is to be found in the woods at Caerhays Castle in Cornwall, which in 1991 measured 15m (50ft). Above Camp 2 it reached 9m (30ft), though stumps of felled trees suggested it might be capable of a greater height. Bark striations were distinct but less obvious than those of *A davidii* nearby. Like that species, the crown of *A forrestii* was wide spreading with long, arching branches curving downwards at the extremities. The leaves were characteristically three lobed, the middle lobe the larger and longer, tapering gradually to a tail-like point. As in *A davidii*, the leaves are double toothed but coarser, while the main veins lack the bold parallel effect of the other. Tufts of reddish-brown hairs occur in the axils of the main veins beneath. On young trees and strong growing shoots the leaves were more variable, generally larger, more coarsely and boldly toothed and with two extra smaller lobes at the base. The most distinctive characteristic of the leaf, however, is the stalk (petiole), which is coloured a conspicuous rhubarb-red and it is this, together with the three-lobed blade, that makes *A forrestii* so easily

recognisable. Indeed, the only other maple I have seen with similar leaves is the east Himalayan *A pectinatum* to which *A forrestii* is closely related.[23] Like *A davidii*, Forrest's maple was flowering, the tiny brownish-green flowers in short red stalked tassels arching above the leaves.

The Chinese ivy *Hedera nepalensis* variety *sinensis* was plentiful in many of the larger trees as well as covering large areas of woodland floor and old stumps. Mature growths were heavy with orange-yellow fruits in dense clusters. Another shrub climbing here was the evergreen currant relative, *Ribes laurifolium*, which we found growing as an epiphyte on the mossy stem of an evergreen oak at 3,050m (10,000ft). Male and female flowers are borne on separate plants, the male flowers being larger in longer clusters. Where both sexes are present the female flowers are occasionally followed by small downy fruits which are purplish-black when ripe. Seeing this plant in the wild put me in mind of my student days at the University Botanic Garden, Cambridge, where I first encountered this dwarf shrub. It was a regular teaser in the plant identification tests and a favourite of the then director, John Gilmour.

23. Current opinion favours both *A forrestii* and *A laxiflorum* as sub species of *A pectinatum*.

Dryopteris wallichiana, in the Cangshan above Dapingdi demonstrating its shuttlecock habit and its bold decorative fronds. (May)

Dryopteris wallichiana, Yunnan, Cangshan. (May)

One of the most impressive sights in the woodland were the ferns, which occurred in great numbers and included the silver-backed *Plagiogyria taliensis* a most ornamental species and *Dryopteris wallichiana* with dark scaly stipe and rachis. They were accompanied by a host of herbs in which *Paris* and *Arisaema* species were prominent, as was the giant lily *Cardiocrinum giganteum* variety *yunnanense*, which frequented damp depressions and which, maddeningly, was still only at bud stage.

By far the most common ground cover, however, was provided by two evergreen thornless creeping brambles, *Rubus tricolor* and *R buergeri*. In places they swamped lesser vegetation in a great green tidal wave that lapped at the perimeter of our camp.

R tricolor is now commonly cultivated in Britain, having first been introduced by E H Wilson in 1908, although it was Delavay, again, who first discovered it. The name, I presume, refers to the three main colours found on the plant: the dark glossy green of the leaves above, the white felted undersurface and the red bristles that clothe the stems and leaf stalks, these later turning brownish. The best tricolor effect can be seen in the unfolding shoots. By contrast, the white flowers produced in the upper leaf axils are not so noticeable, though they do give way to red fruits, which are not only edible but tasty as well.

Compared with this, *R buergeri* is a more subdued plant with softly downy stems and leaves. It differs most markedly from *R tricolor* in its leaves, which are kidney-shaped or rounded with five shallow lobes and small marginal teeth. They are bright green above with a wrinkled (rugose) surface, while beneath they are clothed with pale, silky hairs that are almost silvery on the emerging leaves. I am not aware that *R buergeri* is in cultivation in the West but, were it to be introduced, it would be every bit as hardy and effective as *R tricolor*, especially as a ground cover in shade.

Of the many evergreen shrubs that flourished in the understorey I shall mention just a few. *Camellia pitardii* variety *yunnanica* was not uncommon, with specimens up to 4m (13ft) of relatively compact habit with attractive bronze-coloured young leaves. One plant even carried a few late pink

Rubus tricolor illustrating the three colours alluded to in the second name (specific epithet). It formed a dense evergreen cover in parts of the woods above Shangchang. (May)

The brilliant crimson young growths of *Pieris formosa* on the ridge above Camp 2 at Shangchang. It was from this location, or nearby, that Forrest's original introduction of variety *forrestii* was probably made. (May)

Pieris formosa variety *forrestii* here growing in the woodland garden at Clyne Castle near Swansea, S. Wales. (May)

flowers to remind us of the display we had missed. Rhododendrons in variety included *Rhododendron sinogrande*, some specimens up to 12m (40ft) and into one of which I again climbed at the end of a particularly exciting and tiring day. From my perch I could hear the sounds of camp activity as supper was being prepared and once I caught sight of Peter Cox among the rhododendrons on a nearby hillside. I watched him until the light began to fade when all I could see was his white hat quartering the ground like a lone barn owl. Like the rest of us, Peter was in his element and determined to eke out every minute of this marvellous experience.

One day we climbed the wooded slope above camp in an attempt to reach the ridge track above. For two hours or more we forced our way through dense undergrowth and huge boulders only to meet with defeat at the base of a high rock face. We did however find R *sinogrande* in extensive thickets, seedlings mainly, crowding the upper slope in company with a ubiquitous bamboo. Not far from this place R *maddenii* subspecies *crassum* grew,[24] with its distinctive bold, glossy-green leathery leaves, bluish-green (glaucous) beneath. Unfortunately, we were too early for flower.

The most abundant evergreen in the woods, after the rhododendrons and the rubus, was *Pieris formosa*. In places, these formed trees to 15m (50ft), although two individuals we estimated at 20m (65ft) with girths at 1.5m (5ft) of 147cm (58in) and 138cm (54in). Some of these were in flower, the flowers variable in size, carried in the usual

drooping clusters. The young growths varied in colour from copper to coppery-red and combined effectively with the white flowers. One day, while returning along the ridge above camp, we came across an area of scrub on the woodland fringe occupied by a form of P *formosa* in which the young growths were a brilliant crimson, as rich in their effect as the plant discovered and introduced by George

24. This rhododendron was originally discovered in the Cangshan by Delavay in about 1885 and introduced by Forrest twenty years later. Although not suited in cultivation to very cold areas this subspecies is hardier than R *maddenii* and I remember plants of it surviving quite happily on a rather exposed situation in the Hillier Arboretum in Hampshire.

Members of the expedition on a ridge track above Camp 2 in the Cangshan Mountains. (May)

Forrest to which the name P forrestii was originally given.[25] The plants we saw that day lacked the robust habit and leaf and flower size of what is at present grown in cultivation as P formosa variety forrestii 'Wakehurst', but they were, nevertheless, just as striking in their initial growth. No one is quite sure exactly where and when Forrest collected the original seed although it is likely to have been in 1905/6.

Close by the thicket in which we found our crimson-tipped pieris, there passes a well-worn track which, since early times, has afforded herdsmen, woodsmen, hunters and others a route from Yangbi in the valley to the summit ridge of the Cangshan. It would have been known to Forrest and his collectors and possibly used by them to gain access to the higher slopes. Did he travel this way in 1906, noting the pieris in flower and returning to collect the seed? It is a question to which we shall probably never know the answer.

Today, in garden circles certainly, Forrest's famous pieris

is regarded as a distinct variety of the more widespread P formosa, which occurs from east Nepal in the west to central China in the east. Pieris formosa variety forrestii is regarded as one of the most impressive of all flowering evergreens for acid soils, especially in the selected form 'Wakehurst'. It is not suited to cold exposed areas and in severe winters can be cut to the ground, sprouting again from the base. Nevertheless, among those with woodland or large sheltered gardens its admirers are on the increase.

The evenings we spent at Camp 2 were some of the most memorable of the expedition. After the regular chore of changing the paper in the presses had been completed and notes written up, we would sit round the fire discussing the day's events or planning tomorrow's. Sometimes we would exchange songs with the Chinese or, with the help of Clyde, small talk until the fire burned low. Most nights we watched the sun setting over the eastern rim of the Mekong river valley while, from the valley immediately below, banks of mist rose gently and imperceptibly, their tops red-tinted in the fading light. Most nights, too, we could see the flickering of fires high on distant hillsides marking the activities of hill people burning and clearing areas of forest for the cultivation of crops such as buckwheat and maize. What a destructive and short-sighted activity this is, criticised by local authorities who seem unable to control it, let alone to stop it. Another problem occurs on the grazing areas, which are burned periodically to keep them free of woody growth. These fires inevitably run unchecked for a period, eating further into the remaining forest. When

25. P forrestii was described in 1914 from a cultivated plant and on the herbarium sheets of the type specimens at the Royal Botanic Garden, Edinburgh, the only reference to the seed's origin being the word 'Yunnan'. If the plant described in 1914 was already substantial enough to justify being described as a new species, it suggests that the 1905/6 collection date was correct and this is further substantiated by Forrest himself in an article, 'Notes on the Plants of North West Yunnan', published in the Journal of the Royal Horticultural Society (volume 42, 1916/17). In writing about the Tali Range he makes the following comment: 'That part of the range [the western flank] has never been explored to any extent, and, judging by the results of two short and hasty journeys in 1906 and one in recent years, the collections of which are so far undetermined, it carries many interesting and new species'. Forrest then goes on to describe a selection of the plants he found there. They include Diapensia bulleyana, Pleione delavayi and P forrestii, all of which we also saw in 1981. He then writes: 'There, also, in moist open situations, amongst scrub, was found the beautiful Pieris forrestii with its pure waxy-white fragrant blooms'. Here then is proof of his finding this plant not only in the Cangshan but on the western slopes.

The evenings at Camp 2 were among the most enjoyable of the expedition. Here, a setting sun lights the western sky, while behind the long dark ridge on the horizon lies the Mekong river valley. (May)

George Forrest visited the Cangshan in the early part of the 20th century he found the western flank 'heavily timbered'. He later wrote: 'On the west the vegetation is principally arborescent, so dense in places as to be almost impenetrable, it attains a much greater altitude [than on the eastern flank], and is carried right to the base'. How soon this situation was to change! If Forrest were to return today he would be as devastated as the slopes he once knew. Of course, there are areas of untouched forest; according to the Yangbi elders, sixty

per cent of the county is still forested, but it is increasingly confined to deep ravines and steep hillsides. Elsewhere, the forest has been cleared, too often for temporary gain.

Our camp was ideally placed for botanising, for not only was it surrounded by interesting plants – some even grew between our tents! Above the kitchen area, for instance, flourished an evergreen holly, *Ilex dipyrena*, 7.5m (25ft) high, while close by a bold-leaved buddleja had us all puzzling over its likely identity. Several names were proposed but, in the

The densely wooded slopes of the Changshan's western flank as first seen and photographed by George Forrest in the early 1900s. A good deal of the tree cover has since been destroyed as a result of man's activities.

Deutzia calycosa, a common shrub in the Cangshan, especially around Camp 2 at Shangchang. It was reintroduced to western cultivation in 1981, and is quite hardy in Britain. (May)

Deutzia calycosa 'Dali'. A seedling from the Cangshan growing in the author's garden. It has large pink-tinted flowers. (June)

absence of flowers, it was merely guesswork, although the young shoots we noted were remarkably quadrangular and winged. It was a tree of 6m (20ft) with a single trunk and long drooping seed heads. Seed was collected and the resultant plants have proven quite vigorous, and one specimen against the south-facing wall of my house has reached 5.5m (18ft). The leaves put me in mind of those of *Buddleja colvilei*, but the flowers in late summer are quite different, being small, pale lilac with an orange eye and densely crowded in pendulous tapering heads. In some respects it is closely related to *B forrestii*, differing, however, in its longer, narrower flowers, which are downy on the outside, and in its denser, spike-like flowerheads, which droop like a whippet's tail. I believe it to be *B macrostachya* and, although it has no great beauty of flower, its handsome foliage and impressive habit should earn it a place in specialist collections and botanic gardens. In cold areas it is subject to winter damage, but providing a woody framework has been

established it has the ability to break out again the following spring producing growths 2m (6ft) long or more. The leaves on strong shoots can be as much as 43cm (17in) long.

Several other plants collected in the the Shangchang area have proved new to western cultivation. Most of these we found growing in the many clearings and disturbed areas of woodland. One of the most interesting is *Viburnum chingii*, a relative of *V erubescens*, and described for the first time as recently as 1966, but first discovered in this location in 1940 by the Chinese botanist R C Ching, after whom it is named. It is fairly widespread in Yunnan and favours forest margins and thickets, where it is often stunted and gnarled from browsing. Left alone it makes a shrub of around 2m (7ft), the leaves deciduous or semi-evergreen in a mild winter. The tubular, fragrant, white flowers, pink-tinted on the lobes, are 8mm (⅓ in) long and carried in loose downy clusters at the tips of the branchlets in spring. They are replaced by shining, purplish-black fruits. A plant from the Cangshan was introduced to the

Hypericum latisepalum, a recently named hypericum from the Cangshan. This is a strong-growing shrub with large leaves and large, cup-shaped, rich yellow flowers. It has settled down well in western cultivation, the above specimen flowering in the author's garden in 1987. (July)

Royal Botanic Garden, Edinburgh, and a sucker from this is already more than 2m (6ft) high in my garden, where it thrives. The leaves, which are foetid when bruised, vary from as much as 3.5-9cm (1½-3½in) long, being oval or ovate in shape, toothed and slightly leathery in texture. In my garden in autumn they become tinted above with wine-purple, a most attractive bonus. Having said that, the flowers, although pretty, are lacking in size and substance for it to challenge others of its kind.

The open pastures and cleared woodland areas are a home from home for the many hypericums of the Cangshan. *Hypericum acmosepalum* we found commonly associated with another species, whose bold appearance marked it out as something special. It was a strong-growing shrub of 1.5m (5ft) with comparatively large broad ovate leaves, especially prominent on the main branches. Seeds collected at the time have produced vigorous seedlings that are free-flowering with bold cup-shaped flowers from late summer into early autumn.[26]

One of the most popular and adaptable groups of flowering shrubs for gardens in cool temperate regions are the deutzias, named after the Dutchman, Johan van der Deutz (1743-1788), a friend and patron of the Swedish botanist Carl Thunberg. Most are hardy and easy of cultivation on chalk or acidic soils, flowering mainly in June. It is sometimes argued that these shrubs when not flowering have nothing else to offer the gardener, but this criticism does not take into account the attractive peeling bark of

many species, the elegant habit of some and their reliability. There are several excellent species and hybrids in cultivation and few other shrubs exceed them in 'flower power'.

We were reminded of these qualities several times in the Cangshan, especially in the vicinity of Camp 2 where we found a most attractive deutzia frequent in thickets and clearings. It was a shrub of loose spreading growth to 2m (7ft) high, many specimens just starting into flower. These varied in size and colour, though basically white with some degree of pink or rose-purple staining on the backs of the petals. At first we thought it might be *Deutzia purpurascens*, but on our return to Britain it was identified as *Deutzia calycosa*, a related species, *calycosa* referring to the large sepals of the calyx. Seed was collected from the old capsules of a wide selection of plants and, as expected, the resultant seedlings have proven equally variable in flower.[27]

Viburnum chingii, a species first described in 1966, although discovered in 1940. A relative of the Himalayan *V erubescens*, it was frequent in the Shangchang area and was successfully introduced into western cultivation in 1981. (May)

26. When first examined, this plant was considered by Dr. Norman Robson to be a subspecies of *H bellum*. Subsequently, he described it as a new species under the name *H latisepalum*.

27. In June 1984 at Birr Castle, home of the Earl of Rosse in Co Offaly, Ireland, I was allowed to select two particularly good seedlings of ours for vegetative propagation. One had flowers of good substance, richly stained on the outside, while the flowers of the other were larger, 2cm (¾ in) across, with a shade paler staining. At first we believed our introduction to be the first of this species into western cultivation, but recent evidence suggests that five old plants growing in Peter Cox's garden at Glendoick, Scotland, are the same. These were grown from seed collected by Peter's father and Reginald Farrer in upper Burma in 1919. I should not be at all surprised if Forrest also introduced this shrub, possibly under the name *D purpurascens* or even *D discolor*. Another seedling much admired by visitors in my own garden I have been persuaded to name 'Dali' after the city of that name.

Salix guebrianthiana, a large deciduous shrub or small tree with remarkably long male catkins, grew on the woodland margin close to Camp 2 at Shangchang. (May)

Cladrastis sinensis growing in a ravine below Camp 2 at Shangchang. Peter Hutchison who found it is standing beneath. (May)

Salix guebrianthiana, Cangshan above Camp 2, the female tree with equally long though less ornamental catkins. (May)

Cladrastis sinensis. A rare tree in cultivation here seen in full flower in a garden in Hampshire. (July)

New to cultivation, if only we had succeeded in introducing it, was a most remarkable willow, Salix guebrianthiana, a deciduous shrub or small tree to 6m (19ft) with lance-shaped leaves. What was so special about this willow was the length of its slender, yellow male catkins, which measured as much as 21cm (8in), nor were the females far short of this. It was quite common in clearings and on forest margins at Shangchang and elsewhere in the Cangshan. One handsome specimen by a stream below Camp 2 was growing through the lower branches of a large spreading tree

with bold, deeply divided (pinnate) leaves. On closer examination this turned out to be a wingnut, Pterocarya delavayi, a most handsome species, the downy leaves, 30cm (12in) or more long, made up of fifteen to seventeen leaflets. This tree differs most noticeably from its eastern Chinese counterpart P stenoptera in its non-winged leaf stalk (rachis). In the new Flora of China, P delavayi is now regarded as a variety of P macroptera.

I remember Peter Hutchison scrambling down the gully towards me as I contemplated the wingnut and asking me if I had any idea what a nearby tree might be. This, too, had

Professor Feng and members of the expedition discuss the finding of a rhododendron that Feng believed was R *gastum*, but that David Chamberlain regarded as a hybrid R *arboreum* subspecies *delavayi* x R *decorum*. A flowering specimen is being examined by Tien-lu Ming (standing right). (May)

pinnate leaves but of a different size, texture and appearance and the flowers, which were still in the bud stage, were carried in branched terminal heads rather than in pendulous tassels. It was *Cladrastis sinensis*, a member of the legume family and a Chinese counterpart to the yellow-wood C *kentukea* (C *lutea*) of the south-eastern United States.

C *sinensis* is a superb small- to medium-sized ornamental tree curiously rare in British cultivation. I first met with it in Hilliers old West Hill nursery at Winchester, where it had reached 10m (32ft) on a shallow chalk soil. I remember it flowering in July, every branch tip supporting a large erect conical head (panicle) of white pea flowers that, on closer examination, possessed a faint blush. They were scented, too. It is one of the last trees to break into leaf in spring, while a further characteristic is the swollen base to the leaf stalk (petiole), which conceals a small bud. In my experience it is hardy in British cultivation and is a tree worth considering by gardeners wanting to try something different. E H Wilson, who also found this species in west Sichuan, said that the flowers varied from white to rosy-pink, but I have only seen the white form in cultivation.

Throughout the woods and clearings of the Cangshan there occurred a strong-growing daphne of dense bushy growth that, close to our camp at Shangchang, had produced a specimen of some 4.5m (15ft). It seemed to be evergreen, or partly so, and an early flowerer, for only occasionally did we find the odd white or rose-tinted flower cluster. Once, at Qingbixu on the eastern slopes, we found a plant bearing several orange-red fruits. The Chinese called it *Daphne feddei*, which some recent opinion suggests is no more than D *papyracea*. The latter, however, is native to the western Himalaya, travelling no further east than west Nepal. D *papyracea* is also rare and tender in gardens in Britain, whereas some of the plants of D *feddei* that we saw above Shangchang, and elsewhere at similar altitudes, might prove amenable to cultivation here as is the case with the related and ornamentally superior D *bholua* of the eastern Himalaya.

One of the things that struck us forcibly throughout our time in the Cangshan was the apparent paucity of bird life. Here we were in the breeding season in a range of mountains offering a rich variety of habitats, yet if we saw ten different birds then I am being generous in my estimation. Even the animal life seemed sparse, the largest mammal we saw being a lone red squirrel high on a hillside among the rhododendrons. Interestingly, the bodyguard we had been assigned by the elders of Xiaguan had told us that it was his job to protect us against possible attack by wild animals such as bear, or 'leopard'. With a carbine slung over his shoulder he accompanied our party each time we set out on a trip, even helping us to collect plants on the odd occasion. I never doubted that such animals existed in the Cangshan, it was rugged enough in places, but I fear our numbers must have made the possibilities of encountering such shy creatures rather remote. Indeed, we would have welcomed the

opportunity of seeing a bear certainly – from a safe distance.

The crowning day of our stay at Shangchang was a climb to the summit ridge of the Cangshan. Unfortunately, Bob, having developed a troublesome cough, decided it would be best for him to stay behind, and Clyde who was similarly afflicted kept him company. We left camp at 8am, following a track uphill that skirted the dense forest we had floundered in some days previously. We had intended to reach the secondary ridge above camp as quickly as possible, but plants somehow intervened. One of these was a rhododendron, a tree of some 7.5m (25ft) with rose-coloured flowers in a bold truss. The identity of this tree was the subject of some debate. The Chinese believed it to be R *agastum*, a species first discovered by Forrest north of the Cangshan in 1913. David, on the other hand, thought that the tree was a hybrid between the red flowered R *arboreum* subspecies *delavayi* and R *decorum*, and Peter Cox agreed with him. The lobes of the

A bodyguard assigned to us against possible attack by 'wild animals'. Here above Camp 2. (May)

Rhododendron cyanocarpum was one of the few species flowering on the ridge above Camp 2 at Shangchang. It is related to the Himalayan R *thomsonii* and is, in effect, a pink- or white-flowered version of this well-known red-flowered species. (May)

Viburnum nervosum, a handsome shrub in flower and leaf, occurred as scattered individuals on the ridge above Shangchang and elsewhere in the Cangshan. It is unaccountably rare in western cultivation. (May)

flower varied from five to seven which, David pointed out, showed the influence of R *decorum*. I am not sure what the end result of this argument was but I shall always carry in my mind the scene of the debate. A group of enthusiasts on a high hillside, some standing, pencils and notebooks in hands and, in the centre, sitting on the ground, Professor Feng in full flow, occasionally jabbing his finger at the specimen as it was passed from hand to hand.

It was not long afterwards that we reached the ridge track at 3,050m (10,000ft), whence we had a superb view of the surrounding terrain. We could see Yangbi far below in its valley, west to the hills above the Mekong river and southwards across the intervening ridges to the site of Camp 1 at Dapingdi. Soon we were hard at work climbing the steep hillside, following a track that wound its way through a vast forest composed almost entirely of *Rhododendron* species in which no tree rose much higher than 5m (16ft). It was like a setting from a story by the brothers Grimm, with gnarled and leaning stems clothed with moss and lichen huddled together for protection against the wind. Several species of *Rhododendron* were represented, each giving way to another as we ascended. Since leaving camp we had already seen *decorum*, *yunnanense*, *arboreum* subspecies *delavayi*, *edgeworthii* and *sinogrande*. Now above the tree line there appeared *rex*

subspecies *fictolacteum*, *rubiginosum*, *trichocladum*, *cyanocarpum*, *haematodes*, *heliolepis*, *lacteum* and *selense* subspecies *jucundum*.

Rhododendron cyanocarpum was one of the few species in flower and reminded me of a pink- or white-flowered version of R *thomsonii* that I had first seen in the wild in east Nepal in 1971. Indeed, it is a close relative of that species but confined, apparently, to the Cangshan where it was first discovered by Delavay and later introduced, from the eastern flank, by Forrest. Not for the first time did we feel the great Scotsman's presence. On these exposed slopes R *cyanocarpum*, whose name refers to the bluish-bloomy seed capsules, formed dense thickets up to 4m (13ft) high under which we walked bent almost double at times. Soon R *lacteum* joined the throng, threatening the other's dominance in places and, on one occasion, entirely clothing a north-west facing slope. This is another Forrest introduction, first collected by him from the Cangshan in 1910, though Delavay, again, was its original discoverer.

To full-blooded rhododendron enthusiasts, R *lacteum* is one of the species to grow, principally because of its canary-yellow flowers. The fact that it is not an easy species in cultivation, being slow and fussy, shy at seeding and difficult to layer, serves to make it all the more desirable to its admirers. I remember being approached by such an enthusiast at one of the Royal Horticultural Society's shows

Bergenia purpurascens, previously known under the name *B delavayi*, was common in the Cangshan, here above Camp 2. (May)

in London just before we left on the expedition. He made a request for seed of any rhododendron we might find and above all others of *R lacteum*. His eyes sparkled when I asked 'Why *lacteum* specially?', and he proceeded to tell me of his lifelong interest – love affair almost – in this species. Whether his request was eventually met I know not, for although plenty of seed was collected, I have not met him since.

Seed of *R lacteum* had already been collected by Peter Cox and David above Camp 1, but now Peter, with the assistance of Peter Hutchison, set to work on the rich harvest before us, working as though there was no tomorrow. The flower colour in this species is somewhat variable, there being darker and paler shades of yellow. Indeed the Chinese name for the plant means the 'milky yellow rhododendron'. To our eternal regret *R lacteum* in the Cangshan during our visit was not in flower. Judging, however, by the abundance of seed from the previous year, it must have been, to quote Peter Cox, 'a sight for the gods'. The two Peters did, however, open several swollen flower buds, all but one of them revealing good yellows with or without a red blotch and with no hint of pink.[28]

Leaving our colleagues collecting seed, David and I together with some of the Chinese continued up the track through the pygmy forest. Apart from the rhododendrons, the only other sizeable shrubs present were *Juniperus recurva* variety *coxii*, *Ilex delavayi*, a deciduous holly of limited merit, a stunted *Sorbus* species of the rowan group, and *Viburnum nervosum*. The last named, under the name *V cordifolium*, I had first seen in east

Nepal in 1971, and again as recently as October 1980 on Emei Shan in west Sichuan, its big bold leaves giving rich autumn tints. Here, in the Cangshan – and we saw it on several occasions – it was in flower, the bold dense clusters of white flowers decorating the dark twiggy branches, which were still naked or with the leaves freshly emerged. Often, from afar we saw this plant looking for all the world like small isolated snow patches on the dark hillside.

Beneath the canopy the ground was covered in a rich green carpet of moss in which several dwarf shrubs and herbs flourished. *Rhododendron haematodes* was quite plentiful here as low thickets, though not in flower, nor were any seedlings to be seen, most of those we came across belonging to *R lacteum*.

We found a small creeping evergreen shrublet whose slender erect stems to 10cm (4in) were clothed with tiny bronzed and toothed leaves, 1cm (½in) or slightly longer. It favoured mossy banks and hummocks in sun or shade and resembled *Gaultheria trichophylla*, another of my Nepalese favourites, but it has since been identified as *G cardiosepala*, the name referring to the heart-shaped sepals. It was a pity we did not see it flowering on this occasion, for *G cardiosepala* is distinct among a group of similar species because of its urn-shaped flowers, which are white or sometimes pink tinged. The fruits are apparently variable in colour, from white to blue. Out of flower it differs from *G trichophylla* in its smooth (glabrous) leaves, those of *G trichophylla* being margined with long hairs (ciliate). *G cardiosepala* was collected several times on the Cangshan by Forrest and also by Rock.

Bergenia purpurascens was frequent in the form once known as *B delavayi* with dark purplish-rose flowers, and in one place was accompanied by *Fritillaria cirrhosa*, its slender erect

28. According to Peter Cox, *R lacteum* is susceptible to root rots and does much better when grafted. He has several plants from Cangshan seed growing well raised up on logs in wet ground in his Argyllshire garden.

Notholirion bulbuliferum flowering at the Edinburgh Royal Botanic Garden in 1987 from stock collected in the Cangshan in 1981. (June)

stems carrying a single large nodding bell-shaped flower, pale yellow in colour with a darker freckling within. Another bulbous plant in the rhododendron thicket was *Notholirion bulbuliferum*. At the time it was merely a clump of strap-shaped leaves, but bulbs introduced to the Royal Botanic Garden, Edinburgh, established well, producing strong erect stems up to 1m (3ft) high of drooping pink bell flowers with green mouths, which, according to Ron McBeath, were most attractive. All the more pity that this species tends to be monocarpic (dying after seeding), and therefore needs to be re-established each time from seed or bulbils, which are freely produced round the spent bulb.

Ron McBeath also reported to me the flowering of a gentian – *Gentiana melandriifolia*, seedlings of which were collected in the same area. In its native turf in May it is represented by a basal tuft of long-stalked leaves, in shape not unlike the basal leaves of a campion (Melandrium), giving no hint as to its likely potential. At Edinburgh,

Primula sonchifolia photographed in the Cangshan by George Forrest in the early 1900s. He famously introduced plants packed into bamboo sections encased in ice.

Primula sonchifolia, a native of high mountain pastures in west China and the borders of south-east Tibet and upper Burma. It was plentiful on the summit ridge of the Cangshan, flowering where snow had only recently melted. (May)

Primula sonchifolia, the plump overwintering 'bud' opens in spring to release the foliage and flowers. Here seen near the Cangshan's summit ridge. (May)

according to McBeath, it is quite an attractive plant and different from all the other autumn flowering gentians in its larger leaves, up to 10cm (4in). Its funnel-shaped flowers are a deep clear blue with darker stripes on the outside. It was first discovered and first collected in the Cangshan by Delavay and Forrest respectively.

The real glory of these slopes, however, was provided by a Chinese primula, which occurred both in moist depressions in the rhododendron thickets and in the alpine pastures in between. No ordinary primula this, but *Primula sonchifolia*, one of the loveliest and most aristocratic of a section full of alpine treasures. This species persists through the winter above ground as a plump fleshy resting bud enclosed in broad-based scale leaves with stiff pointed, almost horny, tips. When the snow melts and the soil begins to warm up in early spring these are pushed asunder by a sheaf of jaggedly toothed leaves sprinkled with a fine creamy-white meal (farina). Almost immediately, the flowering stems appear, from one to several per crown, developing slowly at first, lengthening

more rapidly later in the fruiting stage. The flowers begin to open almost as soon as they emerge from the leaf sheath and are carried in a bold loose head, each flower as much as 1.5-2.5cm (½-1in) across and varying slightly in shades of blue with a yellow eye ringed with white. Most of the flowers we saw were ice-blue or lavender-blue and once, above Camp 3, we found a choice white form. Above Shangchang, at 3,500m (11,472ft), in the shade of the rhododendrons, the flowerheads were just emerging, while elsewhere they were fully open. *P sonchifolia* made a sensational sight, especially on those slopes exposed to the sun, for there it flowered in great numbers, spangling the tired brown turf so recently released from winter's grip.

A native of high mountain pastures in western China (Sichuan and Yunnan) and the borders of south-east Tibet and upper Burma, this famous primula was known to most, if not all, the early plant hunters who travelled these regions. At least one of them, Farrer, painted its portrait, and most of them attempted to introduce it as seed. There were many failures until someone realised that success

213

Juniperus squamata, growing in an exposed situation high above Camp 2 in the Cangshan. (May)

would only accompany such attempts if the seed was picked and sent home while still in the 'green' stage, its viability decreasing rapidly afterwards.

The first successful introductions of this plant to western cultivation, however, were as living plants, and there is a famous story concerning Forrest, told to me by Bill Mackenzie, for many years Curator of the Chelsea Physic Garden. As a young man in the propagation department at the Royal Botanic Garden, Edinburgh, he remembered helping to unpack Forrest's plant collections from the seventh and final expedition of 1931/2. These had arrived after news had reached Edinburgh of Forrest's sudden death in the field. The business of unpacking, Bill told me was, as a result, a relatively subdued affair. He remembered emptying baskets of plants in which were lily bulbs packed in red clay to protect and keep them moist. Most intriguing of all was the receipt of *P sonchifolia* crowns (resting buds) that had been crammed into 1m (3ft) lengths of bamboo cane before being packed in ice for the long journey home, a journey that in those days by land and sea could take many weeks, months even.

In cultivation *P sonchifolia* requires a moisture-laden atmosphere if it is to thrive and is ideally suited to peat wall cultivation, especially in the northern areas of Britain where it is most successful. Peter Cox told me his father once established it by a burn in the woodland garden at Glendoick where it flourished for many years, and Peter has since re-established it there.[29]

Finally, the track emerged from the rhododendron thicket on to open slopes with scattered rhododendron scrub mostly low and moulded by the wind. The only other woody plant here appeared to be *Juniperus squamata*. Low and compact in the open, in the shelter of the scrub lower down it reached 2m (6ft) or more, with long ascending arm-like branches tightly crowded with green needle-like leaves giving the branchlets a compact moss-like appearance. These were by far the tallest forms of *J squamata* I have seen, their compact growth no doubt a result of the altitude and exposure.

At last we stood on the summit ridge, which, at this point was 3,840m (12,600ft) above sea level. It was an exhilarating experience and the Chinese and I sang and laughed and danced a little jig, or whatever is the equivalent dance in Yunnan. David, too, was elated but although he posed with us for photographs he could hardly wait to get to grips with the rhododendrons, which formed low islands of leaf, but alas no flower, along the bevelled crest of the ridge.

A cold wind had blown us up the last slope to the crest, but lying down below the crest on the eastern side it was relatively warm and what a wonderful view met our gaze. Far below lay the Er-hai and it seemed to be an easy walk down the eastern slopes, which were bathed in sun and inviting. There appeared to be little if any forest such as we had explored at Shangchang, though our view was necessarily a restricted one. Except for the odd patch in a sheltered ravine, the snow had melted, though only recently, and the ground was still wet. Signs of imminent growth were everywhere apparent and we wondered what flowers would stud the turf in a month's time.

David, meanwhile, had made some initial conclusions about the rhododendrons. There appeared to be a mixture of three kinds, including dwarfed *Rhododendron lacteum* whose leaves seemed little reduced by the exposure. The most common by far was a plant that David and Peter initially suspected was *R roxieanum* variety *cucullatum*, subsequently changing their mind in favour of *R taliense*. This formed a gnarled compact bush up to 1m (3ft) in exposure and up to 1.5m (5ft) in shelter. The leaves were rather variable in size with recurved margins and the undersurface covered with a thick, reddish-brown, woolly pelt of hairs (indumentum). *R taliense* takes its name from the Cangshan (Tali Range), indeed, the Chinese name for this plant, 'da li dujuan', means 'Dali rhododendron'. It was first discovered here by Delavay and later introduced by Forrest.

Our brief sojourn on the summit ridge was followed by a comparatively rapid return, for some of the party at least, and we were still talking of our experience when we retired to our tents that night.

29. It is also flourishing in the garden at Cluny in Perthshire and elsewhere.

View from 3,840m (12,600ft) on the summit ridge of the Cangshan down the east flank to the Er-hai below. Thickets of rhododendrons dwarfed by wind and winter snow comprise several species including *Rhododendron lacteum*, *R taliense* and *R haematodes*. (May)

Rhododendron scrub on summit ridge of Cangshan, windblasted *R lacteum* and *R taliense*. (May)

Some of the team members on the summit ridge of Cangshan with carpets of *Rhododendron* species in the background. (May)

Cornus capitata was common on the dry sun-drenched slopes of the Cangshan below Shangchang. (May)

Myrsine semiserrata, an evergreen tree with remarkably coloured fruits, was fairly common on the hillside below Shangchang. (May)

To Dali and Camp 3

We left Camp 2 for the last time on 10 May, heading down the valley towards civilisation. There was plenty to attract our interest as the track wound through fragments of forest in which many trees and vines flourished. The two snake-bark maples kept us company and we were interested to note one of them, *Acer davidii*, as low as 2,316m (7,600ft), which helps explain why this species is of variable hardiness in cultivation. One tree in my garden from a low level seed collection in the Cangshan persists in growing until well into autumn, these soft extensions invariably falling prey to frost.

With the maples in the thicket grew a large mock orange, *Philadelphus delavayi*,[30] its rich fragrance detectable long before we located its flowers. It was a vigorous shrub of 4m (13ft) or more, with stout smooth (glabrous) shoots and remarkably large leaves, some of which, on strong shoots, measured 15cm by 10cm (6in by 4in). The pure white flowers borne in short racemes along the branches were 2.5-3.5cm (1-1½ in) across with golden anthers and a greyish (glaucous) green calyx. Seed was collected from the previous year's capsules and, from the resultant seedlings, a plant in my garden flowered for the first time in 1985 in late May/early June.

All too soon we were on the hot dry slopes again, a

change made more tolerable by the frequency of a handsome evergreen flowering dogwood, *Cornus capitata*, multi-stemmed shrubs of 5m (16ft) and, once, a single-stemmed tree of 12m (40ft). The dogwoods were in flower, the central knob of tiny green flowers surrounded by the large bracts, four in number, of a pale sulphur-yellow. In the wild this species has a wide distribution from the Punjab along the Himalaya to south-west and central China. It is a

Cornus capitata fruiting in a garden in Hampshire. (November)

30. It is named after the French missionary Jean Delavay who first found it in 1887, introducing it as seed to the Jardin des Plantes in Paris. It was later introduced on several occasions by Forrest.

Indigofera balfouriana, a small deciduous shrub thriving on the dry slopes below Shangchang. It has only recently been introduced to cultivation in Britain. (May)

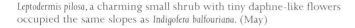

Leptodermis pilosa, a charming small shrub with tiny daphne-like flowers occupied the same slopes as *Indigofera balfouriana*. (May)

magnificent sight when in flower and the succulent red fruit-clusters are also attractive, but in Britain it is only suitable for the warmer areas of the south and west.

Myrsine semiserrata, an evergreen tree of dense leafy growth, occurred fairly commonly around 2,440m (8,000ft) and below, where it reached 3m (10ft). Although this is not hardy enough to be grown out of doors in Britain, except perhaps in the mildest locations, it did bring back for me an amusing recollection. When I first joined Hillier Nurseries in 1962, in the greenhouse containing tender stock plants at the Winchester nursery grew an evergreen shrub that had never been known to flower. It was labelled *Ilex fragilis*. Although a few plants had been grown from cuttings, I am not aware any were ever sold. Then, one year in the late 1960s, it flowered: tiny insignificant greenish-yellow flowers crowded along the branchlets. These were noted by the chief propagator, the late Arthur Prior, who did not think, however, that they merited bringing to anyone's attention and he was right. Then, strangely for a holly whose flowers are normally dioecious (male and female on separate plants), the flowers gave way to fruits. It was not long before Mr Prior asked me to come and look at them for they did not look like any holly he had ever seen. I was surprised, too, for in ripening the berries were changing colour from pink to mauve and then blue, a most striking combination, almost unreal, like some manufactured Christmas decoration. The berries studded the shoots and, though obviously not those of a holly, we could not decide to which genus the plant might belong. Specimens were sent to Kew and back came the answer: *Myrsine semiserrata*! The plants on the hillside below

Camp 2 were also in fruit and quite spectacular, causing much comment and not a little surprise among the Chinese when we were able to name this plant without hesitation.

Not since the hills around Beijing had I seen indigoferas in such profusion. These shrubby members of the pea family are comparatively neglected in British cultivation. They love the sun, and the lower slopes of the Cangshan above Yangbi provided ideal conditions for at least two species, *Indigofera rigioclada* and *Indigofera balfouriana*, both of which appeared variable in height from 1-2m (3-6ft) with dense clusters (racemes) of rose-purple flowers along the length of the stems. The smaller forms were smothered with flowers and quite spectacular.

Accompanying them and obviously relishing the same conditions of heat and a dry stony soil was *Leptodermis pilosa*, a rather twiggy shrub 1.5-2m (5-6ft) high with pairs of small green leaves about 1.5cm (½ in) long and loose clusters of pink-tinted white flowers 1.5-2cm (½ - ¾ in) long. These flowers are absolutely charming when examined closely, the slender curving funnel of the tube spreading wide at the mouth into five lobes, and the pink coloration occurring on the tube and in a pretty star arrangement around the mouth. The flowers also carry a sweet fragrance likened by some to that of a daphne – indeed, the flower is not unlike a little daphne flower. Seen overall, the bush in bloom appears to be sparkling with a myriad of tiny stars. It is native to Yunnan and is yet another example of the old Franco-British 'one-two', Delavay's discovery and Forrest's introduction. It is rare in cultivation, not surprising considering its requirements, but where conditions suit, especially on a chalk or sandy soil, it is

Terraced fields in a valley below Shangchang produce an abstract picture of colour and light. Golden fields of winter wheat await harvesting, while others already flooded and ploughed are ready to receive a crop of rice, the young plants of which fill nursery beds with emerald green. (May)

worth giving a trial. It would certainly find a home from home in places like the Mediterranean and California.

The belly of the valley in its lower reaches was a scene of great activity. Here were terraced fields in many colours and in various stages of cultivation. Gold marked the winter wheat, ripe and awaiting harvesting, green the seedling rice in nursery beds awaiting planting. In between were fields being ploughed, the water buffaloes straining at their yokes, their hides as grey as the mud they trampled, and pulling wooden ploughs with metal plough shares. Then there were flooded fields, their still waters mirroring the sky and passing clouds. Above this band of cultivation the hillsides were desolate, their trees destroyed, their topsoil long since lost to the elements.

That afternoon we were back in Yangbi, and after a meeting with the elders we were treated to a film in the local cinema, an entertainment we were to remember for a long time. No earth-returning astronauts could have enjoyed such attention. Led by the elders and Professor Feng, we walked in single file from our accommodation to the cinema. Every inch of our route was packed with people, young and old, anxious to get a close look at us. Bob's hairy legs were an object of interest and one daring lady actually plucked at them. Seats had been reserved and for two hours or more we were treated to a film about the Bai (a Yunnan minority group) called 'The Five Flowers'. It had been filmed in the Dali area and, naturally, attracted considerable local interest. The dialogue, of course, was in Chinese and we were treated to a continuous whispered translation by Clyde. It was certainly colourful and it was fun and a welcome break from botanical exploration.

On our return to Xiaguan next day, we stopped off at a hot springs baths for a much-needed clean up. It lay close to the road in the Er-hai Gorge and the hot spring was situated in the rocks on the hillside above, its emergent temperature considerably cooled by the time it entered the baths. Each bath was sunk in the ground, measured about 2.5m (8ft) square and was faced with marble. It can accommodate a whole family and probably does, the British team members being allowed the luxury of one each. A continuous supply of water

comes in at one end of the bath and goes out through a hole at the other. One simply blocks the exit with a wooden bung then sits or lies on the floor of the bath and waits for the water level to rise. The depth of immersion is a matter of personal comfort, for the water is piping hot and I suspect fluctuates in temperature from day to day. Certainly, on our three visits, there was one occasion when immersion was barely pleasurable, another when it was a test of stamina and a third when it was impossible. We also took the opportunity, when the water level was low, of washing our shirts and underwear, an operation itself not without hazard as Peter Hutchison found one day when, after an accident with his bung, he was mortified to see various items of clothing disappearing with the water through the hole. He momentarily considered giving chase in an attempt to retrieve them before they reached the river, changing his mind however when his initial shouts attracted a crowd of Chinese into his bathroom.

That night in the guest house dining room in Xiaguan, we were served with a special fish taken from the Er-hai. The fish had first been put in an earthenware pot and immersed in a soup with twenty different kinds of vegetable. That pot was then placed in a larger pot and cooked in an oven. The result was exquisite!

Dali is one of the most famous cities in botanical history and one of a trio of Chinese cities that readily come to mind when botanical exploration in China is discussed. The others are Ichang (now Yichang) in Hubei province and Tachienlu (now Kangding) in Sichuan province. Dali, or Tali-fu as it was previously known, has given shelter to many plant hunters including some of the most famous such as Delavay, Potanin, Forrest, Kingdon-Ward and Rock, as well as botanists like Handel-Mazzetti, Schneider and travellers like Henri, Prince d'Orléans.

In 1905 it was to Dali that George Forrest returned after almost losing his life at the hands of murderous lamas in the mountains of the Mekong-Salween divide. He later wrote: 'After exceptional hardships, extending over a period of twenty three days and hairbreadth escapes, I managed to get down the river to safety, but at the loss of all my collections, and personal belongings. I reached Tali-fu in safety, but in a

A bad case of rust fungus on a hypericum in the hills above Yangbe. (May)

Dali (middle distance) with the Er-hai beyond. Taken from a height of 305m (1,000ft) above the city on the eastern flank of the Cangshan by George Forrest in July 1906. The lower slopes are dotted with Chinese graves, while beyond are the workings of marble quarries

shockingly weak condition about the end of August'. Tragically, two of Forrest's companions at the start of the flight, the French missionaries Père Bourdonnec and Père Dubernard, were later captured by the lamas and horribly put to death. Forrest's original account of the above incident, given in a letter to Sir Isaac Bayley Balfour at Edinburgh, is one of the most exciting and hair-raising real-life adventures I have ever read and vividly illustrates the difficulties some plant hunters in China faced in the early 1900s.

Forrest met with trouble again in 1913, this time in Dali itself. He was returning to the Burmese border after a successful season in the Lijiang (Likiang) area to the north. 'The day I entered the city, the local soldiery, some 3,000 troops, mutinied, shot down their officers when on morning parade and captured the city. I was kept prisoner for fully

three weeks and forced, along with my friend the Rev Mr Hanna, to act as medical attendant to the wounded of the troops, in constant danger of our lives. Fortunately, assistance arrived in time, loyal troops were hurried up from the provincial capital Yunnan-fu [now Kunming], Tali being stormed and after much bloodshed retaken on 24 December'. Not surprisingly, although Christmas Eve, Forrest was packed and ready to leave the next day, no doubt celebrating Hogmanay – in true Scottish tradition – a week later.

Despite the occasional hazards, Forrest used Dali on many occasions, either as a base or as an overnight stop. It stands on the main road north to the famous Yulong Shan or Jade Dragon Mountains above Lijiang (Likiang), another of Forrest's favourite haunts, and carries an important route into Tibet. Of course, Dali was famous long before

The missionaries Père Bourdonnec (left) and Père Dubernard in the French Catholic missionary station at Tseku, north-west Yunnan in 1905. The same year, whilst fleeing (with George Forrest) the approach of lamas on the war path, they were captured and most horribly put to death. Forrest escaped

George Forrest standing beneath a tree of *Prunus majestica* in Dali. This rare cherry is a close relative of the Carmine cherry, *P cerasoides* variety *rubea*, and is not, to the author's knowledge, at present in western cultivation. The photograph was taken by Joseph Rock in May 1922

Two of the Dali pagodas photographed by Joseph Rock in 1922. Three years after the picture was taken the top of the main pagoda (right) was sent crashing to the ground during an earthquake

Dali, the south gate in 1981. The plaque bearing the city's name is made from the local   or 'Dali stone'. This plain design has now been restored to its former glory. (May)

One of the three pagodas near Dali restored in 1978/80. Two of the pagodas, of which this is one, are 1m (3ft) out of perpendicular, presumably as a result of an earthquake. (May)

the age of the plant hunter and explorer. It was the ancient capital of the Bai people, one of Yunnan's several national minority groups. The Bai people had already been living in the Er-hai region for a long time when the western Han Dynasty 206 BC-AD 220 was established. In the eighth century AD the capital city was Taihe, whose ruins lie some 7km (4½ miles) from Dali. Taihe fell into disuse in the tenth century when what is now Dali was established. Three hundred years later came the Mongol conquest and the Bai kingdom was incorporated into Yunnan province. It was during this time that Marco Polo arrived on the scene: 'On leaving Yachi [Kunming] and continuing westwards for ten days, the traveller reaches the Kingdom of Karajang, the capital of which is also called Karajang'. Polo went on to describe one of the 'attractions' of the area: 'In this province live huge snakes and serpents of such size that no one could help being amazed even to hear of them'. He described them as loathsome to behold, ten paces in length and as thick as a stout cask. 'Their eyes are so bulging', he confides, 'that they are bigger than loaves', while 'their mouth is big enough to swallow a man at one gulp'. From the rest of his description, Polo's serpents begin to resemble crocodiles, which is hardly likely; most probably, his was an interpretation of an even older story or legend relating to a great snake or serpent of Er-hai that constantly whipped up the water causing floods in the villages and fields around. A young man named Duan Chicheng vowed to rid the people of this menace. Accordingly, with a sword in each hand and with sharp knives tied to his body, he jumped into the lake to fight the serpent. The monster swallowed him, but was killed by the blades. In gratitude

Dali, the south gate restored to its original state, photographed in 1986. Note free use of 'Dali stone', and the already established weeds on the walls.(Sept.)

to the brave but dead man the local people built a pagoda in his memory.

The Snake Bone Pagoda, built AD 820, can still be seen not far from Dali and when we saw it, it had a tree of some kind growing from its roof and a garnishing of lesser vegetation. It is said to be the oldest pagoda in south China. Also just outside the city is a group of three beautiful cream-coloured pagodas, two leaning, which are all that remain of the Chong Sheng Temple. Built in the Tang Dynasty in the ninth century, this apparently splendid Buddhist temple was once the most important in all China, a magnet to pilgrims from all over the empire as well as from neighbouring countries. The tallest pagoda at 69m (227ft) is divided into sixteen storeys, while the others, situated to north and south are 41m (135ft) high and comprise ten storeys. The two smaller pagodas have been about 1m (3ft) out of perpendicular for four hundred years, presumably as a result of an earthquake. In 1514 a severe earthquake caused a split reaching from top to bottom and 1m (3ft) wide in the main pagoda, and during another earthquake, in 1925, the top of the same pagoda was sent crashing to the ground. After liberation in 1961, the area was declared a protected site and seventeen years later, in 1978, the pagodas underwent major repair and refurbishing, a task completed in 1980, during which many artefacts were found including a small solid gold figure of Buddha.

Today Dali is the principal town of Dali County and part of the Dali Bai Autonomous Prefecture. It is dominated by the Cangshan, but is situated in the middle of a green plain that slopes gently from the foot of the mountains down to the Er-hai. Thus, it was with an air of great expectancy and mindful of its long, colourful and, at times, turbulent history, that we approached Dali on a bright morning on 12 May.

Like Roman cities, Dali was built to a rectangular design

with four stout defensive walls with a gate in each. Sadly, the walls, with two of their gates, the east and west, had been dismantled. Professor Wu, of the Yunnan Institute of Botany, later told us that when he first visited the city forty-one years ago the walls were intact. We asked to be allowed to leave our transport and walk through the massive south gate with its red plastered walls and to this our host agreed. Having entered Dali with due reverence, we reboarded our minibus for the drive to the guest house. We passed along the main street with its wooden-fronted houses, driving slowly because of the people milling around. It was market day and the local shops with wares displayed through open

Dali. A street leading to the west gate and the Cangshan beyond, photographed by Joseph Rock in May 1922. This gate has since been dismantled

Dali, the main street on market day looking south. Photographed by George Forrest in the early 1900s. Note the style of the south gate which has now been restored.

Dali, the main street looking south. As in the earlier photograph (left) the line of the Cangshan can be seen running to the right (west) of the city. (May)

windows were supplemented by numerous itinerant traders whose goods were spread upon the ground. I have never experienced such activity. The bustle and noise was as I imagine a street in medieval England.

There were queer-looking vegetables, potatoes and walnuts in great piles, and fish, chicken and pancakes were being boiled, fried or baked 'while you wait'. We saw craftsmen making and mending shoes and waistcoats, selling bedsprings, pots, kettles and pans, bamboo baskets, hats and firewood. One could buy a potion or a tonic from

a seller of native remedies, or select a slab of marble for one's home. Several people were making coal nobs, mixing coal dust and mud and spooning it out to dry on the pavement. Most people seemed to be dressed in grey, black or faded blue. Indeed, take away the modern tunics, the ubiquitous overhead cables (the scourge of modern China) and the equally ubiquitous planted eucalyptus and I doubt that a returning Forrest would have noticed much amiss.

After a splendid banquet with the city elders, we left Dali intent on reaching the site for Camp 3 before

A meat seller in the main street, Dali. Note the young specimen of *Magnolia delavayi* with the bamboo guard. (May)

A group of Bai women outside a marble workshop in Dali. (May)

nightfall. We were assigned extra personnel including two guides, who doubled as guards – in which capacity they had pistols and carbines. Having driven out of the city through the north gate we turned off the main road to follow a track, our guides called it a 'road', which snaked its way up the Cangshan's eastern slopes. Our 'road' rapidly degenerated into something suspiciously like a dry river bed, which our driver attacked with renewed determination. For several kilometres, we lurched and crashed our way across a rocky treeless terrain, the only colour provided by golden *Stellera chamaejasme* variety *chrysantha*, which was everywhere, and purple *Pleione yunnanensis*, which splashed grassy banks and rills. After several hair-raising escapades, our driver pushed his luck once too often and the bus became well and truly jammed between two large boulders. There was nothing for it but to leave the bus and finish the journey on foot, arriving in camp just as the light was fading.

Camp 3 was situated at the end of a rough road at 3,200m (10,494ft), the highest of our camps, and overlooked Er-hai. Through a deep ravine, along which rushed a stream, we could see Dali some 1,220m (4,000ft) below on the plain. It was, perhaps, our most spectacular camp, surrounded as it was by limestone cliffs and crags with waterfalls and dense forest full of rhododendrons. These included *Rhododendron neriiflorum*, its ruby-red flowers gleaming

A girl in Dali making fuel nobs from coal dust and mud and placing them to dry on the side of the street. (May)

Dali and the Cangshan in early spring. A photograph taken by George Forrest in 1906. Note the lowest limit of the snow and two of the three pagodas – all that remain of the ninth century Chong Sheng Temple

Camp 3 was situated at the end of a rough road at 3,200m (10,494ft) on the Cangshan's east flank overlooking Dali. The slopes above were clothed with scrub in which *Rhododendron trichocladum, Hypericum subsessile, Deutzia subulata* and *Clethra delavayi* occurred. (May)

like jewels in the gloom, and *R sulfureum* and *R edgeworthii* in goodly number, both clinging to precipices and rock stacks and we wondered if seed gathered from this altitude might produce hardier forms than those usually grown.

Immediately above the camp was an extensive area of hillside covered with the deciduous *R trichocladum* in full bloom, dense erect-stemmed bushes 1-1.5m (3-5ft) high, the yellow flowers appearing with, or just before, the leaves. The colour varied slightly and the best forms were a clear yellow with attractively bronzed young foliage as a bonus. We saw this species on several occasions and invariably it occurred in open situations in full sun.

On a moss-covered boulder in the forest one day we found *R dichroanthum*, the typical form endemic to the Cangshan, a low-growing shrub to 30cm (12in), but it was too early for flowering.[31] One of the most exciting finds at Camp 3 was the silver fir *Abies delavayi*, first discovered in the Cangshan by Delavay in 1884. It also occurs in the mountains westwards into upper Burma and north-east Assam. At Camp 3 we saw it as scattered individuals along the ridges forming small woods in steep ravines and gullies. The largest specimens were mostly to be found in inaccessible places, while one we measured on a steep slope above the track was 12m (40ft) with a girth of 204cm (80in) at chest height.

There appeared to be two forms of the fir, no doubt induced by altitude. In the lower parts of its range – around and above our camp – it had pale reddish-brown hairless shoots with similarly coloured slightly resinous buds, which were globose-conical and conspicuous. Second-year shoots were slightly greyer-brown and peeling. The leaves stood up above the shoots, spreading on either side. Those beneath the shoots tended to lie forward, except for a few that spread widely. They varied in length from 2cm (¾ in) on the upper sides of the older shoots to 3.5cm (1½ in) on the previous year's shoots, and were 2mm (⅟₁₆ in) wide on average and notched at the apex. In colour they were a shining dark green above, marked with two conspicuous white stomatal bands beneath. There were a number of smaller leaves clustered around the base of the terminal buds. On some shoots there was an irregular V-shaped depression above, but this was never distinct or obvious. As we climbed higher, we noted a gradual change in branch and leaf form until, at a height of 3,880m (12,724ft), where the last specimens were seen, older trees certainly had the branchlets more distinctly ascending from the branches, while the leaves were shorter, more congested and spread all round the shoot in the manner of the Spanish fir *A pinsapo*. The average leaf length was 18-19mm (¾ in), while the white undersurfaces were less conspicuous due to the strongly revolute margins. On older shoots the leaf margins met beneath, completely concealing the stomatal bands. In cultivation in Britain *A delavayi* is very rare, many of

31. Plants have since flowered at Glendoick Gardens and elsewhere from seed collected above Camp 3.

Abies delavayi growing among limestone crags and cliffs above Camp 3 on the Cangshan's eastern flank. (May)

Below. *Abies delavayi* growing in its type location on the east flank of the Cangshan. The shrub layer beneath mainly comprises rhododendrons of several species. Photograph taken by Joseph Rock in 1922

Abies delavayi, underside of shoot from a tree above Camp 3 on the Cangshan. (May)

Below. The striking blue cones of *Abies delavayi* on a young tree at Glendoick grown from seed collected in the Cangshan in 1981. (June)

Pinus armandii growing in the Waterfall Valley above Dali. (May)

Rhododendron rex subspecies *fictolacteum*; one of the few flower trusses we found in the valleys near Huadianba. Note the richly-coloured indumentum on the leaf undersurface. (May)

the trees so labelled having been reassigned to the closely related *A fabri* from west-central Sichuan. The largest specimen of *A delavayi*, probably from a Forrest collection, grows at Rowallane in Co. Down, N. Ireland. In 2000 this tree measured 21.7m. (71ft.)

Our campsite was situated on one of the numerous lateral ridges running on an east-west axis. Close by a deep, well-wooded valley provided an excellent example of the tree species and their altitudinal sequence. This was especially noticeable with the conifers. *Pinus armandii* came up the valley from lower regions to be replaced by *P yunnanensis*, which, however, did not ascend much more than 100m (328ft) above us. *Tsuga dumosa* was common below and just above our campsite, while *Abies delavayi* began here and gradually assumed dominance the higher it climbed. The company was completed by the presence of two junipers, *Juniperus recurva* and *J squamata*, neither of which was dominant, occurring as scattered individuals. The former we saw on several occasions here, always above 3,000m (9,842ft) and, where it had not been butchered, it made a beautiful tree up to 5m (16ft) with weeping branches densely clothed in rich green leaves, quite the equal to variety *coxii*, if indeed this was not the 'real McCoy'. Nowhere, however, did we see sizeable specimens on the eastern flank, these, no doubt, having been long since felled.

J squamata here was a small spreading or shortly ascending shrub of dense habit. Once, among rocks above camp, we found a low wide-spreading juniper with ascending branches clothed in rich green foliage, the spitting image, I believe, of the plant in cultivation grown as *J recurva* 'Embley Park'. Interestingly, the latter is one of several seedlings once grown at Embley Park, near Romsey, Hampshire, from seed collected by Forrest's native collectors (possibly in the Cangshan) in 1929.

Another plant first discovered here by Delavay – and also bearing his name – is *Clethra delavayi*, which we found in the thicket above camp at a height of approximately 3,400m (11,154ft). Here it formed spreading shrubs up to 2m (6ft) with bronze-coloured young growths. We were, of course, too early for flowers, but last year's seed heads still hung on

the branches.[32] This is one of the most distinguished of flowering shrubs in cultivation where, however, it is somewhat less than hardy. In common with others of its clan it requires an acid soil and in the right conditions can develop into a small tree. In Britain and Ireland it is best seen in the warmer areas and in similar climates elsewhere. It thrives at Wakehurst Place, Sussex, where it is an impressive sight in July with its long one-sided racemes of white flowers thrust out almost horizontally from the branch tips. No such difficulties are posed by *Deutzia subulata* (*D glomeruliflora* var. *forrestiana*) in cultivation where, however, it is rarely seen. This rather slender-stemmed but dense shrub with neatly-pointed leaves was quite common as a companion to the clethra. In requirements, however, it is more amenable and, like most of its clan, it will grow equally well on acid or alkaline soils so long as it is given sun. Plants grown from seed collected at the time have reached 1.5m (5ft), bearing in June neatly rounded clusters of relatively small star-shaped white flowers, which are very pretty with the purple rayed calyces behind continuing to attract after petal fall.

32. According to Peter Cox, this has proved to be the hardiest introduction of this species into cultivation and is performing well.

Rhododendron lacteum (left) and *Rhododendron rex* subspecies *fictolacteum* (right) flowering at Bowood House Gardens near Calne in Wiltshire from seed collected above Camp 3 on the Cangshan's east flank. (May)

Hypericum subsessile, a relict (primitive) species recently named and first introduced from the Cangshan in 1981. Photographed in the author's garden. (July)

In the same area, indeed just outside our tents, grew a most interesting *Hypericum* species that, although not yet in flower, had the most distinctive leaves – oblong to elliptic-oblong in shape, and 5-5.5cm (2-2¼in) long. It was a robust shrub of 1.5m (5ft) with plenty of seed capsules from the previous year. Another characteristic was the absence of flowers, flower buds even, unusual considering that all other hypericums seen so far were either in flower or with flower buds; we concluded that this must be an unusually late-flowering species. We collected no herbarium material, but plants grown in cultivation from seed collected at the time flowered for the first time in 1984 and the following year a plant flowered in my garden. These seedlings have inherited the robust habit of the parents, while the yellow flowers are 3.5-4.5cm (1½-1¾in) across backed by five unequal leaf-like sepals. In truth, this hypericum is more curious than ornamental and I was not surprised, therefore, when Dr Robson of the British Museum pronounced it to be a relict (primitive) species previously known only from herbarium specimens collected by the late Professor Wen pei Fang in Sichuan in 1928 and by Forrest's native collectors, here in the Cangshan, in 1929. Dr Robson has named this new species *Hypericum subsessile*. Apart from its morphological characteristics, it does have another peculiarity – for a hypericum – in that it

flowers late in life, three to four years from seed, most other shrubby hypericums flowering in the second year at the latest. We found H *subsessile* again later on at Huadianba.

Our first day at Camp 3 started bright, but later turned cloudy and windy. We decided to explore the hillside above camp, forcing our way through dense thickets along a track that, at one place, wound its way between impressive rock stacks clothed with vegetation. *Rhododendron cyanocarpum* was plentiful as usual with R *dichroanthum* forming an under-storey. In one place, on a moss-covered rocky mount, we found R *haematodes* in flower – loose trusses of rich red bells from the shoot tips. Here also grew *Rhododendron rex* subspecies *fictolacteum*, trees up to 7m (22ft) high with bold, glossy, green leaves covered beneath with a striking red-brown pelt of hairs (indumentum). One specimen even carried a few flowers, pink in bud, opening white with a ray of purple spots at the base of the throat within.

At one point the track passed the base of a high rock face partially shaded by trees and damp from the presence of a nearby torrent. Here, on mossy ledges, grew a tiny rhododendron, which Peter Cox immediately recognised as R *campylogynum*. It formed loose hummocks and, although not in flower, carried enough seed in last year's capsules to establish it in cultivation. The Cangshan is the most easterly

Diapensia bulleyana, a choice carpeting evergreen growing in its type location in the limestone cliffs above Dali on the Cangshan's east flank. It is named after Forrest's first sponsor, A K Bulley, founder of the nursery firm of Bees. (May)

outpost for this species whose distribution ranges west through upper Burma to the eastern Himalaya (Arunachal Pradesh). It is another plant first found in the Cangshan by Delavay and introduced by Forrest in 1913. It is a gem of a rhododendron with one to two bell-shaped flowers 1-2cm (½ - ¾ in) long, borne on a short thread-like stalk above the

Alpine pastures and scattered scrub at 3,962 (13,000ft) in the Cangshan, photographed by Joseph Rock in 1922. The scattered trees are *Abies delavayi*, and the rhododendron on the left slope is *Rhododendron haematodes*. (May)

leaves. The typical colour is a uniform claret-red with a plum-like bloom and it will be interesting to see if any of our introductions vary from this.[33]

Other plants on the same rock face included a nice form of *Bergenia purpurascens* with luminous pink flowers and *Diapensia bulleyana*. The former belongs to the plant first named *B delavayi* and originally collected by that great French missionary 'above Tali' in 1884. The latter formed tight pads of prostrate stems clothed with tiny glossy evergreen leaves and studded with almost stemless pale yellow tubular flowers with five spreading lobes. It belongs to a genus of only three or four species, one of which, *Diapensia lapponica*, is circumpolar in distribution (that is, ranging from the arctic regions of North America to east Asia including Scotland – on a single mountain in western Inverness where it was first found in 1951). *Diapensia bulleyana* is a choice little shrublet first discovered by Forrest in the Cangshan and named after A K Bulley of Cheshire who first employed Forrest as a plant collector in China. It was growing in the Cangshan in crevices in a semi-shaded rock, its tap root no doubt well established in the rock interior, safe from the fluctuations of heat and cold. In cultivation diapensias are specialist subjects requiring great skill to keep them alive – and perhaps a bit of luck! As far as I am aware, *D bulleyana* has never been successful.[34]

Before leaving this rock face, Peter Hutchison was delighted to find an encrusted mat of tiny leaves, approximately 1cm (⅓ in) long, yellow mealy (farinose)

33. Seedlings at Glendoick have dark plum-coloured heavily bloomed flowers.

34. Some authorities now regard this species as a colour variation of *D purpurea*.

beneath and toothed at the margin. It proved to be *Primula bella*.

The weather had deteriorated to such an extent that it was decided we should have lunch while waiting for improvement. One of our Dali guides set about lighting a fire and we took the opportunity to have a quick search for rhododendron seed. Suddenly we heard shouting and, on running towards its source, saw that the fire had got out of hand and was threatening the surrounding vegetation. With our help it was quickly brought under control and our guide then made a second fire on the track. Even this was badly positioned, for the wind constantly blew the smoke into our faces and we decided to abandon the idea, our guide being admonished by the Chinese. Our lunch, as usual in the field, consisted of hard-boiled eggs, apples, cake and chocolate. This would be supplemented with whatever might be obtained locally, for instance the walnuts at Yangbi.

Our campsite, perched like an eagle's eyrie on the mountainside, afforded us excellent views to the east. Directly below we could see Dali, the original lines of its walls now mostly obliterated. At night its lights twinkled in the dark plain and Bob and I could see them from the entrance to the tent we shared. Across the Er-hai a range of rounded hills, once covered in beech *Fagus engleriana* and now, cleared of forest, lay red-skinned in the sun. The lake itself changed several times a day as clouds and light fluctuated, but was its most alluring early in the morning and evening with the surface washed pink or orange by the sun.

On our last day we set off from the camp to climb Longquan Peak, a high point rising above the head of the nearby valley. It was a glorious morning as we toiled through the dense scrub up the steep hillside. As we had already been this way on the previous day we wasted little time on the first part of our journey preferring to conserve our energies for the ridge area above. We climbed through a region dominated by silver fir, none of great height, the largest 13m (42ft) with a girth of 205cm (81in) at chest height.

We soon passed the previous day's furthest point and continued climbing across a natural stairway of large rough stone slabs that led us through a rather open woodland of fir and rhododendron. Here a most heartening sight met our eyes — *Primula sonchifolia* in flower, covering steep banks and in drifts along streamsides. Here also many *Rhododendron* species converged and we recorded the following: *campylogynum, cyanocarpum, fastigiatum, haematodes, heliolepis, lacteum, rex* subspecies *fictolacteum, selense* subspecies *jucundum, trichocladum, dichroanthum, neriiflorum, rubiginosum, taliense* and *balfourianum*. The last of these seemed similar in effect to *R taliense*, but according to David and Peter Cox it differs in the relatively pale, usually broken indumentum on the leaf undersurface and the large calyx (noticeable on the old capsules). Neither were in flower. *R balfourianum* we later found covering large areas above the tree line. Its patchy indumentum reminded me of a mangy leopard skin coat

One of the several peaks that rise from the Cangshan's summit ridge. Rhododendrons clothe the steep slopes where occasional snow patches defy the sun. They include *Rhododendron balfourianum, R taliense* and *R lacteum*. (May)

compared with the regular orange-red pelt of *R taliense*.

The apparent absence of birch was unusual, for it looked to be typical terrain for these trees, and the same could be said of rowans (*Sorbus* species). Eventually, we emerged from the wood on to an area of exposed rocks where we again found *Diapensia bulleyana* in flower. In

Primula calliantha, a beautiful species growing on an exposed steep rocky slope high above Camp 3 on the Cangshan. Originally discovered here by Delavay in 1883 and introduced to the West by Forrest, it has remained a 'difficult' plant in cultivation. (May)

crevices on the same rocks we found *Primula calliantha*, a beautiful species with tight erect rosettes of green leaves, white and mealy beneath, over which rises a 10-12cm (4-5in) stem bearing a loose umbel of large purple white-eyed flowers 2.5-3cm (1-1¼ in) across. Several rosettes grew together, forming clumps of exceptional quality, their flowers noticeable from some distance. Originally discovered near here by Delavay in 1883 and introduced by Forrest, it has never been an easy species in cultivation; more is the pity, considering its merit.

We reached the summit of Longquan Peak at 4,050m (13,284ft) sometime after midday and decided to eat our packed lunches. From our position we had clear views of Dali and the Er-hai to the east and we could even see the ridge above Camp 1 at Dapingdi to the north west. After lunch we continued for a while along the ridge heading south, Peter Cox lingering to collect rhododendron seed. After a while we stopped to assess our position. The ridge continued in a great arc gradually rising to a high crenulated section, which resembled the backbone of a dragon, ending in the large rounded summit of Malongfeng at 4,121m (13,521ft), the highest point in the Cangshan. Had we had a day to spare and been carrying a bivouac, we could have walked the length of this ridge. It looked so tempting and promising, but time, as usual, was not on our side so, with mist rolling up the western slopes, we reluctantly retraced our steps, on the way picking up Peter Cox's camera, which he had absent-mindedly left by a patch of *Rhododendron balfourianum*. Near here we also collected a prostrate willow, *Salix crenata*, which formed extensive carpets, its slender stems forming a tracery over rocks and banks. On the exposed ridge it was just coming to life, but later, at lower elevations, we saw it in tiny leaf and

studded with charming male catkins like tiny yellow thimbles. It is now established on the peat garden at the Royal Botanic Garden, Edinburgh and elsewhere.

Just as we were leaving the ridge to drop once more into the valley we were surprised to see three men leaving a wooden shack and head along the track towards us. They seemed to be in a hurry and passed us with little more than a nod of acknowledgement. We could not fail to notice that they were armed to the teeth, one with a rifle, another with a carbine and the third with a shotgun. All three carried pistols in their belts and a jingling bunch of metal traps on the end of a string. They also carried a wire cage. We asked Clyde what these men were about and in answer to his enquiry they told him that they were off to catch mice! Later, we met a man with three dead pheasants in a bag. From its green and red plumage I could see that one was a cock Blood pheasant and the others presumably hens of another species. Amherst pheasants are also found in the Cangshan, but the nearest we ever came to these was a bundle of handsome tail feathers from a cock bird being offered for sale in a village.

The next day we returned to Dali via a ridge that began a little way down the road from camp. The camp itself had been dismantled immediately after breakfast and everything packed into bundles for the porters, who had been arriving since early morning. Some of the loads weighed at least 45kg (100lb) and made startling sights, some dwarfing their carriers to such an extent that from behind they looked like giant bundles with legs. The carriers would be travelling the long way, by road, while we had opted to take what promised to be a shorter more interesting route – and so it proved to be.

Our first stop was in a ravine partly sheltered and shaded by trees and thicket. Here were arisaemas in plenty together with *Trillium tschonoskii*, one of two Chinese members of a predominantly North American genus. Some might say that this is one of the least impressive species

Trillium tschonoskii, a member of the lily family possessing a quiet cool charm, was plentiful in wooded ravines in the Cangshan above Dali. (May)

Cypripedium margaritaceum, a most unusual and striking Lady's slipper orchid growing by a track on a ridge above Dali. (May)

Salvia hylocharis, rare if at all in cultivation; we found this attractive species below Camp 3. (May)

with flowers much smaller than the famous Wake robin, T grandiflorum, which is true, but it has a quiet charm and a cool beauty totally at one with these Chinese woods. Each 30cm (12in) stem carries at its summit a trio of large, egg-shaped, horizontally disposed leaves from the centre of which a star-shaped flower rises. Borne on a short stalk, the flower normally rests on the leaf surface so that it appears almost at right angles to the stem. It comprises three oblong pointed white petals backed by three pale green sepals of similar size and shape. Sepals and petals curve outwards to create the star effect. Indeed, in some ways this species resembles a white version of the American T erectum. T tschonoskii is also native to Japan, but in cultivation remains uncommon. We found several colonies in the Cangshan woods and thickets, on one occasion growing with Fritillaria cirrhosa, the two presenting an exquisite combination of green, yellow and white.

In similar situations grew Clintonia udensis, like the trillium and fritillary a perennial herb and a member of the lily family. In this species there are several broad, fleshy, basal leaves above which rises a fleshy stem of 10-15cm (4-6in) bearing at its tip several nodding ice-blue scilla-like flowers. Later the stem increases to as much as 30cm (12in) when the blackish fleshy fruits ripen.

Almost directly above the last, in shady rock crevices, grew what appeared to be a member of the gesneria family (Gesneriaceae). It formed rosettes of downy broad-based leaves and supported a few erect fruiting stems to 12.5cm (5in). It reminded me somewhat of a Ramonda species, but these are strictly European in distribution. In the absence of flowers we could guess no further. Fortunately, we were allowed to collect a few small seedlings and some seed, which have since established and flourished in European

cultivation including the Royal Botanic Garden, Edinburgh, where it has been identified as Ancyclostemon convexus. In the opinion of Ron McBeath it is a nice pot plant for the alpine house with umbels of orange-yellow tubular flowers.

Not far from the track we found low flowering patches of Anemone davidii, a plant not unlike a coarser version of our native Wood anemone (A nemorosa), which I had previously seen on Emei Shan. Shrubs, too, were much in evidence and I was particularly pleased to see Dipelta yunnanensis, an old friend from the Hillier Arboretum. Here it was a shrub of 1.5-2m (5-6ft) with hairy leaves in pairs and pairs of slender pale creamy-yellow foxglove-like flowers spotted orange in the throat, with some specimens having flowers flushed pale pink on the outside. These are hardy shrubs closely related to weigelas and diervillas and resembling them in flower shape. They differ, however, in the bracts at the base of the ovary, which enlarge and become dry, disc-like wings on the fruit.

Our descent continued in very pleasant style, flowers of many kinds attracting our attention – purple pleiones, variously coloured rhododendrons and, once, a herbaceous salvia of 60cm (2ft) with coarsely toothed, hairy, heart-shaped leaves, which were strong smelling when bruised, and with spikes of yellow flowers with a purple tip to the lower lip. Mrs Fang identified this as Salvia hylocharis. Without doubt, however, the most exciting find of the day was a Lady's slipper orchid, Cypripedium margaritaceum.[35]

35. Of this plant Reginald Farrer wrote: 'A very rare species, stemless as in C acaule, with a pair of ridgy purple-blotched leaves from which arises a 10-12.5cm (4-5in) peduncle, carrying a waxen morbid bloom of yellowishness beclouded with maroon and covered in shining purple hairs'. It is not certain that Farrer actually saw this species but Forrest did, and a black and white photograph taken by him is reproduced in The Journeys and Plant Introductions of George Forrest. Forrest found this species on several occasions in Yunnan growing in moist stony situations in pine forests. One collection was made in June at 3,353m (11,000ft) on the eastern flank of the Lijiang (Likiang) range.

Iris collettii, a miniature species we found beneath pine trees on the Cangshan's east flank above Dali. (May)

Iris chrysographes, a distinguished moisture-loving Iris with flowers as dark as any species, here photographed in the Royal Botanic Gardens, Edinburgh. It was plentiful in damp places on the Cangshan's lower slopes. (June)

Farrer states that it occurs on almost pure limestone in pine woods of the Mekong district, which almost certainly refers to north-west Yunnan. We found two flowering plants at the base of a limestone rock close to the track. The two or three boldly-ribbed, ovate leaves were spotted and blotched liver-purple while, in between, nestled a single bloom carried on a 15cm (6in) scape. It was pale greenish-yellow in colour, heavily striped and spotted purple and covered with short erect purple glandular hairs. The rounded pouched lip (labellum) was almost hidden by the petals and sepals, which curved round and over in a protective embrace. A careful search in the surrounding area of grass and loose scrub revealed several unflowered plants, many of which favoured the comparatively dry dappled shade of young pines.

The track several times passed beneath pine trees (*Pinus armandii*), their dead needles covering the bare ground beneath. In one such place, where the light sneaked through the canopy on to a grassy bank, we found a small, almost stemless, iris, since identified by Brian Mathew of Kew as *Iris collettii*. The flowers were no more than 7.5cm (3in) high and slightly over 2.5cm (1in) across, of a pale blue colour with a yellow crest. It was a gem of a plant, what an American friend of mine would call 'a real cutie'.

Both *Rhododendron microphyton* and *R simsii* grew here, the latter with a few late reddish flowers. *R simsii* is the main parent of the indoor azaleas so popular at Christmas and, apart from *R microphyton*, is the only azalea growing wild in western China.

The shady ravines above which we passed were full of good things, especially perennial herbs, some only just emerging. They included *Nomocharis pardanthina*, bulbs of which were introduced to St Andrews University Botanic Garden as well as to the Royal Botanic Garden, Edinburgh, where,

according to Ron McBeath, they have grown with great vigour and flowered very well. Most have inclined saucer-shaped or flattened flowers of pale blush-pink with a heavy spotting, especially on the broad inner segments. These are also sharply and unevenly toothed giving them an attractive fringed appearance. They belong to the form until recently treated as a separate species under the name N *mairei*. Other bulbs we collected elsewhere have apparently produced flowers more in keeping with typical N *pardanthina*. The nomocharis are closely related to the lilies (*Lilium*) and like them are regarded by many as among the aristocrats of the garden. They are hardy plants requiring a deep, moist but well drained soil, preferably in an open site. Although frequently grown in southern gardens they reach their finest proportions in the cooler gardens of the north, especially in Scotland.

Towards late afternoon we finally cleared the forest to find ourselves in an extensive area of rough pasture liberally strewn with boulders and rock slabs. Here grew golden stellera and equally bold clumps of *Euphorbia prolifera* with substantial heads of brassy yellow flowers. Elsewhere, *Iris chrysographes* appeared in damp depressions, large colonies with striking deep purple flowers on 45cm (18in) stems. *Rosa roxburghii* forma *normalis*, with large golden-hearted rose-pink flowers, was plentiful on the banks of ditches, darker in flower and smaller in leaf than the better known *R hirtula* of Japan.

These were just a few of the many plants flourishing among the boulders and pits, left by the marble men of Dali. Dali marble, or 'Dali stone' as it is known locally, is probably the most famous single product of this area. Indeed, elsewhere in China, Dali stone is virtually a synonym for marble. For a thousand years the Bai stone cutters in Sanwanbi village at the foot of the Cangshan have been quarrying the marble that lies under the mountains, and the foothills are pockmarked with craters large and

A marble seller in Dali displaying a container with the distinctive markings for which 'Dali stone' is famous throughout China. (May)

Ponies in the yard of the Dali marble factory waiting to pull a cart stacked with sliced marble. (May)

small where the marble has been excavated. Veteran marble men, it is claimed, can tell with the tap of a hammer at what depth the marble lies within the rock formation. Ancient books refer to the fine grained marble, smooth and cool to the touch, as the 'sobering-up stone', for use after heavy drinking.

Later we were taken round the marble factory in Sanwanbi and, although an interesting experience, we found working conditions there somewhat Dickensian. From here we wandered into Dali spending a happy hour or two exploring the streets. First we walked the main street from the south to the north gate, a distance of 1km (¾ mile). The walls were broken in places, while elsewhere they had become blurred by houses being built on the outside to accommodate the inevitable overflow. We watched for a while a man selling vegetables, weighing them by means of a set of hand-held scales. His customers, mainly old women, haggled and complained throughout the operation in the hope of a better deal.

Walking along one side street Peter Cox and I were

attracted by a courtyard garden seen through an open door. Further investigations were cut short by the sudden appearance of a fierce dog, which chased us back into the street barking all the while. Eventually, we found a small tea house known as the Art Garden. It was owned by Wang Yuangseng, a local artist, who proved a genial host, serving us with tea and a plentiful supply of sunflower and melon seeds. His little garden had walls decorated with, to our eyes, garish paintings. Among the many plants in tubs there were young grafted *Camellia reticulata*, *Agapetes lacei*, a small plant with a large turnip-like base (lignotuber), and *Clematis florida* var. *flore-pleno* with double pale greenish flowers.

In a dark corner of the tea house, which had several rooms, sat an old man who, whenever we looked his way, began counting up to ten in English and shouting 'yes' and 'let's go'. His words served to remind us that time was flying and we would soon have to report to the guest house where our transport was waiting. That night, back in our rooms at Xiaguan, we made preparations for our fourth and final camp in the Cangshan.

Meeting of the ways, an assembly area for agricultural workers and transport in Dali. (May)

Huadianba, a farming village situated at 2900m (9,513ft) towards the northern end of the Cangshan. This was the site of our final camp from which we explored the hills and valleys around. (May)

To Camp 4

We awoke as usual to a musical 6.30 reveille broadcast on the Tannoys, followed by the international news in Chinese. We could not follow the action, but it put a stop to further sleep most effectively. After a breakfast of rice porridge and fried eggs, we collected our belongings and boarded our coach for the 50km (31 mile) drive north beyond Dali. Leaving the transport by the main road we began a 19km (12 mile) walk to Huadianba, heading west into the mountains.

For the first hour it poured, some of the heaviest rain we had experienced, and we cursed as our feet slipped about on the muddy track. We first made our way past a village where we noted *Sophora davidii* being used as a thorny hedge around the fields and vegetable plots. After a relatively flat stretch we began to climb a steep hillside, a climb that took us over 305m (1,000ft) above the valley bottom. The erosion was horrific, with no forest to hold the topsoil, and we passed many ravines where there was no vegetation at all. Elsewhere, the red earth supported a few small plants including some nice patches of *Persicaria capitata* (*Polygonum capitatum*), a pretty, prostrate species with small rounded heads of pink flowers and leaves with a dark V-shaped

The author on the road to Huadianba. (May)

Persicaria capitata was common on the dry slopes and eroded hills on the road to Huadianba. Its tiny pink pill-like flower heads are distinct. (May)

Clematis chrysocoma was plentiful in the sunny, dry foothills of the Cangshan where it is generally found as a dwarf, shortly scandent shrub with satiny-pink flowers. (May)

Severe erosion in the hills above Dali on our journey to Huadianba. (May)

marking, which I had last seen in the wild in east Nepal in 1971. Plants derived from seed collected that year still survive in several sheltered gardens despite the hard winters, while elsewhere it is grown each year from cuttings and overwintered under glass.

In the same family is *Rumex hastatus*, a sort of shrubby Sheep's sorrel, whose pink flowers were giving way to reddish fruits. We had seen this plant, often in vast quantities, all the way from Kunming to Xiaguan and it

Incarvillea arguta loves sunny, dry situations and is commonly found growing among rocks, from crevices in cliffs and in steep ravines. It was abundant on the dry eroded eastern foothills of the Cangshan. (May)

seemed to favour poor soils and river shingles. It is also common in the Yangtze valley. Two other plants of interest grew commonly on these slopes, both of which we were pleased to see. *Incarvillea arguta* is a loose-habited dwarf plant of 30cm (12in), shrubby at the base, producing pinnate leaves and long, one-sided sprays (racemes) of funnel-shaped pink flowers. It, too, flourished in these poor soils and was so common that it created pink splashes as far as the eye could see. It occurs in the wild from west China along the Himalaya to the Punjab, preferring the rain shadow regions and the dry valleys between. It is not entirely hardy in British cultivation, even in the south, and is best grown outside in a crevice in a dry sunny wall like the Californian zauschnerias or in a pot in a cool house. Treated as a half-hardy perennial, it makes an unusual and long-flowering bedding subject as long as new plants are grown each year from cuttings or from the abundantly produced seed.

Sharing these slopes with the incarvillea was a most attractive dwarf clematis – *Clematis chrysocoma*, which here varied in height from 30-60cm (1-2ft), its stems and leaves covered in short dense golden hairs, hence the name. The leaves are divided into three-stalked leaflets that are soft to the touch. But the real merit of this plant lies in its flowers, which are borne singly on long, erect stalks. They are 5-6cm (2-2½ in) across and comprise four petals (correctly tepals) of an almost satiny-pink that is quite outstanding. *C chrysocoma* is apparently only found in Yunnan and was first discovered by Delavay in 1884, who

Osmanthus delavayi was common in the hillside scrub on the trail to Huadianba. Here photographed in the author's garden. (April)

Enkianthus deflexus on the road to Huadianba. It remains an uncommon species in western civilisation. (May)

sent seed home to Paris to be grown by the nursery firm of Vilmorin. It was later introduced again by Forrest, and others no doubt, as it is widespread across the Yunnan plateau and presumably elsewhere in suitable locations. We saw it several times in the hills around Kunming and plants were collected on the dry slopes below Camp 1 at Dapingdi.

It is in some respects a puzzling plant. Seed from plants growing at Hua Hong Dong near Kunming have in cultivation produced seedlings with a tendency to climb and that produce white or pink-tinged flowers. Delavay's original collection was a dwarf pink-flowered plant such as the ones we saw in the Cangshan, but we also noted there, plants with longer stems to 1m (3ft) that had begun to twine in contact with a supporting shrub. Further study in the wild and in cultivation is needed to sort out this species and its variability. What is certain is its tender nature. Like *Incarvillea arguta* it thrives on warmth and a well-drained soil; not surprisingly, earlier Forrest introductions succumbed to cold winters. It would make an attractive cool house subject in a pot but needs more heat to ripen its growth than our summers can presently supply. Like many of the plants of the Yunnan plateau and similar situations elsewhere in the province, it should thrive in Mediterranean regions and in the south-west of the United States.

Not all the ravines on the hillside were devoid of vegetation, although where trees such as pines occurred they were usually heavily butchered. The accompanying scrub, however, was full of good things and gave us some idea of the riches of these slopes in former times. Two camellias were frequent here, neither, of course, in flower. *Camellia pitardii* variety *yunnanica* we had previously seen near Kunming, but *C yunnanensis* was new to us.[36] Professor Feng pointed out to us the essential differences: the smooth (glabrous), red, young shoots and coppery, young growths of the former and the finely downy, young shoots, leaf undersurfaces and leaf stalks

of the latter. The leaves of *C yunnanensis* were also noticeably broader than those of the other. Its flowers are said to be variable in size, 2-4cm (¾-1½ in) across and white with a conspicuous boss of golden stamens. Botanically the two belong to separate sections of the genus, but, as an ornamental, *C yunnanensis* sounds to be inferior.

At about 2,700m (8,858ft) the scrub contained *Dipelta yunnanensis, Corylopsis yunnanensis, Deutzia calycosa, Gaultheria forrestii, Osmanthus delavayi, Stachyurus chinensis* and *Helwingia japonica* over which a powerful climber *Holboellia latifolia* scrambled, and so it continued. We found another *Leptodermis* species, this time *Leptodermis forrestii*, a dense twiggy shrub of 1m (3ft), its slender branches alive with

Porters carrying heavy loads of split canes on the road to Huadianba. (May)

36. Both Forrest and Rock collected *C yunnanensis* in the Cangshan but neither was its original discoverer, that honour going to who else but Delavay?

Rosa sericea, showing its exquisite cup-shaped flowers, which open wide as they age. It was common on the road to Huadianba, a village towards the northern end of the Cangshan. (May)

Leptodermis forrestii, a dense, low, twiggy bush liberally studded with small, star-shaped flowers, was frequent on dry slopes above the track to Huadianba. It would require plenty of summer sun and heat to flourish in western cultivation. (May)

white flowers that were lavender-pink on the outside. It was quite easily the finest species we had seen to date, both in size of leaf and flower, and a shrub well worth introducing to gardens in warmer countries of the West, especially California and the Mediterranean. It is also possible that it would grow in milder parts of Britain and Ireland. Growing well and flowering well, however, do not always go hand in hand and there is no doubt that leptodermis thrive on plenty of sun and warmth. In the past, several species have been grown successfully at the late Colonel Stern's garden at Highdown, Sussex, the dry chalk soil and maritime sun obviously to their liking.

An enkianthus with bold drooping clusters of cream-coloured, bell-shaped flowers heavily striated red was later identified as *Enkianthus deflexus*, a species I had seen giving a brilliant autumn leaf display on Emei Shan in October 1980. Here it only reached 1m (3ft) on an exposed bank, but its branches were packed with flower. In normal conditions it would reach two to three times this height. Several of the hypericums we had previously seen occurred commonly by the track and across the hillside, *Hypericum latisepalum* and *H henryi* being the two most abundant. We even found a few specimens of *Philadelphus purpurascens*, a shrub of some 2m (6ft) with purplish-brown flaking bark on the older stems and bold clusters of cup-shaped white flowers full of yellow stamens. Although only 2.5cm (1in) across, the flowers were most conspicuous and attractive besides giving off a sweet scent. This shrub is closely related to *P delavayi* and was first found in west Sichuan by E H Wilson who introduced it to Britain, since when it has remained in cultivation without ever being as widely grown as its merit deserves, no

doubt having been passed over in favour of the many first-rate especially French hybrids available. Most of the Chinese species of *Philadelphus* are hardy and easy in cultivation as are the wild rose species.

I mention roses because of *Rosa sericea*, which we saw everywhere on the hillside that morning. Here it was a vigorous shrub to 2m (6ft) or more, with erect thorny stems and numerous slender spreading branches clothed with most attractive ferny leaves. The flowers were saucer-shaped, 4-6cm (1½ -2½ in) across with four cream-coloured or pale sulphur-yellow overlapping petals. They were carried singly, all along the branchlets, either inclined or nodding, while the stems, especially the young ones, were clothed with a mixture of prickles and bristles. Some time later we found a single specimen of the form known as *pteracantha*[37] in which the young stems are clothed with conspicuous broad-based and flattened blood-red prickles. Other than the prickles and the clear white flowers, it was similar in height and leaf to the typical plant. *R sericea* is one of the most widely distributed rose species, occurring from the Himalaya east through north-east India, north Burma, south-east Tibet to west and central China. Not surprisingly, it is somewhat variable and several forms or varieties have at various times been named. Perhaps the most well known is subspecies *omeiensis* from west Sichuan and north-west Yunnan, which differs only in minor characteristics from the typical plant. The form *pteracantha* is distinct enough, but the large thorns are a random feature

37. I was interested to learn that this curious form was originally collected in this part of Yunnan by Delavay in 1890. He also introduced at the same time seed of *R sericea* itself to France, where it was grown in the famous Arboretum des Barres of Maurice de Vilmorin.

Magnolia wilsonii, occurred as scattered individuals and was regularly cut over by villagers, resulting in strong regrowth. (May)

Magnolia wilsonii in the wild near Huadianba. This is the form originally collected by Forrest and named M *taliensis*. (May)

and its appearance among populations of the type haphazard. All these forms are hardy and robust and suitable for the larger garden where they will thrive on most soils.

At one point on the track we met a man coming down from the hills carrying an enormous bunch of *Rhododendron decorum* in flower. They varied in colour from white to blush and were a fine sight to see. So, too, was Peter Cox's face when he saw them and it was with renewed energy that he climbed the rest of the slope.

Our track brought us over a ridge into a deep east-west valley. We soon found ourselves on a mountain road, rough at times but a road nevertheless. From here on the journey was much easier, with no more climbing. Not for the first time on this expedition Bob and I had a sing-song, a duet, which amused the Chinese, especially Professor Feng, but not, I fear our British companions who held their hands to their ears in mock disgust. I have always enjoyed singing in the hills, especially where there is no one around to complain and one can sing as loudly as one likes. Indeed the British Consular official A R Margary, when travelling alone in the wilds of China in the 1870s, found the best cure for loneliness and homesickness was to get out in the open and sing all the old songs he knew at the top of his voice, ending with 'God Save the Queen'.

The late Len Beer and I often sang during our time in the mountains of Nepal in 1971, usually when we were either elated or down. Bob had known Len well and shared his penchant for uninhibited singing. Len Beer died tragically young in 1976 and during our time in the Cangshan his name often came up when Bob and I reminisced. Len did not survive to enjoy the reopening of China but we had no doubt that had he been spared, he would have been here in the thick of it.

About midday we sat by the road to eat our packed lunch. The group had become scattered along the road as each of us pursued our individual collecting or photography. Our equipment and supplies, carried by pony and mule, had gone on ahead and we had the rest of the day to reach camp at Huadianba, which lay somewhere near the head of the valley. The valley itself had now widened considerably and began to look more and more like the Western Highlands of Scotland. For a start, the mountains on either side were round-topped with bevelled ridges in between, very different from the sharp crags and cliffs above Dali. Even the valley bottom was wide and relatively flat, with many streams and bogs containing rushes and sedges. But it was no good our Scottish contingent beginning to feel at home, because a closer look at the vegetation revealed a richness of wild species that in Scotland could only be found in some of her famous gardens.

It was while eating lunch that we noticed a nearby hillside that seemed to be flecked with white paper. We debated whether to investigate for we still had a long way to travel. In the end, we decided in favour of a quick look and were thankful we had. Like most of the hillsides in the valley, this one was treeless, the forest having long since been destroyed. In its place, a dense scrub or thicket had developed. Even this we decided was subject to a periodic lopping. No matter, for the shrub flora was virtually intact and full of good things. The white papers turned out to be the unmistakable flowers of *Magnolia wilsonii* and, since there was considerable excitement at this discovery, we spent some time taking photographs.

On closer examination we found that the flowers were being carried on suckering stems up to 2m (6ft) tall, sprouting from the stumps of larger specimens that had long since been felled. It was curious to see such short stems flowering when, in cultivation, one is used to seeing them borne on specimens up to 6m (22ft) high. The

Paeonia delavayi forma *lutea*, an unusual and attractive form with a bold multi-rayed red eye to the cup-shaped flowers. It was frequent in the scrub above the road to Huadianba. (May)

flowers were typically nodding and saucer-shaped, up to 10cm (4in) across, the nine overlapping white tepals setting off the crimson-purple central cluster of stamens, through which protruded the green female cone (torus). Of course, they were deliciously scented and recalled memories of warm, early summer days in an English woodland garden, which is where I first set eyes on this lovely magnolia.[38]

The magnolia was quite common as scattered individuals across the hillside and was accompanied by several other plants familiar from cultivation. Most exciting after the magnolia was a tree peony, *Paeonia lutea*, now generally regarded as a form of the blood-red flowered P *delavayi*. P *lutea* was first discovered in Yunnan by Delavay who also introduced its seed.[39] Here it was a small shrub or sub-shrub of 1-1.5m (3-5ft) and appeared to be suckering. The handsome, large, deeply-divided leaves in no way detracted from the nodding to inclined, cup-shaped, golden-yellow flowers, which were 6cm (2½in) across and borne singly on erect stalks from the upper leaf axils. Normally the petals are clear yellow, but on several plants we found petals with a red basal stain on the inside, giving the flower a dark eye. In one form the stains were so pronounced as to form an eight-pointed star arrangement round the boss of stamens. Interestingly, according to Bean, of the three plants raised from Delavay's original seed, one differed enough in flower to warrant the name 'Superba', but the reddish-maroon colour they exhibited was borne by the stamens rather than the petals.

Another shrub of merit growing with the last two was *Lonicera setifera*, its erect, bristly and hairy stems reaching 2m (6ft). The leaves too were bristly and hairy, those of the young vigorous stems variably lobed. This is a winter-flowering species and the branches were now loaded with 1cm (⅓in) long fruits like small red, ovoid gooseberries. Plants grown from this seed are now well established in Britain, one of them flowering for the first time in my garden in February 1985. I was particularly pleased to see this species having long known it in cultivation where it is not common. My first encounter with it was late in the

hard winter of 1962/63 at Hillier's old West Hill Nursery, Winchester, and during one of the few spells of sunny weather it produced clusters of tubular, daphne-like, sweetly-scented flowers on the naked shoots.[40] In colour these were white, tinted pink on the tube. In the nursery it grew in a border beneath the wall of Winchester Prison, and there was a story current at the time that an escaping prisoner had once almost destroyed the plant in dropping on it from the wall top.

More recently, I have seen L *setifera* growing on the eastern flanks of the Yulong Shan or Jade Dragon Mountains above Lijiang in north-west Yunnan.

Other shrubs we encountered in the scrub, none of them above 2m (6ft), included *Osmanthus delavayi*, just past flowering, *Dipelta yunnanensis*, *Rhododendron yunnanense*, *Spiraea miyabei*, *Leptodermis forrestii*, *Stachyurus himalaicus*, *Corylopsis wilsonii*,

38. Native both to Yunnan and Sichuan, this species was first discovered by E H Wilson and is generally regarded as one of his finest introductions to western cultivation. He collected it in west Sichuan, but the plants we now admired belonged to the form once treated as a species, M *taliensis*, having first been found in the Tali Range (Cangshan) by Forrest. If it differs at all from typical M *wilsonii* it is in the leaves, which are less hairy beneath, the hairs confined to the midrib, veins and leaf stalk – a trivial detail.

39. P *delavayi* forma *lutea* is not often grown now in western cultivation, where it has largely been replaced by the larger flowered and more robust – up to 2m (6ft) or more – P *ludlowii*, first introduced from the vicinity of the Tsangpo Gorges in south-east Tibet by Ludlow and Sherriff in 1936. P *ludlowii* certainly deserves its popularity, but if the smaller P *delavayi* forma *lutea* could be introduced in some of its better forms I have no doubt it would become much sought after, especially by those with small gardens.

40. According to the original label the Hillier plant had been raised from seed No 13520 collected by Joseph Rock. From this number we deduce it was collected during his 1925/26 expedition to north-west Gansu. It was apparently also collected by Kingdon-Ward (No 5688) in the Assam Himalaya in 1924, thus giving the species a wide distribution. It is surprising that L *setifera* is not better known in cultivation considering its winter flowering qualities. There are at least two specimens of the Rock collection in the Hillier Arboretum as well as one of my own from Sichuan. All flower well but are economical in fruit.

Paeonia delavayi, showing its rich crimson flower. A plant growing in the author's garden grown from seed collected in the Jade Dragon mountains or Yulongshan above Lijiang in N.W. Yunnan. (May)

Cypripedium flavum, a magnificent Lady's slipper orchid, was frequent on the slopes above the Huadianba road. It flourished in open grassy areas among the scrub. (May)

Berberis levis and *Leycesteria formosa*, an old friend from Nepal days. Over all this scrambled a variety of vines and creepers, the most abundant of which were *Holboellia angustifolia*, *Clematis montana*, *Aristolochia moupinensis* and *Schisandra rubriflora*. There were few trees, however, other than dense prickly mounds of an evergreen oak, *Quercus monimotricha*, and the occasional heavily butchered lime, probably *Tilia chinensis*.

The crowning glory of the hillside, however, was a magnificent Lady's slipper orchid that occurred singly and in clumps in open grassy places among the scrub. Originally known as *Cypripedium luteum* (a name now assigned as a synonym to the North American *C parviflorum* variety *pubescens*), this is now more correctly *Cypripedium flavum* and is common in west China. Farrer, Forrest, Kingdon-Ward and Wilson[41] all saw and admired it, one of them – it had to be Farrer – even giving it an English name,

41. The first westerner to discover *C flavum* was the French missionary Père David in Baoxing (Mupin), west Sichuan in June 1869. A few years later Delavay recorded it as being abundant around Dali at 3,000m (9,842ft). Ernest Wilson first collected it in north-west Hubei, where it is extremely rare, though he later found it much more common on the Chinese-Tibetan borderland, where it occurred on the margins of thin woodland and thickets and also on scrub-clad boulders stranded in bogs. Around Songpan in north-west Sichuan he found it was abundant in thin woods of spruce and silver fir and near margins of glacial torrents, an observation I can confirm from my own experience in 1986. George Forrest found it growing in shady stony situations in pine forest at 3,048-3,352m (10,000-11,000ft) on the eastern flank of the Lijiang range in north-west Yunnan. In his book *Pilgrimage for Plants*, Kingdon-Ward tells us that *C flavum* was one of the first plants he collected on his first plant hunt in Yunnan where he saw it growing in woodland at 3,352m (11,000ft) on a steep hillside. He describes its flowers as 'chrome-yellow with the cool glaze of Chinese porcelain'.

'Proud Margaret'. In typical vein, Farrer writes of his finding this species during his Gansu (Kansu) expedition with William Purdom: 'We went our way onwards into the darkening narrows of the gorge, here darkened yet more by a fir forest, with Proud Margaret, for a rare eccentricity, growing happily in the moss heaps round the roots of each tree in that eternal twilight'. This account from *The Eaves of the World* is accompanied by a black and white photograph of a flowering plant showing the typically lush foliage and bold bulbous slipper.

A few days later we found *C flavum* again in hillside thickets at 3,150m (10,335ft) above Huadianba. It is indeed a most striking orchid, its erect stems 30-45cm (12-18in) tall with five or more broad, boldly ribbed leaves. The solitary bloom 6-9cm (2½-3½in) across possesses a large conspicuous bulbous lip over which the dorsal sepal curves, protecting the reproductive organs from unfavourable elements. The petals spread laterally reflexing at the tips, while the united lateral sepals fit snugly beneath the lip. The lip is a clear, pale yellow in colour and the petals and sepals have the same ground colour sometimes tinted green and variously blotched and spotted reddish-purple. The staminodes are large and coloured a conspicuous chocolate-purple so that, seen face-on, the flower appears to have a single purple eye, like a cyclops. All parts of the plant, except the petals and lip, are downy.

Naturally, we found it difficult to tear ourselves away from this botanical paradise, but the calls of Professor Feng reminded us of the distance we still had to travel, so we returned to the road to continue our journey. After a while the road passed through an area of peat bogs and memories of Scotland and the west of Ireland returned. We even saw places where the peat was being cut for burning and I almost imagined I was in Co Kerry, but associated with typical peat bog vegetation – grasses and rushes and even White beak sedge (*Rhyncospora alba*) – there were colonies of *Iris chrysographes* and a candelabra primula, *P poissonii*. The iris had dark purple flowers and formed extensive patches, while the primula was more scattered, its tiers of magenta flowers just starting to open. Both plants flourished in damp depressions and by streams throughout the area.

Equally common and forming extensive colonies was *Euphorbia griffithii*, an herbaceous creeping perennial with erect stems to 1m (3ft) high clothed with long willow-like leaves and terminal heads of flowers set among brilliant orange-red bracts. This is a popular plant in British cultivation where it is mainly represented by the selection 'Fireglow' made by the late Alan Bloom of Bressingham, Norfolk. Another form, 'Dixter', has been introduced by the late Christopher Lloyd from a seedling raised by the late Hilda Davenport-Jones. The stems are red, while the leaves are dusky with a purplish bloom beneath and, although the flowers are a rich burnt orange, they are less brilliant than 'Fireglow'. *E griffithii* also differs from 'Fireglow' in its taller,

Primula poissonii. Named for a French botanist Jules Poisson, this striking species was common by the roadside near Huadianba. (May)

Roscoea tibetica, a charming hardy member of the mainly tropical ginger family, *Zingiberaceae.* It was introduced from Huadianba in 1981 and is now established in British cultivation. (May)

Right. *Euphorbia griffithii* was common around Huadianba, colonising pastures and slopes, especially between stands of rhododendron. (May)

more 'floppy' growth and more invasive habit. All forms colour vividly in autumn before dying down.[42]

We ended the day on a high note, finding a lovely flowering herb studding the emerald green of a grassy mound not far from the road. It was a member of the ginger family, *Roscoea tibetica,* a charming little plant not unlike an orchid at first glance. The single, long-tubed flower was raised some 5cm (2in) above a single, shiny green, broad-based leaf with parallel veins. It comprised a broad dorsal petal curving forward, shell-like at the tip and with two narrow, wide-spreading laterals, a deeply two-lobed lip and two erect petal-like staminodes. In colour it was purple with a white tube. There must have been hundreds on this mound and others in the vicinity. The stems of these plants continue to grow until they are anything from 10-18cm (4-7in) or, occasionally, as much as 30cm (12in) tall with three to four stem leaves. It is found in the wild over a wide area: west China, upper Burma, south-east Tibet and Bhutan. A plant introduced to the Royal Botanic Garden, Edinburgh, produces stems eventually to 30cm (12in) and seedlings from this have been widely distributed.

Huadianba, when we finally arrived, we found to be a farming village scattered across the valley floor at 2,900m

42. Although first discovered in 1887, E *griffithii* was not successfully introduced into cultivation until 1949 when Ludlow, Sherriff and Hicks collected it in Bhutan.

Rheum palmatum variety *tanguticum* was being cultivated for medicinal purposes at Huadianba. It was a most ornamental large perennial with rich red stems and leaf stalks and bold, jaggedly-toothed leaves. (May)

Malus yunnanensis. A fruiting tree of wild origin from W. Yunnan, here photographed at Hergest Croft in Herefordshire. (October)

(9,513ft). In earlier days a road connected this village with the Er-hai plain, but extensive erosion had washed away major sections in the steep-sided valley and these had not been restored, hence our having to walk to our destination. All supplies are brought in by pack mule and pony, and herds of goats are brought up to pasture in the grassy areas. We were told that the authorities had tried to bring a large population and agriculture to this remote valley, but the altitude had proved to be too high for most crops, and now only the farm and a few Bai people remain.

The farm was mainly concerned with homeopathic medicinal crops, which were being cultivated and carefully tended around the main farm area and at several outlying communities. The crops included *Aconitum carmichaelii, Angelica sinensis, Fritillaria cirrhosa, Rheum palmatum* variety *tanguticum* and *Saussurea lappa.* The dried lateral roots of aconitum are used in combination with other herbs in the treatment of colds, rheumatoid arthritis, chest and stomach pains and anorexia. The dried root of the angelica is well known as a folkloric remedy for diabetes, hypertension and nephritis, as well as for cancer. It has also been used with other herbs to treat anaemia, constipation and venous thrombosis. Dried bulbs of the fritillaria have long been used in the treatment of chronic coughs, hacking, chronic bronchitis and tuberculosis. We were told that the bulbs could also be boiled in water and the water drunk to ease troublesome coughs. The use of rhubarb to aid the digestion has long been practised in the West and for even longer in China. The dried rhizomes of this Chinese rhubarb, *Rheum palmatum* variety *tanguticum,* decocted with the fruit of *Citrus aurantium* (orange), and the dried bark, etc, of *Magnolia officinalis,* are used in the treatment of intestinal and stomach 'fever' and constipation as well as diarrhoea. With other herbs, rhubarb is also used to treat acute hepatitis and jaundice.

I had last seen *Saussurea lappa* growing wild in the mountains of Kashmir. In China the dried root is used with other herbs in the treatment of dyspepsia, dysentery and abdominal pain. It also has a wider reputation in the treatment of many other disorders.

At Huadianba we were accommodated in a long, low,

two-storeyed building with whitewashed walls: rumoured to be the hospital. The walls, roof and floor were of wood and the whole structure had a medieval look. Each room had three hard trestles on which to sleep and metal bowls were provided for washing. A room below was made available for the work of recording and pressing specimens, and electric light was provided by an ancient generator that was not yet working, so the first night we worked by the light of candles, sitting around a charcoal fire that had been built in the centre of the room. Our shadows danced on the walls as we beavered away, while mugs of steaming green tea served to keep out the cold. After two hours, supper was served in a splendid, large wood-beamed hall that doubled as a cinema. That night, I found sleep impossible with so many images and experiences crowding my mind.

Our hostelry was situated approximately in the centre of the valley. To the south lay hills of granite with wooded valleys, while to the north were limestone scrub-covered hills with grassy plains in between grazed by yaks. Over the next four days we explored selected hills and valleys on both flanks of Huadianba, reaping rich rewards each day, but nothing in my mind will ever compare with our first day when we climbed the slopes to the north and saw our first alpine rhododendrons in flower and *en masse.*

The scrub was, as usual, full of interest, and included many of the shrubs we had seen the previous day. *Rhododendron yunnanense* was common everywhere, its flowers varying in colour from white to lilac, lavender, pink and pale purple. *R decorum* and, higher up, *R irroratum* were equally abundant, some of the former still carrying bold heads of pink-budded, white flowers. All had suffered hard pruning. *Cornus hemsleyi* here reached 5m (16ft) in gullies, but was not in flower. I remembered first having seen this dogwood at Werrington Park in north Cornwall many years ago. There it had dark red shoots, but, apart from its rarity value, it did not impress me as an ornamental.

Two crabs were in flower, both small trees of 5-6m (16-20ft), occurring as scattered individuals in the thickets. One was *Malus yunnanensis* and the other *M hupehensis,* and their close proximity to one another made comparison convenient. Both had developed sharp, pointed spurs on their main

Rhododendron yunnanensis, was common throughout the Cangshan, always free flowering in a generous range of pastel shades of pink and mauve. (May)

An alpine paradise above Huadianba. The slope was filled with flowers, among which those of the dwarf *Rhododendron fastigiatum* (mauve-purple) and *R cephalanthum* (white) were outstanding. Note the Yak-grazed plain below. (May)

Incarvillea mairei at 3,200m (10,500ft) in the northern Cangshan. This bold-flowered perennial was common in the hills above Huadianba. (May)

themselves, these trees lack the open-branched habit and 'flowery-armed' effect of the true M *hupehensis*, which, apparently, is still grown in parts of the United States.

M *hupehensis* was first introduced to the West from Hubei by Wilson, who considered it the finest deciduous flowering tree he had introduced. Another name, M *theifera*, refers to the use in Hubei of its leaves to make a beverage called 'red tea'. M *yunnanensis*, which also occurs in Sichuan and Hubei, was also a Wilson introduction though it had previously been found by Delavay.

branches. However, in M *yunnanensis* the branches were decidedly upright while those of the other were spreading and irregular. The flowers of M *yunnanensis* were 1.5cm (½in) across, cream-coloured and carried on downy stalks in erect, flattened clusters (corymbs) on short, leafy shoots. Those of M *hupehensis* were larger, 2.5cm (1in) across, cup shaped, pure white, pink tinged in bud, fragrant and carried on white, downy stalks 4-4.5cm (1½-1¾in) long in loose clusters on short spurs all along the branches. The juvenile leaves of M *yunnanensis* are often lobed, a characteristic absent in M *hupehensis*. Even from a distance the two crabs were easy to tell apart: the upright crown and scattered creamy flower clusters of M *yunnanensis*, and the spreading crown of M *hupehensis*, its long branches wreathed with white blossom. Both are in cultivation, although the true M *hupehensis* as described above had, until recently, become rare in Britain, its place and name having apparently been usurped by at least one if not two trees of uncertain origin. While attractive enough in

Tien-Lu-Ming with *Rhododendron trichocladum*, forming dense thickets above Huadianba in the northern Cangshan. (May)

In between the areas of scrub and thicket were grassy banks and clearings. These were liberally studded with rock outcrops in which grew a bold and colourful perennial plant, *Incarvillea mairei*. From a clump of deeply divided (pinnate) leaves with large terminal leaflets, rose from one to four erect stems 20cm (8in) high, each bearing several large, trumpet-shaped, crimson or carmine flowers with yellow throats. It was quite spectacular and occurred scattered over a wide area, even following us up the hill into the plains where it was widespread. There seemed to be some variation in stem height not altogether associated with flowering stage or growing conditions. Some plants of lower altitudes had stems to 30cm (12in), while those at higher altitudes had consistently short stems.[43] Carmine was the typical colour, but on one occasion we found a plant with creamy yellow flowers slightly smaller in size than those of the typical form close by.

Lyonias appeared again in the thicket, both *Lyonia villosa* and *L ovalifolia* in various forms being common in the Huadianba area. Their almost protean nature we had long since come to terms with and we were rarely surprised when some new variation turned up. We came to refer to them as the 'masters of disguise'. Sharing the thickets with them were *Pieris formosa* and the bold *Gaultheria griffithiana*, which I had previously seen in east Nepal in 1971, loaded with bunches of black fruits. These two were almost swamped in a sea of scrubby evergreen oaks of several kinds, through which poked rhododendrons, aspen (*Populus rotundifolia* variety *duclouxiana*), and a most attractive rowan of shrubby growth to 4m (13ft) with neatly divided (pinnate) leaves composed of numerous small leaflets. Even the white-budded flowers were carried in elegant slender-stalked clusters. This plant was introduced to the West as seedlings and produced pink-tinted white fruits. Originally it was identified as *Sorbus rufopilosa*, but according to Dr H McAllister of the University of Liverpool Botanic Garden, Ness, Cheshire, it is an unnamed species closely related to the more familiar *S vilmorinii*, which was originally discovered in north-west Yunnan and introduced to France by Delavay. It was also later introduced by Forrest during his last expedition. *S vilmorinii* remains one of the best rowans for the garden, and is particularly suitable for small gardens, where its domed crown of elegant arching branches looks well in a lawn or bed.[44]

At about 3,100m (10,170ft) we breasted the ridge and gazed down the other side into what looked like a gigantic

Sorbus pseudovilmorinii. A recently named species of rowan with elegant foliage. Here a suckering specimen rises from a dense scrub above Huadianba. Note *Populus rotundifolia* variety *duclouxiana* top left. (May)

basin, the bottom of which was a vast grassy plateau on which yaks grazed. This was surrounded by hills, mostly round topped, rising 300-400m (984-1,312ft) above our present position. The plateau was an unremitting green, the surrounding slopes anything but. It was as if a giant had stood in the centre with brushes and paints and coloured the slopes with bold strokes and occasional dabs. As far as the eye could see these slopes were covered in alpine rhododendrons, mostly in flower, and creating colourful tapestries of blue, purple, pink, white and yellow. For a while we could only stand and stare, then we slowly descended the near slope towards the plateau. For the next hour we wandered alone through the rhododendrons, each enjoying our personal dreamworld.

After a while I sat down on the grass, high up on the slope with a wide view of the plateau and the scattered white-hatted figures of my colleagues. The most common rhododendron here was undoubtedly *Rhododendron fastigiatum*,

43. *I mairei* is fairly common in cultivation in the West where it is hardy and reliable in a moist but well-drained soil, and especially one that is deep and rich. In cultivation, too, its flowering stems are generally taller – up to 30cm (1ft) or more. A plant collected at the time now growing at the Royal Botanic Garden, Edinburgh, produces stems as much as 60cm (2ft). It is native mainly to Yunnan, but has also been recorded from west Sichuan and Gansu. First discovered by Delavay and later by Maire (after whom it is named), it was recorded by several other collectors, of whom Forrest was the first to introduce it into western cultivation.

44. This new species has since been described and published under the name *S pseudovilmorinii*. In October 2005 I saw well fruited trees at the University of Liverpool Botanic Gardens, Ness in Cheshire.

Slopes above Huadianba clothed with *Rhododendron fastigiatum* and the taller-growing pale yellow flowered *R trichocladum*. (May)

Rhododendron cephalanthum flourishing in limestone rubble above Huadianba. (May)

which formed tight, low, flat-topped mounds and hummocks plastered with small clusters of lilac, mauve-purple or bluish-purple flowers. Less common, but plentiful in a few areas, was *Rhododendron cephalanthum*, hummocks of gnarled stems, each twig bearing at its tip a neat rounded cluster of white flowers like those of one of the more desirable daphnes. In scattered areas, *R racemosum* appeared, dwarf and compact, its short stems and white-backed leaves crowded with bright pink flowers. The yellow was contributed by *Rhododendron trichocladum*, dense thickets of which we found in association with *R fastigiatum*, generally as a backdrop, the purple and yellow of the two a cheerful sight. Indeed, Peter Cox found a likely hybrid of these two in which the few flowers left were a pink-tinged yellow.

Where *R cephalanthum* occurred, its dense mounds sometimes merged with those of *R fastigiatum*, a striking combination of purple and white. The amazing thing was that all these rhododendrons were growing on limestone. Indeed, several old and healthy plants of *R cephalanthum* we found growing in almost pure lime rubble with a pH of 8.1 and an organic content of 3.2 per cent.

Lime and rhododendrons was a subject on which George Forrest had strong opinions. He once wrote that most of the rhododendrons he had collected in west and north-west Yunnan grew directly in or on pure limestone. According to Forrest, many of the smaller rhododendrons have their roots embedded in the crevices of the limestone rocks or cliffs, or in the limy rubble at their base, while the taller tree species, though with more or less of a bed of humus for support, have their smaller roots similarly placed. Having seen rhododendrons among the limestone crags of Emei Shan in Sichuan and here in the Cangshan I can only agree. The limestone at Huadianba, however, is

dolomitic and a soil analysis indicated that the calcium and magnesium ions are not readily available to the plant. The pH reading of 8.4, therefore, is not a true reflection on the growing conditions. Moreover, the pH reading at Huadianba seemed to be an extreme for, elsewhere in the Cangshan, soil samples taken from rhododendron sites proved to have a much lower pH and a higher organic content. These ranged from pH 3.7 with an organic content of 24.3 per cent for *R lacteum* growing on the ridge above

Rhododendron racemosum. Its low domes crowded with pink to rose-pink flowers were widely scattered on slopes above the plateau. (May)

Rhododendron trichocladum. Its delicate pale yellow flowers appear with or before the new leaves. (May)

Camp 2 at Shangchang, to pH 5.5 with an organic content of 14.9 per cent for R *arboreum* subspecies *delavayi* growing near Camp 1 at Dapingdi. As Peter Cox has since concluded, natural rhododendron soil is, as we suspected, generally very acid and comparatively low in nutrients. Do we, therefore, over fertilise our rhododendrons in cultivation?

We ate our packed lunches among the alpine rhododendrons, still preferring the quiet of our own company at this magical hour. I lay back, resting my head on a natural cushion of rhododendron and closed my eyes. Shortly, I heard the song of a skylark, then two, three, four, singing their hearts out somewhere above. Then I heard another song, far away it seemed, down on the plateau. I opened my eyes as I sat up and sure enough, on the green

Rhododendron fastigiatum and R *cephalanthum* growing together to form a colourful low mound above Huadianba. (May)

Rhododendron cephalanthum on limestone rubble above Huadianba. (May)

plain, following a barely discernible track, was a group of yaks, three of them in line, and lying on their backs three children. They were unaware of our presence among the rhododendrons on the slopes and as they trundled towards us their singing grew louder. It was a wild wind-blown song with occasional chanting that eventually died away as the yaks passed behind a hill and were gone. For me, both the dream and the wonder of the Cangshan experience reached fulfilment in this high place next to the sky. Within a week we would be back in Kunming and this experience would be a memory.

It was time to be moving on and with some reluctance I picked my way down the slope to join my colleagues who had also been mesmerised both by the rhododendrons and the chanting yak-borne children.

The rhododendrons were only part of the plant scene for, growing in the grass areas between them, was a superb range of alpine herbs, most of them in flower and so giving a colourful speckling effect to the green turf. Most plentiful was a small anemone with blue or white buttercup-sized flowers. It looked like a version of *Anemone obtusiloba*, a feature of alpine pastures in the Himalaya,

Anemone trullifolia. A beautiful relative of the Himalayan *A obtusiloba*, which was abundant in grassy areas among alpine rhododendrons above Huadianba. Here photographed by J. Jermyn in cultivation. (May)

Corydalis curviflora variety *rosthornii* with its flower spikes of an electric blue was scattered among the alpine rhododendrons above Huadianba. (May)

Euphorbia regina, similar at a glance to the European *E polychroma*, was frequent on steep exposed slopes above Huadianba. It is not to the author's knowledge in present day cultivation in the West. (May)

especially Kashmir, and, indeed, it turned out to be a close relative: *A trullifolia*.[45]

One of the most highly prized of all alpines in cultivation is *Corydalis cashmeriana* from the Himalaya. Its tufts of rich green, finely-divided leaves and 10-15cm (4-6in) stems bearing spurred flowers of the most dazzling blue never fail to attract comments of admiration at Alpine Garden Society shows in May. I have several times seen this species in Kashmir and Nepal and thought I was renewing our acquaintance on the alpine slopes above Huadianba, for here grew the most beautiful example of the same, or similar, species. It was larger, however, in all its parts although the flowers were the same unforgettable blue. Not surprisingly it proved to be different and was later identified as *Corydalis curviflora* variety *rosthornii*.[46] Its brilliant spikes studded the turf that day creating an effect I shall never forget. Several small plants were collected, some of which are established in cultivation in Scotland, and Ron McBeath at the Royal Botanic Garden, Edinburgh, informed me they have one strong plant in a raised bed in semi-shade, which sends up 15-20cm (6-8in) spikes of brilliant blue flowers in spring and again in late summer without, however, setting a single seed.

In the 1880s Père Delavay discovered in north-west Yunnan a lovely new primula, which was named *Primula vinciflora*, meaning 'with flowers like *Vinca*' – the periwinkle, although, as Farrer remarked, they more resemble those of some exaggerated violet or butterwort (*Pinguicula* species) than a periwinkle. Later, this (and several other similar species) was transferred to a new genus – *Omphalogramma* – as *O vinciflora*. They are not easy to cultivate and, like the corydalis, are best seen in the cooler, moister gardens of northern Britain. More commonly they are grown in pans in the alpine house or cold frame. We were reminded of all this when admiring the blue corydalis, for *O vinciflora* was frequent here, too, its violet, long-tubed flowers borne singly on slender, downy, 15cm (6in) stems above a basal rosette of hairy leaves. It was a thrill to see these two choice alpines together. They occupied a grassy slope in full sun, no doubt impeccably drained, but already well supplied with moisture from the showers, which were a precursor of the rains soon to come.

The steeper slopes were host to a rather fine spurge, which, in its dwarf bushy growth and bold terminal heads of yellow flowers and bracts, reminded me strongly of *Euphorbia polychroma*, a native of Europe and one of the most popular herbaceous garden spurges. Ours was every bit as good and was later named by the Chinese *Euphorbia regina*.

45. Plants were introduced to the Royal Botanic Garden, Edinburgh, where it has thrived and is regarded as an attractive species. It has since become available from nursery sources and hopefully will be seen more frequently in cultivation in future.

46. *C curviflora* itself was first discovered by the Russian botanist Przewalski in Tibet in 1880. It is recorded that he also introduced it to cultivation, and if he had any success then he was luckier than Reginald Farrer who once wrote of it: 'A gloriously lovely species with loose showers of purest azure blossom, in all the scrubby places of the ranges up the Northern Marches of Tibet'. He added: 'I failed to introduce it, alas!' As to the variety, it is named after A von Rosthorn, an Austrian who, according to Augustine Henry, 'made collections of plants in Sichuan, through natives'.

Salvia campanulata, a bold ornamental sage with whorls of large straw-yellow flowers. (May)

Androsace spinulifera, one of the most distinct of its kind growing among rocks in the hills above Huadianba. (May)

Cotoneaster procumbens, an evergreen species, plastering rocks and slopes in the hills above Huadianba. (May)

Lonicera adenophora. A curious deciduous shrub with hairy leaves and paired flowers of sombre hue. (May)

Unfortunately, it was not introduced. A bold ornamental sage also flourished on these slopes, forming clumps of large velvety leaves, greyish-white beneath, and with downy stems to 30cm (12in) high carrying whorls of large, straw-yellow, hairy, two-lipped flowers. We saw it again later in similar sites and it proved to be *Salvia campanulata*, which is now found in British cultivation.

Some slopes were occupied by a bold fern, *Osmunda claytoniana*, a relative of the Royal fern (*O regalis*), but distinct in that its fertile fronds start and end with sterile leafy sections (interrupted). It formed stiff, bronzed clumps over a wide area, favouring damp depressions where the snow had lain longest. This is another of those plants with a circumpolar distribution, from North America eastwards to north-east Asia, but here it seemed a far cry from the hills above Montreal in Canada, where I first saw it wild in 1980.

The many rock outcrops with their attendant debris provided another interesting plant habitat. Here, for instance, grew *Draba yunnanensis*, a tiny, yellow-flowered gem, up to 10cm (4in) tall, with a pad of hairy rosettes. It was accompanied by two androsaces: *Androsace rigida* variety *minor* and *Androsace spinulifera*. The former was a prostrate perennial with mats of hairy rosettes studded with pink flowers on short 2cm (¾in) stems. Unlike *A spinulifera*, it has proved difficult to flower in cultivation.

A spinulifera was far more attractive with loose umbels of soft, pink, yellow-eyed flowers on downy 15cm (6in) stems. The tufts of grey-green, downy leaves vary in form, non-flowering rosettes resembling a small, grey, downy houseleek (*Sempervivum*), the leaves imbricated and ending in a short, sharp point (mucro). The erect leaves of flowering rosettes are longer, looser and without mucro points.

The rocks, too, were plastered with the branches of two prostrate shrubs, one the evergreen *Cotoneaster procumbens*, the other a deciduous willow — *Salix acuminata* variety *microphylla*. The tiny white flowers of the former and the small yellow male catkins of the latter created many bright splashes of colour and could occasionally be found growing with their stems interwoven over the same rock that they encased like a coat of chain mail.

In our excitement over finding these alpine treasures we had, as usual, forgotten the time. It was Professor Feng, yet again, who reminded us we must start on the homeward trail. I remember Bob and I heading for a thicket of shrubs to have a final search, attracted there by a sweet perfume. It came from the pale pink flowers of a lilac, *Syringa yunnanensis*, which here reached 3m (9ft). With this grew two shrubby honeysuckles: *Lonicera inconspicua* (*stenosiphon*) was a deciduous bush of 1.5m (5ft) with pairs of yellow flowers pendulous from the upper leaf axils; *Lonicera adenophora*, on the other hand, was a robust shrub to 2.5m (8ft), with glandular-hairy young growths. The leaves were quite large, up to 10cm (4in) long or more, and glandular hairy beneath. The most striking feature about this shrub, however, was its flowers, which were rather small but of a dark, sombre liverish-purple or dark wine-red and glandular downy on the outside. They were borne in pairs on a slender curving stalk from the upper leaf axils, poised beneath the leaf above like two miniature crows. According to Rehder this species is capable of reaching 6m (20ft) in height. As far as I am aware it is not at present in cultivation in the West where, I suspect, it would be regarded as more interesting than ornamental. *L adenophora* is now considered by most authorities to be the same as *L webbiana*, a Himalayan species. If this course is followed then the latter name has precedence.

That night we had yak meat for supper and, although somewhat tough, it made a change from chicken and fish. We washed it down with beer and lemonade, while those of us who had become hardened to it partook of Professor Feng's Moutai nightcap. The meal was followed by another film show: an epic in black and white with a happy ending.

For some time before the film was due to begin, people had been filing into the hall. They were mainly Bais, many of them in their colourful native dress, which they also wear at work in the fields, preferring it to the Han style denim jacket and trousers. Some of these people had travelled long distances in the dark from their scattered communities, finding their way with the aid of torches or paraffin lamps.

It seemed to us that whole families were present, for several of the women cradled babies in their arms while

Piptanthus nepalensis, an excellent, free-flowering form of the so-called 'evergreen' laburnum. A single bush was found in the shingle by the side of a stream near Huadianba. (May)

Piptanthus nepalensis, a single specimen of excellent form found by a streamside near Huadianba. (May)

older children and a few grandparents were also in evidence. They sat in rows on wooden forms, some of them warming themselves over small metal baskets of hot charcoal that they had carried with them suspended on wire. Robert Fortune once described a similar method of keeping warm that he encountered at Ningbo (Ningpo) in Zhejiang province, east China, during the winter of 1843/44. According to Fortune 'the ladies sometimes use a small brass stove, like a little oval basket, having the lid grated to allow the charcoal to burn and the heat to escape; this they place upon their tables or on the floor, for the purpose of warming the hands and feet. Nurses also carry these little stoves in their hands under the feet of the children'. The Huadianba 'stoves' were less elaborate but apparently just as effective. After the show, the Bai audience did not linger but left in good humour and melted into the night. Some time later, as I stared across the fields towards the north west, I could see pin pricks of moving light like distant fireflies.

The following two days we spent exploring the side valleys south of Huadianba. Here the influence of granite showed in the vegetation, which included birch for the first time, mountain ash in variety, maples and a more limited selection of *Rhododendron* species, including *irroratum*, *facetum*, *edgeworthii*, *rubiginosum* and *cyanocarpum*. Most of the lower slopes as well as the comparatively level areas at the base are covered with scrub in which grow a variety of trees and shrubs. Most of these we had already seen elsewhere. Of those new elements I was pleased to see *Ilex yunnanensis*, tall, erect, evergreen shrubs with small, neatly-toothed leaves and purplish, young growths; *Berberis dictyophylla* with white, bloomy shoots and leaves; *Litsea cubeba*; and *Lindera obtusiloba*, with rounded leaves. Both the last two we had seen all through the Cangshan. The grey-leaved *Buddleja agathosma* (now included in *B crispa*) was also here, as was

a bold-leaved form of *Hydrangea heteromalla* that the Chinese called variety *mollis*. It reached 2-2.5m (6-8ft), its handsome leaves grey and woolly beneath. Later, in a wooded valley, we found it up to 6m (20ft) high spreading widely across a stream.[47] One of the most abundant plants in the scrub, both here and elsewhere in the Cangshan, is *Piptanthus nepalensis* (*laburnifolius*), a rather coarse, wide-spreading shrub up to 2m (6ft) high and twice as wide, with silky young shoots, leaves with three pointed leaflets, dark green above and loose clusters of yellow pea flowers. It is found from west China into upper Burma and from Bhutan to Simla in the Himalaya. Because of its relatively untidy habit and its dislike of frosts it is normally grown in cultivation against a south- or west-facing wall – certainly in colder areas – where it provides a cheering sight in May when in flower. One day we found an excellent form of this shrub growing by a stream. Its stems were fairly erect, up

Populus yunnanensis, a handsome strong-growing balsam poplar not uncommon by streams around Huadianba. Here photographed at the Royal Botanic Garden, Edinburgh, from wild origin. (May)

Hydrangea heteromalla variety *mollis*. A large shrub found in thickets above Huadianba. Here photographed in the author's garden. (June)

Rodgersia aesculifolia variety *henricii*, a plant introduced from Huadianba, here photographed in the Royal Botanic Gardens, Edinburgh. (June)

to 1.5m (5ft), and its habit compact, while the leaves were almost hidden by the ample nodding flower clusters that literally wreathed the stems from top to bottom. It was a marvellous sight and would have been a popular introduction if cuttings had been feasible.

Where streams ran down from the side valleys they formed a system of waterways, often with swamp in between. These permanently wet sites suited those trees like the willows, poplars and alders, which are universally associated with such places and are sometimes the dominant force there. The local alder was *Alnus ferdinandi-coburgii*, which was plentiful here, often a thicket of stems by streams and along tracks. It is a straight-stemmed tree of some 10m (32ft) or more with angular brown shoots of the previous year and obovate pointed leaves 10cm (4in) or more long. These were shining green above and serrulate, with up to thirteen pairs of veins, downy on emerging, soon becoming smooth except on the midrib and main veins beneath. The fruiting cones were 1cm (⅓ in) long, borne singly on a stalk 1.5-2cm (½ -¾ in) long. The young flower clusters were noticeable at the base of the current year's shoot. I had not encountered the species previously and I am not aware of its presence in cultivation.

There were three different poplars of which the most common was the aspen *Populus rotundifolia* variety *duclouxiana*, which formed dense suckering stands in places. Less common, and occurring as isolated specimens or occasionally in small groups, was *P yunnanensis*, a balsam poplar with sticky buds on angular shoots. It had pale bark and ovate leaves (the typical poplar shape), which were pointed at the tip and had small gland-tipped rounded teeth. They were grey-green beneath. The tallest specimens we saw were 18m (60ft). The third poplar was not common, indeed we only saw three or four trees widely scattered along streams. It was, however, the most imposing, one large stump having a girth of 376cm (148in) at chest height. The leaves were bold, ovate to almost rounded and up to 25cm (10in) long, of which the flattened, red-tinged stalk was half.

They were toothed (serrate), light green and, after the initial floss had been shed, quite smooth. There was no

sign of old fruiting catkins and, although we have attempted to match this tree with specimens in the herbarium, efforts to name it have failed.

An herbaceous plant favouring damp places, particularly roadside ditches and streamsides, was *Rodgersia henricii*,[48] a species closely related to *R aesculifolia* and usually confused with it in cultivation. This is hardly surprising considering the features by which they are separated. According to Dr James Cullen of Edinburgh, an authority on the genus, the leaves of *R aesculifolia* are downy on the main veins and also on the teeth beneath, while those of *R henricii* are downy on the veins only. Another difference concerns the sepals of the flowers. In the former species they are conspicuously enlarged after flowering, while in the latter this is not the case, or scarcely so. In the wild, *R aesculifolia* is more northerly

47. A plant of this once grew in my garden where it flourished. The flowers are typical large lace-caps with creamy-white marginal florets. In leaf it reminds me of a plant once grown at the Hillier Arboretum, and although this was received as *H robusta*, an east Himalayan species of marginal floral merit, we decided it belonged to *H heteromalla* and we gave it the cultivar name 'Snowcap'. Sadly, I suspect it may now be lost to cultivation. It was an impressive shrub of its kind.

48. Interestingly, the name of this plant commemorates two famous people, Rear Admiral John Rodgers (1812-1882), a distinguished American naval officer who in 1852-1856 commanded a Pacific expedition during which the first species of the genus, *R podopylla* was discovered in Japan, and Prince Henri d'Orléans (1867-1901), a French explorer who collected in western China and first discovered the above plant, which is now regarded as a variety of the more widespread *R aescolifolia*.

Betula utilis, an excellent form with richly-coloured peeling bark growing in the woods near Huadianba. (May)

Betula utilis - the richly-coloured peeling bark of young trees in a wooded valley above Huadianba. (May)

in its distribution, being native in Gansu, Hubei and Sichuan, while R *henricii* has a more southern distribution, native to Yunnan and upper Burma. The two species do come together, however, in south-east Tibet. As we saw it at Huadianba, R *henricii* clearly resembled R *aesculifolia* in general appearance, the numerous leaflets arising from a common point at the summit of a stout, green, hairy stalk, as in *Aesculus*, the horse chestnut. These leaflets are abruptly pointed, boldly veined and held

Rodgersia pinnata was common in ditches and by streamsides around Huadianba, but not yet flowering. (May)

horizontally or are slightly drooping. The flowerheads on plants at Huadianba were pink tinted but otherwise still in bud. According to Cullen the open flowers can vary in colour from creamy white to a rich rose-pink and Kingdon-Ward once described them as being 'very fragrant'. A plant introduced to the Royal Botanic Garden, Edinburgh, has since flowered, and has proved strong and easy, growing 1-1.3m (3-4ft) tall with pale pinkish-white flowers.

R *henricii* was not the only species of this genus that we found in the Cangshan. More abundant by far was R *pinnata*, especially in the Huadianba area where it sometimes shared the same shady ravines as R *henricii*. It was a robust plant with boldy-veined, rather leathery leaflets on dark stalks above which the dense flowerheads protruded. These, however, were still in bud though attractively suffused, like the leaf stalks, with bronze-red. We had previously seen R *pinnata* in shady moist ravines on the eastern flanks of the Cangshan above Dali and were not surprised to learn later that others had found it in this region. Delavay and Forrest both collected it in the Cangshan, Forrest twice at least on these very slopes. The leaves of R *pinnata* are pseudopinnate, ie with a variable number of leaflets staggered along a long or short rachis.

Another plant that shared the occasional streamside with the rodgersias was *Beesia calthifolia*, a member of the buttercup family (*Ranunculaceae*). Its main ornamental attribute seemed to be its long-stalked, heart-shaped, pale-marbled leaves, not unlike those of a large kingcup (*Caltha* species), but more pointed. A plant introduced to the Royal Botanic Garden, Edinburgh, has since flowered although the event, according to Ron McBeath who noted it, was nothing out of the ordinary, a few modest, five-petalled, whitish flowers towards the summit of an erect stem. The generic name commemorates the nursery firm of Bees of Chester, England, founded by the industrialist, and patron of Forrest and Kingdon-Ward, A K Bulley.

The one and only birch we found was *Betula utilis*, and this as scattered individuals in the valleys. They possessed a

Rhododendron rex ssp. *fictolacteum*, the leaves beneath clothed with a rich rusty-red indumentum. Here growing in the woods above Huadianba. (May)

Fritillaria cirrhosa, a graceful species here growing in a bamboo thicket above Huadianba. (May)

gorgeous rich coppery-orange, papery bark that peeled freely, causing bunches to hang beneath the base of the main branches. The young shoots were glandular downy, while the ovate and abruptly pointed leaves, which were 5cm (2in) long, had nine to fourteen pairs of veins. The tallest specimens were in the region of 12m (40ft) with slender trunks, but stumps of larger trees were much in evidence.

One valley, which we entered in pouring rain, contained a host of rhododendrons that had Peter Cox and David very excited. The first to confront us was a 5m (16ft) shrub of *Rhododendron facetum* (*eriogynum*), its trusses of red flowers almost open. Later it was found in full flower, its superb, waxy, scarlet bells glowing like hot coals in the gloom. Next to it was another rhododendron with pink flowers spotted red within, which David was convinced was a hybrid between R *irroratum* (whence the spots) and R *facetum* (the basic colour). Mr Ming, however, seemed unconvinced. Further up the valley in a deep ravine above a stream we found R *sinogrande*, again in some quantity and so obviously happy that the banks above the track and, indeed, the woodland floor around, were covered with its seedlings of all sizes.

Nearby, we found seedlings of R *edgeworthii* equally abundant, enough to set a rhododendron nurseryman watering at the mouth. Peter Cox, in particular, was astonished by these thickets of seedlings, which shared their moist dappled world with a host of other tree and shrub seedlings including *Tsuga dumosa*, *Daphne feddei* and several linderas and hollies. These moist banks were also home to several gaultherias including *Gaultheria cardiosepala* and G *sinensis*. The former was crowded with tiny, white, pitcher-shaped flowers, while the latter was an evergreen decumbent and creeping shrublet with bell-shaped white flowers. I remembered G *sinensis* from the peat garden at the Hillier Arboretum where it used to produce comparatively large, rich blue fruits crowding the leafy shoots.

Another valley we explored, this time in better weather, proved less exciting botanically than the previous one. We approached along a dried stream bed that afforded the only access. A new (for us) maple proved to be *Acer caudatum* variety *georgei*, a multi-stemmed tree of 8m (26ft) with shoots of the previous year a dark red. The leaves had three to five lobes (palmate), the lobes jaggedly lobed and toothed and tapering to a slender point. They were downy, especially on the veins below and in the vein axils. The greenish flowers (red tinted in bud), were carried in erect spike-like clusters from the tips of side shoots.[49]

Interestingly, unlike the previous valley we had explored, this one contained no *Rhododendron sinogrande*, its place being taken by R *rex* subspecies *fictolacteum*, which in some places was dominant, forming thickets with individual trees up to 8m (26ft). Many of these were ancient specimens thickly clad in green moss and grey lichen. Shortly after seeing them we were forced to scramble up a very steep, almost vertical stream gully densely covered with vegetation that gave way to bamboo through which we had to crawl on our hands and knees. The bamboo covered the summit of a hill – Wutaishan – at 3,400m (11,154ft), and here we decided to eat our lunch perched above the bamboo in the branches of *Rhododendron cyanocarpum*. The last named occurred in quantity, its splendid pink cinnamon, flaky-barked stems up to 6m (20ft), its grey-hued leaves topped with flowers ranging in colour from white to a good deep pink.

Later, in crawling out of the bamboo, we encountered two interesting perennials one of which, *Fritillaria cirrhosa*, we had seen on several previous occasions. Here it grew in some numbers on slender 30cm (12in) stems with a whorl of narrow leaves and a nodding yellow bell, occasionally bronzed on the outside and spotted red within. The other perennial was a relatively small curious

49. This is a variety of a Himalayan maple whose name, *A caudatum* according to Bean, should be discarded in favour of *A papilio*. Named after George Forrest, the above variety is interesting in its erect flower clusters, but is not in the front rank of ornamental maples for the garden. The Chinese referred this maple to subspecies *georgei* which is not recognised by many western authorities. According to Peter Cox, who is growing it from this source, it has a striking look, like a pale *A griseum* and since having seen it myself I can only agree.

Arisaema omeiense growing on a wooded ridge above Huadianba. Note the two large, ear-like lobes at the base of the striped mouth and the lobed and toothed leaflets. (May)

Arisaema species, which was identified by the Chinese as *Arisaema auriculatum* but has since been named *A omeiense*, a variable species especially in leaf shape and flower colour. Its leaves were composed of three stalked leaflets lobed and toothed at the margin. The slender-tubed flowers were all green except for some darker flecks on the outside. The spadix had a long slender appendage that curved from out of the mouth and upwards, looking for all the world like the tail of a mouse. The most unusual characteristic of the flower, however, was its two long appendages or lobes at the base of the mouth.

So absorbed was I in photographing this plant that I inadvertently sat on a dwarf prickly-leaved mahonia that formed a colony of suckering stems to 1m (3ft) high. It was not the first time we had seen this shrub, which had finger-like racemes of yellow flowers in terminal clusters and leaves 17-23cm (7-9in) long with eleven to thirteen glossy, green leaflets. It looked interesting and was later identified by the Chinese as *Mahonia veitchiorum* variety *kingdonwardianum*, though this has subsequently been challenged by various authorities.[50]

On a bank below the mahonia we found *Daphne retusa*, a dwarf evergreen shrub up to 35cm (14in) high, showing a tendency to sucker and forming colonies on moist mossy banks in dappled shade. This is one of the most reliable shrubs of its kind in gardens: hardy, amenable to most soils and situations and regularly producing its terminal clusters of white flowers stained rose or purple on the outside in April and May when, at the same time, they give off a sweet perfume. In some years there is a second flowering in late summer and a plant in my garden regularly gives me this bonus.

As we descended the hill we found a juniper and a mountain ash of particular interest. The former, which the Chinese called *Juniperus gaussenii*, is a little-known species described in 1940 by the botanist W C Cheng who likened it to *J chinensis*. Here it was a tree of 4m (13ft) with wide-spreading bright green, needle-like leaves, spreading branches and branchlets nodding at the tips. It looked to my mind not unlike *J formosana*. The mountain ash was identified by the Chinese as *Sorbus rehderiana*, though I have my doubts about this. It was a tree up to 6.5m (22ft), of spreading habit with conspicuous leafy stipules on the young shoots and below the flowerheads. The leaves were pinnate, averaging 19cm (7½ in) long with a noticeably grooved stalk (rachis) above and seventeen to twenty-one leaflets 3.5-5cm (1½ -2in) long. These were glossy, green and smooth above, paler and downy beneath, toothed at

Mahonia polyodonta, a dwarf evergreen shrub found in the hills above Huadianba and elsewhere in the Cangshan. (May)

Geranium yunnanense, introduced for the first time to western cultivation from the wooded hills above Huadianba in 1981. Here it is seen flowering in 1987 in the Royal Botanic Garden, Edinburgh. (June)

Ulmus bergmanniana, the coppery-red young foliage seen against a sunny cloudless sky at Huadianba. (May)

Ulmus bergmanniana, a rare elm with handsome, conspicuously veined leaves, Huadianba.(May)

the tip or at most in the upper quarter. The flowers were white in broad, flattened or low-domed heads. A noticeable characteristic was the pale brown, hairy veins and rachis beneath. The fruits are said to mature white with or without a pink flush.

One of the most popular groups of perennials in British gardens today are the hardy geraniums, which are available in great variety, differing in habit, leaf and flower. I have several species and hybrids in my garden all of which are reliable and free flowering. I was very pleased, therefore, to see a new (to me) species in the wooded valley above Huadianba that day. It was not in flower but seedlings introduced to the Royal Botanic Garden, Edinburgh, have since flowered and proved to be *Geranium yunnanense*, which, in the opinion of Dr Peter Yeo, botanist at the Cambridge University Botanic Garden and world authority on hardy geraniums, is probably the first time this species has been cultivated in the West. It is a clump-forming perennial with long-stalked, deeply five-lobed leaves and, in summer, nodding or inclined rose-pink, bowl-shaped flowers 2.5-3.5cm (1-1½ in) across. Ron McBeath of the Royal Botanic Garden, Edinburgh, told me that this species had done well in the summer with a mass of rose-pink flowers over a long period. He cautioned, however, that there was a tendency for it to attract mildew in autumn and that it may dislike winter wet. A plant in my garden flowered from June through to August 1986, and I particularly admired the feathered white base to the petals against which the blackish-purple anthers are striking. From my experience it takes full sun, but thrives best in a cool soil in semi-shade.

On our final day at Huadianba we were asked by Professor Feng if we had any preference as to which direction we should head. He proposed taking the road through the valley and beyond the medicinal plant farm to explore another of the side valleys. While this sounded promising, one or two of

us were anxious to spend our last day, a sunny one at that, back in the alpine pastures to the north, continuing where we had left off on the first day. In the event, we agreed to divide our forces and while Bob and David set off with the Professor and his group, the two Peters and I with two of our Chinese companions returned to the hills.

The Professor's party had several new finds including a large leaved elm, probably *Ulmus bergmanniana*. It was a single tree of 5m (16ft) with the most impressive leaves. These were 7.5-10cm (3-4in) or more long, obliquely rounded at the base, abruptly slender pointed at the tip and double toothed. They had beautiful parallel veining in sixteen to eighteen pairs, were coppery-red when young, maturing green. The smooth, reddish young shoots matured to grey the second year. From the downy nature of the leaves I suspect this tree to be the variety *lasiophylla*.

The Professor's party also found another mountain ash

A party of George Forrest's native collectors in the field in north-west Yunnan. The man on the left is Forrest's head man Lao Chao. Note the plant press as well as the guns and dogs, which were used in the hunting of game as well as for protection. Such parties were trained by Forrest to work independently and were responsible for collecting seed of many fine plants, especially in the Cangshan. This particular group was photographed by Forrest in the early 1900s

50. This plant, which grows in my garden is regarded by some to belong to the variable *M polyodonta*, which in the wild enjoys a distribution from N.E. Guizhou, W. Hubei, Sichuan, Yunnan and Burma.

Gentiana ternifolia. A superb autumn-flowering species, which was common in the hills above Huadianba. Here photographed by J. Jermyn in cultivation. (October)

growing by a stream with the elm. It was 5m (16ft), had dark second year shoots and relatively smooth (glabrous), pinnate leaves with eleven to thirteen leaflets of a characteristic sea-green colour above, grey-green beneath. The leaves averaged 3cm (1¼ in) long and were toothed only at the rounded apex. The white flowers were carried in loose, long-stalked heads (corymbs) with no sign of stipules beneath.[51]

Professor Feng's party also found *Tilia chinensis* again, a tree 7.5m (25ft) high, and smaller trees of *Styrax perkinsiae.* Meanwhile, our party once more climbed the hillside heading for the alpine rhododendrons. With fewer diversions it did not take us long and soon we were descending the inner slope on to the plain of the yaks. The

first plant of interest we found was a gentian with narrow leaves rather like *Gentiana sino-ornata.* It was growing as a turf, with loose tufts of prostrate slender stems, some of which we collected and introduced to the Royal Botanic Garden, Edinburgh. It has since flowered – pale blue trumpets with darker stripes on the outside – and been identified as *G ternifolia.* According to Ron McBeath at Edinburgh, it has proved an easy, compact and colourful autumn flowerer, similar to some of the *G x macaulayi* hybrids, and is now available in two clones – 'Cangshan' and 'Dali' – from several nurseries. Indeed, at a Royal Horticultural Society show in London in October 1986, Edrom Nurseries from Berwickshire, Scotland, staged an exhibit of gentians in which pride of place was given to a spectacular drift of *G*

Incarvillea mairei, a single bloom with raindrops, in the hills above Huadianba. (May)

Cypripedium flavum, its bulbous greenish-yellow flowers have a dark cyclopean eye (staminodes). (May)

Cryptothladia chlorantha, an all-green species growing on a rocky ledge in a ravine above Huadianba. Sadly, the expedition was unsuccessful in introducing this choice perennial to western cultivation. (May)

Meconopsis lancifolia, a small monocarpic (dying after flowering and seeding) poppy related to the widespread *M horridula*. A single plant was growing in a small ravine in the hills above Huadianba. (May)

ternifolia in full flower. To no-one's surprise, it attracted a great deal of attention and won a Gold Medal.

We crossed the rim of the valley heading in a north-westerly direction, away from the scene of our previous exploration. *Iris chrysographes* occurred in large non-flowering colonies and *Incarvillea mairei* stained the slopes all around with magenta. *Rhododendron fastigiatum* continued as the dominant dwarf shrub, its massed flowering creating a purple haze on distant slopes. We decided to explore a narrow ravine – a wise decision for here we met with *Cypripedium flavum* again, its bold flowers a real show stopper.

Growing on rocky ledges we also found a green morina

Acanthocalyx delavayi, like *Cryptothladia*, a close relative of *Morina* under which genus both were formerly included. It is a small perennial growing in stony places in the hills above Huadianba. (May)

appropriately named *Morina chlorantha*. From a basal clump of long, narrow, toothed leaves rise several stems to 30cm (12in), smooth below and clothed above with a white woolly down. The upper half of the stem supports several dense whorls of small, green flowers in the axils of bracts. These bracts are probably more attractive than the flowers for they are broad based and clasping, with a weakly spiny point and a charming bicolour effect, the lower half white, the rest jade green. Apart from the weakly prickly basal leaves, the plant is relatively soft and easy to handle. It is a most unusual plant, quite unlike *M longifolia*, which is the species more commonly grown in cultivation; I was not at all surprised to learn that it has since been placed in a separate genus as *Cryptothladia chlorantha*. This is a name gardeners need not worry themselves with at present for the species is not to my knowledge in cultivation, though it would most assuredly prove a popular introduction with alpine enthusiasts.

On the same subject it is worth mentioning another morina we found above Huadianba where it favoured grassy slopes and stony, well-drained places. According to Mrs Margaret Cannon of the British Museum (Natural History), an authority on morina and its allies, this small perennial herb, previously named *Morina delavayi* or *M bulleyana*, should now be known as *Acanthocalyx delavayi*. It is a fragile looking

51. To me it resembled a tree in cultivation long grown as *S hupehensis*, a species with a complex history recently discussed in his book. *The Genus Sorbus* by Dr. Hugh McAllister. From the evidence available, I am inclined to believe the above tree to be the recently named *S carmesina* based on trees collected as seed above Huadianba by Chris Brickell and Alan Leslie in 1987. It is reported as having pink fruits and good autumn colour.

Lloydia species, almost certainly *L. yunnanensis*, a relative of *L. serotina* – the Snowdon lily – one of our rarest natives. (May)

Pinus yunnanensis, Rhododendron yunnanense and an evergreen oak *Lithocarpus* sp. share a hillside position above Huadianba. (May)

An exposed hilltop at 3,150m (10,332ft) above Huadianba. The woody vegetation is mainly provided by dwarfed *Pinus yunnanensis* and *Quercus monimotricha* forming dense mounds with scattered *Rhododendron yunnanense* in flower. The carpeting evergreen in the foreground, right, is *Juniperus squamata*. (May)

plant with a basal rosette of narrow bristle-toothed leaves and from one to three erect or curving, slender, reddish stems to 15cm (6in), occasionally more. The rose-purple flowers are 2.5-4.5cm (1-1¾in) long, have a slender curving tube and are carried in a dense cluster from the tip of the shoot. I am not aware that this plant is in cultivation in the West, although it was collected in the Cangshan by Forrest who may have sent home seed. It would require a well-drained sunny situation in cultivation or, even better, a pot or pan in the alpine house or cold frame.

While I was examining and photographing this gem, Peter Hutchison was wandering along the bottom of the ravine just beneath me. Seeing that I was on the move again, he called to me to come and see what he had found. It was the most lovely poppy, a single plant growing on a stony, partially-shaded bank beneath a large rock. From a basal rosette of bristly leaves almost hidden in the grass rose a single dark stem to 20cm (8in) high carrying three bristly, nodding flower buds and a terminal, saucer-shaped flower. I have seen meconopsis before, several species wild in the mountains of Nepal and, of course, in cultivation with blue, white, yellow and red flowers, each impressive in its own way, but never have I seen a poppy as beautiful as this. The flower was about 5cm (2in) across, with six rounded, overlapping petals of a Royal purple. In the centre, a corona of yellow anthers on dark purple stalks (filaments) surrounded the green stigmas. According to the

Chinese, who collected and dried this plant, it belonged to *Meconopsis lancifolia*, a variable monocarpic (dying after flowering) species, related to *M. horridula*. It has a wide distribution from south-west Gansu to south-east Tibet, north-west Yunnan and northern upper Burma. It was originally discovered by Delavay in Yunnan and has been collected since in one form or another by many great plant hunters, including Forrest, Kingdon-Ward, Farrer and Rock.

The ravine continued for 200m (650ft) or more and we examined nearly every inch of it without finding anything else of interest other than a *Lloydia* species, almost certainly *L. yunnanensis* sprouting from a rock crevice. This is related to our native Snowdon lily (*L. serotina*), but with slightly larger flowers, pink tinted on the outside. From here we headed towards a round-topped hill some distance away, passing through an area of dense thicket in which the Yunnan lilac (*Syringa yunnanensis*) flowered, its white, pink-flushed trusses scenting the air around.[52]

We reached the hill and climbed to its summit at 3,150m (10,332ft). It was covered in scrub, low mounds of the evergreen, prickly-toothed, golden-backed oaks, *Quercus monimotricha* and *Q. longispica*, and equally dumpy specimens of *Pinus yunnanensis*. Colour was provided by *Rhododendron yunnanense*: wind sculptured, compact and plastered with flower. The golden oaks, the dark pine and the pastel shades of the rhododendron created a magnificent patchwork quilt that swept from this hill westwards to a distant horizon.

Among the oak and the pine occurred even lower mounds and carpets of *Juniperus squamata*. There appeared to be two distinct forms: adult plants with compact tightly-packed branches and congested green adult, scale-like foliage, comparatively soft to the touch. Male and female flowerheads (strobili) – and even fruits – were present on separate plants. What appeared to be juvenile plants were plentiful, too, low and diffuse in habit with long slender branches projecting

52. A plant grown from seed collected from Huadianba is flourishing at Glendoick Gardens in Perthshire, producing flower panicles of excellent quality.

Quercus monimotricha, a common evergreen scrub oak in the hills above Huadianba. Here photographed with male catkins in the author's garden. (June)

Thermopsis alpina variety *yunnanensis*, a dwarf creeping herbaceous member of the legume family, formed colonies on steep slopes in the hills above Huadianba. (May)

from the central mass and ascending at the tips. These were covered with needle-like leaves, prickly to handle and bluish-green with conspicuous white bands of stomata. The adult form was superb of its kind, some specimens as much as 3m (9ft) across, yet only 30-60cm (1-2ft) high at the domed centre. The only other woody plants competing with the above were the tiny, green, rushy-stemmed *Ephedra likiangensis* and the equally small *Berberis taliensis*, a species closely related to *B replicata* first discovered in the Cangshan by Forrest who introduced it into cultivation in 1922. Here it was a suckering shrub forming mounds of congested thorny stems up to 60cm (2ft). The evergreen leaves are shining green, bronze-red tinted when young and rolled over (revolute) at the margins almost hiding the silvery undersurface. It was common on the hilltop creeping among the rocks and stones and was crowded with yellow flowers borne in clusters in the leaf axils. I am not aware of this species in present day cultivation, although it used to be grown by Hilliers into the early 1970s. If it is still represented in British gardens it is only in botanical and specialist collections.

After an hour on the hill we turned for home, choosing a slightly different route than that of our approach. We found few plants we had not already seen and the most interesting was the creeping *Thermopsis alpina* variety *yunnanensis*, which looked superficially like a dwarf herbaceous piptanthus. Its downy shoots and leaves, divided into three leaflets, were overtopped by clusters of large, yellow pea flowers. Though no higher than 10cm (4in), its far-reaching underground stems had established this pretty plant over a considerable territory of stony

Mr Zong, the head man of Huadianba, and his wife, who is wearing the traditional Bai costume

Butterfly Spring in the mountains north of Dali is a popular tourist attraction. Here, every year in April and May, large numbers of butterflies congregate on the branches and leaves of the trees above a pool. The trees belong to *Neocinnamomum mekongense*, a close relation of the camphor tree (*Cinnamomum camphora*)

ground at the base of a hill.

For the last time we crossed 'Yak Valley', a blue sky above, skylarks singing and hillsides covered with purple alpine rhododendrons and golden stellera. The yaks were there in great numbers, up to six hundred of them grazing the emerald turf. We stopped momentarily to watch an eagle being mobbed by an Alpine chough then, with one final lingering look at paradise, descended into the valley. Bai girls colourfully dressed were hard at work in the fields, some of them hoeing between the rhubarb, which is, in fact, quite an attractive ornamental with its rich red stalks and stems and jaggedly lobed leaves.

Before breaking for supper that night we had made a start to our day's recording, and at the meal we fêted the elders of Huadianba, including Mr Zong and his wife, who had looked after us so well. Some of the elders had arrived clutching bottles of lemonade and when, at the end of the meal, Professor Feng produced the inevitable Moutai I wondered how they would decline without offending him. To my surprise they responded eagerly and several toasts later the bottle was empty. Now the various elders began passing round their lemonade and I allowed my glass to be filled, secretly thankful to be spared further punishment. "Ganbei!" [Bottoms up!] Mr Zong declared, and down the hatch in one went my lemonade. My eyes bulged and I almost choked as the drink burned its way into my stomach, for this was no lemonade but a home-made concoction reputedly stronger than Moutai. The Chinese could not believe it and laughed

and applauded as I slumped into my seat prepared to meet my doom. Professor Feng had other ideas and, after much hand shaking, thanks and warm farewells, we made our way back to our quarters to finish the recording. For evermore, a

A villager on the Huadianba road wearing a home-made palm fibre cape to keep out the wind and rain. (May)

The head of the valley at Quingbixu in the eastern foothills of the Cangshan. The trees are mainly *Pinus armandii*, while the white flecks proved to be flowering plants of *Rhododendron pachypodum*, *R edgeworthii* and *R maddenii* subspecies *crassum*. (May)

abduct a Bai girl. Her lover, a young hunter, intervened and, in attempting to pull the girl from the despot's clutches, the hunter and the girl fell into the pool and were changed into butterflies. A more scientific explanation suggests that the butterflies' keen sense of smell draws them to feed on the secretion of a camphor tree relative, *Neocinnamomum mekongense*, which has been planted around the pool. Although it was relatively late in the season great numbers of butterflies remained in the trees, though none were attempting to form living columns.

Professor Chen-yih Wu, Director of the Yunnan Institute of Botany in Kunming, had arrived to share with us two final day trips in the field. The first of these was to a waterfall that lay in a deep valley on the eastern slopes of the Cangshan at Qingbixu. We saw many interesting plants and I shall confine myself to a handful of the best.

The cliffs and rocks at the head of the valley were covered in dense, low vegetation in which grew masses of *Vaccinium delavayi*, *Rhododendron maddenii* subspecies *crassum*, *R pachypodum*, *R edgeworthii* and the purple *R microphyton*. The rhododendrons were all in flower and impressive, even though the first three occurred only as scattered individuals. From a distance we could see their white blooms shining through the mist that swirled down from the heights. At one point I found a plant of *R edgeworthii* growing through another of *R pachypodum*, both were in flower and filling the air with a heady perfume.

Pinus armandii clothed the higher ground and looked to be intact and in good health. A low hydrangea on a mossy bank proved to be *Hydrangea scandens* variety *chinensis*. It was a densely-

page of scrawled notes in our field book will serve to remind me of that night. The information contained is accurate enough, but written in a hand influenced by what must be one of the world's most potent spirits.

We returned down the valley the next day, sad to leave Huadianba knowing that it was our last contact with the interior of this mountain range. On our way we again saw several villagers wearing rough, waterproof jackets or cloaks made from the fibre of a palm *Trachycarpus fortunei*. From a distance they resembled strange creatures, half man- half beast. A few days remained in Xiaguan before we were due to return to Kunming and we spent some of the time preparing and packing our belongings, plant specimens and seed.

One day we were taken to a famous location in the mountains north of Dali to see the Butterfly Spring. Here, every year in April and May, millions of butterflies congregate, hanging on the leaves of trees and forming close-packed columns between the tree branches and the surface of a crystal clear pool beneath. According to popular legend, a local despot in ancient times tried to

Professor Chen-yih Wu, Director of the Yunnan Institute of Botany in Kunming, joined us on field trips to locations near Dali and Xiaguan. (May)

Jasminum officinale growing on a rocky hillside in the Cangshan above Dali. (May)

branched, wide-spreading shrub, 1.5m (5ft) tall, with lance-shaped, toothed leaves up to 25cm (10in) long. The terminal heads (corymbs) of blue or green fertile flowers with white ray florets were not, however, especially ornamental.

Veratrum taliense we found on grassy slopes; a non-flowering crown introduced to the Royal Botanic Garden, Edinburgh, has since proved strong growing with stems to 1m (3ft) or more

A shrine in the hills above Dali. Such are not uncommon on the lower slopes of the Cangshan. (May)

Hypericum forrestii in its type location on the eastern slopes of the Cangshan, here growing among the stones of a grave above Dali. It was first introduced to western cultivation by George Forrest in 1906. (May)

bearing spikes of greenish-white flowers. A pink-flowered begonia that we found in the same area, growing on a shady bank, proved to be *Begonia taliensis*. *Jasminum officinale* was everywhere in dense, tangled growths with clusters of sweetly-scented flowers a rich vinous purple in bud – a colour that remained on the outside of the open flower. It seemed to be smaller in leaf and flower than the plant in general cultivation, but its colour more than compensated for this.

Between the mouth of the valley and the main road lay green grassy foothills that gave way to cultivation as one approached the road. Here were roses in abundance, *Rosa roxburghii* forma *normalis* being especially common on the banks between the fields. The rose-purple flowers were impressive but already the prickly hips were forming, and we were told by Professor Wu that these, when mature, would be used locally to make a rather pleasant wine. *R banksiae* variety *normalis* was also present; the same prickly stemmed plant we had seen all the way between Kunming and Xiaguan.

By far the most common flowering shrubs, however, were the hypericums. *Hypericum lancasteri* and *H curvisepalum* favoured the steep banks and slopes higher up the valley, and I shall always count the red or coppery-pink tinted young growths of *H curvisepalum* as being one of the most attractive and memorable ornamental effects we had seen during the entire expedition. A third species also grew here and was particularly common on and around the raised stone graves that are scattered all along these lower slopes. It had to be *Hypericum forrestii*, a most ornamental shrub, here forming low mounds to 1m (3ft) high, with broad-based leaves and comparatively large, saucer-shaped, golden-yellow flowers 3.5-6cm (1½-2½ in) across, containing a crowded ring of short stamens. Elsewhere *H forrestii* is capable of 1.5m (5ft) and it will certainly reach this in cultivation.[53] My determination to

Rhus delavayi growing among rocks in a valley near Dali. Contact with the sap can produce a painful rash. (May)

A strikingly-coloured butterfly seen in the hills above Dali. (May)

collect specimens of hypericums for Dr Robson of the British Museum (Natural History) was a subject of great interest and not a little amusement to the Chinese. Finally, and inevitably, it was the subject of a prank perpetrated by Professor Feng.

In walking up the valley to the waterfall we had passed many holes and depressions filled with water from

Indigofera pendula, an unusual and striking shrub common on hillsides at Santaipo south of Xiaguan. (May)

overnight rain. Suddenly, the Professor called out to me, "Hypericum, new species!" I eagerly walked to where he was standing and, following his pointing finger, saw a plant of H forrestii growing in a water-filled hole, the entire plant submerged. "New species," he repeated, "*Hypericum aquaticum!*"

Our visit next day to Santaipo in Weishan County, 17km (11 miles) south of Xiaguan was equally productive. Between 2,100 and 2,550m (6,890 and 8,366ft) we found a rich variety of plants including *Styrax grandiflora*, first seen near Camp 2 above Yangbi. Here it was a shrub or small tree up to 3m (9ft) tall with clusters (racemes) of white, yellow-anthered flowers 2cm (¾in) across. *Gaultheria forrestii* was abundant on the hillsides, its characteristic milk-white inflorescences – stalks as well as flowers – closely followed by fruits exhibiting an extraordinary colour range of blue, mauve and purple. The four most impressive plants here, though, were a mahonia, an indigofera, a milkwort and a rose.

The mahonia was a bold shrub 2m (6ft) high, each stem supporting a handsome ruff of pinnate leaves up to 60cm (2ft) long with nineteen or more narrow, spine-toothed leaflets. The conspicuous blue, bloomy berries were carried in crowded drooping spikes up to 25cm (10in) long. It was subsequently identified as *Mahonia longibracteata*.

The indigofera was *Indigofera pendula*, an unusual and striking shrub with erect stems to 3m (9ft), and with large pinnate leaves principally gathered towards the ends of the branches from which hung long, slender, tapering, wisteria-like racemes of small pea flowers. These were an attractive reddish-purple, pale lilac on the outside. Sadly, we were unable to introduce this species to cultivation on this occasion but it is now established from subsequent

53. It was first found on these very slopes by Forrest who introduced it to gardens in 1906 and again later. Despite the rise in popularity of the hybrid H 'Hidcote', this hardy and amenable species remains one of the best shrubby hypericums for general cultivation, even though, like most other species, it flowers only once in the season. A seedling in my garden gives rich autumn colour.

Rosa longicuspis, a lovely form with flowers changing from white to pink to rose-red as they age. This plant was common on the hillsides at Santaipo south of Xiaguan; the leaves of this specimen were powdered with dust from a dirt road. (May)

Polygala arillata, a strikingly colourful shrub in flower, and a far cry from the humble milkwort (*P vulgaris*) of British chalk and limestone downs and pastures. It was quite conspicuous in the hillside scrub at Santaipo south of Xiaguan. (May)

collections. It thrives best in sunny sites in warmer areas.

Just as exciting was *Polygala arillata*, a handsome shrubby milkwort 2m (6ft) tall here, but capable of 5m (16ft) in sheltered sites. Its leaves were fairly large, up to 12cm (4¾ in) long, and pointed, while at the tips of the branches bold racemes of slender, yellow, red-flushed flowers appeared. It was quite one of the most attractive shrubs of its kind I have ever seen, a far cry from those prostrate, wiry-stemmed, blue-flowered milkworts of British chalk downs and heaths.[54]

The rose was perhaps the most spectacular of all. It was a big, bold rambler – its long thorny stems closely packed or flung widely into the air. No doubt, given support, it would climb to 5m (16ft) or more. The white, golden-anthered, tea-scented flowers were 5cm (2in) across, and were produced along almost the entire length of the stems. The most enchanting characteristic of this rose, however, was the way the petals turned to pink then rose-red with age, several colours present at one time, creating a stunning effect. Professor Wu told us it was *Rosa longicuspis* and this has since been confirmed. Its leaves, however, are shorter than those of the typical plant and have a short rather than a long point (cusp).[55]

It was on this day that David found a leech on his head! The rainy season was about to begin and by the time we left Yunnan we had experienced several wet days. Our last night at Xiaguan was celebrated with a grand banquet with lots of speeches, all of which we toasted with wine or Moutai. The food included tendons of animals unknown and, as a special 'treat', chicken soup with caterpillars!

The final days were spent in Kunming and were filled with packing and preparations for our departure. Seed, plants and dried specimens were sorted and shared and last minute identifications made. There was time to visit a few local 'tourist' spots and make a trip to the theatre, where I somehow became involved in one of the acts helping a magician to saw

54. I have yet to see *Polygala arillata* grown outside in a British garden, though it would make a colourful conservatory subject.

55. This characteristic led the botanist Boulenger to treat it as a separate species under the name *R yunnanensis*, whilst Handel-Mazzetti regarded it as belonging to *R lucens*. Whatever its true identity, there is no denying its qualities. Plants grown from seed collected at Hua Hong Dong near Kunming in 1980 are now established in cultivation, and in July 1986 I was pleased to see two flowering in the University Botanic Garden, Cambridge. They were growing in an open border in full sun and showed little or no evidence of winter damage. I have also observed well established specimens in several Cornish gardens where they have been trained into trees to splendid effect when in flower.

Even plant hunters enjoy a break from their labours as this photograph taken by George Forrest in April 1919 records. Forrest, left, captioned the photograph 'The Boozers' Club, Tengyueh'. Tengyueh (now Tengchong), a town on the Burma road in south-west Yunnan, was Forrest's main base in China and must have been like a second home. Britain maintained a consulate there, and it was the first or last place that travellers like Forrest returning from or heading for the wilds of north-west Yunnan could expect to enjoy the company of fellow westerners, and catch up on news from home. The man on Forrest's left is Consul Affleck, but he gave no hint as to the identities of his other companions

a woman in half. Then, all too soon, came the farewell banquet attended by all our colleagues from Kunming. There were more speeches and toasts, and more strange foods: bears' palms, elephant's nose and gorillas' lips (all fungi), compared with which the frogs' legs were child's play.

It was with genuine sadness that we embraced each other at the airport the next day. It had been, for the British members certainly, the experience of a lifetime. The way we had worked together as a team, and a happy and successful one at that, made our parting all the more difficult. We could only hope that the chance of repeating the experience might one day present itself.

We came home with over three thousand dried specimens, a total of seven hundred plants representing 180 species, and 213 lots of seed. If it had not been for the expert and meticulous packing of the plants by the two Peters and the VIP treatment given them by Lady Maclehose

in Hong Kong, few would have survived the journey. The dried specimens were deposited for future study in the herbaria of the Royal Botanic Gardens at Edinburgh, Kew and the University of St Andrews. A further set was given to the herbarium of the Arnold Arboretum, Massachusetts.

The living plants and seed went initially to the Royal Botanic Garden, Edinburgh, the former into quarantine. After plant health requirements had been satisfied, the material was then shared with Kew, St Andrews and other scientific establishments as well as with individuals concerned with specialist research. From these sources those plants from the expedition having ornamental merit have gradually found their way into general cultivation. Wherever they are grown they will serve both as a record of one of the most lasting benefits of Sino-British co-operation as well as, for the British members in particular, continued reminders of the days we walked in the footsteps of Forrest!

Most plant hunters after a long absence abroad look forward to returning home and to sharing with fellow plant enthusiasts the thrills of seeing new or even well-known garden plants in the wild. George Forrest was no exception and his stories and descriptions, not to say his recommendations to gardeners, must have held many an audience enrapt. In this photograph, c.1930, Forrest (left) is shown in a garden, probably that of Lord Headfort near Kells, Co Meath, Ireland, talking to a group of Ireland's most distinguished horticulturists. The group on the right comprises, from left to right, Hugh Armytage Moore of Rowallane, Lady Moore, wife of Sir Frederick Moore, the former Keeper of the National Botanic Gardens at Glasnevin, Dublin, and Lord Headfort, a personal friend and patron of Forrest. Behind Forrest, is Mr J A Boyle, Lord Headfort's gardener

Chapter Five

The Peak and the Poppy

Minya Konka

'Early one morning we got our first glimpse of mysterious Mount Koonka, rising high in white majesty and regretted the lack of time that made it impossible for us to make a reconnaissance. The altitude of this mighty peak is unknown, but there are those who claim that it rises more than 30,000ft and is the highest in the world.' Thus wrote the Roosevelt brothers, Kermit and Theodore, in 1929, giving the majority of Americans their first inkling of a major mountain in China's little-known western marches.

The statement appeared in *Trailing the Giant Panda*, an account of a zoological expedition made by the Roosevelts with a friend, Suydam Cutting, into Yunnan and Sichuan earlier that year. The book included a map on which the mountain was clearly shown with the Roosevelts' estimated altitude. The Roosevelts, of course, were not the first to have seen this mountain. The first European believed to have travelled in this region was a Catholic priest, probably Dominicus Parennin, a Frenchman who, in the early eighteenth century, indicated the mountain on a map he prepared for the Emperor Qing Kangxi's Imperial atlas. It was not until 1879, however, that the first scientific observation of the mountain was made by an expedition led by the Hungarian Count Bela Szechenyi. The observation took place on a journey made from Chengdu in Sichuan to Batang (at that time in Tibet) and thence south into Yunnan; the members of this expedition estimated the mountain's altitude to be 7,600m (24,936ft). However, it remained very much a mystery, despite continued, though occasional, sightings of it by travellers, missionaries and, on one occasion, by the explorer and plant hunter Frank Kingdon-Ward. Indeed, some maps of the period made no mention of it. Then, in 1923, an Australian, James Edgar, made sketches of the peak from a point some 40km (25 miles) to the north west, which he published in the *Journal of the West China Border Research Society* together with an article in which he declared 'nothing but a scientific measurement will make me give up the 30,000ft hope'. So the rumour of a mountain higher than Everest germinated and took root in the minds of some explorers and adventurers.

One of them was Dr Joseph Rock, an American of Austrian birth who first visited Yunnan in 1922. He was a man of many talents, not least of which was a passion for natural history and plant hunting. In the same year as the Roosevelt expedition, Rock was again in Yunnan with an expedition financed by the National Geographic Society. One of his briefs was to explore the 'Mount Koonka' region and determine the altitude of its main peaks.

Rock has described how he first set eyes on this remote range in June 1928, while exploring the Konkaling mountains to the north west of Muli in south-west Sichuan. 'I beheld from a ridge, at 16,300ft [4,968m] elevation, a series of snowy ranges, one of special interest far to the north east. My Tibetan guides said this was Minya Konka'. The meaning of the name in the local language, Rock later ascertained, was the 'Great Snow Mountain of the Minya Region'. From Rock's position, this range lay some 160km (100 miles) away and could only be seen through field glasses, but there appeared at its southern end a white pyramid that had Rock gasping. 'I decided then and there to spend the following year exploring Minya Konka', he declared.

True to his word, Rock reached the Minya Konka range in spring 1929 and beheld the 'Great Snow Mountain' in all its glory. Because of the difficulties of travel at that time of the year, he deferred further exploration until the summer and headed north east to Kangding where his party rested. With an improvement in conditions he returned to the range and began his survey of its peaks and other features.

There is no indication in his diaries or elsewhere that Rock believed the main peak to be a world beater, but on 27 February, 1930, the National Geographic Society at its headquarters in Washington received a cable which read: 'MINYA KONKA HIGHEST PEAK ON GLOBE 30250 FEET ROCK'. Its receipt undoubtedly caused great excitement, but the Society was not totally convinced and decided to await Rock's return and the opportunity to study his notes and calculations. Rock duly arrived, bringing with him a mass of superb photographs of the mountain, some of which have never been bettered. In discussion with officers of the Society he conceded that some of his methods of establishing the measurements were, of necessity, relatively crude, due to a lack of elaborate surveying equipment. He did not even possess a theodolite, he complained. Gradually,

A.E. Pratt (left) and J.A. Soulie (right) camping in a valley in the mountains above Tachienlu (now Kangding) in 1889.

Rock revised his calculations until, by the time he published his findings in the October 1930 number of the *National Geographic Magazine*, the height of Minya Konka had shrunk to 7,803m (25,600ft). The early doubts were vindicated two years later in 1932, when an American team not only made the first ascent of Minya Konka, but also surveyed the area using the most up-to-date equipment and instruments available at the time. Their verdict? That the altitude of Minya Konka was 7,590m (24,900ft), only a few metres less than Szechenyi's 1879 estimate. Current Chinese sources give the height as 7,556m (24,788ft).

For years after, Minya Konka was a source of embarrassment to Rock who, not surprisingly, tried to forget the whole affair and concentrate his energies on other matters. These included an intensive study of the Nakhi tribesmen of the Lijiang (Likiang) area of north-west Yunnan and, of course, plant collecting. He was, like Delavay and Forrest before him, a prodigious collector and it must have been a great disappointment to him that comparatively little of what he collected was new. E H M Cox (*Plant Hunting in China*) regarded him as a praiseworthy collector noted for the quality of seed sent home and the many fine forms of plants previously introduced by Forrest and Kingdon-Ward.

It was thoughts of Rock's exploits, and Minya Konka in particular, that filled my mind when, in October 1980, I stood on the summit of Emei Shan (Mt Omei) in west Sichuan, shivering in the early morning light. I had risen early in order to see the sunrise, which I had read could be spectacular from this mountain. In the event, it was brief and rather disappointing due to the low cloud layer. It did, however, last long enough to allow me a first glimpse of the Minya Konka range, snowy white and lying low on the western horizon. Just under a year later I was on the other side of that range as leader of a group of enthusiasts intent on studying and enjoying the abundant flora to be found there.

Before I describe our experiences, let me set the scene a little more with regard to the area and its botanical history. On some modern maps Minya Konka appears as Gongga Shan or Mount Gongga. It lies on latitude 29° 36′N, longitude 101° 52′E, in west Sichuan and is the highest peak of the Daxue Shan or Great Snow range at the juncture of Kangding, Luding and Jiulong counties. The Daxue Shan is, in fact, part of a vast system of mountain ranges that run on a north-south axis through the western parts of Sichuan and Yunnan and neighbouring Tibet and Burma. It is a region noted for its high peaks and ridges with deep valleys and ravines between. Its main peak is covered with snow the year round. From Minya Konka eastwards to the Dadu river and southwards to the Yalong river, the distances are only 30 and 105km (18 and 65 miles) respectively, but the difference in altitude is as much as 6,000m (19,685ft). The intervening area is one of the few in the world with such a complete and complex climatic spectrum, ranging from frigid through cool and warm temperate zones to subtropical. To the north of the mountain lies Kangding (Tachienlu) on the old highway from Beijing via Chengdu to Batang and Lhasa. Based on Kangding, several western botanical collectors and plant hunters have explored the neighbouring valleys and mountains, including such notables as Grigori Potanin, Prince Henri d'Orléans and, of course, E H Wilson.

The American plant hunter Joseph Rock 4th from left with escort to the Konkaling Mountains. He made a famous exploration of the Minya Konka area, obtaining an excellent photographic record that has never been bettered

Our varied group of enthusiasts together with staff of the Chinese Mountaineering Association pose for a photograph on the pass across the Erlang Shan in Sichuan province. (October)

Sixty years ago, while the area north of the Minya Konka range was relatively well known, those to the east, south and west were less so. Rock approached Kangding from the south from his base in Lijiang in north-west Yunnan, collecting in the country west of the range. Wilson travelled through the territory to the east, but did not venture to the western side of the range. It was to this area that our party was heading in September of 1981. Our ultimate destination was the valley of the Pa La river where we intended camping close to a Tibetan village called Liuba. To reach it, we would be journeying from Chengdu, capital of Sichuan, south west to Ya-an and Hanyuan, thence north west up the valley of the Dadu river to Luding and Kangding and, finally, south to Liuba.

In Chengdu we stayed at the same hotel, the Jinjiang, at which I had stayed in 1980 when I led a similar party to Emei Shan. On that occasion I had my first meeting with the great authority on the Sichuan flora, Professor Wen-pei Fang. In 1981 he again honoured us by his presence, pleased to renew our acquaintance and eager for news of old friends and correspondents in Britain and the United States.

We were a varied party representing five countries. Among our number were several professional horticulturists, including three Americans: Paul Meyer, Curator of the Morris Arboretum in Philadelphia, Peter Bristol, Curator of the Holden Arboretum in Mentor, Ohio, and Tim Brotzman, a nurseryman from Ohio. An English nurseryman and noted authority on clematis, Raymond Evison, was also with us, as was Carla Teune, later to become the first woman Curator of the University of Leiden Botanic Garden in The Netherlands. All were friends of long standing and their collective expertise

contributed greatly to the success of our journey. The arrangements for our visit had been made by the Chinese Mountaineering Association whose staff accompanied us, organising transport, meals and accommodation.

To the Dadu river, Kangding and beyond

We left Chengdu early on the morning of 9 September, travelling in two minibuses and accompanied by a jeep and a truck. We drove beneath an overcast sky across the famous Chengdu Plain where rice was being harvested in the fields. The entire area was a scene of intense human activity. Great piles of water hyacinth, *Eichhornia crassipes*, were being raked in from ponds and hauled away in oxen carts, no doubt to be used as pig fodder.

Pigs were plentiful on the road, mostly trussed up and lying on their backs in carts or barrows heading for market. The road was also thronging with people heading for, or

A pig eating water hyacinth in a farmyard on the Chengdu Plain, Sichuan. (September)

Stooking the rice in the fields on the Chengdu Plain, Sichuan. (September)

A primitive but very effective pedal-operated threshing machine, Chengdu Plain. (September)

A villager walking a pig to market in the mountains on the Yaan to Hanyuan road, W. Sichuan. (September)

returning from, the fields with hoes and tools of various descriptions carried over their shoulders. Others, by hand or by bicycle, were hauling carts full of cabbages, kale and other vegetables, while ponies strained to move trucks heavily laden with bricks or coal. We saw several collectors of 'night soil', pulling hard on the handles of their two-wheeled carts on which were mounted elongated barrel-shaped containers with access via a hole on the upperside. These are taken to storage tanks situated between the fields and the liquified contents used later to water and fertilise growing crops. All along the road rice grain had been spread to dry in golden pools, sometimes on straw mats, and it required skilful driving in order to avoid crushing or scattering them.

Crops other than rice are plentiful in this fertile soil and include beans of many kinds, giant radishes, melons, pumpkins and related cucurbits. Oil seed rape and green leaf crops of several kinds were much in evidence, as was sugar cane, jute (for fibre) and tobacco.

Brick kilns were common on the side of the road, the native purple-brown clay a cheap and readily available medium. Outside the kilns, stacked layer upon layer and sandwiched between straw, were the bricks themselves forming miniature hills.

Away from the villages and towns we saw the common Chinese wingnut, *Pterocarya stenoptera*, an ultimately wide-

All along the Chengdu road freshly harvested rice grain had been spread to dry. (September)

Pterocarya stenoptera. One of several Chinese species of wingnut tree here photographed at the Cambridge UBG. (July)

Alnus cremastogyne. An unusual species of alder with characteristic long-stalked fruits, here photographed at Ness Gardens in the Wirral in Cheshire. (October)

Aralia chinensis, with the low-branched fruiting head normally associated with *A. elata,* growing by the Ya-an to Hanyuan road in west Sichuan. (September)

Osmanthus fragrans forma *aurantiacus,* its branches crowded with small, richly-fragrant flowers. Photographed in the garden of the late Vicomte de Noailles at Grasse in the south of France. (September)

spreading often multi-stemmed lush-foliaged tree, growing by ditches and ponds, a situation sometimes shared with the common alder of Sichuan, *Alnus cremastogyne,* a tree commonly of 12-18m (40-60ft) with shining, green, obovate leaves up to 14cm (5½in) long. The most distinctive characteristic of this alder are the solitary, ovoid, fruiting cones, 2cm (¾in) long, which are borne on the end of an axillary stalk up to 8cm (3in) long. The tree is plentiful in suitable situations throughout the province, but at no great altitude, which makes it less than hardy in Britain except in the warmer areas. Even then it is a rare species in cultivation though instantly recognisable in fruit.[1] Another commonly planted native tree here is *Camptotheca acuminata,* a handsome foliage tree – especially the pinkish young growths – though of no merit in flower and fast growing. Here we saw straight-stemmed specimens of 21m (70ft) with smooth grey bark. *Camptotheca* is of botanical interest, being a monotypic genus in the same family as the tupelo *Nyssa.*[2]

Our first night was spent in Ya-an (previously known as Ya-chou Fu), a city of some 200,000 inhabitants and famous for its tea production in the mountainous districts to the south and north west. In this area, according to Wilson, tea is recorded as having been grown since early times. Ya-an was also a centre for the manufacture of the famous 'brick tea', which is still made in factories there.

In the garden of the Government guest house where we stayed, grew several trees 6m (19ft) high of *Osmanthus fragrans,* its orange flowers marking it out as the form *aurantiacus.* The more commonly cultivated form, which we saw elsewhere, has white flowers, while in another they are yellow. Whatever their colour, these flowers, although individually tiny, give off a sweet perfume so powerful that a flowering sprig will fill a room with its fragrance in a very short time. The dried flowers have, from time immemorial, been used to add perfume to the so-called 'jasmine tea'. The true

1. Large well-established trees are to be found at Ness Gardens in Cheshire and Hergest Croft Gardens in Herefordshire.

2. Being tender when young it is not best suited to British gardens, though it is worth trying in frost-free areas.

Rosa roxburghii, flowering in the author's garden in 1987 from seed collected in west Sichuan in 1981. This wild form is known as forma *normalis*. (June)

jasmine, which is also used for the same purpose, is *Jasminum sambac*, a native of India. Its white fragrant flowers are double and much larger than those of the *osmanthus*. Although *O fragrans* is wild in parts of China, it has long been cultivated there for its flowers, especially in temple gardens. Unfortunately, it is too tender to flourish out-of-doors in Britain, though it can be seen in Mediterranean gardens and, no doubt, in areas enjoying a similar climate in the southern coastal states of America. It has been crossed with the hardier Japanese species *O heterophyllus* to produce *O x fortunei*, a handsome, broad-leaved, spine-toothed shrub of dense habit, and there is a less hardy variegated form once attributed incorrectly to *O heterophyllus* as 'Latifolius Variegatus'.

We ventured into the main shopping area of the city before supper in search of a bookshop, which we eventually found, but our progress through the streets attracted so much attention that we were forced to beat an early retreat.

Another early rise next morning saw us out of Ya-an and heading through terraced fields from which maize had just been harvested. Walnuts and white willows were common by the road in company with the ubiquitous planted robinia and eucalyptus. Native plants were also apparent, although we were still at the comparatively low altitude of 700m (2,290ft). From the bus we caught sight of a hydrangea, probably *Hydrangea aspera* (Villosa Group), as well as *Buddleja davidii* and an *Aralia* species. The latter plant resembled *A elata*, the Angelica tree, in its suckering thickets of erect, spiny stems to 5m (16ft) and large, much-divided leaves. Its shining, black, berry-like fruits, similar in size to those of an elderberry (*Sambucus nigra*), were borne in stalked clusters from a multi-branched head (corymbose-paniculate). Seeds were later collected and the resultant plants have proved vigorous in British cultivation, though subject to damage from winter cold. *A elata*, the common species in western cultivation, is native to Japan, Korea, east Siberia and north-east China and is not found in Sichuan. *Aralia chinensis*, a similar species, is more widespread in China including Sichuan, but differs from our plant, and *A elata* for that matter, in its inflorescence, which is a panicle with a long central stem (axis). Later, on the Erlang Shan, we saw plants answering to *A chinensis*, but I rather suspect that this species is more variable in its inflorescence than some authorities suggest.

At an altitude of 1,000m (3,280ft) we stopped in order to make our first examination of the native vegetation, which was becoming increasingly varied. *Rosa roxburghii* was plentiful here, a robust dense-growing and suckering shrub 2-2.5m (6-8ft) high and across, with crisp, rich green ferny leaves and equally ornamental pale, flaking bark on the older stems. Its crowning glory, however, were the fruits: large, yellowish, prickle-clad hips from whence the English names Burr or Chestnut rose originate. The fragrant flowers in May and June are large and rose-pink or rose-purple with a golden boss of anthers in the centre. When mature, the fruits fall to form a thick carpet on the ground and smell of

Rosa roxburghii forma *normalis* with its large prickly fruits, which give rise to its English names of Burr or Chestnut rose. It was common by the Ya-an to Hanyuan road in west Sichuan. (September)

273

Miscanthus sinensis. A popular ornamental grass in Western cultivation, where numerous named cultivars are grown. It is native over a wide area of East Asia from China to Japan. (September)

apples ripening in a loft. It is named after William Roxburgh, Superintendent of the Calcutta Botanic Garden from 1793 to 1813, in whose garden this rose in a double form was first described, having been introduced there from a garden or nursery in Guangzhou (Canton). The wild, single-flowered rose of the name is represented by two races, which have been referred to variety *hirtula* from Japan and forma *normalis* from China. In cultivation the Japanese version, which is my favourite, is the most common and the more ornamental with larger leaves and leaflets and flowers of a paler colour.[3] Recent introductions of seed from the Chinese form, however, have established this in cultivation; one in my garden, for instance, has

flourished and flowered. The Chinese plant was collected by several of the famous plant hunters, including Forrest and Wilson, who referred to it under the name *R microphylla*.

An ornamental grass, *Miscanthus sinensis*, crowded the hillside above, its rose-plumed heads brightened by the morning sun, while the thickets were crowded with familiar plants including *Lonicera nitida*, *Ampelopsis brevipedunculata*, with its brilliant turquoise fruits (once seen never forgotten), *Cornus controversa* and *Acer davidii*, all of which I had seen elsewhere in Sichuan. A new tree for me, however, was a Chinese walnut, *Juglans cathayensis*, which occurred as scattered individuals between the road and the river below. They were trees of some 9m (30ft) with wide,

Ampelopsis brevipedunculata. A most ornamental vine in fruit, the various colours marking the differing stages of ripening. (September)

Sorbus megalocarpa. A distinct and easily recognised small tree with handsome foliage and large fruits. Here photographed at Knightshayes Court in Devon. (October)

spreading crowns and bold, pinnate leaves, which were 60cm (2ft) long, longer on saplings, mainly gathered towards the ends of the branches. They were composed of eleven to seventeen finely-toothed and downy leaflets and gave the tree an imposing appearance. The large, downy, green, egg-shaped fruits hung in strings from the branches.[4]

Litsea populifolia was plentiful by the roadside, a tall shrub or small tree as much as 10m (32ft), but generally half this height, with leaves 5-10cm (2-4in) long, of a characteristic shape, more like that of a cotinus than a poplar, but firm in texture and long stalked. It also grows on Emei Shan and is no doubt common throughout these mountains. This would be a most desirable introduction to cultivation where, however, it would only be suitable for the mildest areas of Britain and Ireland and warmer countries elsewhere. The ditches in this area were filled with *Ligularia dentata* (*clivorum*) forming bold stands of long-stalked, large, leathery, heart-shaped and strongly toothed leaves overtopped by erect stems 1.2m (4ft) high, branching above to support a wide platform of big, orange daisy heads. It was a cheering sight to come across such flamboyant flower power in the teeth of autumn with its fruit and early leaf tints. This handsome hardy perennial has been a favourite in gardens ever since Wilson introduced it from Sichuan in 1900. Several selections have been made over the years, of which 'Desdemona' (raised in 1940) is more compact in growth with leaves rich dark brownish-green above fading to metallic green, while beneath they are a rich mahogany-red. 'Othello', an early selection raised in 1915, is very similar, while 'Moor's Blood' ('Mohrenblut')

from Germany has still darker leaves. All are easy and hardy and especially suited to waterside or bog gardens.

We reboarded our buses and climbed another 1,000m (3,280ft) until we reached a promising piece of roadside where bamboo had run amok. Eagerly we walked up the road away from our vehicles all the while scanning the thicket, and we hadn't gone far before an old friend presented itself. It was a most unusual sorbus with large, obovate, double-toothed leaves, 10-18cm (4-7in) long. We could only find a single small tree of 5m (16ft), but I knew beyond doubt that it was *Sorbus megalocarpa*, a rare tree in cultivation. Apart from its bold, green, parallel-veined leaves, it is unique I believe, for a sorbus, in flowering before the leaves appear in late winter. The flowers are a creamy-white or creamy-yellow in colour, borne

Sorbus megalocarpa flowering in the Hillier Arboretum in 1976. This particular specimen was grown from seed collected by Wilson in west Sichuan. The flowers, which appear before the leaves, are particularly striking when seen against a blue sky. (March)

3. The Japanese plant is now generally treated as a species *Rosa hirtula* (Regel) Nakai.

4. Wilson described this as the common wild walnut of west China and he ought to have known. He was the first to introduce it into cultivation when collecting for the firm of Veitch in 1903. The tree's nuts are of little value for eating and it is purely as a foliage tree that it is cultivated in the West, where it is not common. The largest tree in Britain grows at Hergest Croft, in Herefordshire. Planted in 1912, when measured in 1995 it was 17m (56ft) high.

Sorbus scalaris. A most handsome wide-spreading tree here photographed at Lisle Court Cottage in Hampshire. (October)

Rhus chinensis, a common large shrub or small spreading tree in the valleys of west Sichuan. Its winged leaf-rachis and large heads of late creamy-white flowers are characteristic. (September)

in dense, woolly, stalked heads (corymbs) at the ends of the stout shoots in February or March depending on the weather.

We used to grow this species in the Hillier Arboretum and the trees are still there. I shall never forget my first sight of the flowers on stark, bare twigs against a blue sky. Out-of-doors there is no discernible scent, but cut a flowering twig and bring it indoors and it will gradually fill the room with a rather pungent aroma, unpleasant to some. The Hillier plants were propagated by grafting from two trees growing at Werrington Park in north Cornwall. These had been grown from seed collected by Wilson for the firm of Veitch in 1903. The russet-brown fruits are remarkable for their size, 2-3cm (¾-1¼in) long, looking for all the world like small partridge eggs. It was hardy in Hampshire, but early leafing can invite frost damage in exposed situations.

This was not the only sorbus found that day, for further up the same road we examined several specimens 8m (26ft) high or more of S scalaris, a member of the same section as our native mountain ash (S aucuparia). These trees seemed typical of the one in general cultivation, which was also a Wilson discovery and introduction, this time in 1904. It has long been one of my favourite fruiting trees, ideal for the medium-sized to large garden because of its relatively low but wide-spreading crown. Other points in its favour are its fern-like leaves, bronze-purple when young, becoming shining green above with numerous leaflets, toothed only near the tips and conspicuously veined, colouring richly in autumn. These occur plentifully along the long branches and especially on the short, flowering twigs where they tend to form a rosette beneath the flowerhead. This is a particularly effective backing for the small, orange-red fruits, which are carried in large, dense, flattened clusters that last for a considerable time before attracting the attention of birds.

Soon we were on our way again over several ridges and into a deep, arid-looking valley where Rhus chinensis, with its grey-green, pinnate leaves with a winged rachis and bold, creamy-white plumes of flower, crowded the roadside, enjoying the shelter and dry conditions. We could see several villages by the river below us and in side valleys opposite and were told that coal mining occurs here on a small scale. According to Wilson, the German geologist Baron von Richthofen estimated the coal-bearing ground in Sichuan to exceed in size the total coal mining area of every other province in China, though at the same time he pointed out that the bulk was too deeply buried ever to be of practical value.

When I first began working at the Hillier Arboretum in Hampshire during the 1960s I was amazed one day to see a small willow flowering on the scree beds in front of Jermyns House. It was a shrub no higher than 1m (3ft) and its rather stiffly arching shoots were greyish and hairy, as were the small leaves that crowded them. The catkins too were greyish and erect, to 2.5cm (1in) long. Nothing

Salix bockii, a female plant growing by the Ya-an to Hanyuan road in west Sichuan. It is unusual for a willow in bearing its catkins in autumn. (September)

unusual about this some might say, except that it was early autumn! *Salix bockii*, which is what our willow proved to be, is unusual among willows in flowering in late summer or early autumn on the growing shoots. I was reminded of this fact that day in the valley because here S bockii grew quite commonly by the roadside and on the dry slopes around. Of course, it was in flower, male and female catkins on separate plants, and nowhere above 1-1.5m (3-5ft) high. Some authorities claim a height of as much as 3m (9ft) for this willow, but I suspect this relates to another species, S variegata (duclouxii), which, to all intents and purposes, is a taller growing version of S bockii. I had seen the former in west Yunnan only a few months before and a companion, Professor Guo-mei Feng, told me that he believed the two to be the same. Wilson apparently introduced S bockii into cultivation as cuttings in 1908.[5]

We stopped for a few minutes to study the willow and I took the opportunity of collecting a small fragment of a shrubby hypericum that occurred among the willows by the roadside. It was a small shrub to 1m (3ft) on average,

5. Cuttings collected in 1984 provided plants of a female form now established in British cultivation.

A riverside village in a valley of the Daxiang Shan. Note the terraced and cultivated slopes above which lies a wild scrubby area regularly cut over for fodder and other uses. (September)

of untidy habit with slender, arching branches supporting elliptic, blunt-tipped leaves and shallow, saucer-shaped, yellow flowers, 3-4.5cm (1¼-1¾ in) across, though these were mostly finished. When seen by Dr Norman Robson of the British Museum (Natural History) it was determined to be *Hypericum lagarocladum*, since published as a new species. This was not, however, its first finding. It had previously been collected in Sichuan, as well as in Yunnan, Guizhou and Hunan. According to Robson, it is related to *H acmosepalum*, differing in a number of characters including the arching, open habit of branching and in the usually shallowly incurved petals and relatively shorter stamens.[6]

Towards midday the road snaked its way up a steep hillside covered in a rich scrub and we thought that we would suffer withdrawal symptoms if we were not allowed at least a brief contact with it. Fortunately, having

reached a pass over the top of the hill, it was announced that packed lunches would be taken by the roadside. We discovered that the area of hills through which we were passing was known as the Yiba Shan and that the pass was situated at an altitude of 2,400m (7,873ft). We had about two hours before moving on and the sight of several plant-struck individuals cramming food down as fast as possible is something I shall never forget.

Soon we were meandering through the scrub on the slopes below, occasionally in little groups but mostly alone, all the better to taste the excitement of discovery. *Rhododendron pachytrichum*, *argyrophyllum* and *calophytum* were plentiful in some places, the last named smaller in size and leaf on these exposed slopes than when I had seen it the previous year in the woods on Emei Shan. Two other members of the same family (*Ericaceae*) we found here were *Gaultheria hookeri* and *G nummularioides*, both abundant in open places. The former has a distribution through the eastern Himalaya from Sikkim to west China. Plants from the Chinese end of the range were originally named *G veitchiana* after the firm of Veitch whose former collector, E H Wilson, first introduced it to the West from Sichuan in 1907, though by that time Wilson was employed by the Arnold Arboretum. In the Yiba Shan it was a low evergreen shrub up to 60cm (2ft) with leathery leaves up to 8cm (3in) long. Its underground stems created extensive patches, carpeting the ground in places to the exclusion of all other plants. It was an impressive sight, the stems

6. *H lagarocladum* is now in cultivation as a result of a curious chance. It happened on one of my visits to the Natural History Museum to review the herbarium (dried) specimens of recently collected hypericums. It was when Dr Robson showed me a specimen of the above mentioned *H lagarocladum* that I realised I had not collected any seed. There was, however, a small quantity of seed escaping from the old capsules on the specimen before me and some of this I took away with me and sowed. To my surprise, despite the seeds – and the specimens for that matter – having undergone a fumigation process to kill insect pests, two seedlings subsequently appeared and these are now established in my garden. Here it has developed a loose mound approximately 1 x 1.3m (3 x 4¼ft) with abundant flowers in loose heads at the ends of the slender, arching branches. It has suffered no winter damage during two cold winters but, like most of the newer hypericum introductions, its hardiness will undoubtedly vary according to area. Plants have already been established from cuttings and it is hoped that this attractive species will soon be better known.

Maize cobs hung out for winter use beneath canopies of farmer's houses in a village in the Yiba Shan. (September)

Rosa sericea forma *pteracantha* growing in the Yiba Shan of west Sichuan. It is often grown in western gardens where it is admired for the broad, blood-red thorns of the first year shoots. (September)

crowded with clusters of pea-sized, oblong fruits varying in colour from purple to a startling indigo or China blue.

The second species, *G nummularioides*, was quite different in appearance. It was a much smaller evergreen to 10cm (4in) with patches of slender, arching, bristly stems, layer upon layer. These were clothed with small, leathery, heart-shaped leaves 1.5cm (½ in) long borne in two opposite ranks decreasing in size towards the tips of the stems. The small, bluish-black fruits were crowded beneath the stems and not so easily seen as those of *G hookeri*. *G nummularioides* is a charming shrublet, which I first saw in east Nepal in 1971. It demands in cultivation a moist, but well-drained, acid soil that does not dry out in summer. The best colony of *G nummularioides* that I remember in cultivation grew on a shady bank in the woods at Caerhays in Cornwall. Unfortunately, this has since perished as a result of a dry summer following a severe winter. In the wild these plants would almost certainly have the protection of snow cover during winter.

An evergreen holly, *Ilex ciliospinosa*, shared the hillside with *Berberis gagnepainii*, the latter a strong-growing, dense-habited shrub 2m (6ft) or more high and as much across. In cultivation this is, or used to be, one of the most commonly planted of the evergreen berberis. Its bold clumps of erect stems and arching branches, densely clothed with narrow, dark, dull green, wavy-edged, spine-toothed leaves up to 7.5cm (3in) long, were a familiar sight in public parks and council plantings in general. This is not surprising in view of its easy and hardy nature, free flowering with clusters of yellow flowers at the end of May followed by bloomy black fruits. In addition, its spiny stems made it an ideal candidate for those defensive, informal hedges once commonly planted along busy roads and in similar sites. Seeing this shrub in its native scrub brought back memories for me of early years as an apprentice working in the parks of the Lancashire industrial town of Bolton. All that now seemed to be light years away. Interestingly, this species was introduced from

west Sichuan by Wilson in 1904.

While *B gagnepainii* occurred as scattered individuals, *B wilsoniae* was abundant in places as a dwarf hummocky shrub, similar in all respects to plants seen previously in the hills above Kunming in Yunnan. Prickly stems are not by any means the prerogative of berberis; roses were plentiful here, too, and none more so than *Rosa sericea* forma *pteracantha*, which, unlike the isolated plant seen previously in west Yunnan, occurred here in some numbers. The blood-red, fin-like spines on the young shoots, for which this rose is famous, were superb and the branches were beset with globular, dark crimson hips.

A second shrubby rose was *R davidii*, a vigorous, but rather lax-stemmed shrub up to 3m (9ft) tall. Seed of this rose produced several plants in British cultivation, two of which were raised by Desmond Clarke in his garden in Surrey. One of these, he tells me, is a robust form of the species with

Rodgersia aesculifolia. The bold foliage of this hardy perennial well illustrates the choice of name referring to those of the horse chestnut *Aesculus.* Here growing wild in the Yiba Shan of W. Sichuan. (September)

Rodgersia aesculifolia. A magnificent plant photographed in the Van Dusen Botanic Garden in Vancouver. (July)

attractive dogrose pink flowers 5cm (2in) across, borne in clusters of five to twelve. It is equally impressive in fruit with long, bright red, flagon-shaped hips in large pendulous bunches. The third rose we found that day in the Yiba Shan has since proved to be R *rubus*, a great loose mound of arching and flopping, thorny stems that effectively barred our way into several small ravines in the hillside.[7]

The Americans in the group discovered a styrax, which

was later considered as being close to *Styrax bodinieri.* Seedlings raised at the Morris Arboretum in Philadelphia, however, are reported to be slow growing and not entirely happy. To complete a quintet of sorbus for the day we found the white-fruited *Sorbus setschwanensis,* the red-fruited S *sargentiana,* both mountain ashes, and S *aronioides,* a relative of S *keisleri,* with toothed, but otherwise entire, green leaves.

Just as interesting were a bold-leaved deciduous oak,

Populus lasiocarpa. A most handsome and easily grown ornamental poplar with its red-stalked bold foliage. A female tree growing at the Abbotsbury Subtropical Gardens, Dorset. (June)

Neillia thibetica flowering at Inverewe in Scotland. First discovered in the Kangding area by the naturalist A E Pratt in 1890, it was later introduced to western cultivation by E H Wilson. (June)

A valley in the Yiba Shan between Ya-an and Hanyuan. The more accessible lower slopes are extensively cultivated, the native forest being confined to the ridges and steep upper slopes. (September)

Quercus dentata, and the even more impressive *Populus lasiocarpa*.[8] The poplar was represented by several fine trees up to 12m (40ft) or more, their big heart-shaped, red-stalked leaves hanging on the stout shoots. They were individuals, scattered across the immediate slope and standing proud of the scrub, which swept in a richly-textured blanket up and down the hills. Some autumn colour was already beginning to appear, mainly enkianthus and maples.

By this time I had descended the slope into the valley bottom where a stream meandered through an area of rough grass and scrub. Here were several moisture-loving plants including large colonies of *Rodgersia aesculifolia* now in seed, and *Ligularia wilsoniana*[9] with rounded or kidney-shaped, long-stalked leaves and erect stems, to 1.5m (5ft), crowded with golden-yellow daisies.

In a ravine close by the ligularias grew several large wingnuts, trees of some 12m (40ft) or more with long spreading branches, large buds and pinnate leaves composed of fifteen to seventeen finely toothed leaflets. Although toothed, the leaf rachis lacked the wings so characteristic of the common Chinese species *Pterocarya stenoptera*. In some respects it was not unlike the Caucasian wingnut, *P fraxinifolia*, and may well have belonged to *P macroptera* var. *insignis*, a tree that is, to the best of my knowledge, rare if not absent from western cultivation.[10]

In a nearby thicket grew a familiar plant in *Neillia thibetica*,[11] a shrub of some 2-2.5m (6-8ft) with widely arching stems and sharply toothed and lobed leaves. This close relative of the spiraeas is not as common in gardens as its beauty would merit. Under its synonym, *N longiracemosa*, I

7. Seed collected at the time has produced plants of tremendous vigour with downy young shoots and leaves comprising five leaflets, purple tinted when young. The white, sweetly scented flowers in summer are carried in dense clusters followed by small globular red fruits. Its passing resemblance to a bramble *Rubus* species in leaf and flower is referred to in its name. This species was introduced by both Wilson and Farrer, though it was first discovered by Augustine Henry in Hubei. It is hardy but unaccountably scarce in cultivation.

8. The finest example of *Populus lasiocarpa* in British cultivation that I know of grows in the Bath Botanic Garden. It is a superb tree of its kind and in 2005 measured 26m (85ft).

9. I was pleased to see the ligularia as it gave me a chance to check out one of its characteristics. The leaf stalks are supposed to be hollow, and so they were, differing in this respect from the very similar *L veitchiana* whose leaf stalks are solid. Both were discovered and introduced into cultivation by Wilson in the early 1900s and both are still with us, or are they? Plants grown by Hillier in the 1960s under these names always proved to be the same species – *L veitchiana*. Time and again I would slice through the leaf stalks of plants received or seen under one name or the other always to find them solid. If *L wilsoniana* is still in cultivation it must be rare and may even be growing under the wrong name.

10. This – along with several other Chinese species – has since been introduced into western cultivation e.g. the Howick Arboretum in Northumbria where they are so far proving hardy.

11. *N thibetica* was originally discovered by the English naturalist A E Pratt near Kangding in 1890. Before he left that city he met the young Frenchman Prince Henri d'Orléans, recently arrived from Tibet. Unknown to Pratt, the prince had also collected specimens of the same neillia in the same area and these, together with other specimens collected on his journey, he entrusted to Pratt who delivered them to the French legation in Shanghai on his way home. Pratt's specimens were deposited at Kew on his return. Here they were examined by the great botanist W B Hemsley who, in 1892, described Pratt's neillia as a new species, naming it *N longiracemosa*. Under this name it was distributed in Britain. Unknown to Hemsley, the same neillia collected by Prince Henry d'Orléans had been named the year before by the French botanists Bureau and Franchet who chose the name *N thibetica*. Many people doubted that the two were different but it was not until 1963 that they were united under the name *N thibetica*. In keeping with the International Code of Botanical Nomenclature, whose Rule of Priority states that the first validly published name for a plant shall be deemed the correct name. If nothing else, this story explains one of the reasons why a familiar name is sometimes dropped in favour of another. It also illustrates the problems that faced botanists charged with determining the many unfamiliar and often new plants pouring in from China in the late nineteenth and early twentieth centuries.

Ligustrum lucidum, the Chinese tree privet, an excellent example of this popular ornamental species, here photographed in a garden in Winchester, Hampshire. (August)

first saw this shrub at the Cambridge Botanic Garden where it flowered freely, the long, slender, tail-like spikes of rose-pink flowers crowding the branches in May and June. Considering that it is hardy and easy in almost any soil, reliable and satisfying in flower, and ornamental in habit and leaf, I am surprised that it is not grown more often. Its flowering shoots exhibited at a recent Royal Horticultural Society Show in London won for this shrub an Award of Merit and numerous new admirers. Like many other tall shrubs of this family, some of the spiraeas in particular, N *thibetica* can become dense and crowded over the years and thus lose its elegance and appeal. Young growths, therefore, need to be encouraged to shoot from the base by pruning away the old flowering wood immediately after flowering. This should be cut to near ground level when, at the same time, any dead or weak growth should be similarly removed.

A commonly occurring and colourful annual herb on these slopes was *Halenia elliptica*, a relative of the gentians but differing in its flowers, which have four slender spreading spurs at their base. The flowers are borne in loose clusters (panicles) on erect stems 20-50cm (8-20in) tall and look most attractive in the mass. The plants we saw had relatively large conspicuous flowers and most probably belonged to the variety *grandiflora*. Apart from white, it occurred in various shades of blue as well as blue and white bicolours and caught the eye of all members of our party, especially where it occurred in drifts by the

road or track. *H elliptica* is a wide-ranging species occurring from west Asia eastwards along the Himalaya to north and west China. Its variety is particularly common in west Yunnan and west Sichuan, but neither, as far as I am aware, are presently in cultivation. More is the pity for they would make useful late summer additions to the rock garden. Their flowers, by the way, can be mistaken at a glance for those of a tiny upturned aquilegia, but on closer examination their true affinity becomes apparent.

In September 1971, when plant hunting in East Nepal, I had the good fortune to find that curious climbing member of the gentian family, *Tripterospermum volubile*. Previously classified under *Gentiana* and by some authorities under *Crawfurdia*, this charming perennial fascinated me with its drooping clusters of blue, or greenish-blue, tubular, bell-shaped flowers in the axils of smooth, paired leaves. It climbed by means of its slender, twining stems and reached 3m (9ft) at least. We collected some of its curious purple fruits, like tiny succulent radishes, but I am not aware that the resultant seedlings remained for long in cultivation. I was reminded of this in the Yiba Shan that day when we found T *volubile*, or something very similar, flourishing in several places, its rich blue flowers studding the twining stems. It is an interesting and attractive plant and I can only assume that it shows some intransience in cultivation, otherwise it would assuredly be encountered more often.[12]

I cannot leave mention of the Yiba Shan without

reference to the ferns that grew in abundance and variety in the shady ravines. Several familiar genera were represented, but there was one fern above all others that impressed by its ornamental qualities. This was a shield fern, *Polystichum squarrosum*,[13] which formed bold clumps of handsome, deeply divided fronds, 45cm (18in) or more long, carried on stalks (stipes) densely clothed with rich brown, papery scales. The segments of the fronds were leathery in texture with spiny teeth almost prickly to the touch. In colour they were dark green above, paler and attractively veined beneath, both surfaces glossy.

Late that afternoon we arrived at the small town of Hanyuan (Fulin), which is situated on a low lying plateau close by the Dadu river at an altitude of only 900m (2,952ft). In the gardens of this town and in those of neighbouring hamlets we found a surprising variety of plants grown for food as well as for ornamental purposes: walnuts were common, paulownias, their flowers long gone, loquats, castor oil (*Ricinus*), sunflowers and soya beans. Amaranthus, red and green, are grown here, for their flowers and, possibly, for their leaves too, which are cooked as a spinach. Giant bamboo clumps were frequent as well as Tallow trees (*Sapium sebiferum*), China trees (*Melia azedarach*), dahlias, *Salvia splendens* and cannas. One of the most commonly planted trees in this area is the Chinese tree privet, *Ligustrum lucidum*. Here it is found in village plots as well as on roadsides and field margins. Its presence in these parts is mainly due to its former importance in the breeding of the famous Chinese white wax insects (*Er1icerus pela*). For centuries, the white wax insect[14] has been bred on ash and tree privet in south-west China for the commercial production of wax.

It is the males who exude the commercial wax. On a heavily infested branch the wax deposited over a three month period can be as much as 6.3mm (¼in) thick. They prefer lower elevations and *Fraxinus chinensis* as their host plant. In these conditions they produce wax most prolifically and develop most successfully. The females, however, prefer higher altitudes of 1,000-3,000m (3,280-9,842ft) and

Ligustrum lucidum, the abundant flowers give off a rich fragrance, cloying to some noses. Here photographed at the Hillier Arboretum. (September)

Ligustrum lucidum, the striking bloomy-black fruits are a feature of trees grown in continental gardens. Here photographed at Bergerac, France. (December)

Ligustrum lucidum as their food plant, probably producing the largest number of eggs in spring with a greater proportion of females reaching maturity. For this reason, in the past, broods of white wax insects were produced in privet plantations and transferred by carrying large quantities of scales to ash plantations lower down.[15]

12. I have yet to see a plant well established outside in a British garden. Ron McBeath of the Royal Botanic Garden, Edinburgh, informs me that a plant grown from wild-collected Nepal seed flourishes in the Temperate House there. Trained upon wires it has reached 3m (10ft) or more and flowers profusely. Attempts to grow it out of doors have met with less success. Several Chinese species are now in cultivation from recent introductions, though none is common.

13. Spores of this species were collected by one of my colleagues, Alan Lesley, and the resultant plants are now established in a number of collections. It is undoubtedly a valuable addition to the ferns in cultivation and seems set to enjoy a bright future. It has since been introduced from other locations.

14. Chinese white wax insects belong to the scale insect family (Coccidae). Gardeners in the West will be familiar with scale insects, several of which are pests of both ornamental and economic plants such as camellias, orchids, peaches, apples, roses, citrus fruits. They are, however, hardly recognisable as insects, for they are wingless and legless. They remain motionless, like soft-shelled tiny limpets or barnacles attached to their host plant by their snout (stylet), through which they suck sap from the plant's vascular system. They often exude wax to prevent them from desiccating and to give them protection from natural enemies. There is one generation per annum. Eggs are laid by the sedentary adult females on twigs and branches in early spring (April). According to the Japanese researcher I Kuwana, the greatest number of eggs laid by a single female is 15,028 and the smallest 3,372. The eggs remain protected underneath the pear-shaped scale of the adult female

until they hatch up to two months later (June). The females hatch first and the young crawlers (the only mobile stage, when the insects have rudimentary legs) make their way to the upper leaf surface where they settle to feed. The males hatch a few days later and crawl to the lower leaf surface where they settle to feed in clusters. After a period of feeding both sexes move to two- to three-year-old twigs and branches, where they finally settle. The females undergo two moults and the males three before achieving adulthood in the autumn when the males mate with the females, dying shortly afterwards. The females overwinter on the twigs and branches till the following spring.

15. Introducing the insects from the privet to the ash involved a most extraordinary operation each year beginning at the end of April. At this time, scales were carefully removed from the branches of the privets in the Anning river valley, packed into paper packets and made up into loads, sixty packets per load of 27kg (60lb). These were then carried on the backs of porters through several mountain ranges, principally via Hanyuan, to Leshan. It was an amazing operation and the trouble taken by those involved to ensure the safe travel of the insects in their care is almost unbelievable. Imagine the porters carrying their precious loads of scales, travelling only at night or on dull days when temperatures were lower in order to slow the insects' development and their untimely emergence. They even unpacked their loads at each resting place, placing the packets of scales in the coolest places. The scales were then suspended in little leafy cradles close beneath the branches of the ash. Later, on escaping from the old scales and from their cradles through holes punched in the leaf, the young crawlers would move up the branches to feed on the leaves.

Pyrus pyrifolia variety *culta*, this large fruited form of a wild Chinese pear is grown in many named cultivars in China. Here photographed at Larchwood in Norfolk. (November)

In Sichuan, the main breeding centre for the insect on privet was in the valley of the Anning river, a tributary of the Yalong in the south of the province. Over 321km (200 miles) to the north, in the vicinity of Leshan (Chiating), was situated the centre of white wax production as an article of commerce. Here, Chinese ash (*Fraxinus chinensis*) was cultivated specifically as a host for the insects. This is not as strange as it may seem given that the ash and the privet are members of the same family (*Oleaceae*).

The ash was grown in great numbers between fields, on village plots and on the lower slopes of hills, pollarded periodically to keep the trees to a manageable size and to encourage lush foliage. A hundred days after introducing the insects to the ash trees, wax production would be completed and the branches of the trees would be lopped and as much of the wax as possible removed by hand. This was placed in boiling water, the wax melting and rising to the surface to be skimmed off.

White wax has been prized by the Chinese for centuries and was first made known to the West by the Jesuit missionaries in China in the early seventeenth century. According to notes compiled by Matthaeus Ricci, published by Christiana de Trigault in 1615, 'This white wax is superior in quality to ordinary wax, for it is less sticky and burns with a brighter flame'. Alexander Hosie, writing in 1869 after a special study of the industry in Sichuan, claimed that in western China 'Its sole use is for coating the exteriors of animal and vegetable tallow candles and for giving a greater consistency to these tallows before they are manufactured into candles. Insect white wax', he pointed out, 'melts at 71°C [160°F], whereas animal tallow melts at about 35°C [95°F]'. He also reported that in other parts of China white wax was used for imparting a gloss to silk, and as a furniture polish. Several of the plant hunters, Forrest in particular, coated seeds such as magnolia and camellia in tallow, but whether this was the ordinary kind or insect white wax I do not know.

As an ornamental, the Chinese tree privet, *Ligustrum*

lucidum, is one of the best of its kind and has long been a special favourite of mine. Its dense, rounded head of dark, polished green leaves is unmistakable, and when the bold conical heads of creamy-white flowers appear in August and September the whole canopy becomes alive with bees and other insects. They are, of course, attracted by the nectar and no doubt the scent, which is like that of any other privet: sweet and rather cloying.[16]

Having spent the night in the local guest house we drove out of Hanyuan next morning along a road[17] that followed closely the north bank of the Dadu river, which Wilson would have known as the Tung river. This is one of the longest rivers in Sichuan, having its source in south-east Qinghai province, eventually joining with the Min river near Leshan and thence to the Yangtze, east of Yibin. At Hanyuan there is a considerable flood plain of shingle and stones and in several places along the road we negotiated heaps of debris and large boulders deposited by the numerous torrents that rush down from the steep hillsides above. The proximity of water brought an abundance of birds, especially wagtails, while cliff swallows, family parties no doubt, whizzed through the air above the water. People were already on the roads, porters mainly, and we passed several carrying huge bamboo baskets, six or seven at a time one inside another. In the old days Hanyuan was famous for its pears, which, according to A E Pratt who passed this way in 1889, were

16. It is a tree most suited to the southern and western areas of Britain where it is tolerant of most soils as long as they are not waterlogged. It is especially good on the chalk soils of Winchester in Hampshire where it is found in a number of gardens in and around the city. Some of these are of good height, but the famous tree on Winchester Cathedral Green, at one time the best in Britain and a lovely specimen over 15m (50ft), was fatally damaged in a gale in 1970. A replacement there is already a handsome specimen. The largest specimen in Britain is now a tree of 17.5m (58ft) at Thorn House in Devon (1977). Two variegated forms, 'Excelsum Superbum' and 'Tricolor', are in cultivation. Both are striking foliage trees but subject to damage in severe winters as is the type. Typical *L lucidum* is commonly planted in the southern states of the United States where it is known as Waxleaf privet.

17. This road, potholed and dangerous in 1981, has since been replaced by a more modern metalled version running from Chengdu to Kangding.

Valley of the Dadu river (formerly Tung river), the main route from Beijing to Lhasa in Tibet. At the time of our visit, its brown waters were filled with logs from trees felled from rapidly diminishing forests in some remote valley. (September)

very fine but suitable only for cooking. We saw a number of pear trees being cultivated in gardens here. They bore large, rounded fruits with a hard, gritty flesh and belonged to *Pyrus pyrifolia* variety *culta* of which there are many selections grown in Chinese orchards.

Another common tree along the river valleys around Hanyuan is the Tung oil tree, *Aleurites fordii*, the seed of which produces an oil valuable in the manufacture of varnish and high-quality paint. As a drier it is claimed to exceed linseed oil and for centuries has been China's principal wood oil. It is cultivated in many of the big river valleys of west and central China, being especially common along the Yangtze river. Although a handsome foliage tree it is far too tender to survive out-of-doors in Britain, requiring a subtropical climate. According to W T Stearn, a more recent use of Tung oil, as far as western medicine is concerned, is in the treatment of leprosy.

The river was high and moving swiftly, coloured light brown from the topsoil it carried, washed from the treeless slopes along its course. It also carried logs in large numbers, trees felled from rapidly diminishing forests in some remote watershed valley.

The road along the Dadu river valley near Shimian. The hillsides are full of interesting plants which kept us occupied for several hours. This road has now been replaced by a modern metalled version. (September)

Shimian, on the Dadu river. A small town in one of Sichuan's major river valleys. (September)

Clearing away a rock fall on the Hanyuan to Kangding road near Shimian. Such falls are not uncommon in the steep-sided valleys of west Sichuan, especially after heavy or continuous rain

The team of volunteers who cleared the road. They had left their various jobs in Shimian to come to our aid and spent the next several hours working non-stop. (September)

A village huntsman preparing to fire his crossbow on the road near Shimian in the Dadu river valley. Such weapons are effective for more than 100m (330ft), and were once commonly used by many of the tribal people of the south-west. (September)

Some hours after leaving Hanyuan, we rounded a bend to find ourselves confronted by a man waving his hands for us to stop. He told us that a rock fall had occurred on the hillside ahead blocking the road with a huge pile of boulders. We all got out of the buses and continued on foot to view the obstruction. It was an impressive pile and with no way round it we resigned ourselves to a long delay. Help was on the way from the town of Shimian on the other side of the river, and in the meantime we were taken across a bridge to have some lunch in a restaurant there. On our return we found a large gang of people tackling the obstruction with shovels, crowbars and picks, carting away the rocks in wheelbarrows. At this rate, we reasoned, it would take at least a day to clear. For a while we sat by the roadside entertained by a fur-hatted huntsman with a crossbow. Several times he demonstrated his skill, firing a bolt at various targets on the grassy bank on the other side of the

road. His final shot had us on our feet and scattering when the bolt, deflected by a rock, headed back in our direction, narrowly missing a passing chicken.

Ducks in some numbers were being carried along the road on bicycles. Some were in bamboo baskets while others were in large bunches tied by their feet to the back of the saddle. Mostly they were heading for, or returning from, a local market.

Just when we were beginning to get itchy feet our guides suggested we might like to go up on the slopes to look for flowers. We needed no persuading! The road at this point lies at 1,000m (3,280ft) and for the next few hours we climbed the hillside above, ascending some 244m (800ft) in the process.

The vegetation was patchy, mainly scrub with trees that appeared from below to be some kind of fir. We were delighted when it turned out to be *Keteleeria evelyniana*. They were not the best of specimens, 10m (32ft) at most, the

Keteleeria evelyniana is spectacular with its large, erect. cylindrical cones 12cm (4¾ in) long, their broad scales recurved at the tips. (September)

At many points along the road we met villagers cycling to market with live ducks in bamboo cages or trussed up by their legs in noisy feathered bunches. (September)

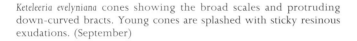

Keteleeria evelyniana cones showing the broad scales and protruding down-curved bracts. Young cones are splashed with sticky resinous exudations. (September)

narrow leaves 2.5-4cm (1-1½ in) long, compressed and short pointed with two pale grey-green bands of stomata on each surface. They were crowded mainly on the upper side of the shoot rising upwards and slightly forwards with a small proportion loosely arranged beneath. Some trees carried cones on their upper branches, slender and cylindrical in shape, 12cm (4¾ in) long with broad green scales rounded and slightly recurved at the tip. It seemed to be fairly widespread though scattered across the hillside and no doubt was once dominant here.

As we had found in Yunnan the previous spring, *Keteleeria evelyniana* appear to thrive in a well-drained soil on slopes that enjoy a great deal of sun in spring and autumn. During summer these slopes must be running with water as there is little in the way of ground vegetation to hold the majority of the rainfall. Wilson knew the problems well: 'Unlike the mountains bordering the eastern limits of the Red Basin, which are mainly of hard Carboniferous and Ordovician limestones, those of the west are principally of mudshales and granitic rocks which disintegrate very readily in their exposed parts and erosion is rapid'. He added, 'In the deforested parts landslides are general'.

Other trees sharing these slopes with the keteleeria included three different species of oak, *Quercus glauca*, *Q phillyreoides* and *Q variabilis*. The last named is deciduous although its leaves hang on often into the new year. These are quite substantial, 12-17.5cm (4¾-7in) long, with from nine to sixteen pairs of parallel veins ending in bristle-tipped teeth. They are distinct also in their dark green upper surface contrasting with the pale grey or creamy-grey felted undersurface. This is not all, however, for the acorns are almost hidden inside large fuzzy cups. The bark too, of older trees certainly, is greyish-brown, thick and corky with ridges and furrows. This is a widely distributed species, being found in Korea and Japan as well as in northern China. The trees here were relatively small, 10m (32ft), though they are capable of as much as 24m (80ft). *Q variabilis* seems tolerant of extremes, enjoying drought and cold in equal measure and, although not common, has long been cultivated in the West especially in those regions enjoying cold winters and hot summers.[18]

While *Q variabilis* is reasonably well known in British cultivation, *Q phillyreoides* is not. This is an evergreen that I

Quercus phillyreoides, an evergreen oak of dense bushy habit, which is uncommon in cultivation. Photographed here in the Granada Arboretum, Cheshire. (April)

Viburnum congestum, an evergreen shrub with bright red (maturing black) clusters of fruit that, from a distance, remind one of a holly (*Ilex* species). It grew on the steep hillside of the Dadu river valley above Shimian. (September)

first met with in the Hillier Arboretum in the 1960s. I particularly remember its dense, bushy habit and its obovate, leathery, dark green, glossy-topped leaves, toothed (in the upper half) but not prickly. The young growths are coppery or bronze in colour. The trees on the slopes above Shimian were some 4.5-6m (15-20ft) high and equally dense and bushy. They appeared quite at home and, considering its apparently adaptable nature, it puzzles me that this species is not better known and more widely grown in western cultivation. It is free growing once established and can put out long extension growths in some years. Apart from China, this species is native also to Japan from which country it was first introduced to Britain by the Kew collector Richard Oldham in 1861.

Growing with the Q *phillyreoides* we found a large shrub of dense compact habit. At first we mistook it for a holly because of the bunches of red fruits peppering the dark foliage. On closer examination it proved to be *Viburnum congestum*. It was about 3m (9ft) high on average and as

much or more across, the numerous branches densely clothed with elliptic to obovate or rounded leaves 2.5-4cm (1-1½ in) long. These were blunt tipped and dark glossy green above, paler below. The red ellipsoid fruits eventually darkened to black and were carried in conical clusters at the ends of the twigs. Plants raised from these fruits have proven frost tender even in southern England, and it would appear that this species is only suitable for Mediterranean-type climates, such as southern Europe and California.[19] Other woody plants sharing these slopes with the viburnum

18. Q *variabilis* was first introduced to Britain by Robert Fortune in 1861 and later in 1882 from seeds sent from the Beijing area by Dr Emil Bretschneider. One of these trees still grows in Kew Gardens and was 17m (50ft.) in 2001. An even larger tree grows at Hollycombe in Sussex. This was 19m (62ft.) in 1997. Q *variabilis* was also collected by Wilson in west Sichuan and by Forrest in Yunnan.

19. A single example still grows in the Chelsea Physic Garden in London, where it is much admired by visitors. It is a shrub of 1.7m (5½ft.) or more, each year producing from May into June terminal clusters of scented white flowers, greenish in bud.

Osyris wightiana, a small- to medium-sized semi-parasitic shrub related to the Bastard toadflax (*Thesium humifusum*) of British chalk downs. We found it on a hillside above the Hanyuan to Kangding road. (September)

included *Osyris wightiana*, *Rhus chinensis*, *Debregeasia longifolia* and two pistachios, *Pistacia chinensis* and *P weinmanniifolia*. We also found *Abelia schumannii*, a small shrub, 1-1.3m (3-4ft), the lilac flowers with an orange flare in the throat borne singly in the leaf axils. It is a pretty little long-flowering shrub, and although in British cultivation subject to damage in severe winters, it normally shoots from the base again the following year. The herbaceous vegetation, such as it was, seemed to be on the wane but seed collected from an iris has since produced plants determined by Brian Mathew at Kew as *Iris leptophylla*.[20]

It was while climbing one of the keteleerias to examine

Our bus squeezes through the cleared road after a delay of seven hours. (September)

the cones that I heard an explosion. It was followed at intervals by others and they seemed to be coming from the road below. When we returned to the buses we were told that the rock fall had been cleared by dynamite and, sure enough, a gap had been made just wide enough for our transport to squeeze through, to the cheers of a watching throng. Those who assisted in the operation clapped and smilingly allowed themselves to be photographed.

The delay had cost us seven hours and our drivers now pressed on, anxious to make up as much time as possible. The valley deepened and we had to crane our necks to see the steep slopes above. Both slopes and riverside were littered with large red sandstone boulders and rocks. Keteleerias continued as isolated groves while the long-needled *Pinus yunnanensis* became dominant. By the river and along the side streams *Alnus cremastogyne* reigned supreme. Soon we were passing through deep gorges with high rock walls and an angry and powerful river below.

Darkness fell and still we sped on, climbing away from the river up the high slopes, our height emphasised by the tiny specks of village lights way down in the inky black of the valley. Sometimes the outside wheels of our bus seemed to be turning in space as we swept perilously close to the edge of the road and several members of our party vacated their seats on the precipice side of the bus in favour of those across the gangway; I couldn't blame them.

20. This species was first collected in Sichuan by Limpricht in 1922 and in the opinion of Mathew appears to be a vigorous version of *I decora* with flowers 5-6cm (2-2½ in) across. It is now grown in the Alpine and Herbaceous Department at Kew where it is regarded as 'very nice, like a superior *I decora* with a better, richer colour'.

The ornate entrance to the Iron-chain Bridge over the Dadu river at Luding. Our first visit took place late at night when all that was visible of the river was the white froth kicked up by the water's rush. (September)

We arrived at Luding around nine that night and persuaded our guides to allow us to spend the night here rather than continue to Kangding as originally intended. It was in a village near Luding, in 1889, that A E Pratt found an inn which 'for filth, discomfort and the quantity of vermin that it contained was entitled to take the cake'. Leaving at an early hour the next morning he concluded that this inn would remain fixed in his mind as containing the most varied collection of disagreeable things he had ever met with at one time. Chinese inns were notorious in the old days, especially those in remote areas, and most western travellers and plant hunters who wrote on the subject had their own horror stories concerning their experiences in such places. Nowadays of course, the situation is much improved, though there remain some 'country' guest houses whose most memorable feature concerns the state and smell of their latrines.

We were all tired after a long and eventful day but not so tired as to miss a chance of seeing the famous Iron-chain Bridge. Before the internal combustion engine and the building of a modern bridge across the Dadu river, all who travelled this important route between China and Tibet crossed the river by this suspension bridge. It is

The Iron-chain Bridge over the Dadu river at Luding, showing the arrangement of the wooden planks. (September)

The Iron-chain Bridge, Luding. A huge mural depicting a celebrated communist action here is housed in the local museum. (September)

The Iron-chain bridge over the Dadu river at Luding, looking down on the town from the mountains above the south bank. (September)

mentioned by all the plant hunters who ever came this way and it is said to have changed little in the last two hundred years. It is made of hand-forged links, each 20cm (8in) long, almost 2.5cm (1in) thick, joined in thirteen chains to span the river 45m (150ft) below. Two chains on either side, the highest at 1.3m (4ft), are designed to prevent one from falling over the brink. The floor is made of wooden boards laid across chains like railway sleepers. These in turn support a central cat-walk of boards laid four abreast plus two flanking cat-walks each of two boards' width. In between the boards are gaps and, at the time of our visit, there were a good number of broken or missing boards. The bridge is a little over 3m (9ft) wide and 102m (336ft) long. It is said that the Emperor Qing Kangxi in 1705 ordered 12,000 families to work on building this bridge and it has been repaired many times since. Not surprisingly, it was once of great strategic importance and featured in the Long March of Mao Zedong's (Mao Tse-tung) armies who won a major victory in Luding against the Nationalist forces of Chiang Kai-shek. A huge mural in the local museum depicts the action on the bridge in glorious colour.[21]

Although it was late, a number of us trooped down the street to the bridge entrance, an ornate wooden structure lit by large lanterns. Boldly we set off for the other side, Carla Teune leading the way, but before we had gone very far we became alarmed by the bouncing and clanging caused by our determined tread. We stopped until the bridge came to rest and then proceeded, stopping and starting at intervals all the way over and back again. All we could see of the river was the white froth kicked up by the water's rush, but we could hear its voice, a wild crashing sound which almost drowned our attempts at conversation. I was reminded of the experience of A E Pratt who, when he crossed this bridge on 2 June, 1890, was 'heartily laughed at by the natives, for the oscillation was so great as to cause

me some alarm, there being no hand rail'. Pratt at least crossed the bridge during daylight, though we were by no means the first westerners to attempt a night crossing.

One of the most scary night-time crossings was that made by Arthur Emmons, a member of the successful American team that climbed Minya Konka in 1932. As a result of frost-bite suffered on the mountain, Emmons's feet had become gangrenous. Having returned to Kangding he was faced with an eight-day journey to Ya-an and the nearest hospital. Due to his incapacity, Emmons was carried in a litter on the shoulders of two porters, and due to the slowness of these men the party was often travelling until well after dark. It was on such an occasion that they approached Luding. Emmons later wrote about the experience. 'At last, towards midnight the lights of Lutingchiao [Luding] came into view. The town lay on the far side and the bridge must be crossed that night'. At first his men, being exhausted, refused to cross the bridge. 'Finally, they plucked up courage, and with the spare man carrying a dim, smoky lantern in front, we started over. The footing even in the daylight was treacherous enough but at night the chance of stepping on a rotten board or where one was entirely missing was much too great for comfort. We reached the middle of the river and the bridge began to sway badly. The men staggered crazily in the darkness and my litter swung violently from side to side with the gyrations of their shoulders. They began to shout hysterically to each other in a panic of fear'. Emmons, laced tightly in a sleeping bag between two stout bamboo poles, took one look at the boiling torrent below and prepared to save himself by grabbing one of the chains. Fortunately, the men had sense enough to halt until the bridge stopped swinging. 'Again they proceeded, and when the chains began swinging stopped a second time. In this way, after what seemed a veritable eternity, we got safely across'.

Despite little sleep that night, we were on the move again at six the next morning, crossing the Dadu river by the modern bridge and driving away from the river towards Kangding. Luding lies at an altitude of 1,400m (4,592ft) and we were surprised, therefore, to see a Prickly pear cactus, Opuntia dillenii,[22] growing in some quantity on the hillside above the road. It was a most extraordinary sight: a native plant of South America flourishing in a remote corner of China! It was seen in this area by E H Wilson who claimed that it covered many miles of barren rocky slopes, but he could not offer a solution as to how it arrived here.

After some distance the road entered a deep gorge or canyon-like valley through which ran the Kangding river,

21. Recent published accounts have tended to play down this event as little more than a skirmish.

22. This plant, which has been widely planted and naturalised elsewhere in China as well as in the Himalaya, is now regarded as being Opuntia monacantha (Willd.) Haw., a native of South America. It has been identified in the past with both O vulgaris and O dillenii.

Buddleja nivea growing in the author's garden from seed collected in the Kangding river gorge in 1981. The rather small flowers and white woolly young growths are characteristic. (August)

formerly the Lu, on its way to the Dadu. We were intrigued by the apparently dry nature of this (and neighbouring) valleys where much of the scrub seemed almost xerophytic with a great number of spiny shrubs and sun-loving subjects. *Incarvillea arguta* thrived here in crevices in the cliffs and in the rock rubble beneath them. They were still flowering, their pink trumpets painting the pale stone behind. *Vitex yunnanensis* was common here, a lax shrub up to 2m (6ft) the leaves with five smooth-edged leaflets. The branched heads of tiny, pale lavender-blue flowers are less ornamental than those of the more widespread *V negundo*. Equally plentiful was the small pale blue flowered *Ceratostigma minus* and the powder-blue flowered *Caryopteris incana*, a low shrub and a parent of the popular garden hybrid *C x clandonensis*. The *ceratostigma* I remembered from the Hillier Arboretum where it once grew in a warm sunny border close by the entrance porch to Jermyns House, home of the late Sir Harold Hillier. It is a tender dwarf shrub in British cultivation and far less ornamental in my opinion than the well-known *C willmottianum*, which I saw in the Min river valley in 1986.

Buddleja davidii was everywhere in company with a second species *Buddleja nivea*. Seed of the latter has produced large vigorous shrubs with slender woolly spikes of pale violet flowers. As a flowering shrub this species is not worth growing; on the other hand, the dense, white, woolly floss on the young shoots and leaf undersurfaces is most appealing especially in spring.

Possibly the two most brightly coloured plants flowering in the gorge that day were climbers, both with long twining stems scrambling over the roadside vegetation. One of these, with racemes of brilliant blue trumpet flowers and arrow-shaped leaves, looked to be a Morning glory (*Ipomoea* species) or a close relative, while the other proved to be *Apios macrantha*, a member of the pea family (*Leguminosae*). It was a handsome plant with ash-like (pinnate) leaves and racemes of pale yellow flowers, in shape not unlike those of a monkshood (*Aconitum* species) with a strongly curved spur-like keel. I have never heard of this climber being grown in western cultivation, though it was first made known in 1890 by Augustine Henry, one of whose Chinese collectors found it in Sichuan. It would undoubtedly require a warm, sunny, well-drained situation to thrive and given that it would make a most ornamental if vigorous attraction.

In the cliffs grew a small gesneriad, an *Oreocharis* species with a basal rosette of long-stalked fleshy oval leaves with scalloped margins. Above these rose several slender erect stems to 12.5-15cm (5-6in) bearing several nodding purplish-brown bell flowers. Not far away we found a hypericum that caused great excitement when I presented a small dried fragment to Dr Robson. He declared it to be an unnamed species that had previously been collected on only three occasions, all in the Kangding area. The last specimen had been picked in 1938 by native collectors in the employ of the Hon H D McLaren, 2nd Lord

Hypericum maclarenii flowering in the author's garden from seed collected in the Kangding river gorge in 1981. According to Dr N K B Robson of the British Museum (Natural History) who named it, this is a relict (primitive) species. Its ornamental merit was acknowledged by the Royal Horticultural Society in 1986 when flowering material exhibited from Nymans, Sussex, received an Award of Merit. (July)

Aberconway. Dr Robson has since named this species *Hypericum maclarenii*, in reference to the above collection.[23]

One of our buses had been giving trouble and although this caused delays it did at least allow us the occasional unscheduled stop. On one occasion, towards the upper end of the Kangding river gorge, we walked for some distance up the road stopping finally to admire a magnificent fruiting specimen of *Viburnum betulifolium* (with leaves like *Betula*, the birch). It was 4m (13ft) high by as much across and almost every branch was bowed by the weight of the fruits like brilliant redcurrants in large drooping bunches. There were several others around but none compared with

Deutzia vilmoriniae photographed in the author's garden grown from seed collected in the Kangding river gorge, W. Sichuan. (June)

Viburnum betulifolium flowering in author's garden grown from seed (left) collected near Kangding in 1981. (July)

Viburnum betulifolium with its large drooping bunches of redcurrant-like fruits was frequent among the scrub in the Kangding river gorge. It was a shrub of some 4m (13ft), its branches bowed by the sheer weight of fruit. (September)

this. With it grew *Deutzia vilmoriniae*, 2m (6ft) high with wide spreading branches packed with seed.[24]

Both deutzia and viburnum were growing among thick scrub that now covered the steep sides of the gorge. At intervals, streams tumbled from the heights above and the whole 'feel' of this place was moist and cool compared with the drier, sun-baked lower parts of the gorge.

It was here, in the gorge below Kangding, that we saw *Polygonum aubertii*[25] in its original location; it is fairly plentiful in the mountains around the city. It was in flower, the thin white tassels wreathing the scrambling stems, creating impressive streamers on top of the scrub or climbing into trees to hang its flowering stems from the canopy like bunting.

Kangding, formerly Dardo, Tatsien-lu or Tachienlu, is one of the three most famous towns in the history of botanical exploration in west and central China, the others being Dali in Yunnan and Yichang in Hubei. Once known as the 'Gateway to Tibet', Kangding lies on one of the major routes from Beijing to Lhasa, a route which was as important in Marco Polo's day as it is today. It is situated in a deep valley at an altitude of 2,600m (8,529ft) on latitude 30° 03´N, longitude 101° 58´E. The latitude is approximately the same as Cairo and New Orleans. It is surrounded by high mountains and, according to Wilson, was rebuilt on its present site in the early nineteenth century when its predecessor, situated about 1km (½ mile) above, was totally destroyed by a landslip due to a moving glacier. As befitted a 'wild and woolly' frontier town, Kangding was once a 'mean and dirty' place with many ramshackle wooden buildings and narrow streets covered with mud. On the other hand, it was for travellers an exciting place where

23. From a botanical standpoint this is an important plant, regarded by Robson as an isolated relict species. Plants in cultivation grown from seed collected in 1981 are rather dwarf, 60-90cm (2-3ft), with comparatively narrow pointed leaves and star-shaped golden yellow flowers 4-5cm (1½-2in) across. It is an attractive shrub in flower and has suffered no harm outside in my garden despite two winters when -10℃ (14°F) was recorded. Indeed, its quality was recognised by the Royal Horticultural Society in August 1986 when an Award of Merit was given to flowering material exhibited from Nymans Garden in Sussex.

24. A pinch of this has resulted in a large number of plants in cultivation, one of which in my garden produced its pure white, honey-scented flowers in handsome bunches in June 1984. An even larger flowered seedling was raised at Nymans Garden, Sussex, and is being vegetatively propagated. *D vilmoriniae* was first discovered by the French missionary Paul Farges in Sichuan in 1897, who sent seed to the famous nurseryman Maurice de Vilmorin after whose wife it is named.

25. *Polygonum aubertii* was first introduced to Western cultivation (Paris) from Kangding in 1899 by the French missionary Georges-Eliosippe Aubert. In cultivation it has long been confused with the closely related *P baldschuanicum* of south Tadzhikistan introduced to Britain via St. Petersburg in 1883. So alike are the two that many authorities regard them as the same species and in most modern floras they are treated as such under the name *Fallopia baldschuanica* with *F aubertii* as a synonym.

Chinese from the east met Tibetans from the west across a border that moved according to the political fortunes of local warlords. It was, and to some extent still is, an important political, military and commercial centre and scene of uncountable major and minor dramas, some of which have been related by Victorian and Edwardian visitors.

Kangding was a city well known to several plant collectors and naturalists, including the English naturalist A E Pratt who stayed here in the summer of 1889 and again from April to July of the following year. During these periods he explored the mountains and valleys around, collecting a good number of dried plant specimens that he deposited at Kew on his return home. As Bretschneider has pointed out, Pratt was principally a zoological collector and was only persuaded to collect plants by Augustine Henry, whom he had met at Yichang on his way up the Yangtze. Pratt took with him a Chinese collector trained by Henry and among the plants new to science he collected were *Neillia thibetica* (as *N longiracemosa*), *Sorbus prattii*, *Rubus cockburnianus* and *Primula cockburniana*, the last two named in honour of the members of the Cockburn family domiciled in China.

During his first stay in Kangding, Pratt met the French missionary Jean André Soulié who also collected in the Kangding area and in south-east Tibet. On Pratt's second visit to Kangding he met the Frenchman Prince Henri d'Orléans recently arrived with his party at the end of an incredible journey across central and eastern Asia. The young prince (he was only twenty-three at the time) had been making botanical and other collections throughout his journey, and on his arrival in Kangding made further collections (all dried specimens) which he persuaded Pratt to take with him to Shanghai for despatch to the Paris Museum and Herbarium.

However, the most famous of the early collectors to make Kangding his base was the Russian explorer Grigori

The town of Tachienlu (now Kangding) photographed in 1929 by Joseph Rock. Here two rivers join to form the Kangding River, which flows through the Kangding Gorge to join the Dadu River above Luding. For many years Kangding was the base for plant-hunting expeditions into the surrounding mountains as well as a major staging post on the Beijing to Lhasa road. Here, tea from China was exchanged for hides, furs, wool and gold from Tibet.

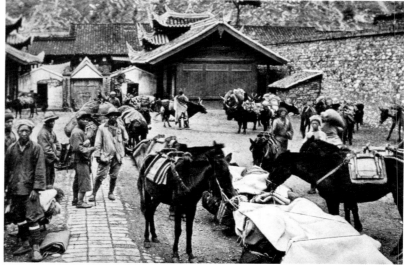

Members of Rock's entourage at the China Inland Mission, Tachienlu (now Kangding), west Sichuan in 1929, preparing for the journey to Minya Konka. Photograph by Joseph Rock

Nicolaevich Potanin. He travelled widely in central and eastern Asia, making four great journeys between 1876 and 1894, which resulted in thousands of specimens of all kinds including dried plants. In 1892 he spent several months in Kangding, from April to July exploring and collecting in the mountains around.

Despite the close attentions of these collectors the turn of the 20th century saw another influx of plant collectors anxious to visit Kangding, or at least to use it as a base for exploration further afield. A German, Dr Wolfgang Limpricht, was there in 1914, and in 1922 it was the turn of Dr Karl August Harald Smith (Harry Smith), a Swedish botanist. Smith returned there in 1934 but, according to Cox, found the area disappointing botanically, regretting that he had wasted so much time there. Maybe Rock felt the same when in spring 1929 he spent only two weeks in the city before returning to Minya Konka.

The problem no doubt was that by the 1930s, the area around Kangding had been examined so many times by so many people that there was little in the way of new plants remaining. Fifty years after Harry Smith we found the hills around Kangding full of interesting plants, no new species admittedly, but old friends from cultivation which, as far as I am concerned, gives me as much pleasure as finding something quite new. Plants apart, we found it exciting enough travelling a road made famous in botanical history by such notables as Potanin and, of course, Wilson. Perhaps more than any other, Wilson is the plant collector one immediately recalls when the name Kangding or Tachienlu, as he would have known it, is mentioned.

During the first decade of the 20th century Wilson found himself in Kangding on several occasions and he devoted a chapter to it in his book *A Naturalist in Western China*. His description of the city as it was at the turn of the 20th century is well worth reading. He collected a large number of plants and, more importantly, seeds in the area and on journeys to the north, east and west. As far as I am aware, he did not travel to the south west and was unaware of Minya Konka, although he remarked on the ranges of high mountains south of Kangding, which he regarded as part of the 'Chino-Tibetan Borderland', a name he coined for this wild, relatively unexplored region.

Wilson's most remembered visit to this area, however, was in 1903 during his second expedition for the firm of Veitch. His main objective was to collect seed of the yellow poppywort, *Meconopsis integrifolia*, which Pratt had reported as growing in the alpine pastures above Kangding. In this endeavour Wilson was successful and the poppy was duly introduced to cultivation.

Due to the delays we had suffered we did not stop in Kangding but drove into the city and out the other side. One of our buses had to be left behind for repairs, its passengers crowding into the second bus with an overspill into the jeep. Soon we were climbing steeply, following the road to Batang

Hypericum pseudohenryi growing above Kangding quite close to the main road into Tibet. It was first collected in this area by Ernest Wilson in 1908, and is a most ornamental shrub for the garden with its free-flowering habit and red-tinted capsules. (September)

and heading for the Zheduo Pass. It was here that we had our first sight of the peaks that lie to the north of the Minya Konka range, sharply cut and covered with snow.

Sambucus adnata, the Asiatic cousin of the European Dane's elder, (*S ebulus*), was plentiful by the road, its suckering stems forming extensive colonies of bold leafy stems 1-1.5m (3-5ft) high, topped by the plate-sized heads of red berries. It was collected from this area by Pratt, but only as a dried specimen. Nearby we found *Hypericum pseudohenryi* growing in some quantity. It was from this area in 1908 that Wilson first introduced this species as seed, and it was tempting to believe that these plants may have been descendants of those he found. This is an excellent late summer flowering shrub for the garden, 1-1.5m (3-5ft) tall, its rounded habit crowded with golden-yellow flowers with wide-spreading petals. The pointed fruit capsules are prettily red tinted as a bonus. It was flowering its heart out as we passed, and on our return I gathered some seed from which many plants have been raised and are now well established in British gardens.

We were allowed a stop at around 3,000m (9,848ft) and immediately made for the nearby hillside, which, like others in the neighbourhood, was covered with a dense mixed

Rosa moyesii, flowering in 1986 at Nymans, Sussex, from seed collected above Kangding in 1981. Both this rich pink and the more familiar blood-red flowered form were reported by Ernest Wilson when he first introduced this species from the Kangding area in 1903. It is named after the Rev J Moyes, a missionary who accompanied Wilson on a journey into east Tibet. (June)

scrub in which grew roses, philadelphus, deutzias, buddlejas, viburnums, spiraeas, sorbarias, indigoferas and rhododendrons, plus many other well-known genera. The common rhododendron was *Rhododendron decorum*, which I had seen in great quantity in western Yunnan a few months previously, while the buddleja proved to be *Buddleja stenostachya*.

I collected here the seed of a rose, a shrub of some 3m (9ft) with tall, loose, prickly stems and slender bottle-shaped red hips. I guessed it to be *Rosa moyesii*, which had first been found in the Kangding area by Pratt in 1893. Wilson collected it ten years after and it is from this seed and a later batch that *R moyesii* was established in cultivation. With its blood red flowers (even better in the selection 'Geranium'), this is one of the most famous and desirable of all rose species, although it is rather too vigorous for smaller gardens. Plants grown from the 1981 seed flowered for the first time in 1985 and instead of being blood red, as I had expected, were a rich pink with a white central zone. Apparently *R moyesii* does vary in flower colour and some pink flowered seedlings were raised from Wilson's original collection.[26] The name, incidentally, commemorates the Rev J Moyes, a missionary in west China known to Wilson.

The sorbaria proved to be *Sorbaria arborea*, a name that aptly describes this large, sometimes tree-like shrub with bold, pinnate leaves. On these exposed and, no doubt, cut-over hillsides it grew no higher than 3m (9ft), but from the size and number of its seed heads it must have presented an impressive picture in July when its plumes of white flowers would have been at their best.

Like a giant spiraea, this is a vigorous hardy, bold and free-flowering shrub in cultivation, suitable for most soils, but not for the small garden. Like others of its clan it responds well to hard pruning, which encourages a regular crop of stout shoots with outsize leaves and flowerheads. According to Wilson, it was used in some parts of west Sichuan as a hedge around fields and village plots.

Malus kansuensis an uncommon species in cultivation here seen in the wild above Kangding. (September)

Scattered through the scrub was a crab-apple, *Malus kansuensis*, a small tree with three-lobed leaves, pale and downy beneath, with slender, reddish-purple stalks and similarly coloured veins. The small fruits were egg shaped, yellow flushed with red. Although a pretty species, this crab is rarely seen in western cultivation outside botanic gardens and arboreta. It is perfectly hardy and floriferous, producing its white flowers in clusters (corymbs) during May.

We were about to return to the bus when I spotted a

Berberis verruculosa well known in cultivation having been first introduced by E. H. Wilson in 1904 and again later from above Kangding. Here it is photographed in cultivation. (April)

Allium cyaneum. A pretty little bulbous perennial, common on rocky slopes above Kangding. (September)

Rocky hillside by the road above Kangding, a rich habitat in plant life supporting many ornamentals. Here we found species of *Berberis*, *Cotoneaster*, *Rosa*, *Lonicera*, *Sorbaria*, *Rhododendron*, *Allium*, and many more. (September)

dwarf, compact evergreen berberis fairly widely distributed on the slopes above. It was an old garden favourite, *Berberis verruculosa*, with its spiny, minutely warty (verruculose) shoots and almost blackish-green, silver-backed leaf clusters. On these slopes its dense mounds were no higher than 1m (3ft), but it is capable of almost twice this height elsewhere. It was first introduced to western cultivation by Wilson in 1904 and again from the Kangding area in 1910.[27]

One of the few herbs we found in flower was a wild onion, *Allium cyaneum*, a small tuft of slender green leaves and equally slender stems nodding at the tip to support a cluster of rich blue flowers. It was a gem and seemed quite common among the rocks.

We continued the long climb, stopping at regular intervals to allow the engine to cool. The last of these enforced stops, on a section of the Zheduo Pass, was long enough for us to have a scout around on a hillside quite different to those lower down. Here, at 3,900m (12,792ft), the scrub was much smaller, more compact and of a different character. Most abundant were the tiny leaved alpine rhododendrons of the Lapponicum section. None were in flower, of course, but their tight hummocks, no more than 60cm (2ft) high, dominated large areas especially on the slopes. *Potentilla arbuscula* was equally dwarf and compact and sported the occasional, late, large golden flower, the size of a fifty pence piece. There was also a

prostrate cotoneaster, a deciduous shrub whose stems followed closely the contours of the rocks and hillocks on which it grew. The small, rounded, polished green leaves set off the comparatively large, rounded, sealing-wax red fruits. It was undoubtedly *Cotoneaster adpressus* and later proved quite common in the hills around Liuba. This has been in cultivation for over eighty years and remains one of the best dwarf berrying ground cover shrubs for small gardens.

One of the most commonly occurring shrubs on the high plains and pastures of west Sichuan is an interesting spiraea relative called *Sibiraea angustata*. Interesting is the word, for there is little ornamental value in its early summer clusters (panicles) of small white flowers, though

26. According to Martyn Rix, who has travelled widely in S.W. China, the pink flowered plant is the most common form in the wild. Trust Wilson to introduce the less common and more desirable red form.

27. B *verruculosa* (with B *candidula*) is a parent of a number of hybrids in cultivation mostly of Dutch origin such as 'Amstelveen' and 'Telstar' raised for their compact evergreen nature and their tolerance of neglect and pollution. At one time they were widely planted in inner city areas, still are in some countries of Europe.

Cotoneaster adpressus formed carpets and hummocks on the hillsides above Kangding, its branches studded with red berries. (September)

Gentiana farreri, or a closely related species, growing in alpine pastures, often in damp depressions or on the margins of bogs, on the Zheduo Pass above Kangding. (September)

its deciduous, glaucous green, fleshy leaves have some value in the collector's border. It was a sturdy-stemmed bush up to 1.5m (5ft) forming wide-spreading clumps among the low scrub for as far as the eye could see. It is regarded by some authorities as a variety of *S laevigata*, a native of Russia, which I remember first seeing in the University Botanic Garden, Cambridge, in the early 1960s.

With it grew dwarf gnarled bushes of a shrubby honeysuckle *Lonicera rupicola* (*thibetica*). A few red fruits collected at the time have produced plants that, although they retain the small leaves and small lilac flowers, are too coarse growing to be of real value in the garden. One plant I was especially pleased to find here was an ornamental rhubarb, *Rheum alexandrae*.[28] It was common in damp

Lonicera rupicola, a dwarf shrub when wind-blasted and browsed, but of untidy habit in cultivation. It was common on the hillsides above Kangding. (September)

depressions and on stream banks, its bold rosettes of shining, dark green leaves crowded into colonies, some of the older leaves already turning orange and red. Its flowering was long since past. Wilson knew it in these mountains and described it as 'the most striking of all the herbs, an extraordinary plant, with a pyramidal inflorescence, 3-4ft [1-1.2m] tall, arising from a mass of relatively small (for a rhubarb), ovate, shining sorrel-like leaves and composed of broad, rounded, decurved, pale yellow bracts overlapping one another like tiles on a house roof'. He further observed that it preferred 'rich boggy ground where verdure is luxuriant and yak delight to feed'. I wonder how many gardeners in the West could provide such exacting conditions? It is in cultivation, in Britain certainly, where, not surprisingly, it is regarded as a tricky plant. I have yet to see it growing anything like as well as it does in the wild and the same can be said for its Himalayan cousin *R nobile*. Kingdon-Ward saw *R alexandrae* in Sichuan: 'A magnificent field of this species numbering hundreds of plants, like slender porcelain pagodas standing shoulder to shoulder'. He complained that plants in cultivation had too much green in the bracts and lacked the sharp yellow colour they enjoyed at an altitude of 4,267m (14,000ft).[29]

Around many of the damp depressions where the rhubarb grew there also occurred a most lovely gentian. It was a prostrate plant with slender shoots clothed with narrow leaves. At the tip of each shoot was borne a single, large, up-turned funnel-shaped flower of a startling Cambridge blue paling to white at the base and with long green bands

28. *R alexandrae* was first discovered above Kangding on 13 June, 1893 by Grigori Potanin and named in memory of his wife Alexandra, an intrepid woman who accompanied her husband on his travels assisting with the collection and preparation of botanical specimens. She was taken ill in Sichuan during his fourth and last expedition and, although Potanin made all haste to get her to hospital at Chongqing (Chungking) on the Yangtze, she died when only two days away from that city. Potanin had her body sent overland to be buried in Russian soil.

29. I have since seen it growing and flowering something near to perfection in the rock garden at the RBG Edinburgh and it doubtlessly flourishes equally well elsewhere particularly in cooler northern gardens.

Gentiana veitchiorum. Its rich blue trumpet flowers decorated many areas of alpine pasture and hillside above Kangding and, like *G farreri*, seemed to enjoy rather dampish situations. (September)

bordered with dark violet on the outside. It looked very much like the gentian Reginald Farrer introduced from Gansu – *Gentiana farreri*.[30] Its very narrow leaves (up to 1mm broad), short flower stalks, and long recurved filiform sepals certainly echoed Farrer's description of this plant, as did the luminous blue of the corolla, which bulged noticeably above half-way giving it a slightly bell-shaped appearance. Several flowers I measured were 7-7.5cm (2¾-3in) long and 3cm (1¼in) across the mouth, and as each plant produced numerous radiating flowering shoots, the resultant effect was extraordinary with pads and pools of blue trumpets scattered across the otherwise tired-looking brown alpine pastures.

Although Farrer's original discovery was made in Gansu, I see no reason to doubt that *G farreri* might also occur in similar situations to the south west in Sichuan. If the plant growing on the Zheduo Pass is not *G farreri* then it must at least be a close relative.

Almost as common, was a gentian of similar habit, but

with shorter broader leaves. The trumpet-shaped flower, moreover, was a rich deep blue. It has since been identified as *Gentiana veitchiorum*,[31] a species considered among the finest of the dark blue autumn flowering kinds, excelled only by the matchless *G sino-ornata*.

30. Ever since its first public appearance at a Royal Horticultural Society Show in London in 1916, when it caused a sensation, *G farreri* has been a regular recipient of verbal and literary accolades. Farrer himself regarded it as 'by far the most outstandingly beautiful of its race', and G H Berry in his book on gentians, published in 1951, devoted ten pages to its cultivation. Berry considered it the 'gentian of all gentians, a classic, the King of the Himalayas'. It is little wonder, then, that with so many growers besotted with the beauty of this plant, its apparent demise in cultivation has caused widespread dismay. If the pundits are right, then all the plants bearing the name *G farreri* in cultivation are no more than hybrids of the same with other related species. It is not that these plants are worthless, many of them are beautiful in their own right, just that the peculiar qualities of the real McCoy have been at best dissipated, at worst lost. According to a recent monograph by Ho Ting-nong and Liu Shang-Wu (2001), *G farreri*, referred to here as *G lawrencei* variety *farreri*, occurs in alpine meadows between 2,400 and 4,600m (7,900 and 15,000ft.) over a wide area of S.E. Tibet, W. Sichuan, Qinghai and S.W. Gansu.

31. *G veitchiorum* has been crossed with others to produce a host of hybrids for the peat or alpine garden. There are many named forms producing a galaxy of trumpeted flowers varying in size, shape and shade. They all demand a lime free soil.

Rheun alexandrae, named for Alexandra, wife of the Russian plant explorer Grigori Potanin. This magnificent ornamental rhubarb is photographed here at the RBG, Edinburgh. (May)

Zheduo Pass above Kangding, a magnificent mountain landscape with the Minya Konka range to the right. It is in these alpine pastures that on 18th July 1903 E.H. Wilson first set eyes on *Meconopsis integrifolia*, the yellow poppywort. (September)

South to Liuba

By mid-afternoon, our bus finally made it to the summit of the Zheduo Pass at a height of 4,150m (13,615ft). The view was spectacular to say the least. To the south soared the peaks of the Minya Konka range doomed to eternal snow, while northwards lay a cold grey waste of shattered rock and scree. Below us, ranging westwards into Tibet marched a succession of rounded hills, their slopes greened like algae on the fluted bark of a fallen tree. Apart from grasses and the flattened pads of an alpine campion, *Silene* species, there was little to be seen on the exposed summit.

We did, however, find three interesting alpines in flower. One was a stonecrop with golden yellow star-shaped flowers surprisingly large for the size of the plant. It was later named *Sedum oreades*. With it grew an annual gentian, *Gentiana tongolensis*, which formed dense flattened pads of slender stems terminating in small, star-shaped flowers of pale primrose.[32]

By far the most curious plant here, however, was *Saussurea stella*, a squat perennial with a rosette of leaves flattened against the ground, their stalks enlarged towards the base and coloured a pale purple. In the centre of the rosette was a dense cluster of tiny white-crowned flowerheads like miniature shaving brushes. Its second name, *stella*, means star, and this plant indeed resembled a small, multi-rayed, starfish nestling in the turf.

Since leaving Luding early that morning we had ascended approximately 2,743m (9,000ft) and the comparatively thin air of the summit caused several of our party to suffer headaches. After a short lunch break, therefore, we continued along the road, which snaked steeply down through broad green valleys where herds of yak and the black yurts of nomadic Tibetan herdsmen were the only signs of life. We had left the main road to Batang and from now on our route would take us through territory seen by relatively few westerners. From wild, windy pastures the road passed by villages where the distinctive remains of stone towers stood like squat

32. This species was first discovered in the alpine pastures above Kangding in the 1890s by the French missionary and plant collector Jean André Soulie, who in 1905 met with a violent death at the hands of Tibetan monks. Interestingly, a pinch of seed collected from another gentian long since flowered and given to the Alpine Departments of the Royal Botanic Gardens at Kew and Edinburgh has since germinated and flowered. It proved to be *G trichotoma* and, according to Ron McBeath at the latter garden, has superb blue flowers. It is rather unusual in producing an erect stem as much as 30cm (12in) tall, with whorls of narrow leaves at intervals in the axils of which two to three erect flowers 2.5cm (1in) long are borne, creating a spire-like effect in May and June.

Sedum oreades, a small prostrate species with large flowers, common on the summit of the Zheduo Pass. (September)

Gentiana tongolensis, an annual species, its stems flattened against the windswept turf on the Zheduo Pass. (September)

chimneys above flat Tibetan roofs. The exact significance of these towers, which can be square, hexagonal or octagonal in shape, is still uncertain. Wilson suggested that they may have had several uses as store houses, watch towers and harbours of refuge in times of trouble. They were built apparently when this area was part of the Chiala Kingdom, a semi-independent state between China and Tibet ruled by a king who resided at Kangding. The state was considerable, bounded by the Dadu valley in the north, the Yangtze valley to the east and the valley of the Yalong in the west. It included the whole of the Minya Konka range.

Streams and torrents appeared seemingly from nowhere, their shingled banks and islands clouded by tamarisk and willow. Gradually we dropped into a long, deep, well-forested valley, its myriad greens a startling contrast to the bare heights above. It had been an exciting and exhausting journey and the day was fast drawing to a close when we entered the valley of the Pa La river, finally halting by a meadow above the water's edge.

Saussurea stella, a curious alpine with the leaf bases flattened and coloured and spreading like the arms of a starfish. The small flowerheads form a dense central cluster. It was common on the alpine pastures above Kangding and on the Zheduo Pass. (September)

Tibetan village south-west of Kangding with stone tower. E.H. Wilson was of the opinion that these towers once served as store houses in peace time, and as refuges or watch towers in times of trouble. (September)

Pi Ho valley village. The river is flanked with *Hippophae* and willow *Salix* species. (September)

The Pa La river valley, a rich scrub of woody plants including Cotoneaster, Berberis, oak, shrubby honeysuckle and juniper crowded the road and river side supporting Clematis species and *Rosa saulieana*. (September)

We erected our tents in the dark and what a pantomime that proved to be. We were all dog tired and what with searching for level sites, unravelling the tents and hunting around for rocks with which to hammer in the guy rope pegs and weigh them down, the situation, not surprisingly, proved a little overwhelming for some. Eventually, we were all settled in and, after a snack meal eaten cold because of cookhouse problems, we retired to the damp privacy of our tents.

Our camp was situated at an altitude of 3,500m (11,482ft) on latitude 29° 28′N, longitude 101° 32′E. Here we were to spend the next five days, with treks on foot and pony into the surrounding hills and valleys. It was an idyllic place hemmed in by steep-sided mountains clothed with forest and scrub. Tibetan hamlets lay scattered along the main valley, the nearest Liuba, only a ten minute walk further east. The Tibetans are a naturally curious people, and to have a party of westerners encamped on their doorstep must have been the nearest thing to having a circus in town. For the duration of our stay we were objects of interest, our camp regularly visited by adults and children happy to pass the time of day observing us. They would stand or sit in groups on the slope above, talking continually, discussing our every move, occasionally laughing loudly at our embarrassment as when

The small Tibetan village of Liuba in the Pa La river valley. To the villagers we were an unexpected source of interest and entertainment. (September)

some of us tried to mount unwilling ponies. The bolder individuals would stroll through our camp eager to touch any new object – especially pieces of equipment – examining it carefully with a serious gaze.

They were a fine looking race, the men tall and sturdy, the young women rosy cheeked and handsome. Both men and women had strong faces, and those of the old people were especially full of character. The old women seemed to spend much of their time winding woollen thread on to sticks, carrying their work with them on walks to the fields or the next village. Most of them wore traditional clothes, usually some loose-fitting wrap-around garment tied at the waist. These tended to be dark in colour as were other items of everyday wear such as jackets and waistcoats. Occasionally we met a man wearing a sheepskin-lined gown worn casually over one shoulder, the other arm hanging free.

Boots, too, were Tibetan style with high woven uppers tied below the knee with lengths of material. A broad brimmed trilby was the favourite headgear of both sexes, though caps were worn by a few. The overall drabness of their clothes was often brightened by lengths of colourful yarn around the waist or by a tunic shirt of red, blue or mulberry purple. The women liked to wear colourful tassels or braids in their oiled, black hair which was often plaited and wound around the head, and most wore bright jewellery in the form of earrings, beads, bangles and rings. In the short time we were with them the people seemed friendly and blessed with a good sense of humour, and whenever we passed through their villages or fields we were invariably greeted with broad smiles or maidenly giggles.

Our camp above the Pa La river, a little to the west of the village of Liuba. (September)

Tibetan children from the village of Liuba (September)

Tibetan woman in traditional dress on the outskirts of Liuba. (September)

Tibetan woman at Liuba. (September)

Quercus longispica showing the long tassled male catkins. Photographed at the Hillier Arboretum in Hampshire, the only plant grown from seed we collected above Liuba. (July)

Quercus longispica, an evergreen oak, was common as dense scrub on the hillside of the Pa La river valley. The leaf undersurface is covered with a dense, yellowish down. (September)

Quercus longispica showing the almost spineless adult foliage and the long peduncled acorns. (September)

The Pa La river valley was well wooded, the trees a mixture of conifers and deciduous, with a rich understorey of shrubs and herbs. The greatest density and variety occurred in the valley bottom, gradually thinning out and giving way to scrub higher up. Much of this scrub consisted of an evergreen oak, *Quercus longispica*, a species new to me. The hard leathery leaves are a dark polished green above and covered beneath with a yellowish down. In common with many scrub oaks the leaves are prickly toothed on young or sucker shoots, gradually losing the teeth in maturity. The fruits are borne in spikes, several together along a slender stalk. In sheltered ravines this oak was a small, stout, short-stemmed tree of 6-9m (20-30ft) with a spreading, heavily-branched crown. Elsewhere it surged up beneath the spruce canopy and continued above the tree line as a dense chest-high scrub until, at around 4,000m (13,123ft), it gave way to the ubiquitous dwarf lapponicum rhododendrons. Although the oak occurred on both sides of the valley, there was a marked preference for the south-facing slopes where it occurred in vast quantities, dominant above the tree line, the yellow undersurface of the leaves from a distance giving a golden glow to the hillside, especially noticeable in sun. On closer examination, there appeared to be at least two different scrub oaks in these hills. Seeds collected at the time have resulted in a single bushy tree, which appears to be flourishing, at the Hillier Arboretum.

South-facing slopes of the pa La river valley are covered with a scrubby golden-backed oak *Quercus longispica*. (September)

307

Valley of the Pa La river looking east from above our campsite near Liuba. The conifers in the background belong to *Picea balfouriana*. (September)

Valley of the Pa La river looking west from above our campsite near Liuba. *Picea balfouriana* is the common tree conifer here. (September)

On the cooler north-facing slopes of the valley the rôle of the oak was taken by *Rhododendron decorum*, equally common beneath the canopy and on the edge of the tree line above which, however, it was not inclined to venture. At this point another species was common, no flowers, of course, but large leaved, up to 15cm (6in) long, covered beneath with a buff-coloured indumentum. It was a bold shrub of 2-3m (6-9ft), and on several occasions we found lone individuals in small gullies well above the tree line. Photographs were taken and a small fragment collected to assist identification. Later it was confirmed by Dr David Chamberlain at the Royal Botanic Garden, Edinburgh to be *R phaeochrysum*. The flowers are said to be white flushed pink with crimson flecks.

The most widespread trees in the valley were conifers, of which there were several kinds. A handsome spruce was dominant on the north-facing slopes and on the lower regions of those opposite. It proved to be *Picea likiangensis* variety *balfouriana*,[33] which formed tall columns of 24m (80ft) or more with thick, deeply-furrowed bark and short, spreading branches clothed with short, blunt, densely-crowded and overlapping leaves varying in colour from green to blue-grey. The young cones were a striking plum-purple maturing to greyish-brown.

Sharing the valley bottom with the spruce was a large juniper. It was particularly common by the river, where grew trees of all sizes including some ancient, large-boled specimens 15-18m (50-60ft) high with grey or greyish-green scale-like leaves and small black fruits. At one time we considered this to be *Juniperus potaninii*, but more recent opinion suggests it is *Juniperus tibetica*, a rare species native to west Sichuan and adjacent Tibet. Plants from seed collected at the time are now established in cultivation.

Another juniper, *J ramulosa*, we found one day in an isolated grove near a stream in the valley above our camp. They were trees of 9m (30ft) or more with dark flaky bark, their scale-like leaves dark green and carried in long, arching sprays. Most Chinese authorities regard *J ramulosa* as a synonym of the closely related *J convallium*.[34] Apart from the two tree junipers described, a third species, *J squamata*, was common above the tree line. There it was dwarf and spreading, but, compared with others I have seen of this species, it was of little ornamental merit.

Picea balfouriana, with its colourful cones, was the dominant tree in the Pa La river valley. Some specimens were 24m (80ft) or more high. (September)

Picea balfouriana. A handsome young tree, in cone, grown from seed collected in the Pa la river valley, near Liuba. Photographed at Bolham Orchard, near Tiverton in Devon. (July)

Juniperus tibetica in the Pa La river valley. Plants grown from seed collected here in 1981 are now in western cultivation. (September)

33. This is now generally regarded as a species in its own right – *Picea balfouriana* Rehder & Wilson. It was first discovered and introduced by Wilson from somewhere west of Kangding and, although it has been with us for over seventy years, it remains uncommon in cultivation, which is curious considering its undoubted merit. I first saw it in the Hillier Arboretum, two young trees of slender conical habit with leaves of a striking grey-blue colour. They are still there and growing strongly. According to Wilson, it is the tallest of the Chinese spruces. It was named for F R S Balfour, 'a lover and enthusiastic planter of trees on his estate at Dawyck, Scotland, as a slight return for his substantial assistance to the Arnold Arboretum in its second Wilson Expedition to China'. The tallest tree of this species is a specimen at the Dawyck Botanic Garden which in 2005 measured 22m (72ft.)

34. These species were identified by the late Laurie Gough of the South Bank Polytechnic in London, whose special interest in conifer resins led him to examine anew the taxonomy of junipers both wild and cultivated. He examined all my Chinese junipers over the years, and his untimely death in 1984 was a sad loss to his many friends in the conifer fraternity.

Larix potaninii, its large handsome cones conspicuous on the upper sides of the branches. This was a common tree in the Pa La river valley, although nowhere did we find it the dominant species. (September)

The cones of the *Larix potaninii* note the broad scales and the protruding bracts. (September)

Two other large conifers were found in the Pa La river valley, both as scattered individuals. One was a larch, *Larix potaninii*,[35] a tree here of 9m (30ft) with pale yellow or straw-coloured shoots, green or sea-green leaves to 2.5cm (1in) long, and egg-shaped cones 5cm (2in) long lining the upper sides of the branchlets. The cones were quite substantial with long, pointed, recurved bracts protruding from between the broad, pale brown scales. Later we saw much taller examples of this larch in greater quantities in neighbouring valleys. In the Pa La river valley, however, there was evidence that larger specimens had been felled in the past. It is known locally as Red fir, its wood esteemed as the most valuable of all timber in west Sichuan for construction work.

The other conifer growing in the valley was *Pinus densata*, a relative of the North China pine *P tabuliformis* of which it is, by some authorities, considered a variety. In the valleys west of Minya Konka, it is a strong, tall, open-crowned tree, which in more exposed places it is often squatter and denser in habit. Some specimens in the neighbouring valley of the Pi river were 15-18m (50-60ft) or more, while higher still on the more exposed slopes they were less than half this size. Some cones were collected and from their seed plants have been established both in England and the United States.

It was in the neighbouring valley of the Pi river that the last conifer we encountered on the expedition, a fir, grew. *Abies ernestii*,[36] an identification since confirmed by the Arnold Arboretum, occurred here in some quantity as a tree of 18-21m (60-70ft) or more with dark grey fissured bark. We had first noted it late in the afternoon of our arrival and saw it again on a return visit. In some parts of the valley above the river it formed dense stands

occasionally with Balfour's spruce. A wind-blown branch we found among the rocks had cones attached. These were shortly stalked, 7-10cm (2¾-4in) long, cylindrical, broadening slightly towards the base, of a violet-brown colour with broad overlapping rounded scales and no protruding bracts. The current year's shoots were ridged, without hairs and of a shining orange-brown becoming grey the second year. The buds were broad based with a blunt tip, greenish and covered with a layer of clear resin. The firm, short, pointed leaves were crowded above the branchlets, the shorter leaves steeply ascending, those on the flanks spreading widely to 2-3cm (¾-1¼in) long. There was no V-shaped parting above and only a small proportion of leaves spreading below. In colour they were dark glossy green above and marked with two broad, pale, glaucous bands of stomata beneath.

The two most abundant groups of deciduous trees in the Pa La river valley were birch and mountain ash. Of the former we found two species, *Betula utilis* and *Betula szechuanica*, the latter previously referred to as *B japonica* variety *szechuanica*, or as *B platyphylla* variety *szechuanica*. They tended to occupy distinct zones. *B utilis* was the common birch of the valley bottom ascending the slopes – north-facing slopes especially – for some distance before giving way to the other species that preferred the upper reaches of the forest, even occurring as isolated groups or individuals

35. This is another conifer first introduced from the Kangding area by Wilson, although the name honours Potanin who first discovered it in the same area in 1893. The largest specimen of this larch in British and Irish cultivation is a tree at Headfort, Co. Meath, which measured 16m (52ft) in 1980.

36. *A ernestii* is extremely rare in cultivation, though it was distributed in the early 1940s by Hilliers from seed received from a Chinese source. It is named after Ernest Wilson who found it in the mountains north east of Kangding in 1907.

Betula utilis, the common birch of the Pa La river valley and neighbouring valleys. The bark was richly coloured and peeling on the main stems, giving them a decidedly shaggy appearance. (September)

Betula szechuanica occurred with B utilis around Liuba, though ascending to a higher elevation. Its bark was a conspicuous silvery-white by contrast with B utilis. (September)

above the tree line. All the trees of B *szechuanica* we saw had silvery-white bark and sharply-toothed, few-veined leaves dotted with glands beneath. Seed from these trees has germinated freely in cultivation and grown strongly. From their growth so far these saplings seem about to justify Bean's remark that this is 'a vigorous but rather graceless tree'. From what I saw in the wild it is the nature of the beast. B *utilis*, on the other hand, was extremely ornamental, varying in the colour of its peeling papery bark from cream with pink tints to a rich coppery-brown, the same variation incidentally, that one sees in this birch in the Himalaya. Some trees we found in the woods by the river were quite sizeable, up to 12m (40ft) with impressive girths and crowns. One of our number, Tim Brotzman, climbed into a tree in order to shake down some seed and this, together with seed from other trees, has produced a host of promising saplings in cultivation in Britain and the United States. It is not impossible that the two birches in the valley hybridise, which might explain some of the trees with bark of an intermediate character, but until the Chinese form of B *utilis* has been more thoroughly studied, these will remain an unknown quantity.

Pinus densata was quite plentiful in the Pa La river valley, young trees growing strong and erect in the more sheltered sites. (September)

Sorbus gonggashanica. A new species common in the Pa La river valley area of W. Wichuan, here photographed near the village of Liuba. (September)

Sorbus gonggashanica, a handsome and most ornamental species here growing in the author's garden. (September)

Sorbus rehderiana, a young tree photographed by H. McAllister at Ness Gardens in Cheshire from seed collected in the Pa La river valley, W. Sichuan. Note the glossy foliage and erect fruit clusters. (September)

Of mountain ash we saw three or four species at least, one of which was Sorbus rehderiana, a white-fruited tree first found by Carla Teune in the valley above camp. Later we found it elsewhere. This species is distinguished from its closest allies by its slow growth, stout, stiff dark twigs, glossy, relatively smooth leaflets and upright clusters of small fruits. It has a wide distribution from S.E. Tibet, through Burma and Yunnan to W. Sichuan (Gongga Shan). Two other species had smaller leaves with smaller, neater leaflets prettily toothed, and drooping bunches of white fruits. They were plentiful both in the main valley and in all the ravines, often clinging to steep banks, their branches spreading or hanging over the rushing streams. One of these two Sorbus species, with white fruits like

Sorbus pallescens, a member of the whitebeam group, was widespread in the Pa La river valley and in neighbouring valleys. The silver-backed leaves and comparatively large red and green fruits make this a most ornamental small tree for gardens. (September)

Sorbus pallescens, photographed in the Pi river valley showing its bold foliage and fruits. (September)

Acer cappadocicum variety *sinicum*, the shoot of a young tree growing in the author's garden. Note the rich tint of the new leaves. (April)

pearls, seemed very close to S *koehneana*, but Dr Hugh McAllister, of the Liverpool University Botanic Garden at Ness in Cheshire, is of the opinion that both represent new species.[37] His opinion is based on dried specimens, plus seed and seedling characteristics. Young trees of both are in cultivation and should prove useful additions to those already well established here.

Another sorbus widespread in these valleys is *Sorbus pallescens*, a member of the whitebeam group. One tree of 9m (30ft) that we found above the road in the Pi river valley, was thick stemmed with a large spreading crown clothed with broad, toothed, silver-backed leaves. The fruits were like small crab apples, rounded, pale green with a bold red cheek and covered with a thin, pale bloom. They were carried in heavy bunches from the short twigs all along the branches. Seed from this tree has produced strong trees with leaves somewhat narrower than those of the adult tree. Young trees are of upright habit becoming broader and more spreading in maturity.

Growing with the whitebeam above the Pi river was a magnificent specimen of *Acer cappadocicum* variety *sinicum*, a

tree of 9m (30ft) with five to seven lobed leaves and crowded bunches of red fruits. As we saw it that day, seemingly hovering above the rushing waters of the river below, it was quite one of the loveliest maples I have encountered. Its leaves are smaller and, by comparison, less coarse than those of the type, while from a distance the red-tinted fruits gave the impression of flowers. Young trees in cultivation are growing strongly and produce coppery-red young leaves.[38] As if one maple was not enough, there grew on the hillside above the road a 6m

Tibetan girls near the village of Liuba in the Pa La river valley. Whenever we passed through the villages or fields we were invariably greeted with broad smiles or maidenly giggles. (September)

37. The first of these and the most common in the Minya Konka area has become well established in British cultivation, where it has made a multi-stemmed small tree or large shrub to 3.5m and has relatively large white fruits in pendulous bunches. It has been named S *gonggashanica* after the mountain range in which it is found. The second species, named S *parva*, is a much smaller, stiffer shrub with glossy leaflets and white fruits.

38. A tree in the author's garden had achieved close on 12m (40ft.) in 2006.

Prunus serrula – the bark of a tree growing by the Pa La river showing its characteristic gloss. We were surprised to see this ornamental cherry being cut for firewood, but it is, in fact, highly flammable and burns fiercely when dry. (September)

(20ft) tree of *A davidii* with gracefully arching branches packed with red-winged fruits. Both maples occurred elsewhere in neighbouring valleys.

Due to their height – 2m (6ft) plus – two of our Americans, Paul Meyer and Tim Brotzman, were the centre of attention wherever they went. Tim is a broad-shouldered man with a big bushy beard and moustache; understandably, he was a sensation with the Tibetans who looked at him with something akin to awe. A blue handkerchief with white spots tied round his head gave him the air of a swashbuckling pirate. Whenever we set off along the road with Tim and Paul in our midst we attracted people like bees to honey. Young women working in the fields of barley would drop everything and come rushing towards the road, stopping short to peer at us through gaps in the fence, giggling whenever we looked at them and running away as fast as their legs would carry them when Paul or Tim made as if to approach them.

The river, with its accompanying dirt road, was the thread that bound this and neighbouring valleys and villages together. We could hear it chattering as we lay in our tents at night, and early each morning we washed in its ice-cold shallows. On its banks we discovered a rich selection of woody plants, among which the Tibetan cherry *Prunus serrula*[39] was the most eye catching. The sight of it brought back to me the times I have seen this tree in cultivation, never dreaming that one day I should see it in the wild! It was common here along the river bank, bushy specimens with the characteristic polished, peeling mahogany-red bark. Nowhere, of course, did we see the

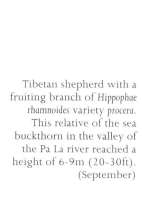

Old Tibetan woman of Liuba winding in a ball of wool. (September)

Tibetan shepherd with a fruiting branch of *Hippophae rhamnoides* variety *procera*. This relative of the sea buckthorn in the valley of the Pa La river reached a height of 6-9m (20-30ft). (September)

stout-stemmed specimens so familiar in gardens. This is because the cherry is valued here only for its use as fence stakes and for firewood, for it is highly flammable and burns fiercely. Most of the trees we saw were in the 4.5m (15ft) range, but in less accessible places elsewhere in these mountains trees of 7.5m (25ft) are not uncommon.

A variety of the sea buckthorn *Hippophae rhamnoides* known as *procera* also grew by the river and by streams in several of the side valleys. It was strong growing, making a tree of 6-9m (20-30ft), with a dense, spreading head of spiny branches. These were densely clothed in narrow, silver-backed, willow-like leaves and crowded with orange-yellow berries, juicy and extremely acid to the taste. One day we found a tree recently felled by a herdsman to provide a meal for his sheep who pulled and chewed on the shoots, their tails wagging furiously. The spiny branches are also used by the villagers as a defensive top to their walls and later, at Liuba, we saw great quantities of old branches bleached by the sun topping the walls of animal compounds and cultivated plots.

By the river we also found a wild crab, *Malus toringoides*, a small, erect-branched tree with deeply five-lobed leaves and clusters of ovoid yellowish-green fruits with a reddish cheek. This is a crab of reasonable merit rarely seen in cultivation, in Britain certainly, though there are occasional impostors that pass for it. It is easily distinguished by its deeply-lobed leaves, the lobes on some leaves going almost to the midrib. Only the closely-related and far more ornamental *M transitoria* has leaves more deeply and more narrowly lobed. This latter species first introduced to cultivation by William Purdom from Gansu in 1911 is easily recognised by its glossy foliage and pea-sized, golden yellow fruits. Strangely, for a river valley, there was a dearth of willows and poplars. Willows were present, but not in the quantity and variety one would have expected and none of those seen were of any note.

Of poplars we saw just a handful, all belonging to the one species, a bold foliaged tree of 18-21m (60-70ft) with a close grey bark and large heart-shaped grey-green leaves up to 20cm (8in) long on green stalks. We decided it was *Populus wilsonii*, a rare tree both in the wild and in cultivation where it is hardy enough and ornamental but

Populus wilsonii, a rare poplar noted for its large grey-green to sea-green leaves on green stalks. Here photographed in the Hillier Arboretum. (June)

difficult to propagate.[40]

Being relatively late in the season, most of the early flowering streamside perennials were in seed, and it was only when some of these germinated and flowered in cultivation that we could confirm their identity. *Trollius pumilus* was one such. Its remains we found in moist grassy places by the Pa La river and in similar places by streams in some of the side valleys. Plants grown from seed have produced dense tuffets of deeply-cut leaves and 15-20cm (6-8in) slender stems topped by yellow flowers with spreading petals. In the Alpine Department at Kew this collection is regarded as 'outstanding, very dwarf, easy and seeding readily'.

In similar sites grew several primulas one of which, *Primula sikkimensis*, still sported the occasional late umbel of nodding yellow flowers on 30-60cm (1-2ft) stems. It was a robust plant with bold clumps of long, toothed leaves. After flowering the flower stalks (pedicels) straighten out and become erect as the seed capsules develop. This is a common species in the mountains of Asia with a distribution from west China westwards through southeast Tibet, north-west Burma, Bhutan, Sikkim and Nepal. I first saw it in the Jaljale Himal of east Nepal in 1971 and it is a well-known and easy plant in cultivation.

Another species almost as common as the above around

39. Although Wilson introduced this tree in 1908 from the Kangding region, it was discovered much earlier by Delavay in north-west Yunnan, and was introduced from the same region by Forrest in 1913. As an ornamental tree it is grown principally for one reason – neither in flower nor leaf does this cherry impress, its sole claim to fame resting on its bark with which no other cherry can compare. In some parts of Britain the bark can be marred by algal growth, which can, however, be removed with a scrubbing brush. That famous gardener and plantsman A E Bowles, it is said, used to encourage visitors to his garden to pat and stroke the stem of his Tibetan cherry to maintain a gloss and, furthermore, periodically he would take a scrubbing brush and a bucket of warm water to his tree and give it a good clean up. The largest specimen in British cultivation is a tree of 17m (56ft) at Endsleigh in Devon (2003).

40. I remember a tall specimen of this tree growing in the former Hillier nursery at Chandlers Ford in Hampshire in the 1960s. Although by no means a bestseller, demand always exceeded supply. The current British and Irish champion is a tree at the Batsford Arboretum, Gloucestershire that had attained 15m (50ft.) in 2003 and there are younger trees elsewhere.

Arisaema ciliatum variety *liubaense*, a specimen with unripened fruit growing among rocks close by the Pa La river near Liuba. The fruits later turn a bright, shining red. This recently named variety is based on plants found at Liuba during our expedition to Minya Konka. (September)

Arisaema fargesii, a species found close to our camp near Liuba. Here photographed in the author's garden. (July)

Liuba had much smaller leaves and seeding stems. When it flowered in cultivation the whorls of small neat orange-red flowers identified it immediately as P *cockburniana*, a species first discovered in the Kangding area or nearby by A E Pratt. In cultivation, and possibly in the wild too, it tends to be short lived and should be raised from seed each year. In some moist pastures it occurred in vast numbers, often in the company of *Trollius pumilus*, which must make for a striking combination when the two are in flower.

One other primula we found in seed has since proved to be P *watsonii*,[41] a relative of P *vialii*. Several plants grew on a damp shady bank across the river from camp. From small rosettes of lightly downy and toothed-green leaves rises a slender stem 10-15cm (4-6in) tall bearing a short spike of small, deep blue, deflexed flowers. They are not particularly striking, but are pleasantly clove scented.

Another plant that appeared to relish the damp grassy areas close to the water was a royal blue trumpet gentian not unlike *Gentiana sino-ornata*. It had the same large funnel-shaped flowers produced singly at the ends of loose trailing shoots radiating from the rootstock. The leaves

were longer and narrower – 2-3mm (up to ⅛ in) broad – than in the previously seen G *veitchiorum* and, of course, the flowers were larger, tapering evenly to the base. It was frequent around Liuba and in one place it flourished in a boggy area close by the river, its long leafy growths threading their way through spongy moss. Although originally discovered by George Forrest in north-west Yunnan, G *sino-ornata*, according to the Chinese, also occurs in west Sichuan and south-east Tibet.

Gentians were everywhere, and between Kangding and Liuba we must have seen up to ten species, only a few of which we have been able to name. When one examines the lists of plants discovered in the Kangding area and beyond by Potanin and others, one finds the names of numerous gentians, few of which, to my knowledge, are in present day cultivation. It may be that some of these names have been made synonyms of others, but, from a horticultural point of view, I wouldn't mind betting that the plants they represented are different enough to be worth growing. I have seen autumn-flowering gentians before, in east Nepal where G *ornata* and G *depressa* stud the

Triosteum himalayanum, a curious herbaceous relative of the honeysuckle, produces attractive perfoliate upper leaves and brightly coloured berries. It was common in the Liuba area. (September)

Incarvillea lutea, a robust perennial with outstanding yellow trumpet-shaped flowers. Here photographed on a roadside verge in Muli, S.W. Sichuan. (June)

last of the season's turf before the onset of winter, but even that experience pales in comparison to the gentians of the Minya Konka country.

Gentians and primulas, lovely as they are, were not the only perennials to attract our attention that week. The woods, banks and hillsides bore evidence of a rich variety, most of which, however, were long past flowering. In a thicket close to the river one day we found the giant lily Cardiocrinum giganteum variety yunnanense, a mixture of young, non-flowering rosettes and current year plants, their tall stems full of ripe seed capsules. Another member of the same family, Notholirion bulbuliferum, occurred in the same thicket, and, again, the tall seeding stems spoke of flowers long blown.

An Arisaema I supposed to be A consanguineum was the most frequent of several Arisaema species seen. That species is one of the tallest and strongest of the genus, in the wild certainly, and I have seen its green and brown mottled stems 1m (3ft) tall. The green-hooded flower with brownish stripes and a long, brown, tail-like appendage is modest compared with those of some other species, but the fruits that follow are spectacular. They are green at first, becoming red at maturity, and are borne in a large, dense, conical head whose weight eventually causes its supporting stem to bow like a swan's neck, finally, hanging limply. It was not uncommon in the Pa La river valley.[42] Another species, found by Carla Teune, had larger, bolder leaves with just three broad leaflets. Seed from this plant collected by Teune was germinated by several enthusiasts in the West, and has been identified as A fargesii.[43] Both the above plants preferred open sunny sites among boulders and scrub as well as half shade on woodland margins.

Similar sites were chosen by that unusual herbaceous relative of the honeysuckle Triosteum himalayanum (hirsutum). It is a softly bristly plant in all its parts, a low clump of erect

stems to 45cm (18in) high, though usually less, and broad-paired leaves, which are narrowed and joined at the base. The uppermost pair are larger and perfoliate, from the centre of which a cluster of small pinkish or pale yellowish flowers emerge. These are of little or no ornamental merit, but they are replaced by a knob of juicy red berries similar to those of the common honeysuckle and the plant is then worth its place in the woodland garden.

On a bank high on the slope across the river we found an Incarvillea species in fruit. It had a basal rosette of pinnate leaves with unequal sized leaflets and a tall stem fully 1m (3ft) high. It almost certainly belonged to I lutea, a magnificent yellow-flowered species that has proven slow if not difficult to flower in cultivation.

Seed of Delphinium tatsienense was collected on a hillside in the Pa La river valley. Its finely-cut basal leaves and slender sprays of rich deep blue flowers with a creamy centre make this a little charmer for the garden, despite its relatively short life. Like Primula cockburniana, it should be grown regularly from seed.

On the same hillside grew a bold perennial salvia with large, heart-shaped, basal leaves and purple flowers in

41. Reginald Farrer mentioned this species in a brief but scathing description in his book The English Rock Garden: 'P watsonii is the most worthless species of the Grape Hyacinth group. It makes rosettes of shaggy oblong foliage, and sends up rather tall bare fat stems that end in a spike of small wizen flowers ridiculously insignificant at the top of such a powdered maypole'. Plants from the above seed have been flowered by the Royal Botanic Gardens at Kew and Edinburgh, as well as by Dr Ron Mackenzie at Shilton in Oxfordshire. It was identified by Dr. John Richards.

42. This plant has since flowered in cultivation from a Carla Teune collection and has been named as a new variety liubaense of A ciliatum. Both the species and its variety differ from A consanguineum in their long, running underground stems.

43. The first flowering that I heard about occurred in the United States in the garden of Judy Glattstein of Connecticut, in 1985. Her plant produced a hooded flower exhibiting a striking combination of white, green and blackish-purple stripes. The spathe curved forward and downward at the tip ending in a tail-like point, while the spadix was poker like, greenish and contained within the spathe.

whorls up the stems. The entire plant was covered in sticky hairs like the European *Salvia glutinosa*. It has since been identified as *Salvia przewalskii*, and plants in cultivation from seed we collected are robust and floriferous with stems up to 1m (3ft).

On the day we returned to the Pi river valley to examine more closely the maples growing by the road, we were delighted to discover a lovely, tall thalictrum with bold, open heads of lilac flowers with creamy-white anthers. Its stems reached 1.5m (5ft) above dainty divided foliage and we recognised the plant as being *Thalictrum delavayi*.[44] It was not common here, just a few clumps growing among scrub above the road, but it really made our day.

Once included in the same family (*Ranunculaceae*) as the thalictrum, but now given independent status (*Paeoniaceae*), are the peonies of which several are native to western China. In several places in the Pa La river and Pi river valleys we found an herbaceous peony which we suspected to be *Paeonia veitchii* – plants grown from seed have since flowered in my garden and are undoubtedly this species. Our plant was clump forming, up to 30cm (12in) or slightly more, with quite handsome shining green, deeply

divided leaves and a single nodding fruiting head. It was fairly common on shady banks on the edge of the forest and I was interested to read later that P *veitchii* had been found in the Minya Konka area by Joseph Rock in July 1929. His field note records it as growing on grassy slopes among bushes and as having pink to purplish flowers. It was first introduced to cultivation by Wilson in 1907 and is very hardy and reliable in western cultivation, though not in the same flower league as most other species.

Rock also found *Geranium pylzowianum* growing in meadows in this area, and we also found this species growing on a grassy bank by a track. Seeds from these plants have germinated and plants are now in cultivation, although it was already being grown from an earlier Farrer introduction from Gansu (Kansu). It is a slender-stemmed perennial up to 15cm (6in) tall, sometimes taller, spreading by means of thread-like stolons to which are attached small tubers. The leaves are kidney shaped and deeply lobed, while the wide, trumpet-shaped flowers are 2.5cm (1in) across, deep rose-pink with darker veins and a whitish centre. It is a choice little plant, best in a well-drained sunny site on the rock garden. Plants from our seed at Kew increase very readily and it is regarded there as a 'charming plant'.

'Charming' is a term used by Brian Halliwell (Assistant Curator in charge of the Alpine and Herbaceous Department at Kew) for another plant collected as seed in the Pa La river valley that day. It was growing there among moss-covered rocks on the edge of a wood and I mistook it for a columbine (*Aquilegia* species). Only when plants flowered in cultivation did I realise that it was a close relative – *Semiaquilegia ecalcarata* (*simulatrix*). I have a plant in my own garden, which for three years has grown quite happily in a sandy loam of no special merit. It produces prettily-divided leaves of typical columbine shape but smaller and in keeping with the size of the plant. It flowers in May and June, the dainty nodding flowers atop slender, downy, purple-flushed stems 25-38cm (10-15in) high. Each flower consists of a ring of five sepals, which spread widely to form a five-pointed star 2.5cm (1in) across. Below this is a bell-shaped skirt of five obovate petals rounded at the tips. Both sepals and petals are a lovely dusky mauve-purple, darker on the backs of the sepals and on the inside of the petals. S *ecalcarata*, which is widely distributed in the Far East, was once included

44. This species is well established in cultivation, occasionally under its synonym T *dipterocarpum*. There is a double form, 'Hewitt's Double', raised by the now defunct nursery firm Hewitt of Solihull, north of Birmingham, where E H Wilson once worked in his youth. Whether this form was raised from seed of the type given to his old firm by Wilson is not known. Both single and double forms are worth a place in the garden, but I much prefer the flowers of the former for the contrast between petals and anthers, those of the double being of rosette form without anthers.

Salvia przewalskii growing in a dry stream bed above our camp in the Pa La river valley. A large-leaved, stickily hairy perennial, it was found in several locations in the Liuba area. (September)

Iris ruthenica var. *nana* growing in a pasture in the Pa La river valley. I had previously seen this iris in the hills above the Great Wall north of Beijing. (September)

within *Aquilegia* as *A ecalcarata* and still is by Chinese botanists. It differs, however, in the petals having a small swelling at their base (gibbous) rather than the conspicuous spur so typical of the columbines. Reginald Farrer in *The English Rock Garden* refers to this plant as having the 'subtle charm of Japan'. The plant he described, however, had flowers of a 'burnt-sienna brown', quite unlike the plant from the Pa La river valley. Not too far away we found a diminutive blue-flowered iris, *Iris ruthenica* variety *nana*, which I had previously seen growing in the hills above the Great Wall north of Beijing.

Our Chinese guides were very anxious for our safety and, although we found the restrictions they placed on our movements at times irksome and frustrating, we appreciated their concern given that we were a group of

The author seed sorting in the schoolroom at Liuba. We were given permission to stay here after heavy rain rendered our leaky tents unsuitable.

mixed ages and physical abilities. Late one afternoon two Tibetans marched into camp carrying a dead Himalayan Black bear strung from a pole. The bear had been shot in the forest at the head of the valley above camp and our guides seized on this incident to justify their concern. We should all have liked to see a living bear, and the sight of this handsome creature lying dead and trussed up on the ground really depressed us. Wild birds and animals were scarce here we concluded, either that or they kept their heads down and stayed out of sight. We did, however, one day see a snake among rocks on the hillside that the Chinese told us was a dangerous kind of viper.

The weather, after a bright start, had turned wet and for three days running we had rain. This did not matter so much during the day when we were active, but at night it was a different story. For one thing, our tents leaked and it became difficult if not impossible to keep anything dry. Another factor that did not help matters was the lack of a hot breakfast to start the day. We had a hot dish for the evening meal but for breakfast, as for lunch, it was biscuits, apples, hard-boiled eggs and salted peanuts with some chocolate. It was nutritious, of course, but we would have given almost anything to have started the day at least with a bowl of hot porridge – even the rice-based variety. Nor were things made any easier by the fact that we were beginning and ending the day in wet clothes and boots, with the inevitable consequences. Several of our group contracted colds, troublesome enough in some cases to confine those afflicted to their tents. The Chinese guides for some reason would not light a fire and there was nowhere we could dry our clothes, let alone our bones. In the evenings, therefore, all attention focused on a large fire made by a group of Tibetans above

Euonymus porphyreus, a most ornamental Chinese spindle with winged capsules on thread-like stalks. It was quite common in hillside thickets in the Pa La river valley. (September)

Lonicera deflexicalyx branches well-studded with brilliant orange, shining berries. Although hardy, it is rare in western cultivation, though established in many collections from the above seed. (September)

our camp who had encamped there with their ponies so as to be ready should we require them. They were a jovial lot and some of our party spent the odd evening seated with them around their warm crackling fire swapping food and songs. It is at such times that one wishes one could remember all those school and communal songs that were such fun as a child. As it was, we rounded up enough between us to keep our hosts laughing until drowsiness intervened and sent us to our sleeping bags.

Tibetan youths with well-fruited branches of a shrubby honeysuckle, *Lonicera deflexicalyx*, a common roadside species in west China. It bears yellow two-lipped flowers in pairs in June. (September)

At the end of our third day of rain, with no change in sight, we asked to be allowed to sleep somewhere in Liuba — a shed, a stable, anywhere out of the rain. In the event we were billeted in the village school. It was to be our base for only two more nights, but it was bliss and allowed us to dry out. It was also a move warmly welcomed by the village children as it gave them an unexpected holiday. The children, by the way, were given their lessons in Chinese by a most likeable and good-humoured young man who resided in the school house.

Our travels over the last few days had taken us in several directions and we had seen many plants. What we had achieved, however, was merely a drop in the ocean, so vast was the landscape. The valleys we had explored were but a handful in a huge complex, each valley doubtless offering its own specialities. The shrub flora here was outstanding and many of the most popular genera in western gardens were represented by at least one species. *Berberis dictyophylla*, for instance, was plentiful by the road, its stems, leaves and berries coated in a white bloom, giving them almost a ghostly appearance in the gloom. *Cotoneaster* was present in the form of *Cotoneaster acutifolius* or similar with shining black fruits, while a larger, bold-leaved, black-fruited shrub reminded me of the Himalayan *C affinis*. A third black-fruited species proved to be *Cotoneaster kongboensis* Klotz. The red-fruited *C adpressus*, meanwhile, was also common as a ground cover.

In the thickets a fine spindle was prominent with its four-winged crimson capsules strung along the spreading branches. It was a strong growing shrub of 3m (9ft) or more and proved to be *Euonymus porphyreus*. It is in the same group as *E macropterus* and *E planipes*, with similar fruits. Seedlings of *E porphyreus* are now established, perhaps for the first time in cultivation, although this species was previously collected by Wilson, Forrest and others. Its flowers are described as purple-maroon by Forrest and as greenish by Rock who found it in the Minya Konka area

The author ready for another day's exploration in the valley of the Pa La river south-west of Kangding in west Sichuan. The scrub on the hillside behind is principally evergreen oak (*Quercus longispica*) and juniper (*Juniperus tibetica*) while the trees by the river in the background are Balfour's spruce (*Picea balfouriana*). (September)

Daphne retusa. In British gardens a popular dwarf evergreen shrub of compact nature. Here photographed in the Pa La river valley. (September)

in 1929; it is also found in Hubei province. The name *porphyreus* is from the Latin and means 'purple in colour', presumably referring to the flowers.

The flowers of the spindle are of little ornamental consequence; this cannot be said of *Syringa tomentella*,[45] a lilac that we also found growing among thickets. It was a shrub of about 3m (9ft) with relatively small leaves, downy beneath, and dense terminal heads of purplish-flushed white, sweetly-scented flowers. The flowers we saw, however, must have been a second late crop, for this species normally flowers in June.

The Tibetans were intrigued by our interest in their flora. Although they love colourful flowers, sometimes wearing them in their hair or hats, their main interest in plants naturally concerns their economic use, in particular their medicinal or food value. Occasionally they brought us samples to look at, offering suggestions on how we should use them. On one such occasion two youths approached us carrying branches of a shrubby honeysuckle with pairs of long, narrow, hairy leaves and sporting clusters of brilliant, almost translucent orange berries. We asked them where they had found such a prize and they led us along a stream below their village to where a large bush, some 3m (9ft) high and as much across, glistened in the sun. It was *Lonicera deflexicalyx*, a deciduous shrub rarely seen in cultivation outside specialist collections. Its yellow, two-lipped flowers are borne in axillary pairs all along the arching branches in May and June. Bean thought very highly of this shrub, describing it as 'notably elegant, free-growing, very hardy and floriferous'. Plants grown from seed collected near

Liuba are growing strongly in cultivation but have yet to live up to their fruiting potential in the wild.

Throughout our journey to Liuba we had seen lots of deutzias and philadelphus, mostly in thickets on hillsides. They occurred in the Pa La river valley as well, and from one of these, a wide-spreading shrub of 2.5m (8ft), seed was collected. From some of this seed, plants were produced at Nymans Garden in Sussex and flowered for the first time in June 1985. The blooms were 2.5cm (1in) across, white and richly scented, the green calyx having a dusky tinge near the tips of the sepals. It proved to be *Philadelphus purpurascens*, an easy and hardy shrub related to *P delavayi* and worth growing for its powerful fragrance. The best forms of this species have dark purple calyces that provide a striking contrast with the expanded flowers.

One of my favourite groups of shrubs, however, are the daphnes. There are a number of species recorded from Sichuan, but the only one we found in the Liuba area was the dwarf evergreen *Daphne retusa*, which I had previously seen in west Yunnan. It also occurs westwards, as far as east Nepal where the late Len Beer found it in 1974. In the Pa La river valley it was frequent on the edge of forest and in scrub, often on steep banks in ravines. Some plants carried red fruits. This species was first discovered by A.E. Pratt in the Kangding area and was first introduced from the same area by Wilson in 1901 during his first expedition for the firm of Veitch.

45. *Syringa tomentella* is not all that common in cultivation even though it was first introduced by Wilson from Kangding as long ago as 1904. It had been previously collected from the same area as dried specimens by both A E Pratt and Prince Henry d'Orléans.

Cornus macrophylla, here flowering in the Hillier Arboretum, was frequent in the more sheltered valleys south-west of Kangding. It is a most ornamental small tree or large shrub, too little seen in western cultivation. (July)

Satyrium ciliatum, a distinct and late flowering terrestrial orchid, here growing in the Pa river valley. (September)

One day we revisited the valley of the Pi river through which we had driven on the day of our arrival. We were particularly keen to see the firs and maples, which I have already described, but there were also other plants, especially shrubs, to attract our attention. *Cornus macrophylla*,[46] for instance, was plentiful, a big wide-spreading shrub or small tree of 4.5m (15ft) and as much or more across. The branches were freely covered with flattened heads of dark blue-black fruits. This is not unlike another Chinese species, *C controversa*, in general habit, although the latter has a more distinctly tiered habit of branching. *C macrophylla* differs most markedly in its opposite leaves, whereas those of *C controversa* are alternate, as is the case with the eastern American *C alternifolia*. With the dogwood grew *Lindera glauca*, a free-growing shrub to 5m (16ft) with leaves glaucous beneath and small black fruits. In China this and several other species are employed in the manufacture of incense sticks. It also occurs in Taiwan, Korea and Japan.

On the steep hillside above the river, growing among pines, was a rhododendron of free growth with comparatively small, pointed leaves, 3-5cm (1¼-2in) long, brown and densely scaly beneath. It was common here, a shrub of some 3-4m (9-13ft), often in groups and loaded with seed.[47]

Sharing the slopes with the rhododendron I was pleased to find a rather attractive shrubby potentilla of 1m (3ft) with silky, silvery leaves. It was not in flower but had a remarkable resemblance to *Potentilla* 'Vilmoriniana', a popular shrub in cultivation. We found several plants all alike, and I came to the conclusion that it could only be *P arbuscula* variety *albicans*, a plant of which was originally grown in western cultivation from seed collected by Wilson in the Kangding area. Similar plants had apparently previously been collected from the same area by both Soulié and Pratt. In places, the silver of the potentilla contrasted beautifully with the blue flowers of a small perennial, *Dracocephalum tanguticum*. This was a charming plant forming clumps up to 30cm (12in) or more of slender stems with finely cut aromatic leaves and two-lipped flowers in erect spikes. We found it again later on dry, stony, sunny slopes, which it appeared to relish.

Growing on the same slopes and, likewise, flourishing was a most attractive terrestrial orchid, *Satyrium ciliatum*. It is a far flung relative of a genus mainly based in South Africa and is closely related to *S nepalensis*, which I had previously seen in east Nepal in 1971. It was a most distinctive plant with dense spikes of rich pink flowers as much as 30cm (12in) tall. The flower has a bold,

Rosa soulieana, flowering its heart out in the University of Cambridge Botanic Garden in 1986, grown from seed collected in the Pi river valley south-west of Kangding. The sea-green leaves are almost completely hidden by the flowers, which are creamy-yellow in bud. Once established, this vigorous scandent shrub quickly covers its support with a blanket of growth. (July)

drooping, taper-pointed lip that presses close to the spike, giving it a narrow poker like appearance. We also found an orchid of a very different appearance in *Spiranthes sinensis*, an Asian relative of the European Autumn ladies' tresses – *S spiralis*. Indeed, with its erect wiry stems and spiralling flower spikes it very much resembles this species, differing most obviously in its pink rather than white flowers. This charming little orchid, in its variety *amoena*, enjoys a truly remarkable distribution in the wild from Afghanistan, along the Himalaya to China and Japan, thence southwards to Malaysia (I once found it in the Cameron Highlands of Malaya) and Australia.

The two most commonly seen groups of woody-stemmed plants on our journey to Liuba had been roses and

clematis. The roses occurred everywhere in great variety, both shrubby and climbing. The most abundant species in the Pa La river valley was *Rosa sericea* subspecies *omeiensis*, the swollen footstalks of the yellow, or red and yellow, hips giving them a slender pear-shaped appearance. *R sericea* forma *pteracantha* with its large, flattened, bloodied shark's fin thorns was also present in some numbers. There were many roses of a climbing or rambling nature among which *R rubus* has already been mentioned. In the valley of the Pi river grew *Rosa soulieana* scrambling over low scrub on a sunny hillside. Its pale, thorny stems, 3-4m (9-13ft) long, were clothed with typical sea-green or greyish-green leaves, while the small egg-shaped hips were an attractive orange-red.[48] Most other climbing roses we saw have yet to be named, though some that we

46. As a flowering subject Bean gives short shrift to *C macrophylla*, which I think is unfair. It does not compare with the so called 'flowering dogwoods' such as *C kousa* and *C nuttallii*, but among those dogwoods with typically dense-headed flowers (corymbs) it is one of the best. I shall never forget it flowering in the Hillier Arboretum during the hot summer of 1976. Two bushy trees there of some 6m (19ft) plastered their leafy branches with broad heads of creamy-white flowers that proved a magnet for insects. At that time I considered this species one of the loveliest trees in the arboretum. Even when out of flower its habit and foliage is not to be sneered at. The small but attractive blue, berry-like fruits are a bonus. Hardy and easy on most soils it is a curiously underrated species and in North America is virtually unknown. According to Michael Dirr it has shown a tolerance of dry soils and has a potential for urban planting. It has a tendency to produce several main stems from low down, developing a broad rounded habit. The largest example in British cultivation is a tree of 12m (40ft.) at Greyswood Hill in Surrey (1998).

47. Young plants in cultivation from seed collected in this location have produced small clusters of mauve-blue flowers. It certainly belongs to subsection Triflora and both Peter Cox and the late Alan Hardy identified it as *Rhododendron tatsienense*, a close relative of *R davidsonianum*. *R tatsienense* was first discovered in the Kangding (Tachienlu) area by the French missionary Soulié.

48. Seed collected at the time has produced vigorous plants some of which have already flowered. These are creamy-white and 4cm (1½ in) across in July. In July 1986, I saw two impressive large plants from the above collection growing in a sunny border in the University Botanic Garden, Cambridge. Each was a dense mound 2m (6ft) high and wide and literally plastered with flower and abuzz with bees. As the name suggests this rose is named after the Abbé Soulié who sent back to France dried specimens and seed collected in the Kangding area in 1895.

Orostachys species, a rosette-forming monocarple succulent related to and sometimes included under *Sedum*. Occasional on rocks in the Pa La river valley above Liuba. (September)

Clematis rehderiana, a strong-growing, blanketing species with cowslip-scented flowers that we found in the scrubby hills above Kangding. (September)

collected as seed should flower during the coming years.[49]

In the opinion of Raymond Evison, our clematis expert, we saw on our journey to and from Liuba some twenty-five different species and forms of this genus. In the Liuba area, for instance, grew a puzzling array belonging to *Clematis akebioides*. These were variable, to say the least, with finely cut green, grey or blue-grey leaves and long-stalked, nodding lantern-flowers of pale to dark yellow, sometimes with brownish or reddish suffusion. They clambered over lesser fry, especially in thickets, often swamping their support.

In the valley above camp we found *Clematis lasiandra*, a slender-stemmed climber with small, pendulous bell-shaped flowers 1.5cm (½ in) long of an unusual coppery-brown. These were borne in clusters of two or three from the leaf axils and were packed with silky, hairy styles. A white flowered form had also been seen on the hillside above the landslip at Shimian and again in the Kangding river gorge. Bean remarked that this was not one of the most promising species which, if compared with most other species, is true. It does, however, possess what catalogue writers call 'a quiet charm' and will undoubtedly appeal to clematis enthusiasts.

Growing in the same valley, its long stems scrambling

over surrounding vegetation, we found *C potaninii*. It was a distinct species, the leaves divided into five main segments, each of three downy, coarsely-toothed and lobed leaflets.[50]

In the Kangding river gorge too were found several other *Clematis* species, of which *C connata* and an as yet unnamed species were the most common. The former is a strong growing species with relatively coarse foliage and showers of bell-shaped soft yellow flowers in autumn. Seed collected at the time has produced plants with larger flowers than those of the form previously in cultivation. The leaf stalks, which in this species are characteristically flattened and joined at the base, are even more so in the Kangding plants, so broad in fact that they form a green, saucer-shaped structure through which the stem passes. These plants are, however, slightly tender.

Related to *C connata* is *C rehderiana*, which has similar, though normally larger, cowslip-scented flowers and similar leaves, except that the stalks are not flattened at the base. We found this on the hillside above Kangding in which area it was originally discovered by the French missionary Père Aubert in 1898. Aubert also introduced it as seed to France and thence to England. It was also collected in the same area by Wilson some years later. I could just picture Aubert standing chest high in the thicket gathering the silky seed tufts of this plant, having no doubt detected the sweetly-scented flowers from the road. There are still flowers when the first seeds are ripening, and its late blooming habit is most useful in gardens where this species is occasionally seen covering a fence or wall or growing into a tree. Plants

49. One of these, an extremely vigorous species, still grows in the author's garden. Its large heads of small, sweetly-fragrant white flowers and equally large heads of tiny red fruits identified it as R filipes.

50. Plants grown from seed collected at the time have flowered at Kew (May 1986) and elsewhere. According to Brian Halliwell, then Assistant Curator in charge of the Alpine and Herbaceous Department at Kew, the flowers are distinct in possessing six pure white tepals that make for a flower of rounded outline some 5cm (2ins) across or slightly more. They are borne either singly or in threes from the leaf axils.

51. C gracilifolia was introduced by Wilson from west Sichuan, by William Purdom from Gansu and by Forrest from Yunnan. The plant in present cultivation, according to Raymond Evison, was introduced by the Swedish collector Dr Harry Smith from west Sichuan in 1935. It is a beautiful and sometimes floriferous species less vigorous than C montana and flowering earlier.

Syncalathium souliei, a curious rosette-forming composite growing on screes in the valley of the Pa La river above Liuba. (September)

grown from seeds of our Kangding plant flowered for the first time at Burford House, Shropshire, in autumn 1984 and were a clear primrose-yellow colour. It is a fine form and according to Evison should prove hardy. At Kew, apparently, its flowers are eaten by earwigs!

Growing in the scrub above Kangding on the same hillside as *Rosa moyesii* we found *Clematis gracilifolia*,[51] which at first glance resembled *C montana*, but with more graceful leaves, consisting of three to seven coarsely toothed or lobed leaflets. Seed was collected and plants first flowered at Burford House in spring 1984. These were 4-5m (1½-2in) and white.

Liuba is a village of a single street and some twenty or twenty-five houses. These are solidly built from the local stone, dark and rough hewn around a wooden superstructure – larch or spruce probably. Most of the windows have a whitewashed U-shaped surround, while their wooden shutters and frames are occasionally decorated with colourful geometric patterns or floral designs in which a semi-double white tree peony is sometimes featured. The roofs of the houses are gently sloping, their wooden boards weighted down with rocks. Some houses had adjoining buildings with flat roofs on which to dry and store barley. These were often protected by an overhang where hay was kept for the livestock in winter.

The strong stone-walled structure of a house in the village of Liuba. The wooden boards of the roof are weighed down with rocks. (September)

Father and son peering from a window in Liuba. The stylised white flower decorations above the window probably represent tree peonies. (September)

Ponies in Liuba being made ready for our group. (September)

Women and children of Liuba sheltering from the rain in the yard of the Liuba 'guesthouse'. (September)

Tibetan women and children outside the village of Liuba with the author who has just demonstrated his one and only conjuring trick, the disappearing coin. (September)

One wet morning we were allowed to see the 'official' guest house, a large wooden structure in the centre of the village. The courtyard had a hard-packed earth floor, muddy now from the passage of carts and livestock. It was enclosed on three sides by a two-storeyed building. The fowls and livestock were housed at ground level with the carts, trailers, ploughs and other equipment. The upper

storey was reached by a flight of stairs that led on to a balcony with dwellings leading off. The large single rooms we peeped into were clean and tidy with a central hearth and the glimmer of copper pots and pans in the gloom. The village also had a store which, as far as we could see, had little for sale, as well as a square-towered Buddhist temple, which was closed and locked.

For our last full day at Liuba we decided to cross the river and climb the north-facing hillside in the hope of seeing Minya Konka. Our prayers for a fine day were answered, and it was with light hearts that we set off that morning across the ramshackle wooden bridge spanning the Pa La river west of the village. At first we followed a track that led us through the forest, mainly spruce, birch and rhododendron. Then we climbed steeply until the trees began to thin out. Here, in the shelter of *Rhododendron phaeochrysum* and with a scattering of birch we found *Cassiope selaginoides*, a dwarf creeping evergreen forming tufts and mounds of erect shoots 10-15cm (4-6in) high, densely clothed with tiny scale-like leaves, not unlike a little whipcord *Hebe* species. It was fairly common on banks, and later we found it among rhododendrons along the upper reaches of the forest. Its white, bell-shaped, nodding flowers are borne singly on thread-like stalks and are produced when the alpine rhododendrons are blooming. *C selaginoides* is a

Our party crossing the Pa La river below Liuba. (September)

Upper Pi river valley with Tibetan dwelling. Note the dense forests of *Picea balfouriana* and other conifers. (September)

Pa La river valley. Our camp is sited far side of river (lower left), whilst the village of Liuba is just off the picture right. (September)

choice little plant suitable for a cool pocket in the peat garden.

The forest gave way to open hillside clothed in a low dense cover of small-leaved alpine rhododendrons of the Lapponicum section. There appeared to be several distinct kinds, one of which was probably *Rhododendron intricatum* with its dense-mounded, intricately branched habit. Other plants had looser, erect branches up to 1m (3ft), even taller beneath the trees lower down. Their leaves were up to twice as long as those of *R intricatum*, similarly covered beneath with pale yellowish scales and with a grey, almost silvery, cast above. One specimen we found had a few unseasonal trusses of small, lavender-blue flowers. A dried specimen was later identified by Dr David Chamberlain at the Royal Botanic Garden, Edinburgh, as *R hippophaeoides*. This species is one of the most popular and satisfactory of its group in cultivation, flowering in April if not before. It is native to north-west Yunnan and south-west Sichuan and was collected by most of the plant hunters in these areas, in particular by Forrest, Rock and Kingdon-Ward. They often found this species inhabiting wet places, and we too found it several times in damp depressions, bogs even, but it was by no means confined to these places. *R intricatum* was first discovered by the French missionary the Abbé Soulié in 1895 somewhere to the west

of Kangding and first introduced some nine years later by Wilson. Its flowers are lilac, darker in bud.

These rhododendrons flower after the snow melts in late April and May. At that time the hills and alpine plateaux resemble a series of patchwork quilts in which purple, lilac, blue, yellow, pink and white predominate. The nearest we have to this effect in Britain are the heather moors of the north, which, although impressive, are limited to shades of purple. More colourful are the heathlands of southern and western Britain where the heather is joined by red and pink heaths (*Erica*) of several kinds plus the gold of the dwarf or the western gorse (*Ulex minor* and *U gallii* respectively). Even this cannot match the mountains above Kangding when winter loosens its grip.

The rhododendrons, although little more than knee high, were so dense and tangled that our progress was considerably slowed. We found a number of erect 15cm (6in) stems poking through the low cover, each terminating in a seed capsule. I guessed it to be a species of fritillary, but plants grown from this seed by Dr Martyn Rix, a noted authority on this genus, are, in his opinion, more likely to be a lily, *Lilium lophophorum*, a curious little species first discovered in west Sichuan by both A E Pratt and Prince Henri d'Orléans.

327

Minya Konka or Gongga shan rising majestically head and shoulders above its neighbours. When he first surveyed this mountain, the plant explorer Dr. Joseph Rock declared it to be higher than Mt. Everest, a grave miscalculation. (September)

Members of the group resting at an altitude of 4,200m (13,776ft) above the valley of the Pa La river. Liuba is in cloud shadow, while away on the horizon rises the Great Snow Mountain – Minya Konka, 7,590m (24,900ft). (September)

Liuba village, the first sprinkling of snow heralds the approach of winter. (September)

Liuba village, note the dense thicket of *Hippophae* along the wall top. (September)

Finally, at an altitude of 4,200m (13,776ft) we sat down in the midst of the rhododendrons to eat a lunch of apples, chocolate and nuts. We could not have chosen a better vantage point, for directly below us stretched the Pa La river valley where, in the green mouth of a side valley, we could see the coloured specks of our camp and the village of Liuba to the east. To the north-east stretched wave upon wave of mole-coloured hills and beyond them, rising head and shoulders above its neighbours, the majestic white pyramid of Minya Konka.

Early next morning we awoke to find the hillsides above Liuba dusted with the first snow of winter. The air was colder and autumn tints had appeared where, at the beginning of the week, all had been green. The camp was dismantled and after a quick breakfast we were on the road again heading for the valley of the Pi river and the Zheduo Pass.

Lunch was taken at the roadside in the alpine pastures. Some distance away there was a group of black yurts out of which several Tibetans emerged. On spying us they came running in our direction, jumping like deer the numerous streams in between. Soon they were among us, watching as we ate, joking and giggling. There were four or five women, one of them, possibly a girl in her late teens or early twenties, had a smooth, rounded face with flattened rosy cheeks and a disarming smile.

Not long after we climbed out of the bus to have a final look into Tibet from a point just below the summit of the Zheduo Pass. We all scattered, anxious to enjoy a last search for alpines in the wilderness of rock and grit around us. Suddenly Tim Brotzman was shouting, Paul Meyer too, and the rest of us ran towards them. Before I reached their position, I saw the object of their excitement, the most lovely

Young Tibetan woman on the alpine pastures on the Zheduo Pass above Kangding. (September)

Tibetan women on the Zheduo Pass above Kangding. (September

Stony alpine pastures at 3,800m (12,460ft.) on the Zheduo Pass, home of the yellow poppywort *Meconopsis integrifolia*. It is in this general area that Ernest Wilson first encountered this remarkable plant in 1908. (September)

The fort-like village of Liuba seen from a window. (September)

yellow poppywort – *Meconopsis integrifolia*. There were two plants in flower and a careful search revealed many others in seed. By rights there should have been no flowers so late in the year, but our eyes were not playing tricks. The entire plant, excepting the flower, was clothed in long golden hairs, soft to the touch. From out of the rosette rose an erect stem of 20cm (8in) bearing at its summit a large globular clear yellow blossom made up of several broad-based overlapping tissue-paper-thin petals. It was a breathtaking experience and we could not believe our good fortune.[52]

That night we stayed in a hostel in Kangding. Because of restrictions on the movements of foreigners we were not allowed out of the city, nor were we even allowed to photograph it, but our previous experiences helped make this disappointment more bearable.

The next morning we were heading down the gorge of the Kangding river reaching Luding in time for lunch. The plan was to push on that afternoon back the way we had come as far as Hanyuan, where the night would be spent. There was one big problem, however. News came in that a huge landslip further down the valley had taken away a section of road and that it would take weeks to clear. In order that our guides could have time to discuss the situation with the local authorities, we were given permission to look round the town for an hour or two. I headed straight for the Iron-chain Bridge to take photographs. This being done and finding myself on the south side of the Dadu river, I decided to explore the steep hillside above.

One of our party, a German named Wolfgang Kletzing,

Meconopsis integrifolia, the yellow poppywort, a late-flowering plant in the alpine pastures just below the summit of the Zheduo Pass. (September)

Indigofera szechuanensis, a flowering shoot of a plant growing at the Royal Botanical Gardens, Kew, from seed collected in the Pa La Ho. Photographed by Brian Schrire. (September)

had joined me and, together, we began the climb. Conditions were fairly dry and the vegetation was typical of such places in these mountains. There were roses in quantity, *Incarvillea arguta*, and indigoferas. *Abelia schumannii* was plentiful as also was *A engleriana*, like *A schumannii* a bushy shrub but taller, to 1.5m (5ft), with small shining, privet-shaped leaves and pairs of funnel-shaped, rose-coloured flowers with an orange flare in the throat. The flowers were smaller than those of *A schumannii*, 1.5-2cm (½-¾ in) as against 2.5-3cm (1-1¼ in). The most interesting plants on this hillside, however, were the lilies, not in flower, of course, but in seed. They were nowhere abundant, occurring as scattered individuals over a very wide area. There appeared to be two distinct species and our guess was confirmed some years later when seed we introduced into cultivation produced plants that have flowered.[53]

Our second lily proved to be *L sargentiae*, and we were delighted when it was later confirmed, for this was one of Wilson's finest introductions, its name honouring the wife of Professor Charles Sargent, his 'chief' and Director of the Arnold Arboretum in Massachusetts. An even greater cause for pleasure was the news that it was above here, in the valley of the Dadu (Tung) river around the village of Luding

52. Near here, on 18 July, 1903, E H Wilson first found the yellow poppywort. He later wrote of the event: 'I am not going to attempt to record the feelings which possessed me on my first beholding the object of my quest to those wild regions. Messrs Veitch dispatched me on this second and very costly journey to the Tibetan border for the sole purpose of discovering and introducing this the most gorgeous alpine plant extant'. Most of the plants seen by Wilson that day were already past flowering, but later he saw it again and this time 'Above 11,500ft [3,505m] altitude, the gorgeous *Meconopsis integrifolia*, with huge, globular, incurved, clear yellow flowers, emblazon miles of mountain-side. On stems from 2-2½ ft [60-75cm] tall, myriad flowers of this wonderful poppywort presented a magnificent spectacle'.

Seed from the Zheduo Pass was widely distributed in cultivation on our return and has given renewed pleasure each year since. Though this is not a true perennial (odd plants may survive to flower a second year), itt produces such an abundance of seed, and is so easy to grow, that there is no reason why it should not be maintained in the garden indefinitely. In cultivation it prefers a moist, but well-drained acid soil and is ideal in the peat garden. Cultivated plants are known to produce flowers sometimes 15cm (6in) across: real show stoppers. Wilson, by the way, was not the first to discover this species. That honour goes to Nicolai Przewalski, of Przewalski's Horse fame, a Russian who collected dried specimens in Gansu in 1873. It was also collected as seed by Forrest in north-west Yunnan

53. One of these, in the garden of Mr and Mrs Martyn Simmons, Quarry Wood, near Burghclere in Berkshire, produced a slender stem, between 60 and 90cm (2 and 3ft) tall, bearing long, narrow leaves and terminating in a single, nodding, bell-shaped flower about 7cm (2¾ in) across the spreading and recurving segments. It was ivory coloured, freely speckled red within and green tinted without. The bold anthers were a brilliant orange-yellow. In addition, the flower was slightly fragrant. It proved to be *Lilium bakerianum*, a species with a wide distribution, its northern limit, according to Wilson, just east of Kangding. Indeed, I suspect that Wilson may well have been referring to these slopes above Luding when he wrote 'East of Tachienlu [Kangding] between 4,000 and 6,000ft [1,219 and 1,828m] altitude, I found it in plenty on steep slopes among shrubs and grasses in loam overlain with leaf soil of good depth'. The only difference was the absence of a good depth of leaf soil.

Lilium bakerianum flowering at Quarry Wood in Berkshire from seed collected above Luding in 1981. (July)

Salix magnifica, remarkably like a magnolia in leaf, is not uncommon in west Sichuan. Here it is pictured with the author in the Wolong Valley, north-west of Chengdu, in 1986. (September)

(Luting-chiao), that Wilson first collected this lily. Wilson well describes its habitat in these valleys where the climate (compared with further east in the Emei Shan area) is drier, in some quite arid, and the winters long and cold. Here, Wilson believed, this lily is seen at its best, growing among rank grasses and scrubby woody growth on granite, slate and mud shales where it enjoys good drainage and blossoms in June and July. Flowers produced by our seedlings in cultivation are typically funnel-shaped and fragrant, pure white within, purple flushed without. Interestingly, Wilson found that the flowers of L *sargentiae* were commonly collected by the locals, boiled and dried in the sun, then minced, fried with salt and oil, and eaten in the same way as preserved cabbage.

These valleys of west Sichuan are something of an El Dorado as far as lilies are concerned, for several species are found here. Wilson considered L *sargentiae* a noble lily and worthy of a place in every garden. It usually opens its flowers about two weeks later than L *regale* and the two lilies Wilson considered worthy companions. The Regal lily many people regarded as Wilson's best introduction. He found it restricted to about fifty miles of the narrow semi-arid valley of the Min river in conditions much like those described for the valley of the Dadu river.[54]

On returning to the Iron-chain Bridge we found a wild clematis swamping scrub above the river. It reminded us of the European *Clematis vitalba* and was equally rampant. It proved to be C *grata*, presumably the variety *grandidentata*, which has white flowers 2.5cm (1in) across in axillary and terminal clusters in May and June.

It was late afternoon by the time we returned to Luding, entering the guest house to the news that we would be staying the night. There was still no decision on

how we were to return to Ya-an, so we made the best of the situation and had a party in Carla Teune's room. There was plenty of food, which several members of our party had bought in the local market, and I contributed a large bag of walnuts. Someone, I cannot remember who, provided several bottles of ginseng brandy, at least that is what it said on the label. Whether it tasted of ginseng I cannot say, but I can certainly testify to its potency.

The following morning at breakfast we were told that permission had been obtained for us to return to Ya-an via a road that climbs out of the Dadu river valley downriver from Luding and crosses a shoulder of the Erlang Shan, a mountain of 3,550m (11,646ft) altitude, overlooking and east of Luding. Because of the landslip this was the only road into Luding and therefore to Kangding from the east and was, as a result, full of traffic. Having reached the head of the pass at 3,000m (9,840ft) we made our way down a valley on the north-eastern flank. The difference between the two flanks was spectacular. The dry, scrubby vegetation of the Dadu river valley had now given way to a lush, dense forest rich in species. For several kilometres we crawled along behind a military convoy, frustrated by the variety of plants passing by and our inability to make contact. The slow pace at least allowed us to identify a few plants and some of us were thrilled to recognise *Cotoneaster horizontalis*, its characteristic fan-like branches covering rocks above the road.

Cercidiphyllum japonicum and *Hydrangea heteromalla* were also identifiable. There were several plants we had previously seen, among which *Rhododendron calophytum*, *Pterocarya macroptera* var. *insignis* and *Populus lasiocarpa* were particularly impressive. It was here, by the roadside, that we saw an *Aralia* species whose fruiting heads had a distinct central axis as described for *A chinensis*. We also saw a large-leaved magnolia of some 12m (40ft). Several trees grew in a grove and may have been *Magnolia sargentiana*. It is possible, if not probable, that Wilson would have travelled over the Erlang Shan on his way to or from Kangding and, if so, would most likely have seen these magnolias or rather their predecessors.

On the one occasion we were allowed to get out of the buses, when the convoy in front had come to a halt, we

Hypericum forrestii, a fine autumn- colouring shrub in the author's garden grown from seed collected on the Erlang Shan in W. Sichuan. (October)

immediately found two most interesting plants. One resembled a magnolia in leaf and was believed to be so when first found by Wilson. Having been brought up with this shrub in the Hillier Arboretum, however, I recognised it as that most remarkable willow *Salix magnifica*. Several large shrubby specimens of 3-4m (9-13ft) grew on the slope below the road, their bold grey-green leaves with a pale bloom above. It is generally hardy in cultivation, though the young growths in spring are liable to be damaged by a late frost; otherwise it is impressive in foliage and a guaranteed teaser in gardening circles.

The other plant that caught my attention was a maple that, at first glance, resembled a small leaved *Acer davidii*, which also occurred in these hills. It was a small tree of 6-7.5m (20-25ft) with pale, striated bark and gracefully arching, densely leafy branches. The leaves were rather thin in texture, ovate and rounded or shallowly heart-shaped at the base and ending in a remarkable tail-like point. The margins were sharply toothed and shallowly lobed (lobulate) in the lower half. Some of the leaves I measured were 14cm (5½ in) long, of which the tail-like point was as much as 4cm (1½ in). The most distinctive character, however, apart from the tail point, were the tufts of coffee-coloured hairs in the vein axils beneath. A dried fragment from this tree I compared with specimens in the Kew Herbarium on my return and matched them with *Acer laxiflorum*.[55] The last plant I examined that day was *Hypericum forrestii*, a robust form which in the author's

garden regularly colours a rich red in autumn.

The convoy moved off and we reluctantly boarded the buses. Judging by what we saw in a limited area and time the Erlang Shan would certainly repay a detailed search. For the rest of the day we crawled down the valley, dropping through the contours, squeezing past heavily laden timber lorries and sundry other obstacles. It was evening when we reached Ya-an and our accommodation. Although we had another day's drive to reach Chengdu our journey, as far as the adventure was concerned, was at an end. We felt a little sad not to have had the opportunity to explore the Erlang Shan, yet it would have been churlish to complain. To have trodden in the footsteps of Rock and Wilson and to have seen the peak and the poppy that brought them respectively embarrassment and pleasure is an experience we shall long remember.

Acer laxiflorum, showing the distinctive tail-like point to the leaf. It is related to *A forrestii* and *A davidii*, and is not uncommon in the mountains of west Sichuan. This specimen was photographed in the Wolong Valley, north-west of Chengdu, in 1986. (September)

54. In June 1993 I realised a dream when I saw the Regal Lily growing in its classic site in the Min valley.

55. This species was originally collected as dried specimens near Kangding by Pratt as well as on Emei Shan by Ernst Faber, and later by Wilson south east of Kangding in 1908. It is in cultivation at Trewithen in Cornwall from whence a young grafted tree was established in the Hillier Arboretum and is now growing strongly. Several more recent collections are now in cultivation.

Chapter Six

North of the Yangtze

*S*ince the events described in this chapter there have been major changes in the Yangtze Gorges brought about by the Three Gorges Dam project. Begun in 1992 and due for completion in 2009, the dam is claimed to be the largest construction project in China since the Great Wall itself. When filled to capacity, the resultant reservoir will be approximately 360 miles (580km) long and 574ft (175m) deep, allowing the passage of 10,000-ton freighters as far as Chongqing. One estimate suggests that approximately 243 sq miles (629km²) of land will be submerged and 1-2 million people displaced. The long-term effects of all this on the immediate environment and those displaced is unknown. Deidre Chetham gives an evocative and informative account of the history of this region up to the beginning of the dam project in her book Before the Deluge – The Vanishing World of the Yangtze's Three Gorges (see Bibliography).

This chapter provides a glimpse of how the Three Gorges appeared to me on my first visit in 1983.

One of my favourite ornamental trees is a Chinese mountain ash – *Sorbus hupehensis*. I first came to know it many years ago in a park in the north of England, its branches each autumn

bowed beneath the weight of its white, red-stalked fruits.[1] I was an apprentice then, green behind the ears and with no reference books of my own. I remember struggling with the pronunciation of the second word and wondering what on earth it meant. I was duly informed by my foreman that it meant 'Hupeh', a province in south-central China, and that the correct pronunciation was 'who pay'. The name stuck in my head and I soon came to identify the province, along with those of Yunnan and Sichuan, as being one of the richest sources of ornamental plants for western gardens.

Hubei, as it is now spelt, has long been a happy hunting ground for botanists and plant hunters, which is not surprising considering its position and its physical features. It lies between latitude 30° and 35°N, its boundaries shared by six other provinces including that of Sichuan to the west. It is crossed by two of China's most important rivers, the Han Shui (Han river) in the north and the Chang Jiang in the south. The last named is better known, in the West certainly, as the Yangtze, China's longest and most famous river. From

The sheer magic of the Yangtze Gorges almost defies description at times, especially when morning mist softens the often sharp outlines of the mountains rising steeply above the river. Entrance to the second or Wu gorge at Wushan. (May 1983)

its birth in the middle of the Tanggula Shan (Tanggula mountains) on the Qinghai-Tibet Plateau, it travels some 6,380km (3,964 miles) across China to the East China Sea. From west to east, its course takes it through Qinghai, Tibet, Yunnan, Sichuan, Chongqing (Municipality), Hubei, Hunan, Jiangxi, Anhui, Jiangsu and Shanghai.

At the time of our visit it was navigable for a good distance along its course, ocean-going vessels up to 10,000 tons could sail upstream for 1,000km (620 miles) as far as Wuhan, and steamers and small cruise ships even further to Yichang and Chongqing. Above Yichang the river flows through the 193km (120 miles) of the Yangtze Gorges, considered by many as one of the natural wonders of the world. Since time immemorial, the Yangtze has served as a highway between the eastern maritime provinces and the interior. It was once the classic route used by most western travellers to Yichang and Chongqing and thence overland to Chengdu and beyond. It was also used by those heading for Kunming in Yunnan.

To the north and south of the Yangtze Gorges are high mountains culminating in the 3,105m (10,187ft) Wuming Peak (Peak with No Name) and the slightly less high, but better known, Dashennongjia at 3,052m (10,013ft) to the north west of Yichang.[2] Despite the dramatic results of forest clearance and erosion in these mountains there remains a rich and varied flora.

On the northern fringe of these mountains, towards the north-west corner of Hubei, lies a lesser range known as the Wudang Shan, which, although in no way comparable botanically, contains much of interest to the plantsman, including many old garden friends.

In May 1983 I led a party of plant enthusiasts on a visit to the Wudang Shan, travelling there by way of Beijing, Chongqing and Yichang. Apart from the usual forays in the vicinity of the capital and another in the Chongqing area, our contact with wild plants was mainly confined to the four days we spent in the Wudang Shan.

We had left Beijing late morning after a four-and-a half-hour delay due to an engine fault on our plane. The flight to Chongqing in south-east Sichuan took about two-and-a-half

A minor river joining the Yangtze. (May 1983)

hours, and we touched down in sunshine and a high humidity, having descended through dense low cloud. We were met at the airport by a guide from the local branch of the Chinese International Travel Service who welcomed our tired, hot and frustrated party with the news that we were to visit the Chongqing No 1 Rubber Tyre Factory.

We were anxious to see something of the countryside, so we asked if it might not be possible to forgo the factory on this occasion and head somewhere else instead. Fortunately, our guide appreciated our feelings and suggested that we visit the Northern Hot Springs Park (Beiwenquan), which lies to the north of the city. It sounded more promising than a tyre factory, and with undisguised relief we climbed aboard a waiting bus. What we did not know was that the hot springs lay some two-and-a-half hours away!

The climate is warm temperate, bordering on the subtropical, and this produced a few surprises, such as *Chrysanthemum indicum*, a rather weedy herb with single yellow daisy flowers. This is fairly widespread in China, certainly in the warmer southern and eastern parts. Although in itself of little ornamental merit, it has achieved fame as being one of

1. To the confusion of many gardeners, Dr. Hugh McAllister, in his recent book *The Genus Sorbus*, has suggested that the tree originally collected by E H Wilson in W. Hubei in 1906 and named *S hupehensis* belonged to another species *S dicolor* and is no longer in cultivation. Meanwhile, the trees long grown and well known in cultivation as *S hupehensis* (blue-green leaves and white fruits) and *S hupehensis* variety *obtusa* (blue-green leaves and pink-flushed fruits) he has renamed *S glabriuscula* and *S pseudohupehensis* respectively.

2. In 1980 the area was the scene of international botanical activity when a Sino-American Botanical Expedition, the first of its kind, spent the months of August and September in the Shennongjia Forest district. This was the first expedition of its kind and proved highly successful, both from a botanical and a horticultural point of view. It was successful, too, in enhancing relations between the botanical fraternities of the two countries. Before this joint venture, however, these mountains had been explored by a number of Chinese botanists, the first of whom, S S Chien and R C Ching, spent two months in 1922 collecting many dried specimens. They were followed in 1944 by Z. Wang. Long before these explorations, however, the Yangtze Gorges and their surrounding mountains had been the subject of continual scrutiny by a stream of western travellers, botanists and plant hunters, among which two in particular stand supreme – Augustine Henry and E H Wilson.

335

Lysimachia paridiformis var. *stenophylla*. Like the type plant left, this handsome variety best enjoys a cool, moist, preferably woodland site. Here photographed in the author's garden. (July)

Lysimachia paridiformis, a striking Chinese relative of the yellow loosestrife, a common British native herb of marshes and lakesides. It was originally introduced to Kew Gardens by Augustine Henry in 1889, but has long been absent from western cultivation. (May)

the parents of the florists' chrysanthemum.[3]

According to Alice Coates, *Flowers and Their Histories*, these hybrids have been cultivated in China for at least 2,000 years, having been mentioned by Confucius in about 500 BC. Their cultivation spread to Japan at the end of the fourth century AD,[4] and in 797 the chrysanthemum was made the personal emblem or crest of the Mikado.[5] Today it is one of the most popular of all cultivated flowers, represented by a staggering number of named garden varieties, which are continually being added to. Mindful of the more exotic garden varieties one sees being exhibited at shows in the West, it was hard to

believe that the humble flower I found near the Northern Hot Springs could have any possible connection and yet, when I handled the plant, bruising its leaves in the process, it had that unmistakable aroma. It is the aroma of chrysanthemums, which I find so evocative. It brings back memories of my days as an apprentice with a northern parks department and, in particular, the annual chrysanthemum show in the town hall.

The Northern Hot Springs are believed to have been in use for 1,500 years. There are now forty individual baths and three Olympic-style pools filled with calcareous water at a temperature of 28°-35°C (82°-95°F). Not surprisingly, some of our party were tempted by these facilities and enjoyed a leisurely soak. The rest of us headed for the nearest hillside, reached by a track on the far side of the road.

One of the first plants we found was a viburnum – probably *Viburnum hypoleucum*. It was a medium sized deciduous shrub related to our native Wayfaring tree – *V lantana*, and possessed little or no ornamental merit. Other shrubs included a buddleja with grey, downy leaves and tiny, mauve flowers – *Buddleja crispa* perhaps – and a viciously thorny bramble, *Rubus pungens*, with pinnate leaves and red fruits.

More interesting than these, however, were three perennial herbs, two of them quite common on the woodland floor. *Houttuynia cordata* preferred ditches and damp spots especially near streams where it formed an extensive ground cover. This is a curious plant with long-nosed, white-petalled flowers and heart-shaped, pointed,

3. According to a recent study by Shiro Kitamura, the origins of the modern chrysanthemums lie with two wild plants, *Chrysanthemum indicum* variety *procumbens* and *C zawadskii* variety *latilobum*. The ranges of these two varieties abut in central China, where natural hybrids seem to have occurred. From these, the ancestors of the well-known florist's flower were developed.

4. According to a recent work on the *History and Principle of Traditional Horticulture in Japan* by Kashioka and Ogisu, the introduction of the first chrysanthemum hybrids from China to Japan occurred during the Nara period (710-794). Some writers on the subject believe that an earlier date is likely, though no records exist.

5. According to a more recent Japanese source, the chrysanthemum flower was adopted as the crest (on banners, livery, palanquins, etc) of the Imperial house (lineage). It is still in use today as the crest of the Imperial household (in informal representation as a 16-rayed double chrysanthemum flower) and as the crest of the household(s) of the Imperial prince(s) (in formal representation as a14-rayed single chrysanthemum flower as seen from below (proximally)). Several unsuccessful attempts were made to introduce chrysanthemums to Europe in the late 17th century, but it was not until 1789 that three cultivars were successfully imported from China into France. One of these, later named 'Old Purple' survived and it arrived in England in 1790. New cultivars continued to

arrive and by 1825 about 60 were being grown in Britain.

6. *Houttuynia cordata* has been cultivated in the West apparently since 1820 and is commonly seen in British gardens where, because of its fast moving underground stems, it 'spreads like the plague'. There is a curious and certainly more attractive double form, 'Flore Pleno', with cone-shaped tiers of petals, and 'Chameleon', a striking variegated form in which the leaves are green and yellow with pink tints, intensifying in autumn.

7. *L capillipes* was first discovered by Augustine Henry near Yichang, and shortly after in 1887 by the Rev Dr Ernst Faber in the Chongqing area.

8. *L paridiformis* was first discovered by the French missionary Paul Perny in Guizhou and later by Augustine Henry near Yichang. From seeds sent by Henry to Kew in 1889, a plant was raised and flowered.

9. *L paridiformis* has now been introduced to Western cultivation. Even more ornamental, however, is the variety *stenophylla* whose numerous long, slender-pointed leaves are borne in a dense terminal ruff from the heart of which in July appears a crowded cluster of golden-yellow flowers. Each spring a plant in my garden produces a crop of new shoots forming a low mound up to 30cm (12in) or so.

The Yangtze River valley at Leibo. The river here forms the boundary between Yunnan (far shore) and Sichuan. The rich colour is a result of erosion and soil run-off. Note the low level cultivation, including potatoes, in the foreground. (June 1993)

dark green leaves. The leaves when bruised have a strong smell of Seville oranges that is not to everyone's taste.[6]

The yellow loosestrifes, *Lysimachia* species, are a large genus with a surprisingly limited representation in western cultivation. In the woods above the hot springs we found no less than four different kinds, two of which were, in my opinion, highly desirable. The first of these – *L capillipes*, was a slender-stemmed, multi-branched herb with small leaves and equally small yellow flowers. The 'airy' nature of the plant, together with the daintiness of its flowers carried on thread-like stalks really appealed to me and I look forward to seeing this plant in cultivation one day.[7]

Very different was *Lysimachia paridiformis*, a squat perennial with single fleshy stems up to 15cm (6in) bearing a rosette of four broad, rounded or egg-shaped, handsomely-veined leaves.[8] Plumb in the centre was a rounded nugget of golden yellow flowers. It was startling in its effect and in leaf reminded me of some exotic version of our native Herb Paris – *Paris quadrifolia*, but the flowers were something quite different. To the best of my knowledge neither of these loosestrifes are in cultivation in the West where they would require a moist, shady position.[9]

We arrived in Chongqing well after dark and headed straight for the Renmin Grand Hotel, an extraordinary pseudo-palace with rather mean rooms. At least those *we* occupied were small and poky and tucked away at the back of the hotel where loudly knocking pipes, high humidity and mosquitoes kept some of us awake most of the night.

To the Yangtze Gorges

We were up and breakfasting at half past five the next morning, leaving the hotel an hour later for the drive to the steamer departure point on the Yangtze below. It was already warm and sticky and, although the sun had yet to appear, the day promised to be a scorcher. The river was covered by a mantle of fog through which moved the ghostly shapes of river craft. Moored at the end of a wooden pier lay a steamer of the 'East is Red' line, one of several plying between Chongqing and Wuhan. The journey takes three days down stream to Wuhan and five days for the return. Our party was only going as far as Yichang, however, which lies less than two days away.

We were to spend a night on board the steamer, accommodated in small but adequate cabins at deck level. There were other passengers, of course, Chinese mostly, representing a wide spectrum of the population: soldiers in green uniforms, school children with white or blue blouses and red neckties, college students, and mothers with babies, all of whom seem to have crowded on deck to watch the steamer's departure, achieved midst a great clattering of gangplanks and the loud blast of the steamer's siren. Slowly the engines throbbed into action and we pulled away from the shore heading for mid-stream. Now we could see Chongqing, or a good deal of it, on the slopes above the northern shore. There was hardly any ground that did not support houses or buildings of some kind and even the steepest sections bore signs of man's past or present activities.

337

A steamer of the East is Red line waiting to take on passengers at Chongqing. This is one of several steamers that ply the Yangtze between Chongqing, Yichang and Wuhan. (May 1983)

River craft on the Yangtze at Yichang. (April 1988)

Caesalpinia decapetala, a common thorny scrambler among scrub in the Yangtze Gorges. (April 1988)

Winter wheat ripened in the fields above the Yangtze. (May 1983)

Top right. A village nestling in the hills below terraced fields, Yangtze Gorges. (April 1988)

Bottom right. Pagoda with attendant vegetation on a hilltop in the Yangtze valley below Chongqing. The scattered fields support winter wheat awaiting harvesting, while the heavily lopped trees belong to the Funeral cypress *Cupressus funebris*. (May 1983)

By mid-morning we were cruising in brilliant sunshine, the shorelines some distance apart and changing all the while. We passed towns and villages perched on top of rocky outcrops, some of them with pagodas still intact. In many places people were gathered by the waterside washing clothes or bathing, while others we saw in the fields gathering in the winter wheat. Here, we were told, the climate is such that two wheat and three rice crops could be grown in a year, while maize and oil seed rape were also grown as cash crops. On the steep hillsides the fields were in strips or terraces that ran row upon row from riverside to summit, giving an attractive banded effect to the landscape.

On some hillsides we saw great green rippling banks of bamboo, while the only trees we could see were planted pines – *Pinus massoniana*, camphor – *Cinnamomum camphora*, Australian gum – *Eucalyptus robusta*, and Funeral cypress – *Cupressus funebris*. The last was most plentiful, often in groves and invariably lopped into a column or a mop head, very different to the well-grown weeping pot specimens once commonly grown in Victorian and Edwardian conservatories as decorative plants for the large country houses. We used to grow this conifer on Bolton Parks

Department for use on civic occasions such as the annual Mayor's Ball. The flattened sprays of foliage once resulted in this species being regarded as a *Chamaecyparis* until resin analysis proved otherwise

Brown stains on distant banks turned out to be stacks of earthenware pots and urns awaiting shipment. These are

A gaggle of river craft moored in the early morning at Chongqing. (May 1983)

Earthenware pots being transported down the Yangtze below Chongqing. These are used, among other things, for salting down vegetables. (May 1983)

Sheer rock walls in the Qutang Gorge or 'Windbox', the first of the three main gorges below Fengjie on the Yangtze. (May 1983)

used, among other things, for salting down vegetables. Several times we saw small boats loaded so heavily with earthenware that they appeared about to sink at any moment.

The variety of river craft was enormous and I wondered if anyone had ever made a special study of them. Birds were surprisingly sparse here, and we saw nothing all day apart from a solitary cormorant that sat sunning itself on a rock; with its dark, shining wings outstretched it reminded me of some ancient pterodactyl.

We spent the night on the river at Wanxian, a city on the northern shore, reputedly a charming place at one time, now rather drab looking though its setting is impressive enough. The steamers would lie up here rather than navigate the gorges in darkness. At this point we were still in Sichuan province and some distance before the border with Hubei. Wanxian's famous free market was still in full swing late that night. Here a wide range of goods could be bought: fruits and vegetables, herbs and native medicines as well as manufactured articles, in particular handicrafts and plaited bamboo ware, from baskets and fans to wicker chairs and screens.

At half past six the next morning we passed the town of Fengjie, beyond which lay the first of the three main

Adiantum reniforme variety *sinense*, in the Yangtze Gorges near Wanxian. Photographed by M Ogisu. This plant and others like it have probably now been lost beneath the rising waters of the Three Gorges Dam. (April)

An ancient trail beneath overhanging rocks in the Qutang Gorge. (May 1983)

gorges, the Qutang (Chutang) Gorge, known as the 'Windbox' because of the rushing wind funnelled through its high cliffs. This gorge was 8km (5 miles) long and was entered in Fengjie County where the mountains seemed suddenly to close in, leaving only the narrow entrance to the gorge. It was the shortest and the most dramatic of the three gorges, the sheer precipices on either side less than 100m (328ft) apart in places forming a colossal gate. 'The mighty river is suddenly contained like a thousand seas poured into one cup', as the Song Dynasty poet Su Dongpo aptly described the spectacle.

The 'Windbox' certainly lived up to its name for, as we entered the gorge, a wind appeared as if from nowhere and blew so strongly that it was all we could do to stay on our feet and two unguarded hats were blown into the air. All three gorges were flanked by towering cliffs of rock, largely carboniferous limestone, 152-610m (500-2,000ft) or more high and commonly 152-305m (500-1,000ft) or more sheer. In the old days passage through the gorges was an adventure, to put it mildly. Some found it a terrifying experience because of the uncertainties of the currents and the hazards of rock and shallows, not to mention rapids and whirlpools.

341

River craft with sail hoisted, Yangtze river. (April 1988)

Lime kilns in the Yangtze Gorges. (May 1983)

The first power-assisted boat ascended the gorges in 1898, but for a long time afterwards most large non-powered boats made the journey only with the help of trackers, men employed to haul the boat by rope or hawser through the most difficult sections. A guidebook account of a passage through the gorges in 1915 mentions the use of hundreds of trackers (four hundred sometimes) to haul up a large junk (a dozen or more would be needed in the case of small craft), these men 'straggling over irregular boulders with their hawsers 1,200 ft [365km] long and as thick as one's arm, all the time yelling, shouting or chanting, their movements directed by the beating of a drum or gong – a veritable pandemonium in the midst of extreme danger'. Not only trackers, but divers were sometimes engaged to release the tracking line should it become entangled among rocks in the river. There are innumerable accounts by Westerners of adventures in the Yangtze Gorges, especially in the latter half of the nineteenth century. Alexander Hosie, who

made his first journey shortly after Christmas 1881, describes how, when there was no suitable ground for tracking, the oars would be brought into use. 'An aged musician would sing his boat songs, the whole crew joining loudly in the choruses, the echoes reverberating from cliff to cliff'. His journey from Yichang to Chongqing took a whole month!

Another Victorian who braved the gorges was Mrs J F Bishop (generally known today under her maiden name, Isabella Bird), an intrepid lady who spent several years travelling in the Far East, often in out-of-the-way places. Later, in an account of her experiences, *The Yangtze Valley and Beyond*, she related some of the stories told to her concerning the dangers of the journey: 'Of people like Consul Gardener, finding their boats disappearing from under them, or like the missionary, who, coming down with his wife's coffin, came to grief, the coffin taking a lonely and ghostly voyage to a point far below'. 'Signs of disaster', she continued, 'abounded. There

All hands to the oars, a craft passing close to the south shore in the Yangtze gorges. (May 1983)

A log raft on the Yangtze river. (May 1983)

Another steamer of the East is Red line on its way upriver to Chongqing. Compared with the journey in the early 20th century, travel through the Yangtze Gorges in the latter part of the century was relatively tame, though the visual rewards remained. (May 1983)

Descending the rapids in the Yangtze Gorges, a terrifying experience for some. Photograph taken by E H Wilson in the early 1900s

were masts above water, derelicts partially submerged in quiet reaches, or on some sandy beach being repaired, and gaunt skeletons lay here and there among the rocks which had proved fatal to them'. Of the trackers she wrote: 'No work is more exposed to risks to limb and life. Many fall over the cliffs and are drowned; others break their limbs and are left on shore to take their chance; severe strains and hernia are common, produced by tremendous efforts in dragging, and it is no uncommon thing when a man falls that his thin naked body is dragged bumping over the rocks before he extricates himself'. One of the most moving accounts of a passage through the gorges is to be found in *The Crippled Tree* by Han Suyin where the author describes a journey made by her father in 1903. The terrors of the rapids, the chants and songs of the boatmen and their ultimate relief are poignantly recalled from her father's diary entries.

Modern-day passage through the gorges in the 1980s was tame by comparison. The trackers were no more and the infamous rapids now a thing of the past. This was partly due to the elimination of more than a hundred danger spots by blasting, excavating and retrenching, and even the seasonal rise in the river level had been controlled by the Gezhouba dam below the eastern entrance to the gorges. With just a little imagination, however, one could relive the thrills of the early travellers through these gorges and marvel at the grit that marked those trackers of old.

Hypericum monogynum, a low shrubby species with bold foliage and flowers, is native in the Yangtze Gorges and elsewhere in south-east China. Its flower mounds could be seen on steep slopes and grassy ledges high above the river. (May)

Wushan or Wuxia,the middle of the three gorges, was 40km (25 miles) long and contained the celebrated 'twelve peaks of Wushan', all of them in excess of 305m (1,000ft), making huge walls on the north side of the gorge. Here we saw Black kites and birds like Sand martins, but without the white rump, possibly cliff swallows.

The third gorge was the Xiling, at 76m (45 miles) the longest gorge; like the others it supported a scrubby vegetation in which a long scrambling rose (possibly *Rosa banksiae* variety *normalis*) was common. The only other flowers we could detect on the cliffs, and then only by use of binoculars, were those of a low shrubby hypericum with relatively large yellow blooms. This proved to be *Hypericum monogynum* (*chinense*), native in the gorges, having been recorded here by Henry, Wilson and others.[10] It is widely distributed in south-east China and has been introduced several times to cultivation, which explains in part why this species has proved of variable hardiness, some forms from warmer areas being more subject to winter damage than others. Nevertheless, in cold areas of

Britain it is worth giving it some form of protection in order to enjoy its attractive bold-stamened flowers on low mounds of substantial foliage.

Another distinctive plant, even without flowers, is the Chusan, or windmill, palm – *Trachycarpus fortunei*, which we saw here on cliffs above the river. It looked wild enough but this species is so widely cultivated in China, and no doubt naturalised too, that its true distribution as a native has become somewhat blurred.[11] It is the hardiest palm of its kind, though it is not happy when exposed to cold winds.[12]

For a time, in the lower part of the gorges, our steamer was accompanied by a flight of seven Lesser egrets, their snow-white plumage mirrored in the mud-brown water. They flew some 60m (200ft) away on a parallel course for almost 1.5km (1 mile) before veering off into a side valley.

The most frustrating aspect of our passage through the gorges was our inability to examine the vegetation. 'So near, so far', was a regular cry. We would dearly have liked to explore any one of the numerous side valleys where, according to Wilson, 'to walk in the early morning or after

344

a slight shower, when the air is laden with the soft delicious perfume from myriads of rose flowers, is truly a walk through an earthly paradise'.

The scenery in the gorges Wilson found to be all and more than any writer had described it as being. 'The journey from Ichang to Chunking and beyond', he later wrote, 'has been described so often that the subject is threadbare'. This was probably true at the time, but Wilson was reckoning without the poet's eye and pen of Reginald Farrer who, with William Purdom, descended the gorges in 1915 on his return from Gansu (Kansu). Although physically and mentally tired from his exertions in the north west, Farrer, in his inimitable style, managed a brief but classic commentary on the experience to end his book *The Rainbow Bridge*. His opening sentence, describing their approach to the entrance of the Qutang Gorge, brilliantly sets the scene: 'A flotilla of junks approached to meet us, ahead of the Great gate, phantasmal as a floating flight of moths in the grey of dawn against the towering grey of the cliffs behind'. Even when fatigued, Farrer's imagination did not desert him.

Shortly after two in the afternoon we reached the Gezhouba dam complex and passed through the huge lock to the river below. Soon after, we arrived at Yichang where the temperature was over 37°C (98.5°F). Later that afternoon we were taken to the East Hill, now a park, from the top of which we had a commanding view of the city and the river beyond. It was disappointing to say the least, a large industrial sprawl with no redeeming features that

Trachycarpus fortunei, the Chusan palm, here photographed on Isola Bella on Lake Maggiore in Italy. It was common in places in the Yangtze Gorges, though whether it is native there or originally planted is now hard to ascertain. (June)

10. *Hypericum monogynum* (*chinense*) was introduced into Britain as long ago as 1753 and later, in 1793, by Sir George Staunton and David Nelson who accompanied Lord Macartney's mission. According to Philip Miller, seeds of this shrub were brought in 1753 to His Grace, the Duke of Northumberland, and were sown in His Grace's curious garden at Stanwick'. It was later grown in the Chelsea Physic Garden, where Miller wa curator.

According to Dr N K B Robson of the British Museum (Natural History), the form introduced by Staunton and Nelson was collected in coastal Guangdong province, though it is also found in eastern Hubei and Jiangxi. It is a lowland form widely cultivated in the warmer regions of the world but tender in Britain and suitable only for the mildest areas. In 1881 another somewhat hardier form of *H monogynum* was introduced to European cultivation by the Kew collector Richard Oldham who collected it in Japan, to which country it had been introduced from China. This form is a native of upland regions of central China (Shaanxi, Sichuan and western Hubei) whence it has spread (partly by introduction) into coastal lowlands from Fujian north to Shandong. This form is widely cultivated in Europe, North America and other temperate regions where it is more or less hardy. The name *monogynum*, by the way, refers to the styles, which, although typically five in number, are almost completely united into a column.

11. A box of young plants was sent to Kew Gardens in 1849 by Robert Fortune who first saw this palm on the islands of Chusan (now Zhoushan) off the coast of east China in Zhejiang province and again, later, in the hills south-east and north-west of Ningbo (Ningpo) in the same province. Although Fortune's was not the first introduction of the palm into Europe (a Bavarian eye surgeon and plant collector Philipp von Siebold sent seed from Japan to Holland in 1830) it was certainly the most successful, and its establishment in cultivation in Britain was consolidated when Fortune sent a further consignment, this time of seeds, in the 1850s, the resultant plants being put up for auction in 1860. Interestingly, trees from Fortune's introductions are still alive and well outside at Kew, in the gardens of Osborne House in the Isle of Wight and elsewhere. One of the Kew trees had attained 8m (26ft) in 1984, while two later introductions planted at Trebah in Cornwall and Abbotsbury Subtropical Garden in Dorset had reached 12m (40ft) in 2003.

12. The most commonly planted palm in Britain, where it is fairly widespread, it thrives best in the warmer areas of the country, particularly in a sheltered or woodland situation. The Chusan palm is widely planted on the west coast of the USA in California and, occasionally, as far north as Oregon. On the east coast it is grown as far north as North Carolina. It is also commonly planted in southern Europe and the Mediterranean region, where it is every bit as ornamental as the many other exotic palms cultivated there.

The west end of the city of Ichang (now Yichang) on the Yangtze, photographed by Ernest Wilson in March 1908

345

Rosa chinensis variety *spontanea*, the wild China rose here photographed by Mikinori Ogisu in 1983 on a hillside in the Yangtze valley region of Leibo County in S. Sichuan. Both Henry and Wilson reported having seen, if not collected, specimens of this historical rose, but it is not known to have been successfully introduced, as seed, to the West until 1987 when the Japanese botanist and plant explorer Mikinori Ogisu obliged. It is a strong growing climber best suited to warmer climates. It grew well for me, reaching 6m (20ft.) on the south wall of my house flowering for the first time in May-June 1996. (May)

we could see. A heavy pall of smog hung in the air from countless factory chimneys and I found it hard to reconcile this city with the Ichang of the plant hunters.

In the history of western botanical exploration in China, Yichang is to Hubei what Dali and Kangding are to Yunnan and Sichuan respectively. The first botanical notable to visit Yichang was the great French missionary-naturalist Armand David, who stayed here, albeit briefly, on his way to Sichuan in 1868. As far as I am aware the only collections he made in the area were in the gorges. Ten years later Thomas Watters, an Irishman from County Down, came to Yichang as Acting Consul. He stayed for two years during which time he collected dried specimens and living plants many of which he sent to Kew. Although plant collecting was not an important activity in his life, he managed to find thirteen plants that were new to science, the most interesting of which, from an ornamental point of view, were *Pyracantha crenato-serrata* (now P

Augustine Henry in a Chinese courtyard towards the end of the 19th century. During seven years stationed at Yichang he collected several thousand dried specimens of plants growing wild in the mountains north and south of the Yangtze Gorges. Henry first made known to the West the riches of the flora of central China, paving the way for professional collectors such as Ernest Wilson, who introduced many of them into cultivation

fortuneana), *Viburnum utile*, *Primula sinensis* and *P obconica*.

Another visitor at this time, Charles Maries, also concentrated his attentions on the gorges, where, according to Bretschneider, he had a glorious time. Maries was an Englishman in the employ of the nursery firm of Veitch in Chelsea, and by the time he arrived at Yichang in 1879 he had already collected in Fortune's old territory around Ningbo in Zhejiang province, as well as in the Lushan mountains in Jiangxi province. In addition he had been to Taiwan and twice to Japan. He was, therefore, an experienced collector who was not afraid to travel in wild places, and it is curious that he did not follow Père David's lead in heading for greener fields in Sichuan. As far as is known, he did not even venture into the mountains above the gorges but stuck to the accessible glens, possibly in the company or on the advice of Watters. (It may have been Maries who encouraged Watters into collecting plants himself.) Although he was responsible for introducing several plants of note, including *Primula obconica* from the Yangtze Gorges, and *Hamamelis mollis* from Jiujing (Kiukiang) in Jiangxi, Maries has been berated by some garden historians for the plants he failed to collect. Poised as he was, at Yichang, with a treasure chest of new ornamental plants just waiting to be unlocked, he chose to spend his time in the gorges before hot-footing it back to Japan where, one suspects, he felt more at home than in China. Even his employers regarded him as 'high in enthusiasm but lacking in staying power', a criticism deemed unfair by other writers.

According to Bretschneider, that other great French missionary-botanist Jean Delavay also passed through Yichang and the gorges on his way to Yunnan, but whether he collected plants here Bretschneider does not say. Like Père David before him, he had other pastures in mind.

Up until now a good number of people had visited Yichang and collected plants, mostly in the gorges. No one, it

13. In the twenty years Henry spent in China, he is said to have collected a total of 158,000 dried herbarium specimens representing 6,000 species, of which almost 1,500 were new to science.

The Daning River Gorge off the main Yangtze Gorge near Wushan. These narrow gorges are possessed of a rich flora. (April 1988)

appears, had either the time or the inclination to explore the flora of the mountains beyond. Then an Irishman, Augustine Henry, appeared on the scene to change all that. Henry had joined the Imperial Chinese Maritime Customs Service in 1880, and in 1882 he was appointed to Yichang as a medical officer (he was a trained physician) and Assistant Customs Officer. Although Yichang is about 1,609km (1,000 miles) from the sea, it was, in Henry's day, an important treaty port as the head of steam navigation on the Yangtze. Henry

remained in Yichang until March 1889 when he was transferred to Hainan Island. During this time he was to collect and send to Kew several thousand dried specimens of plants collected in the mountains north and south of the Yangtze Gorges. They included no less than five hundred new species and twenty-five new genera, a remarkable achievement for a man who, when he first arrived in Yichang, had no special knowledge of botany and no particular interest in wild plants other than in their medicinal properties.[13]

For a European, Yichang in the 1880s had little to offer in the way of social activities: mainly card playing, tennis and shooting. Henry, on his own admission a poor shot, took to hiking in the mountains, gradually moving further and further afield until he was spending several weeks of his leave on single journeys. His hikes, which started as healthy exercise, gradually became more productive as he developed an interest in plant collecting. Very soon he became thoroughly absorbed in his new pastime, and the parcels of specimens sent to Kew, who naturally encouraged him, increased in content and regularity. Henry not only collected dried specimens, but plants and seeds too, most of which he also sent to Kew. He also learned the Chinese language, which helped enormously in his relations with the ordinary people with whom he was very popular.

Towards the end of his time in Yichang, Henry had the brief company of the Rev Dr Ernst Faber and A E Pratt. The former, an accomplished sinologist and an able botanist much travelled in China, arrived in Yichang in 1887 on his way to West Sichuan, where he became the first botanist to climb Emei Shan (Mt Omei). Pratt also arrived in Yichang in 1887, together with his wife and family, for whom he found accommodation before setting off to explore the countryside on both sides of the river. He was a zoologist by choice, but he was eventually persuaded to take with him a plant collector trained by Henry, an arrangement that was to prove successful and satisfactory to all concerned. During 1888 and 1889 Pratt travelled widely in Sichuan – including Mt. Omei (Emei Shan), Wa Shan and Tachienlu (Kangding) – collecting specimens of around 500 plant species, of which 150 were new to science. He left China for England in October 1890.

One of the dried specimens sent by Henry to Kew was

Davidia involucrata, the Chinese Dove tree, a variety of which, *vilmoriniana* was found by Augustine Henry in the mountains south west of Yichang. He sent seed to Kew, which, apparently, no one considered sowing. Photographed in the Hillier West Hill Nursery, Winchester, Hampshire. (May)

E H Wilson's houseboat *The Harvard*, which he used on the Yangtze during his third expedition, the first on behalf of the Arnold Arboretum of Harvard University, 1906-1908.

E H Wilson (bearded figure seated) and staff on his houseboat *The Harvard*; the flat-capped man is the zoologist Walter Zappey.

the remarkable Chinese Dove tree – *Davidia involucrata* var. *vilmoriniana*. He had collected this from a single tree growing near the hamlet of Ma-huang-po in the mountains south-west of Yichang. Interestingly, he also sent to Kew seed of this tree, which, however, no one in the herbarium considered sowing, pickling them instead. Many years later, when stationed at Simao (Szemao) in south Yunnan, he found himself recounting this story to an eager young man who had just arrived from England. That man was E H Wilson, who was to become to Henry what George Forrest in some respects was to Jean Delavay. Employed first by Veitch of Chelsea and Coombe Wood, and then by the Arnold Arboretum in Massachusetts, Wilson made four expeditions to central and western China introducing, it has been estimated, over a thousand ornamental plants new to western cultivation. He covered much of the ground travelled previously by Henry, successfully introducing seed or live material of many plants first discovered by the Irishman. Using Yichang as a base between 1900 and 1911 Wilson explored the wild mountainous country of western Hubei and adjacent Sichuan, often following little known tracks once used by salt smugglers. Wilson's exploration in the Yichang area began with a disappointment when the Dove tree, for which he had express instructions to collect seed, was found to have been felled to provide timber for a native house. Having followed Henry's directions implicitly, his heart must have fallen as heavily as the tree on beholding the solitary stump. He continued the search, however, and some days later found more Dove trees elsewhere. These proved to be the type, *D involucrata*.

Wilson last stayed in Yichang in February 1911 on his return from the Min valley in north-west Sichuan where he had sustained a broken leg. Since Henry and Wilson, no other collectors have made their mark in west Hubei in quite the same way. As a theatre manager might have observed, theirs was a hard act to follow. The impact of their activities in this area is nicely summed up by a remark made by the Dutch-born American collector Frank Meyer

on his first visit to Yichang in 1917: 'I am now on *Terra Sancta*', he wrote in a letter to David Fairchild, his chief at the United States Department of Agriculture. 'Mr Wilson and Dr Henry had Ichang as headquarters for many years. I feel like a Christian in Palestine or a Mohammedan in Mecca'.

Like Meyer, our party felt a strong sense of the 'magic' these two men had invested in Yichang. Of the city itself, however, we could only sympathise with Farrer who found it lying 'sad and flat and forbidding – looking grey under a grey sky, with nothing but grey flatness filling all the world around'. Our only contact with wild plants on our brief visit was on the East Hill where we found mugwort – *Artemisia vulgaris*, Wild carrot – *Daucus carota*, and Buxbaum's speedwell – *Veronica persica*, three plants that any British wild flower enthusiast would have recognised, no doubt introduced by Europeans years ago.

Saruma henryi, a curious herbaceous perennial related to *Asarum* originally discovered by Augustine Henry in the Yangtze gorges. Here photographed in the author's garden. Its generic name is an anagram of *Asarum*, to which it is related. (April)

There was a wide range of vegetables and other foodstuffs on sale at the Xiangfan free market. Clockwise from top left: Chinese spinach; ginger and garlic; bean curd; preserved eggs, which are prepared by dipping fresh eggs in a mixture of lime, clay and water, then coating with rice husks and leaving for a month before eating; lotus tubers, *Nelumbium lotus*; bean sprouts being weighed out by a stall holder; and sweet potatoes, *Ipomœa batatas*. (May 1983)

Yichang, like the plant hunters, was already a memory that evening, as we sat in the crowded compartment of a train heading north east to Xiangfan, a city of some 330,000 population, situated north east of Yichang on the Han river (Han Jiang), a tributary of the Yangtze. The next morning we visited a free market where a wide range of vegetables and other foodstuffs was on sale. Red-leaved amaranth, lotus tubers, ginger, garlic, sweet potatoes and bean sprouts were all popular items, as also were pressed bean curd and pea powder jelly. One man was preserving eggs by dipping fresh eggs into a mixture of lime, clay and water. These are then coated with rice husks and left for one month before eating. Live food was available in the shape of ducks, chickens, white rabbits and sharp-nosed terrapins.

We were taken to see the last fragments of the old city wall, with the North Gate reputedly 1,500 years old. Here, on waste ground, we saw a wide selection of weeds of cosmopolitan distribution among which were several familiar from Britain. They included Creeping thistle – *Cirsium arvense*, Petty spurge – *Euphorbia peplus*, Shepherd's purse – *Capsella bursa-pastoris*, Fat hen – *Chenopodium album*, chickweed – *Stellaria media*,

Xiangfan, the name of the city above the West Gate. (May 1983)

and a rather splendid dandelion. I dried a specimen of the latter sending it on my return to 'Dr Dandelion', J Richards of the University of Newcastle upon Tyne, who identified it as *Taraxacum eriopodum*.

In a small workshop in the old part of the city we watched mattresses being stuffed with fibre removed from the leaf bases of the Chusan palm. We even slept on such mattresses in Xiangfan finding them comfortable enough, though probably a haven for insects.

Xiangfan, the North Gate, reputedly 1,500 years old. This gate and a fragment of the north wall are all that remain of the old defences that suffered many assaults, including that by Kublai Khan and his Mongol forces in the 13th century. (May 1983)

Opposite: *Metasequoia glyptostroboides*, a strong-growing, young tree demonstrating an ornamental muscular base. Here growing in The Hillier Arboretum, Hampshire. (April 2005)

Eriobotrya japonica, commonly planted on the streets of Xiangfan. Here photographed in Spain. (May)

There was considerable evidence of tree planting in the city and a surprisingly varied selection had been tried. They included *Metasequoia glyptostroboides*,[14] *Ligustrum lucidum, Trachycarpus fortunei, Paulownia tomentosa, Populus tomentosa, P x canadensis, Platanus x hispanica, Eriobotrya japonica, Juniperus chinensis, Livistona chinensis, Camptotheca acuminata, Cedrus deodara, Magnolia grandiflora, Photinia serrulata, Lagerstroemia indica, Ailanthus altissima, Melia azedarach* and *Robinia pseudoacacia*. These trees seemed to thrive in this climate, which brings temperatures as low as -5°C (23°F) in winter and up to 35°C (95°F) in summer. Annual precipitation, we were told, varies from 1,600mm-2,159mm (63-85in). The soil hereabouts seemed to be a sandy clay and supported crops of excellent quality.

14. In 1944, in E. Sichuan province, Z. Wang made the first collections of herbarium (dried) material of the so-called Dawn Redwood *Metasequoia glyptostroboides*, officially named and published in 1948. This beautiful deciduous conifer, described as a living fossil, had first been discovered, but not collected, by a forester T. Kan in 1941. Following in Wang's footsteps, C J Hsueh made further collections of this unique conifer in 1946, and it is on Hsueh's (type) material that the species is based. After a successful expedition by an American- funded Chinese party in 1947 seed was made available the following year via the Arnold Arboretum to botanical gardens and other institutions around the world.

Metasequoia glyptostroboides, the type tree on which the name is based, growing near the village of Modaoqi in E. Sichuan (now in Hubei). Standing in the foreground are members of the Sino-American Botanical Expedition to W. Hubei in 1980 at which time the tree had a diameter (above buttressed base) of 167cm (65⅝in.). It was established in 1977 to be around 450 years old. The Americans, from left to right, are: David Boufford, James Luteyn, Bruce Bartholomew, Stephen Spongberg and Theodore Dudley.

Metasequoia glyptostroboides. The rich reddish bark of this tree, one of a group of three, is highlighted by the overnight snow. Stanley Park, Vancouver (February 1989)

The artificial lake above the Han River dam. (May 1983)

Carter and his best friend, below the Han River dam project. (May 1983)

That evening we left Xiangfan and headed north west to Junxian, just south of the border with Henan province. This is the site of a huge dam project on the Han river known as the Danjiangkou (Dan river) Dam, it was completed in 1974, and we were to spend the night there as guests of the dam authorities. I took it as a good omen that a nightingale, or something very much like it, was singing in the scrub beneath the guest house as we sank into sleep.

The next morning we were given a tour of the dam and the power house, which, to non-specialists certainly, was most impressive. The Han river has a long history of flooding, resulting in massive loss of life and property. The last serious flooding in 1935 covered ninety-six per cent of Wuhan County and eighty-eight per cent of the neighbouring county. It is estimated that 80,000 people died. We were told that since the dam project started in 1958, little or no flooding had occurred and that it was now possible for boats to travel all the year round between Wuhan on the Yangtze and Shaanxi province to the north west. From the level of the artificial lake behind the dam to the river below was a fall of 68m (223ft), boats of up to 170 tons moving up or down via a cradle-lift in a giant lock.

The Han River Danjiang-kou Dam, Hubei Province. (May 1983)

Our first sight of the Wudang Shan across the Han lake in north-west Hubei. The highest peak, known as the 'Pillar of Heaven' rises to 1,611m. (5,286ft) (May 1983)

The Wudang Shan

We were back at the dam after lunch, ready to continue our journey on the lake by launch. Two main rivers, the Han and the Dan, flow into the lake, which covers an extensive area of low-lying ground. Our journey, in ideal conditions, took three-and-a-half hours during which we were able to relax and enjoy the scenery. The low hills flanking the lake were richly grassed, and for the first time in my visits to China I saw dairy cattle. We were heading in a north-westerly direction through a rather gentle landscape, but on the horizon we could see a long range of mountains emerging from the haze of the plain. Gradually, they loomed larger and we could see quite clearly what appeared to be a row of sharp, craggy teeth, irregular but continuous, lying parallel with the lake. It was the Wudang Shan range.

Eventually, we changed direction and turned south west into an inlet that ended in a small bay where green pastures sloped gently to the waterside. On stepping ashore we could hear a cuckoo calling, a reminder of home, and on the telegraph wires along the road perched a Black drongo, a bird that, to the best of my knowledge, never reaches our shores. As usual, a bus was waiting to take us to our base for the next four days, a guest house at Laoying built on the site of an old military camp of the Ming Dynasty.

The facilities at the guest house were rather spartan, but adequate enough for our purposes. The rooms, which we shared, had little in the way of furniture and the pillows were stuffed with wheat chaff, which proved more comfortable than the sand-filled variety we had used on our overnight train journey from Yichang to Xiangfan.

On the night of our arrival we were visited by an old man selling walking sticks made from the wood of a shrub known to the Chinese as Long-life bush. We had to smile at this sales ploy but most of us bought one. Mine had a handle fashioned in the shape of a bird like a kingfisher.

The land between the Wudang Shan and the lake was intensively cultivated and, apart from a low range of dry hills, appeared relatively flat. The Wudang Shan range stretches for 260km (161 miles) on a south-east/north-west axis. Its highest point, the so-called 'Pillar of Heaven', rises 1,611m (5,286ft) and lies on latitude 32°14′N, longitude 111° 01′E. Around this peak are many strangely shaped rocks and crags, while high cliffs and deep ravines are another common feature. Much of the rock appeared to be of limestone with some sandstone and in parts of the lower hills, where the forest had been destroyed, there was considerable erosion. The soil in these mountains, we were informed, is a yellow-brown forest soil with a pH of 6-7, while in the highest regions is found a brown forest soil with a pH of 4.5-6.

From our necessarily brief observations, these mountains appeared to enjoy a warm temperate climate with evidence of several microclimates in the deep ravines and valleys. The lower slopes supported an extensive scrub that contained many well-known shrub genera, such as *Deutzia, Philadelphus, Rosa* and *Indigofera*. The only virtually intact

Both Augustine Henry and Ernest Wilson botanised in the mountains south of the Wudang Shan. Here is the native support team that accompanied Wilson on a 965km (600 mile) journey through north-west Hubei into Sichuan in 1910. Photograph by E H Wilson

The Japanese botanist and plant explorer Mikinori Ogisu who introduced the wild China rose *Rosa chinensis* variety *spontaneau* to Western cultivation in 1987, here seen at the type location of *Epimedium ogisui* and *Euphorbia lancasteriana* in Baoxing, W. Sichuan. (June 1993)

forest we saw was restricted to the steeper slopes in the higher regions and in deep ravines and similarly inaccessible sites elsewhere. Even here, most of the really large timber had been removed, apparently during the 1950s. The forest consisted almost entirely of deciduous trees with just two pine species supported by a mixed deciduous and evergreen shrub understorey.

Distributed among these mountains are temples and other buildings of the Daoist faith, constructed, some of them, five hundred years ago. Daoism, a religion developed by the Han people (China's majority nationality), stems from the ancient worship of gods and nature. It arose toward the end of the Eastern Han Dynasty in the second century and acquired a wide following in the Ming Dynasty (1368-1644). In 1411 the Ming emperor Cheng Zu put 300,000 artisans and soldiers to work on a huge project in the Wudang Shan – an ensemble including forty-six temples

and halls, seventy-two grotto shrines, thirty-nine bridges and twelve pavilions and terraces. The work took six years to complete and cost the imperial treasury a sum equivalent to the tax receipts of thirteen provinces for the same period. Not surprisingly these mountains attract a great number of Chinese visitors, including some genuine pilgrims.

As far as I am able to ascertain, no western plant hunters had botanised in the Wudang Shan before our visit, although both Henry and Wilson travelled through the mountains to the south as far as Fangxian (Fang Hsien). Doubtlessly, the Wudang Shan would have been of little interest to them compared with the higher mountains with their cool-temperate flora to the west. In 1980, or thereabouts, a party of botanists from Wuhan University visited the Wudang Shan collecting a large number of dried specimens. A list of their collections had kindly been made available to me and proved of great help during our visit.

With the tourist potential in mind, a new road was being constructed to take traffic from the main road near Laoying up to the major concentration of temples and pavilions. At the time of our visit, work on this road had only recently begun, and we were taken up the old route, a dirt road that climbed a zigzag course from the valley to a height of 1,000m (3,280ft), after which a track continued the ascent via several steep flights of stone steps to the main peak, the Pillar of Heaven. Each day, for three days our party travelled up and down the dirt road in a battered bus, skilfully and fearlessly driven around curves of intestinal complexity by a man from Laoying.

On the first day we decided to climb the main peak and set off in the bus into the hills with great expectations. The lower slopes we found rather dry and dusty with a dense scrub, through which poked specimens of the South China or Masson's pine — Pinus *massoniana*, mostly hard pruned and grotesque. Other trees here included two oaks — *Quercus variabilis* and *Q acutissima*, likewise mutilated, and the low-spreading mounds of *Rhus chinensis*, the Chinese sumach, which in cultivation is one of the last small deciduous trees to flower (in September), sharing the honour with *Aralia elata* and a few others. The rhus thrives best in regions enjoying hot summers, especially in parts of the north-eastern United States. *Coriaria nepalensis* was plentiful, as was *Paliurus hemsleyana*, a relative of the Christ's thorn — *P spina-christi* of the eastern Mediterranean. Its viciously thorny stems were almost impossible to move through and many of them supported the coils of a familiar climber, *Wisteria sinensis*. This seemed to be everywhere on these slopes, its stems often swamping the undergrowth, yet, curiously, hardly anywhere in flower, due perhaps to the regular lopping of the scrub by villagers.

Wisteria sinensis a familiar twiner from gardens was common among scrub on the lower slopes of the Wudang Shan. (May 1983)

Left: *Indigofera
amblyantha*. A
spreading shrub of
medium size
sometimes seen in
western
cultivation, though
not as commonly
as it deserves. It
was plentiful on
the dry lower
slopes of the
Wudang Shan.
(May 1983)

Below: *Indigofera
carlesii*, a dwarf
species with long
tapering racemes,
was common on
the dry sunny
lower slopes of the
Wudang Shan. It is
not, to my
knowledge, in
Western culti-
vation. (May 1983)

We were told by a local guide that much of the forest that once covered these slopes had been felled as recently as the 1950s, and I could not help but wonder if the wisterias had then climbed into trees. Considering their abundance, they must have presented a marvellous sight when allowed to flower. *W sinensis* is considered native in central and eastern China. Wilson, and others before him, found it plentiful in western Hubei from river level to 1,005m (3,300ft). It was particularly common in the Yangtze Gorges, and Wilson mentions a semi-bush form as being the more common. Maybe the plants of the Wudang Shan were of this form.[15]

Growing with the wisteria on these hillsides was a rather attractive dwarf indigofera up to 1m (3ft) high with bold, lax, long-tapered racemes of pink pea flowers. It was later identified as *Indigofera carlesii*,[16] a plant that I have never

encountered in cultivation, though the rarely grown I *decora* is somewhat similar in effect. Higher in these hills, on exposed slopes and in ravines, we found two other species thriving in the summer heat. One of these, *Indigofera amblyantha*, I consider one of the loveliest of its kind in gardens. Here it was 2m (6ft) by 3m (9ft) across, its spreading branches sparsely clothed with small, pinnate leaves and sporting slender, tapering racemes of pale salmon-pink pea flowers like candelabra from late May onwards. These curve gracefully upwards from the slender shoots and an established bush in full flower is a most lovely sight. I *amblyantha* is sometimes seen in gardens in Britain where it occasionally masquerades under the name I *potaninii*, a related species with very long racemes of coral-pink or reddish flowers from April or May until the first frosts. The other species common here has been identified by Kew as I *pseudotinctoria*.[17]

At about 800m (2,623ft), *Pinus massoniana* gave way to P *tabuliformis*, which was prominent, though nowhere dominant, for the rest of the climb. Both these pines enjoy a wide distribution in the wild, P *massoniana* preferring warmer, lower altitudes. Into some of these pines scrambled the long, thorny stems of *Rosa multiflora* variety *cathayensis*, a rose which, lower down, was content to throw a cloak over banks and scrub. In a landscape bereft of bright colours, the fragrant pink blossoms of the rose, fading to white with age, were especially welcome. Wilson reported this rose as being 'very common in rocky places beside streams everywhere in western Hupeh', adding that the 'flowers are always pink and larger than the type'.

The road at one point traversed a narrow neck of land with views of deep valleys uncomfortably close on either side. Some of our party closed their eyes, while those unlucky enough to be occupying the rear seats found

Rosa multiflora variety cathayensis was abundant on the lower slopes of the Wudang Shan, often scrambling into the lower branches of pines. (May 1983)

The track leading to the summit of the Wudang Shan at 1,611m (5,286ft). The upper slopes and ravines were filled with trees and shrubs familiar to gardeners in the West. (May 1983)

themselves being tossed about in all directions as our bus ground its way in and out of ruts and holes caused by rainwash and poor maintenance. Eventually, at an altitude of 1,000m (3,280ft), the road came to an abrupt end in a flat open area attended by a huddle of tea houses. From here we followed a track that descended a slope for a short way, before setting off up an ever-increasing incline eventually to disappear in the forest. Far above protruded a 'thumb' of rock, the Pillar of Heaven. So rich was the flora on both sides of the track that it took some of us a good hour to cover the first few hundred metres. At this point, trees were relatively small and isolated, but they increased in size and number as we gained height.

A Chinese Horse chestnut – Aesculus wilsonii, was quite common here and with it, though less frequent, a Chinese Sweet chestnut – Castanea henryi, its smooth green leaves

lined with bristle-tipped teeth.[18] Neither was in flower.

Other trees growing on these slopes included Euptelea pleiosperma, much cut over, the strong sucker growths producing showers of attractive, rounded, shining, green, toothy leaves with a characteristic tail-like point. This is a tree of little beauty in flower, having clusters of red stamens on the leafless shoots in early spring. Its long-stalked leaves, however, have a distinct and delicate effect and are an attractive reddish-purple when young, sometimes colouring well in autumn.[19]

A Pterocarya species – possibly P hupehensis – with some trees up to 12m (40ft), was plentiful, as was Liquidambar

Euptelea pleiosperma is common in the mountains of west and central China, but only occasionally met with in Western cultivation. The reddish-purple young leaves are the greatest attraction of this tree. Photographed here in young fruit in W. Sichuan by Martyn Rix (June)

15. Wisteria sinensis was apparently first introduced to Europe (Britain) in 1816, brought from a garden in Canton (now Guangzhou) by a Captain Wellbank on the East Indiaman Cufnells and grown in the peach house of Charles Hapden Turner of Rooks Nest in Surrey. It was followed, a few days later, by a second plant, which was grown by a Thomas Carey Palmer of Bromley in Kent, with whom it flowered for the first time in 1819. From these and subsequent introductions, this species was to become one of our most exotic and popular garden climbers.

16. Indigofera carlesii was named after W R Carles (c1848-1929) of the British Consular Service in China who, in gardening circles, is mainly remembered for the plants he collected in Korea (eg Viburnum carlesii), where he was stationed from 1883 until 1885.

17. Indigofera pseudotinctoria was similar in some respects to I amblyantha and almost equal to it in garden merit. Both these species were known to Wilson, who was the first to discover I amblyantha in west Hubei in 1907, and both are easy of cultivation, thriving especially in a well-drained soil in full sun. They were grown to perfection on the chalk soil of Winchester in Hilliers old West Hill Nursery. The finest specimen of I amblyantha I ever saw grew in a wall bed on the sandy soil of the late Gerald Coke's garden at Jenkyn Place in Hampshire. When I last saw it, it measured somewhere in the region of 2.5m (8ft) by 4m (13ft) or more across, a splendid sight when in flower.

18. Castanea henryi is a rare species in cultivation where, in Britain certainly, it is not the happiest of trees. A specimen at Kew attained only 5m (16ft) in forty-five years, which, for a tree capable of up to 24m (80ft) in the wild, is extremely slow. It also grows in the Hillier Arboretum and appears now to be growing more freely than it did in the 1970s, when its unripened growths were regularly killed in winter. In the Wudang Shan its shoots obviously enjoy the summer ripening so often lacking in Britain.

19. Euptelea pleiosperma is hardy, but not commonly seen in western cultivation. A tree on the chalk of Hillier's old West Hill Nursery in Winchester reached a height of 9m (30ft) in the 1960s. It differs from the Japanese E polyandra in its more rounded, abruptly pointed, less jaggedly-toothed leaves.

Dipelta floribunda, an erect growing shrub common in the Wudang Shan. Here photographed at La Vastérival in Normandy, France. (May)

almost any soil, though preferring good drainage and full sun. The best specimen I ever met with grew on the chalk soil of Hillier's old West Hill Nursery in Winchester. When I first saw it in the early 1960s, it was already 6m (20ft) tall, and when it flowered in May and June it was admired by staff and visitors alike.

Not far from the dipelta at the West Hill Nursery was a large specimen of a Chinese Plum yew[22] – *Cephalotaxus fortunei* (growing in the shade of *Torreya californica*) and I thought it one of the most handsome of hardy evergreens with its long, glossy, dark green leaves arranged either side of the shoot like a parting through the middle of the hair. I never dreamed then that one day I should see this yew relative in the wild state, yet here it was in the Wudang Shan, large bushes up to 5m (16ft) and almost twice as broad. In some places in the wild it is recorded as reaching 20m (65ft).

Cornus kousa variety *chinensis* is regarded by many gardeners, myself included, as one of the best all-rounders in cultivation.[23] Its tiered habit of branching is attractive at all times and when, in June, these are coated with the white flowerheads, like cream on a cake, the effect is breathtaking. As if this were not enough, the leaves in autumn become suffused with a rich wine-purple or red and the tree glows like a bonfire. The tiny green inconspicuous flowers are borne in tight, rounded heads and are attended by four large, pointed, white bracts that give the flower its beauty. Like all dogwoods, if one

formosana.[20] The last named is widely distributed in China and Taiwan, both as a native and as a cultivated tree. Those found in west Hubei and east Sichuan were previously regarded as different enough to be treated separately (variety *monticola*).[21]

The thicket on the hillside was packed with good things and we could not get over the fact that many of them could be examined without having to leave the track. Garden notables such as *Dipelta floribunda*, *Cephalotaxus fortunei* and *Cornus kousa* variety *chinensis* rubbed branches with lesser-known plants like *Hypericum longistylum* and *Meliosma dilleniifolia* subspecies *flexuosa*, and our heads swam with names. The dipelta occurred as scattered bushes of 3-5m (9-16ft) or more with strong, erect stems and clusters of fragrant, funnel-shaped, pale-pink flowers with yellow throats crowding the branches of the previous year. The bark of the older stems was pale brown and flaking in a most attractive manner. This is one of the finest of all flowering shrubs for the larger garden, hardy and easy on

20. In cultivation in Britain *L formosana* is relatively uncommon, being mostly found in botanical gardens and arboreta. A fine specimen of 22m (72ft), the largest in Britain, grows at Killerton, Devon (2001). The autumn colour of *L. formosana*, however, can rival that of the better known and more commonly planted American species – *L. styraciflua*. Its leaves are distinctly three-lobed and in some forms turn to rich orange and red before falling. Like the American tree it is variable in autumn effect and would repay careful selection. As far as I am aware there are no named forms of the Chinese tree in cultivation excepting 'Afterglow', a selection made in the United States, which is described as having lavender-purple new growth and rose-red autumn colour.

21. Trees in cultivation now referred to as Monticola Group are reliably hardy in Britain and colour well in autumn.

22. In cultivation in Britain, despite *Cephalotaxus fortunei* having been introduced from a Shanghai nursery by Robert Fortune as long ago as 1849, it is rarely seen above 5m (16ft). The largest recorded specimen in Britain grows at Cuffnells, Hampshire. In 1980 it was 9m (30ft) high.

23. Typical *C kousa* is native to Japan. Indeed, the word *kusa* (French transliteration kousa) is the Japanese name for this tree in the Hakone region of Honshu. The variety *chinensis* is native to central China and was first introduced to cultivation from west Hubei by Wilson in 1907. It differs but little from the type, indeed, allowing for natural variation, there seems to be no watertight character on which to separate the two. For what it is worth, plants of the Chinese variety I have seen in cultivation, presuming them to be true to name, have tended to be freer growing with larger flowers and larger bracts. The leaves have lacked the smudges of chocolate-coloured down in the axils of the main veins beneath, a characteristic commonly, if not always, present in the leaves of the Japanese tree.

24. Both *C kousa* and its variety *chinensis* are commonly grown in gardens in Europe and North America and elsewhere. They are also responsible for a host of named selections varying in habit, size, leaf colour, autumn colour, and shape and colour of floral bracts, as well as freedom of fruiting.

Cornus kousa variety *chinensis* was frequent in the Wudang Shan especially on the margins of woodland and in glades where full sun encouraged maximum flowering. This flowering specimen was photographed in the Hillier Arboretum. (June)

Below left: *Cephalotaxus fortunei* a large shrub of spreading habit in the Wudang Shan (May 1983)

Below right: *Hypericum longistylum*, a small shrub with frondose branches, small neat leaves and small flowers with conspicuous stamens. It was common in thickets in the Wudang Shan. (May)

tears a leaf gently apart, the lower portion will hang suspended, apparently without support. Closer examination, however, will reveal the hair-like vascular strands connecting the two halves. It is a trick that never fails to amuse children.

I was interested to note that the leaves of the Wudang Shan trees were quite smooth beneath. Unfortunately, we were just too early for their flowers, which were still green and expanding. The trees on the open hillside were 6m (20ft) high, probably taller in the forest. In cultivation, both *C kousa* and its variety seem happiest in a well-drained acid soil, preferably in full sun. In the wild, the best flowering displays are often from specimens on the margins of forest or streams where the light can reach them. Another bonus of this tree are the attractive pendulous red fruits that follow in a warm summer. Though edible, they have little other than novelty value as a dessert.[24]

Pinellia ternata a curious but charming aroid growing beneath a rock in the edge of woodland in the Wudang Shan. (May)

It is worth mentioning that three other dogwoods were found in the Wudang Shan that day. Both *C macrophylla* and *C controversa* were frequent in the thicket and in the forest, while below the summit of the Pillar of Heaven we were delighted to find 9m (30ft) specimens of *C chinensis* (not to be confused with *C kousa* variety *chinensis*), the Chinese relative of the European *C mas*.

I wish that we could have introduced *Hypericum longistylum*. I searched hard for seed capsules of the previous year, but, unusually, there were none remaining. It was a small shrub up to 1m (3ft), with frondose branches clothed with small leaves and studded with neat golden-yellow flowers the size of a buttercup, crowded with conspicuous long stamens and styles. Most plants were still in bud, yet, even at this stage, they were pretty.

On a bank above the track we found a clump of a charming, albeit curious, aroid, the leaves with three coarsely-toothed, pointed leaflets. The slender, funnel-shaped flowers were green with paler stripes and dusky purple within. Even more curious was the long, green, tapering rat's-tail of a spadix that emerged from the flower through the folded tip of the spathe. It proved to be *Pinellia ternata*, a close relative of the arisaemas. This plant has long been used in Chinese traditional medicine as a cancer remedy and in the treatment of vomiting and chest pains.

The thicket supported a number of climbers and vines, including *Rosa henryi*, its long, sparsely-prickled stems with

Rosa henryi, rare in cultivation but common enough on the margins of woodland in the Wudang Shan. (May)

Pilgrims and tourists climbing the steep flights of steps leading to the summit of the Wudang Shan. (May 1983)

ample leaves comprising five sharply-toothed leaflets. The flowers were white and fragrant. Very different were the twining stems and dark green leaves of *Akebia trifoliata*, which in places cast sombre green nets over surrounding shrubs, occasionally clambering into the lower branches of neighbouring trees. Even more impressive were the powerful, far-reaching stems of *Actinidia deliciosa*, the Chinese gooseberry, better known in the West as Kiwi fruit, which was plentiful both in the open and in the forest's shade. It was from west Hubei in 1900 that Wilson first introduced this plant to cultivation. He also introduced *Schisandra sphenanthera* from west Hubei, and this, too, was a

common twiner on these slopes, its greenish flowers orange-red within. *Rosa henryi*, by the way, was not the only rose species in the thickets. A slender-stemmed shrub of some 1.5m (5ft) with neat foliage and small pink flowers 2cm (¾ in) across proved to be R *giraldii*.

By now we were in the forest and ascending the first steep pitch of stone steps. The track followed a ravine for much of the way, crossing and recrossing via small bridges or boulders. Conditions here were shady and moist and the vegetation changed as a result. A gleam of purple on the mossy ledges of a rock face across the ravine proved, with the aid of binoculars, to be a ground orchid, possibly *Pleione bulbocodioides*.

Sinowilsonia henryi with immature fruiting spikes, here photographed at the Cambridge University Botanic Gardens. (July)

Rubus phoenicolaceus. A strong rambling, red-fruited species above the trail in the Wadang Shan. Known as the wineberry in cultivation, it is here photographed at Bolham Orchard, Tiverton in Devon. (July)

Several perennial plants thrived in the gloom, including three yellow-flowered stonecrops: *Sedum aizoon*, *S amplibracteatum* and *S lineare*. Equally popular with rock garden enthusiasts in the West are the saxifrages, and we were delighted to find two species enjoying the same cool, shady conditions as the stonecrops. One of them was a plant that I first saw grown in a pot in the window of a cottage in Lancashire, and since then in gardens in many places. It was Mother of thousands – *Saxifraga stolonifera*, with its rounded long-stalked leaves, red thread-like stolons and showers of white flowers on hairy, 25-30cm (10-12in) long stems. The other species we found that day was *S sibirica* variety *bockiana*, an attractive fleshy-stemmed plant with white flowers on 10-20cm (4-8in) stems; the leaves were fan shaped and toothed. It favoured the moss-covered tops of boulders in or alongside the stream bed where it

formed small colonies, its flowers gleaming in the shadows. Typical *S sibirica* I remembered having admired in the mountains of Kashmir in 1978. On a bank close to the track we also found a close relative of the saxifrages in *Chrysosplenium macrophyllum*. In Britain we have two native species in *C oppositifolium* and *C alternifolium*, the so-called golden saxifrages, but neither could hold a candle to this one, which formed dense low carpets of large obovate leaves up to 15cm (6in) long in bold rosettes. I thought at first that we had found a small hairy-leaved bergenia, but the fruiting heads gave the game away. If the flowerheads, which are typically early, are in any way equal in merit to the leaves, this would be well worth introducing for shady streamsides in gardens in warmer regions of the West.[25]

It was while ascending yet another flight of steps that I walked into a leafy branch hanging from a tree above my

Deutzia rubens with substantial clusters (corymbs) of white flowers was fairly common alongside the track climbing the steep hillside towards the summit of the Wudang Shan. (May 1983)

Acer franchetii, a large leaved tree maple in the Wudang Shan. (May 1983)

head. From the shape and hairiness of the leaves I immediately thought we had found a witch hazel – *Hamamelis mollis*. However, on following the branch through, I realised it was attached to a tree 18m (60ft) high and there were others of similar dimensions. No ordinary witch hazel this, I told myself. I then noticed the tell-tale drooping grey-green flower tassels that identified these trees as *Sinowilsonia henryi*,[26] the name neatly commemorating both E H 'Chinese' Wilson, who first introduced it to cultivation, and Augustine Henry, who first discovered it in the wild here in north-west Hubei!

In the same vicinity grew *Forsythia giraldiana*,[27] now well past flowering, but distinct enough with its long, dark stems and narrow, entire, slender-pointed leaves.

Two other shrubs from this general area are worth mentioning. One is *Deutzia rubens*, which was fairly common alongside the track, flowering freely despite the shade, its flowers white with conspicuous stamens shedding their pollen on the slender-pointed leaves beneath. The other plant was a hydrangea with leaves that were large and roughly hairy and the plant was like no other species I had ever seen.[28]

On our way through the fringe of the forest we had found the evergreen maple *Acer oblongum* and between this point and the summit we were to find a further eight species. *A cappadocicum* variety *sinicum* and *A flabellatum*[29] were the most frequent, followed by the inevitable *A davidii*, and its subspecies *grosseri*, and the big-leaved *A franchetii*. New to me was *A amplum*,[30] also large leaved and related to *A cappadocicum*. More impressive than any of these, however, was *A henryi*, many trees of 12m (40ft) or more with typical leaves comprising three downy-veined leaflets that were boldly toothed above the middle. This is a lovely tree in cultivation, often giving good autumn colour and is yet another example of a Henry discovery and a Wilson introduction.

25. This species is now in cultivation, in Britain certainly, from recent introductions

26. My first experience of this rare tree in British cultivation was a flat-topped bush in the Cambridge University Botanic Garden, a pygmy compared with these trees. There are better specimens in North America, and in 1985 I saw a small spreading tree of 7.5 by 10.5m (25 by 35ft) in the Brooklyn Botanic Garden in New York. Its rarity in cultivation is partly due to its lack of ornamental merit and also the difficulty of propagation. Peter Dummer, an experienced propagator at Hillier's Nurseries, once told me he had several times attempted to graft it without success but had subsequently rooted it from cuttings. My mistaking this tree for a witch hazel is perhaps not surprising, for it is, after all, in the same family: *Hamamelidaceae*. Wilson found this species common in the sheltered valleys and ravines of north-west Hubei. 'In general appearance', he once wrote, 'It resembles a witch hazel'. I was in good company it seems.

27. *Forsythia giraldiana* was named for the Italian missionary Giuseppe Giraldi, who collected plants in Shaanxi province. I first saw it as a student in the Botanic Garden at Cambridge, where its solitary, pale yellow flowers regularly appeared in February or early March, well in advance of others of its clan.

28. Back home, I grew a plant germinated from a seed capsule dropped by one of the Chinese hurrying down the track. I guessed that he must have picked it absent mindedly from a bush somewhere above us. The seedling was very distinct in the dark, rough hairs on its stems and leaf stalks. In July 1987 this plant flowered producing lace-cap heads of tiny, pale-blue, fertile flowers surrounded by larger white ray florets. A specimen sent to the Royal Botanic Garden, Edinburgh, was identified as *Hydrangea aspera* subspecies *robusta* (*H robusta*), which I had previously seen in a larger, broader-leaved form in East Nepal.

29. Now regarded as a subspecies of *A campbellii*.

30. Now regarded as *A longipes* subspecies *amplum*.

Acer griseum. A young tree in woodland in the Wudang Shan. Nowhere did we find trees of substantial girth, though some are known to exist. (May)

Acer griseum. The author with tree grown from Wilson's seed in the gardens at Dyffryn near Swansea, formerly home of the late Reginald Cory (July)

Acer griseum. A young, exceptionally well-barked tree in the Reflections Nursery, Seattle, Washington, USA, No wonder Kelly Dobson the owner is pleased. (November)

I was really thrilled to see this maple in the wild, but better was to come. I had stopped to get my breath back at the top of a particularly steep pitch in the track. Without looking, I leaned against the nearest tree while waiting for several other members of my party to catch me up. One of them appeared round a bend below and likewise stopped for a breather. She looked up at me and then asked me the name of the curious tree that was supporting me. I turned around and nearly fainted, for the peeling papery cinnamon red

bark could only belong to one tree: the Chinese Paperbark maple – *Acer griseum*.[31] It was not a large tree, some 5m (16ft), but there was no doubt about it being the real McCoy. A brief search of the area revealed several more, mostly slender-stemmed up to 10m (33ft), some with a dark 'close' bark, less attractive than the form admired in cultivation.

It is rumoured that this maple is now endangered in the wild, and from the few specimens we saw, spindly ones at that, this may well be the case.

The surprises did not end with *A griseum*, for growing not ten metres further up the track we found a superb Snakebark maple with pale, striated bark and a graceful head of arching branches to 10.5m (35ft). The long, pointed, broad-based leaves bore two distinct basal lobes, and on some leaves a second much smaller pair.

Our track was shared with a large number of Chinese, many of them in student groups, some of whom moved up at a steady jog. Our party, meanwhile, was well strung out, those intent on reaching the summit well ahead while the keenest plants people brought up the rear. At one point we stopped to look at a number of trees growing in the forest that had curious V-shaped grooves cut into the bark of their

31. *A griseum* was discovered by Wilson in west Hubei and introduced by him in 1907. Wilson described seeing many fine specimens of this maple in the area, one a tree of 18m (60ft). *A griseum* is one of the most admired trees in western cultivation, where its warm-coloured peeling bark and rich autumn foliage tints are greatly admired. Although relatively slow growing, it is hardy and easy enough on most soils, acid or alkaline, and appears only to dislike badly-drained conditions. There are many fine specimens in European and North American gardens, especially in the Arnold Arboretum in Massachusetts, which, according to Michael Dirr, are worth a trip to see in any season. Dirr regards this tree as 'assuming with age a dignity unmatched by other trees', and there are many who would agree with him. Two of the finest specimens in Britain grow at Dyffryn Gardens, the former home of Reginald Cory near Cardiff. Both are Wilson originals planted in 1911. One is now 10m (33ft) with a girth of 185cm (73in), and the other 11.5m (38ft) with a girth of 130cm (51in). Other, taller specimens are found in East Bergholt in Suffolk, and Hergest Croft in Herefordshire, whilst the tallest is a tree of 18m (59ft) at Arley Castle near Bewdley in Worcestershire (2003). On a visit to Edinburgh in 1983 I was interested to see an old specimen of this maple growing in the garden of George Forrest's former home.

Lindera obtusiloba, exhibiting the variably-lobed leaves. The leaves are often wine-purple when young and give butter-yellow tints in autumn. (*left*: Wudang Shan, (May 1983); *right*: author's garden, October)

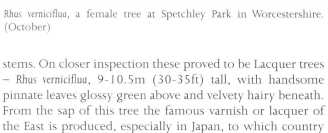

Rhus verniciflua, a female tree at Spetchley Park in Worcestershire. (October)

Rhus verniciflua, the Lacquer tree. The owl-eyed scars on the trunk are the result of incisions made during resin tapping. From this resin the lacquer of the East is produced. (May 1983)

stems. On closer inspection these proved to be Lacquer trees – *Rhus verniciflua*, 9-10.5m (30-35ft) tall, with handsome pinnate leaves glossy green above and velvety hairy beneath. From the sap of this tree the famous varnish or lacquer of the East is produced, especially in Japan, to which country

this tree was introduced from China many centuries ago. It has a wide distribution in the wild, from China to the Himalaya, and is much cultivated elsewhere in eastern Asia and Malaysia for its sap.[32] When crushed, the fruits of this tree provide a fatty oil used for making candles.

368

Rhododendron simsii growing on steep banks and cliffs in the Wudang Shan. It is widely distributed in the warmer areas of China, but is too tender for cultivation outside in Britain. (May 1983)

Mother and baby with sprays of *Rhododendron simsii* in the Wudang Shan. (May 1983)

R verniciflua is uncommon in western cultivation where it is mainly found in botanic gardens and arboreta. It is a bold-foliaged tree, impressive when mature. The flowers are tiny and of little ornament, but the yellowish fruits, which are the size of a small pea, are attractive. These are borne in large loose heads on female trees but need a male companion and a warm summer to fruit well. Like most other sumachs (*Rhus* species) its sap is poisonous and liable to cause a severe rash when in contact with the skin. Pratt found that sap tappers in Hubei suffered from this problem.[33]

Growing with the Lacquer tree in the Wudang Shan we found a sharp spined hawthorn, probably *Crataegus hupehensis*, that, in Wilson's day certainly, was largely cultivated as a fruit tree in some districts of Hubei. Much more exciting, however, was a lovely member of the bay family (*Lauraceae*) – *Lindera obtusiloba*. This was plentiful in the forest, the trees 6-9m (20-30ft) high, with handsome leaves, broad and rounded at the base and with a pointed apex. Some leaves were distinctly three lobed at the tip and all the recently emerged leaves were a striking coppery-red or wine-purple colour, paling to green with age. This species, which is widely distributed in the wild from west China to Korea and Japan, was first introduced to the West by Maries from Japan in 1880 and later by Wilson from west Hubei.

It is one of the loveliest and most desirable woody plants for sheltered woodland gardens, especially on well-drained acid soils where it makes a large bush or small tree. In spring, before the leaves appear, the shoots are crowded with dense clusters of small mustard-yellow flowers, while in autumn the leaves turn a rich butter-yellow often with red or orange tints before falling.

Rounding a bend in the track we came upon a small tea house where we stopped for a drink and a packet of Chinese biscuits. A large Mock orange (*Philadelphus* species) grew on a bank, its branches spreading over the track. We could not resist picking a few of the previous year's seed capsules and in 1985 plants grown from this seed flowered for the first time at Nymans in Sussex. They proved to be *Philadelphus sericanthus*, their flowers white, 2.5cm (1in) across and produced in racemes. Although disappointingly lacking in fragrance, they are attractive enough and freely produced in June.

From the tea house we could see red stains on the limestone crags above and when we looked at these through binoculars we found they were the common red evergreen azalea – *Rhododendron simsii*. As a shrub of 1-2m (3-6ft) it was plentiful in the upper regions of the forest and crags and on cliffs in ravines. It was, incidentally, the only species of the genus seen by us in the Wudang Shan.[34]

32. From May, at the earliest, in the trunk and main limbs, incisions are made from 10-30cm (4-12in) long, below which shells or similar shallow containers are then fixed. The sap, which when fresh is the colour and consistency of thick cream, then flows slowly in to the containers, which are carefully emptied into a wooden bucket every day. The 'bleeding' is continued for up to fifty days, the incision needing to be repeated every week. The quantity of sap produced from each incision is very small, and it takes a long time to half fill the bucket. Tapping for sap starts when a tree has attained a diameter of only 15cm (6in) and continues at intervals of five to seven years until the tree is fifty to sixty years of age. The process is well described by the English naturalist A E Pratt, who studied it in an area not too distant from Yichang in 1887.

33. For many years a large specimen of this tree grew in Hillier's old West Hill Nursery at Winchester, where it was admired by all who saw it. One autumn the leaves turned a rich bronzy-purple and the then nursery foreman decided to cut a few branches for an exhibit at the Royal Horticultural Society's Great Autumn Show. Before the end of the day, the skin of his arms and face was beginning to itch and by the following morning he was in agony: his arms, face and neck were red and swollen. In the end he had to go into hospital and it was a month or more before he was fit enough to resume work. The champion specimen of *R verniciflua* grows in the Abbeyleix estate in Co. Laois, Ireland. When measured in 2000 it was 19m (63ft) tall. A similar sized, but ailing, tree grows in the University Botanic Gardens, Cambridge.

34. This evergreen or semi-evergreen species of the Tsutsusi section has a wide distribution in the wild from N.E. Upper Burma, Thailand, Indo-China, W. to E. China, and extreme S. Japan. It is a tender species best known as the chief parent of the common indoor or "Indica" (a misnomer) azaleas so popular with florists and garden centres, especially at Christmas.

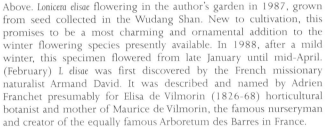

Above. *Lonicera elisae* flowering in the author's garden in 1987, grown from seed collected in the Wudang Shan. New to cultivation, this promises to be a most charming and ornamental addition to the winter flowering species presently available. In 1988, after a mild winter, this specimen flowered from late January until mid-April. (February) *L elisae* was first discovered by the French missionary naturalist Armand David. It was described and named by Adrien Franchet presumably for Elisa de Vilmorin (1826-68) horticultural botanist and mother of Maurice de Vilmorin, the famous nurseryman and creator of the equally famous Arboretum des Barres in France.

Top right. *Magnolia biondii* photographed by Mikinori Ogisu at Lichuan, Hubei. (April)

Right. *Magnolia sprengeri*, a beautiful pink-flowered species here photographed by Mikinori Ogisu in the mountains of S.W. Hubei. This species was first discovered in the Wudang Shan. (April)

After our refreshments we moved on, climbing all the while, the undergrowth full of familiar plants such as *Ilex pernyi*, *Iris tectorum*, *Decaisnea fargesii*, *Rodgersia aesculifolia* and *Viburnum sargentii*, the last named a Chinese version of our native Guelder rose – *V opulus*. These were interspersed with plants unfamiliar to me, such as *Stephanandra chinensis*, which is no improvement ornamentally on the familiar *S tanakae* from Japan. There were several viburnums and loniceras that we could not name, one of the last being particularly ornamental with its brilliant orange berries. This shrub, some 2m (6ft) in height, I found particularly interesting. Its early fruiting indicated an even earlier flowering, and yet it was quite plainly unrelated to the winter-flowering *Lonicera fragrantissima* and *L standishii*, and even to *L setifera*, which I had seen previously in Yunnan. The puzzle was not resolved until 1987 when a 1m (3ft) specimen grown from seed collected in the Wudang Shan flowered for the first time in my garden in late March. Specimens were later examined by a Kew botanist and determined as *Lonicera infundibulum* variety *rockii*.[35] The fragrant flowers appear with the emerging shoots from late January until early April. They are borne in pairs on a pendulous stalk from the axils of the lowest pair of leaves. The young shoots, leaf stalks, flower-stalks,

ovaries and bracts are glandular hairy, while the latter are often pink tinted. The individual flowers are funnel-shaped and sparsely hairy, 2cm (¾ in) long with a slender tube swollen (gibbous) at the base and flared at the mouth into five wide-spreading, almost equal, lobes. In colour they are pale primrose yellow, pink-tinged on the outside. As far as I am aware, this is the first occasion this shrub has appeared in cultivation. Its hardiness, early flowering, fragrance and attractive fruits combine to make it a distinctive and ornamental addition to the shrubby honeysuckles already established in western gardens. During the mild winter of 1987/8 it was flowering quite freely in January.

Among the trees were individuals in leaf, but not in flower, over which we puzzled long and hard. These included crabs, cherries and hornbeams. The most common oak was the deciduous *Quercus aliena* variety *acuteserrata* with bold, obovate, regularly-lobed leaves. It was a tree here of 12-15m (40-50ft), occurring as scattered individuals or occasionally in groves.

35. The specific epithet refers to the funnel-shaped flowers, while the varietal name commemorates Joseph Rock who first found this variety in western Sichuan in 1925. This name has since been replaced by *L elisae* to the relief all those gardeners now growing this charming shrub.

Iris tectorum in the Wudang Shan, N.W. Hubei. Commonly grown on walls in China and Japan. (June)

One of the hornbeams proved to be *Carpinus cordata*.

By the side of the track we found a magnolia, a tree of about 9m (30ft), and there were others of similar size in the forest below. We presumed them to be *Magnolia sprengeri*, which is native to west Hubei and east Sichuan (the Wudang Shan is where this species was first discovered, the type location). Our local guide who had accompanied us up the mountain had brought along another man who described himself as a sort of forest ranger with special responsibilities for the Wudang Shan. His knowledge of its flora was considerable, although he did not know their Latin names. He knew the Chinese names for most of the plants we saw, however, and told us that the magnolia flowered before the leaves and that they were white, a fact later confirmed by the owner of the tea house, which leads me to believe the above tree may well have been *M biondii*, said to be the most northerly occurring species in China.

371

Walking stick sellers by the track to the Golden Summit of the Wudang Shan. (May 1983)

A pilgrim on the track to the Golden Summit, Wudang Shan. (May 1983)

Our forest ranger also knew the Chinese name for a plant growing by the track above the magnolia. We recognised it as a Plume poppy – *Macleaya microcarpa*, a familiar herbaceous perennial from gardens. Its juice is orange and stains the skin, and when I was a boy I used to pretend it was iodine. My grandfather had a large clump with its bold-leaved stems and pale pinky-buff flowers in his garden, possibly the only one in Bolton at that time. Imagine my surprise when, on enquiring of the ranger whether this plant had any native uses, he plucked off a leaf, dabbed the juice from the broken stalk on my hand and told us (through our guide) that it was used as an antiseptic for bites, stings and cuts!

For the next half hour or so our track was full of walking stick sellers spaced out at regular intervals. Their products exhibited a variety of handles, some carved, some not, their shafts painted in bright colours or coated with a clear varnish. They were so persistent in their entreaties that those of our party who did not already possess a stick very soon acquired one. Some of the sticks had dragon-head handles and we were told of a legend that explains their origin. All the peaks in the Wudang Shan lean respectfully towards the main peak, the Pillar of Heaven, that is all except the Jiang Peak or 'Obstinate Peak' which refused. Infuriated, the Emperor Zhen Wu (a deity or spirit worshipped by Daoists) stormed at it: 'Since you refuse to

Lonicera tragophylla is one of the most admired honeysuckles in cultivation, its glaucous-backed leaves and bright golden-yellow flowers in summer rendering it extremely showy. Unlike most other species it grows best in comparative shade, either on a wall or even better, into a tree such as an old apple or similar. Photographed here in Maurice Foster's garden at White House Farm near Sevenoaks in Kent. (June)

Maackia chinensis below the summit of the Wudang Shan. The silvery, silky young growths of this small, spreading tree are its most notable feature. (May 1983)

Maackia chinensis, photographed here in flower at the Hillier Arboretum, Hampshire, England. (August)

Helwingia japonica is a deciduous member of a curious genus of evergreen and deciduous – often suckering – shrubs up to 2m (6ft). The tiny flowers, male and female on separate plants, are borne at the end of a slender stalk, which, due to its fusion with the midrib, appears to be sprouting from the upper leaf surface. The dark, shining flowers of H *japonica*, especially when seen in sunlight, have the appearance of a fly resting on the leaf surface. When pollinated – presumably by small insects – small, black shiny, berry-like fruits (drupes) are produced. Here photographed at the Royal Botanic Garden, Edinburgh. (May 2006)

lean, I shall have 3,000 hairs plucked from your body every year'. And indeed, during the annual pilgrimages in the past, 2,000-3,000 branches of trees on the peak were cut to make walking sticks, each carved at one end into a dragon head. Today their manufacture and that of other sticks still adds to the income of the local people.

The track ended at the base of a rocky pinnacle, at the foot of which lay a temple. On the hillside just below the crag was a dense thicket in which a host of interesting plants seemed to be fighting for survival. It was indeed a glorious tangle in which we could see *Kerria japonica*, a prickly-leaved evergreen oak, possibly *Q spinosa*, *Spiraea blumei*, *Cotoneaster dielsianus*, *Hydrangea heteromalla*, *Helwingia japonica* and *Symplocos paniculata*. Scrambling over these were several climbers of which *Clematis montana*, *Lonicera tragophylla*, *Celastrus*

hypoleucus (*hypoglaucus*) and a climbing monkshood (*Aconitum species*) were prominent. The two most exciting finds here, however, were *Maackia chinensis* (*hupehensis*) with its striking silvery, silky, young growths just emerging, and *Syringa microphylla* almost, but not quite, in flower. The maackia was a small, spreading tree up to 6m (20ft) high, while the lilac reached 2m (6ft). Both are in cultivation, the latter commonly grown and a favourite with gardeners, while the maackia is rarely seen outside botanic gardens and specialist collections. Its dense, erect, crowded racemes of dull white pea flowers are of little ornamental merit. All enjoyed their well-drained situation in full sun, exposed to the elements. The altitude here is 1,550m (5,085ft) and, according to the forest ranger, the temperature can drop to -10°C (14°F) in winter.

The south-east ridge of the Wudang Shan seen from the Golden Summit 1,611m (5,286ft). This wooded ridge was full of trees and shrubs of ornamental merit that had survived because of the religious significance of the mountain as well as the precipitous nature of the terrain. (May 1983)

Members of our group pose for the obligatory photograph on the Golden Summit. No less than three of those present were over seventy. (May 1983)

Climbing the Heavenly Stairway on the Wudang Shan. Nine flights of stone steps up the Heavenly Pillar take the visitor to the Golden Summit at 1,611m (5,286ft). (May 1983)

Platycarya strobilacea displaying its male catkins at the University of Cambridge Botanic Garden. In the Wudang Shan we saw trees of 15-18m (50-60ft). Rarely seen in western cultivation, this unusual tree is a relative of the more familiar walnut. (May)

With regular stops it had taken us four hours to cover the 8km (5 miles) from the end of the road. The Pillar of Heaven is bounded at its base by a 1.5km (1 mile) red stone wall built in 1423. It is pierced by four gates only one of which, the South Heavenly Gate, allows access to the summit through the Tai-he Palace. It is said that when building this palace, the Emperor Cheng Zu had in mind the Forbidden City in Beijing. It was built in 1416 and is a conglomeration of pavilions and courtyards set out on a chess-board design. Following a narrow cliff corridor, we emerged above and to one side of the palace at the base of a vertical rock face. Here one is faced by the famous Heavenly Stairway, nine flights of steps, 120 in total, leading up to the Golden Summit. These steps are about a metre in length, but only deep enough to hold the ball of one's foot so that the heel almost touches the face of the person behind. It is like a climbing a series of stone ladders and the only assistance provided is a strong iron chain set into the low flanking wall. For the remnants of our weary party the staircase almost proved to be the straw that broke the camel's back, but we made it and in the group that then posed for a photograph stood three members over seventy years of age!

The hall that crowns the Golden Summit has a two tiered roof. It stands 5.5m (18ft) high and is constructed entirely of gilded bronze, so that it gleams even on the dullest day. Even the altar and statues inside are of bronze; the main statue, with loose hair and leg lifted, is the Emperor Cheng Zu, who is flanked by the 'Golden Boy' and the 'Jade Girl'. The whole bronze structure, together with its contents, is said to have been welded without a seam. It weighs 5,000kg (98cwt) and has survived this exposed position since the fifteenth century. So small was the Golden Summit and so crammed was it with people who were arriving by the minute, that we had the distinct feeling of being the occupants of some heavenly bird table. Any minute we expected to be pushed off the edge by the press of bodies and so, having paid our respects and posed for the obligatory photographs, we began our descent.

Not surprisingly, on our way down we saw a number of plants missed on the way up. Two of these were trees: *Populus adenopoda* and *Platycarya strobilacea*. The poplar, a tall slender-stemmed tree of the aspen group varied in height from 18-20m (60-65ft); its long-stalked, ovate or rounded, slender-pointed leaves were margined with shallow rounded teeth. Two conspicuous glands at the junction of the petiole and leaf blade were another feature.

Arisaema engleri growing in woodland shade below the summit of the Wudang Shan. (May 1983)

into three stalked, sharply-toothed and pointed leaflets above which rose a single funnel-shaped flower with a long, pointed limb that curved forward and downward to protect the mouth. The club-shaped spadix, meanwhile, was hidden within the tube. Its colour scheme was a dark chocolate-purple with whitish longitudinal stripes on the back of the limb.

On the day after our summit climb we once more drove into the mountains to the end of the dirt road. This time we were heading for the South Crag Temple, reached by a track heading away almost at right angles to the summit track. There was no forest here, but rich scrub supporting many of the plants seen the previous day. A small flowered white deutzia was not uncommon here and I believe it to have been *Deutzia setchuenensis*. This is represented in western gardens, in Britain certainly, by the variety *corymbiflora*, a superior plant to the type with larger flower clusters (corymbs) and broader leaves.

One of my favourite whitebeams, *Sorbus folgneri*, grew here as a small tree 4.5m (15ft) high with a graceful head of slender, arching branches.[37] The leaves were lance shaped, long, pointed, dark green above and contrasting silvery-white felted beneath. This is probably the most elegant of its group, quite hardy and happy on most soils.

The track we were following eventually led us downhill

Interestingly, these leaves were quite smooth (glabrous), while those of young suckering plants seen later were most certainly downy beneath.[36] I have noticed a similar variation in the leaves of *Populus tomentosa* in the Beijing area. The platycarya I had seen on a previous occasion in the hills above the West Lake at Hangzhou in Zhejiang province. In the Wudang Shan it appeared less abundant but it made a taller tree of 15-18m (50-60ft), no doubt drawn up by competition from neighbouring oaks. In western cultivation Platycarya, a monotypic genus of the walnut family (*Juglandaceae*), is not common although quite hardy. I first saw it in the Hillier Arboretum in the 1960s where its cone-like fruits always puzzled students. I have since seen several good-sized trees in the Arboretum des Barres in France and in several other botanical collections in Europe and N. America.

At one point on our way down the track we stopped to eat a packed lunch and, in wandering through the forest nearby, I found a large colony of the Giant lily – *Cardiocrinum giganteum* variety *yunnanense*, only a week or two from flowering. Just as abundant, if not more so, was a striking aroid – *Arisaema engleri*. Its long-stalked leaves were divided

The dragon head incense burner in the Nanyan Hall. In years past, pilgrims wishing to offer incense to please the deities had to make the perilous journey along the stone neck clutching burning joss sticks. (May 1983)

36. In *Trees and Shrubs Hardy in the British Isles*, Bean refers to the hairy nature of the juvenile leaves of this species and quotes Wilson in saying that although wild trees seem to vary in hairiness, the leaves of old trees are always glabrous at maturity.

The South Crag Temple, which clings to a rock face in the Wudang Shan, houses many fine sculptures. (May 1983)

into the remnants of the Nanyandain, or South Crag Temple, which dates from 1413. There are said to have been 640 rooms in the temple, most of which were destroyed by fire in the late Qing Dynasty. There is still enough remaining to appreciate how impressive it must once have been. Impressive too are the monastery buildings, which cling to the face of a high precipice with rocks projecting overhead and a deep ravine below. One can reach these buildings via a narrow path and it is certainly worth the effort. At the end of the cliff is a granite structure beautifully carved. It houses many fine sculptures, while the reliefs on the pillars and walls depict five hundred Daoist images. The *pièce de résistance*, however, is the incense burner on the head of a stone dragon jutting

out from the building on a neck 3m (9ft) long and 40cm (16in) in diameter! In days past, pilgrims wishing to offer incense to please the deities had to make the perilous journey along the stone neck, clutching burning joss sticks and trying not to look at the yawning abyss beneath. Needless to say, there were some who did not make it.

37. There are several seed-grown trees in the Hillier Arboretum, some decidedly more ornamental than others. Seedlings vary in the whiteness of the leaf undersurface and I have seen some forms in cultivation with broader, coarser leaves that were grey rather than silvery-white beneath. The clusters of white flowers in April or early May are followed by small reddish fruits that are late ripening and often retained into early winter. A seedling with yellow fruits raised in the Hillier Nurseries in the 1960s we named 'Lemon Drop'. Given time and suitable growing conditions *S folgneri* can reach a good size. The largest in British cultivation is a tree at Caerhays in Cornwall which measured 20m (65ft) in 1984.

Epimedium stellulatum 'Wudang Star', a charming evergreen species photographed here in the author's garden in Hampshire. (May 1996)

In peeping over the parapet to one side of the incense burner, I was delighted to see a beautiful maple, probably *Acer cappadocicum* variety *sinicum*, growing on the slope below. It must have been every bit of 18-21m (60-70ft) with a good stem and neatly five-lobed, slender, pointed leaves. The crevices between the stone blocks of ruined walls and buildings supported a flora of their own in which ferns were prominent. Other plants included *Delphinium anthriscifolium* with slender stems, finely-cut leaves and small, brilliant blue flowers. Even more plentiful was an *Epimedium* species, with toothy shining leaves and airy branched heads of small star-shaped white flowers.[38] It literally filled the cracks and was equally common in rocky places around.

The Wudang Shan has been described by many knowledgeable Chinese as 'Nature's Treasure House of Medicine', and around the South Crag Temple, in particular, many important medicinal herbs are said to grow. China's great physician and pharmacologist Li Shizhen (1518-1594), after searching the country 'north and south' for the mandrake, finally found it here, or so legend has it. Of the 1,800 medicinal ingredients listed in his *Compendium of Materia Medica*, over four hundred are found in these mountains.

From the temple ruins we descended the hillside and followed a track that led to an attractive small pavilion

perched at the end of a rock promontory. It was quite narrow and perilous in places, but there were many interesting plants on either side. A *Keteleeria* species, probably *K davidiana*, sharp-needled conifer, was one of them, a small isolated specimen of 6m (20ft). *Staphylea holocarpa* and its variety *rosea* grew here as well as in the forest. The typical form has white or slightly pink-tinted flowers and green or bronze-green emerging leaves. The flowers of the variety, as we saw them, were a good pink, while the young leaves were a vinous purple, almost with the intensity of the purple-leaved plum (*Prunus cerasifera* 'Pissardii').

38. This proved to be a previously undescribed species, and was described and named E *stellulatum* (meaning flight of little stars) by the late Professor W.T. Stearn. Plants in cultivation from the above source bear the cultivar name 'Wudang Star'.

From the South Crag Temple in the Wudang Shan a narrow path leads to an attractive small pavilion perched on the end of a rock promontory. The pines are *Pinus tabuliformis*. Here we also found *Tilia henryana*. (May)

Acer cappadocicum variety *sinicum*, a superb example of this lovely maple growing below the South Crag Temple, Wudang Shan

Hosta ventricosa, showing its bold, beautifully veined and glossy foliage, photographed in the author's garden. (May)

Hosta ventricosa, a plant of wild origin here flowering in the author's garden. (August)

Hosta ventricosa was plentiful in the undergrowth, but too early for flower, of course. However, the plants that most thrilled me here were several specimens of a handsome lime – *Tilia henryana*, which stood 6-9m (20-30ft) high. Having seen this species in cultivation in the Hillier Arboretum and at the Arboretum Kalmthout in Belgium, it was easy to recognise with its characteristic leaves, sporting bristle-like teeth and a lovely coppery or reddish colour when young.[39]

After a rather greasy lunch in a village inn, we drove down the road to where a stream descended through a rocky ravine, passing beneath the road to join the river lower down. We were at an altitude of about 610m (2,000ft) and the scrubby vegetation on the hillside gave way to more sizeable specimens by the streamside. Conditions here were equally dry and parched and we spent a hot hour or so working down the ravine to the river. It was worth it, however, for apart from the indigoferas already mentioned there were many other things to occupy our attention and not only plants; on clambering down a steep slope below the road, we disturbed a Blue rock thrush, a male bird with dark blue plumage.

Ramie – *Boehmeria nivea*, was common here, 1-2m (3-6ft) tall clumps of hairy stems clothed with bold, rounded, sharply-toothed leaves that were silvery-white beneath. A member of the nettle family (*Urticaceae*), this herbaceous perennial is an important fibre plant in China. It is cultivated over much of the country and is wild in the warmer regions. It is a common plant on village plots, in Sichuan and Hubei certainly, and in some places it is, or used to be, cultivated on a large scale. The fibre is contained in the 'bark' of the stem, which is stripped and separated. In Sichuan and Hubei it is woven into 'grass cloth' and used mostly on a local basis. In the seventeenth century ramie fibre was widely used for summer clothing, curtaining and mosquito netting etc. The cloth is said to be rather coarse and much inferior to that obtained from ramie in the southern provinces.[40]

In the scrub we found *Lonicera nitida*, a familiar shrub from cultivation, and *Kolkwitzia amabilis*,[41] known as the

Beauty bush in the United States where it is more commonly grown than in Britain. It is a large shrub of bushy habit eventually as much as 5m (16ft) high and across. The paired flowers are produced in clusters all along the arching branches in May and June when this shrub is a lovely sight, well deserving its American name. In shape

39. Named after Augustine Henry, who first discovered this species, *Tilia henryana* was later introduced to cultivation by Wilson from west Hubei. Wilson described this tree as being the largest of the limes in central and western China and recorded specimens as tall as 24m (80ft). Indeed, he found a tree of such dimensions in west Hubei at the top of a pass, the name of which, Ten-shu-ya or 'Lime Tree Pass', was taken from this giant. It had a girth of 8m (27ft) at chest height and, though hollow, appeared to be in good health. It is not uncommon in British and European cultivation, mainly in arboreta and specialist collections, where it does not always produce a strong leader or a shapely tree, though such exist. A tree of 12.5m (41ft) grows at Birr Castle in Co. Offaly, home of the Earl of Roses, which was received as seed in 1938 from the Lushan Botanic Garden in China's Jiangxi province. A tree of similar size, planted about 1940, grows in the Arboretum des Barres in France.

40. Robert Fortune, in the middle of the nineteenth century, reported on the use of ramie fibre in Chusan (now Zhoushan) for making ropes and cables. A fuller account of the preparation of ramie fibre is given by Alexander Hosie in his book *Three Years in Western China*, published in 1897. According to William Stearn (*A Gardener's Dictionary of Plant Names*), ramie is one of the strongest fibres known, but owing to technical difficulties it is not widely used commercially in the West, its principal use being in the manufacture of gas mantles. Perhaps this is why Queen Victoria, it has been said, offered a reward of 100 guineas to whoever could invent a method of preparing the fibre for wider use. The reward, it is rumoured, has still to be claimed.

41. Kolkwitzia was named after Richard Kolkwitz, Professor of Botany in Berlin around 1900, while *amabilis* means lovely. It is apparently confined in the wild to Hubei on the watershed of the Han river and the Yangtze and was introduced to cultivation by Wilson in 1901 when collecting for the Veitch firm.

Tilia henryana, photographed at Marwood Hill in. N. Devon. This handsome lime was native in the woods of the Wudang Shan. Note the coppery-red young foliage. (September)

Kolkwitzia amabilis, the Beauty bush, was common on dry slopes and in ravines in the Wudang Shan. This flowering specimen was photographed in the Chelsea Showground, London. (May)

Tilia henryana, showing the characteristic bristle-tipped leaves, here photographed at Marwood Hill, Devon. (September)

Tilia henryana. The foliage is silvery-green or grey hairy on first emerging. Photographed at the Granada Arboretum, Cheshire. (April)

381

Acorus gramineus, growing in a river bed in the Wudang Shan. This species has spawned a large number of cultivars, especially in Japan where it is popular. (May 1983)

and size the flowers are not unlike those of an abelia, to which kolkwitzia is related, but the sepals, and later the fruits, are clothed in pale bristles, giving the flower and fruit clusters a fuzzy appearance. The flowers themselves are pink with a yellow stain in the throat. Flowers on the Wudang Shan plants seemed mostly to be pale pink and I have seen

Loropetalum chinense flowering in a Mediterranean garden in the South of France. An evergreen shrub with flowers resembling a white witch hazel (*Hamamelis*) to which family it belongs. It is too tender for all but the warmest gardens in Britain but makes an excellent cool greenhouse subject. It was abundant on the lower slopes of the Wudang Shan. (February)

such plants in cultivation, but there are also available selections with flowers of a clearer pink, of which 'Rosea' and 'Pink Cloud' are two of the best. The Beauty bush is well worth growing for its flower, but its large size and ultimately untidy habit mark it as a mixed border subject or as a specimen in a large lawn. Its size can be controlled by removal of the old flowering stems immediately after flowering. It is an easy, hardy and reliable shrub on most soils (especially chalky), and is worth considering for all but the smallest gardens. It does, however, need full sun to promote free and regular flowering.

A huge specimen of the Beauty bush used to grow on the chalk soil of Hillier's old West Hill Nursery in Winchester and was a picture when in flower. Nearby, in the same border, grew an evergreen viburnum – *Viburnum utile*, that produced its rounded clusters of white flowers from the ends of the branchlets in May. These were not scented unfortunately, but desirable nevertheless, and together with its relatively open habit and ovate or oblong leaves, shining dark green above, it was a shrub of some quality. *V utile* was also frequent among the scrub in the ravine, where it reached 1.5-2m (5-6ft) with the typical open, some would say straggly, habit of growth. Its flowers were almost over but had been produced in some quantity, obviously revelling in the sun and shelter of its situation.[42]

One of the loveliest members of the witch hazel family is *Loropetalum chinense*, which was plentiful in the ravine and elsewhere on these sun-blasted slopes.[43] It is an evergeen shrub of dense, fairly compact habit to 1-1.5m (3-5ft) or more, with hairy leaves 2.5-5cm (1-2in) long, prettily bronze or coppery-red tinted when young. It does not appear to have anything in common with a witch hazel (*Hamamelis* species) until it flowers and one notes the

42. This is another Wilson introduction from west Hubei that is curiously uncommon in western cultivation, perhaps as a result of its use as a parent in several ornamental and successful hybrids, of which the most well known is *V x burkwoodii* and its cultivars. These have the decided advantage of fragrance, which is inherited from the other parent *V carlesii*. A more recent hybrid is *V x pragense*, in which *V utile* has combined with the large leaved *V rhytidophyllum* to produce an attractive and useful shrub of extreme hardiness with leaves intermediate in size between those of the parents. It is a hybrid of considerable potential in the colder areas of Europe and North America. Even more recently, in the United States, *V utile* has been used in a cross with a cultivar of the hybrid *V x carlcephalum* to produce two first-class hardy shrubs of compact habit: 'Chesapeake' and 'Eskimo', neither of which is commonly grown in British gardens

43. Wilson was familiar with this shrub in west Hubei where he found it abundant on the tops of cliffs, among loose conglomerate and limestone boulders, forming a well-nigh impenetrable scrub. 'In full flower', he wrote, 'they look like patches of snow at a distance'. First discovered by Clarke Abel in 1816 growing on the city walls of Nanking, and introduced to cultivation by Maries in 1880, *L chinense* is rarely grown outside in Britain due to its tender nature. Elsewhere, in the Mediterranean region and in the warmer southern regions of the United States, especially the SE and SW, it flourishes and is much admired. In recent years *L chinense* has become much better known in Britain and N. America as a pot plant for the conservatory or cool greenhouse. This is mainly due to the introduction from China of a range of new cultivars differing in their coloured foliage – red, purple, green – and in their variously coloured flowers, from white through pink to red, as well as pink and white bicolours.

Loropetalum chinense 'Song Dynasty', with pink flowers and purple leaves. A cultivar of Chinese origin introduced to Western cultivation via Japan. (February)

Loropetalum chinense 'Ming Dynasty', with red flowers and purple leaves. Introduced to the West from China via a Japanese nursery. (February)

characteristic strap-shaped petals. Even then, they are white rather than yellow, produced in dense clusters on the slender twigs in February and March. It was long past flowering here, but I have seen it flowering in cultivation when it is very impressive. It is fairly widely distributed in the warmer regions of China. I had seen it previously on warm exposed rocky hillsides above the famous West Lake at Hangzhou in Zhejiang province. Where it flourished in the company of an evergreen holly — *Ilex cornuta*, and a scrambling rose — *Rosa cymosa*.

Rosa cymosa, a common scrambling small-flowered but fragrant rose in the Wudang Shan. Here photographed above Hangzhou in Zhejiang province. Note the numerous small buds and flowers. (May 1983)

Above and below. *Pteroceltis tatarinowii*, an old, multi-branched tree photographed in the Morris Arboretum, Philadelphia. The grey and cream peeling bark is a notable feature, especially in winter. The tree was frequent on dry slopes and in ravines in the lower half of the Wudang Shan. (April)

Much of the scrub in the ravine consisted of a prickly-leaved evergreen oak – *Quercus* species, over which, in places, scrambled an evergreen honeysuckle – *Lonicera similis*, with pale yellow flowers, looking like a rather superior *L japonica*.

When I first joined Hillier's in 1962 and began work at the old West Hill Nursery, I used to spend most of my lunch breaks checking through plants growing in the nursery. There were two long borders flanking the main drive, both packed with trees and shrubs many of which had been grown from wild collected seed. One of these was a thorny shrub – *Zanthoxylum americanum*, known in North America as the Prickly ash or Toothache tree. The bark and fruits of this plant and others of its kind have a pungent, acrid taste and a popular name for this species supposedly refers to their use by certain North American Indians who chewed on them to alleviate toothache. I remember chewing a twig to test this story and found the juice had a numbing effect on my tongue and lips. If anyone is tempted to try this for themselves, it should be remembered that the twig or the fruit, which is the size of a peppercorn, need only be nibbled not chewed, and on no account should it be swallowed.

Growing in the ravine was a Chinese version of the Toothache tree – *Z armatum*, distinct in the winged leaf stalks and flattened spines borne in pairs on the same plane. I told our guide about the American Indians' use of the twig and fruits and asked that he relate it in Chinese to the forest ranger who listened carefully and then began to smile and nod. He then told us that this Chinese shrub is used in the same way by villagers in the area. The name *zanthoxylum* derives from the Greek *xanthos* meaning yellow and *xylum* wood, referring to the yellow heart-wood of some species.

The ravine contained two interesting trees, which were by no means confined here. One of these was *Gleditsia sinensis*, which, according to Wilson, is quite common and widespread in the Yangtze valley and similarly warm valleys elsewhere in Hubei. It can reach 12-15m (40-50ft) in some places, but here it was about half this height, its stem and main branches literally bristling with vicious branched woody spines several centimetres long. The leaves were pinnate up to 25cm (10in) long with up to fourteen glossy topped leaflets, increasing in size towards the tip. There was no terminal leaflet. The timber of this tree according to Wilson was once used in general carpentry and furniture making.

Its fruits (pods) were also used as a soap in general laundry work, producing a good lather in either hot or cold water. The saponaceous fat, which produces the lather, is contained in the pod itself rather than the seeds, these being discarded when the pod is crushed. This and several other trees with similar uses are referred to by the Chinese as Soap trees. Currently there is some doubt as to the true identity of this Hubei tree, some authorities suggesting it may belong to another species. Unfortunately, there was neither flower nor fruit available at the time of our visit.

The second tree to catch our attention was far more widespread, commonly bushy and part of the general thicket, occasionally producing a main stem to 4.5-6m (15-20ft). In leaf it reminded us of a nettle tree (*Celtis*), but the few small nut-like fruits that remained were winged like those of an elm (*Ulmus*) and born singly in the leaf axils of the current year shoots. It was undoubtedly *Pteroceltis tatarinowii*, a monotypic genus (only one species).[44]

A common undergrowth beneath the trees in the ravine, and indeed in many places on these dry slopes, was a prickly bramble – *Rubus corchorifolius*, with leaves shaped like those of an elm and single heads of orange fruits. We tasted some of these finding them quite palatable and sweet and were not surprised to read later that Wilson, who first introduced it to western cultivation, considered it one of the three best of the edible Chinese kinds. Wilson hoped that by hybridising them, some of the *Rubus* species he introduced would help evolve a new race of berries to add to the soft fruit then in cultivation. I am not aware that this particular dream ever came true.

Having descended the ravine we found ourselves by the so called Sword river crossed by the Sword Bridge built in 1413. Parts of the river bank were flanked by rock walls and cliffs,

which, we noticed, supported a rich variety of self-clinging climbers. Here was Chinese ivy – *Hedera nepalensis* variety *sinensis*, and *Trachelospermum jasminoides* fighting it out with *Euonymus fortunei*, a species widespread in China, Korea and Japan, represented in Western cultivation by a multiplicity of cultivars. I shall never forget seeing this euonymus and the trachelospermum climbing the stems of trees in the hills above the West Lake in Hangzhou, Zhejiang province, in May 1979. They appeared as solid columns of green up to 9m (30ft) or more, the latter plastered with sweet-scented flowers. In the United States the trachelospermum is known as Star jasmine and is especially popular in Californian and Arizonan gardens.

44. The name *pteroceltis* (winged *Celtis*) referring to the form of the fruits, and *tatarinowii* after Alexander Tatarinov, a Russian botanist and medical man who spent ten years in Beijing in the 1840s. During this time he collected dried specimens of plants in the region, one of which was this tree. It is interesting that this species should be recorded in areas so far apart. Central China appears to be its main home. Wilson saw it in west Hubei on several occasions and it is said by the Chinese to occur in Sichuan, Guizhou and Tibet. There is a particularly fine specimen of this tree in the Morris Arboretum in Philadelphia, Pennsylvania. Measuring 9-10.5m (30-35ft) in 1976, this was probably grown from seed sent to the United States Department of Agriculture by Frank Meyer in 1907 and collected in Shandong province. Older specimens, including the Morris Arboretum tree, exhibit attractive flaking bark, while the leaves often turn a clear yellow in autumn.

The Sword Bridge crossing the Sword river in a valley of the Wudang Shan. Built in 1413, it is still used by the inhabitants of a nearby hamlet to reach the new road above. (May 1983)

Parthenocissus henryana is especially attractive in autumn. Here growing on a west-facing wall in the author's garden. (November)

Dregea sinensis, which we found in the Wudang Shan twining its way through hillside scrub. Photographed here flowering on a wall at Jenkyn Place, Hampshire. (July)

The only deciduous, self-clinging climber in this area of the Wudang Shan seemed to be a vine – *Parthenocissus henryana*, which shared the same rocks as the euonymus. A handsome species with its reddish-purple young growths and pale, veined leaflets, it reaches its peak of ornamental perfection in autumn when its foliage exhibits rich red and scarlet tints. Twining, rather than self clinging, *Dregea sinensis* (*Wattakaka sinensis*) was another climber that we found to be plentiful in the thicket.[45]

That night after dinner we were treated to a film show in a nearby hall. To our surprise, much of the action in the film, a Chinese 'thriller', was set among the rhododendrons on Emei Shan in Sichuan. I shared a room that night with a man who had spent much of his life with trees and forestry. He was also keenly interested in birds and identified many of those we saw during our visit. One of the most irritating of these was an Indian cuckoo. It never seemed to stop calling from a hillside behind our guest house. Even at night we would sometimes wake to hear its call, which, according to a recent book on the subject, is 'ko-ko-ta-ko', but to us it sounded like 'one more bottle'. Despite its English name it is found through much of south-east Asia.

On our final day in the mountains we decided to visit the Purple Clouds Temple. This is the largest of the temples in the Wudang Shan. Built in 1413, ten years earlier than the Forbidden City in Beijing, it comprises 860 halls and pavilions, the sloping roofs with green glazed tiles and finely sculptured porcelain birds and beasts standing along the ridges. Inside, the main hall of the temple is illuminated by great lanterns and draped to the floor with yellow-ochre tapestries, while bluish smoke from burning incense twirls around the gold-painted clay figure of the Jade Emperor with his golden pages and jade maids at his side.

The main hall is supported by thirty-six red cedar pillars, while the ceiling is decorated with paintings of figures, birds and flowers. Four colourful pearl lanterns hang from the ceiling. The temple is, in effect, a museum of articles from the Yuan, Ming and Qing dynasties and, although much of what we saw was covered in dust and in need of renovation, there was no doubting the importance of the temple in China's heritage.[46]

We found the Purple Clouds Temple, like so many temples and monasteries in China, a haven for fine trees. For a start, there was a huge spreading Horse chestnut – *Aesculus wilsonii*, dominating one corner of a courtyard.[47]

Aesculus wilsonii, a fine spreading tree in the corner of a courtyard in the Purple Clouds Temple, the flower trusses are within two weeks of opening. (May 1983)

The main hall of the Purple Clouds Temple in the Wudang Shan with a protected woodland on the hillside behind. It was built in 1413, ten years earlier than the Forbidden City in Beijing. (May 1983)

Aesculus chinensis. This is a spectacular species in flower, but slow growing in British cultivation where it is rarely seen. Photographed in Hangzhou, Zhejiang province. (May 1979)

Though its long, tapered flower 'candles' had developed, they would not be opening for another week or two. It is closely allied to the Indian Horse chestnut – A indica, having similarly elegant foliage (not coarse as in A hippocastanum and its allies) and flowerheads. It is said also to be closely related to A chinensis, a native of northern China, which is commonly planted in the Hangzhou area of Zhejiang province, differing in its large leaves.[48]

45. Dregea sinensis (Wattakaka sinensis) was discovered in west Hubei, north of Yichang, by Augustine Henry in 1887 and by the Rev Ernst Faber in Guizhou in the same year. It was Wilson, however, who first introduced it to cultivation from west Hubei. It is not a striking ornamental but interesting in being an almost hardy relative of the hoyas, which, in Britain certainly, are greenhouse subjects. The fragrant cream-coloured red-streaked flowers are carried in nodding clusters in June or July. Both Dregea and Hoya belong to the milkweed family (Asclepiadaceae) and have the characteristic milky-white sticky sap. One of the best specimens of the former grew on the warm south-facing wall of Jenkyn Place, home of the late Mr and Mrs Gerald Coke in Hampshire. Coincidentally, it was accompanied there by Trachelospermum jasminoides, both climbers flowering exceptionally most years.

46. According to one legend, the temple is also the home of Taijiquan (T'ai Chi Ch'uan) or shadow boxing. During the years of transition between the Yuan and Ming dynasties (around 1368), a great boxing master Zhang Sanfeng took refuge in the Wudang Shan to pursue his study of the boxing arts. Through assimilations of animal movements, mainly from the tortoise, snake, deer and crane, he evolved the world-famous Taijiquan, a school of boxing that diverts hard blows with subtle deflections, thereby infusing the Daoist philosophy into boxing. He also developed a series of Taiji (T'ai Chi) forms using sword, broadsword, staff and spear, thus founding the famous Wudang School. Anyone visiting cities such as Beijing, Shanghai or Hong Kong will have seen Chinese people in parks and other relatively quiet places practising Taijiquan. In 1984 the champion of this art was Pu Huan; brother of the last Emperor of China, Pu Yi. Today Taijiquan (more commonly know in England as T'ai Chi) is popular throughout the West, from city parks to village halls, as a gentle form of exercise.

47. First introduced to the Arnold Arboretum by Wilson in 1908, this impressive species is rarely seen in cultivation. There is a tree of about 19m (62ft) in the woods at Caerhays in Cornwall originally received from the Arnold Arboretum, but the largest in Britain is a tree of 21m (68ft) at Melbury Park, Dorset (1980).

48. Aesculus chinensis was originally introduced to cultivation by William Purdom from the Beijing area in 1912 and is represented at Kew by a tree that in 2001 measured some 12m (39ft). A tree of similar size can be found in the Hillier Arboretum in Hampshire. I shall never forget, on my first visit to China, marvelling at Aesculus chinensis in the grounds of the Hangzhou Hotel by the West Lake. There were two trees in the hotel garden, the larger around 20-21m (65-70ft) high. The bark of the stem was dappled grey and brown and flaky like an old sycamore (Acer pseudoplatanus). The white, long-stamened flowers were carried in densely packed cylindrical or slightly tapered heads (panicles) up to 45cm (18in) long. These were arranged horizontally or gently ascended from the shoot extremities. Judging by its performance in Zhejiang and further north, I believe it to be best suited to those countries enjoying a continental climate of hot summers and cold dry winters. According to Bean the young growths of this species are subject to damage by late spring frosts, a problem that ceases as the tree matures. The fruits of A chinensis are rounded compared with those of A wilsonii, which are ovoid or pear-shaped and have a thinner shell.

387

Pseudocydonia sinensis, an old tree in a courtyard of the Purple Clouds Temple. (May 1983)

Pseudocydonia sinensis, in a courtyard of the Purple Clouds Temple. The ornamental bark is well displayed. (May 1983)

On a higher tier above the courtyard in a raised bed at the Purple Clouds Temple, was the best specimen I have ever seen of *Pseudocydonia sinensis*, the Chinese quince.[49] It was easily 9m (30ft) with a stout stem clothed with a strikingly dappled flaking bark, like that of a plane (*Platanus*).

Outside the temple walls grew *Cudrania tricuspidata*, now *Maclura tricuspidata*, and *Eucommia ulmoides*, both presumably planted. The former is a thorny-branched tree with shining green, entire to three-lobed foliage and tight, ball-like heads of tiny, green flowers, male and female borne on separate plants. It is in the same family as the mulberry (*Moraceae*), and its leaves are similarly used in China for feeding silkworms. *Eucommia* is not only a monotypic genus, but also belongs to a monotypic family (*Eucommiaceae*). It is a deciduous tree allied to the elm (*Ulmus*) and widely cultivated in China for its dried bark, an infusion from which has for 2,000 years or so been valued as a tonic. According to Chinese sources, it is also useful in the treatment of impotence, lumbago and leg or knee weaknesses. Infusions of eucommia have also been used in the Soviet Union in the treatment of hypertension, reportedly with good results.

Another attribute of this tree is the rubber it contains, which, however, is of an inferior quality to the real thing. How many times have I demonstrated the gentle tearing of a leaf into two apparent separate halves, only to see the look of puzzlement on students' faces when the lower half refuses to fall. This is because the two halves remain attached by slender strands of rubber from the veins. *Eucommia ulmoides* is the only tree hardy in our climate known to produce rubber. Although it has latex in the leaves, bark and seeds, the rubber content is only three per cent of the dry weight, an insufficient quantity for commercial purposes.[50]

49. A close relative of the common quince (*Cydonia oblonga*), this tree is not commonly seen in gardens in Britain. It is hardy and will flower and fruit here, but there is no doubting that it does best where summers are consistently warmer. The best specimens in cultivation are found in Europe, especially in the Mediterranean region, where its soft carmine flowers in spring give way to huge fruits, up to 18cm (7in) long, which ripen to lemon-yellow. In Britain these fruits too often remain green and hard. In the United States this tree is rarely seen outside botanic gardens and arboreta. There are good specimens in the Morris Arboretum in Philadelphia and the Brooklyn Botanic Garden, New York. Two bushy specimens, grown from seed received from the Shanghai Botanic Garden, grow in neighbouring gardens to mine and regularly produce substantial fruits.

50. On a visit to the Sukhumi Botanical Garden, Georgia, in the then Soviet Union in 1979, I was told by the director about a project that had been undertaken in the garden in the 1920s. At that time rubber had been produced from eucommia equal in quality to that of Indonesian rubber. Despite this success, on orders from Moscow, production had not been taken up because, at the time, it was cheaper to produce synthetic rubber. According to Bean, fossils found in tertiary brown-coal deposits in Germany, known as 'monkey's hair', derive from the leaves of some extinct species of eucommia. Not only that, but they are well enough preserved to burn when a match is put to them, giving off a smell of rubber. The largest *E ulmoides* in British cultivation is a tree of 20m (65ft) at Hergest Croft in Herefordshire (1995).

Pseudocydonia sinensis fruit in a Hampshire garden. These can be used to make a delicious jelly or preserve. (October)

Pseudocydonia sinensis showing the large leaves and the soft pink flowers. Here photographed in a Hampshire garden. (May)

Pseudocydonia sinensis fruiting in Brooklyn Botanic Gardens. (October)

Eucommia ulmoides, with characteristic drooping leaves, here photographed in the Hillier Arboretum. (October)

Far left. *Firmiana simplex*, the Chinese Parasol tree with its large handsome maple-like leaves. A young specimen growing at the Morris Arboretum, Pennsylvania, USA. (August)

Left. A female Daoist monk at the Needle in the Well Temple

Opposite: *Catalpa fargesii* forma *duclouxii*, a tall tree below the Purple Clouds Temple, Wudang Shan. (May 1983)

The Purple Clouds Temple is situated at the base of Zhanqi Peak, which is well covered in trees including pine, and with vast thickets of bamboo. Because of the proximity and religious nature of the temple, the forest on the hillside behind is untouched and supports a range of beautiful trees with fine stems. Here grew an uncommon dogwood – *Cornus walteri*, several trees of 9m (30ft) with a roughly creviced, dark bark like an alligator hide, and ovate to elliptic slender-pointed leaves up to 10cm (4in) long, hairy beneath. The crowded heads of small, white flowers at the tips of the branches were not quite open, but, from the quantity present, these trees would be a rare picture in a week's time.[51]

The forest here was a joy to see, masses of maples (*Acer cappadocicum* variety *sinicum*), oaks (*Quercus aliena* variety *acuteserrata*), aspen (*Populus adenopoda*) and *Firmiana simplex*. The last named, the Chinese Parasol tree, reached 15-18m (50-60ft), its smooth greyish-green barked stems straight as gun-barrels, supporting large crowns of bold, maple-like foliage. Unfortunately, this tree is not entirely suited to Britain, although a young tree in my garden survived three cold winters without any harm before finally being blown down in a storm. It is undoubtedly a tree that requires warm summers to ripen its shoots and can then take the cold. It is commonly planted in Beijing and other Chinese cities enjoying a continental climate. It also grows well in similar conditions in European cultivation and no doubt in North America too. The red glutinous inner bark of this tree is powdered by the Chinese and used in rice porridge.

Other trees in the wood included *Cunninghamia lanceolata* – the China fir, *Pinus tabuliformis* and *Keteleeria davidiana*, all of 15-18m (50-60ft) and present in some numbers. The most spectacular tree of all, however, was *Catalpa fargesii* forma *duclouxii*. This was plentiful and flowering in the wood and elsewhere in the valley, sometimes growing in the vicinity of villages where it may have been planted. It was a tall, stately tree, mostly over 18m (60ft),

two trees much more, maybe 24m (80ft), the ground beneath them littered with the darkly-spotted, lavender blossoms. Wilson first collected seed of this tree from the Fangxian area south of the Wudang Shan in 1907.

Due to its strategic position, the Wudang Shan has often been used as a base by revolutionary forces. The peasant leader Li Zicheng (1606-1645), who rose in revolt at the end of the Ming Dynasty, assembled his army here. The ruins of Laoying Temple, burned by Li's forces before they were forced to retreat, still stand at the foot of the mountains.

In 1856, during the Qing Dynasty, peasant insurgents from Hubei and Henan provinces, known as the Red Turbans, entrenched themselves in this area. An inscription chronicling their suppression by the Qing government is engraved on a rock at the South Crag Temple. In more recent times, the Chinese Red Army fought here. In 1931 the 2nd Army Group of the Red Army, under its commander He Long, marched north west from Hong Hu (Lake Hong) in southern Hubei to the Wudang Shan and set up his headquarters in the Purple Clouds Temple.

My bird spotting colleague was having a whale of a time: fine trees on the one hand, birds on the other. A jay was seen in the wood, very similar to our native bird, and another Blue rock thrush, this time a female, put in an appearance. In the temple compound a tame Peking robin followed us around, while outside, across the valley, another cuckoo, the Large Hawk cuckoo, teased us with its repetitive cry 'beer fever, beer fever'. Like the Indian cuckoo near our guest house, it must have been suffering from a hangover.

51. This is a hardy and easy tree, curiously rare in Western cultivation, in Britain at least, where it is normally found only in botanic gardens and arboreta. True, it is not spectacular in the same way as *C kousa* or *C nuttallii*, but it is a tree of substance and potential and ought to be more widely grown. It was originally introduced from west Hubei by Wilson in 1907. The largest specimen in Britain is a tree of 15m (50ft) growing at Wakehurst Gardens in Sussex (1997), and there are several fine trees elsewhere.

On our return down the mountain we stopped to visit the Needle in the Well Temple where practising Daoists are in residence. Legend has it, that the Emperor Zhen Wu, tired of meditating alone in the mountains to attain immortality, decided to go back to the world of men. On his way down he came upon an old woman beside a well grinding away at a thick iron bar. 'What are you doing', Zhen Wu asked. 'Making a needle for my embroidery', the woman replied. Seeing Zhen Wu's astonishment, the old woman – actually an incarnation of a Bodhisattva or Buddhist saint – smiled and said, 'With perseverance, even an iron bar can be ground into a needle'. Chastened, the emperor returned to his meditation in the mountains. The well can still be seen today. A building nearby houses a bronze statue of the old woman holding an iron bar and smiling at visitors, while her words have become a well-known proverb in China.

Our final day was spent in the plain towards the lake. First we were taken to the village of Jinghua to see an ancient tree – *Juniperus chinensis*, which had had its top blown out by lightning sometime in the 1950s. It was, nevertheless, quite impressive with a girth of 313cm (122in) at chest height. We were told a curious story by a villager who said that in 1952 this tree blossomed one morning with five different colours, the phenomenon lasting for eight days. It was a miracle for which we could offer no answer.

An ancient Chinese juniper tree, *Juniperus chinensis*, in the village of Jinghua. (May 1983)

Opposite: *Juniperus chinensis.* The trunk of the ancient tree in the village of Jinghua girthed 313cm (122in) at chest height. (May 1983)

Old stone well near the village of Jinghua, N.W. Hubei. (May 1983)

The Paper mulberry – *Broussonetia papyrifera*, was plentiful here and, we were told, still used for paper, producing an off-white product, while the leaves are fed to the pigs.[52] In the same village, *Toona sinensis* (*Cedrela sinensis*) was cultivated for its young shoots, which have a taste of onions and are used in cooking. Native to the western and northern areas of China, this tree is widely cultivated and is occasionally seen in temple gardens as a stately tree after the manner of an ailanthus. It is also much planted in industrial areas of China south of the Yellow river because it is strongly resistant to, and tolerant of, aerial pollution. It is capable of reaching 24m (80ft) or more, eventually.[53] Its large, pinnate leaves have a resemblance to those of *Ailanthus altissima*, the Tree of Heaven, but the leaflets of the latter bear at their base gland-tipped teeth and lack the characteristic onion odour of the toona; while the leaves of the toona frequently lack the terminal leaflet.

Several times we were invited to sit down by villagers who were eager to engage us in conversation. A woodworker showed us a coffin he had just made out of cypress (almost certainly the China fir *Cunninghamia lanceolata*), which he told us was the best for such use, though expensive. He would be lacquering it with varnish

from *Rhus verniciflua*. Timber of the Empress tree – *Paulownia tomentosa*, stacked nearby was to be used for furniture.

Outside the village, in a dry ravine, we found a Chinese wingnut – *Pterocarya stenoptera*, and also *Ehretia corylifolia*, a tree I had last seen in the dry hills of Kunming in 1981. *Pterocarya stenoptera* is less commonly cultivated in Britain compared with the United States where, in the south-west especially, it is regarded as a good-looking tree with only one real virtue: it succeeds well in compacted, poorly aerated soils in playgrounds and other high traffic areas. Aggressive roots make it unsuitable in lawn and garden and it is best accommodated in parks and similarly well-trodden sites.[54] Native to western China and commonly planted elsewhere, it shares with the introduced London plane and the American Black locust (*Robinia pseudoacacia*) a remarkable tolerance of suburban problems including pollution, soil compaction and bad pruning (hacking).

Having recently seen *Akebia trifoliata* in the mountains, we now found another species – *A. quinata* – scrambling about over scrub. Its leaves are divided into five short-stalked leathery leaflets that lack the lobing of the other species. Both are in western cultivation, usually trained against a wall, fence or hedge. Their purple flowers are

A coffin newly made from 'cypress' wood (*Cunninghamia lancealata*) waiting to be treated with varnish from the Lacquer tree *Rhus verniciflua*. (May 1983)

Toona sinensis, a young well-shaped example at Saling Hall, Essex. (July 1989)

Toona sinensis 'Flamingo', demonstrating its shrimp-pink young growth. Here photographed at the RHS Garden, Wisley, Surrey. (May)

52. This is another tree that thrives on hot summers and cold winters and I have in mind a huge multi-stemmed specimen of 12-15m (40-50ft) in the Brooklyn Botanic Garden in New York.

53. Trees of this calibre are found in a number of European collections such as the Arboretum Kalmthout in Belgium and the Arboretum von Gimborn in Holland. The largest specimen in Britain grows at Hergest Croft in Herefordshire and, in 1995, measured 23m (75ft). However, apart from a few notable specimens, *Toona sinensis* is not common in British cultivation despite it being a hardy tree. Indeed, it is the one hardy member of the mainly tropical mahogany family (*Meliaceae*). The only species of its genus, it has, to the best of my knowledge, only one named selection, 'Flamingo', in which the young growths are a striking shrimp-pink rather than the reddish-purple of the typical tree. This cultivar originated in Australia and was introduced into New Zealand in the 1930s. It is particularly common in the Auckland area of North Island where I saw it in 1985. More recently it has been introduced to British cultivation, its growth has shown remarkable tolerance to frost. 'Flamingo' received an Award of Merit from the Royal Horticultural Society in October 1986.

54. One of the finest specimens of this wingnut in Britain grows at the Royal Botanic Gardens, Kew. In 2001 it measured 24m (78ft) high, whilst there are several trees elsewhere of 20m (65ft) or so.

Ilex cornuta, the Horned holly with its curiously spined evergreen leaves. We found both male and female plants in dry ravines below the Wudang Shan. The fruits ripen to red. (May)

Ilex cornuta. A selected seedling heavy with ripened fruits, here growing at Calloway Gardens, Georgia, USA. (January)

often hidden beneath the leaf canopy, while the curious sausage-shaped fruits are only borne, in Britain certainly, after a long warm summer and even then but sparingly.

The ravine contained several plants of the Horned holly – *Ilex cornuta*, with its polished green, hard, rectangular five-to-seven spined leaves.[55] It is slow growing and compact in habit, all the plants we saw were 1-1.5m (3-5ft).

As we walked alongside a stream cascading down the ravine we saw a flash of brilliant turquoise, like a flying neon tetra fish. It was the Blue-eared kingfisher, which is related and very similar to our native bird. Almost the last plant we saw that day was a terrestrial orchid – *Bletilla ochracea*, an erect perennial with arching, sword-shaped leaves and several pale yellow flowers on a slender stem; it was a lovely plant. As we stood admiring it from across the stream, a line of water buffalo came tramping through the ravine, one of them heading straight for the orchid. Luckily, at the very last minute, it turned away to browse

some choicer morsel. What really surprised me were the conditions in which the orchid grew. The soil was stony, loose and naturally well drained, with little in the way of organic matter, while the ravine itself was a sun trap from which we were happy to escape.

The last plant we examined, believe it or not, was a dandelion (*Taraxacum* species). After all the exotic and exciting plants we had seen over the last few days it seems ironic that when I sent a dried specimen of this plant to Dr Richards in Newcastle upon Tyne, he declared it to be a new species! To my knowledge this has still to be named.

55. Although introduced to Britain as long ago as 1846 by Robert Fortune, this holly has never been common in gardens here. It is much more popular in the United States, or at least its cultivars and hybrids are, the species now less so, and appears to thrive best in areas enjoying a continental climate. In some years its fruiting is spectacular. It is much more commonly grown in gardens in the south east of the USA and on the West Coast, where it is represented by numerous cultivars and hybrids.

Water buffalo came within an ace of eating the *Bletilla*, left. (May)

Bletilla ochracea, a terrestrial orchid growing in a ravine. Shortly after finding this lovely plant it just missed being destroyed by a water buffalo, which, luckily, turned away at the last minute! (May)

Xuanyue or Gateway to Wudang Shan. (May 1983)

Chapter Seven

The Long White Mountains

In a remote area of north-east China on the border with North Korea stretches a mountain range known as the Changbai Shan or the Long White Mountains. Nearly four hundred years ago, from a valley on the outskirts of these mountains, there came a Manchu chieftain Nurbachi (1559-1626) who challenged the power of China, and whose son Abahai, after a determined struggle, conquered the Celestial Empire to found the Qing (Ching) Dynasty, which lasted from 1644 until 1911. For much of this time the Changbai Shan was regarded as sacred to the ancestors of the Manchus and, in theory at least, it was considered a sacrilege to trespass there. Indeed, a large area was reserved as an Imperial hunting park.

View of the upper Song Hua valley and waterfall under cloud. (July)

The mountains straddle the border at latitude 41° 40′N and longitude 128°E, their southern half in North Korea, their northern half in the Chinese province of Jilin (Kirin). The highest point is the Baitou Shan (White-headed Mountain), an extinct volcano of 2,749m (9,018ft), which, according to Chinese sources, last erupted in 1702 and previously in 1597 and 1668. Despite being the largest mountain in north-east China and the Korean peninsula, it bears no comparison with some of those in the opposite corner of the country in north-west Yunnan and Sichuan, for it is a gently rising dome of lavas and basalt. Indeed the rise to the summit is so gradual that, from a distance, it seems to be no height at all, hardly catching the eye except in winter when covered with snow. It is its long, low, winter outline that probably accounts for its name. At least that is one explanation, while another refers to the presence on the mountain of white limestone, which, on the Korean side, was once quarried. The outer cone of the volcano is also composed of a pale or whitish grit or pumice that, on a clear day, may well be visible from a distance. Even the Korean name refers to its colour: Paik-do-san meaning White Mountains.

Probably the first Europeans to visit the Changbai Shan were Jesuits who, at the beginning of the eighteenth century, were sent by the Emperor to these regions on a mapping mission. Almost two hundred years were to pass before the next Europeans came this way. This time it was

an Englishman, Henry, later Sir Henry, James of the Bombay Civil Service. In 1886 he made a journey into what was then known as Manchuria with two companions, one of whom, incidentally, was Sir Francis Younghusband, soldier, diplomat and explorer. They approached the mountain by way of Shenyang (Mukden) and Jilin (Kirin) and succeeded in climbing to the crater of the Baitou Shan. Neither James nor his companions had a particular interest in plants, though they did collect some five hundred dried specimens, most of which were sent to Kew for naming.

The first botanist in this region appears to have been the Russian plant explorer Vladimir Komarov in 1897, though his field of operations was south of the Changbai Shan, in North Korea. Likewise, in 1906, the American collector Frank Meyer travelled from Shenyang south to Dandong (Antong), crossing the Yalu river (Yalu Jiang) into North Korea and thence through wild mountainous terrain to the north-eastern corner of this country where he crossed the Tumen river and headed north to Vladivostok. This route must have taken him round the southern half of the Changbai Shan. Unfortunately for gardeners, Meyer was a collector of economic plants and he introduced few, if any, of the ornamental plants he would most certainly have seen on this journey. Since Meyer's time the forests, on the Chinese side of the border certainly, have received a great deal of attention from Chinese botanists and scientists, though with few, if any, benefits to ornamental horticulture in the West.

Mention must also be made of three Japanese botanists, Y Yabe, M Kitagawa and M Noda, all of whom, in the early part of the 20th century, made significant contributions to the study of the flora of this region. Yabe was employed by the South Manchurian Railway Company to carry out a survey of this area. His results were published in 1912. Kitagawa published his *Lineamenta Florae Manshuricae* in 1939 after many years of investigation. Noda made extensive collections on the Changbai Shan, under the Japanese rule of Manchukuo. His results were published (as a Manchurian flora) in 1972. The classic study of the Manchurian flora, however, was carried out

Panax ginseng, perhaps the most famous and expensive herb in Chinese traditional medicine. (July)

by the great Russian botanist Carl Maximowicz between 1854 and 1856, though in truth his work mainly concerned the Amur region on the borders of China (Heilongjiang) and Russia (south-east Siberia).

Today, on the northern side of the Changbai Shan, lies one of China's three world biosphere reserves,[1] which occupies some 1,965km[2] (760 square miles) rising from 800m (2,624ft) in the north west, to the summit of Baitou Shan. The importance of the reserve lies in the fine examples it contains of a whole range of types of forest and mountain vegetation. Here are found many plants enjoying a circumpolar distribution, being found in northern areas of North America, Europe and Asia. Such is its relatively untouched condition that it affords scientists an excellent opportunity to compare conditions here with those of similar areas in Russia, Europe and North America. It is, in short, a paradise of its kind to anyone interested in plants of the boreal (northern) regions.

The reserve, however, is not an island in a sea of cultivation. It is part of a vast region of coniferous and deciduous broad-leaved forest that compares favourably with the coniferous forests of the north-west United States and the Canadian Rockies and with the deciduous broad-leaved forests of eastern North America. They have many tree types in common, especially larch, pine, spruce, fir, maple, oak, poplar, ash, alder and birch. At the beginning of the 20th century, the forests of north-east China stretched in an almost continuous belt northwards from the Yalu river in the border regions of China and North Korea to the Amur river valley (Heilong Jiang valley), a distance of over 1,500km (930 miles). It must have been an extraordinary sight.[2]

When gardening friends heard that I intended travelling to the Changbai Shan in 1984 there were those among them who could not understand why this region should interest me. 'Surely', they reasoned, 'it is to south-west China that you should be heading'. They found it hard to believe that there was more to the Chinese flora than the treasures of the south-west and central provinces. These are the richest and therefore most rewarding areas in terms of

hardy ornamental plants, but the north-eastern provinces have their own special mix that is just as fascinating in its own way. This is particularly true of the Changbai Shan where the familiar and the unfamiliar are represented in almost equal numbers. Here are found many plants first introduced to western cultivation via Korea, Japan and south-east Siberia, where they are often equally common. Then there are plants that are no longer in cultivation and worthy of reintroducing. There are even plants that, to the best of my knowledge, have never been cultivated in the West even though they have undoubted ornamental merit.

Fascinating again, are those plants native here that are familiar to us in the northern areas of Britain, of which Mountain avens – *Dryas octopetala*, Bog whortleberry – *Vaccinium uliginosum* and Twin flower – *Linnaea borealis* are but three examples. Indeed, it is interesting to note that of the five hundred specimens collected by James and his party in 1886, no less than 160 were also to be found in Britain. Another aspect of the flora that is worthy of note is the number of plants native here that have closely related and occasionally look-alike versions in North America. According to recent figures published in China, the plant resources of the Changbai Shan are very abundant, somewhere in the region of 1,300 species of flowering plants and ferns being recorded, representing 122 families and 430 genera. These include three hundred plants of medicinal importance, of which the ginseng (*Panax ginseng*) is the most famous. Indeed, during the Qing Dynasty, if not before, each year the Emperor would send out an expedition to the Changbai Shan to collect roots of this herb for their own personal use.

---

1. The others being Wolong, home of the Giant Panda in Sichuan province, and Dinghushan in Guangdong province.

2. Indeed, a naturalist who visited this region in 1913 was overwhelmed: 'But the forest! Time and again it riveted one's attention as millions and millions of trees appeared, clothing the hills, ridge upon ridge, to the horizon. There was no break in the sea of green, there was no gap visible. It just rolled on and on, seemingly without end'. I seem to recall that something similar was once said about the forests of Eastern White pine (*Pinus strobus*) in the New England states of America. No doubt it could have been said of forests everywhere before man's ignorance and greed changed everything. Certainly, in the north-east provinces of China, massive resettlement projects, especially in the early 1930s, resulted in the large-scale clearance of forest, and we should be thankful that some areas in the Changbai Shan were left virtually intact.

Sweet William (*Dianthus barbatus*), native to S. Europe naturalised in Jilin province and elsewhere in N.E. China. (July)

Though we did not see ginseng growing wild, on our return to Changchun we were taken to the University of Agriculture where it was being cultivated in special plots for research purposes. We were told that it is used in the treatment of certain types of cancers as well as improving the blood circulation and as a tonic. It is also accredited with many other 'cures' and 'benefits', and a thriving business is based on this plant and its innumerable products. In our hotel shop, ginseng products for sale included soap, toothpaste, tablets, pills and a cordial.[3]

It is worth mentioning here the climate of the Changbai Shan as this is an important factor in the variety and distribution of its flora. It enjoys long cold winters and short cool summers with an average annual temperature ranging from 3°C (37.4°F) at the base of the reserve to -7°C (19.4°F) at the top. The annual maximum hardly reaches 10°C (50°F) in July, while the lowest temperature ever recorded is -44°C (-47.2°F).[4] Annual precipitation averages between 70 and 140cm (28-55in) according to site, much of it falling as snow or, between June and August, rain. At this time, too, hailstorms are not uncommon. The growing season in this region is, therefore, very short and once winter comes to an end new growth begins immediately and develops rapidly.[5]

In late June 1984, I left Beijing with a small party of plant enthusiasts and flew to Changchun, capital of Jilin province. Our visit had been arranged under the auspices of the Chinese International Tourist Service (CITS) whose guides accompanied us and were a constant help throughout our stay. We spent that night and the following day in Changchun, a rather dull and featureless industrial city set in a broad, flat landscape, much of it intensively cultivated.[6]

The local branch of the CITS had organised a visit to a local township that specialised in the cultivation of vegetables. The total land under cultivation here was 2,801 hectares (6,920 acres), of which just over half was used for vegetables, these being produced from spring through to autumn. Spring brought spinach, Chinese chives, spring onions, Chinese cabbages and radishes, whilst summer was the season for tomatoes, cucumbers, squash, aubergines, green peppers, dwarf green beans, potatoes and more Chinese cabbages. Climbing green beans were a speciality of late summer, while autumn brought turnips, carrots, and more potatoes and Chinese cabbages.

The Pure Moon township, as it was called, had a population of some 20,403 including a labour force of some 7,780, not all being employed on the land. Indeed, this was a well-organised and diverse economy with nine different enterprises, including brick factories, a quarry, a bakery and an animal husbandry farm where pigs, cows, chickens and deer were bred. The Sika deer were bred for their antlers, which were removed when 'in moss' for use in Chinese traditional medicine. They appeared to be well cared for, as were the fruit trees in an orchard nearby. Here, apples, apricots and grapes were being grown. Both orchards and fields in this township, as elsewhere in the Changchun area, are sheltered by trees planted along roadsides and above ditches. The most commonly used tree was the Pekin willow – *Salix babylonica* var. *pekinensis* (*S matsudana*), together with its weeping and umbrella (or globose) forms: 'Pendula' and 'Umbraculifera' respectively. The second year shoots of all three have a shiny, pale grey-brown or olive-brown bark. Both 'Pendula' and the typical tree reach 12m (40ft) or so eventually and are very hardy. Both are planted in Changchun together with a poplar, possibly *Populus cathayana*, which eventually reaches 20m (65ft) or more with a large, spreading crown and a dark, rugged bark. The Pekin willow, by the way, is commonly planted throughout north China especially in the Beijing area where it was recorded by, among other people, E H Wilson who, in 1909, collected cuttings from Tianjin 'near the racecourse'.

The plants for which I shall most remember the township of Pure Moon, however, were three dandelions, all of which grew on a rubbish dump outside the deer compound. They looked to be different from one another, and I was delighted when specimens of two of the three I had collected and dried were declared by Dr John Richards, an authority on these plants, to be new species yet to be named. The third specimen he identified as *Taraxacum platypecidum*.

To return briefly to fruit trees. It was in Jilin province near the old capital of Jilin itself that Frank Meyer located a peach tree said to be highly resistant to cold. It grew in the garden of a Buddhist temple nurtured by a priest who cheerfully allowed Meyer to take cuttings for which he paid $2. Meyer spent a Christmas in Changchun during his first expedition in 1906. He stayed there at the home of an Irish Presbyterian Missionary, which, with others of its kind, he regarded as 'little oases'. His was an opinion shared by other plant explorers many of whom had great cause to be thankful to such people.

We left Changchun at seven in the evening, pulled by a splendid steam engine heading east across the plains towards Jilin, beyond which we would travel south east in the direction of Tumen, the end of the line. We had one last look at the endless crops in their flat landscape

Iris ensata, common in the marshes around the Changbai Shan. (July)

Iris ensata, previously known under the name *I. kaempferi*, with velvety purple blooms. (July)

before closing the curtains of our four-berth compartment and dropping off to sleep.

It was some 350km (220 miles) and ten hours from Changchun to our destination Mingyuegou, a small town set among hills and close to a large dam project. I remember opening our curtains and seeing, in the pale light of dawn, hilly wooded country with valley bottoms speckled with purple irises and orange lilies. It was an exciting contrast to the landscape we had left behind.

We arrived at five in the morning, too early for breakfast in a town just awakening, and so our guides and those who had arrived to meet us from the Changbai Shan Reserve decided to take us to the artificial lake above the dam. This early opportunity to see the native vegetation suited our party down to the ground and we needed no second call to climb aboard the jeeps provided for the journey.

Although the original forest cover had long since been cleared, the low hills surrounding the lake had a dense cover of young trees, all native species, mostly planted I suspect, including oak (*Quercus mongolica*), pine (*Pinus koraiensis*) and larch (*Larix gmelinii* var. *olgensis*), with a prominent shrub layer of hazel (*Corylus sieboldiana* variety *mandshurica*), buckthorn (*Rhamnus davurica*) and hawthorn (*Crataegus pinnatifida*).

The herb layer was even richer and in marshy areas by the lake we found a number of plants familiar from Europe. These included Lesser reed mace (*Typha angustifolia*), Toad rush (*Juncus bufonius*), Water-whorl grass (*Catabrosa aquatica*), Amphibious bistort (*Persicaria amphibia*) and galingale (*Cyperus longus*), all wetland subjects in

Britain. In the drier herbage *Lilium pumilum* was plentiful, its orange Turk's cap flowers brilliant in the grass. As in the hills around the Great Wall near Beijing, it was accompanied here by the yellow trumpeted day lily (*Hemerocallis minor*). Equally impressive was a plant that reminded me of a rather refined version of the popular Sweet William (*Dianthus barbatus*) of our gardens at home. Its dense, domed heads of purple single flowers seemed to be everywhere, carried on sturdy erect stems in the grass. Although native of southern Europe, the Sweet William is known to have been introduced and naturalised (gone wild) in a number of far flung parts of the world including, apparently, north-east China. Who introduced it I wonder? Perhaps a homesick missionary was responsible. It was common enough here and looked quite at home among herbs of more certain native origin.

The silky seed heads of a Pasque flower – *Pulsatilla cernua* variety *koreana*, caught my eye. It was plentiful in grassy sections over a wide area. The leaves were quite unlike those of the British native species *P vulgaris* in being larger with broader segments and quite smooth (glabrous) except for some hairs on the leaf stalks.[7]

Where streams slipped into the lake occasionally, large areas of flanking bog and similarly wet areas occurred, some of these intersected by smaller streams. It was a home for a variety of perennials one of which, *Iris ensata*, dominated the scene with its bold flowers.[8] This was the big purple flower that we had seen from the train that morning, splashing the green marsh grass like some vast Monet canvas.

3. I was interested to read in a report on herbal pharmacology in China, prepared by the American Herbal Pharmacology Delegation to China in 1974, the following statement regarding its analysis of this plant: 'None of the many pharmacological activities, reported in over 500 original literature reports on *Panax ginseng*, would account for the uses stated for this plant in traditional Chinese medicine'. Nevertheless there are those even in the West who would swear by it.

4. This is a relatively mild situation compared with the average temperatures for Jilin province as a whole which are -18°C (0.4°F) in winter (January) and 20°C (68°F) in summer (July).

5. This is particularly noticeable in woody plants, especially trees, and explains why some species at least are unsatisfactory under British conditions, where their newly emergent growths are subject to damage by spring frosts. This is less of a problem in northern areas of North America, especially in the north east of the United States and Canada where many of these trees and shrubs find a home from home.

6. Changchun was once home to Pu Yi (1905-1967) the last of the Qing emperors. For seven years, until his death, he worked as a gardener in the Beijing Botanic Garden.

7. It became established in British cultivation from seed collected from Mingyuegou. Two plants once growing well in an acid sandy soil in my garden, while plants in the rock garden at Kew flowered for the first time in 1986 producing nodding lavender-purple silky bells on erect stems.

8. Previously known as *I kaempferi*, this is one of the most spectacular and popular of its kind in western gardens where it is normally planted in moist situations, such as the margins of pools and streams. There are now many named selections available in cultivation, varying in size and colour, many of them originating in Japan where this plant has long been admired and grown. Its beauty has caused many a plantsman poet to put pen to paper, including that great gardener A T Johnson who referred to *I ensata* and its forms as 'those miracles of beauty and infinite grace which leave all who behold them agasp in silent awe'. Had Johnson seen this iris wild in these northern marshes I believe he would have been lost for words. *I ensata* is also found wild in North Korea, eastern Siberia and Japan.

Lilium dauricum. Brilliant blooms on grassy slopes and roadsides. (July)

Lilium dauricum, said to be the first Asiatic lily introduced to Western cultivation in the 18th century. (July)

Here it formed stout clumps of narrow, green leaves topped by the stiffly erect flower stems up to 1m (3ft) tall, each bearing usually a single, large flower 12.5cm (5in) across of velvety Royal purple with a conspicuous golden-yellow flash at the base of the falls.

Almost as common as the iris, but more localised, was a loosestrife – *Lysimachia thyrsiflora*, a perennial forming clumps and colonies of erect stems up to 60cm (2ft) tall with pairs of lance-shaped leaves. The yellow, star-like flowers were quite small, borne in long-stalked clusters (thyrses) in the leaf axils at the middle of the stems. This plant particularly interested me because it is also a rare British native found mainly in northern England and southern and eastern Scotland. It has an extensive distribution in the cool temperate regions from North America across Europe into Asia. It was the first of many plants that we were to find in and around the Changbai Shan enjoying what plant geographers call a circumpolar distribution. This species grew in shallow water and in wet places generally, while on banks, hillsides and in less watery places we found *L clethroides*, a loosestrife of a very different kind.[9] This also formed patches from its far-creeping underground stems (rhizomes), but the leafy stems, up to 1m (3ft) tall, ended in a dense spike of white flowers arching like a swan's neck.

From Mingyuegou to the lodge in the Changbai Shan Reserve is a distance of some 160km (100 miles). Our route lay south over ranges of rolling hills and through wide valleys where large areas of cultivation surrounded villages and the occasional small town. Wherever the road passed through hills, the native vegetation filled ravines and clothed steep hillsides and it was in such an area that we made our first stop. For some time we had glimpsed a large, bright orange flower in the roadside herbage and, being unable to identify this plant in passing, we requested a short break. The flower in question turned out to be a lily – *Lilium dauricum*. It was a stout-stemmed, leafy plant, up to 76cm (30ins) tall, with a terminal umbel of five to six large, erect, cup-shaped flowers, the segments spreading and a brilliant orange-scarlet, darkly spotted within. It was, together with *Iris ensata*, the most striking flower we saw during our visit.[10] It was common in sunny, grassy places throughout our journey and, in places, we saw it growing on slopes above marshes where *Iris ensata* flowered. The bold orange of the one and the purple of the other made an unforgettable picture.

Matching the lily in brilliance, but with flowers of a very different size and shape, was *Lychnis fulgens*, a superb campion that shared the same grassy areas as the lily, especially by the road. These flowers were 5cm (2in) across, the five spreading petals deeply divided and a fiery scarlet in colour. Several flowers were borne at the summit of an erect, downy, 30-60cm (1-2ft) long stem. Judging by the limited rootstock and single stem I suspect that this is a short-lived perennial in the wild as it is in cultivation.[11]

9. Unlike *Lysimachia thyrsiflora*, *L. clethroides* is a favourite garden plant for moist soils especially by waterside, though it can form large colonies in time and may need controlling. It is native to Japan and probably North Korea as well as north-east China, and was introduced to western cultivation as early as 1869.

10. *L dauricum* has a wide distribution in north-east Asia. It was probably the first Asiatic lily to be introduced into western cultivation, being grown in the garden of Peter Collinson at Mill Hill, London in 1745, introduced, it is said, from Siberia.

11. Although long cultivated in the West it is now something of a rarity, most often represented by one of its hybrids. Of these, *L x haageana* (*L coronata x L fulgens*) and *L. 'Arkwrightii'* (*L chalcedonica x L x haageana*) are not uncommon. Most of these hybrids have the same short-lived tendency as *L fulgens* and need to be grown fairly regularly from cuttings. They do, however, produce plenty of seed resulting in seedlings with equally brilliant flowers. Probably the best of these hybrids is 'Arkwright's Vesuvius', which has large orange-red flowers and dark brownish foliage on 30-45cm (12-18in) stems. It is also somewhat longer-lived than *L fulgens*, though equally beloved by slugs.

Lychnis x haageana in a Birmingham garden. Like its parents (*L coronata* x *L fulgens*), this famous hybrid can be short lived, shorter still should slugs or snails locate it. (June)

Lychnis fulgens with fiery scarlet flowers, shared the same grass verges and banks as *Lilium dauricum*. Plants of this splendid campion grown from seed collected at the time were, for a while, grown in the author's garden. (July)

Lychnis fulgens in the author's garden, one of the brightest of all campions. (July)

Matteuccia struthiopteris at Dawyck Gardens, Scotland. It is well named the Shuttlecock or Ostrich Plume fern. A common fern in the Changbai Shan. (June)

In a moist roadside ditch we found an attractive Globe flower – *Trollius ledebourii*, combining very effectively with drifts of the Shuttlecock or Ostrich-plume fern – *Matteuccia struthiopteris*. The last named is found throughout the northern areas of the cool temperate zone and I had seen it previously in Canada and north-east Turkey. It is hardy and easy especially in a moist soil where it suckers freely, in time forming extensive colonies. The stout clumps of bold fronds look exactly like giant green shuttlecocks. *Trollius ledebourii* here reached 30-45cm (12-18in) with multi-petalled, pale orange or orange-yellow flowers. The other perennial to catch our eye, though hardly ornamental, was

Paris verticillata growing in forest at the foot of the Changbai Shan. It is similar in some respects to P *polyphylla* of the Himalaya and south-west China. (July)

Veronicastrum sibiricum, in the Changbai Shan. It is rare in cultivation where it is replaced by the North American *V. virginicum* and its cultivars. (July)

Paris verticillata, similar in some respects to the Himalayan P *polyphylla* with numerous leaves forming a whorl or ring around the stem, but more closely related to P *quadrifolia*.

Here too by the roadside flourished stout clumps of *Veronicastrum sibiricum*, a relative of *Veronica* with 1m (3ft) tall stems, whorls of long leaves at intervals and a slender terminal spike of blue flowers. Of the woody plants we found during this initial foray, I shall mention just a few, beginning with the most obvious – *Sorbaria kirilowii*.[12] In some respects like a giant spiraea, this strong-growing shrub forms large thickets of suckering stems up to 2.5m (8ft), with large pinnate leaves up to 30cm (12in) long and bold terminal plumes of creamy-white flowers.

Competing with the sorbaria in flower was a lilac – *Syringa reticulata* variety *mandshurica* (*S amurensis*).[13] It was a large shrub or small tree to 6m (20ft) forming bold clumps and thickets on the forest margins, especially in damp areas. The leaves are slender pointed, not unlike a Black poplar in shape, while the creamy-white, privet-scented flowers are crowded into irregular heads up to 15cm (6in) or more long.

In the woodland just above the road we found two trees that caused us a lot of pleasure. One of these was the Manchurian walnut – *Juglans mandshurica*.[14] It was a widely branched tree up to 12m (40ft) with stout, glandular

Sorbaria kirilowii, a giant relative of spiraea with suckering stems up to 3m (9ft) or more. These are clothed with deeply divided (pinnate) leaves similar in shape to those of a Mountain ash – *Sorbus*, hence *sorbifolia*. (July)

Acer triflorum in author's garden. In some years the autumn leaves can be yellow and in others orange or red tinted. (November)

hairy shoots and pinnate leaves up to 60cm (2ft) long. These were made up of some thirteen to nineteen toothed and slender-pointed leaflets downy beneath. Some of the young trees, especially two- to three-year-old seedlings, had longer leaves still and later appeared very conspicuous in the thicket, especially near streams and along the gravelly banks of rivers, in which places this walnut seemed particularly abundant. Although inferior in quality to those of the Persian or English walnut (*J regia*), the nuts of *J mandshurica* have been eaten in north-east China and the Amur region of Siberia where it grows wild.

Even more exciting than the walnut however was *Acer triflorum*, which, ever since I first set eyes on it in the Hillier Arboretum in Hampshire in the 1960s, has remained one of my favourite maples. Here it occurred as scattered individuals of some 6-7.5m (20-25ft). Apart from north-east China, it is native to North and South Korea and has been introduced from there several times in recent years by various American expeditions. Few maples in my opinion can match *A triflorum* in autumn when its foliage, in some forms certainly, turns from yellow to a brilliant orange-red or crimson, equal if not superior to that of *A griseum*. Like that species, *A triflorum* has leaves with three leaflets, while the bark, although peeling when mature, is darker and vertically fissured.[15]

---

12. This is a tough, hardy, reliable, free-flowering shrub, adaptable to most soils and situations. It is not, however, suited to small gardens or restricted areas in larger gardens, its suckering habit being difficult to contain. It is rare in British cultivation, if present at all.

13. This is rarely seen in cultivation in the West, being inferior to the type – *S reticulata*, a native of Japan. It is also less satisfactory, being subject to frost damage in spring except in colder more northerly regions. It is more often seen in cultivation in the United States and Canada where its winter hardiness is particularly appreciated by gardeners in the more northerly states and provinces.

14. Due to its hardiness, it is able to tolerate colder climates than *J regia*, and is said for this reason to be cultivated in parts of Russia, northern Europe and the Canadian plains. It is not, to my knowledge cultivated except as an ornamental in the United States, despite having been introduced by Meyer in 1916. He believed it to be of value as a hardy shade tree, possibly also as stock for the Persian walnut in colder areas. The tallest specimen recorded in Britain is a tree at Syon Park in London, which measured 17m (55ft) in 2002.

15. *Acer triflorum* prefers an acid soil and is comparatively slow growing, developing a relatively compact head of branches, making it a good lawn specimen. In addition to its habit, autumn foliage and winter bark, it is a hardy tree, though unhappy in exposed situations. A tree in my garden in Hampshire – planted in 1984 from seed wild collected in S. Korea – is now over 6m tall. It colours richly in November and is equally attractive, in a more subtle way, in spring. A specimen at Dunloe Castle Hotel Arboretum, Killarney, Ireland, measured 12.5m (41ft) in 2002.

Village on the road to Changbai Shan. (July)

Many of the houses in villages we passed through had curious chimneys made from hollowed tree trunks, sometimes with a metal casing or supporting bands. (July)

Populus tremula variety davidiana, a Chinese variety of the European Aspen. (July)

Some of the villages we drove through in the early part of our journey were occupied by people of Korean nationality. Many of their houses had curious chimney stacks made from a hollowed tree trunk, sometimes with a metal casing or supporting bands. This structure stood separately from the cottage and was connected to the hearth within by an underground flue. Chickens, ducks and livestock wandered at will, often occupying the main road, sections of which were unsurfaced and deeply rutted. Fringing the road in places, and in wet areas generally, grew an aspen – Populus tremula variety davidiana (P davidiana), a Chinese version of our native species differing principally in the shallower teeth of the leaves. It was a tall, smooth, pale-barked, slender-stemmed tree of 12-18m (40-60ft), its leaves in constant motion and was first discovered in the mountains north-east of Beijing, by the French missionary-naturalist Armand David, after whom it is named. Curiously, it also grows wild in west-China and south-east Tibet.

Around midday we arrived at the town of Antu where we stopped for lunch in a local guest house. Afterwards, I was challenged to a game of table tennis by our national guide, a young, slenderly-built man who showed remarkable agility in soundly defeating me.

Three of the most abundant roadside shrubs over much of our journey were Spiraea salicifolia, Rosa acicularis and the Amur maple – Acer tataricum subspecies ginnala. The first of these is a vigorous shrub of 1.5m (5ft), sometimes more, suckering to form dense extensive colonies in the same way as S alba and S latifolia in north-eastern North America, and S douglasii on the American Pacific coast. The leaves of Spirea salicifolia are green, lance shaped, sharply toothed, up to 8cm (3in) long, and densely clothed the erect, smooth shoots, many of which ended in an erect, crowded head (panicle), some 10cm (4in) long, of rose-pink flowers. It has a remarkable distribution in the wild, occurring from central Europe, through Russia and Mongolia to north China, Korea and Japan.[16]

Acer tataricum subspecies *ginnala*, the Amur maple. A fruiting branch of a bush growing by the road near Antu in south-east Jilin. Both leaves and fruit colour richly in autumn. (July)

Clematis ianthina, a slender-stemmed climber growing in roadside scrub near Antu in south-east Jilin. (July)

Rosa acicularis, like the spiraea, is a suckering shrub forming thickets of 2m (6ft) stems, the older ones densely clad with slender spines and bristles. Both flowers and young fruits were present, the former 3-5cm (1¼ -2in) across and rose-pink or reddish in colour. The hips were small, rounded and orange with spreading entire sepals. Apart from at the roadside, it was widespread by ditches and field margins and appeared to be the most common rose in the area.[17]

Not surprisingly, considering its northerly distribution, the Amur maple – *Acer tataricum* subspecies *ginnala*, is seen at its best in the colder regions of the world, though it is adaptable to a wide range of soils and situations. In southern Jilin it seemed to be everywhere, taking the role of our native Field maple (*A campestre*) as a field margin shrub as well as occurring in a variety of other habitats. It tended to be shrubby in growth, forming large dense mounds, clumps and thickets up to 4m (13ft) or more with occasional multi-stemmed trees of 5 to 6m (16 to 20ft). Some were crowded with pendulous clusters of red-tinted immature fruits that highlighted the otherwise green leafy branches. The leaves were coarsely toothed and typically three lobed, the middle lobe longest and slender pointed, glossy dark green above, paler below. In the wild, apart from north China, it is found in central China, Korea and Japan.[18]

At one point, not long after leaving Antu, we stopped to examine a climber garlanding the roadside scrub. It turned out to be *Clematis mandshurica*, an herbaceous species closely related to *C terniflora* (under which species it is sometimes included as a variety), and to the European *C recta*. Supported by the scrub, its stems reached 2m (6ft), with deeply divided (pinnate) leaves and showers of small, white, narrow-tepalled flowers that gave off a heavy perfume. It was an attractive plant of its kind and seemed quite common in south-east Jilin.

Different again was *Clematis ianthina*, which also grew in roadside thickets and scrub. This too seemed to be herbaceous or semi-herbaceous in growth, its stems reaching 2-3m (6-10ft) with support. Its leaves were pinnate and in the axils of some of these occurred a single nodding flower on a short stalk. Compared with most other clematis, the flowers of this plant are unusual in being pitcher-shaped, 2.5-4cm (1-1½ in) long and woolly hairy on the outside. They comprise four deep-purple tepals that are pointed and recurved, the whole resembling a curious elfin cap. It was the first time I had seen this variety in the flesh. It is closely related to *C fusca*, which I remember seeing at the Hillier Arboretum in the 1970s where it grew for several years on a pergola. *C. ianthina* was once regarded as a variety of this species (*C. fusca* var. *violacea*).

16. Like many of its clan, this is a tough, hardy shrub responding readily to hard pruning each year in February, the resulting shoots bearing larger flowerheads. Left to its own devices, it quickly overruns lesser fry and its flowerheads are smaller and less effective. It is not suitable for small gardens or restricted sites and, so long as it can see the sun, is best used in those sites where other shrubs have been tried and failed. Spirea salicifolia has been cultivated in Britain since the sixteenth century and in some places has escaped and naturalised, especially on roadsides. It is sometimes referred to in Britain as Bridewort, presumably because its flowers were once popular as bouquets for summer brides.

17. Although attractive in flower and free fruiting, this rose is inferior in merit to the similarly suckering *R rugosa*. Its hardiness and suckering habit, however, are worth considering in cold northerly areas where it has some use as a hedge. It must also be a strong candidate for planting on steep banks to help arrest erosion. It is widespread in the wild from northern Europe, eastwards to Siberia, north China, Korea and Japan. It is also found in North America, and I was reminded of these Jilin thickets in October 1985, when in Alberta, Canada, I saw it equally common in similar situations.

18. In cultivation this is a free-growing maple, though lacking the grace of *A palmatum* and its relatives. There are other attributes, however, apart from its hardiness, the most ornamental being its autumn colours, mostly yellows or reds. In common with other maples grown for their autumn display, it is variable in this respect, some seedlings being better than others. In North America, where this maple is more commonly grown than in Britain, seedlings have been selected for the brilliance or reliability of their autumn colour. There is also, in cultivation, a dwarf, densely-branched bushy form reaching 1.5m (5ft) and capable of rich tints in autumn; named 'Durand Dwarf', it originated in the Durand Eastman Park, Rochester, New York before 1955.

In British gardens, it is sometimes seen growing in shade, which it can tolerate quite well. The best autumn colours, however, are encouraged by warmth and sun; the finest display I ever saw was on a specimen growing in a sunny exposed situation on the acid sand of a garden in Norfolk, England. Perhaps its best use in cultivation is as a background planting. Several plants in a group will, in time, form an impressive mound of lush, glossy green summer foliage. The largest specimen in British cultivation is a tree at Gatton Park in Surrey, which measured 10.5m (35ft) in 1977.

View from the guest lodge in the Changbai Shan Reserve looking towards the waterfall at the head of the Song Hua valley. The woodland is almost entirely birch – *Betula ermanii*. In the distance, left of centre, the tip of the Baitou Shan can just be seen. (July)

The Changbai Shan Reserve

We made no further stops that afternoon although we were often tempted. Towards the end of the day we found ourselves following a long, straight dirt road that was dry and dusty. Eventually we pulled up outside the main entrance to the Changbai Shan Reserve, which here, certainly, had a high post and wire boundary fence. After the formalities were seen to, we were allowed to drive through the gates into the reserve. Now the road climbed steadily through dense forest in which grew many exciting plants. Once we stopped to speak to another British group of naturalists who, like ourselves, were visiting the Changbai Shan to see her flora and fauna. Their botanical leader was an old acquaintance of mine, General Secretary of the Royal Society for Nature Conservation, Dr Franklyn Perring, who was at that time engaged on the monumental *Atlas of the British Flora*. His party was also staying at the reserve lodge and during the next few days, we had several meetings, usually late at night, when we discussed plants seen and swapped

information and opinions.

The lodge was a relatively new building of two storeys situated in the valley of the Song Hua river at an altitude of 1,700m (5,577ft). Conditions were relatively spartan but quite adequate for our purposes. Our meals revolved around eggs, fried or boiled, rice or vegetable soups and various fish and chicken dishes. These were often cooked with local herbs and accompanied by various green vegetables plus one or two concoctions of uncertain origin.

The lodge was our home for eight nights and each morning we would set out to explore a different area. The valley of the Song Hua river is on a north-south axis, and from the main entrance to the reserve at 985m (3,229ft), it is possible by means of road and track to ascend through four distinct zones of vegetation to the summit of Baitou Shan itself at 2,749m (9,018ft).

The largest zone is one of mixed coniferous and broad-leaved deciduous forest that occurs below 1,000m (3,300ft). Over much of the area the soil is a brown forest soil, fertile and deep. The most abundant conifer in

The main road to the Changbai Shan Reserve, a strip of dust in summer flanked by forest of variable quality. (July)

The guest lodge in the Changbai Shan Reserve is situated in the valley of the Song Hua river at an altitude of 1,700m (5,577ft). It is surrounded by birch forest – *Betula ermanii*, in which spruce, fir and poplar occur mainly in groves or as scattered individuals. (July)

Pinus koraiensis at the Morris Arboretum, Philadelphia. This is the common pine of the Changbai Shan. (April)

this zone is the Korean pine — *Pinus koraiensis*, a magnificent tree here, sometimes dominant, but mainly sharing land with other tree species.[19] Occasional specimens we saw approached 30m (100ft) in height, but they were mostly in the region of 21-24m (69-79ft) tall. Trees in isolation were often shapely in habit with horizontally spreading branches and a reddish-grey, rough and scaly bark. Elsewhere, it was in a highly competitive situation and less shapely as a consequence. The needles of this pine are carried in bundles of five, spreading and 8-13cm (3-5in) long. They are triangular in cross section and finely toothed, green on the outer surface and bluish-white from the lines of stomata on the two inner surfaces. The cones, which we did not examine, are said to be short-stalked, 9-14cm (3½ -5½ in) long, blue-green when young turning to grey-brown on ripening. This must be one of the most abundant pines, occurring in Japan (Honshu), Korea, north-east China and east Siberia. A valuable timber tree in north-east Asia, its wood being

compared with the Eastern White pine (*P strobus*) of North America, the Korean pine has suffered much from exploitation in the past and continues to be felled in great numbers in some places. We were told that many of the best trees outside the Changbai Shan Reserve had been removed during the Japanese occupation in the 1930s.[20]

This pine has another economic use in its edible nuts or kernels. These have been used since time immemorial wherever the tree occurs in the wild, and in recent years they have been exported by the Chinese to the United States and elsewhere. According to some authorities, these Chinese pine nuts are inferior to those of the European pignolia (*P pinea*) but are desirable nonetheless.

There was another pine in this lower zone, around 700m (2,295ft), much less common and more localised in its occurrence, and one we immediately recognised from the warm reddish-brown or orange-brown bark of its upper stem and main branches as *P densiflora*. Not unlike *P sylvestris*, it was a fine looking tree, often growing on low red sandy hills, where it occasionally reached 24m (80ft) or more in height.[21]

There grows here another conifer, a rather attractive spruce — *Picea koraiensis*, isolated trees growing to 20m (65ft) with a spire-like crown and blue or grey-blue foliage. The young shoots are green, smooth on strong leading shoots, glandular downy on laterals, becoming greyish-brown and grooved in the second year. The leaves are linear, 1.5-1.7cm (½- ¾ in) long (on side shoots), with a sharp point (prickly to the touch), slightly compressed, four sided, with lines of stomata on all surfaces but conspicuous only on young leaves. They are widely parted below the shoot, densely crowded and lying forward above. Restricted in the wild to North Korea, north-east China and east Siberia (in the Ussuri region), it is a distinct and ornamental spruce now much planted in parks and city areas in north China.

Picea koraiensis; the prickly grey-blue foliage of this attractive spruce. We saw occasional trees in the Changbai Shan area, and it is much planted in parks and city areas in north China. (July)

Ulmus laciniata, a distinctive elm here in Hokkaido, Japan. (October)

Handsome though these conifers were in isolation, it was the deciduous trees that dominated. They occurred in great numbers and in fascinating variety, oaks, limes, elms, maples and birch being particularly common. The oak was *Quercus mongolica*, the Mongolian oak, which is distributed in the wild over a wide area of north-east Asia, including Korea and northern Japan.[22] It was a handsome tree, specimens of 20m (65ft) and above being common. No doubt even finer specimens outside the reserve had long since been removed. Some trees had superb straight stems with a thick, dark, fissured bark. The bold leaves were obovate, regularly lobed and with two ear-like lobes (auricles) at the tapered base. They varied in size from 10-15cm (4-6in), those of sucker growths up to 25cm (10in) or more.

Of elms we saw two species, whilst a third, *Ulmus macrocarpa*, we had seen plentifully at various points on our journey from Mingyuegou. The most common species in the lower zone was *U japonica* (*propinqua*), a tree of 9-15m (30-50ft) with smooth, grey shoots liberally marked with small lenticels. The buds were small with brown outer scales. Its leaves were obovate up to 11cm (4¼ in) including a short, downy stalk. They had a slender-pointed apex and a noticeably oblique base, one side cuneate, the other rounded. The margins were double toothed while the surfaces were smooth and shining above, paler and smooth beneath except for tufts of white

Quercus mongolica showing the characteristic fissured bark of the trunk. Nowhere did we see a large specimen, these presumably having been felled many years ago. (July)

hairs in the vein axils. It was particularly common by the roadside and in the fringes of the forest.[23]

Remarkably distinct in leaf was *U laciniata*, which occurred here mainly as a small tree of 9m (30ft). From an oblique rounded base, the leaves gradually broadened to the apex where there occurred from three to five tail-like projections or prongs. Both surfaces were roughly hairy (scabrid), more especially above. This curious

19. In cultivation *P koraiensis* is one of the hardiest pines with a loosely conical habit of growth. In Britain, where it is rare, it appears to grow best in the north and west. In southern districts it is often slow growing and sickly looking. Certainly this is how I remember several young specimens at the Hillier Arboretum in Hampshire in the 1970s. In North America it is more successful, in colder areas at least, and is accordingly more widely planted. The largest specimen in British cultivation is a tree at Crarae, Argyll, which measured 22m (72ft) in 1994.

20. One recent source refers to the presence in the 1920s of pines up to 50m (164ft) tall.

21. *Pinus densiflora* is native to a wide area of N.E. China as well as Korea (North and South), Japan and the Russian Far East. It has been referred to by the Chinese under *P. sylvestris* as var. *syvestriformis* and closely resembles the Scots pine in leaf, bark and cone. In cultivation it is less tolerant of alkaline soils. The largest example in Britain and Ireland is a tree of 21m at the RHS Gardens, Wisley (2000).

22. The Mongolian oak was first recorded by Lord Macartney's Embassy to the Emperor Qian Long in 1793. According to Sir George Staunton, it was one of two oaks seen on their journey from Beijing to Chengde (Jehol), where the Emperor had a

summer residence. This is a rare tree in British cultivation where it is noted for its remarkably large leaves. It is usually represented by a Japanese variety, *grosseserrata*, which is rather more adaptable to our climate than the type. Even so, both are better represented in northern areas of the United States, especially in New England where the variety certainly thrives, there being an excellent specimen in the Arnold Arboretum, Massachusetts, which in 1972 was 18.5m (61ft) with a girth at chest height of 200cm (79in). One of the best specimens of *Q mongolica* I have seen in Europe grows in the Arboretum des Barres at Nogent-sur-Vernisson in France. Visiting the arboretum on my honeymoon in 1978, I picked from under this tree a dead leaf fully 30cm (12in) long. The tallest tree in British cultivation is a specimen at Arley Castle, Worcestershire, which measured 15m (50ft) in 1992.

23. *Ulmus japonica* (*propinqua*) is native to north-east Asia including Japan, where it reaches 30m (100ft) or more. Even before Dutch Elm disease, this was a rare species in the West, despite having been introduced to the Arnold Arboretum, Massachusetts, as long ago as 1895. The tallest example of this elm in British cultivation is a tree of 15m (50ft) measured on Sussex University Campus in 2002. A similar tree grows in the Hillier Arboretum in Hampshire where it shows no effects of Dutch Elm Disease (I hope I am not tempting fate).

Bee hives in a clearing in the Changbai Shan. (July)

A bee keeper in the forest outside the Changbai Shan Reserve. A nomadic people, the bee keepers come here each year when the limes (Tilia species) are in flower. (July)

species is related to our native Wych elm (U glabra), but is confined in the wild to north-east Asia including Japan. I have never met with it in cultivation, where its leaves would immediately distinguish it. Not all the leaves, however, were conspicuously pronged though all were toothed. Most specimens by the road and along ditches had been coppiced, resulting in a large head of strong shoots with large leaves some of which were quite striking in effect.

Equally striking were the leaves of the Manchurian lime – *Tilia mandshurica*, which was fairly well distributed throughout the hills below 1,200m (3,935ft).[24] This is the north-east Asian version of the European Silver lime (T tomentosa), and like that species has its leaves covered beneath with a close, silvery-white felt. It is, however, an ultimately smaller, more graceful tree, less stiffly branched and with leaves more coarsely toothed with long-pointed teeth. The largest trees we saw were in the region of 15m (50ft), but most were only half this with strongly arching branches almost weeping at their extremities and clothed with bold, lush foliage 8-15cm (3-6in) long, beneath which the fragrant, creamy-white flowers hung. In the wild this is the most widespread of east Asian limes, especially in eastern Siberia.

Accompanying this tree in the Changbai Shan was T *amurensis*, the Amur lime, a splendid stately tree of broad columnar habit when isolated. We saw several specimens of 18m (60ft) or more but these were in the forest and their shape consequently uneven. More pleasing were small trees growing on the forest margins or in clearings, where their spreading branches curved gracefully downwards at the extremities. The leaves are relatively small and neat, not unlike those of our native Small-leaved lime (T cordata), to which species T amurensis is closely related. Its fragrant white flowers are borne in clusters above and below the leaves. It is found in the wild in eastern Siberia, north-east China and Korea in which places, together with T mandshurica, it is an important bee tree. Indeed, in the forests outside the Changbai Shan Reserve, we saw many clearings where hives had been set up for the lime flower season. We were told by our local guide that the bee keepers are a nomadic people who each year in June arrive from many parts of China with their bees. They stay until the limes finish flowering before moving elsewhere. Their hives, unlike the curious hollowed logs I had previously seen in Yunnan, are similar to the common British version, made of slatted wood with flat roofs.[25]

24. The Manchurian lime is rarely seen cultivated in Britain, being confined to a few arboreta and specialist collections. A tree introduced to Kew in 1871 eventually grew to 13.5m (45ft) before dying in 1921. Its young growths in early spring were frequently damaged by frost, a common problem in Britain with many trees from these northerly regions. A replacement, however, has grown, though sporadically. It is a tree that undoubtedly grows best in a continental climate. A fine example of this lime grows at Thorpe Perrow Arboretum in Yorkshire, which in 2004 measured 15m (50ft). It is just one of several species planted there in a remarkable lime avenue.

25. T amurensis is rarely seen in British cultivation; it is less successful than T cordata and T japonica, which are equal in merit and flourish better in our climate. A tree at Birr Castle in Co. Offally, Ireland measured 11m (36ft) in 1990.

26. This maple is rare in western cultivation where it is a hardy and free-growing tree

especially suited to shade. I remembered it from the Hillier Arboretum in the 1970s where young trees, from northern Japan probably, grew fast and furious.

27. A tegmentosum has the same bold beauty as the moosewood and serves the same purpose in the garden. Like A pensylvanicum, it is shade tolerant and is an excellent woodland or understorey tree on slightly acid soils. It is, however, curiously rare in cultivation, in Britain certainly, where it is found in a few collections. This is another tree that I first saw in the Hillier Arboretum, which, when I last saw it in 2006, was 8m (26ft) and seemed happy enough. In the United States there are said to be fine specimens at the Arnold Arboretum and in a few other collections. It is native to east Siberia, north-east China and Korea and was first discovered and named by the Russian collector Carl Maximowicz, who found it in the Amur region in the 1850s. Indeed, this famous collector was responsible for collecting and naming a great number of the plants of north-east Asia, many of which are found in the Changbai Shan area.

Acer caudatum ssp. *ukurunduense*, a small- to medium-sized maple of the understorey with sycamore-like leaves and unusual erect candle-like flower racemes. It was common in woodland on the lower slopes of Changbai Shan. (July)

The maples of this zone are several, each attractive in its own right. At the time of our visit *Acer caudatum* ssp. *ukurunduense* was in bloom, its small greenish-yellow flowers carried in erect, downy, candle-like clusters (racemes) 9cm (3½ in) long on 4-5cm (1½ -2in) long stalks above the branches. The leaves were densely hairy beneath and five-lobed, rather coarsely toothed especially on sucker shoots when they resembled those of a sycamore (*A pseudoplatanus*). This is the north-east Asian counterpart of the eastern American Mountain maple *A spicatum*, and is very similar except that the leaves of the latter are more usually three-lobed and glabrous. It was common in the forest where it made a large shrub or small, multi-stemmed tree to 7.5m (25ft) with wide-spreading branches spaced almost in tiers. Where competition was fierce occasional specimens reached as much as 15m (50ft).[26]

Another maple that was common in the forests of the lower areas of the reserve, was *A tegmentosum*, which is the north-east Asian counterpart of the eastern American moosewood – *A pensylvanicum*. It was of similar size 4.5-6m (15-20ft), occasionally up to 10m (32ft) high, with branches stiffly ascending at first, spreading and becoming more graceful with age. The younger shoots were smooth

and pale green, while bark of the stem and main branches was pale green with silvery striations. The leaves were up to 17cm (6½ in) across with three large lobes and two smaller basal lobes, all coarsely toothed and slender pointed. The leaves of vigorous shoots and sucker growths were often larger. They were green and smooth on both surfaces, the axils of the veins beneath with small plugs or protuberances.[27]

A tegmentosum was almost as common as *A caudatum* ssp. *ukurunduense* in the forest and wandering through these trees I was reminded of my first visit to Canada in 1980 when, in a forest above St Adel near Montreal, I first saw *A pensylvanicum* and *A spicatum* growing together in the wild. The Changbai Shan forests, however, were far richer in maples, for four other species were growing here fairly commonly in glades and on margins.

Acer tegmentosum, a common understorey species in the forests of the Changbai Shan. (July)

Acer pseudosieboldianum, a common understorey maple in the woodlands of the Changbai Shan. (July)

A pseudosieboldianum was also a common understorey, especially in moist places where it was a multi-stemmed shrub up to 8m (26ft) high and across.[28] Its rounded leaves, 12.5cm (5in) long including stalk, with a heart-shaped (cordate) base, were nine lobed to half way or more, the

lobes oblanceolate, long pointed and jaggedly double toothed. In autumn these colour brightly before falling.[29]

A barbinerve and *A tschonoskii* are two small tree maples that occur scattered through these forests. The former reaches 7m (22ft) with elegant arching branches not unlike some Japanese maples of the *A palmatum* group. The downy, reddish shoots carry broad-based, three-lobed leaves to 7cm (2¾ in) long on bright red, downy stalks up to 9cm (3½ in) long. The leaves are softly downy, especially beneath where whitish hairs clothe the veins and crowd the vein axils – hence *barbinerve*. This maple had already flowered and carried pendulous clusters of downy-stalked fruits with wide-spreading wings. *A tschonoskii* was also a graceful tree of similar size to the last, with arching branches and bright red, slender shoots that, like the leaf stalks, are smooth (glabrous). The latter are much shorter than those of *A barbinerve*, 3-4cm (1¼ - 1¾ in), while the leaves are three to five lobed, coarsely toothed and bright green and smooth except for the brownish curly hairs on the veins beneath.[30]

A barbinerve is restricted to north-east China, while *A*

28. The long second name comes from the Greek *pseudo* – false, while *sieboldianum* refers to a Japanese maple, *A sieboldianum*, which *A pseudosieboldianum* resembles in leaf.

29. E H Wilson also saw *A pseudosieboldianum* in Korea and wrote: 'In autumn its foliage assumes wonderful tints of orange, scarlet and crimson and is responsible for much of the autumn beauty of the forest'. It is not uncommon in cultivation, requiring similar conditions to *A japonicum*, that is a moist but well-drained site sheltered from cold winds.

30. Neither of these maples is common in western cultivation though they are generally represented in specialist collections. Both are hardy and ornamental in habit and leaf and their relatively small size qualifies them for the small garden where they would make charming specimens for the lawn.

Acer pseudosieboldianum, showing the characteristic rich autumn colour, here seen in Peter del Tredici's garden, Massachusetts, U.S.A. (October)

Acer barbinerve, flowering in cultivation at Herkenrode, Belgium from seed collected in the Changbai Shan. Photographed by Philippe de Spoelbirch. (April)

Acer tschonoskii variety *koreanum* with its characteristic slender red leaf stalks and attractive lobed leaves. (July)

Acer tschonoskii variety *koreanum*. A group of young trees growing on the edge of woodland near the main entrance to the Changbai Shan Reserve. It is an elegant small tree and quite hardy. (July)

Acer mono in cultivation from seed collected in the Changbai Shan. (July)

tschonoskii is also found in Japan. In fact, the Japanese tree is regarded as the typical species, while that in north-east China and North Korea (the one we saw) is regarded as *Acer tschonoskii* subspecies *koreanum* (variety *rubripes*), differing in its reddish leaf stalks and young shoots, its longer, more tapering leaf lobes and the more spreading wings of the fruit.

A mono completed the maple representation in these forests. Here it was a small tree, often shrubby, though reaching 15m (50ft) or more on occasions, with long-stalked leaves that were quite smooth except for hairs on the veins beneath. The leaves had three large and two smaller, slender-pointed lobes, the central lobe being the largest. They were shallowly heart-shaped (sub-cordate) at the base, and nowhere did we see the straight based (truncate) leaves so typical of the related *A truncatum*.[31]

Before I deal with the birches of the forest I should like to describe three other trees that are plentiful in this zone, each very different from anything that has gone before. Like the oaks, the ashes are represented here by a single species, *Fraxinus mandshurica*, the Manchurian ash, a tree in places 21-24m (70-80ft) high or more, with a dark, fissured bark, grey shoots and dark brown buds. The leaves we examined were 36cm (14in) or more long with from seven to thirteen stalkless, toothed and downy leaflets. It occurred fairly commonly, but scattered, in forest clearings and margins as well as by the road.[32]

Maackia amurensis and *Phellodendron amurense* are, as their names suggest, associated with the Amur region of north-east China and east Siberia. First discovered there by Maximowicz in the 1850s, he also first introduced them to western cultivation via St Petersburg. Both have bold, deeply divided (pinnate) leaves, but here the resemblance ends. *Maackia amurensis* was a large shrub or small tree up to 9m (30ft) with a wide, spreading head of branches. The leaves are alternate, grey-green in colour and have a swollen base to the stalk that does not conceal the bud. Later, dense terminal finger-like clusters (racemes) of dull white pea flowers are produced. These are of no great beauty although they are said to smell of new-mown grass. This is a tough and hardy tree, very common on the lower regions of the Changbai Shan and the surrounding areas.[33]

Maackia amurensis in cultivation at Wisley. The silvery, silky young foliage is characteristic. (May)

The bark of *Betula platyphylla* is covered by a white powdery deposit that rubs off on the hand like chalk

The Amur Cork tree, *Phellodendron amurense*, belongs to the same family as rue (*Ruta graveolens*), its leaves having a strong smell of turpentine when bruised. They differ from those of maackia in being opposite and glossy green. The leaf stalk has a similarly swollen base that does, however, conceal the tiny white bud. It reached 9-12m (30-40ft) here, older trees especially showing their characteristic ridged and furrowed corky bark. The flowers of phellodendron are small and insignificant, male and female on separate trees. They are replaced on female trees by shiny black berry-like fruits carried in bold bunches that ripen in October and are carried well into winter.[34]

In the lower regions of the Changbai Shan it was a common tree, especially by roadsides and on dry sandy hills, often growing with the maackia and so making comparison that much easier. The dried bark of *P amurense* has many uses in Chinese traditional medicine, along with other herbal ingredients it is used in the treatment of dysentery, jaundice, eczema, dermatitis, lumbago and night sweating.

The birches, like the maples, are represented by several species in the Changbai Shan area. We found five species all told, all but one in the lower zone. By far the most abundant and widespread here is the Manchurian birch *Betula platyphylla* (*mandshurica*). It was dominant in places, forming vast forests, the white stems almost dazzling the eyes when lit by the sun. Like that of the related Sichuan birch – *B szechuanica*, the bark is covered by a powdery deposit that rubs off on the hand like chalk or whitewash. Some trees we noted were stocky and 15m (50ft) or more in height, but the majority were less and slender stemmed. Most of the best trees outside the reserve had long since been removed we were told. The leaves were slender pointed with up to seven pairs of lateral veins, downy only on the veins beneath.[35]

31. *A mono* is native over a wide area from central to north China, east Siberia, north-east China, Mongolia, Korea and Japan. It is not as common in cultivation as its merit deserves and this may in part be due to the matching qualities of the better known *A truncatum*, though this too is hardly planted outside specialist collections. Both are excellent maples for cold areas and are especially appreciated in the north-eastern states of America. Indeed, the noted American plantsman Michael A Dirr considers *A mono* one of the most beautiful trees in the Arnold Arboretum – praise indeed! The largest specimen in British cultivation grows at Hergest Croft in Herefordshire, and in 1985 measured 25m (82ft). A young tree grown from seed collected in the Changbai Shan is well established in a school's grounds near my home. Its foliage turns a rich yellow in autumn.

32. *Fraxinus mandshurica* is rare in cultivation in Britain due to its flushing too early in spring when it is liable to frost damage. It is better suited to colder more northerly climates.

33. *Maackia amurensis* is named after Richard Karlovich Maack, a Russian naturalist who travelled in the Amur and Ussuri regions between 1855 and 1860 making botanical and zoological collections. The largest specimen recorded in Britain is a tree at the National Arboretum Westonbirt, Gloucestershire, which measured 10m (32ft) in 2002.

34. *P amurense* is not as successful in Britain or Ireland as it is in a continental climate, although a tree at Belgrave, Cobh in Co. Cork, Ireland had reached 19.5m (64ft) when measured in 2004, and there are other, smaller specimens elsewhere. With us it usually breaks too early and is often damaged by frost. One of the most impressive specimens I have seen in Europe was a tree in the city park at Bochum in Germany. It was a sunny autumn afternoon and the tree was loaded with fruits, while its leaves were turning a rich gold prior to falling. There are many fine specimens in the colder areas of the United States and Canada, where it is much admired for its rugged grey-brown bark, which is particularly impressive on the stems of old trees, especially in winter. It is mainly suited to large gardens and parks with space enough to develop its broad crown.

35. Typical *B platyphylla* is only found in mainland north-east Asia and is rare in western cultivation, its early leafing tendency being a problem except in cold northerly areas. In Britain certainly it is most usually represented by the variety *japonica* from Japan, which is far more satisfactory here and in North America where it is apparently less susceptible to the bronze birch borer, a scourge of white-stemmed birches on that continent.

Betula platyphylla. The slender white stems of this birch covered vast areas around the foot of the Changbai Shan. It is not best suited to British cultivation. (July)

Betula costata. A tall-stemmed specimen of this handsome birch on the edge of forest dominated by Manchurian birch B platyphylla. Changbai Shan Reserve. (July)

In the 1960s, when I first worked at the Hillier Arboretum, there was a rather fine birch with creamy-white bark there labelled Betula costata. It had been distributed widely in the trade by the Hillier Nurseries and was much admired. On closer examination, however, this tree proved to be wrongly named and it has since been identified by Dr P C de Jong of Utrecht University as a form of B ermanii.[36] I was delighted, therefore, to see the real McCoy in the forests of the Changbai Shan where it grows with B platyphylla, usually as scattered individuals. Young trees there have a pale orange-brown or creamy-brown, pink-tinted, exfoliating bark that gives the stem a soft shaggy appearance. On mature trees the bark of the main stem is dark greyish-brown and flaking, while on

the upper stem and branches it is comparatively smooth, creamy-white and peeling. The leaves are narrowly ovate and slender-pointed, with ten to fourteen pairs of veins, and are carried on slender, downy shoots. Small but distinct tufts of pale brown hairs are found in the axils of the veins beneath. In every way this is a distinct species, its bark characteristics not unlike those of the river birch − B nigra of eastern North America. Like the American tree, B costata varies in its bark effect, some individuals developing a smoother, whiter bark than others. Indeed, seed of such trees has been introduced from South Korea by several recent expeditions.[37]

It is worth recording that B costata in the wild is one of the largest of all birches. We saw many fine trees in the Changbai Shan, but the prize went to a magnificent specimen on the forest edge close to the main entrance to the reserve. This tree must have been 30m (100ft) at least, with a tall, clear, dark stem and a spreading crown. It towered head and shoulders above its neighbours, mostly Manchurian birch, and was visible from a considerable distance.

The early leafing habit of some provenances of B costata is

Betula costata, detail of stem. (July)

418

Viburnum sargentii, a close relative of the European Guelder rose *V opulus*, was common in swampy places in the lower reaches of the Changbai Shan Reserve. Its leaves and fruits in autumn contribute colourful splashes to the woodland scene. (July)

Salix raddeanna, a common willow in the Changbai Shan area, here a female form with ripening catkins. (July)

shared by another birch in the Changbai Shan area, namely B *dahurica*. It was a tree of 5-7m (16-23ft) with a rich purplish-brown, papery bark flaking away to reveal the pinkish-white new bark. The bark on older stems was thick and spongy forming a patchwork of ash-grey and brown flakes. The slender, spreading branches were arched at their extremities, while the young shoots were both glandular-warty and hairy. These were furnished with small, downy, unequally-toothed leaves to 4.5cm (1¾ in) long, gland dotted, pale and downy beneath.[38]

Very different is B *fruticosa*, a shrubby small-leaved birch of 2m (6ft) with ovate leaves 2-3cm (¾ -1¼ in) long with six to eight pairs of veins, which are hairy beneath. It favoured boggy or swampy places and was occasionally abundant there, forming extensive thickets. In one place, where both B *fruticosa* and B *dahurica* were present, we found a tree of 7m (23ft), which we believed to be a hybrid between the two. It had the habit and bark characteristics of B *dahurica*, while the leaves resembled more those of B *fruticosa*. B *fruticosa* is rare in cultivation in the West, where it is replaced by the very similar B *glandulosa* and B *glandulifera* of North America and B *humilis* of north Europe and north Asia. Ornamentally, there is little to choose between them, and all are hardy and easy, especially in wet acid soils. Many alders and willows also enjoy wet conditions and we were interested to see *Alnus hirsuta* growing commonly by roadside ditches and rivers. It is a large-leaved version of the European Grey alder (*A incana*) and reaches a similar size.

Of willows we saw many. Most common was a vigorous 'pussy willow' like a large-leaved version of our native *Salix caprea*. This, we decided, was probably S *raddeana*. There was also a narrow-leaved willow, possibly S *gilgiana*, as well as S *koriyanagi*, an east Asian version of our native purple willow (S *purpurea*), and another with white-bloomy shoots that may have been S *acutifolia*. All of these were mainly shrubby

in habit, the first and last named occasionally making small trees of 9-12m (30-40ft).

Sharing many of the wet and watery places with the willows was *Viburnum sargentii*, an east Asian version of the European *V opulus* or Guelder rose, and the American *V trilobum* or Cranberry bush. It is no more attractive than *V opulus* and if it differs at all it is in its more vigorous habit and coarser growth. There is also in cultivation a yellow-fruited form of *V sargentii* called 'Flavum' and, from the National Arboretum in Washington, two fine selections in 'Onondaga' and 'Susquehanna'. None of these in my experience, enjoys a dry situation, but, given sufficient moisture at the root, they are easy, hardy, ornamental and entirely satisfactory. Another viburnum frequent here, though preferring a drier situation, was *V burejaeticum*. It belongs to the same group as our native Wayfaring tree (*V lantana*) and is of similar garden merit.

Two hawthorns are plentiful in these forests. One is *Crataegus pinnatifida*, with deeply-lobed, smooth and glossy

36. Most trees in cultivation belong to the clone 'Grayswood', a most attractive tree for the garden.

37. In the wild it is distributed through Korea, north-east China and south-east Siberia. Trees of the more northerly provenances have generally proven early leafing in western cultivation and, not surprisingly, are rare and little known in British gardens. Recent introductions of this birch from South Korea, however, are proving more satisfactory and I look forward to seeing it more widely established and better known. A tree of 10m (32ft), when measured in 2005, grows at Bridge Gardens, Hungerford in Berkshire.

38. A native of north-east and north China, Korea and north Japan, this birch is rare in British cultivation, where it sometimes appears as an unsightly stunted tree due to repeated frost damage to its young growths. What may be a different clone of this species is represented by a tree of 20m (65ft) at Hergest Croft in Herefordshire. This does not suffer damage, at least not on a regular basis, and is a relatively fine tree as a result. Trees of similar merit, possibly from the same provenance, grow in the Arboretum des Barres in France. It is worth growing for its bark, which, on a healthy tree, is as good as that of the American B *nigra*. Recent introductions from South Korea and north Japan, if later leafing, may well see this species becoming more widely established in cultivation. In North America this birch is well suited to the cold winters and hot summers of the north, especially the north east. A seventy-six year old tree in the Arnold Arboretum, Massachusetts, is over 10.5m (35ft) or more. According to one observer there, this species does better on dry soils than most other birches and is resistant to the bronze birch borer.

Sambucus sieboldiana, a relative of the European red elderberry *S. racemosa*, common in thickets in the Changbai Shan. (July)

Philadelphus tenuifolius, a small-flowered species not uncommon in roadside scrub and forest margins in the Changbai Shan. (July)

leaves, and the other *C maximowiczii*, with less deeply-lobed, downy, obovate leaves. Indeed, not only leaves but also the shoots and young fruits are downy. Both species are shrubby and broadly spreading in habit, reaching 4.5m (15ft) or more in height.

Corylus sieboldiana var. *mandshurica* and *C heterophylla*, were plentiful in thickets; the nuts of both these hazels are commonly found for sale in town and city markets in north China in autumn and winter. Also plentiful was *Sambucus sieboldiana*, already loaded with red berries in dense clusters. It belongs to the same group as the European Red elder (*S racemosa*).

We were interested to find a wild Mock orange – *Philadelphus tenuifolius* – growing quite commonly on the forest margin and in roadside thickets. It was a shrub of about 2m (6ft) with large leaves and comparatively small white flowers of limited ornamental merit.

Of shrubby honeysuckles we saw several including *Lonicera chrysantha*, a shrub of 3m (9ft), its branches crowded with orange fruits eventually turning red. Its flowers in May are pale yellow darkening with age and are quite attractive *en masse*. Indeed, this is one of the most satisfying of its kind in British conditions and well worth considering for the larger garden. Even more interesting, however, was *Lonicera caerulea* variety *edulis*, a small shrub of 1-1.2m (3-4ft) with slender, spreading, downy branches and softly hairy leaves. Nothing remarkable up to now one might say, until one sees the

fruits. These are oblong, 1.5cm (⅗ in) long, succulent and covered with a bluish bloom. The varietal name *edulis* describes their edible nature, and on trying a sample I found them in taste not unlike a blueberry (*Vaccinium corymbosum*). This honeysuckle was dominant in places, forming a low understorey, sometimes sharing a glade with a curious spindleberry – *Euonymus pauciflorus*. This shrub varied in height from 2-4m (6-13ft), and while of no obvious ornamental merit was very distinct in its minutely warty (verruculose) shoots and softly downy short-stalked leaves 6-7.5cm (2¼ - 3in) long which ended in a slender almost tail-like point. The small pale purplish four-petalled flowers were borne in pairs on long thread-like stalks from the leaf axils and lay pressed flat against the leaf upper surface.

In the thickets and scrub by the road many of the above named shrubs came together in a dense tangle joined by *Deutzia parviflora*, *Spiraea chamaedryfolia*, *Aralia elata* and *Berberis amurensis*, the last named a close relative of the European *B vulgaris* but altogether a more robust shrub, larger in all its parts, especially in the leaves, which can be as much as 10cm (4in) long. Apart from the local use of its red berries, the dried roots of this berberis are used

39. Apart from north-east China, it is also native to east Siberia, Korea and Japan. First introduced to western cultivation from the latter country in 1830, it is now relatively common in gardens, though not to the extent it deserves. It is a hardy plant in all bar the coldest areas where, in severe winters, unripened shoots may be cut to the ground. Normally, however, these sprout anew from the spreading underground rootstock. Hard pruning the stems in late winter encourages even stronger growths with larger leaves.

Lonicera caerulea variety *edulis*, a dwarf shrub favouring woodland shade. Its sizeable fruits are edible and have a taste not unlike those of a blueberry (*Vaccinium corymbosum*). (July)

Euonymus pauciflorus, a curious spindleberry with warty shoots, was frequent in the forest at the foot of the Changbai Shan. (July)

in Chinese traditional medicine in the treatment of conjunctivitis, either as a decoction or an eye wash. A garden selection 'Flamboyant' is known for its brilliant scarlet autumn leaf colour.

Aralia elata is the Angelica tree, a pithy, thorny-stemmed shrub or small tree, which here formed clumps and thickets up to 5m (16ft) or more.

Its huge, much divided leaves, often crowded towards the ends of the stems and branches, together with its large, branched heads of creamy-white flowers, make this one of the most handsome and effective of all hardy deciduous woody plants. It is especially valuable for its late flowering in August and September and for its architectural quality, its bold habit associating well with buildings. It is, incidentally, remarkably tolerant of urban conditions and is equally happy on acid or alkaline soils. The flowers are followed by small shining black fruits beloved by birds and hang from the tips of the branches in luscious bunches. The leaves, and to a lesser extent, the flowerheads, bear some resemblance to those of the giant biennial herb angelica (*Angelica archangelica*), hence the English name.[39]

These scrub and grass areas by the road had another

Aralia elata, fruiting in the Hillier Arboretum. The fruits are approximately the size of an elderberry but are not edible except to birds. (October)

Actinidia kolomikta showing the curious and ornamental leaf variegation. (July)

Paeonia obovata in fruit in the woodlands of the Changbai Shan. Note the broad obovate terminal leaflet. (July)

occupant that we were anything but pleased to see. The ubiquitous tick was ever ready to attach itself to passing animals, human or otherwise, and at the end of each day spent in the lower regions of the reserve, de-ticking was a regular operation before retiring to bed.

Of climbing plants there were several, but none more common nor more spectacular than *Vitis amurensis* and *Actinidia kolomikta*. The former I had previously seen in the hills around Beijing. It is a noble foliaged vine, related to *Vitis vinifera*, but distinct enough in appearance and well worth growing in the larger garden where its vigour can be accommodated. Here it scrambled over shrubs and into the lower branches of trees forming bold curtains of growth. Elsewhere it scrambled over the ground providing, in places, extensive carpets. It must be a fine sight when its leaves colour in autumn.

Actinidia kolomikta I had seen previously in west Sichuan in 1981 (variety *gagnepainii*), but in the Changbai Shan forests it was more plentiful and spectacular, scrambling into trees and swamping lesser fry. The curious and striking colour combinations exhibited by its leaves are well enough known in cultivation, but they are somehow more impressive in these forests where some plants attain heights of 6-9m (20-30ft). The leaves, or some at least, are tipped with white, like a cat's tongue dipped in cream. Sometimes half or occasionally the

Opposite: Actinidia kolomikta scrambling into the lower branches of trees in a woodland clearing at the foot of the Changbai Shan. The common trees here are *Tilia amurensis*, *Acer mono* and *Pinus koraiensis*. (July)

entire leaf is white and this is not all, for another colour, pink, creeps in to stain the white or the green creating a lovely tricolour effect that brightens the gloom of the forest.

Nowhere did we see this climber flourishing in heavy shade. It was usually found in glades, on forest margins and in stream gullies, where at least some light was available. In cultivation it is not uncommon and, despite suggestions to the contrary, seems suited to any aspect.[40]

Among the rich selection of woody plants in these forests it was a joy to find an equally rich representation of perennials. There has been no better introduction to the perennials of this region than that written by Henry James (in *The Long White Mountain*) when he passed through these forests on his way to the Changbai Shan in 1886.[41] James was no plantsman and even less of a poet, yet something of the colour and flavour of this area is captured in his description. One can only imagine what a Farrer would have made of it.

Some of James's perennials we had already seen on our journey to the Changbai Shan, now others presented themselves. Some of these had yet to flower while others were already blown. One such was *Paeonia obovata*, which we

40. A fine specimen at Kiftsgate Court in Gloucestershire flourishes on a south-facing wall, while an equally flourishing specimen at Newby Hall in North Yorkshire grows just as well on a north-facing wall. It was originally introduced to western cultivation around 1855.

41. 'The lower slopes are covered with forests of birch and pine, but these gradually grew less dense, until we emerged on a delightful grassy plateau dotted with trees. It was like being transported into the Garden of Eden. In the forests, fine Turk's cap lilies, orchids and blue-bells had lit up the gloom, now rich open meadows, bright with flowers of every imaginable colour, where sheets of blue Iris, great scarlet Tiger lilies, sweet scented Day lilies, huge orange buttercups or purple monkshood delighted the eye'.

Clintonia udensis an unassuming member of the lily family producing dark-blue fleshy fruits in autumn. (July)

Iris setosa was common in swamps around the foot of Changbai Shan, its grey-green flag-like leaves and slaty-blue flowers an effective combination. The Changbai Shan is its only location in China. (July)

Iris setosa, detail of flowers showing the beautifully marked falls. (July)

found common but scattered among scrub in sun or shade.

This beautiful herbaceous species enjoys a widespread distribution in N.E. Asia, including China, Korea, E. Siberia and Japan, where it is found in woods and scrub, usually on mountains. The leaves are biternate, each set of three broad leaflets with a slender-stalked obovate terminal, hence the name. Its flowering stems can attain 60cm (2ft), with large bowl-shaped blooms up to 7cm (3in) across. The tepals can vary in colour from white through cream to rosy-purple, and are set around a corona of golden-yellow stamens with

a crimson centre. The form most usually found in British cultivation − variety *alba* − is a highly rated ornamental swooned over by connoisseurs. Sadly we arrived too late to see its flowers, though the smooth blue-bloomy seed capsules were present.

In the dappled shade of the forest we found several plants of the lily family including *Clintonia udensis* in flower and fruit. *Paris verticillata*, *Trillium kamtschaticum* with small but attractive white flowers, and Lily of the valley − *Convallaria majalis*, were also present, the latter treated by some authorities as a distinct species under the name *C keiskei*. Even more interesting, though sadly not yet in flower, was a Turk's cap lily, *Lilium distichum*,which occurred as scattered individuals in forest glades and on stream banks. It produced a stout stem up to 1m (3ft) tall, supporting a single whorl of leaves and terminal buds.

Another two weeks and this lily would have been flowering. The flowers are described as nodding or horizontal, up to 7.5cm (3in) across with recurved segments, pale orange-red in colour with darker spots. Several flowers are borne in a fan-like (distichous) arrangement from the top of the stem.[42]

In marshy sites in sun or shade we often found the Sensitive fern, *Onoclea sensibilis*. This has a wide distribution in northern Asia and North America, where it forms extensive patches in suitable sites in sun or shade. It is one of my favourite hardy ferns and is fairly common in cultivation by pools and in bog gardens where its handsome deeply-

Rubus arcticus, a small herbaceous species found in the northern (boreal) regions of N. America, Europe and Asia. (July)

Potentilla fruticosa. A widely distributed variable species occurring in North America, N. Europe (including N. England and W. Ireland) and Asia. Here growing in the Changbai Shan. (July)

divided, fresh green fronds turn a pleasant foxy-brown in autumn. The spore cases are borne either side of an erect stem, their bead-like appearance providing the alternative name: Bead fern.[43]

Two other ferns we found in the forest we recognised as native to Britain and other parts of the northern regions. These were the Oak and Beech ferns, *Gymnocarpium dryopteris* and *Phegopteris connectilis* respectively, lovely and delicate as ground cover in shade.

According to our local guide, this lower forest zone is home not only to ginseng, which we did not see, but also for a large number of wild mammals including the Manchurian tiger of which there are rumoured to be at least twenty in the reserve (although another source claims that the last tiger in the reserve was killed in 1980). There are also lynx, Red and Sika deer, sable, otter, squirrels and the Yellow weasel. These forests also contain the Chinese Forest frog (*Rana temporaria chensinensis*) from which a high-grade nourishing tonic, known in Chinese traditional medicine as 'Forest frog oil', is obtained.

One day we journeyed out of the reserve to visit a lake, the Yuan Chi, or Original Pool, situated not very far from the North Korean border. On the way we passed through a vast, fairly level terrain in which bogs, swamps and pools were commonplace. One of the most attractive swamp perennials was *Iris setosa*, a bold species with clumps or colonies of erect, sword-shaped leaves up to 2.5cm (1in) across. Above these were carried the flowers on 60-90cm (2-3ft) stems

branching in their upper parts. These were 6-9cm (2½ -3½ in) across and of a lovely slaty-blue with a white basal patch on the falls, veined purple and blue. It was very common over a wide area in ditches and bogs, sometimes accompanied by the big purple *I ensata*. *Iris setosa* has a vast distribution in the wild in north-east Asia and in North America. It also shared these bogs with the pale pink flowered herbaceous *Rubus arcticus* and *Osmunda cinnamomea*. On a nearby track we came across the shrubby *Potentilla fruticosa* and the herbaceous *Hypericum ascyron*, whose pale yellow petals resembled the blades of a propeller.

42. Native of eastern Siberia, north-east China and Korea, *Lilium distichum* is not often seen in western cultivation, although it was collected by E H Wilson and more recently by Richard Lighty (of Longwood Gardens) in Korea. Wilson described it as 'a delightful waif of the forests'.

43. Its popular English name derives from the fact that its fronds crumple at the first touch of frost

Hypericum ascyron. An herbaceous species of erect habit. Note the characteristic petals like the blades of a propeller. (July)

Polemonium caeruleum widespread in the Boreal regions including the Peak District and the Yorkshire Dales in England, where it is found on limestone. (July)

Syringa wolfii, a large shrub related to *S villosa*, with richly fragrant flowers. It was common in the lower reaches of the Changbai Shan Reserve. (July)

In the ditches alongside the road a large-flowered lilac flourished despite the regular lopping it endured. Untouched, it was a robust shrub of 3-4m (9-13ft) with leaves up to 15cm (6in) long and dense, conical, terminal heads (panicles) of sweetly fragrant lilac or pinkish-lilac flowers, paler within. Each of the four lobes of the flower had a tiny recurved point on the outside. It was variable in flower colour and quality, but there were many forms I would have been happy to accommodate in my garden. We identified it as *Syringa wolfii*, which is related to the well-known *S villosa*, and even more closely related to the Hungarian lilac *S josikaea*.[44] Beneath it, in the grassy ditch, grew Jacob's ladder *Polemonium caeruleum*, which I first saw as a wild plant in the limestone country near Malham Cove in the Craven District of Yorkshire.

In many bogs, especially where scattered birch provided shelter and light shade, grew *Ledum palustre*, a dwarf evergreen shrub in the heather family (*Ericaceae*). It mainly grew to 50cm (20in) high and twice as much across, forming twiggy mounds clustered with small, dull-green leaves covered with white woolly hair beneath. Tight rounded clusters of white flowers terminated the twigs and a bush in full flower was pretty to say the least.

There appeared to be two forms, one of which had smaller flowers and flower clusters and narrower leaves. The two often grew together and where their numbers were considerable, they creamed the ground like snow from a distance.[45]

When we reached Lake Yuan Chi we found a pleasant stretch of water surrounded by marsh in which grew brilliant orange Globe flowers – *Trollius ledebourii* and purple iris *I ensata*. A new shrub for us was *Rhododendron parvifolium*

44. Native of North Korea, eastern Siberia and north-east China, *Syringa wolfii* is a rare species in western gardens even though it was first introduced as long ago as 1907. It is bold and colourful in flower, vigorous in growth and very hardy, which is sufficient reason why it should not be confined to specialist collections. It was named after Herr Egbert Wolf, dendrologist and Director of the Gardens of the Imperial Forestry Institute at St Petersburg around the turn of the 20th century.

45. This is probably the plant that Henry James saw in 1886: 'We climbed the slope up to our waists in luxuriant wet grass full of tiger lilies and other gorgeous flowers and across a stretch of moorland perhaps two or three miles broad, covered with a dwarf white rhododendron'. Ledum is not unlike an alpine rhododendron and is regarded as such by several authorities.

46. *Rhododendron parvifolium* is, by some authorities, regarded as a group within *R lapponicum* ie. *R lapponicum* Parvifolium Group. It is native to the Pacific coastal areas of Japan, Korea and Siberia, and is much more amenable to cultivation, in Britain certainly, where it is generally early flowering from January to March, frosts permitting. *R parvifolium* was first described in 1834 from plants growing around Lake Baikal in Siberia and introduced to cultivation in 1877.

Ledum palustre formed low hummocks in bogs and on the margins of pools and lakes around the foot of the Changbai Shan. Here it shares a site with the white stemmed *Betula platyphylla* and *Larix gmelinii* variety *olgensis*. (July)

(confertissimum), a twiggy erect bush up to 1m (3ft) tall forming low thickets in the marsh, often growing with *Betula fruticosa*. There were just a few rose-purple flower clusters remaining. According to the Philipsons and other authorities, R *parvifolium* is insufficiently distinct botanically from R *lapponicum* to be retained as a separate species. From a gardener's point of view, however, it is very distinct in habit compared with the prostrate R *lapponicum*, which we later saw in the alpine regions of the Changbai Shan, and here, certainly, favoured wet peaty places such as bogs and lake margins, rather as Sweet gale – *Myrica gale* – does in Britain and Ireland.[46]

Ledum palustre (right), and the narrower leaved form (left). Both are equally abundant in the bogs of the Changbai Shan. (July)

Trollius ledebourii growing in the marshes around Lake Yuan Chi at the foot of the Changbai Shan. It was probably the flowers of this species to which Henry James referred in 1886 as 'huge orange buttercups'. (July)

Pyrola incarnata, a handsome wintergreen for a cool peaty soil. It was frequent on banks and on the edge of woodland in the Changbai Shan Reserve. (July)

In a nearby thicket grew a solitary bushy crab apple, *Malus baccata* variety *mandshurica*, as well as several perennials, many of them familiar from Britain, like Marsh fern (*Thelypteris palustris*), Round-leaved sundew (*Drosera rotundifolia*) and Common cotton grass (*Eriophorum angustifolium*). We were particularly enchanted, however, by a bold wintergreen, *Pyrola incarnata*, with basal clusters of rounded, shining, green leaves above which rose several stems carrying pink, bell-shaped nodding flowers.[47]

Above the lower forest zone, from 1,100 to 1,800m (3,600-5,900ft), lies the second zone. This is one of coniferous forest in which spruce, fir, pine and larch are dominant in various combinations, the larch occurring where the spruce-pine forest has been disturbed by fire. None of these conifers are entirely restricted to this zone, of course, there being some spillage into zones above and below. Nor is this zone exclusive to coniferous trees as we shall discover. The soil here is described as a brown Taiga soil. The pine is Korean pine, *Pinus koraiensis*, which I have already described. It is mainly found in the lower part of this zone. The fir and the spruce one sees here in great numbers, the rich, glossy green of their evergreen spires covering the slopes in a dense canopy, among which in autumn the reds and yellows of poplar, larch and maple "explode" like firecrackers.

Abies nephrolepis has several common names, among which Amur fir and Siberian fir offer us a clue to its native home. Of several Chinese names for this tree, Manzhou-lengshan (Manchu fir) gives yet another clue, for this tree ranges from the Russian far east, Korea and N.E. China, south to Shaanxi and the Hebei provinces. It is said, however, to be most abundant in the Changbai Shan. At one time its occurrence within this range was much greater even than today, large-scale felling having severely reduced its numbers, in some areas more than others. It is a tall tree of narrowly conical habit, the bark grey and smooth on young specimens, becoming darker and shallowly fissured on old trees. This is especially noticeable in the lower stem region. The new shoots are green and downy, becoming grey and smooth later. Along these the leaves are arranged, widely parted below the shoot, crowded and stiffly ascending above and pointing forwards. Individual leaves are narrow (linear) 2-2.5cm (¾ -1in) long, with a rounded tip in which a shallow notch occurs. In colour they are shining green above, marked with two bands of stomata below, the stomata white on new leaves, becoming pale green by the second year. Most of the trees we saw were 15-18m (50-60ft) in height, while occasional specimens in deep, moist

The cones of a puzzling larch (*Larix* species) in the Changbai Shan Reserve. It appears to be *L mastersiana*, a rare species from north-west Sichuan, presumably planted here by a forester. (July)

Picea jezoensis, showing the contrasting colour of the upper (top) and lower leaf surfaces. This spruce was plentiful in the Changbai Shan Reserve, often sharing the same site as the Amur fir. (July)

Abies nephrolepis, the Amur fir, showing the characteristic dappled grey, shallowly fissured bark of the lower stem. It was common, sometimes dominant, in the lower zones of Changbai Shan Reserve. (July)

but well-drained soils in sheltered ravines or on steep slopes lower down were at least 21-23m (70-80ft) or more.

The Ezo or Jezo spruce – *Picea jezoensis* – was equally attractive as a young tree, narrowly conical with a spire-like upper crown. In height it matched the Amur fir, the best specimens being those on deep well-drained soils in sheltered sites. The young shoots are green and smooth, becoming pale brown then greyish. The leaves are compressed, narrow (linear), 10-11mm (⅓ in) long, ending in an abrupt sharp point. They are shining green above, marked beneath with two bluish-white bands of stomata, and are densely crowded, lying forward above the shoots and widely spreading on either side. Early flushing is a characteristic of this spruce. [48]

According to some accounts I have read, the common larch of the Changbai Shan should be the Dahurian larch, *Larix gmelinii*, which extends over a wide area of north-east Asia from east Siberia, south to north-east China and North Korea. Several varieties further extend its range into north China, the Kuriles and south Sakhalin. Current Chinese opinion, however, favours the Changbai Shan larch as belonging to *L gmelinii* variety *olgensis* (*L olgensis*), which is distributed through north-east China in Jilin and Liaoning into Korea, as well as the Russian far east. [49]

47. *Pyrola incarnata* is occasionally seen in cultivation in the West but not as often as its beauty merits. In the opinion of the late Alfred Evans, formerly Assistant Curator in charge of the Herbaceous and Alpine Department at the Royal Botanic Garden, Edinburgh, the species of *Pyrola* are among nature's aristocrats, their presence in the garden indicating not only the interested plantsman, but also a successful cultivator. He recommends a cool position for them underneath the north side of a rhododendron in the peat garden.

48. One grew for many years in the Hillier Arboretum, but compared with its Japanese variety – *hondoensis*, it was a poor tree, stunted from repeated frost damage and slow-growing as a consequence. Typical *P jezoensis* is found in the Russian far east as well as in north Japan, in Hokkaido and north Honshu. *Abies nephrolepis* has a similar distribution to the spruce but is absent from Japan. Although rare in British cultivation, it seems to have grown rather better than the spruce, there being specimens of 18m (60ft) in several collections, and one of 23.5m (77ft) when last measured at Stourhead, Wiltshire in 1977.

49. Although first introduced into Britain as long ago as 1827, *L gmelinii* variety *olgensis* has never proved entirely successful due to its habit of early flushing. A tree of 16m (52ft), when last measured in 1983, grows at Warnham Court in Sussex.

Prunus maackii growing with a slender-stemmed *Betula ermanii* on Baitou Shan. The shining orange-brown bark is the most ornamental feature of this Bird cherry. (July)

The Changbai Shan larch averaged 18-21m (60-70ft) with taller specimens in more sheltered places, especially in the bottom lands. It was a lovely sight in its summer green, conical in outline and with a dark-grey, flaky bark when young, more spreading and uneven in habit and with a reddish-brown bark when old.[50]

Apart from the larch, there were a number of deciduous trees associated with the evergreen conifers just described. Several of the maples found in the lower zone also entered this one, especially *Acer caudatum* ssp. *ukurunduense*, *A tegmentosum*, *A tschonoskii* variety *koreanum* and *A barbinerve*. These gave a light and airy look to the many glades and clearings dominated by the more funereal shades of the spruce and fir. Often accompanying them were two Bird cherries and a rowan or mountain ash. Of the former, *Prunus padus* variety *pubescens* was the most frequent, a small- to medium-sized tree with slender clusters (racemes) of white flowers. This is a Far Eastern

Prunus maackii, a twin-stemmed tree in the woods of the Changbai Shan. (July)

Prunus maackii 'Amber Beauty' in a garden at East Ruston, Norfolk. In this selection the bark is of a brighter colour. (September)

form of our native Bird cherry *P padus*.[51]

The other Bird cherry in the Changbai Shan is *Prunus maackii*, the Manchurian Bird cherry, better known in cultivation than the last though not as common as its merit deserves. It occurred here as scattered trees up to 9m (30ft) or more, mostly on the margins of the forest or in clearings or ravines where its crown could see the sky. The bark of its stem and main branches was typically orange-brown, smooth and shiny. The white flowers in comparatively short, spike-like clusters (racemes) 5-7.5cm (2-3in) long had finished the previous month to be replaced by small, rounded, green fruits, which would turn black later. Wherever it occurred, its warm, shining bark stood out in the

thicket, and on one occasion it flourished alongside an equally attractive creamy-stemmed birch *Betula ermanii*.

It normally develops in time a rounded crown while its bark can be variable in tone, on some specimens peeling attractively. Although generally easy in most soils and sites it is especially notable in areas enjoying a continental climate, as in parts of the United States and Canada. Apart from eastern Siberia and north-east China, it is also found in the wild in Korea. Botanically it is interesting in bearing its flowers on the previous year's shoots rather than the shoots of the current year as do other Bird cherries.[52]

The rowan growing in the Changbai Shan is a widely branched tree up to 9m (30ft) in the forest but just over

50. For some reason, I did not examine the cones of these trees, maybe because earlier in the week I had already photographed a branch with cones on a tree growing below the reserve lodge. These cones were reddish purple and conical, with conspicuous protruding and reflexed bracts. The leaves of the tree were green and 2-2.5cm (¾-1in) long. After a lecture I gave eighteen months later, the late Alan Mitchell, the well-known tree authority, queried the name of this larch. On checking the cones I realised that they had nothing to do with *L gmelinii*, nor even variety *olgensis*, and seemed to have more in common with *L potaninii* from west China. Since then, my slide has been seen by Christopher Page at the Royal Botanic Garden, Edinburgh, who came to the conclusion that the cones seemed identical with those of *L mastersiana*, a rare *Larix* species found by E H Wilson in west Sichuan in 1908. In a more recent letter from the conifer authority Aljos Farjon, late of the RBG Kew, he confirmed Page's identification, but could offer no answer as to how this rare species came to be in the Changbai Shan other than as a result of a deliberate planting by the Chinese.

51. *Prunus padus* var. *pubescens* is very similar to a tree growing in the Hillier Arboretum under the name *P padus* variety *commutata*. This tree flourishes and although ornamentally no improvement on the typical form, it flushes three to four weeks earlier. Curiously, I have never seen it damaged as a consequence.

52. First discovered by R.C. Maack, in the Amur region in 1856, *P. maackii* was introduced to western cultivation via St Petersburg in 1910. It is hardy and easy in cultivation, where it has attained a large size, a specimen at the Bute Park Arboretum in Glamorgan, Wales, being the largest recorded in Britain at 17m (56ft) in 2005. It is said to be a "fine spire-shaped tree". A selection known as 'Amber Beauty', of Dutch origin, well describes the bark colour, though, like its Tibetan counterpart *P serrula*, it benefits from an occasional cleaning of algae.

Sorbus pohuashanensis flowering in the birch woods on Changbai Shan. It is closely related to the European rowan *S aucuparia* and has similar red fruits in autumn. (July)

Populus maximowiczii, showing the conspicuous net (reticulate) venation of the leaves and their characteristic twisted tip. A tall and handsome poplar, it occurred singly or in small groups by rivers and in ravines in the Changbai Shan Reserve. (July)

half this height in clearings, ravines and in forest margins. Here it was plentiful but scattered, displaying its flattened heads of white flowers to advantage above its bold foliage. In view of the confusion surrounding this species in cultivation, it is perhaps worth giving a few more details of the Changbai Shan trees. The older shoots are brownish-purple, shining and lenticelled, while the young shoots are covered with a dense grey hair (tomentum). The leaves are pinnate up to 20cm (8in) with up to fifteen leaflets. These are 4-6.5cm (1½ -2½ in) long, lance shaped, slender pointed, obliquely rounded at the base, sharply toothed (serrate) except at the base, green above with scattered grey hairs and bluish-green (glaucous) beneath with a dense pelt of hairs. The flowerheads (corymbs) have densely hairy branches and are closely attended beneath by leaves with deeply-toothed (lacerate) stipules, which, however, are soon shed. The buds are densely covered with white hairs. When we first found this tree we thought it belonged to S *amurensis*, a native of north-east China, east Siberia and Korea, but no less an authority than the late Dr T T Yü told me that the Changbai Shan tree is considered to be S *pohuashanensis*.[53]

Before leaving the subject of trees, there are two others found in this zone which need describing. The first and

the least common is *Populus maximowiczii*, a magnificent tree that grew mainly by the Song Hua river and in similar places elsewhere. We encountered a good number of young trees and a handful of really big trees up to 30m (100ft) or more with magnificent stems and bold, spreading crowns. The bark of young trees and of branches on larger trees was smooth and grey or pale greyish-green, while the lower stem region of older trees

53. In 1874 the noted German botanist Emil Bretschneider visited the Po-hua Shan range of mountains (now the Bai Hua Shan), some 75km (46 miles) west of Beijing. Among the interesting plants he collected was a mountain ash, similar in many respects to our native European species *Sorbus aucuparia*. Indeed, some authorities now regard it as no more than a geographical form. It was named S *pohuashanensis* after its location. Some eight years later, Bretschneider introduced this species as seed to several gardens in the West. It was later again introduced by Frank Meyer from the Wu Tai Shan, a range of mountains south west of Beijing, in Shanxi (Shansi) province. (The Wu Tai Shan is the southernmost locality in China for a number of Siberian and north-east China trees and shrubs and the most westerly point reached by many Korean species.) Meyer had gone to the Wu Tai Shan at the request of his chief, David Fairchild of the United States Department of Agriculture, who had ordered the trip as a favour to Professor Sargent of the Arnold Arboretum. Meyer found these mountains comparatively barren, the result of massive deforestation. He did, however, find the mountain ash and, on a subsequent visit in 1913, collected its seed. Whether Bretschneider's or Meyer's original introductions are any longer in cultivation in Britain is doubtful, though plants derived from Meyer's collection may well survive. Plants in present day cultivation under this name are among the heaviest fruiting of all rowans and among the most ornamental of their kind.

54. It was quite most handsome large poplar I had ever seen, a view shared, I have since discovered, by E H Wilson who wrote: 'This poplar grows to a larger size than any other species of eastern Asia, and ranks with the largest trees that are grown there'.

Wilson saw it in Korea and it is also native to Japan and eastern Siberia. I remembered this species from the Hillier Arboretum where it flourished, a strong-growing, early-leafing, healthy-looking poplar with a large, well-balanced crown. Small wonder that it has been used as a parent for a number of hybrids of which the American raised 'Androscoggin', 'Geneva', 'Oxford' and 'Rochester' are the most well known. In cultivation, it is said to be susceptible to bacterial canker, but the Hillier tree was never troubled in my time there nor do I recall having seen any of the Changbai Shan trees so affected, although the canker may well be absent from this relatively isolated area. It is, apparently, highly thought of in those parts of North America where it is grown. The largest specimen of this poplar in British and Irish cultivation is a tree at Mount Usher in County Wicklow, Ireland, which was recorded as 27.5m (90ft) in 1989.

55. In the wild, B *ermanii* has a wide distribution in north-east Asia including Japan and Korea. Some of the early introductions from mainland locations apparently proved early flushing in cultivation and suffered as a result, in Britain certainly. Trees grown from Japanese sources, however, have generally proven more satisfactory as illustrated by the superb specimen at Grayswood Hill, Surrey, from which numerous progeny have been produced by grafting.There is no proof that the above tree is of Japanese origin, but it seems most likely. The largest recorded specimen in Britain is a tree of 22m (72ft) recorded in 2002 at the National Arboretum, Westonbirt, Gloucestershire. Trees of similar size occur elsewhere. There is no doubting that B *ermanii* is one of the best ornamental barked birches for general cultivation, suitable to most soils and situations except the very small garden.

Betula ermanii, the most abundant tree in the Changbai Shan, dominant in the higher regions and mingling with *B platyphylla* on the lower slopes. (July)

was darkly fissured. The leaves on stout, smooth shoots were elliptic with a short, abrupt, twisted point and a rounded base. They measured 10-13.5cm (4-5½ in) long, including the rounded stalk of 2.5cm (1in), and were matt green and noticeably net-veined (reticulated) above, white and net-veined, the veins raised, beneath.[54]

The most abundant deciduous tree in this zone,

however, is the birch or rather birches, for there are two species represented. One is *Betula platyphylla*, which ascends the slopes from the lower zone to about 1,219m (4,000ft). From there the other birch — *Betula ermanii* — takes over, increasing in numbers until it becomes the dominant tree in the next, higher zone.[55]

B ermanii is a lovely tree in every respect, although in the

433

Rosa davurica, is the most commonly occurring rose in the Changbai Shan Reserve, its flowers varying from white through pink to deep rose. (July)

Rosa davurica, a lovely white-flowered form. (July)

wild it is variable in bark quality. On Changbai Shan trees the bark is creamy-white with pinkish tints, freely peeling, sometimes in large sheets especially at the base of major branches, where it sometimes hangs in bunches rustling in the wind. Older trees often develop a grey or dark grey bark, particularly on the lower stem. The bark of young branches is a shiny orange or orange-brown, becoming cream later. Young shoots are glandular warty and rough to the touch, while the leaves are triangular-ovate, 6-7.5cm (2½ -3in) long, including a stalk of 1.5-2cm (½ - ¾ in), sharply double-

toothed, green and smooth (glabrous) except for hairs on the midrib and on the seven to eight pairs of veins beneath.

At the lower end of its range, especially in the mixed broad-leaved deciduous and conifer forest, B ermanii is often single stemmed and tall, up to 20m (65ft) or more, becoming stockier and sometimes multi-stemmed higher up. Birches are well known to be promiscuous in cultivation and I could not help but wonder whether any hybrids had occurred between B ermanii and B platyphylla where these two meet. Although I examined a number of trees in this area I found nothing suspicious.

Compared with the lowest zone, this one had fewer shrub species, most of which were of general distribution. They included a rose, *Rosa davurica*, probably the variety *setacea*, a loose-stemmed bush of 2-3m (6-9ft) in height and width. The flowers were 5cm (2in) wide and variable in colour, from apple-blossom-pink to red, with a white 'eye'. Occasional plants had pure white flowers and there were many attractive shades in between. A characteristic of the flowers were the long sepals, two to two-and-a-half times longer than the flowers in bud, including the leafy appendage. Both sepals and flower stalks were bristly and glandular hairy, while the big, broad stipules at the leaf base were glandular ciliate. It was the most common rose in these mountains, especially memorable on the forest margin and by road and river bank.[56]

Rosa koreana, a small suckering shrub related to the European Scotch or Burnet rose *R pimpinellifolia*, with sea-green foliage and white flowers pink-washed in bud. We found it on several occasions in the Changbai Shan, where it appeared to favour steep banks. (July)

Even prettier was *Rosa koreana*, a small suckering shrub to 1m (3ft), the slender young stems densely beset with reddish bristles and spines, turning a shining chestnut brown the second year. The leaves, in keeping with the size of the plant, were small and neat to 6.5cm (2½ in) long, with nine to eleven sea-green leaflets. The flowers are borne singly on slender, reddish, glandular hairy stalks on the upper sides of the branchlets. They are 3cm (1¼ in) across with white, deeply-notched petals, blush-pink in bud. Filling the open flower is a ruff of yellow-tipped stamens. This is a delightful little rose, obviously related to our native Scotch or Burnet rose (*R pimpinellifolia*), but less dense and rampageous. We saw it only in two or three places on banks above the road and on each occasion we stopped to admire it. As far as I am aware it is not at present in western cultivation, though someone surely must have introduced it in the past either from north-east China or Korea. It is possible, of course, that this rose is another 'early flusher', which might explain its apparent absence in cultivation, in Britain at least.

In the birch woods behind the reserve lodge there occurred a mix of shrubs that we found fairly typical of this situation. The ground throughout was covered by an almost solid impenetrable carpet of *Rhododendron aureum* (*chrysanthum*). The individual plants were 30cm (12in) high on average, but much broader; their branches intermingled with those of their neighbours. These plants had already flowered, but we later this species in full flower at higher altitudes. Their leaves were variable in size and shape, generally elliptic to elliptic-oblong, 6-10cm (2½ -4in) long with recurved margins, green above and slightly glossy, paler beneath. In this evergreen carpet few other shrubs thrived, but those that did were present in good number, such as *Lonicera caerulea* variety *edulis*, which was one of the most abundant understorey shrubs in the Changbai Shan area.

Several small straggling currants and gooseberries were

Ground cover in the birch woods behind the guest lodge in the Changbai Shan Reserve. *Rhododendron aureum* (recently flowered) dominates, while *Juniperus communis* subspecies *saxatilis* and small-leaved *Vaccinium uliginosum* play supporting roles. (July)

also found here, of which the most curious was *Ribes horridum*, well named with its brown, densely bristly and prickly stems and small, lobed and toothed leaves. It was a low-spreading shrub up to 1m (3ft) and reminded me in some ways of the North American Swamp gooseberry (*R lacustre*).

Another shrub sharing the rhododendron's territory here was the dwarf form of our common juniper – *Juniperus communis* subspecies *saxatilis*. This must be one of the most widely distributed of all conifers, being found in high latitudes of North America, Europe and Asia and in high mountains further south. I first saw it growing on the northern coast of Scotland in Sutherland, where its creeping stems formed curtains on the sea cliffs of the Kyle of Tongue. It is also found on moors and mountains in North Wales and the north of England and in lowland bogs in the west of Ireland. Not surprisingly, considering its distribution, it has been given many names of which the following are perhaps

56. Beyond north-east China it occurs in Korea and eastern Siberia.

435

Lycopodium annotinum, the Interrupted clubmoss, formed dense hummocks and carpets in the cool shade of fir forest in the Changbai Shan Reserve. (July)

Linnaea borealis, the Twin flower, one of the most charming and delicate of north temperate flowers. Its name honours the great Swedish naturalist Carl von Linnaeus (1707-1778) whose favourite it was. (July)

the most well known: J communis subspecies nana and J communis variety montana. In north-east Asia it is known to Chinese botanists as J sibirica.

However much one admires the great forests in this zone and they are, after all, the dominant feature, the early summer belongs to the perennials, which occur here in great variety. Ornamentally, they belong to two groups. The first of these comprises what might be called plants of quiet charm, those with small or delicate flowers or interesting foliage which please rather than assault the eye. Of these there were several, mostly common and favouring the cool, dappled shade of the forest or mossy banks above stream and road. When I think of these plants, I remember especially our last day when we explored an area of forest some way below the reserve lodge, between the road and the river. The trees were mainly tall, dark fir with some birch and larch, conditions varied from heavy to dappled shade with the occasional glade spotlit by shafts of sun. The ground throughout was covered with a dense emerald pelt of mosses, several different kinds, deep and spongy in places and sprinkled with dead leaves.

Here, too, we found Rhododendron mucronulatum, a slender branched shrub to 1.5m (5ft). In late winter its clusters of rose-purple flowers must create lovely pools of colour in the gloom. Its Chinese name means 'welcome red rhododendron', and the pleasure these flowers must give travellers through the snow-covered landscape is easy to imagine.[57]

Growing in the moss, at first glance resembling a robust version of Polytrichum commune, grew a fern relative, the Interrupted clubmoss – Lycopodium annotinum. It was quite common, forming tufts and carpets, its shining green leaves adding yet another shade to the forest floor. Two wintergreens were plentiful here: Pyrola renifolia had small greenish-white flowers sprinkled along a short erect stem, while Moneses uniflora – the One-flowered wintergreen – carried a single nodding white flower atop a slender stem. For such a tiny unassuming herb, the latter has a tremendous distribution in the wild: in northern Europe and Asia from Iceland to north Japan, south to the mountains of north-east Spain, Corsica, Italy and northern Greece, and in North America from Newfoundland to Alaska, Pennsylvania and New Mexico. It is a rare native in Scotland, mainly in the eastern half of the country, and I well remember first seeing it in the 1950s in the Scots pine woods of the Rothiemurchus Forest near Aviemore. I had gone there in search of Crested tits and, having found a nest site, I sat down in what I hoped would be a suitably concealed position in a mossy depression. It was only when I laid my field glasses on the ground that I noticed this charming little flower, which came as an unexpected bonus.

Another fragile herb that I first saw in Scotland was the Twin flower – Linnaea borealis. This is also found in northern Europe and Asia and is represented by the variety longiflora in North America. In north-east Asia it is referred to as forma arctica, but the plants I examined in the forests of the Changbai Shan seemed to me no different from the plant I have since seen widespread in Sweden and Norway. On these moss-covered banks the Twin flower sends forth numerous thread-like stems with pairs of small, neatly-toothed leaves at intervals, and slender ascending shoots bearing at their tips a pair of nodding, white, bell-shaped flowers speckled and streaked pink within and almond scented. It is one of the loveliest wild flowers I know and I can well understand it having been a favourite of Linnaeus, the great Swedish naturalist after whom it is named. It can be naturalised in the woodland garden so long as it is given a moist, acid, leafy soil in semi-shade.

Trientalis europaea, a delicate little herb spreading by long, slender, creeping, underground stems (rhizomes). (July)

Dryopteris crassirhizoma in the author's garden. This is a common fern of woodlands in N.E. China, Korea and Japan. (July)

The 'moss forest', as we came to refer to it, had many other treasures, some of which we found elsewhere. I saw here two more old friends in *Trientalis europaea* and *Maianthemum bifolium*, Chickweed wintergreen and May lily respectively. The former has long white, thread-like underground stems (rhizomes), which produce patches and pools of slender, leafy shoots 10-15cm (4-6in) high, with a ruff of leaves above which appears a single, erect, seven-petalled, white flower on a slender stalk. It is a most delicate, totally unsophisticated perennial and one suitable for naturalising in woodlands (especially pine woods) on acid, sandy soils.

The same could be said of *Maianthemum bifolium*, with its slender stems bearing two heart-shaped leaves one above the other, and a slender, elongated cluster (raceme) of tiny, fragrant, white, star-shaped flowers. This, too, is a runner, forming extensive patches and is equally happy on acid or limy soils. The Changbai Shan plant belongs to ssp. *kamtschaticum*.

The forest also supported a wealth of ferns, including three I hadn't previously encountered: *Dryopteris crassirhizoma*,[58] *Athyrium acrostichoides* and *A crenatum*. There were woodland grasses, too, including one of my favourite British native species: *Milium effusum*, the Wood millet.

When it comes to the main display of summer

57. *Rhododendron mucronulatum* maintains its early flowering in cultivation, where this species and its various forms are just as welcome, frost permitting, in January or February. Two of the best selections available in cultivation are 'Winter Brightness' and 'Cornell Pink', both the recipients of awards from the Royal Horticultural Society. *R mucronulatum* was first introduced to the Arnold Arboretum, Massachusetts, from Beijing in 1882 by Emil Bretschneider.

58. I now grow this beautiful fern in my garden, where it has developed a bold shuttlecock clump of bright green fronds, which survive through winter before being replaced by the new fronds.

Aruncus dioicus ssp. *kamtschaticus* and *Trollius japonicus*. Both perennials favoured moist grassy places and ditches in the Changbai Shan. (July)

Filipendula palmata, a well-known perennial in Western cultivation, here in the Changbai Shan reserve. (July)

Thalictrum aquilegiifolium variety *sibiricum* (above) and *Valeriana officinalis*, an eye-catching combination in the ditches and woodland glades of the Changbai Shan. (July)

438

flowers, this second zone of the Changbai Shan is breathtaking. Rarely before have I seen banks and ditches so crammed with flowers, nor woodlands so carpeted with them. They flowed down the slopes from the subalpine meadows, a rich tidal wave of colour thronging the many glades and clearings in the forest. In one 3m (9ft) stretch of ditch alone we counted twenty different flowering herbs including the bold, white-plumed Goatsbeard (*Aruncus dioicus* variety *kamtschaticus*), the pink-headed *Valeriana officinalis*, the large white candy-floss heads of *Thalictrum*

aquilegiifolium variety *sibiricum*, and the pale pink frothy heads of *Filipendula palmata*. Bold perennials were everywhere, and I was particularly impressed with a stately white flowered False hellebore – *Veratrum oxysepalum*.[59] Not far away we found a rather handsome dandelion *Taraxacum cuspidatum* with deeply and sharply cut leaves.

59. This must be a close relative of the more familiar *V album*, which is little enough seen in cultivation where it generally excels, especially in northern gardens such as at Raby Castle in Durham, England.

Taraxacum cuspidatum, a Chinese dandelion, one of many species we saw in the north east of the country. (July)

Veratrum oxysepalum, a close relative of the False hellebore *V album*, growing in a woodland clearing in the Changbai Shan. The yellow flowers beneath belong to *Trollius japonicus*. (July)

Ligularia sibirica, a robust perennial common in moist places and streamsides in the Changbai Shan. (July)

Equally impressive in the Changbai Shan was *Ligularia sibirica*, a bold clump-forming perennial, with long-stalked, large, rounded, leaves and tall poker-like heads (racemes) of yellow daisy flowers. This species is not unlike several others well known in cultivation, but totally new to me, and quite unlike any other I have seen was *Ligularia jamesii*, first discovered here by Henry James after whom it is named. The long-stalked leaves are arrow-shaped and jaggedly toothed, while the large golden-yellow daisy heads 7.5cm (3in) across are borne singly on a 30-60cm (1-2ft) stem. Interestingly, the basal leaves of this plant are small and rounded or kidney-shaped, 2.5-3cm (1-1¼ in) across with a neatly scalloped edge.

L sibirica occurred as stout clumps or colonies in grassy glades or on slopes above the river. *L jamesii*, however, was

Below left and right. *Ligularia jamesii* was first discovered in the Changbai Shan region by Henry James in 1886. It differs from most other species in its combination of arrow-shaped leaves and stems bearing a single flowerhead. (July)

Aquilegia flabellata var. *pumila*, the exquisite flowers of this choice perennial, which is also found in N. Japan. (July)

Aquilegia flabellata var. *pumila*, an outstanding perennial that favoured the cooler higher woodland areas of Changbai Shan. (July)

usually single stemmed and occurred as scattered individuals throughout the birch woods and in ditches by the road. I have no doubt that should L *jamesii* be introduced to western cultivation it will be regarded as a desirable addition to the woodland garden or perennial border, where it will likely as not form clumps.

I have always been an admirer of the Grannies' bonnets or columbines of the old cottage gardens. These are mainly derived from the European columbine *Aquilegia vulgaris*, but there are many other wild species scattered across the northern temperate zones, some of which are cherished garden plants for the border or rock garden. The Changbai Shan supported at least two species in *Aquilegia oxysepala* and *flabellata* var. *pumila*. The former was a green-leaved plant with loosely branching stems up to 75cm (2½ ft) with typically nodding flowers. These were variable in colour. Some we saw in pastel blues, lilacs and yellow, while others had mahogany-red sepals and apricot-yellow petals. Occasional plants had white flowers that were tinted with pale green. It was widely distributed throughout the lower zones of the reserve in contrast to the strikingly blue-flowered *Aquilegia flabellata* var. *pumila*. This columbine seemed to prefer the higher, cooler regions and was particularly fond of damp moss-covered boulders and banks in the birch woods above the reserve lodge. Here it produced compact clumps of attractively divided green foliage, above which rose sheaves of stems 30-40cm (12-16in) tall bearing showers of relatively large nodding flowers of deep blue, the inner 'skirt' of petals were white-tipped or entirely white. Each petal ended in a spur, curling inwards at the tips. (*A. flabellata* was described from a cultivated plant now represented in gardens by many hybrids and seed strains. *A. flabellata* var. *pumila* is the wild phase, which is also found in N. Japan, S. Kuriles, Sakhalin and N. Korea.) Botanically, *A oxysepala* is not far removed from *A vulgaris*, and is by some authorities regarded as no more than a variety of that species. A pinch of seed from *A oxysepala* was collected and established in cultivation.

Aquilegia oxysepalum, variable in flower colour, was common in moist shade in the Changbai Shan. (July)

441

Geranium eriostemon variety *reinii* was common in the Changbai Shan where it flourished on roadside banks, in ditches and woodland clearings. (July)

Trollius japonicus, a handsome dark-stemmed Globe flower abundant in the Changbai Shan. In its rich yellow buttercup-shaped flowers it is quite unlike the more familiar European species *T europaeus*. (July)

I have already mentioned my interest in the hardy geraniums, so, naturally, I was delighted to find in these forests a plant new to me. From a fairly compact clump of five-lobed, downy leaves rose downy, branching stems up to 40cm (16in) long with flattened, pale violet-blue

Campanula punctata, a bold, large-flowered perennial growing in the woods of the Changbai Shan where it favoured pumice soils. Its alternative though incorrect name, *C nobilis*, better describes this plant's ornamental merit. (July)

flowers paling to white at the centre that were 2.5-3cm (1-1¼ in) across. It was quite common in glades, on grassy banks, ditches and by roadsides. At first, I suspected it to be *Geranium maximowiczii*, but a dried flowering specimen has since been identified by Dr Peter Yeo of the Cambridge University Botanic Garden as *Geranium eriostemon* variety *reinii*.[60]

The dark-stemmed *Trollius japonicus* (*riederianus* variety *japonicus*), whose yellow flowers with spreading petals resembled those of a large handsome buttercup was, perhaps, the most common perennial flowering at this time and occurred in large numbers over a wide range of habitats, not all of them wet. Its bright flowers speckled the woods and meadows throughout this zone and it was especially common in ditches and on banks by the road. Other woodland perennials that attracted our attention included *Cimicifuga simplex*,[61] *Cacalia robusta* and *Aconitum kamtschaticum* (*maximum*), none of which, however, were in flower.

In the lower part of the zone, growing on pumice

The waterfall at the head of the Song Hua valley seen from the screes above the hot springs. An alpine yellow poppy (*Papaver pseudoradicatum*) is frequent on these steep stony slopes. Birch (*Betula ermanii*) and alder (*Alnus mandshurica*) provide the main shrubby vegetation. (July)

soils, we found a superb bellflower – *Campanula punctata*. It is a free-growing perennial of 30-60cm (1-2ft) with long-stalked, heart-shaped basal leaves and large, pendulous, creamy-white tubular bells 7.5cm (3in) long, hairy on the outside and speckled darkly within. Obviously enjoying free drainage and full sun, it often dominated banks above the road, its roots delving into ancient ash and cinders.[62]

The Song Hua river has its beginning in a beautiful lake that fills the old crater of the Baitou Shan. It escapes from the lake through a gap in the north side of the crater wall and descends from there via a spectacular waterfall into the valley above the reserve lodge. Several times we had caught sight of the waterfall through gaps in the trees and at the first opportunity we headed in its direction.

A great deal of activity was taking place along the road, many people engaged in the construction of buildings of one kind or another to accommodate the increase in visitors the Chinese tourist authorities envisaged. Naturally, local stone was much in evidence in

60. This variety differs from the type in the deeper, more elongated leaf divisions. Typical *G eriostemon* is native over a wide territory from east Tibet to west China, and from east Siberia to north-east China, Korea and Japan. The variety *reinii* is supposed to be restricted to Japan, but the Changbai Shan plants have proved otherwise. It is hardy and lovely in flower, while the richly tinted autumn foliage is a bonus. Plants are now established in British cultivation from Changbai Shan seed.

61. Current opinion now regards *Cimicifuga* as belonging to the genus *Actaea*, in which case this species would be known as *A simplex*.

62. Although by no means rare in western cultivation, *C punctata* is more often represented by its hybrids *C* 'Burghaltii' and *C* 'Van Houttei', both of which are similar in habit with similarly shaped flowers. Those of the former, however, are an unusual pale greyish-lilac, while those of 'Van Houttei' are darker. Both are lovely and well

worth a place in the garden.

C punctata is native to eastern Siberia, north-east China, Korea and Japan, and was introduced to western cultivation as long ago as 1813 from Siberian seed. It was again introduced in 1844 by Robert Fortune, probably from a Shanghai nursery. Fortune's plant turned out to have pale purple flowers and was given the name *C nobilis* by John Lindley, botanist and Secretary of the Royal Horticultural Society. It is a name befitting the plant in flower, but the name *C punctata* (describing the spots within the flower) had already been given to this species by the eminent French naturalist Lamarck in 1783. It was only later that Lindley's *C nobilis* and Lamarck's *C punctata* were found to be one and the same species and the latter name, having priority, was retained as the correct one. In Fortune's day, this bellflower was, apparently, a great favourite with the Chinese in the northern parts of the country, being grown in gardens or in pots. The closely related *C takesimana* of Korea, with flowers of a rich lilac-white, is equally invasive, though commonly grown and popular in many British gardens.

443

A stonemason taking a breather while his colleagues work on the screes behind. (July)

these new structures and on a nearby scree we watched several men engaged with hammers and cold chisels, shaping the stone into manageable blocks. In the vastness of the scree they appeared like ants, their grinning faces regularly obliterated in a cloud of dust and flying rock splinters.

Here the forest was almost entirely of birch – *Betula ermanii*, trees of 9-12m (30-40ft) tall, mostly branching

Stonemason at work. The dust and fragments thrown up seemed not to trouble him and he wore no protection. (July)

low, some individuals already assuming weird shapes fashioned by the wind sweeping down off the screes. They grew among boulders, some of which towered like miniature crags, topped by rowans or seedling birch. The whole rock landscape beneath the trees was dappled with green velvety moss in which grew columbines, cranesbills, Globe flowers and the yellow-rayed *Ligularia jamesii*. In one grassy place we found *Sanguisorba officinalis*, the Great burnet, with its deeply-divided (pinnate) leaves and tall branching stems bearing crimson flowerheads. This was another old friend from British meadowlands. Nearby, grew another species, *S sitchensis*, in bold mounds of lush apple-green foliage, in the midst of which rose 60-90cm (2-3ft) stems bearing attractive tapering poker-like spikes of tiny white flowers bristling with long white stamens. Later we completed a trio when finding *Sanguisorba parviflora*, a charming multi-stemmed perennial to 75cm (30in), with a myriad erect white-stamened heads smaller than a thimble. The last two are now in cultivation from seeds collected at the time.

Close by a stream we found *Saxifraga punctata* growing among wet rocks. It reminded me of *S rotundifolia* with its rosettes of long-stalked, kidney-shaped leaves, though the white flowers in dense clusters were of no special merit.

Since leaving the lodge we had been following a pipeline that ran on supporting stone piles alongside the road. When we finally reached its source we discovered an area of hot springs further up the valley. The steaming water was being transported down the valley to supply various facilities including hot baths near the reserve lodge. Hot water was bubbling out through holes and fissures in the rock between the main river and a small tributary, and the area was clouded with steam that drifted down the valley and through the trees. It was probably these springs that Henry James referred to in 1886 as being at a temperature of about 80°C (175°F), hot enough for local hawkers to boil eggs and for visitors to take therapeutic dips in steamy pools.

I was surprised to see how close to the springs the vegetation grew, its growth apparently in no way affected

Sanguisorba sitchensis, a handsome perennial with tapered, poker-like flower spikes above mounds of sea-green foliage. (July)

Sanguisorba parviflora forms a neat clump of deeply divided leaves above which are delicate white flowerheads borne on slender stems. It was common on Changbai Shan in moist grassy areas. A flowering clump in the author's garden. (July)

Hot springs in the Song Hua valley, Changbai Shan. Many plants grew within splashing distance of steam vents and hot water

Mossy boulders with birch trees in the woods of the upper Song Hua valley. (July)

Erigeron or *Aster* species. An unidentified species by the Song Hua river, below the waterfall Changbai Shan. (July)

Campanula glomerata variety *dahurica*. A striking dwarf free-flowering bellflower, close by the hot springs in the Song Hua river valley. (July)

by the heat. One of the plants flourishing here was a bellflower, *Campanula glomerata* variety *dahurica*. This is, in effect, a robust and spectacular version of our native Clustered bellflower, which gives such a lovely show on chalklands of the south and east. In this variety, the bold, crowded heads of erect, purple-blue flowers are carried on stout stems 30cm (12in) tall above leafy piles.[63]

In the shingle and stones by the edge of the stream grew several alpine plants that had found here a congenial home. A creeping white-flowered campion, *Silene repens*, was plentiful and an even more attractive chrysanthemum, *Chrysanthemum zawadskii* variety *alpinum*. I am not sure which name is the more impressive. The plant itself is quite attractive. From low mats of grey deeply-cut foliage rise slender stems, bearing aloft a single, relatively large, pale pink daisy. Some plants were well-established pads of 30cm (12in) or more across.

Growing in the shingle, their flowers viewed against the dark running waters of the stream, they were a memorable sight. Whether this plant will retain its charm in cultivation, where it will require a well-drained sunny situation, remains to be seen.[64] Close by we found a most handsome alpine *Erigeron* species with pink rayed flowers.

From the hot springs, which are situated at 1,800m (5,904ft), we scrambled up the screes towards a rim of

63. It is not uncommon in cultivation where, in suitable conditions, it seeds around to form, in time, considerable patches. It was once grown on a scree bed at the Hillier Arboretum in Hampshire where it was much admired in flower. Eventually, its spread threatened other less robust plants and it had to be drastically reduced.

64. In writing of this charming plant, I am reminded of Reginald Farrer's dismissive comment about *Chrysanthemum zawadskii* itself. Comparing it with *C nipponicum* he wrote: 'Though much smaller [*C zawadskii*] is a rather leafy thing of about 9 inches or a foot, whose flowers it is flattery to describe as "rose clair", for they are in reality, as a rule, of a rather pallid dim tone'. I wonder what he would have said of variety *alpinum*?

Silene repens, a pretty little campion with creeping rootstock forming patches and colonies in riverside gravel. (July)

Chrysanthemum zawadskii variety *alpinum* growing in the stony margin of a mountain stream on Changbai Shan. (July)

447

crags high above. Here, among the jumble of rocks and rubble, we discovered several plants of great interest. *Rhododendron aureum* was again plentiful, carpeting the ground in many places and sporting an occasional truss of pale sulphur-yellow flowers. Mixed in with this shrub was the delightful *Phyllodoce caerulea*, a low tuffety shrublet, its stems crowded with heath-like shining evergreen leaves and terminating in loose clusters of pitcher-shaped, deep pink-purple flowers, each on a slender stalk.[65]

Photographing *Phyllodoce coerulea* on screes above the hot springs in the Song Hua river valley. (July)

Phyllodoce coerulea and *Rhododendron aureum* (centre) flourished on the screes above the head of the Song Hua valley, Changbai Shan. (July)

Phylodoce coerulea, a charming member of the heather family *Ericaceae* formed patches and hummocks on the slopes of the Baitou Shan. (July)

The best was yet to come, however, for in open areas of established scree and on firmer ground nearby, grew the most charming little alpine plant I have seen for a long time. It was a creeping shrublet forming mats and carpets of shortly ascending shoots clothed with small, narrow, oblong, green and glandular ciliate leaves. Above these hovered like butterflies rose-coloured flat-faced flowers with five petals, the two lowermost parted to accommodate the short, bent style. It was an impressive sight and we puzzled long and hard over its identity. It reminded us in some ways of *Rhodothamnus chamaecistus*, while *Rhododendron camtschaticum* also came to mind. In the end we decided it belonged to a rhododendron listed in a guide to Changbai Shan plants as *Rhododendron redowskianum* and this identification has since been proved correct. The Chinese name for this little plant means 'in the clouds rhododendron', a most appropriate reference.[66]

65. This species is also a rare British native, being found in a few remote locations in the mountains of Westerness and Perthshire in Scotland. It is, however, widely distributed in northerly and Arctic regions of Europe, North America and Asia from Iceland to Japan and from Greenland to Quebec and the mountains of New Hampshire in the United States. It is also found, though rarely, in the Alps and Pyrenees. Plants of the European form are said not to be easy in cultivation. Several times we lost this form in a peat garden at the Hillier Arboretum, but maybe this was simply a dislike for our relatively warmer, drier southern climate. There is, however, a plant, known as variety *japonica* (a name for which I can find no authority), which is said to be more amenable to general cultivation. From a description and a coloured photograph in Alfred Evans's book, *The Peat Garden and its Plants*, it would appear to be the same as the plant we saw in the Changbai Shan. It formed patches in places, its flowers contrasting most effectively with the pale yellow of the rhododendron.

66. I am not aware that this plant, which has a restricted distribution in north-east China, south-east Siberia and North Korea, has ever been in cultivation. Judging by its habitat, it would require a freer draining, sunnier position than the related *R camtschaticum*, which is in cultivation and much admired. According to Peter Cox of Glendoick this rare species is best considered as a difficult-to-please smaller flowered dwarf version of *R redowskianum*. Ivan Ivanovich Redowsky (1774–1807), the Russian botanist who first discovered it and for whom it was named, was shot on suspicion of being a spy.

Rhododendron redowskianum formed extensive carpets on the screes above the head of the Song Hua valley, Changbai Shan. (July)

Rhododendron redowskianum is a choice alpine deciduous shrublet restricted in the wild to north-east China (Changbai Shan), south-east Siberia and North Korea. (July)

The waterfall at the head of the Song Hua valley. The foreground scrub is composed of *Betula ermanii* and *Alnus mandshurica*. (July)

Both R *redowskianum* and R *camtschaticum* are deciduous and have been said to differ from typical *Rhododendron* in their inflorescence, which is a raceme, bearing in its lower part persistent leafy sterile bracts, the few flowers being confined to the apex of the raceme. The bracts below the flowers of typical rhododendrons are not persistent. Due to this characteristic, a botanist by the name of Small regarded R *camtschaticum* and R *redowskianum* as belonging to a separate genus, which he named *Therorhodion*; connoisseurs will be relieved to know that most other rhododendron authorities do not agree with this separation, nor even the character on which it is based.

From our position high on the screes, we looked across a wilderness of rock to the waterfall, a magnificent feature in a stark grey and brown setting of basalt cliffs. According to Henry James, the fall is approximately 45.5m (150ft) and flows from spring until winter when

Opposite: Valley of the Song Hua river in the Changbai Shan Reserve below the Reserve Lodge, looking south to the waterfall, which flows from the crater lake. The conifers in the foreground are *Picea jezoensis* and *Abies nephrolepis*. (July)

Right: The basalt cliffs and screes at the head of the Song Hua valley. The stream that feeds the waterfall flows via a deep ravine from Heaven's Lake, which fills the old crater of Baitou Shan. The pilgrims' path winds up towards the fall before climbing steeply to the right and reappearing along the foot of the cliffs above. (July)

Crossing the Moon Bridge over the Song Hua river. (July)

Crossing the Song Hua river by way of a fallen *Populus maximowiczii*. For some people hands and knees offer the safest way across such obstacles. (July)

Dianthus superbus with its bold feathered petals was frequent in the rocks and shingle by the upper Song Hua river. It enjoys a wide distribution in the mountains of Europe and northern Asia. (July)

Rhododendron aureum forming a low impenetrable ground cover. (July)

the lake, which feeds it, freezes.[67] Our local guide, Ma Qiyan, told us that the crater lake, known as the Tianchi or Heaven's Lake, had long been regarded as sacred. Henry James said that the lake was called Long Wang Tan – or Dragon Prince's Pool – by the hill people, and was sacred to the Dragon, the God of Rain. Mr Ma also told us the following story concerning the ancestors of the Manchus. Seven maidens were swimming one day in Heaven's Lake when a bird flying overhead dropped a 'ginseng nut' (presumably a root). One of the maidens on eating the nut became pregnant, later giving birth to the first of the Manchu race. In 1905, a shrine or temple was built on the slopes above the lake with access by a narrow track from the Song Hua river valley. This, however, had been destroyed during the Cultural Revolution in the 1960s. Even so, a great number of Chinese and Korean pilgrims and others continue to visit the site. In order to reach it, they follow the track up the valley to the waterfall via a charming stone-built Moon Bridge, beneath which the river rushes in a froth of white foam. Gradually the track climbs steeply to the right, then turns left to skirt the base of a high cliff above the fall. From here pilgrims proceed along the ravine to Heaven's Lake. Due to the unstable nature of the cliffs, it is not uncommon for accidents to occur and one evening after supper we saw a man being carried into the lodge having apparently been struck by a falling rock. It was good enough reason for our guides to refuse us permission to visit the temple site.

Some of the visitors tramp up to the waterfall in casual clothing and nothing more than flimsy slippers or sandals on their feet. Hiking in itself is not a popular pastime here, hence the lack of suitable clothing and footwear, but Chinese people young and old will endure considerable hardship in order to visit buildings or sites of historical importance or religious significance in out of the way places.

Just across the river from the reserve lodge, on the hillside opposite, is found a shaded pool known as Little Heaven's Lake. It is surrounded by birch woodland with a scattering of poorly shaped spruce. To reach this we crossed the river via the stem of a fallen poplar, *Populus maximowiczii*. It was easier to cross this on hands and knees than risk a dunking or worse in the angry torrent beneath.

On the far side was an extensive open area of boulders and stones in which grew several small plants some of which, the silene and the *chrysanthemum*, we had seen previously by the hot springs. Another plant I was pleased to see here was the Mountain sorrel, *Oxyria digyna*, which I first encountered on a visit to the Grampian Mountains of Perthshire in Scotland as a youth in the 1950s. I learned then that its fleshy, rounded leaves were pleasantly acid to the taste, quenching one's thirst like sorrel does on a hot day.

The crowning glory of these river shingles, however, was *Dianthus superbus*, which has a wide distribution in the mountains of Europe and northern Asia.[68] It is not especially neat in habit, but the wide-spreading, branching stems carried sprays of rich pink fragrant flowers with a reddish central zone and deeply cut petals giving a fringed appearance to the flower. Somehow, it was not a plant I expected to see in this wild place, but it was obviously well established and flourishing here.

The birch woods were something close to paradise and we would cheerfully have spent the rest of the day here had we not wanted to climb to the pastures above. *Rhododendron aureum*, as usual, formed a ground cover, but not so dense that it excluded other plants. Chickweed

67. A more recent travel guide describes the waterfall as 68m (223ft) high, a significant difference.

68. *Dianthus superbus* is a well-known plant in western cultivation having been grown in European gardens, it is said, since the thirteenth century and introduced to British cultivation in 1596. The Changbai Shan plant had more richly-coloured flowers than the typical European form, which are pale or lilac-pink.

wintergreen and May lily carpeted the ground in places, and an alpine strawberry, *Fragaria orientalis*, was frequent, as was *Clintonia udensis* and *Lilium distichum*. The lake itself I found disappointing and there was nothing heavenly about it that I could detect, it being too shaded and stagnant.

We continued our climb, following a winding track, which at one point emerged in a grassy glade. Here we stopped, our eyes almost popping out of our heads, for sprinkled throughout the glade, held clear of the grass, were the myriad flowers of a Lady's slipper orchid – *Cypripedium guttatum*. Each plant bore two boldly-ribbed green leaves above which rose a 15cm (6in) downy stem carrying a single bloom 3cm (1¼ in) across. In colour it was white, heavily spotted and blotched rose-purple on the inside and on the pouched lip. It was a gem of a plant and there must have been several hundred of them in this and neighbouring clearings.[69]

Unlike the more familiar clump-forming *C calceolus*, *C guttatum* has a system of far creeping stems (rhizomes) that wander and zigzag over or just under the ground, making collecting, according to Farrer, a difficult task. His answer to the problem would have given today's conservationists palpitations, and rightly so. 'Our chief hope', he reasoned, 'must lie in collecting wide unbroken sods of it from its native forests, and bringing them into cultivation as they are'. He was by no means alone in this attitude towards plant collecting, which was not uncommon in his day. Regrettably, in some quarters it has continued

Cypripedium guttatum, handsome in leaf as well as in flower. The famous plantsman and writer Reginald Farrer described this orchid as a 'fairy among its kind, filling the dreary birch forests and lone pinewoods of the far North with beauty'. (July)

Cypripedium guttatum carpeting the ground in a woodland glade above the Song Hua river, Changbai Shan. (July)

Alnus mandshurica, the Siberian Green alder, a large shrub with boldly-ribbed leaves and conspicuous, cone-like fruiting heads. (July)

until the present day, with obvious results.

Having left the Lady's slipper glade far behind, we found ourselves threading our way through birch woodland with an understorey of Siberian Green alder – *Alnus mandshurica*, which is a north-east Asian version of the Green alder, *A viridis* of the mountains of Europe. It looks very much like it, too, being a multi-stemmed shrub to 5m (16ft) or more with boldly-veined green leaves and erect clusters of green fruiting 'cones' 1cm (½ in) long.

We had now entered the third vegetational zone in the Changbai Shan, which occurs between 1,800 and 2,000m (5,900 and 6,500ft). Birch, *Betula ermanii*, is the dominant and virtually the only tree, forming pure stands in places. The soil is a podzolic forest soil, with rather poor fertility. Many of the birch are sparse and misshapen at the upper limit, mainly due to the thin soil and exposure.

As soon as we reached the alders our guide, Mr Ma, began searching the ground in their vicinity and we imagined he was looking for some kind of fungus. Eventually, after an hour or so, he yelled triumphantly and called us to come and see what he had found. It was a strange looking plant, like an elongated caramel-coloured spruce cone, 7.5-10cm (3-4in) tall with numerous overlapping scales. Peeping from between the upper scales we could see tiny purple flowers. There were two flowering spikes joined at the base by a stout 'plate' or 'foot'. It looked to me to be a relative of the broomrapes (*Orobanche*), root parasites, several species of which are native in the British Isles, and that is just what it turned out to be. It was *Boschniakia rossica* and was parasitic on the roots of the alder.

69. We were not the first people to have been dumbstruck by this plant. Even Reginald Farrer must have been rendered temporarily speechless at the sight of this orchid, which has a wide distribution in the northern regions from the Urals across Asia to Siberia, Korea and north-east China south to the Himalaya; it is also found wild in Alaska. His experience of it in Gansu (Kansu) elicited the following typical description: 'C guttatum is a fairy among its kind, filling the dreary birch forests and lone pinewoods of the far North with beauty…away over the dim expanses of the Siberian woodland, dance those ample broad-hooded blossoms of pure white, with their swelling lip that is blotched and marbled most fantastically with rose'.

Betula ermanii and *Trollius japonicus* in the Changbai Shan. (July)

Mr Ma, our guide in the Changbai Shan, with *Boschniakia rossica*, which is growing in a carpet of Bog whortleberry (*Vaccinium uliginosum*), but is actually parasitic on the far reaching roots of a nearby alder (*Alnus mandshurica*). (July)

Boschniakia rossica, a member of the broomrape family (Orobanchaceae) and an important Chinese medicinal plant. Its tiny, purple flowers can be seen protruding from the brown, fleshy scales. (July)

According to Mr Ma, this is an important medicinal plant used to treat, among other things, kidney complaints and problems of the joints and back. It is also a general tonic, supposedly giving great strength and long life – in other words, an aphrodisiac. Mr Ma told us that only the basal part or 'foot' is used and this is soaked in alcohol for twenty-four hours until the liquor is yellow. A tipple is then each taken day. It sounded to be a medicine with great potential, but did it work? Mr Ma would not be drawn, but judging by his fitness and bright smile…

We spent a little time searching for more boschniakias, locating several, one with four flowering stems in a cluster. We then left the woodland and entered a grassy, treeless pasture. Here were more Lady's slippers and a tiny, white-flowered annual gentian. We also found Frog orchid, *Coeloglossum viride*, and Quake grass, *Briza media*, both familiar plants of chalk or limestone pastures in Britain, although they are by no means restricted to such. We also found Mountain avens – *Dryas octopetala*, which is also normally found on basic soils.

When we climbed higher we could have been on a Scottish moorland, for the Alpine clubmoss (*Lycopodium alpinum*) appeared together with the evergreen Cowberry (*Vaccinium vitis-idaea*) and the deciduous Bog whortleberry (*Vaccinium uliginosum*). Both vacciniums have an extensive distribution in the northern hemisphere including the British Isles. *V uliginosum* is quite distinct with small, blue-green leaves. The small, juicy, black berries, covered with a bluish (glaucous) bloom are edible in small quantities and, according to Mr Ma, are used to make the sweet red wine we had been drinking each night.

We wound our way through one last area of birch wood where the trees were lying almost horizontally, no doubt as a result of fierce wind and winter snow. Then we were standing on the lip of the Song Hua valley, looking

Betula ermanii flattened by the weight of winter snow. (July)

The upper reaches of the Song Hua valley. Above can be seen the northern rim of the crater, while below the vast screes are gradually being invaded by birch and alder scrub. (July)

The waterfall at the head of the Song Hua valley seen from the screes above the hot springs. The pilgrims' path can just be discerned snaking across the scree to the right of the waterfall before ascending the cliffs and skirting the base of the higher cliffs above. (July)

down on to the waterfall. We could see right down the valley to the reserve lodge and beyond that to the periphery of the reserve. From this height it was easy to see the extent of the forest, which stretched well beyond the reserve, to some 50km (31 miles), a vast sea of trees in varied tones of green.

We could also see above the waterfall and there was the young Song Hua river running through its austere cindery ravine. We could not, however, see the Heaven's Lake. The snow apparently begins falling here towards the end of September or early October, though isolated snow

showers are not uncommon even in June. In winter according to our guides, the whole of Jilin province is covered in snow except for the hot springs area.

Having had lunch, we began the long trek back to the lodge, heading first for an area of birch wood on a steep slope. In the rough grass above the wood we found a lovely alpine monkshood – *Aconitum monanthum*. This had a tuft of deeply- and narrowly-lobed, glossy, green leaves and short stems bearing one to three large, bluish-purple, helmeted flowers 2.5cm (1in) high on long stalks from

Aconitum monanthum, a curious little alpine monkshood in the grassy pastures above the tree line. (July)

Clematis ochotensis, a low-growing scrambling species closely related to the European *C alpina*, was frequent in the alpine meadows and woodland margins on Baitou Shan. It is rare in western cultivation. (July)

the upper leaf axils. The flowers were a third of the total height of the plant, but later we saw more plants in the valley with stems up to 16cm (6¼ in).

Nearby, we found an equally attractive clematis that Chinese and Japanese botanists refer to as a species – *Clematis ochotensis*, but that some other authorities consider a variety of the European mountain species *C alpina*, as

variety *chinensis*. It was a scrambling, slender-stemmed plant up to 3m (10ft), its leaf clusters dwarfed by the single nodding blue-purple flowers.[70]

We ended this day of days singing our way back through the woods to the river and the lodge beyond, stopping several times for an impromptu concert of songs and dancing, to which everyone contributed.

The alpine pastures on Baitou Shan. *Rhododendron aureum* was plentiful in stream gullies, its pale sulphur flowers creaming the slopes. (July)

458

Tofieldia coccinea, a miniature species of the iris family in damp depressions. (July)

Unquestionably, the most enjoyable day of our week in the Changbai Shan, was a visit to the crater of Baitou Shan to see Heaven's Lake. We left the lodge early, taking packed lunches and drove in the jeeps down the valley. After a while, we turned right and climbed up a steep dirt road that wound its way through dense forest of tall fir and spruce. Gradually, these evergreens began to thin out and birch (*Betula ermanii*) took over. Many of these were short-stemmed, wide-spreading specimens, reminding me of ancient olive groves or apple orchards, except that these trees had cream and pink bark that was peeling in large sheets.

The ground beneath was crowded with flowers, especially *Ligularia jamesii*, and there were great drifts of *Aconitum kamtschaticum*, not yet in flower, filling the glades just as *A laeve* does in the birch woods in the mountains of Kashmir. At around 1,900m (6,200ft) we emerged from the birch into subalpine pastures, their rich green speckled with colour as far as the eye could see.

Hedysarum ussuriense was plentiful, a low-spreading herb with pinnate leaves and one-sided clusters (racemes) of long, creamy-yellow pea flowers carried above the mounds of foliage on long stalks. A bright single daisy flower reminded me of our native Field fleawort, *Senecio integrifolius*, but proved to be *S alpinus*. A *Persicaria* species, with its pale pink poker-like flowerheads, resembled our native *P. vivipara*, and growing with it by a streamside we found a tiny perennial with a tuft of miniature iris-like leaves and short, dark, slender stem tipped with a small cluster of pale pink star-like six-petalled flowers with reddish ovary. It proved to be *Tofieldia coccinea*, a member of the Iris family.

Senecio alpinus, a small species we found peppering the mountain slopes over wide areas. (July)

70. This species has a wide distribution in north-east Asia, including east Siberia, north-east China, N. Korea and north Japan. It is now in cultivation in Europe, represented by several selections and hybrids, all of which are of garden merit.

Papaver pseudoradicatum, one of a large complex of Arctic poppies. (July)

The road began to climb the steep hillside in a series of gigantic curves and most vegetation hugged the ground or the rocks and boulders above it. We had now entered the highest (fourth) zone on the Changbai Shan, the alpine tundra zone above 1,980m (6,500ft). In loose scree areas and on bare patches on the steeper slopes grew a beautiful alpine poppy, *Papaver pseudoradicatum*, its large, pale sulphur blossoms in constant motion above a basal tuffet of deeply cut, grey, downy leaves. In suitable places it occurred in some numbers, exposed to the elements, especially the wind, which blew continuously from out of the Song Hua river valley. According to some authorities, this poppy is just one of a host of so-called Arctic poppies found across the northern regions of Europe, North America and Asia. The name *P. radicatum* has been used to describe the species in the broadest sense. It has contributed as a parent to the Iceland poppies of gardens, a colourful but short-lived race of hybrids.

There were three species of Rhododendron in these high pastures. *R redowskianum* I have already described. It was plentiful here, mainly on the lower slopes. It gave way higher up to another dwarf creeping species – *Rhododendron lapponicum*, whose stems plastered banks, often following the contours of hummocks or rocks. Its slender branches were covered with small, pale green leaves 1cm (½ in) long, densely brown and scaly beneath. The tiny flowers, rose-purple in colour, were borne in neat, small but conspicuous terminal clusters. It was a tough, wiry shrublet and made a charming picture, especially when it shared the same bank or boulder top as the Mountain avens – *Dryas octopetala*, with its small, creamy-white, golden-centred flowers, like miniature roses.[71]

71. *Rhododendron lapponicum* has a wide distribution in the northern hemisphere, especially in the Arctic regions. It was first described from Lapland by Linnaeus (hence the name *lapponicum*, from Lapponia, the Latinised version of Lapland). Typical *R lapponicum* was first introduced to gardens from North America in 1825. Sadly, in Britain certainly, it has not proved amenable to cultivation and does not persist for long.

Papaver pseudoradicatum, a lovely alpine poppy, frequent on screes and in bare or stony areas on the slopes of Baitou Shan. (July)

Dryas octopetala or Mountain avens growing amongst *Rhododendron redowskianum* on Baitou Shan. (July)

Purple-flowered *Oxytropis anertii* growing with creamy-white *Dryas octopetala* on the slopes of Baitou Shan. The former even ventured on to the remnants of the ash cone of the summit. (July)

Rhododendron lapponicum, a well-established plant hugging an exposed rock high on Baitou Shan. (July)

Rhododendron lapponicum growing on a moss-covered boulder on Baitou Shan. Although long known from northern Europe, it has proved difficult, to say the least, in cultivation. (July)

Rhododendron aureum with *R lapponicum* (bottom left) on Baitou Shan. These two species shared the higher slopes of the mountain. (July)

Third in the trio of rhododendrons was the ubiquitous *R aureum* (chrysanthum).[72] This was, without doubt, the most common flowering woody plant in the upper zones of the Baitou Shan, extending from the woods below the lodge (where it was past flowering), to the upper limits of the mountain just short of the ash cone itself. In these alpine pastures it was spectacular, the low evergreen hummocks plastered with loose trusses of pale sulphur-yellow, funnel-shaped flowers. Long bands of yellow marked its progress up steep gullies, and its predilection for streamsides and wet depressions here contrasted with its blanket distribution in the birch woods below. Some days before in Changchun we had visited a man who produced fascinating carved figures from the gnarled roots of this rhododendron.

The road petered out near the top of the mountain and we walked the rest of the way on foot. We were now on the outside of the ash cone or what remained of it and the 'soil' consisted of pale pumice and cinder. Here the poppies appeared again and I was reminded of Henry James's comment: 'Even here, on naked pumice, were clumps of wild yellow poppies, dwarf saxifrage, a vetch and other botanical treasures'. The saxifrage was probably *Saxifraga laciniata*, which resembles in some respects our native Star saxifrage – *S stellaris*, its basal rosette of toothed leaves giving rise to an erect, branching stem bearing showers of small, white, star-like flowers, each petal with two yellow and one red basal spot.

72. *R aureum* is a close relative of *R caucasicum* from north-east Turkey and adjacent parts of the Caucasus in similar situations. Apart from north-east China, *R aureum* occurs widely in the Siberian-Mongolian mountains west to the Altai Mountains and south to the high mountains of north Japan and Korea. It is said to be very low growing as a young plant in cultivation, and its dwarf habit and wind tolerance, according to Peter Cox, might well ensure for it a future as a parent of a new race of dwarf hybrids.

View north from the summit of Baitou Shan. In the foreground stretches the pale pumice and cinder of the ash cone, or what remains of it after several centuries of weathering. It is hard to believe that some plants found a home here. (July)

Streamsides on the slopes of Baitou Shan stained yellow with the blooms of *Rhododendron aureum*. (July)

Rhododendron aureum mass flowering. In mid-summer this species is conspicuous from afar. (July)

Oxytropis anertii, an attractive low carpeting perennial of the pea family, here growing in loose pumice and ash on the summit of Baitou Shan. (July)

Rhodiola atropurpurea, a purple-flowered relative of our native Roseroot *R rosea*, was frequent among rocks and in crevices on Baitou Shan. (July)

Salix polyadenia variety *tschangbaischanica*, a tiny willow creeping in the ash and pumice of the summit cone of Baitou Shan. It is closely related to *S herbacea*, the dwarf willow, which has a wide distribution in northerly regions of North America, Europe and Asia. (July)

Henry James' vetch was almost certainly *Oxytropis anertii*, a prostrate perennial forming mats of grey-green hairy stems and divided leaves above which are borne dense terminal heads of bluish-purple pea flowers. Of his 'other botanical treasures' we found a stonecrop (*Rhodiola atropurpurea*, a purple-flowered relative of our native Roseroot *R rosea* common in our northern and western mountains), a small white flowered *Androsace* species, possibly *A lehmanniana*, with rosettes of hairy leaves, *Potentilla nivea* with trifoliolate toothy leaves white hairy beneath. Its myriad flowers in summer stain the alpine pastures yellow for miles around, and a minute willow not far removed from our native *Salix herbacea*. This had slender creeping stems threading through the ash to form loose mats with small, rounded leaves and tiny, erect catkins consisting of a few flowers. It proved to be *Salix polyadenia* variety *tschangbaischanica*. It seemed incredible that these last few should find a home and choose to live on this uncompromising site exposed to the elements.

Potentilla nivea, in places this alpine perennial grows in huge numbers and is one of the flowers Henry James noted on his visit to the Changbai Shan in 1886. (July)

High projection shaped like a salmon's head on the lip of the caldera

Opposite above: Heaven's Lake in the caldera of Baitou Shan fair took our breath away. According to one legend, this is where the first of the Manchu race was conceived. It is also sacred to the Koreans. (July)

Opposite below: The Tianchi, or Heaven's Lake, in the caldera of Baitou Shan. The Chinese border with North Korea cuts across the lake, the hills on the far (south) side of the water being in the latter country. (July)

When, finally, we breasted the rim of the caldera, our chatter about plants was silenced as our eyes fell at last upon a sight that transcended all that had gone before. Tianchi (Heaven's Lake), is the name given by the Chinese to the body of water that now fills the caldera of the Baitou Shan. On a clear day these calm waters share the blue of the sky, changing from turquoise to ultramarine, depending on the intensity of the sun and its position. At other times, clouds gather over the mountain, and the water becomes a Stygian pool. All of us, Europeans and Chinese, stood quietly gazing into the depths of a lake starkly ringed with ochre-coloured crags and dark precipices. The border between China and North Korea passes right through the middle of the lake; through field glasses we could see figures standing on the far (Korean) side of the caldera, no doubt, like us, marvelling at the wonder of the scene.[73]

It was indeed a superb spectacle. We judged the lake to be about 2.5km (1½ miles) broad and 10 or 11km (6 or 7 miles) in circumference. I was interested to read in a

73. It is worth recounting Henry James's reaction to the same scene almost a century earlier: 'At last we got to the top and looked over the edge, and lo! at the bottom of a crater on whose brink we were standing, about 350ft [106m] below us, we saw a beautiful lake, its colour of the deepest, most pellucid blue, and though the wind was howling above, its surface as still as Lake Leman, reflecting the crown of fantastic peaks with which the rugged top of the mountain was adorned'.

recent account (2005) that this is China's deepest lake.

James and his companions attempted to descend the crater, but were cautioned by their guide who warned that anyone who did reach the bottom would not be allowed to return by the spirit of the lake. Fortunately, good sense prevailed and after a brief attempt they returned to base.

We would dearly love to have stayed on the edge of the crater until evening, but our guides were pressing for our return and, with storm clouds now obliterating the sun, we reluctantly turned away. Rather than drive back down the road, we requested that we be allowed to return on foot through the alpine pastures. It was one of the most memorable descents of a mountain I have ever made.

A myriad flowers in a spectacular landscape filled the next two hours of our lives and left us with an experience to remember. Just as we reached the shelter of the birch woods the heavens opened and the rain came hard and fast, drawing a curtain over the slopes we had so recently explored. It was an ominous but somehow fitting end to our adventure in the Long White Mountains.

At the end of the week we began the long dusty return to Mingyuegou, making several stops, once to admire a powerful large-leaved Dutchman's pipe – *Aristolochia mandshuriensis* – scrambling into trees by the roadside. Only a few yards away on a shady bank we found carpets of *Asarum sieboldii* (*heterotropoides* variety *mandshuricum*) with bold kidney-shaped leaves attractively marbled on the upper

Heaven's Lake on the Baitou Shan; the foreground slopes are covered with the massed yellow blooms of *Potentilla nivea*, an alpine species widespread in northern regions of the northern hemisphere. Photographed by Kim Jung Myoung.

A high slope on the Baitou Shan stained with the rose-coloured flowers of *Rhododendron redowskianum*. Photographed by Kim Jung Myoung.

surface. This is an important plant in Chinese traditional medicine, the dried parts combined with other herbs treating common colds, headache and stuffiness. It is also used in the treatment of chronic bronchitis, mouth ulcers and nasal catarrh. Almost the last plant we examined was a day lily, *Hemerocallis middendorffii* with clusters of orange-yellow flowers. Seed was collected from old capsules and one of the resultant seedlings flowered in my garden in 1988.

That evening we celebrated with a Korean farewell banquet, a sumptuous affair consumed with gusto amid toasts, singing, and the sound of rain beating a tattoo on the restaurant's tin roof. We were served a total of seventeen separate dishes before the final course – a bowl of steaming Korean-style noodles. The meal was accompanied by several drinks including a rather syrupy red liqueur made from the fruits of a hawthorn (*Crataegus pinnatifida* 'Major').

A final candle-lit sing-song in the railway station waiting room was interrupted by a shrill whistle and the sound of a steam engine closing in. Grabbing our belongings, we dashed across the rainswept platform to board the train. I remember, on entering our compartment, wiping a peephole in the misted window through which to wave to our guides as they receded – their hands waving vigorously – into the night.

Chinese Place Names

Since the Chinese language does not possess an alphabet it has long been a problem for the non-Chinese reader to render in his or her mother tongue the sound represented by each Chinese character. For most readers of English or other western European languages this has meant simulating the sounds using the Latin alphabet, a procedure known as romanisation. In the early days of plant exploration in China, foreigners often had to invent their own spellings of place names, especially in little-known and previously un-mapped areas. Eventually a system of romanisation, the Post Office system, was devised which covered the regions, provinces and all but the smallest towns. In many cases, the spelling of the place name was based on the local dialect, thus giving us towns such as Amoy and Swatow.

In 1942 the Post Office system began to be replaced by the Wade-Giles system, which is commonly found in western books concerning plant exploration in China. This was the system most widely used in the West until comparatively recently. It is characterised by the use of apostrophes to distinguish initial sounds, and in some instances may appear illogical. Thus P is pronounced like B. The usual P sound is represented as P'. K is pronounced as J, and so on. When this system is grasped, the present day rendition of Peking as Beijing does not appear such a drastic transformation!

In 1958 the Chinese began to popularise their own system known as Pinyin (spelt sound), and since 1979 this has become the official system of transcribing Chinese names and places in publications in western European languages printed in China.

On the whole, I have used the Pinyin system in all but a few well-known names, such as Tibet and the Yangtze river. Where relevant, the Wade-Giles spellings have also been given in parentheses.

Pinyin spellings in this book have been taken from the *Zhonghua Renmin Gongheguo Fen Sheng Dituji* (*Atlas of China by Provinces*) published in Beijing in 1974. The following lists compare the Pinyin and Wade-Giles/Post Office versions for some of the more important locations in China.

Terms used on modern Chinese maps and atlases

bei	north
bulag	spring
bulak	spring
chi	lake
co	lake
dao	island
ditu	map
dong	east
feng	mountain, peak
gang	harbour, port
gu	valley
guan	pass
hai	sea, lake
he	river
hu	lake
jiang	river
ling	mountain, range, ridge
murun	river
nan	south
nur	lake
po	lake
qu	river
quan	spring
shamo	desert
shan	mountain, peak, range
shankou	pass
sheng	province
shi	city, municipality
shui	river
ul	mountain, range, ridge
xi	west
xian	county
zangbo	river
zhong	central
zizhiqu	autonomous region

Provinces and autonomous regions (AR)

Pinyin	Wade-Giles/Post Office
Anhui	Anhwei
Fujian	Fukien
Gansu	Kansu
Guangdong	Kwangtung
Guangxi	Kwangsi
Guizhou	Kweichow
Hainan	Hainan
Hebei	Hopeh
Heilongjiang	Heilungkiang
Henan	Honan
Hubei	Hupeh
Hunan	Hunan
Jiangsu	Kiangsu
Jiangxi	Kiangsi
Jilin	Kirin
Liaoning	Liaoning
Nei Monggol	Inner Mongolia (AR)
Ningxia	Ningsia (AR)
Qinghai	Tsinghai
Shaanxi	Shensi
Shandong	Shantung
Shanxi	Shansi
Sichuan	Szechuan
Taiwan	Taiwan (Formosa)
Xinjiang	Sinkiang Uighur (AR)
Xizang	Tibet (AR)
Yunnan	Yunnan
Zhejiang	Chekiang

Important cities and towns in botanical exploration
(M = municipality)

Pinyin	Province	Wade-Giles/Post Office
Adunzi	Yunnan	A-tun-tze
Aomen	Guangdong	Macao
Badong	Hubei	Patung
Baoxing	Sichuan	Mupin
Beijing	(M)	Peking
Changchun	Jilin	Changchun
Chengde	Hebei	Jehol
Chengdu	Sichuan	Chengtu
Chongqing	(M)	Chungking
Dali	Yunnan	Tali, Tali-fu
Fuzhou	Fujian	Foochow
Guangzhou	Guangdong	Canton
Guilin	Guangxi	Kweilin
Guiyang	Guizhou	Kouy yang
Hangzhou	Zhejiang	Hangchow
Harbin	Heilongjiang	Harbin
Huangpu	Guangdong	Whampoa
Kangding	Sichuan	Tachienlu, Tatsien-lu
Kashi	Xinjiang	Kashgar
Kunming	Yunnan	Kunming, Yunnan-fu
Lanzhou	Gansu	Lanchow
Leshan	Sichuan	Chiating
Lhasa	Xizang (Tibet)	Lhasa
Lijiang	Yunnan	Likiang, Lichiang
Lüda	Liaoning	Talien
Luding	Sichuan	Luting Chiao
Mengzi	Yunnan	Mengtze
Nanjing	Jiangsu	Nanking
Ningbo	Zhejiang	Ningpo
Qingdao	Shandong	Tsingtao
Shache	Xinjiang	Yarkand
Shanghai	(M)	Shanghai
Shenyang	Liaoning	Mukden
Simao	Yunnan	Szemao
Suzhou	Jiangsu	Soochow
Taibei	Taiwan	Taipei
Tengchong	Yunnan	Tengyueh
Tianjin	(M)	Tientsin
Ürümqi	Xinjiang	Urumchi
Xiamen	Fujian	Amoy
Xianggang	Guangdong	Hong Kong
Yaan	Sichuan	Ya-Chow
Yichang	Hubei	Ichang
Zhangjiakou	Hebei	Kalgan
Zhoushan	Zhejiang	Chusan

Important mountains in botanical exploration

Pinyin	Province	Wade-Giles/Post Office
Anyemaqen Shan	Qinghai	Amni Machen
Cangshan, Cang Shan	Yunnan	Tsangshan or Tali Range
Daba Shan	Sichuan	Tapashan
Emei Shan	Sichuan	Mt Omei
Erlang Shan	Sichuan	Erhlang Shan
Gongga Shan	Sichuan	Minya Konka
Lu Shan	Jiangxi	Lu Shan
Taibai Shan	Sichuan-Shaanxi	Taipai Shan
Yulong Shan	Yunnan	Lichiang Range

Important rivers in botanical exploration

Pinyin	Wade-Giles/Post Office
Chang Jiang	Yangtze (lower)
Dadu He	Tung
Han Jiang	Han
Heilong Jiang	Amur
Huang He	Yellow or Huang
Jinsha Jiang	Yangtze (upper)
Lancang Jiang	Mekong
Longchuan Jiang	Shweli
Min Jiang	Min
Nu Jiang	Salween or Salwin
Qinghai Hu (lake)	Koko Nur
Wusuli Jiang	Ussuri
Yalu Jiang	Yalu
Yarlung Zangbo Jiang	Yalu Tsangpo

Trees and Shrubs
in Chinese Cities and Towns

Most large centres of population are well endowed with trees, the majority planted during the last seventy to eighty years. These comprise native as well as foreign trees, though the latter are generally predominant. The following lists, compiled mainly from my own observations, are by no means comprehensive.

Beijing (Imperial City)

Trees, shrubs and climbers

Aesculus chinensis
Asparagus sprengeri (in pots)
Broussonetia papyrifera
Campsis grandiflora
Catalpa fargesii variety *duclouxii*
Cedrus deodara
Celtis bungeana
Diospyros kaki
Diospyros lotus
Firmiana simplex
Ginkgo biloba
Jasminum mesnyi
Juniperus chinensis
Magnolia denudata
Malus spectabilis
Metasequoia glyptostroboides
Morus alba
Paeonia suffruticosa
Parthenocissus tricuspidata
Philadelphus pekinensis
Phyllostachys species
Platycladus orientalis
Plumeria acutifolia (in tubs; taken under glass in winter)

Prunus mume
Prunus persica 'Alba Plena'
Prunus persica 'Rosea Plena'
Prunus persica 'Rubra Plena'
Prunus triloba 'Multiplex'
Punica granatum
Rosa xanthina
Rosa xanthina forma *spontanea*
Salix babylonica var. *pekinensis* 'Umbraculifera'
Sophora japonica
Sophora japonica 'Pendula'
Syringa oblata
Syringa oblata variety *affinis*
Wisteria sinensis
Xanthoceras sorbifolium
Ziziphus jujuba variety *inermis*

Perennials

Agapanthus orientalis variety *praecox* (in pots; taken under glass in winter)
Hemerocallis fulva
Hosta plantaginea
Paeonia officinalis 'Rubra Plena' and other cultivars and hybrids
Pinellia ternata

Weeds

The walls, cobblestones, flowerbeds and waste places in the Imperial City have long been a home for wild plants many of which, when in flower, add their own colourful contribution to this exotic location. The following list is merely a selection of those seen and identified during several visits since 1979. It could easily be extended.

Abutilon avicennae
Amaranthus retroflexus
Asparagus davuricus
Calystegia subvolubis
Campylotropis species
Capsella bursa-pastoris
Cheilanthes argentea
Chenopodium album
Conyza canadensis
Lemna polyrhiza

Lepidium ruderale
Lycium chinense
Medicago sativa
Melilotus parviflora
Myosotis peduncularis
Orychophragmus violaceus
Oxytropus bicolor
Plantago asiatica
Portulacca oleracea
Potentilla supina
Rehmannia glutinosa
Rubia cordifolia
Salvia plebeia
Scorzoneria austriaca
Setaria viridis
Solanum nigrum
Viola mandshurica

Beijing (streets and highways)

Trees and shrubs

Acer truncatum
Albizia julibrissin
Amorpha fruticosa
Diospyros kaki
Euonymus bungeanus
Forsythia suspensa
Fraxinus chinensis
Fraxinus pennsylvanica variety lanceolata
Ginkgo biloba
Juglans regia
Juniperus chinensis
Koelreuteria paniculata
Lagerstroemia indica
Ligustrum sinense

Pinus bungeana
Pinus tabuliformis
Platanus x hispanica
Populus x canadensis
Populus tomentosa
Robinia pseudoacacia
Rosa xanthina
Rosa xanthina forma spontanea
Salix babylonica var. pekinensis
Salix babylonica var. pekinensis 'Pendula'
Salix babylonica var. pekinensis 'Umbraculifera'
Sophora japonica
Sorbaria sorbifolia
Syringa oblata
Syringa oblata variety affinis

Beijing (Summer Palace)

Trees, shrubs and climbers

Albizia julibrissin
Amorpha fruticosa
Ampelopsis aconitifolia
Buxus microphylla variety japonica
Buxux microphylla variety sinica
Catalpa fargesii variety duclouxii
Cercis chinensis
Chaenomeles speciosa
Diospyros kaki
Ginkgo biloba
Jasminum nudiflorum
Juglans regia
Juniperus chinensis
Juniperus chinensis 'Kaizuka'
Magnolia denudata
Magnolia liliiflora
Malus spectabilis
Phyllostachys species
Picea koraiensis

Pinus bungeana
Pinus tabuliformis
Platycladus orientalis
Prunus triloba 'Multiplex'
Pseudocydonia sinensis
Salix babylonica var. pekinensis 'Pendula'
Sambucus williamsii
Sophora japonica
Sophora japonica 'Pendula'
Sorbaria sorbifolia
Syringa oblata
Syringa oblata variety affinis
Ulmus macrocarpa
Ulmus pumila
Viburnum erubescens variety gracilipes
Vitis amurensis
Wisteria sinensis

Perennials

Hosta plantaginea
Iris decora
Paeonia hybrids

Chongqing (streets and highways)

Trees

Ailanthus altissima
Campthotheca acuminata
Cinnamomum camphora
Firmiana simplex
Ligustrum lucidum

Melia azedarach
Nerium oleander
Paulownia tomentosa
Platanus x hispanica
Robinia pseudoacacia

Guangzhou, Guangdong province (streets and highways)

Trees

Acacia confusa
Aleurites moluccana
Bauhinia blakeana
Bauhinia purpurea
Bauhinia variegata
Bombax ceiba
Casuarina equisetifolia
Cinnamomum camphora
Delonix regia
Eucalyptus citriodora
Eucalyptus robusta
Ficus microcarpa

Grevillea robusta
Hibiscus tiliaceus
Jacaranda mimosifolia
Lagerstroemia speciosa
Litchi chinensis
Livistona chinensis
Melaleuca leucadendron
Melia azedarach
Michelia alba
Psidium guavana
Sterculia nobilis
Swietenia mahogani

Nanjing, Jiangsu province (streets and highways)

Trees and shrubs

Cedrus deodara
Cinnamomum camphora
Euonymus japonicus
Ginkgo biloba
Juniperus chinensis
Lagerstroemia indica
Ligustrum japonicum

Magnolia grandiflora
Metasequoia glyptostroboides
Pittosporum tobira
Platanus x hispanica
Sapium sebiferum
Sophora japonica

Shanghai (streets and highways)
Trees

Ailanthus altissima
Cedrus deodara
Cinnamomum camphora
Firmiana simplex
Ginkgo biloba

Juniperus chinensis
Paulownia tomentosa
Platanus x hispanica
Robinia pseudoacacia
Salix babylonica
Taxodium distichum

Wuhan, Hubei province (streets and highways)

Trees and shrubs

Ailanthus altissima
Cinnamomum camphora
Firmiana simplex
Ginkgo biloba
Juniperus chinensis
Ligustrum lucidum
Pittosporum tobira

Platanus x hispanica
Populus x canadensis
Pterocarya stenoptera
Robinia pseudoacacia
Trachycarpus fortunei
Viburnum awabuki

Xian, Shaanxi province (streets and highways)

Trees and shrubs

Acer buergerianum
Acer truncatum
Catalpa ovata
Cedrus deodara
Firmiana simplex
Juniperus chinensis
Ligustrum lucidum
Paulownia tomentosa (mostly in backyards)

Platanus x hispanica
Populus x canadensis
Populus simonii
Populus tomentosa
Robinia pseudoacacia
Salix babylonica var. pekinensis 'Pendula'
Sophora japonica
Thuja orientalis

Yichang, Hubei province (streets and highways)

Trees and shrubs

Broussonetia papyrifera
Cinnamomum camphora
Citrus species
Jasminum mesnyi
Melia azedarach
Nerium oleander

Paulownia tomentosa
Photinia serrulata
Platanus x hispanica
Populus x canadensis
Punica granatum
Salix babylonica

475

A Select Glossary

acuminate — tapering at the end, long pointed, as in the leaves of *Buddleja forrestii*

acute — sharply pointed, as in the leaves of *Cotoneaster acutifolius*

anther — the pollen-bearing part of the stamen

apomictic — seeds produced solely by the mother plant without fertilisation. The seedlings of an apomictic plant will be as similar to the parent as plants propagated vegetatively by cuttings or grafting. Several genera of the family *Rosaceae*, including *Cotoneaster*, *Malus*, *Amelanchier* and *Sorbus*, share this characteristic, though not <u>all</u> the species are so.

auricles — ear-shaped appendages at the base of a leaf or petal

bipinnate — twice pinnate, as in the leaves of *Aralia elata*

bract — a modified, usually reduced leaf at the base of a flower, often coloured as in *Euphorbia griffithii*

bullate — blistered or puckered, as in the leaves of *Cotoneaster bullatus*

calyx — the outer part of the flower, the sepals

capsule — a dry, several-celled pod, as in the fruits of Iris

ciliate — fringed with hairs, as in the calyx of *Rhododendron pachypodum*

connate — united, joined into one organ as in the leaf stalks of *Clematis connata*

cordate — shaped like a heart, as base of leaf, as in the leaves of *Cardiocrinum giganteum* var *yunnanense*

corolla — the inner, normally conspicuous part of a flower, the petals

corymb — a flat-topped or dome-shaped flowerhead with the outer flowers opening first, as in *Hydrangea aspera*

cuneate — wedge-shaped, as in the leaf base of *Meliosma cuneifolia*

cyme — a flat-topped or dome-shaped flowerhead with the inner flowers opening first, as in *Sedum aizoon*

dioecious — male and female flowers on separate plants, as in holly (*Ilex*), willow (*Salix*) and poplar (*Populus*)

distichous — two-ranked, as in the branches of *Cotoneaster horizontalis*

downy — softly hairy, as in the leaves of *Clematis rehderiana*

elliptic — widest at or about the middle, narrowing equally at both ends, as in the leaves of *Rhododendron rufum*

entire — undivided and without teeth, as in the leaves of *Magnolia denudata*

exfoliating — peeling off in thin strips, as in the bark of *Prunus serrula* and *Acer griseum*

exserted — projecting beyond (as with stamens from corolla), as in the stamens of *Rhododendron spinuliferum*

farinose — a mealy or powdery deposit often white or yellow, as on the young leaves of *Primula sonchifolia*

ferruginous — rust-coloured, as in leaf undersurface of *Rhododendron rex* ssp *fictolacteum*

filaments — the stalk part of the stamen to which the anther is attached

filiform — thread like, as in the sepals of *Gentiana farreri*

floriferous — free flowering

frondose — frond-like, as in branching habit of *Hypericum henryi*

gibbous — swollen on one side, as in the flowers of *Semiaquilegia ecalcarata*

glabrous — hairless, as in the leaves of *Paeonia delavayi*

glandular — with secreting organs (glands), as in the leaves and stems of *Rehmannia glutinosa*

glaucous — covered with a bloom, bluish-white or bluish-grey, as in the stems of *Rubus biflorus*

hispid	beset with rigid hairs or bristles, as in the shoots of *Rubus tricolor*
indumentum	dense hairy covering, as in leaf undersurface of *Rhododendron rex* ssp *fictolacteum*
inflorescence	the flowering part of the plant
involucre	a whorl of bracts surrounding a flower cluster or a single flower as in most members of the thistle and daisy family (*Compositae*)
labellum	the third petal of an orchid flower, usually enlarged (the lip)
lacerate	torn or irregularly cleft
lanceolate	lance-shaped, widening above the base and gradually tapering to the apex, as in the leaves of *Prunus serrula*
lenticelled	small, slightly raised interruptions of the surface of the bark through which air can penetrate to the inner tissues, as in the bark of *Prunus serrula*
linear	long and narrow with nearly parallel margins, as in the leaves of *Lilium pumilum*
lobe	any protruding part of an organ (as with leaf, corolla or calyx), as in leaves of *Quercus dentata*
lobulate	divided into small shallow lobes
midrib	the central vein or rib of a leaf
monocarpic	dying after flowering and seeding, as in *Meconopsis integrifolia*
monoecious	male and female flowers separate on same plant, as in pine (Pinus) and most other conifers, birch (Betula) and oak (Quercus)
monotypic	a genus with one species, as in ginkgo (G biloba)
oblanceolate	lanceolate but broadest near the apex
oblique	unequal-sided, as in the leaf base of *Ulmus macrocarpa*
oblong	longer than broad, with nearly parallel sides, as in the leaves of *Acer oblongum*
obovate	inversely ovate, as in the terminal leaflet of *Paeonia obovata*
obtuse	blunt (as with apex of leaf or petal), as in the leaves of *Hypericum forrestii*
orbicular	almost circular in outline, as in the leaves of *Cotinus coggygria* var *cinerea*
ovate	having an outline like a hen's egg (broadest below the middle), as in the leaves of *Prunus maackii*
palmate	lobed or divided in hand-like fashion, usually five- or seven-lobed, as in the leaves of many maples, eg *Acer palmatum*
panicle	a branching raceme, as in the inflorescence of *Pieris formosa*
pedicel	the stalk of an individual flower in an inflorescence
peduncle	the stalk of a flower cluster or of a solitary flower
penjing	Chinese name for Bonsai
perfoliate	a pair of stalkless opposite leaves or bracts of which the bases are united as in the uppermost leaves of *Lonicera tragophylla*
petal	one of the separate segments of a corolla
petiole	the leaf stalk
pinnate	with leaflets arranged on either side of a central stalk, as in *Sorbus sargentiana*
pistil	the female organ of a flower, comprising ovary, style and stigma
plumose	feathery, as the down of a thistle, or as in the inflorescence of *Cotinus coggygria*
prostrate	lying flat on the ground, as in the stems of *Cotoneaster microphyllus*
pruinose	bloomy, as in the berries of *Berberis pruinosa*
pseudobulb	the thickened or swollen stem of certain orchids, as in *Pleione*
pubescent	covered with short, soft hairs, downy, as in the shoots of *Spiraea pubescens*
raceme	a simple elongated inflorescence with stalked flowers, as in *Prunus maackii*
rachis	an axis bearing flowers or leaflets, as in the main stem of a fern frond such as *Matteuccia struthiopteris*
revolute	rolled backward, margin rolled under (as with leaf), as in the leaves of *Ledum palustre*
rhizome	rootstock of root-like appearance, the apex sending up stems or leaves, as in *Euphorbia griffithii*

477

rib	a prominent vein in a leaf
rufous	reddish-brown, as in leaf undersurface of *Rhododendron rubiginosum*
rugose	wrinkled, as in leaf surface of *Rosa rugosa*
scabrid	rough to the touch, as in the leaves of *Crataegus scabrida*
scale	a minute leaf or bract, or a flat gland-like appendage on the surface of a leaf, flower or shoot; sometimes woody as in the cone scales of a conifer
scandent	with climbing stems, as in *Rosa rubus*
scape	a leafless flower stalk or inflorescence stalk arising usually from ground level, as in *Primula florindae*
sepal	one of the segments of a calyx
serrate	saw-toothed (teeth pointing forward), as in the leaves of *Sorbus pallescens*
serrulate	finely toothed, as in the leaves of *Osmanthus serrulatus*
sessile	not stalked, as in the leaves of *Cunninghamia lanceolata*
spadix	a flower spike with fleshy axis found in aroids and palms, as in *Arisaema elephas*
spathe	a large bract enclosing one or several flowers, as in the hood of *Arisaema elephas*
spike	a simple, elongated inflorescence with sessile flowers, as in *Hedychium spicatum*
spur	a tubular projection from a flower, as in the flowers of *Halenia elliptica*, or a short stiff branchlet as in *Malus toringoides*
stamen	the male organ of a flower comprising filament and anther
staminode	a sterile stamen or similar structure inserted between the corolla and the pistil, as in the flowers of *Corylopsis*
standard	the upper broad petal(s) of certain flowers especially in *Iris* and legumes such as *Cercis*, *Robinia* and *Sophora*
stigma	the summit of the pistil which receives the pollen, often sticky or feathery
stipe	the lower stalk of a fern frond as in *Dryopteris wallichiana*
stipule	appendage (normally two) at base of some petioles, as in rose (*Rosa*) and Pea (*Lathyrus*)
stolon	a shoot at or below the surface of the ground which produces a new plant at its tip, as in *Saxifraga stolonifera*
stomata	breathing pores in leaf surface
strigose	clothed with flattened fine, bristle-like hairs, as in the leaves of *Hydrangea aspera* ssp *strigosa*
style	the middle part of the pistil, often elongated between the ovary and stigma
tepals	petals and sepals of similar appearance, as in flowers of *Clematis* and *Magnolia*
thyrse	a compact narrow panicle as in the inflorescence of *Lysimachia thyrsiflora*
tomentose	with dense, woolly pubescence, as in the leaf undersurface of *Paulownia tomentosa*
tomentum	dense covering of matted hairs, as in the leaf undersurface of *Anemone tomentosa*
trifoliolate	a leaf with three separate leaflets, as in *Acer griseum*
type	strictly the original (type) specimen on which a name is based, but sometimes used in a general sense to indicate the typical form of the species
umbel	a normally flat-topped inflorescence in which the pedicels or peduncles all arise from a common point, as in the flowerheads of *Angelica sinensis*
vein	a strand of vascular tissue in a leaf
venation	the arrangement of the veins
verruculose	minutely warty, as in the shoots of *Berberis verruculosa*
villous	bearing long, soft hairs, as in the stems and leaves of *Meconopsis integrifolia*
whorl	three or more flowers or leaves arranged in a ring, as in the leaves of *Paris polyphylla*
xerophytic	drought tolerant as in *Prinsepia utilis*

Botanists, Plant Explorers and Others Associated with the Chinese Flora

Clarke Abel

Abel, Clarke, 1780-1826   *Abelia chinensis*

Born in England. Died in Cawnpore, India.

English physician and naturalist. Accompanied Lord Amherst's Embassy to the Chinese Court in 1816-1817. Collected dried specimens in several areas of China including Hong Kong, north China, especially the Beijing area, Nanjing and the lower Yangtze valley, and finally Guangzhou in south China. On his returning to England, the ship foundered in the Gaspar Straits between Sumatra and Borneo, and all Abel's specimens were lost. Fortunately, a small duplicate collection had been given to Sir George Thomas Staunton, who also accompanied the Embassy as third Commissioner, and these were saved, including those of the *Abelia*, which bears his name, and *Loropetalum chinensis*. After his return, Abel published an account of his travels, *Narrative of a Journey in the Interior of China in 1816-1817* (1819)

Baber, Edward Colborne, 1843-1890   *Euodia baberi*

Born in Dulwich, London. Died in Bhamo, Burma.

British consular official. Joined British Consular Service in 1866 and posted to Beijing. Served in various capacities in several parts of China. Made several journeys in Sichuan and Yunnan. First Westerner to ascend Emei Shan (Mt Omei). Made no plant collections but reported on many aspects of economic plants including white wax insect.

Isaac Bayley Balfour

Balfour, Sir Isaac Bayley, 1853-1922   *Rhododendron balfourianum*

Born in Edinburgh. Died in Haslemere, Surrey

Noted Scottish botanist. From 1887 to 1921 Professor of Botany at Edinburgh University and Regius Keeper of the Royal Botanic Garden, Edinburgh. Was responsible for naming many of George Forrest's Chinese introductions, especially *Primula* and *Rhododendron*, most of which were first grown in the Botanic Garden. He was instrumental in launching Forrest and, later, Kingdon-Ward on their plant-collecting careers by recommending them to Arthur Bulley.

Bean, William Jackson, 1863-1947   *Hypericum beanii*

Born in Leavening, near Malton, Yorkshire. Died in Kew.

English horticulturist, dendrologist and author. Began his career in private service at several good gardens including Belvoir Castle in Lincolnshire. Entered the Royal Botanic Gardens Kew aged 20 in 1883 as a student gardener, working his way up the ladder eventually to become Curator in 1922. He retired in 1929, after 46 years of service. He became an outstanding authority on woody plants, especially those from China, and was one of the first to grow many of the novelties being sent home by such as Henry, Kingdon-Ward and Wilson. He wrote numerous articles for the horticultural press as well as several books on woody plants, of which *Trees and Shrubs Hardy in the British Isles*, first published in 1914 (presently in its 8th ed.), is still a classic.

W.J. Bean

Bodinier, Emile-Marie, 1842-1901

Buxus bodinieri

Born in Vaiges (Mayenne), France. Died in Guiyang, Guizhou, China

French missionary and plant collector. Collected mostly dried specimens in Beijing area, Hong Kong and for many years in Guizhou. He arrived in Guizhou in 1862 and over many years botanised whenever he found time, sometimes accompanying fellow missionary botanists Pierre Cavalerie and Francois Ducloux. He later moved to Beijing where he was detained for 10 years by mandarins at the Imperial Court. He spent some of this time exploring the Baihua Shan and other mountains close to the capital sending over 900 dried specimens to the Abbé David who passed them on to the Paris Museum. Bodinier discovered several species new to science and eventually returned to Guizhou.

Emile Bodinier, (in 1876)

Bretschneider, Emil, 1833-1901

Bretschneidera sinensis

Born in Riga, Latvia. Died in St Petersburg, Russia.

One of the greatest historians of botanical exploration in China and author, in 1898, of the classic work on the subject *History of European Botanical Discoveries in China*. For seventeen years, 1866-1883, he was physician to the Russian Legation in Beijing, and during this time explored extensively in the country around the capital discovering several plants of horticultural interest. He collected many dried specimens as well as seed and plants, which he sent to European and North American institutions, principally Kew, Jardin des Plantes, Paris, St Petersburg Botanic Garden and the Arnold Arboretum, Massachusetts. He was specially interested in introducing woody plants to cultivation. He also travelled in Japan, India, Java, Sri Lanka and N. America. Between 1882-95 he published *Botanicum Sinicorum* a survey of the flora, vegetation and medicinal plants in China.

Emil Bretschneider

Bulley, Arthur Kilpin, 1861-1942

Primula bulleyana

Born in New Brighton, Cheshire. Died in Neston, Cheshire.

English businessman, horticulturist and the first of the great 20th-century patrons of plant collecting. Made a famous garden noted for its Asiatic plants around his home at Ness, Neston, on the Wirral Peninsula, Cheshire, now the University of Liverpool Botanic Garden, better known as Ness Gardens. Financed several expeditions to the Himalaya and China and helped a number of famous plant hunters in their early careers. Thus George Forrest journeyed to Yunnan on his first expedition in 1904, Frank Kingdon-Ward also visited south-west China sponsored by Bulley in 1911, while R E Cooper explored Bhutan and Sikkim 1911-1913. Bulley also founded the nursery firm Bees of Chester.

Bunge, Alexander Georg von, 1803-1890

Pinus bungeana

Born in Kiev, Ukraine. Died in Odessa, Ukraine

Eminent Russian/Ukrainian botanist of German extraction. Professor of Botany at Kiev; later Director of Dorpat Botanic Garden. Travelled widely in Siberia, Mongolia and north China. Accompanied an ecclesiastical mission to Beijing in 1829, collecting widely and successfully in the plains and mountains around the capital, returning to Russia in 1831. Many of the plants he collected in the Beijing region were species new to science. His son, Alexander Jr (1851-1930) was also a botanist and traveller in China, Japan and Korea.

A.K. Bulley

Carrière, Elie Abel, 1818-1896

Carrieria calycina

Born in May-en-Multien, Seine-et-Marne, France. Died in Montreuil, near Paris, France.

French horticulturist and botanist. From 1852 until his retirement in 1878 he was Chief Gardener of the nurseries at the Paris Museum where so many plants and seeds were being grown from the collections of the French missionaries. From 1866 he was also Chief Editor of the periodical *Revue Horticole* in which he published a great deal of information on ornamental plants, especially those from China cultivated in the museum's garden.

Cavalerie, Pierre 1869-1927
Nothaphoebe cavaleriei

Born in Roussenac (Aveyron), France. Died in Kunming, Yunnan, China.

French missionary and plant collector. Left Paris in 1894 for Guizhou where for many years he travelled widely in the south of the province often collecting dried specimens, which he sent to the Paris Museum. His collections contained a number of species new to science. In 1919 he retired to Kunming in Yunnan where he earned a living as a rice merchant until he was murdered by a Chinese servant.

Chenault, Léon 1853-1930
Ligustrum chenaultii

Born and died in Orleans (Loiret), France.

Famous French nurseryman of Orleans who specialised in rare and recently introduced woody plants. At its peak, his catalogue listed around 3,000 species and varieties. In 1908, he retired and sold his nursery but continued growing and propagating at his new home, the Villa Flora. From then on Maurice de Vilmorin, living at the nearby Arboretum des Barres, used Chenault's exceptional talent to germinate seeds received from the French missionaries in China and those sent by the Arnold Arboretum collected by E.H. Wilson in the same country. Many notable trees and shrubs in the Arboretum des Barres were the result of Chenault's skills. He also was the first to market *Osmanthus delavayi* and the hybrids of *Paeonia lutea* (now *P. delavayi* ssp. *delavayi* forma *lutea*).

Cheng, Wan Chun (Zheng Wan-Jun), 1904-1983
Abies chengii

Born in Jiangsu province, China. Died in Beijing, China.

Distinguished Chinese botanist and Director of the Institute of Agriculture and Forestry in Beijing. Between 1930 and 1950 he collected extensively in Sichuan, writing on a wide range of woody plants, especially conifers, on which he was a leading authority.

Chun, Woon Young (Chen Huan-yong), 1890-1971
Deutzia chunii

Born in Hong Kong. Died in Guangzhou, China.

Chinese botanist. As a young man travelled to the USA to study at the Arnold Arboretum, Harvard University, Boston. Returned to China to teach and was the founder and first director of the South China Botanical Institute, Canton, now Guangzhou. He made a particular study of *Betulaceae* and *Juglandaceae*.

Cox, Euan Hillhouse Methven, 1893-1977
Juniperus recurva variety *coxii*

Born in Westwood, near Glendoick, Perth. Died at Glendoick.

Scottish plant collector, horticulturist and author. One of the last Europeans to see Reginald Farrer alive, accompanying him for the first year of their expedition into upper Burma, 1919-1920. He helped introduce a number of fine plants from the Burma-China border. He also wrote several accounts of plant hunting, of which *Plant Hunting in China* is a classic of its kind. His son Peter and grandson Kenneth have followed in his footsteps: three generations of plant explorers.

Craib, William Grant, 1882-1933
Craibiodendron yunnanense

Born in Kirkside, Banff. Died in Kew, Surrey

Scottish botanist. Regius Keeper of Botany at Aberdeen University. An authority on Asiatic flora, especially *Primula*, *Indigofera* and *Enkianthus*. Made a special study of the flora of Thailand.

Cunninghame (or Cunningham), James, c.1665-1709
Cunninghamia lanceolata

Died at sea returning to England from Java.

Scottish surgeon and first British plant collector in China. First visited China in 1698 in the service of the Honourable East India Company and was stationed for a year on the island of Amoy (now Xiamen). From 1700 to 1703 was again in China, this time on the island of Chusan (Zhoushan). He also collected elsewhere, including St Helena and the Ascension Isles, Cape Province and Malacca. He assembled a large collection of dried specimens most of which he sent to various botanical friends in London.

Alexander von Bunge

Euan Hillhouse Methven Cox

Pierre Cavalerie

Armand David

Armand David, (Paris 1882)

Jean-Marie Delavay

David, Jean Pierre Armand 1826-1900

Davidia involucrata

Born in Espelette, near Bayonne (Basses Pyrenées), France. Died in Paris, France.

French missionary and an energetic and industrious observer and collector of natural history specimens, especially plants. As a boy his father, a doctor, often took him for walks in the mountains to study plants and animals. Trained as a Lazarist priest and in 1862 sent to Beijing where he lost no time in exploring and collecting. The importance of his botanical and zoological activities and achievements led to an exceptional agreement that allowed him to give up his missionary duties in order to spend all his time collecting specimens. In 1866 he travelled to S. Mongolia and in 1868 to Sichuan and S.E. Tibet where he spent almost a year in Moupin (now Baoxing) where he first encountered the Dove Tree *Davidia* and the Panda; he later explored five other provinces. He was, until his death, the link between the French missionary collectors and the Paris Museum. He left China for the last time in 1874. During his three expeditions in China, David collected around 3500 herbarium specimens representing over 1500 species, of which 11 genera and 250 species were new to science.

Decaisne, Joseph 1807-1882

Decaisnea fargesii

Born in Brussels, Belgium. Died in Paris, France.

Belgian horticulturist and botanist. Born in Brussels when Belgium was part of the French Napoleonic Empire, his family settled in Paris when he was 14. His drawing ability helped him gain employment at a laboratory of human anatomy until, at the age of 17, he joined the garden staff at the Paris Museum. A hard and dedicated worker he taught himself horticulture and botany and over a period of years rose through the ranks to become a Professor and Director. He had a special interest in phytogeography and studied the plants collected by botanists in Japan, Timor, Egypt and Arabia. A bachelor, he devoted his entire life to his work, dying "in harness" after two difficult years spent in Paris trying to protect the glasshouses at the Jardin des Plantes from the German artillery during the Franco-Prussian War.

Delavay, Jean-Marie 1834-1895

Magnolia delavayi

Born in Les Gets (Haute-Savoie), France. Died in Kunming, Yunnan, China

French missionary and botanist. Probably the most prominent figure amongst the Chinese missionaries who botanised in China. First sent to China in 1867 to Guangdong province, close to the Vietnamese border where his boyhood experiences trekking in the French Alps stood him in good stead. He collected many specimens in the mountains, sending them to Henry Fletcher Hance, a consular official at Whampoa (now Huangpu) in Guangdong. During a short stay in France in 1881, Delavay was asked by Armand David to collect specimens for the Paris Museum; this he did with a vengeance. For the next ten years, based in the village of Huangping in N.W. Yunnan, north of the Erhai lake, he worked indefatigably as an explorer and plant collector (mainly dried specimens) in the region around.

In 1891 he travelled back to France for treatment suffering from the after effects of bubonic plague but returned to China two years later to begin working and collecting again, this time in N. E. Yunnan where he found the climate more suitable. In all, he collected over 50,000 herbarium specimens belonging to 4,000 species, of which two thirds were new to science. He also sent seeds of plants to the garden of the Paris Museum including several *Rhododendron* species. Many of his discoveries were later introduced to British cultivation by George Forrest.

Diels, Frederich Ludwig Emil, 1874-1945

Cotoneaster dielsianus

Born in Hamburg, Germany. Died in Berlin, Germany.

Eminent German botanist. Professor of Botany and Director of Botanic Garden and Museum in Berlin - Dahlem. Wrote numerous botanical works including *Flora von Zentral China*.

Ducloux, Francois 1864-1945   *Cupressus duclouxiana*

Born in Lyon (Rhone), France. Died in Kunming, Yunnan, China.

French missionary and plant collector. Travelled to Yunnan at the age of 25 in 1889 staying first in Huangping, the same village as Delavay. The two actually met, though Delavay was very ill at the time. Ducloux spent most of his career in Kunming, teaching latin and theology. From 1905 to 1911 he sent seeds he had collected to Maurice de Vilmorin at Arboretum des Barres, many were raised by Leon Chenault. He was one of the longest serving French missionaries, having been in China 45 years by the time of his death.

François Ducloux, 1889

Faber, Ernst, 1839-1899   *Abies fabri*

Born in Coburg, Germany. Died in Qingdao, Shandong, China.

German missionary and botanist. Sent to China in 1865. Travelled in many parts of the country and was the first botanist to climb Emei Shan (Mt Omei), Sichuan province. Collected many dried specimens, most of which he sent to Kew and to Dr Hance at Huangpu in south China.

Wen Pei Fang

Fang, Wen Pei, 1899-1983   *Carpinus fangiana*

Born in Zhong Xian, east Sichuan, China. Died in Chengdu, Sichuan, China.

Distinguished Chinese botanist. Studied at the University of Edinburgh from 1934 to 1937, gaining his doctorate. Travelled widely in Sichuan province for many years, collecting over 20,000 dried specimens, including over 100 species that were new to science and becoming the authority on its flora, especially that of Emei Shan (Mt Omei). Leading authority on *Aceraceae* and *Ericaceae*, especially Chinese species of *Acer* and *Rhododendron*.

Farges, Paul Guillaume 1844-1912   *Epimedium fargesii*

Born in Monclar-de-Quercy (Tarn-et-Garonne), France. Died in Chengdu, Sichuan, China.

French missionary and plant collector. Left for Chengdu in Sichuan in 1867 and from there to N.E. Sichuan where he spent much of his free time collecting dried specimens and seeds in the Daba Shan. In 1893 he was moved to Chongqing, the provincial capital, as chaplain of a local hospital. He had a great passion for plants and came to be regarded by Delavay as one of his heirs in the field of botany. In 1896 he despatched 2,000 dried specimens to the Paris Museum and in 1900 a further 3,500. These contained hundreds of species new to science, including the wild progenitor of the China Aster *Callistephus chinensis*. He also sent seeds to Maurice de Vilmorin at Arboretum des Barres who, in return, sent seeds of vegetables for Farges to distribute to local farmers.

Paul Farges

Farrer, Reginald John, 1880-1920   *Gentiana farreri*

Born in Clapham, Yorkshire. Died in Nyitadi, Upper Burma.

English plant hunter, alpine gardener, botanical artist and author. Famed for his writings on travel, plant hunting and rock gardening, of which *The English Rock Garden* (first published 1919) is a classic. Made only one expedition to China, to Gansu in the north west, with William Purdom, 1914-1916. Collected seed and living plants, especially of alpine and rock plants. It is from this expedition that the well-known garden shrubs *Buddleja alternifolia* and wild source *Viburnum fragrans* (now *V. farreri*) were introduced. On his return home, he published two books describing their travels and experiences, *On the Eaves of the World* (2 vols; 1917) and, posthumously, *The Rainbow Bridge* (1921).

Reginald Farrer

Guo Mei Feng

Feng, Guo Mei (Feng, Kuo-Mei), 1917-2007

Rehderodendron fengii

Born in Yixing, Jiangsu.

Botanist and plant collector. Widely travelled in China, in particular in Yunnan. An authority on *Camellia* and *Ericaceae*, especially the genus *Rhododendron*. Leader of the Sino-British Botanical Expedition to the Cangshan in W. Yunnan in 1981.

Forrest, George, 1873-1932

Pleione forrestii

Born in Falkirk, Stirlingshire. Died in the field in west Yunnan, China

Scottish plant hunter, traveller and botanist. One of the most successful of all plant hunters. Between 1904 and 1932 made seven expeditions to China, mainly in west Yunnan and the mountains of the Sino-Himalaya. Made massive collections of seeds, plants and over 31,000 dried specimens, especially rich in *Primula* and *Rhododendron*, including many new species. He made extensive use of native collectors whom he trained so well that they continued to collect under new employment after his death. All his expeditions were sponsored by private sources, individuals or syndicates, the first of whom was AK Bulley. He was an indefatigable traveller covering a wide area within his chosen territory. He introduced many of the plants first discovered by the French missionary Delavay. Among his most notable introductions are *Pieris formosa* var. *forrestii*, *Rhododendron sinogrande* and *R griersonianum*, *Magnolia campbellii* ssp. *mollicomata*, *Roscoea humeana*, *Buddleja fallowiana*, *Camellia saluenensis* and *Primula forrestii*. Forrest also made collections of mammals, birds and insects, including a number new to science.

George Forrest

Fortune, Robert, 1812-1880

Trachycarpus fortunei

Born in Blackadder Town, Berwickshire. Died in Brompton, London.

Scottish traveller, plant collector and author. One of the most successful of all plant introducers. Sent to China in 1843 by the Royal Horticultural Society, he spent the next three years in the various treaty ports along the coast as far north as Shanghai, buying plants in nurseries and gardens. He returned to China on three subsequent occasions, collecting numerous living plants and seed in the vicinities of the treaty ports and further inland in the provinces of Fujian, Zhejiang and Anhui. During his second and third visits he collected seeds and plants of the tea plant for the Honourable East India Company, which were introduced to north-east India, thus laying the foundation of the tea industry in that country. His fourth and final visit to the Far East, 1860-1862, was mainly spent collecting in Japan, though he again visited Shanghai and, for the first time, Beijing. From his visits he is said to have introduced to Britain for the first time nearly 190 species and varieties of living plants, including *Jasminum nudiflorum*, *Mahonia japonica*, *Cephalotaxus fortunei*, *Clematis lanuginosa*, *Weigela florida* and *Rhododendron fortunei*.

Robert Fortune

Franchet, Adrien 1834-1900

Cotoneaster franchetii

Born in Pezou (Loir-et-Cher), close to Vendôme, France. Died in Paris, France.

Eminent French botanist. Together with the missionary collectors David and Delavay, a member of the French triumvirate who played an important part in the discovery and recording of the Chinese flora in the second half of the 19th century. For much of his career he worked at the Paris Museum where he was responsible for describing and naming many of the collections of plants being sent from China by the French missionaries, particularly those of David and Delavay. He was an acknowledged authority on the floras of China and Japan, publishing numerous papers and monographs on the subject, including the now scarce *Plantae Davidianae* and *Plantae Delavayanae*. He was, it is said, by those who knew him well, a most helpful and modest man who failed to receive due recognition for his work from the French scientific fraternity at the time. He described more than 1,200 species from China new to science.

Gagnepain, François 1866-1952
Berberis gagnepainii

Born in Bois-de-Raveau (Nièvre), France. Died in Paris, France.
French botanist. A farmer's son who began his career as a local schoolmaster with an interest in native plants before being recommended to succeed Adrien Franchet to the Chair of Botany at the Paris Museum. In this he was successful and for the rest of his career worked mainly on the flora of Asia producing 400 publications on the subject. Perhaps his most outstanding achievement was to publish, as sole author, 69 volumes of the monumental *Flore de l'Indochine [Flora of Indochina]*. Described by contemporaries as a likeable man with a great love of social justice, he died accidentally, falling from a train.

Gill, William J, 1843-1882
Quercus gilliana

Born in Bangalore, India. Murdered by Bedouins in Sinai.
British traveller and geographer. Served in the British army in India for several years, after which he travelled in Persia, Transcaspian Russia and then China. In 1877 made a remarkable journey, in the company of William Mesny, through Sichuan, south-east Tibet and Yunnan. Mapped most of his route and made notes on plants seen. Wrote an account of this journey entitled *The River of Golden Sand*.

Giraldi, Giuseppe, 1848-1901
Acer giraldii

Born in Larciano, Italy. Died in Paocheng, Shaanxi, China.
Italian missionary and plant collector. From 1888 until his death collected over 5,000 dried specimens in Shaanxi. He also collected some seed and plants, which he sent to the Botanical Garden in Florence. Among his many discoveries, *Forsythia giraldiana* and *Collicarpa bodinieri* var. *giraldii* are among those still cultivated in Western gardens, the former introduced by Farrer and Purdom.

Hance, Henry Fletcher, 1827-1886
Rhododendron hanceanum

Born in Old Brompton, London. Died in Amoy (now Xiamen), China.
Eminent English botanist and plant collector. Resided for over forty years in China, mainly in Hong Kong and Whampoa (now Huangpu) in Guangdong province as a consular official. His great knowledge of the Chinese flora was of help to a steady stream of botanists and others who collected plants in that country. Many of them sent him dried specimens collected on their travels, often through little known areas. He amassed a collection of 22,437 specimens, which are now housed in the British Museum (Natural History) in London.

Handel-Mazzeti, Heinrich Freiherr (Baron) von 1882-1940
Eurya handel-mazzetii

Born in Vienna, Austria. Died in a car accident in Vienna, Austria.
Austrian botanist, traveller, phytogeographer and plant collector. Son of an officer in the Austrian army, he owed his love of nature, especially plants, to his mother to whom he was devoted, dedicating his monograph on *Taraxacum* (dandelions) to her in 1907. He was a keen climber and hiker in the mountains of Europe and W. Asia and in 1914, in response to the plant discoveries of George Forrest, he was sent to accompany the German botanist Camillo Schneider to Yunnan in China on a journey of plant exploration. They travelled to the Yulong-shan above Lijiang, where they met up with Forrest before continuing their journey. In July of that year they received news of the declaration of war between Germany and the Western Allies. Unable to return to Europe, they continued their exploration until early the next year when Schneider left to take up a position as botanist at the Arnold Arboretum in the USA leaving Handel-Mazzeti to pursue his exploration alone. This he did with immense success travelling through Yunnan, Sichuan, S.E. Tibet and Guizhou to Hunan, from where, in 1919, with the end of the war in Europe, he returned home. He made extensive collections of dried specimens, some 3,000 in total including many species and some genera new to science. He later published an account of his travels and discoveries, recently translated into English as *A Botanical Pioneer in South West China*. He was regarded as one of the greatest authorities on Chinese plants and their distribution with a particular interest in *Primula* and *Lysimachia*.

Adrien Franchet

Henry Hance

Heinrich von Handel-Mazzeti

William Botting Hemsley

Augustine Henry

Joseph Hers

Hemsley, William Botting, 1843-1924 *Styrax hemsleyana*

Born in Uckfield, Sussex. Died in Broadstairs, Kent.

Eminent English botanist. The son of a gardener, Hemsley entered Kew as an apprentice gardener. After six months he was offered temporary work in the Kew herbarium, where he stayed for the rest of his career, rising to become Keeper in 1899. After retirement in 1908 he moved to Strawberry Hill, Twickenham, but continued to visit Kew for some years after. In 1884 he began work on a catalogue of the known plants of China, an impressive work completed in 1905. He named and described many new species from China, including many of EH Wilson's collections.

Henry, Augustine, 1857-1930 *Tilia henryana*

Born in Dundee, Scotland; shortly after his birth his parents moved to Cookstown in Co Tyrone, Northern Ireland. Died in Dublin, Northern Ireland.

Irish physician, plant collector, botanist and author. From 1880 employed for twenty years by the Imperial Chinese Maritime Customs Service. For seven years, 1882-1889, he was stationed at Ichang (now Yichang) on the Yangtze. Here he first began collecting dried specimens and seed from the mountains of west Hubei and adjacent Sichuan, sending them to Kew. He also served in Hainan Island (briefly), Taiwan and for several years in south Yunnan at Mengtze (now Mengzi) and Szemao (now Simao), and continued to collect in these areas. It is said that he sent to Kew over 150,000 dried specimens, representing 6,000 species of which nearly 1,500 were new to science. He introduced a number of plants to cultivation, but many of his best discoveries were later successfully introduced by E H Wilson. On his return to Britain in 1900 he began a successful career in forestry and, together with H J Elwes, wrote the classic *The Trees of Great Britain and Ireland*.

Hers, Joseph, 1884-1965 *Acer grosseri var. hersii*

Born in Namur, Belgium. Died in Louvain, Belgium.

Belgian administrator and amateur dendrologist. First went to China in 1905 to become interpreter to the Belgian Consul in Shanghai. From 1913, on leaving consular service, until 1924, he was General Secretary of the General Company of Chinese Railways and Tramways. One of his duties was to locate timber for railway construction. He also had the opportunity of tracing the route for a proposed railway from the sea to the Gansu border. During this period he was based in Henan but travelled in remote areas of Gansu and Shaanxi as well as Henan and Jiangsu. He made a large collection of dried specimens as well as seeds of many trees, which he sent to the Botanical Garden in Brussels and to the Arnold Arboretum, Massachusetts.

Hu, Shiu Ying, b. 1910 *Ilex huiana*

Born in Zuzhou, China.

Distinguished Chinese botanist. For many years worked at the Arnold Arboretum of Harvard University, Massachusetts. An authority on the genus *Ilex* and Chinese medicinal plants. Published extensively on Chinese plants especially *Philadelphus, Clethra, Compositae* and *Orchidaceae*.

d'Incarville, Pierre-Nicolas Le Cheron 1706-1757 *Incarvillea grandiflora*

Born in Louviers (Eure), France. Died in Beijing, China.

French Jesuit priest and botanist. Sent to Beijing in 1740 where he lived in the residence of the Jesuits in the Imperial Palace. He tried to cultivate the attention of the new Emperor Qianlong, who had an interest in gardens and flowers, but the Emperor was hostile to evangelisation in his country and actively persecuted the Jesuits except those residing in the Forbidden City. Indeed, d'Incarville collected his first dried specimens in the Forbidden City but in 1745, along with his colleagues, he was forced to leave and take up residence elsewhere. He continued to collect specimens in the city and its surroundings as well as seeds of the Kiwi fruit (or Chinese gooseberry) *Actinidia deliciosa, Sophara japonica* and Tree of Heaven *Ailanthus altissima*, which he sent to Paris. Many ornamental plants in Western gardens, including the Bleeding heart *Dicentra spectabilis*, were originally introduced by him. Sadly, it was not until more than a century later that his specimens in the Paris Museum were named by Adrien Franchet, after his attention was drawn to them by Emil Bretschneider.

Kerr, William 1779-1814

Kerria japonica

Born in Hawick, Roxburghshire. Died in Colombo, Sri Lanka.

Scottish gardener and plant collector. Son of a nurseryman who became a gardener in the Royal Botanic Garden at Kew (c.1800). In 1803 he was sent by Kew to Canton (now Guangzhou) in South China where he purchased plants from nursery gardens around the city. Many of these were subsequently grown for the first time in Europe at Kew. They included *Kerria japonica*, a cultivated double-flowered form now known as 'Plena' and the double white Banksian rose *Rosa banksiae* variety *banksiae* ('Alba Plena') or Lady Banks Rose (named for the wife of the then advisor to the Royal Botanic gardens, Sir Joseph Banks). Kerr later collected in Java and the Philippines before ending his days in Ceylon (now Sri Lanka) where he was Superintendent of Gardens on Slave Island and at King's House, Colombo.

Kingdon-Ward, Francis (Frank) 1885-1958

Rhododendron wardii

Born in Manchester. Died in London.

English plant collector, explorer, geographer and author. Often regarded as the last of the great plant hunters in China. The son of a Professor of Botany at Cambridge University, he travelled extensively in West China, S.E. Tibet, Burma and Assam. His first plant hunting expedition to Yunnan in 1911 was sponsored by the Liverpool businessman and gardener A.K. Bulley, who had previously sponsored George Forrest. Kingdon-Ward probably collected plants in east Asia over a longer period than any other explorer, mounting successive expeditions between 1911 and 1956. He introduced dried specimens, plants and seeds especially of *Primula* and *Rhododendron* and famously introduced seed of the Blue poppy *Meconopsis betonicifolia* (as *M. baileyi*) from S.E. Tibet in 1925. He authored countless papers and many books about his travels and collections as well as their cultivation in gardens.

Frank Kingdon-Ward

Kirilov, Porphyri Yevdokimovich 1801-1864

Indigofera kirilowii

Died in St. Petersburg, Russia.

Russian physician and botanist. Studied medicine in St. Petersburg before being appointed physician to a Russian Ecclesiastical Mission to Beijing in 1830 in company with Alexander von Bunge. During a long residence in the Chinese capital he devoted himself to investigating the flora of the Beijing Plain and its adjacent mountains, in about 1835 being the first botanist to visit the celebrated mountain Po-hua-Shan, 60 miles west of Beijing. He left China in 1841 and returned to St. Petersburg where he was appointed Interpreter for Chinese in the Asiatic Department of the Foreign Office. He made large collections of dried specimens and some of living plants and seeds in the Beijing area and Mongolia. These included the first dried specimen of the Chinese Ginseng *Panax ginseng* to be received in Europe from its homeland in China's north eastern provinces.

Bernhard Koehne (Courtesy of Hunt Institute for Botanical Documentation, Carnegie Mellon University, Pittsburgh, PA)

Koehne, Bernhard Adalbert Emil, 1848-1918

Sorbus koehneana

Born in Sasterhausen, Striegau, Germany. Died in Berlin, Germany.

German botanist and dendrologist. Professor in Natural History at the Falk Gymnasium, Berlin. Author of several important botanical and horticultural works including *Deutsche Dendrologie*. An authority on *Lythraceae* and certain genera of *Rosaceae*. He named a number of new Chinese collections made by Wilson, especially in *Sorbus* and *Philadelphus*.

Komarov, Vladimir Leontjevich, 1869-1945

Syringa komarowii

Born in St Petersburg, Russia. Died in Moscow, Russia.

Russian explorer and botanist. Travelled widely in south-east Siberia, especially in the Amur river valley and what was then known as Manchuria, now China's north-east provinces. Reached the Korean border in 1896. Revisited north Korea the following year and returned via Jilin province to the Siberian coast. Collected 6,000 dried specimens between 1895 and 1897, including many species new to science, most if not all of which he took with him on his return to St Petersburg Botanic Garden.

V.L. Komarov

Frank Ludlow

Ludlow, Frank, 1885-1972

Rhododendron ludlowii

Born in Chelsea, London. Died in London.

English naturalist, botanist, traveller and plant hunter. A former teacher who, for twenty years from 1932, in a famous partnership with George Sherriff, explored in the eastern Himalaya, including south-east Tibet, collecting both dried specimens and living plants and seed for British cultivation. Their introductions included many species new to science and were particularly rich in *Rhododendron, Primula* and *Meconopsis*.

Maack, Richard Carl 1825-1886

Maackia amurensis

Born in Arensburg, Isle of Oesel. Died in St. Petersburg, Russia.

Russian naturalist and explorer. Studied natural sciences at St. Petersburg University and in 1852 appointed Professor of natural sciences at the Gymnasium (College) of Irkutsk, later becoming Superintendent of all schools in eastern Siberia. In 1855 he made an expedition to the Amur river region returning the following year. In 1859 he made a journey along the Ussuri river. He published accounts of both journeys, from which he returned with many botanical, zoological, geological and other specimens. His dried plant specimens contained many species new to science including *Prunus maackii* and were described by Maximowicz and others. His later years were spent in St. Petersburg.

Edouard Maire, 1872

McLaren, Henry Duncan, 2nd Lord Aberconway, 1879-1953

Hypericum maclarenii

Born at Bodnant, North Wales. Died at Bodnant.

English industrialist and horticulturist. In collaboration with his mother, Laura, 1st Lady Aberconway, transformed an ordinary garden at Bodnant, Tal-y-cafn, into one of outstanding beauty and botanical interest. For twenty-two years, 1931-1953, President of the Royal Horticultural Society. He supported many plant collecting expeditions to China, especially those of Wilson, Forrest and Kingdon-Ward. After Forrest's death in 1932, McLaren continued for a while to employ his native collectors who sent seed back to Bodnant.

Maire, Edouard 1848-1932

Allium mairei

Born in Trondes (Meurthe-et-Moselle), France. Died in Tung-ch'uan, Yunnan, China

French missionary and plant collector. Sent in 1872 to Yunnan where he spent the rest of his life. In his spare time he collected large numbers of dried specimens, including *Incarvillea mairei* and *Mahonia mairei* and some seed especially in the Kunming area where from 1907 to 1916 he was Pro-Vicar Apostolic of Yunnan province.

Maries, Charles, 1852-1902

Platycodon grandiflorum variety *mariesii*

Born in Hampton Lucy, Warwickshire. Died in Gwalior, India.

English plant hunter. Son of a boot- and shoemaker, who as a schoolboy was tutored in botany by his headmaster the Reverend G. Henslow, who later became Professor of Botany to the Royal Horticultural Society. Maries first worked with his younger brother Richard, who had set up as a florist and nurseryman at Lytham in Lancashire. After seven years he took employment with the famous nursery firm of Veitch of Chelsea, and from 1877 until 1879 travelled on their behalf in Japan, Taiwan and China. He was most successful in Japan, from which country he introduced many ornamental plants, especially maples and conifers. In China he collected mainly in Zhejiang province, especially Ningbo, where Robert Fortune had previously collected, and along the Yangtze as far as Yichang, from where he introduced *Homamelis mollis* and *Primula obconica*. He was one of the first 60 recipients of the Royal Horticultural Society's Victoria Medal of Honour, in 1897.

Charles Maries

Maximowicz, Carl 1827-1891

Populus maximowiczii

Born in Tula, Russia. Died in St. Petersburg, Russia.

Eminent Russian botanist, traveller and plant collector. His illustrious career began in 1845 as a student at the Dorpat University, initially in medicine and then botany. Five years later he was appointed Assistant Director of the University Botanic Garden under Alexander von Bunge. The following year he was appointed Keeper of the herbarium at St. Petersburg Botanic Garden where he was based for the rest of his working life. Between 1853 and 1864 he made a series of extensive journeys on behalf of the Botanic Garden charged with collecting plants, seeds and dried specimens. One voyage took him south to Rio de Janeiro in Brazil, Valparaiso in Chile and to Hawaii, but his main activities concentrated on Japan, Manchuria (N.E. China) and S.E. Siberia, where he explored both the Amur and Ussuri river valleys. From Japan alone he collected 2,500 dried specimens and around 400 living plants. Hundreds of species new to science resulted from these travels and many new plants first cultivated in St. Petersburg Botanic Garden eventually found their way into European cultivation and beyond.

On his return from Asia, Maximowicz was made Chief Botanist and Director of the Botanical Museum. From then on he specialised in the flora of eastern Asia, naming and describing his own collections and those of others in the herbarium as well as subsequent collections made by fellow Russians such as Przewalski, Piasetski and Potanin and from non-Russian sources including Hance and Hancock in S. China and Tchonoski and others in Japan.

Carl Maximowicz

Meyer, Frans (Frank) Nicholas 1875-1918 *Syringa meyeri*
Born in Amsterdam, The Netherlands. Drowned in the Yangtze River, China.

American plant collector of Dutch birth. Arrived in the United States in 1901. From 1905 until his death he was employed by the US Department of Agriculture as a collector of economic plants. He made four major expeditions, which took him into central Asia, Siberia, north Korea and China. He collected and dispatched to America vast quantities of seed, plants and propagation material, especially of fruits, vegetables, cereal and fodder crops, and windbreak trees. He also collected a lesser number of ornamental plants. He is credited with over 2,000 plant introductions, details of which he carefully and painstakingly recorded by hand, including notes on cultivation, propagation and native uses. He had an insatiable thirst for travel and the ability to walk long distances along trails and across rough country, even in winter. His introductions were described by his employers as having changed the landscape and improved the economy of the United States.

Frank Meyer

Monbeig, Jean-Théodore 1875-1914 *Deutzia monbeigii*
Born in Salies-de-Béarn (Pyrenées Atlantiques), France. Died in W. Sichuan, China.

French missionary and plant collector. In 1899 he travelled to Tsekou (now Gongshan) in W. Sichuan and with fellow missionary Père Dubernard founded a mission for new converts. In 1905 anti-foreign riots started along the Sino-Tibetan border in the vicinity of Batong; several missionaries were killed, including Dubernard and Soulié. Monbeig died 10 years later in similar circumstances, on the road from Xinlong (now Yaregong) to Litang. He made a number of collections mainly of dried specimens.

Orléans, Prince Henri d', 1867-1901 *Rodgersia aesculifolia* variety *henricii*
Born in Ham, Surrey. Died in Saigon, Vietnam.

French explorer and naturalist, son of Robert, Duke of Chartres, the grandson of the ousted 'King of the French' Louis-Philippe. In 1889, at the age of twenty-two, he made an extraordinary journey from France to Siberia, and thence south via Chinese Turkestan to Tibet. From here his party continued to Sichuan, Yunnan and into Vietnam as far as Hanoi, which they reached towards the end of 1890. He made geological, zoological and botanical collections (mostly dried specimens), which he presented to the Paris Museum. They included a good number of species new to science. In 1895 he returned to China on a second expedition, this time to south-west China. His main objective was the exploration of the upper courses of the Mekong, Salween and Irrawaddy rivers. He completed this pioneering journey in less than twelve months, arriving at Assam in time for Christmas. Most of his botanical and zoological collections on this journey were made in Yunnan.

Jean-Théodore Monbeig

Paul-Hubert Perny

Perny, Paul-Hubert 1818-1907
Ilex pernyi

Born in Pontarlier (Doubs), France. Died in Garches (now Hauts-de-Seine), France.

French missionary, naturalist and botanist. Began his career as a curate in Besancon before travelling to Guizhou in 1847 where he worked until 1857, returning to France that year for a respite. He then returned to Guizhou where he continued for a few years until 1862 when he moved to Sichuan. He left China for good in 1868, settling in Paris, where the following year he published a French-Latin-Chinese dictionary on spoken Mandarin, to which he later added a lexicon on natural history. Perny was the first European zoological and botanical explorer in Guizhou. In 1850, he sent to Lyon, one of the world capitals of the silk industry, 500 living cocoons of an oak silk worm (*Bombyx pernyi*). When he returned to France in 1857 he brought with him several thousand living plants and animals as well as herbarium specimens, including many species new to science.

G.N. Potanin

Piasetsky, Pavel Jakovlevich, 1843-1919
Vitis piasetskii

Born in Orel, Russia.

Russian army surgeon, naturalist, ethnographer, diarist and accomplished artist. In 1874/5 accompanied Captain Sosnovski's expedition to explore a trade route from Russian territory in Dsungaria into north-west China and the Upper Yangtze area. Made zoological and botanical collections throughout the journey, among which around 36 plants proved to be species new to science, including *Buddleja alternifolia* and *Dipelta floribunda*. These were collected in the provinces of Hubei, Shaanxi and Gansu. In 1880 Piasetsky published an account of the journey entitled *Travels in China*.

Potanin, Grigori Nikolaevich, 1835-1920
Larix potaninii

Born in Yanisheva, Siberia. Died in Tomsk, Siberia.

Eminent Russian explorer and naturalist. Between 1876 and 1894 made four great journeys into eastern Asia, including Mongolia and China, principally in the provinces of Shanxi, Gansu and Sichuan. He made vast collections of zoological and botanical specimens (12,000 dried specimens from his third expedition alone) as well as of seed, which was sent to the St Petersburg Botanic Garden. Potanin's wife Alexandra (after whom *Rheum alexandrae* is named) accompanied and assisted him on all four expeditions, dying on the last. Among his plant collections were many species new to science.

Pratt, Antwerp E, active late 19th/early 20th century
Sorbus prattii

English naturalist and traveller. From 1887 until 1890 explored the upper Yangtze area of Sichuan province and the mountains around Kangding. He was mainly interested in zoology, collecting animals, fish, insects and birds, but at Yichang on his journey up the Yangtze he met Augustine Henry who persuaded him to take a trained native to help him collect and dry botanical specimens. He collected some 500 species, mostly in the Kangding area, including many species new to science.

Przewalski, Nicolai Mikhailovich, 1839-1888
Ligularia przewalskii

Born near Smolensk. Died in Karakol at the start of another journey.

Illustrious Russian soldier, explorer, geographer and naturalist. From 1867 to 1869 collected in the Ussuri River area of eastern Siberia. Between 1870 and 1885 he made four great journeys of discovery in central Asia, collecting large numbers of zoological and botanical (dried) specimens. Many seeds were also gathered, and plants from these were grown in the St Petersburg Botanic Garden and elsewhere in Europe. They included many species new to science.

A.E. Pratt

Purdom, William 1880-1921

Born in Heversham, Westmoreland. Died in Beijing, China.

Allium purdomii

English plant hunter and gardener. As a young man he worked for Messrs Lowe & Co. and Messrs Veitch at their Coombe Wood nursery before joining Kew in 1902 where he "distinguished himself as a propagator and grower of hardy woody plants" becoming subforeman of the Arboretum Nursery and from 1905 a student for two years. From 1909 until 1911 he was in north-west China on a plant hunting expedition financed jointly by the firm of Veitch and the Arnold Arboretum, Massachusetts. He spent most of this time in Gansu, Shanxi, Inner Mongolia and the Tibetan borderland whence he returned with seed, plants and dried specimens. These included *Aesculus chinensis*, *Daphne giraldii*, *Malus transitoria* and *Viburnum fragrans* (now *V. farreri*). In 1914 he returned to China collecting in Gansu with Reginald Farrer. On the latter's return to England in 1915, Purdom remained in China as an Inspector with the Chinese Forestry Bureau. He was given a job organising a tree planting programme for the Chinese Railways, living for much of this time in a converted railway carriage in remote areas. Sadly, the rigours of the job led to his demise following a minor operation at the French Hospital in Peking (Beijing), just one year following the death of Farrer in Burma.

Reeves, John (senior), 1774-1856

Born in West Ham, London. Died in Clapham, London.

Reevesia thyrsoidea

English naturalist. Lived in China from 1812 to 1831, eventually becoming chief Inspector of Tea for the Honourable East India Company in Guangzhou. Collected living plants from local nurseries and gardens, sending them by sea to various individuals and institutions in England, in particular the Horticultural Society of London (now the Royal Horticultural Society). Commissioned Chinese artists to prepare a now famous collection of coloured drawings of native plants. He was the immediate or indirect source of introduction to Britain of the first Chinese azaleas, camellias, tree peonies, chrysanthemums and numerous other ornamental garden plants.

Reeves, John Russell (junior), 1804-1876

Died in Wimbledon, Surrey.

Skimmia reevesiana

English naturalist, son of John Reeves (senior). Lived for thirty years in China as Assistant, then Chief Inspector of Tea in the employ of the Honourable East India Company. Collected mainly dried specimens as well as a number of living plants, such as *Deutzia scabra*, which he introduced to England.

Rehder, Alfred, 1863-1949

Born in Waldenburg, Sachsen (Saxony), Germany. Died in Boston, Massachusetts, USA.

Rehderodendron macrocarpum

Distinguished American botanist and author of German birth. Went to the United States in 1898 and was initially employed as a garden labourer at the Arnold Arboretum of Harvard University, Massachusetts. His botanical training and experience in Germany soon earned him a job in the Arboretum library and herbarium where he rose to become Professor of Dendrology and a world authority on hardy woody plants, especially those of China. He was responsible for describing many of EH Wilson's collections as well as those of other collectors, among them Joseph Rock. He published numerous papers on his subject and will long be remembered for three publications in particular: *Bibliography of Cultivated Trees and Shrubs Hardy in the Cooler Temperate Regions of the Northern Hemisphere*, 1949, *Bradley Bibliography* (a five-volume guide to the Literature of the Woody Plants of the World Published before the Beginning of the Twentieth Century), 1918, and his better-known *Manual of Cultivated Trees and Shrubs Hardy in North America*, 1927.

Nicolai Przewalski

William Purdom

Alfred Rehder

491

Joseph Rock

Charles Sargent

George Sherriff

Rock, Joseph Francis Charles, 1884-1962   *Paeonia rockii*

Born in Vienna. Died in Honolulu, Hawaii, USA.

American explorer, geographer, plant hunter and photographer of Austrian birth. From 1908 to 1919 he lived in Hawaii becoming an authority on the woody flora of those islands. Between 1922 and 1949 he spent a great deal of his time and was very much 'at home' in China, mainly in Yunnan, Sichuan, south-east Tibet and Gansu, financed by various American institutions. He was a man of many talents and a natural linguist, as well as a prolific collector of dried specimens and seed, especially *Rhododendron*. His photographs of Gongga-shan (Minya Konka) in the Hengduan mountains of W. Sichuan have never been surpassed.

Sargent, Charles Sprague 1841-1927   *Sorbus sargentiana*

Born in Boston, Massachusetts. Died in Brookline, Massachusetts.

Distinguished American dendrologist, botanist, horticulturist, plant collector and administrator. In 1873 created the Arnold Arboretum of Harvard University at Jamaica Plain, Massachusetts, becoming its first Director, a position he held until his death. Collected extensively in North America, later compiling his monumental *Silva of North America*. He also collected in Japan in 1892. He was responsible for employing a number of plant hunters to collect in China on behalf of the Arnold Arboretum; these included EH Wilson, William Purdom and Joseph Rock. Their collections and those of others helped make the Arboretum one of the premier collections of Asiatic, especially Chinese, woody plants in the Western world.

Schneider, Camillo Karl, 1876-1951   *Deutzia schneideriana*

Born in Oschatz near Leipzig, Germany. Died in Berlin, Germany.

German botanist, dendrologist and plant collector. Began his working life as a gardener becoming a garden architect in Vienna. Between 1903 and 1912 he wrote his monumental *Illustrated Handbook of Woody Plants Cultivated in Central Europe* (*Illustriertes Handbuch der Laubholzkunde*). After travels in the Caucasus he accompanied Handel-Mazzetti in 1914 on a plant collecting expedition through Yunnan and west Sichuan where they collected large amounts of dried specimens, though little in the way of live plants or seed. When war broke out in Europe he left China via Shanghai, where he was briefly interned and came eventually to the Arnold Arboretum of Harvard University, Massachusetts, where he worked for four years as a taxonomist, describing a good number of EH Wilson's Chinese collections. He was a specialist in the genera *Berberis* and *Syringa*. Went to Berlin in 1919 where he worked as a garden architect and editor. He also began a monograph on the genus *Berberis*, which, however, was unfortunately destroyed by fire during the Second World War, before it could be published.

Sherriff, George, 1898-1967   *Berberis sherriffii*

Born in Larbert, Stirlingshire. Died in Kirriemuir, Angus.

Scottish soldier and plant hunter. From 1932 onwards, in partnership with Frank Ludlow, he made several expeditions into the eastern Himalaya, especially Bhutan and south-east Tibet, whence large numbers of dried specimens and seeds were introduced to Britain. In 1950 made a renowned garden around his home at Ascreavie where many of his introductions, especially *Rhododendron*, *Primula* and *Meconopsis*, flourished.

Simon, Gabriel Eugène, 1829-1896   *Populus simonii*

Born at Metz, France. Died in Paris, France.

French diplomat, agronomist, botanist and plant collector. Between 1860 and 1871 he travelled widely in China, both in an official capacity and in pursuit of his botanical interests. He also visited Japan. During this time he made extensive collections of dried specimens and seed, all of which he sent to the Paris Museum, the seed to be grown in the gardens there. A number of his collections proved to be species new to science.

Smith, Karl August Harald, 1889-1971

Cotoneaster harrysmithii

Born in Stockholm, Sweden. Died in Uppsala, Sweden.

Swedish botanist and plant collector, better known as Harry Smith. Between 1921 and 1935 made three expeditions to China, collecting first in the Western Hills of Beijing. Most of this time, however, was spent in the provinces of Yunnan, Sichuan, Shanxi and Tibet. He made large collections of dried specimens, including a number of species new to science. He also collected seed that he introduced to Western cultivation, mainly through Magnus Johnson Nurseries in Stockholm and the Gothenburg Botanic Garden. He became an authority on the Asiatic species of *Gentianaceae*, *Orobanchaceae* and *Saxifraga*.

Harry Smith

Smith, Sir William Wright, 1875-1956

Primula smithiana

Born in Lochmaben, Dumfriesshire. Died in Edinburgh.

Distinguished Scottish botanist. For many years, 1922-1956, Regius Keeper of the Royal Botanic Garden, Edinburgh, and Professor of Botany at Edinburgh University. An authority on the Himalayan and Chinese floras. Like his predecessor at Edinburgh, Sir Isaac Bayley Balfour, he was involved in naming and describing a great number of George Forrest's Chinese collections. An authority on *Rhododendron* and *Primula*.

Soulié, Jean-André 1858-1905

Rhododendron souliei

Born in Saint-Juery (Aveyron), France. Died in Yaregong, W. Sichuan, China.

French missionary and plant collector. Left France in 1885 for the Tibet mission and was posted to Batang and then Luding, both towns now in W. Sichuan. He later moved to Tsekou (now Gongshan) in N.W. Yunnan joining Père Dubernard until 1896 when he settled in Yaregong (now Xinlong) in W. Sichuan. In 1905 during troubles along the Sino-Tibetan border he was captured by lamas, tortured and put to death. During his time travelling in rough mountain terrain he collected and sent to the Paris Museum around 7,000 dried specimens and some seeds including species new to science.

William Wright Smith

Staunton, Sir George Leonard, 1737-1801

Elsholtzia stauntonii

Born in Cargin, Galway, Ireland. Died in London.

Diplomat and amateur botanist. Secretary to Lord Macartney's Embassy to the Qian Long Emperor in 1792-94. Subsequently, they journeyed south through the eastern provinces and eventually to Guangzhou. Both Staunton and Macartney collected dried specimens, while a gardener attached to the Embassy, probably J Haxton, collected living plants mainly in the Beijing area. Staunton was also accompanied by his young son George Thomas (1781-1859) who from 1799-1817 worked with the Honourable East India Company in Canton and in 1816-1817 travelled with Lord Amherst's Embassy to the Jiajing Emperor as physician and naturalist.

Tatarinov, Alexander Alexeyewich, 1817-1886

Pteroceltis tatarinowii

Born and died in Penza, Russia.

Russian physician and botanist. From 1840 to 1850 attached to the Russian Ecclesiastical Mission in Beijing, during which time he made a thorough study of the flora of the country around the capital. He collected dried specimens both there and in Mongolia on his journey to and from Beijing. Also commissioned a set of coloured drawings of Chinese plants by a native artist.

J. A. Soulié

Turczaninov, Nicolai Stepanovich, 1796-1864

Carpinus turczaninowii

Born in Nikitowka, near Kharkov, Russia. Died in Kharkov, Russia.

Distinguished Russian botanist. Travelled extensively in Siberia and was the first botanist to collect in the Amur river valley in 1833. Became an authority on the floras of Mongolia and north China, publishing many papers on the subject.

H.J. Veitch

Veitch, Sir Harry James, 1840-1924

Paeonia veitchii

Born in Exeter, Devon. Died in Slough, Buckinghamshire.

English horticulturist and nurseryman. Fourth generation of the famous nursery dynasty, and from 1870 Head of the Royal Exotic Nurseries in Chelsea from which came numerous new foliage and flowering plants for the stovehouses and conservatories of Victorian England. Also responsible for several other nurseries in south-east England, including Coombe Wood at Kingston, Surrey, in which were grown hardy ornamentals, including most of EH Wilson's early introductions from China. Veitch employed Wilson to mount two plant-hunting expeditions to China and later helped sponsor William Purdom on an expedition to north-west China (1909-1911). In 1912 he planned and organised the Royal International Horticultural Exhibition held in the grounds of the Chelsea Hospital, for which he was knighted. The success of the exhibition encouraged the Royal Horticultural Society to stage its first Chelsea Flower Show in 1913.

M.L. de Vilmorin

Vilmorin, Maurice Levêque de, 1849-1918

Sorbus vilmorinii

Born in Verrières-le-Buisson (Hauts-de-Seine), France. Died in des Barres (Loiret), France.

Respected French Nurseryman and Dendrologist. Second son of Louis de Vilmorin famous for his research on heredity of cultivated plants. Travelled worldwide and for some years in charge of family business Vilmorin, Andrieux & Cie before retiring in favour of his brother Philippe. In 1894 he began planting his family estate at des Barres with a collection of shrubs from the Arboretum de Segrez after the death of the owner Alphonse Lavallée. It rapidly increased as a result of seeds sent by the French missionaries in China to his good friend Adrien Franchet at the Paris Museum. Thus Franchet was able to study living plants of new species he had described from dried specimens. Some at least of this seed was germinated and grown on by Léon Chenault another friend. Chinese plants were also grown on in the Vilmorin family estate at Verrières-le-Buisson. Many of the trees and shrubs resulting from the French missionaries' endeavours were first grown in Europe at Verrières-le-Buisson and the Arboretum des Barres and, like its English contemporary the Veitch Nursery of Chelsea and Coombe Wood, the Vilmorin Nursery was mainly responsible for these plants entering general cultivation.

J.C. Williams

Williams, John Charles, 1861-1939

Rhododendron williamsianum

Born and died at Caerhays Castle, Cornwall.

English businessman and horticulturist. Made a famous woodland garden - or rather collection - around his home in which he cultivated trees and shrubs, especially those from China. It still exists and is renowned for its outstanding collections of *Magnolia*, *Rhododendron* and *Camellia*. There are also many rare oaks. He subscribed to the expeditions of EH Wilson and George Forrest, and Caerhays has many fine specimens grown from their seed. He gave his name to the now famous hybrid *Camellia* x *williamsii* (*japonica* x *saluenensis*) first raised at Caerhays in 1925 and now represented in cultivation by numerous named cultivars with single, semi-double or double blooms in colours varying from red through shades of pink and rose to white.

Willmott, Miss Ellen Ann, 1858-1934

Ceratostigma willmottianum

Born in Isleworth, Middlesex. Died in Brentwood, Essex.

English horticulturist, garden maker and authoress. First woman member to be elected to the Linnean Society. Subscribed to EH Wilson's expeditions to China. Several of his new introductions were named after her, including *Rosa willmottiae* and *Lilium davidii* var. *willmottiae*. She lived and gardened at Warley Place, Essex and in France.

Wilson, Ernest Henry, 1876-1930

Magnolia wilsonii

Born at Chipping Campden, Gloucestershire. Died, with his wife, in a car accident in Massachusetts, USA.
English traveller, plant collector and author. One of the most successful of all plant hunters. Trained at the Birmingham Botanic Gardens and then the Royal Botanic Gardens, Kew. Engaged by the English nursery firm Veitch of Chelsea and Coombe Wood to journey to China in search of hardy ornamental plants for British gardens. His first expedition lasted from 1899 to 1902 and a second, for the same firm, from 1903 to 1905. He was subsequently employed by the Arnold Arboretum, Massachusetts, to return to China on two further expeditions, 1906-1908 and 1909-1911. Apart from an initial foray into south Yunnan to meet Augustine Henry in 1899, his principal areas of activity were the provinces of Hubei and Sichuan. He introduced a vast quantity of plants and seed to Western cultivation and a large number of dried specimens as well. One estimate puts his introductions of new garden plants at well over a thousand. A good number of these were originally discovered, though not introduced, by Augustine Henry. Wilson was so successful in his chosen profession that he attracted the nickname 'Chinese' Wilson. After his China experiences he travelled again in the Far East to Taiwan, Korea and Japan, introducing more plants. He also travelled to many other countries around the world. He was a prolific author and later became Keeper of the Arnold Arboretum. Among his most notable introductions were *Acer griseum*, *Prunus serrula*, *Rhododendron williamsianum*, *Sorbus sargentiana*, *Primula pulverulenta* and *Lilium regale*.

E.H. Wilson

Yü, Te Tsun, 1908-1986

Sorbus yuana

Born in Gansu province, China. Died in Beijing, China.
Distinguished Chinese botanist and plant collector. Until his death, Senior Professor of the Institute of Botany, Academia Sinica, Beijing. Widely travelled in China collecting dried specimens as well as living plants and seed. In 1937 and 1940 led two British and Irish-backed Chinese expeditions to Yunnan and Sichuan, introducing seeds of many fine plants to Western cultivation. One of the foremost students of Asiatic *Sorbus*, an authority on Chinese *Rosaceae* and primary advocate of renewed and continued co-operation between Chinese and Western botanists.

Te Tsun Yü

A famous line-up of senior botanical staff at the Arnold Arboretum of Harvard University, Jamaica Plain, Massachusetts, USA, in August 1916. All, in one way or another, played a role in the discovery, naming, introduction or cultivation of Chinese plants. All are commemorated in the names of trees or shrubs of Chinese origin. From left: Alfred Rehder (*Rehderodendron macrocarpum*), E.H. Wilson (*Magnolia wilsonii*), Charles Sargent (*Sorbus sargentiana*), Charles Faxon (*Abies fargesii* var. *faxoniana*) and Camillo Schneider (*Zelkova schneideriana*).

495

Appendix 5

A Select Bibliography

Abel, C, *Narrative of a Journey in the Interior of China, 1816-1817*, 1819

Anisko, T, *Plant Exploration for Longwood Gardens*, 2002

Anon, *Flora Hupehensis*, vols 1 and 2, 1976 and 1979

Anon, *Flora Reipublicae Popularis Sinicae*, vol 7, 1978

Anon, *Flora Yunnanica*, vols 1-3, 1977-1983

Anon, *Iconographia Cormophytorum Sinicorum*, vols 1-5, 1980

Anon, *Report on Herbal Pharmacology in the People's Republic of China*, 1975

Aris, M, *Lamas, Princes and Brigands. Joseph Rock's Photographs of the Tibetan Borderlands of China*, 1992

Baber, E C, 'Travels and Researches in Western China', *Royal Geographical Society Papers*, vol 1, p 1, 1882

Bartholomew, B, et al, 'The 1980 Sino-American Botanical Expedition to West Hubei Province', *Journal Arnold Arboretum*, vol 64, no 1, 1983

Bean, W J, *Trees and Shrubs Hardy in the British Isles*; 8th edition revised, vols 1-4, 1970-1980, and *Supplement* by D E Clarke, 1988

Beckett, K, ed., *Alpine Garden Society, Encyclopaedia of Alpines*, 2 vols, 1993

Bishop, G, *Travels in Imperial China. The Exploration and Discoveries of Père David*, 1990

Bishop, J F, *The Yangtze Valley and Beyond*, 1899

Blackmore, S and Tootill, ed., *The Penguin Dictionary of Botany*, 1984

Bretschneider, E, *History of European Botanical Discoveries in China*, vols 1 and 2, 1898

Brickell, C D and Mathew, B, *Daphne - The Genus in the Wild and in Cultivation*, 1976

Briggs, R, *Chinese Wilson*, 1993

Brown, D, *Aroids*, 2nd ed., 2002

Brummitt, R K, *Vascular Plant Families and Genera*, 1992

Brummitt R K and Powell, C E, eds., *Authors of Plant Names*, 1992

Burrell, C C and Tyler, J K, *Hellebores*, 2006

Calloway, D J, *Magnolias*, 1994

Cannon, J and J F M, 'A Revision of the Morinaceae', *Bulletin British Museum (Nat Hist), Botany Series*, vol 12, no 1, 1984

Chamberlain, D F and Cullen, J, 'A Revision of Rhododendron', *Notes, Royal Botanic Garden, Edinburgh*, vol 39, nos 1 and 2, 1980 and 1982

Chang, H T, ed., *Flora Reipublicae Popularis Sinicae*, vol 35 (2), 1979

Chang, H T and Bartholomew, B, *Camellias*, 1984

Chapman, G P and Wang, Y Z, *The Plant Life of China*, 2002

Chetham, D, *Before the Deluge*, 2002

Chung, H H, *A Catalogue of Trees and Shrubs of China*, 1924

Clapham, A R, Tutin, T G and Warburg, E F, *Flora of the British Isles*, 1962

Clausen, K and Hu, S Y, 'Mapping the Collecting Localities of E H Wilson in China', *Arnoldia*, vol 40, no 3, 1980

Coombes, A J, *The Collingridge Dictionary of Plant Names*, 1985

Cooper, R E, et al, *George Forrest*, 1935

Cowan, J M, *The Journeys and Plant Introductions of George Forrest*, 1952

Cowley, E J, 'A Revision of Roscoea', *Kew Bulletin*, vol 36 (4), 1982

Cowley, E J, *The Genus Roscoea*, 2007

Cox, E H M, *Plant Hunting in China*, 1945

Cox, K N E, ed., *Frank Kingdon-Ward's Riddle of the Tsangpo Gorges*, 2001

Cox, P A, 'Plant Hunting in China', *Journal American Rhododendron Society*, vol 36, no 2, 1982

Cox, P A and Cox, K N E, *The Encyclopaedia of Rhododendron Species*, 1997

Cribb, P, *The Genus Cypripedium*, 1997

Cribb, P and Butterfield, I, *The Genus Pleione*, 2nd edition 1999

Cribb, P, Tang, C Z, and Butterfield, I, 'The Genus Pleione', *Botanical Magazine*, vol 184, pt 3, 1983

Cullen, J, 'Taxonomic Notes on the Genus Rodgersia', *Notes, Royal Botanic Garden, Edinburgh*, vol 34, 1975

Cullen, J, *Hardy Rhododendrons*, 2005

Cunningham, I S, *Frank N Meyer - Plant Hunter in Asia*, 1984

Cutting, S, *The Fire Ox and Other Years*, 1947

Davidian, H H, *The Rhododendron Species*, vols 1-3, 1982-92

Desmond, R, *A Dictionary of British and Irish Botanists and Horticulturists*, 1977

Dirr, M A, *Manual of Woody Landscape Plants*, revised edition, 1983

Duan, C, ed. in chief, *Scientific Investigation of the Plants on Cangshan Mountain*, 1994

Elliott, B, *The Royal Horticultural Society – A History*, 2004

Elvin, M, *The Retreat of the Elephants*, 2004

Evans, A, *The Peat Garden and its Plants*, 1974

Evans, R L, *Handbook of Cultivated Sedums*, 1983

Fang, W P, *Icones Plantarum Omeiensium*, vol 1, nos 1 and 2, 1942 and 1944

Fang, W P, ed., *Flora Sichuanica*, vol 1, 1979

Fang, W P, ed., *Flora Reipublicae Popularis Sinicae*, vol 46, 1981

Fang, W P, ed., *Sichuan Rhododendrons of China*, 1986

Farjon, A, *Pines*, 1985

Farjon, A., *World Checklist and Bibliography of Conifers*, 2nd edition, 2001

Farrer, R, *On the Eaves of the World*, 1917

Farrer, R, *The English Rock Garden*, vols 1 and 2, 1919

Farrer, R, *The Rainbow Bridge*, 1921

Feng, G M, *Rhododendrons of Yunnan*, 1981

Fitzgerald, C P, *The Tower of Five Glories*, 1941

Fitzgerald, C P, 'The Tali District of Western Yunnan', *Royal Geographical Society Journal*, vol 19, 1942

Flanagan, M and Kirkham, T. *Plant Hunting on the Edge*, 2005

Forrest, G, 'The Perils of Plant Collecting', *Gardeners' Chronicle*, May 1910

Forrest, G, 'The Flora of North-Western Yunnan', *Journal Royal Horticultural Society*, vol.41, 1915/16.

Forrest, G, 'Notes on the Flora of North-Western Yunnan', *Journal Royal Horticultural Society*, vol.42, 1916/17.

Forrest, G, 'Exploration of North-West Yunnan and South-East Tibet, 1921-22', *Journal Royal Horticultural Society*, vol.49, 1924.

Fortune, R, *Three Years Wanderings in the Northern Provinces of China*, 1847

Fortune, R, *A Residence Among the Chinese*, 1857

Fox, H M, *Abbe David's Diary*, 1949

Galle, F C, *Hollies – The Genus Ilex*, 1997

Gardiner, J M, *Magnolias – A Gardener's Guide*, 2000

Govaerts, R and Frodin, D G, *World Checklist and Bibliography of Fagales*, 1998

Green, P S and Simmons, J B, *Report on a Visit to the People's Republic of China*, Royal Botanic Gardens, Kew, 1978

Green, R, 'Asiatic Primulas', Alpine Garden Society Guide, 1976

Grey-Wilson, C, *Clematis – The Genus*, 2002

Grey-Wilson, C, *Poppies*, revised edition, 2005

Gusman, G and Gusman, L, *The Genus Arisaema*, 2003

Han, Suyin, *The Crippled Tree*, 1965

Handel-Mazzetti, H. (trans. Winstanley, D), *A Botanical Pioneer in South West China*, 1996

Hara, H, Stearn, W T and Williams, L H J, *An Enumeration of the Flowering Plants of Nepal*, vol 1, 1978

Hara, H, and Williams, L H J, *An Enumeration of the Flowering Plants of Nepal*, vols 2 and 3, 1979 and 1981

Haw, S G, *The Lilies of China*, 1986

Heriz-Smith, S, *The House of Veitch*, 2002

Herner, G, 'Harry Smith in China - Routes of his Botanical Travels', *Taxon*, vol 37(2), 1988.

Hillier, J and Coombes, A, consultant eds., *Hillier Manual of Trees and Shrubs*, 2002

Hinkley, D, *The Explorer's Garden*, 1999

Ho, T N and Liu, S W., *A Worldwide Monograph of Gentiana*, 2001

Hosie, A, *Three Years in Western China*, 1897

How, F C, ed., *A Dictionary of the Families and Genera of Chinese Seed Plants*, revised edition, 1982

Howard, R A, 'E H Wilson as a Botanist', *Arnoldia*, vol 40, no 3, 1980

Hsueh, C J and Yi, T P, 'Two New Genera of Bambusoideae from South-West China', *Acta Botanica Yunnanica*, vol 2, no 1, 1980

Hunt, D, ed., *Magnolias and their Allies*, 1998

Hutchison, P, 'Expedition to the Cang Shan Range, 1981', *Quarterly Bulletin Alpine Garden Society*, vol 51, no 2, 1983

James, H E M, *The Long White Mountain*, 1888

Jeffrey, C, *Biological Nomenclature*, 1973

Jiyin, C, Parks, C R and Yueqiang, D, *Collected Species of the Genus Camellia*, 2005

Johnson, O, ed., *Champion Trees of Britain and Ireland*, 2003

Jocelyn, E and McEwen, A, *The Long March*, 2006

Keswick, M, *The Chinese Garden*, 1978

Kingdon-Ward, F, *The Land of the Blue Poppy*, 1913

Kohlein, F, *Saxifrages and Related Genera*, 1984

Kong, W S. and Watts, D, *The Plant Geography of Korea*, 1993

Kuan, C T, ed., *Flora Sichuanica*, vol 2, 1983

Kuang, K Z and Li, P C, eds., *Flora Reipublicae Popularis Sinicae*, vol 21, 1979

Lancaster, C R, 'A Year to Remember', *International Dendrological Society Year Book*, 1980

Lancaster, C R, 'Another Year to Remember', *International Dendrological Society Year Book*, 1981

Lancaster, C R, 'A Plant Hunter in China', *Pacific Horticulture*, 1981

Lancaster, C R, 'Flowers of the Marble Mountains', *Bulletin Hardy Plant Society*, vol 6, no 1, 1981

Lancaster, C R, 'In the Footsteps of Wilson', *The Garden*, Journal Royal Horticultural Society, vol 106, pt 10, 1981

Lancaster C R, *Plant Hunting in Nepal*, 1981

Lancaster, C R, 'Five Orchids of Yunnan', *The Garden*, Journal Royal Horticultural Society, vol 107, pt 11, 1982

Lancaster, C R, 'Flowers of the Cangshan', *Pacific Horticulture*, vol 43, no 4, 1982/83

Lancaster, C R, 'On the Other Side of the Mountain', *The Garden*, Journal Royal Horticultural Society, vol 108, pt 10, 1983

Lancaster, C R, 'The Wudang Mountains of North-West Hubei', *International Dendrological Society Year Book*, 1983

Latham, R, *The Travels of Marco Polo*, 1958

Leeuwenburg, A J M, 'The Loganiaceae of Africa-Buddleja - Revision of African and Asiatic Species', *Medelingen Landbouwhogeschool Wageningen*, Nederland, vol 79, no 6, 1979

Li, G, chief ed., *The Genus Aspidistra*, 2004
Li, H L, *Floristic Relationships between Eastern Asia and Eastern North America*, 1981
Liden, M and Zetterlund, H, *Corydalis*, 1997
Ling, L, ed., *Flora Reipublicae Popularis Sinicae*, vol 75, 1979
Liu, T S, *A Monograph of the Genus Abies*, 1971
Liu, Y H, ed. in chief, *Magnolias of China*, 2002
Lu, G D and Hueng, H T, 'Botany', in Needham, J, ed., *Science and Civilisation in China*, 1986
Lyte, C, *Frank Kingdon-Ward*, 1989

Ma, S, *The Rare Plants and Flowers of Western Sichuan*, 1984
Mabberley, D J, *The Plant Book — A Portable Dictionary of the Higher Plants*, 2nd edition, 1997
Man, J, *Kublai Khan*, 2006
Mathew, B, *The Iris*, 1981
McAllister, H, *The Genus Sorbus*, 2005
McLean, B, *George Forrest*, 2004
McMillan Browse, P, ed., *Gardening on the Edge*, 2004
Mitchell, A F and Hallet, V E, *Champion Trees in the British Isles*, 1985
Mitchell, R J, et al, *Cang Shan — Report of the Sino-British Expedition to China, 1981*, 1984
Mitchell, R J, 'Memorable Trees of Yunnan', *Arboricultural Journal*, vol 8, no 4, 1984
Morley, B D, 'Augustine Henry; His Botanical Activities in China', *Glasra*, no 3, 1978

Nelson, C E, 'Augustine Henry and the Exploration of the Chinese Flora', *Arnoldia*, vol 43, no 1, 1982/83

Philipson, M N, and W R, 'A Revision of Rhododendron Section Lapponicum', *Notes*, Royal Botanic Garden, Edinburgh, no 34, 1975
Phillips, R and Rix, M, *The Quest for the Rose*, 1993
Phipps, J B, *Hawthorns and Medlars*, 2003
Pratt, A E, *To the Snows of Tibet Through China*, 1892

Rehder, A, Manual of Cultivated Trees and Shrubs Hardy in North America, 2nd edition, 1940
Rehder, A, Bibliography of Cultivated Trees and Shrubs, 1949
RHS Plant Finder, 21st edition, 2007-8
Richards, J, *Primula*, 2nd edition, 2003
Robson, N K B, 'Studies in Genus Hypericum - 3', *Bulletin British Museum (Nat Hist), Botany Series*, vol 12, no 4, 1985
Rock, J F, 'The Glories of Minya Koonka', *National Geographical Magazine*, October 1930
Rosengarten, F, Jr, *The Book of Edible Nuts*, 1984

Sargent, C S, ed., *Plantae Wilsonianae*, 3 vols, 1911-1917
Sealy, J R, *A Revision of the Genus Camellia*, 1985
Shengchen, L, ed. in chief, *Wild Flowers of China*, 1996
Shephard, S, *Seeds of Fortune — A Gardening Dynasty*, 2003
Shulman, N, *A Rage for Rock Gardening*, 2001
Stearn, W T, *The Genus Epimedium*, 2002
Stearn, W T, *Stearn's Dictionary of Plant Names for Gardeners*, 1992
Stearn, W T, ed., *John Lindley*, 2005
Synge, P M, *Lilies*, 1980

Takhtajan, A, 'A Revision of Daiswa (Trilliaceae)', *Brittonia*, vol 35, no 3, 1983
Tang, Xiyang, *Living Treasures — An Odyssey through China's Extraordinary Nature Reserves*, 1988
Taylor, G, *An Account of the Genus Meconopsis*, 1934
Thomas, G S, *Perennial Garden Plants*, 3rd edition, 1990
Treseder, N G, *Magnolias*, 1978

Valder, P, *Wisterias*, 1995
Valder, P, *The Garden Plants of China*, 1999
Valder, P, *Gardens of China*, 2002
Vertrees, J D, *Japanese Maples*, 1978

Waddick, J W and Zhao, Y T, *Iris of China*, 1992
Wang, C W, *The Forests of China*, 1961
Wang, D and Shen, S J, *Bamboos of China*, 1987
Wang, F T and Tang, T, eds., *Flora Reipublicae Popularis Sinicae*, vol 14, 1980
Wang, W T, ed., *Flora Reipublicae Popularis Sinicae*, vol 28, 1980
Ward, B J, *The Plant Hunter's Garden*, 2004
Wharton, P, Hine, B and Justice, D, *The Jade Garden*, 2005
Whittacker, P, *Hardy Bamboos — Taming the Dragon*, 2005
Wilkie, D, *Gentians*, 1950
Willis, J C A, *A Dictionary of Flowering Plants and Ferns*, 8th edition revised, 1973
Wilson, E H, *A Naturalist in Western China*, vols 1 and 2, 1913
Wilson, E H, *Plant Hunting*, vol 2, 1927
Wilson, E H, 'Magnolias', *Journal of Magnolia Society*, vol 16, no 2, 1980
Wu, C Y, ed., *Flora Xizangica*, vols 1 and 3, 1983 and 1986
Wu, C Y, and Li, H, eds., *Flora Reipublicae Popularis Sinicae*, vol 13 (2), 1979

Yeo, P, *Hardy Geraniums*, 2nd edition, 2001
Ying, T, Zhang, Y and Boufford, D A, *The Endemic Genera of Seed Plants of China*, 1993
Young, J and Chong, L S, *Rhododendrons of China*, 1980
Yu, D, *The Botanical Gardens of China*, 1983

Index of Plants

The abbreviations of authorities are based on *Authors of Plant Names* (1992) edited by RK Brummitt and CE Powell. Where authorities appear in parentheses, this indicates the authority responsible for originally naming and describing the plant, while the second authority is the one responsible for the present combination (name); eg: Betula szechuanica (*C.K. Schneid.*) *C.-A. Jansson*. Schneider was the first to name this birch as Betula japonica var. szechuanica. Later, Jansson preferred to treat it as a species in its own right, hence Betula szechuanica (*C.K. Schneid.*) *C.-A. Jansson*.

An excellent discussion of the correct use of nomenclature is given in *Biological Nomenclature* by Charles Jeffrey.

Page numbers in **bold** refer to captions and/or illustrations

Index of Arboreta and Gardens

Page numbers in **bold** refer to captions and/or illustrations

Western gardens, arboreta and parks mentioned in this book are all located in Great Britain, unless otherwise stated. Not all the undermentioned are still in exisance or open to the public. Would-be visitors are advised to check before making a journey.

Index of People

Page numbers in **bold** refer to captions and/or illustrations

Index of Locations

Page numbers in **bold** refer to captions and/or illustrations

Following are the more important Chinese locations mentioned and illustrated. Most of the Chinese names mentioned are in Pinyin.

General Index

Page numbers in **bold** refer to captions and/or illustrations